SANSKRIT

An Introduction to the Classical Language

This course in Sanskrit has been devised to enable the student to read Indian classics in the original. The carefully graded chapters explain Sanskrit grammar and style with exceptional clarity. Exercises, most of which use only sentences taken directly from Sanskrit authors, enable the student to check his progress.

This is not only a primer, but also a work of scholarship, for the book contains much new material on Sanskrit syntax and usage. Its explanation of how to use Sanskrit commentaries is especially useful. The text also includes an appendix on prosody, extensive vocabularies both into and out of Sanskrit, and full keys to the exercises.

TEACH YOURSELF BOOKS

SANSKRIT
An Introduction to the Classical Language

Michael Coulson

TEACH YOURSELF BOOKS
Hodder and Stoughton

ACKNOWLEDGEMENT

THE publishers wish to acknowledge the invaluable help of Dr. Richard Gombrich, Boden Professor of Sanskrit at Oxford University, in the preparation of this book.

First printed 1976
Sixth impression 1986

Copyright © 1976
Michael Coulson

This volume published by David McKay Company Inc., 750 Third Avenue, New York, N.Y. 10017.

ISBN 0 340 32389 2

*Printed and bound in Great Britain
for Hodder and Stoughton Educational,
a division of Hodder and Stoughton Ltd,
Mill Road, Dunton Green, Sevenoaks, Kent,
at the University Press, Oxford*

Contents

Preface

THE plan, scope and length of this book have been determined primarily by the aim of enabling students to cope as rapidly as possible with straightforward Classical Sanskrit texts. The material has been drawn almost entirely from the Sanskrit (not Prakrit) prose dialogue of the major dramas, extracted onto cards and then graded according to the main morphological and syntactical features which required explanation. From Chapter 6 onwards all the sentences of the exercises and all the more elaborate examples given in the chapters themselves are taken without change from actual Sanskrit works. While the intention is to provide an introduction to the Classical language in general, because of the nature of the bulk of the material the book is, in the first place, a guide to Sanskrit dramatic prose; and it is probable that I have sometimes incautiously presented as generally valid points of usage which really hold good only of the Classical dramatists.

Existing Sanskrit primers tend to be admirably systematic in their presentation of the complicated morphology of Sanskrit (which includes a mass of verb forms little used by most writers) but rather cursory in their treatment of such basic facts of life as the prevalence of nominal constructions and compound formations. The student may get the misleading impression that Classical Sanskrit syntax is very similar to that of Latin and Greek, and emerge well drilled in the varieties of athematic inflexion and yet quite unprepared, for instance, for such simple discoveries as the fact that someone in a play, speaking from the heart, instead of saying "Thank

God my children are alive' can and does say (literally) 'Thank God I am alive-childed'. In the present book thorough drilling in all the forms of declension and conjugation has been a secondary consideration, and the student will therefore benefit from a certain self-discipline in memorising accurately the paradigms introduced into each chapter. In part this shift of emphasis (though I think it desirable at any rate) has been dictated by the use of real Sanskrit material: second-person dual ātmanepada forms are not particularly thick on the ground whether in plays or in texts of any other kind. Serious inadequacy in this respect is, however, prevented by the fact that grammatical forms once introduced continue to be illustrated and required throughout the book: each exercise contains a natural element of revision of all previous exercises.

It is particularly students without a teacher who need a fuller explanation of Sanskrit syntax and idiom than existing primers give, and so I have been happy to model this book upon the Teach Yourself volumes which I myself in the past have found so helpful and stimulating. At the same time it seemed practical to assume a somewhat greater degree of sophistication in potential students of Sanskrit than in students proposing to teach themselves a language such as French. Someone who has never previously learnt a foreign language will probably find the early chapters rather heavy going unless he is fairly bright. A significant proportion of readers are likely to have some acquaintance with either Latin or Greek, and so I have cited parallels where these seemed illuminating, but knowledge of either language on the part of all readers is in no way assumed. In passing it is perhaps worth stating plainly that the present work is essentially intended to be an entirely 'synchronic' study of Classical Sanskrit: occasional references to the earlier history of the language, whether at the Vedic or Indo-European stage, have been introduced where it seemed that they might help to emphasise or clarify the point under discussion. Undoubtedly some readers would prefer more of such references, others less.

To make the book better adapted for use in university courses, a separate set of English–Sanskrit exercises without key has been provided. These too, from Exercise 6 onwards, are all English versions of Sanskrit originals.

For reasons of both convenience and economy, the use of the nāgarī script is discontinued in the body of the text after the first five chapters. Ample practice in reading and writing the script continues to be provided in the exercises.

Many people have given help and advice during the long and laborious period of preparation of this book. A particularly deep debt of gratitude is due to the following: to Dr. Richard Gombrich, of Oxford, for detailed comment and unfailing sympathy and encouragement over many years; to Mr. C. A. Rylands, formerly of the School of Oriental and African Studies in London, for reading with a quite remarkably sharp eye much of the final draft, and for giving me in many acute observations the fruits of his years of experience as a teacher of Sanskrit; to my colleague at Edinburgh Mr. W. E. Jones, for much patient and careful discussion of the first two chapters; and to Mrs. Elizabeth Kelsall, without whose competent editorial assistance I should still be struggling to get the book finished. Much error has been eliminated with the help of these friends and of the students with whom I have used the work in draft form. I am keenly conscious that many imperfections remain.

Edinburgh, January 1973

Note. Dr. Coulson died before this book could be published. Dr. Gombrich has seen it through the press; he wishes to thank Miss Elizabeth Christie for her help with the proof-reading.

Introduction

SANSKRIT is a member of the Indo-European family of languages to which most of the languages of Europe (including, for instance, English, Welsh, Latin and Greek) also belong. These have all evolved from a single language (or, more immediately, a group of closely related dialects), namely 'Primitive Indo-European' or just 'Indo-European', spoken in about the third millennium BC, of which no direct record remains. The original Indo-European speakers seem to have been tribes inhabiting the plains of Eastern Europe, particularly the area north of the Black Sea (archaeological remains in the South Russian Steppes are in harmony with this supposition), from where migration subsequently occurred in many directions. With the discovery of Hittite, Sanskrit has ceased to be the oldest recorded Indo-European language: but for many reasons, including the fact that Hittite separated early from the main Indo-European stock, Sanskrit remains of central importance to the student of the history of the Indo-European languages.

Sanskrit belongs, more specifically, to the Indo-Iranian branch of Indo-European. The other most important member of this branch is Persian. The earliest Indo-Iranian speakers are conveniently known as Aryans, from the name which they gave themselves (Sanskrit **ārya**, Avestan *airya*—from the latter the modern name Iran is derived, while the name Éire, at the other end of the Indo-European spectrum, may also be cognate). Although it is reasonable to assume that the original homeland of the Aryan tribes was to the north of the Caucasus,

our earliest record of them comes neither from this region
nor from the Indo-Iranian area but from south of the Caucasus, from the Mitanni kingdom of Northern Mesopotamia,
where a ruling dynasty bearing Aryan names and worshipping
Aryan gods such as Indra had established itself in the first half
of the second millennium BC. However, the main movement
of Aryan migration was not south but east into Central Asia,
and from there by separate penetrations into Iran and India.
Thereafter the Aryans of Iran and the Aryans of India went
their separate ways both culturally and linguistically. The
oldest stage of Iranian is represented by Avestan, the sacred
language of the Zoroastrians, and by Old Persian, the dialect
used in the cuneiform inscriptions of the Achaemenian kings.

In India, a highly evolved and urbanised civilisation had
existed long before the coming of the Aryans. This was the
'Indus Valley Civilisation', known to us in particular from
excavations at Harappa and Mohenjo Daro, and dating from
at least the middle of the third millennium. The culture was
stable over a long period, and literate. It came to a sudden end,
and it is tempting in the extreme to attribute its destruction
to the coming of the Aryans. However, an awkward time gap
exists, and has not yet been successfully explained, for the
Indus civilisation seems to have perished in about 1700 BC
and there is no evidence that the Aryans reached India before
the latter half of the second millennium.

The survival in Baluchistan up to the present day of a Dravidian language, Brahui, so far from what is now the main
Dravidian area in Southern India, makes it reasonable to conclude that before the arrival of the Aryans Dravidian was
spoken over a much wider area, and the suggestion has naturally been made that the inhabitants of the Indus cities spoke
a Dravidian language. At present this remains unproved,
unless recent claims of successful decipherment of the Indus
script are accepted, and other non-Aryan language families do
exist in India, most notably the group of Munda languages.
Although the language of the Aryans established itself over
most of Northern India, it seems that in the long run the
Aryans were affected both culturally and linguistically by the

peoples they conquered, and Dravidian and Muṇḍa influences (particularly the former) can be traced in the development of Sanskrit itself.

The speech introduced by the Aryans into India developed and diversified, and the major modern languages of Northern India are descended from it. The generic term for such languages is Indo-Aryan. One may conveniently divide the development of Indo-Aryan into three stages: Old, Middle and Modern.

Old Indo-Aryan is equivalent to Sanskrit only in the widest sense of the latter term, and is divided principally between Vedic and the later Classical Sanskrit. Our record of Old Indo-Aryan begins with the hymns of the Ṛgveda, which date back to at least 1000 BC and are the product of a considerable literary skill. That they were composed a fair time after the arrival of the Aryans in India is shown both by the absence of any reference to a homeland outside India and by divergences, principally phonetic, in the language itself from what can be reconstructed as the common Indo-Iranian tongue. Intermediate between the language of the Ṛgveda and that of the Classical period is the language of the Brāhmaṇas, prose works which seek to interpret the mystical significance of the Vedic ritual, the earliest of them written well before the middle of the first millennium BC. The Upaniṣads are a part of the Brāhmaṇa literature.

With the passage of time the language of even the educated priestly class diverged more and more from that of the sacred hymns themselves, and it became increasingly a matter of concern that the hymns should be transmitted without corruption, in order to preserve their religious efficacy. Consequently, a study began to be made of the principles of linguistic, and more particularly of phonetic, analysis. From this developed a grammatical science which concerned itself not only with the sacred language but also with contemporary educated speech. The grammar of Pāṇini, the **Aṣṭādhyāyī**, usually attributed to the fourth century BC, is evidently the culmination of a long and sophisticated grammatical tradition, though the perfection of his own work caused that of his predecessors to vanish.

In less than 4000 sūtras, or brief aphorisms (supplemented on
points of detail by the grammarian Kātyāyana), he analyses
the whole phonology and morphology of Sanskrit. He anticipates much of the methodology of modern formal grammar:
his grammar is generative and in some respects transforma-
tional. It cannot, however, be compared very directly with
modern grammars, since its form is geared to the needs of
oral transmission, and Pāṇini could not avail himself of the
mathematical symbols and typographical conventions of the
written page. The work was so brief that it could be recited
from beginning to end in a couple of hours. It was so compre-
hensive and accurate that it quickly became the final authority
on all questions of correct usage. By Classical Sanskrit is
meant essentially the language codified by Pāṇini.

The formal differences between Vedic and Classical Sanskrit
are not enormous. Phonologically, the most obvious is a
difference of sandhi, whereby for instance a trisyllable such
as **vīriam** (or **vīriyam**) becomes a disyllable **vīryam**. Morphologically, the wealth of inflected forms is somewhat
reduced, for instance by the disappearance of the subjunctive.
In vocabulary a fair number of ancient Aryan words are lost,
but the loss is far outweighed by the acquisition of enormous
numbers of words from non-Aryan sources. Classical Sanskrit
is based on a more easterly dialect of Old Indo-Aryan than is
the Ṛgveda, as is shown by the fact that it contributes a number of words which preserve an original Indo-European **l**,
where the Ṛgvedic dialect (in common with Iranian) changes
this sound to **r**: thus both Vedic **raghú** 'swift, light' and
Classical Sanskrit **laghu** 'light, nimble' are cognate with
Greek *elakhús*. Other Old Indo-Aryan dialects existed; we
have no direct record of them, but from them various dialects
of Middle Indo-Aryan evolved.

The beginnings of Middle Indo-Aryan antedate Pāṇini, for
the speech of the ordinary people had been evolving faster
than that of the educated classes. The term **saṃskṛta** means
'polished, (grammatically) correct', and is in contrast with
prākṛta '(speech) of the common people'. Just as Sanskrit
interpreted in a wide sense may conveniently stand for Old

Indo-Aryan, so Prākrit, interpreted equally widely, may stand for Middle Indo-Aryan. More narrowly, three stages of Middle Indo-Aryan may be distinguished. The first is represented by Pāli, the only Indian language in which the earliest Buddhist scriptures have been preserved on a large scale, and by the dialects used in the inscriptions of the emperor Aśoka (*c.* 250 BC). The process of morphological simplification which distinguishes Classical Sanskrit from Vedic here continues and is accompanied by drastic phonological simplification, including a reduction in the number of vowels and a simplification of consonant groups (thus Sanskrit **traividya** becomes Pali **tevijja**). These processes continue (for instance, with the loss of many intervocalic consonants) in the second stage, that of the Prakrits proper, including Māhārāṣṭrī, Śaurasenī and Māgadhī, and the various dialects of the Jain scriptures. The third stage is represented by Apabhraṃśa, a generic term for the further popular evolution of Middle Indo-Aryan up to the end of the first millennium AD, foreshadowing the final collapse of the old Indo-European inflexional system and the emergence of the Modern Indo-Aryan languages, Bengali, Hindi, Panjābi, Gujarāti, Marāthi, etc. Hindi in its wider sense denotes a group of dialects spoken from Rājasthān to Bihār: upon one particular dialect are based both the official language of Pākistān, Urdu, and the official language of India, (modern standard) Hindi. The term Hindustāni is sometimes used nowadays to denote the common substratum of these two languages, lacking both the extreme Persianisation of Urdu and the extreme Sanskritisation of Hindi.

The Sanskrit of Pāṇini's time had the *cachet* not simply of being the dialect of the educated classes but also of being much closer than was the popular speech to the language of the sacred scriptures themselves. Naturally the prestige of Sanskrit was resisted by those who questioned the authority of the Vedas, and for this reason the early writings of the Buddhists and the Jains are in varieties of Middle Indo-Aryan; the Buddha is reported to have said that his teachings should be given to the people in their own language. Nevertheless, Sanskrit continued to be cultivated, and not merely by the brahmins. Important evidence of this is provided by the two great Indian epics, the Mahābhārata and the Rāmāyaṇa. They were recited and handed down by non-brahmins (the Sūtas), and their audience was a popular one. Although their origins are no doubt more ancient, they evidently belong in something like their present form to about the beginning of the first millennium AD. Their language is Sanskrit, but of a later kind than Pāṇini's—Classical Sanskrit with an admixture of minor features of Middle Indo-Aryan morphology and syntax. It is Sanskrit composed instinctively rather than according to Pāṇini's rules by men for whom Sanskrit was not too remote from their own informal speech. The advantage of using Sanskrit, in addition to the dignity which it imparted to the verse, lay in its role as a *lingua franca* uniting the various regions of Aryan India. One may compare the way a Londoner and a Glaswegian often find the English of the BBC easier to understand than each other's.

As Middle Indo-Aryan developed and its various dialects drew further apart, this role as a *lingua franca* grew increasingly important, and at a time when brahminical influence was increasing. In the early centuries AD, first in the north and later in the south, Sanskrit became the only acceptable language both for administration and for learned communication. The Buddhist Aśvaghoṣa (second century AD) is a significant figure in the process. While early Buddhist literature had first eschewed Sanskrit completely, then compromised with a hybrid language or at least with a non-Pāṇinian Sanskrit, he himself not merely writes Classical Sanskrit but is a master of Sanskrit literary style, and is as important in the history of Sanskrit literature as in the history of Buddhism.

This is the beginning of the great period of Classical Sanskrit, and it lasted for something like a thousand years (possibly a little less for creative literature, but several centuries longer in various fields of speculative thought). For the early centuries AD our knowledge is sketchy, for much of what was written has perished. Part of the reason for Aśvaghoṣa's literary importance is that he is very nearly the only significant predecessor of the poet Kālidāsa whose work has survived.

Kālidāsa is commonly dated to the early fifth century, and on reading his poetry one cannot doubt that it represents the culmination of a great tradition; yet he is the earliest of the major classical poets. Perhaps, like Pāṇini, Kālidāsa eclipsed his predecessors and made their work seem not worth preserving.

By now Sanskrit was not a mother tongue but a language to be studied and consciously mastered. This transformation had come about through a gradual process, the beginnings of which are no doubt earlier than Pāṇini himself. Something of the true position must be reflected in the drama, where not merely the characters of low social status but also the women and young children speak some variety of Prakrit. Kālidāsa learnt his Sanskrit from the rules of a grammarian living some 700 years before his time. Such a situation may well strike the Western reader as paradoxical. Our nearest parallel is in the position of Latin in Medieval Europe. There is, however, an important difference. Few would deny Cicero or Vergil a greater importance in Latin literature than any Medieval author. Conversely, few Sanskritists would deny that the centre of gravity in Sanskrit literature lies somewhere in the first millennium AD, for all that its authors were writing in a so-called 'dead language'.

On this point it may be useful to make a twofold distinction—between a living and a dead language, and between a natural and a learned one. A language is natural when it is acquired and used instinctively; it is living when people choose to converse and formulate ideas in it in preference to any other. To the modern Western scholar Sanskrit is a dead as well as a learned language. To Kālidāsa or Śaṃkara it was a learned language but a living one. (The term 'learned' is not entirely satisfactory, but the term 'artificial', which is the obvious complementary of 'natural', is normally reserved for application to totally constructed languages such as Esperanto.)

The literary medium of any language contains elements of learned speech. Apart from any tendency to conform to conscious grammatical rules, one may observe a limitation or regularisation of sentence patterns, and a widening of vocabulary by the itemisation of more complex ideas. In the expression

of a given idea, provided that in both cases it is contained
in a single sentence, the syntax will therefore be *simpler* in
formal than in conversational speech. Compare the subject–
verb–object simplicity of 'an unexpected arrival will admittedly
affect our numbers' with the relative syntactical complexity
of 'it's true that how many we're going to be will depend on
whether anyone turns up that we aren't expecting'. (A particular factor affecting the written style of English is the need to
avoid sentences made seriously ambiguous by the lack of an
appropriate voice inflection.)

Living languages, whether natural or learned, change and
develop. But when a learned language such as literary English
is closely tied to, and constantly revitalised by, a natural
idiom, its opportunities for independent growth are limited.
Sanskrit provides a fascinating example of a language develop-
ing in complete freedom from such constraints as an instrument of intellectual and artistic expression. To say that
Classical Sanskrit was written in conformity with Pāṇini's rules
is true, but in one sense entirely misleading. Pāṇini would have
been astounded by the way in which Bāṇa or Bhavabhūti or
Abhinavagupta handled the language. It is precisely the fact
that Sanskrit writers insisted on using Sanskrit as a living and
not as a dead language that has often troubled Western scholars.
W. D. Whitney, a great but startlingly arrogant American
Sanskritist of the nineteenth century, says of the Classical
language, 'Of linguistic history there is next to nothing in it all;
but only a history of style, and this for the most part showing
a gradual depravation, an increase of artificiality and an intensi-
fication of certain more undesirable features of the language—
such as the use of passive constructions and of participles
instead of verbs, and the substitution of compounds for
sentences.' Why such a use of passives, participles and compounds should be undesirable, let alone depraved, is left rather
vague, and while there have been considerable advances in
linguistic science in the past fifty years there seems to have
been nothing which helps to clarify or justify these strictures.
Indeed, Whitney's words would not be worth resurrecting if
strong echoes of them did not still survive in some quarters.

Acceptance of Pāṇini's rules implied a final stabilisation of the phonology of Sanskrit, and also (at least in the negative sense that no form could be used which was not sanctioned by him) of its morphology. But Pāṇini did not fix syntax. To do so explicitly and incontrovertibly would be difficult in any language, given several ways of expressing the same idea and various other ways of expressing closely similar ideas. Certain major morphological simplifications typical of Middle Indo-Aryan were prevented by Pāṇini's codification: thus Sanskrit retains a middle voice and an obligatory dual number. On the other hand, the way Prakrit dealt with all past tenses, replacing them with a past participle and where necessary a passive construction, being a negative procedure could be imitated by Sanskrit (see Chapter 4), and as a result in certain styles of Classical Sanskrit a past finite tense is something of a rarity. Because it did not occur to Pāṇini to prohibit such a construction, or to limit its use to particular circumstances, supposedly 'Pāṇinian' Sanskrit could be written in a quite non-Pāṇinian way, eschewing a whole mass of difficult forms and conforming to the usage of the popular language.

But in other and more important respects the syntactical changes wrought in Sanskrit took it further from popular speech. Indeed, one such may be distinguished which actually depends upon the preservation of the full Old Indo-Aryan case system, namely the increasing exploitation of various cases to represent certain 'abstract' syntactical relationships: instrumental or ablative to express cause, dative purpose, locative circumstance and hypothesis, an abstract accusative with a verb of motion to express change of state, and so on. This development is inseparable from the most striking change of all, the exploitation of nominal composition. In Vedic, noun compounds are hardly more frequent than in Homeric Greek, but their frequency increases throughout the history of the language. More important still, the compounds which occur in the earlier language are seldom of more than two members, whereas in the later language the occurrence in a single short sentence of several compounds of four or five members is perfectly normal, and in certain styles compounds of twenty or more members are not thought excessive. Here again, advantage has been taken of a negative freedom. It is, in fact, an important feature of compounds that, co-ordinatives apart, they are binary in structure (i.e. can be ana-lysed through repeated bisection—see particularly Chapter 7). Pāṇini gives rules for the construction of compounds. By applying these rules recursively, compounds of any length may be built up. At one and the same time Pāṇini is obeyed and bypassed. One may indeed wonder to what extent the style of the grammatical sūtras themselves encouraged this process; evolved to meet very specific scientific needs and utilising cases and compounds in a way quite foreign to the natural language, it may well have served as a partial model for other types of discourse.

The cumulative effect of such changes is certainly startling. The syntax of Classical Sanskrit in many major respects bears little resemblance to the syntax of any other Indo-European language (leaving aside similarities in certain kinds of Middle Indo-Aryan writing). Whitney is typical of many Western scholars who manage to convey contempt for the avoidance of the intricacies of the Old Indo-Aryan verbal system, with a simultaneous contempt for the pedantry of those who flex their grammatical muscles from time to time by using a num-ber of *recherché* forms and irritation at the difficulty of under-standing the ordinary language of the learned. The first two points are of little importance. As to the third, it is certainly true that modern scholars often meet with ambiguities and obscurities in reading Classical texts, and that some of the ambiguities arise out of the use of long compounds. But the texts were not written for us, and there is little to suggest that Sanskrit writers qualified to participate in academic discussion found any difficulty in following the language it was couched in: such a situation would indeed have been perverse. (The use of long compounds in creative literature (kāvyaṃ) is something of a separate issue: there, easy intelligibility might well be at odds with the desire to achieve some particular effect.) What is perhaps true is that such a style does not take kindly to textual corruption. A great burden of information may be carried by a single vowel or consonant, the alteration of which may give an entirely different twist to the meaning of a whole sentence. To this may be added the inadequacy of existing dictionaries for many kinds of Sanskrit texts, and the fact that modern scholarship has still a long way to go in reconstructing the cultural and intellectual presuppositions, the 'universe of discourse' implicit in Sanskrit literature.

Another striking feature of Classical Sanskrit is its wealth of synonyms. First (what is, of course, not quite the same thing), it has a huge vocabulary, a composite store of words from many sources, Aryan and non-Aryan. Secondly, there operates upon these words a tendency, no doubt normal to some extent in any learned language, to blur distinctions between words that to start with were close in meaning but not synonymous. One may compare the way writers of English will ring the changes on various series of words ('way, manner, fashion, mode', 'occupation, employment, pursuit') merely to avoid repeating the same word, not because some other is especially appropriate (the phenomenon of 'elegant variation'). Particularly significant is the way a hyponym (more specific term— 'innovation, development, transformation') will alternate with its superordinate (less specific term—'change') for the same reason, and not because some particular level of precision is being aimed at. The usage of words that are more distinct 'emotively' than 'cognitively' ('hide', 'conceal') may also be assimilated, and this may come about because the literary context (e.g. committee report as opposed to advertising copy) neutralises possible differences of emotional effect.

Poetry written within such a literary idiom does not necessarily seek to reverse these trends. As the literary tradition develops, poets moving towards a classical style build up a useful stock of uncoloured synonyms (*amor, ardor, flamma, venus*; *amour, fers, feu, flamme, soupirs, vœux*) which they can draw on at will, confident that long use has made the words innocuous. Classical poets do not need these extra words because they are technically less competent than poets that stick closely to natural speech: they merely prefer to reserve their energies for other ends. The tendency to treat language in this way, perhaps only faintly observable in the Western tradition, is of central importance in the poetry of Classical Sanskrit. The poet has quite enormous reserves of cognitively and emotively synonymous words to draw upon. What most especially swells these reserves is the possibility of a sort of 'componential' compounding; thus the word **rājan** 'king' may be replaced by an indefinite number of compounds meaning 'lord of men', 'guardian of the people', 'enjoyer of the earth', etc. (the extent to which *any* word with the appropriate sense could be used in helping to form such compounds was partly a question of style; naturally, creative literature in general went further than academic prose, and thorough exploitation of the device was considered a particular characteristic of the Gauḍa (Eastern) poetic style). Because of these resources it was possible to write Sanskrit verse in metres of great complexity and beauty.

Furthermore, because of the long history of the language and the varied sources from which it drew its vocabulary, many Sanskrit words have a number of quite distinct meanings; and this feature, too, is much augmented by compounding (e.g. because it literally means 'twice-born', the word **dvijaḥ** can signify 'brahmin', 'bird' or 'tooth'). Thus punning is made possible on a scale inconceivable in a natural language—on far too large a scale, in fact, to be effective *per se* for any humorous purpose. Instead sustained paronomasia is used in certain literary styles for perfectly serious literary purposes— not (at least in good writers) for empty display or mere playfulness, but to achieve a density of expression that could be attained in no other way: the same words may convey simultaneously the imagery of an idea and the contrasting imagery of a metaphor or simile which comments upon that idea. In this as in other respects it is the peculiar merits of Sanskrit poetry which make it least translatable.

Using This Book

PROVIDED that the main features of Sanskrit phonology described in Chapter 1 are understood, it is not necessary to memorise the whole alphabet before proceeding to Chapter 2. The nāgarī script is complicated, and is best assimilated gradually; most learners need several weeks, even months, to read it with complete fluency. It would be possible to use this book without learning the nāgarī script at all (making use only of the transliterated versions of the exercises). This might suit some experienced linguists, anxious to gain a rapid impression of the langugage. But the ordinary student is advised against such a course. Transliteration has a distorting effect upon Sanskrit phonology, unless interpreted with a knowledge either of the nāgarī script or of phonetics. It is essential to have a sure grasp of the fact that letters distinguished from each other only by small diacritic marks represent totally independent items in the Sanskrit sound system and that **dh**, for instance, is no less a single phoneme than **d**.

Sanskrit is a language with a very different surface structure from that of English. Each chapter deals with a number of its more prominent morphological and syntactical features. The focus of attention should always be firmly upon the Sanskrit structure and not upon the English by which it is represented. Thus in Chapter 4 there should be no danger of an attempt to translate 'literally' into Sanskrit a sentence like 'it was he who made this garden', since neither the relative pronoun nor a verb 'to be' has been introduced at this stage. Such a sentence should be dealt with in the light of what is said in Chapter 4 on the use of the particle **eva**.

Those who do not find committing paradigms to memory an impossible burden would be well advised to learn the grammar for each chapter before tackling the exercises; time spent on this will be saved in doing the exercises themselves. Some may wish to go further, and to learn each special vocabulary by heart. If this is not done, it is at least worth reading slowly through the vocabulary (preferably aloud) before starting the exercises. As the vocabularies grow longer, it will become increasingly important to handle Sanskrit alphabetical order: a note on this is given at the beginning of the general Sanskrit–English vocabulary; the complications caused by the position of anusvāra should not give rise to much difficulty in the (comparatively short) special vocabularies.

It is assumed that the aim of anyone using this book is to acquire the ability to read original Sanskrit texts. The sentences contained in Exercise 6 onwards are all taken from Sanskrit authors. They should therefore be treated as interesting objects of study rather than as hurdles to be overcome. The test of your progress is not whether you have always achieved versions identical with those found in the keys (this is hardly possible) but whether you have fully understood how the key corresponds to the exercise.

A particular difficulty arises over the Sanskrit–English sentences. Deriving from real utterances, they will sometimes seem quirky or obscure when divorced from their literary context. The special vocabularies are designed to reduce this difficulty as much as possible. There is also the question of the more general context, i.e. the cultural background, of the material. In this connection all students of Sanskrit should be aware of the existence of Professor A. L. Basham's scholarly and yet highly readable account of ancient Indian civilisation, *The Wonder That Was India* (Sidgwick and Jackson, hardback; Fontana, paperback).

Those who do not learn languages easily may prefer to work through the book once using both parts of each exercise for translation out of Sanskrit only. Progress could then be consolidated by working through all the English–Sanskrit sentences a second time in the normal way.

Careful attention should be paid to the examples given in the text of each chapter, since these represent the types of sentence to be encountered in the exercises. Because each example is followed immediately by a translation, it has not seemed necessary to exclude an occasional form which anticipates the grammar of a later chapter (as well as grammatical forms dealt with later in the same chapter). These forms are explained in the general vocabulary, where there will also be found any words not listed in the special vocabulary of the exercises.

For clearness and convenience a topic is usually treated as a whole in a particular chapter, even if one or two aspects of it are not applicable until later in the book. Observations which may be passed over rapidly and returned to later are enclosed in square brackets.

Many Sanskrit words have a number of different meanings. The vocabularies in this book are not intended as a dictionary, and generally speaking therefore only meanings relevant to the material used in the book are given either in the special or in the general vocabulary.

Many Sanskrit words are synonymous with several others, at least in certain of their meanings. Such synonyms have often been differentiated by near-synonyms in English. The object of this is merely to guide towards a correct choice of Sanskrit word in a particular sentence (correct in the sense of corresponding to the original). There need be no head-scratching over the difference in meaning between a word translated as 'employ' and a word translated as 'engage': there is none of any consequence.

Conversely, when a Sanskrit word already met with occurs again in a related but slightly different sense, it is not put a second time into the special vocabulary but will be found listed with both meanings in the general vocabulary.

Certain typographical devices have been used in English versions of Sanskrit sentences. These should give no trouble if the following principle is borne in mind: rounded brackets (parentheses) enclose matter not directly represented in the Sanskrit; square brackets enclose what is not wanted in the

English version. A colon implies that what follows is a freer version of what precedes. Thus a sentence is often interrupted by a literally translated phrase in square brackets and with a colon, followed immediately by a more idiomatic or more intelligible rendering of the same phrase. Square brackets are also used in conjunction with an oblique stroke to provide an alternative interpretation of the Sanskrit: e.g. 'he [/she] is going'. Rounded brackets with an oblique stroke suggest an alternative phrasing: e.g. 'he said "that is so" (/that this was so)'.

Students with linguistic aptitude who are particularly impatient to grapple with a continuous text may like to experiment with something simple on their own at any point after Chapter 8. Advice on dictionaries, etc. is given on pp. 277–9. It would be advisable to glance ahead at the main features described in the later chapters, and in particular (if a narrative text is chosen) at the paradigms of the imperfect and perfect tenses.

Chapter 1

BEFORE the introduction of printing into India in the eighteenth century, the script in which Sanskrit was written and taught varied from place to place in India, and was the same, or almost the same, as that used in writing the local vernacular language. Well-travelled paṇḍits might understand many forms of the alphabet, but the basis of Sanskrit tradition lay in recitation and oral communication. The widespread dissemination of printed Sanskrit texts, however, encouraged the predominance of one form of writing, the nāgarī (or devanāgarī) script of central India, in which the modern languages Hindī and Marāṭhī are also written. Today even the most traditionally minded paṇḍits are familiar with it, and Sanskrit publications of more than local interest are printed in no other script.

All the Indian scripts, however much elaborated in their forms, are developments over the course of centuries from a single source. This was the brāhmī script, written from left to right, first known to us from the inscriptions of the emperor Aśoka (third century BC). Its origin is unknown. Many suppose it to be an adaptation of the Semitic alphabet, but by the time of the Aśokan inscriptions the adaptation is already too thorough for positive identification. It reflects with considerable accuracy the phonetic structure of the Indo-Aryan languages. All later Indian scripts inherit its unusual graphic system; they differ from it and from each other solely as to the shapes into which the individual letters have evolved.

Your best way to learn the sounds of Sanskrit is therefore to learn to write the nāgarī script.[1] In this chapter the sounds and the letters are presented side by side. You may think it worth taking the trouble to learn to write Sanskrit well, even if your usual English handwriting is a scrawl: you will never need to cover page after page in a tearing hurry, and in what you do write you can take pleasure in forming the characters slowly and with control. You should use black ink and a pen with a nib capable of producing thick and thin strokes. The most convenient method is to acquire one of the inexpensive fountain-pens to which a variety of nibs can be fitted. For preliminary practice, an ordinary pencil can be sharpened to a broad, flat point.

Because of the way in which an Indian reed pen is cut, the thick and thin strokes lie in the reverse direction to our own Italic script: that is, the thick strokes run from bottom left to top right and the thin strokes from top left to bottom right: /
\. Left-handed writers are thus at less of a disadvantage than in writing the Italic script; and right-handed writers will need to hold the pen at a different angle from usual in their hand and may find it helpful to use a nib with a moderately oblique

[1] It may be wondered why several references are made in this chapter to the values of the nāgarī letters as used for modern Hindī. The point is that basically the values are the same for both languages: spelling of the Indian vernaculars has never been allowed to ossify in the same way as that of Italian and Greek, in which words with a classical spelling (*voce, hugieia*) are given a quite unclassical pronunciation. Thus Sanskrit **karma** 'deed' changed to Prākrit **kamma** and Medieval Hindī **kāma**. These distinctions are reflected in the spelling. Only the latest change, to modern **kām** with final 'a mute', remains unrecorded, and this can be justified both because final a still has a vestigial, 'latent' existence, like French '*e muet*', and because of the extreme inconvenience within the Indian system of writing of marking this particular change. That region which has most altered the traditional sound values of the alphabet, Bengal, shows an exactly parallel deviation in the way its paṇḍits (of the older school) actually pronounce Sanskrit itself. Another reason for mentioning certain features of modern pronunciation is that these may otherwise puzzle the learner when he hears Sanskrit spoken by an Indian.

cut of the sort normally intended for the left-handed. Right-handed and left-handed writers will make each stroke from opposite ends. (In this and what follows it should be emphasised that what is being taught is not traditional Indian calligraphy—for which see in particular H. M. Lambert's *Introduction to the Devanagari Script* (London, 1953)—but its adaptation in one of various possible ways to the modern fountain-pen.) The right-handed writer should hold the pen along the line of the thick stroke and pointing to the bottom left; the left-handed should also hold it along the line of the thick stroke but pointing to the top right. In as many of the strokes as possible the pen should be drawn towards you—up towards the right for the right-handed, down towards the left for the left-handed.

In addition to their distinctive element, most letters in the nāgarī script contain a vertical and a horizontal stroke. The right-handed writer will draw the vertical stroke upwards and the horizontal stroke to the right. The left-handed will draw the vertical stroke downwards and the horizontal stroke to the left. In each letter the distinctive element should be written first.

This is how a right-handed writer might form the sign त ta:

| 1 Distinctive element | 2 Vertical stroke | 3 Horizontal stroke |

This is how a left-handed writer might form the same sign:

This sign is an illustration of the basic principle of the script, which is halfway in character between an alphabet and a very regular syllabary. The signs for the consonants such as t do not stand for themselves alone but possess an inherent short **a** (which is by far the commonest of all Sanskrit vowel sounds). If you wish to represent the consonant **t** without a following **a**, you must add a special cancellation stroke (called a **virāma**) below the letter: त् **t**. Thus the word **tat** meaning 'it' or 'that' is written तत्.

Vowels

To represent vowel sounds other than **a** various marks are added above, below or on either side of the basic consonant sign. There are thirteen vowels in Sanskrit, of which one (ḷ) occurs only in one verb and another (ṝ) is not very frequent. They are given below as written after the consonant **t**. As additional guides to pronunciation, an appropriate IPA symbol is given in square brackets and the nearest equivalent sounds in French and English are added. The French sounds are seldom more inaccurate than the English, and often very much nearer the mark.

SIMPLE VOWELS (LONG AND SHORT)

		English 'equivalent'	French 'equivalent'
त **ta**	[ə]	b*u*t	—
ता **tā**	[a:]	f*a*ther	t*ar*d
ति **ti**	[i]	f*i*t	*i*ci
ती **tī**	[i:]	f*ee*	p*i*re
तु **tu**	[u]	p*u*t	t*ou*t
तू **tū**	[u:]	b*oo*	c*our*t

SYLLABIC LIQUIDS

तृ **tṛ**	[r]	American 'p*ur*dy' (but nowadays pronounced as in English 'p*re*tty')

तॄ t̄ऱ [r:] —(the preceding sound lengthened)—

तॢ tḷ [l] table   table

DIPHTHONGS

ते te (i.e. tē)	[e:]	made (esp. Welsh)	été (but longer)
तै tai	[ai]	bite	travail
तो to (i.e. tō)	[o:]	rope (esp. Welsh)	fausse
तौ tau	[au]	found	caoutchouc

Notes on the vowel sounds[1]

To the British in India, the short **a** sounded like the English vowel sound in the received pronunciation of 'but' and 'duck'—hence spellings such as 'pundit', 'suttee', 'Punjab' (**paṇḍit, satī, Pañjāb**). This English sound may be taken as a reasonable guide to the pronunciation, although the Indian sound is somewhat less open. The corresponding long vowel **ā** is completely open, and thus these two vowels are distinguished not merely in length but also in quality (for standard Western Hindi **a** is half-open, central, unrounded; **ā** is open, forward of central, unrounded). This distinction of quality held good over 2000 years ago and was known to Pāṇini.[2] On the other hand, the long vowels **ī, ū** and **r̄** differ from the corresponding short vowels only in being held longer. This distinction of pure length has been almost lost in modern

[1] The sounds of Sanskrit are known to us with considerable accuracy. But difficulties in mastering the less familiar sounds need cause no great distress. Many western Sanskritists treat Sanskrit entirely as a written language, and when forced to pronounce a few words of it do so without distinguishing, for example, between retroflex and dental, or between aspirates and non-aspirates. How much trouble to take is thus a matter of personal choice, although the tendency nowadays is to pay more attention to such matters.

[2] The final aphorism of his whole grammar is the shortest grammatical rule in the world: simply अ अ a a—i.e. '/a/ → [ə]', 'The sound that (for convenience of grammatical statement) we have treated as differing from /ā/ only in length is, in fact, to be realised as [ə]'.

Hindi, and uneducated people regularly confuse i with ī and
u with ū in their spelling. All three syllabic liquids, ṛ, ṝ and
ḷ, vanished long ago from popular speech, and the memory of
how to pronounce them correctly has faded. Syllabic ḷ occurs
only in some forms of the verb kḷp and may be ignored.
Paṇḍits nowadays tend to pronounce ṛ as if it were ri and ṝ
even more improbably as rī. (Hence the anglicised spelling
Rigveda for ṛgveda.) For convenience you may do the same.
But it is by no means impossible to make [r] a syllable in its
own right: American speakers do so in some pronunciations
of 'pretty' ('pṛdy'), and upper- and middle-class Englishmen
in some pronunciations of 'interesting' ('íntṛsting').[1]

Of the four diphthongs, e and o are known as 'short'
diphthongs, and ai and au as corresponding 'long' diphthongs.
Historically this is justified: while e and o are descended from
normal Indo-European diphthongs, ai and au correspond to
diphthongs of which the prior element was long (as in Greek
ēi, ōi, ēu, etc.). But in Sanskrit at an early stage the long diphthongs shortened to ordinary diphthongs, and the ordinary
diphthongs narrowed into simple vowel sounds. It is extremely
important to remember, however, not only that e and o
despite their pronunciation remain classified as diphthongs
(for reasons that will be apparent when you learn the rules
of sandhi) but also that phonetically and metrically e and o
are not short but *long* vowels. The only reason they are not
usually transliterated as ē and ō is that since short ĕ and ŏ do
not occur at all in Sanskrit (because Indo-European e, o and a
all converge into Sanskrit a) the distinction does not have to
be marked. The process of diphthong narrowing has continued, and modern Indian speakers pronounce ai and au as

---

[1] This example is particularly close, in that ancient phoneticians
analysed syllabic ṛ as consisting of the consonant r with a vocalic
'trace element' before and after it—like the two vestigial 'e's' in
'int'r'sting'. Phonemically, however, ṛ is a short vowel like any other:
a word such as kṛ-ta 'done' is composed of two equally short (or
'light') syllables, e.g. for purposes of verse scansion.

very pinched, closer sounds (cf. the ultra-genteel pronunciation of English 'nice'), some even as monophthongs, so that it is often rather difficult to distinguish ai from e and au from o.

Notes on the vowel signs

Perhaps the most striking is the sign for short i—ि—which is written before the consonant sign, although the vowel sound itself follows the consonant. Originally, in fact, the sign consisted only of the curl at the top, but to distinguish it more clearly from other signs the tail was lengthened into a vertical line. If you are like most Sanskritists, you will often find at first that you have written a consonant sign without noticing that the next vowel is an i, for which a space should have been left.

Note that the four diphthong signs are constructed on a regular principle. The sign for e ॔ is doubled to make ॓ ai; from these o and au respectively are distinguished by the addition of the vertical bar ा, which on its own is used to make ā. Usually the signs are placed above the bar, but very occasionally you may find them above the consonant sign itself, thus: तॊ to and तॆा tau. This does have the advantage of distinguishing तॊ to more clearly from ती tī. Even so, it should normally be quite possible to tell them apart: you may occasionally come across bad printing in which it is difficult. In your own writing you should form the two differently: the ī is a single stroke, the vertical line being once again a prolonged tail. On the other hand, o is made up of two strokes, which should be written separately. First draw the vertical bar ा (upwards if right-handed, downwards if left-handed); then draw the hook ॆ (to the right if right-handed, to the left if left-handed).

Initial vowel signs

Whenever a vowel is preceded by a consonant, the vowel sign

is attached to the consonant, as described above. This applies not only within a single word but also when one word begins with a vowel and the preceding word ends in a consonant. For this reason, in printing Sanskrit in nāgarī (or in any other Indian script), it is not always possible to make a space between one word and the next, and it needs practice to spot where one word ends and the next begins. Even so, a vowel obviously cannot be combined with a consonant (a) when it begins a sentence, (b) when it is itself preceded by another vowel—in Sanskrit this is comparatively rare—and (c) when a word beginning with a vowel is written on its own, as in a dictionary entry.

For use in these circumstances there is a second set of vowel signs—initial (or more accurately 'free-standing') signs. They are:

अ or ऋ a, आ or ऋा ā; इ i, ई ī; उ u, ऊ ū; ऋ r̥, ॠ r̥̄, ऌ l̥;
ए e; ऐ ai; ओ or ऋो o; औ or ऋौ au

Examples for practice एति eti 'he goes'; अतीत atīta 'past'; तितउ titaü 'sieve'.

There are two signs in Sanskrit that have no 'free-standing' form because they represent modifications of vowel sounds, one by nasalisation, the other by adding aspiration.

Anusvāra

This is written as a dot at the top right of the syllable (represented in transliteration by ṃ). It signifies that the vowel sound is nasalised, probably rather in the way that some French vowel sounds are nasalised—although the ancient descriptions are not absolutely clear. Thus तों toṃ and तं taṃ are to be pronounced very roughly as the French *ton* and *teint* respectively.

Examples for practice तं taṃ 'him'; तां tāṃ 'her'; तितउं

titaūṃ 'sieve (*accusative case*)'; अंत **aṃta** less correct spelling of **anta** 'end'.[1]

Visarga

This is written as two dots after the syllable (represented in transliteration by ḥ). Its pronunciation presents more difficulty to a European than that of anusvāra. In theory it is a pure voiceless aspiration like an English 'h', but added after the vowel sound, whereas of course the English aspirate always precedes a vowel. To achieve this you might start by pronouncing it as the *ch* in German *ich*, or even Scottish *loch*, and then refine away the 'rasping' element until only a pure breathing is left. Alternatively, you may, like many paṇḍits, introduce a fainter echo of the preceding vowel sound: e.g. त: **taḥ** as 'tah^a', ती: **tīḥ** as 'tīh^i' (which is like English 'tee-hee' only if you put all the stress on the *first* syllable of the latter).

Examples for practice तत: **tataḥ** 'thereupon'; ता: **tāḥ** 'those women'; तै: **taiḥ** 'by them'; आ: **āḥ** 'ah!'.

Consonants

All the vowel sounds of Sanskrit have now been mentioned. Their number is less than the number of vowel sounds in English. Of consonants, on the other hand, Sanskrit has a far greater number than English. This is principally due to the proliferation of plosive consonants (or 'stops'). These the grammarians grouped into five series according to their place of articulation, each series comprising four stops together with the related nasal consonant:

---

[1] When these less correct (or at any rate less precise) spellings are encountered, they should not affect pronunciation: पंडित **paṃdita** is still to be pronounced पण्डित **paṇḍita**. For a fuller discussion of the ancient value of the anusvāra, see W. S. Allen's *Phonetics in Ancient India*, pp. 40–6.

STOPS AND NASALS

	Voiceless		*Voiced*		
	Unaspirated	*Aspirate*	*Unaspirated*	*Aspirate*	*Nasal*
Velar	क ka	ख kha	ग ga	घ gha	ङ ṅa
Palatal	च ca	छ cha	ज ja	झ jha	ञ ña
Retroflex	ट ṭa	ठ ṭha	ड ḍa	ढ ḍha	ण ṇa
Dental	त ta	थ tha	द da	ध dha	न na
Labial	प pa	फ pha	ब ba	भ bha	म ma

Unaspirated voiceless stops k, c, ṭ, t, p

These really are unaspirated, unlike their English equivalents.
It is often not realised that one of the ways in which, for
instance, the English word 'key' differs from the French *qui*
is that the English *k* is followed by an aspirate, or '*h*-sound'
(which, however, disappears when the *k* is preceded by an *s*,
as in 'skill'). Unless you speak a language such as French in
which the voiceless stops are never aspirated, you may have
difficulty in eliminating this aspiration from your pronunciation.

क **k** as *k* in 'kill'—better, as *c* in French *coup*
च **c** as *ch* in 'chill'—better, as *c* in Italian *voce*
प **p** as *p* in 'pill'—better, as *p* in French *pique*

Retroflex[1] *and dental*

Sanskrit distinguishes two types of *t*, *d*, etc. The dental series

---

[1] A frequent synonym of 'retroflex' is 'cerebral'. This is an unfor-
tunate translation of the Sanskrit term **mūrdhanya** 'made in the
head', itself unusually imprecise. The word 'cerebral' is still in
common use among Sanskritists, but since retroflexion as a phonetic
phenomenon is by no means confined to Sanskrit, I have thought it
wiser to adopt the more accurate term preferred by phoneticians as
being more likely to prevail in the end.

is the type found in European languages other than English. A French *t* or *d* is made by striking the edge of the teeth with the tip of the tongue. (In other words, the place of articulation is the same as for the English *th* in 'thin'.) An English *t* or *d* is made with the tongue drawn a little further back, so that the tip strikes against the front of the palate or the teeth-ridge, instead of against the teeth. This English *t* seems to Indians to be their retroflex ṭ, rather than a dental t—and when transcribing English words into the nāgarī script they employ retroflex consonants instead of dentals: e.g. the English word 'tip' would be written टिप् ṭip. However, the true Indian retroflex consonant is made rather by curling the tongue up and striking the palate (perhaps at a point further back) with the very tip or even the underside of the tongue.

ट ṭ as *t* in English 'try'
त t as the first *t* in French 'tout'

Examples for practice तट: taṭaḥ 'bank'; पीत pīta 'drunk'; पचति pacati 'he cooks'; कूप: kūpaḥ 'a well'.

Voiceless aspirates kh, ch, ṭh, th, ph

These are much *more* strongly aspirated than the English voiceless stops *k*, *t*, etc., which fall between the two stools. However, it is easier to add aspiration than to take it away: pronounce 'up-heaval' first in two distinct parts and then more rapidly, trying to run the *p* on to the following syllable. It should be plainly understood that all these sounds are merely aspirated forms of those in the preceding column: ph is NOT as in 'physic', th NOT as in 'thin', kh NOT as *ch* in Scottish 'loch'.

Examples for practice अथ atha 'hereupon'; पीठं pīṭham 'stool'; फटा phaṭā 'serpent's hood'; खात khāta 'dug up'; क्षोटित choṭita 'torn off'.

Unaspirated voiced stops g, j, ḍ, d, b

This is the simplest series. The corresponding English letters will serve as a guide. The only problem is in preserving the distinction described above between retroflex ḍ and dental d.

Examples for practice गज: gajaḥ 'elephant'; जड jaḍa 'numb'; बीजं bījam 'seed'; ददाति dadāti 'he gives'.

Voiced aspirates gh, jh, ḍh, dh, bh

These are all equally troublesome. They are, of course, aspirated forms of the preceding series. The difficulty is that, since the letters are voiced, the aspiration must be a voiced aspiration. The last letter of the Sanskrit alphabet is ह ha, the Sanskrit *h*, which is also voiced. (The only voiceless *h* in Sanskrit is the rather special visarga, described above.) The key to the pronunciation of all these letters is learning to pronounce a voiced *h* instead of the voiceless English *h*[1] (it is true that some English speakers make voiced *h* a rather infrequent allophone of *h*—e.g. in the word 'in*h*erent').

Voiced sounds are those made with a vibration of the vocal cords. Some consonants are voiced, others voiceless. All vowels are voiced, unless you whisper them. An extremely easy way to tell whether a sound is voiced or not is to put your hands firmly over your ears: start by making a prolonged *sss* sound, which is voiceless; then make a *zzz* sound, which is voiced, and you will hear the vibration of the vocal cords very plainly as a droning in your ears. Lengthen the ordinary English *h* into a prolonged breathing and it will be quite

---

[1] I believe this to be so, from having taught myself in this way before I had ever heard a voiced aspirate pronounced correctly. On the other hand, in India ह ha itself is no longer a voiced sound, and consequently an Englishman I met there, who had lived in the country for several years, had difficulty when asked in producing a plain voiced *h* sound, even though he could pronounce the voiced aspirate stops perfectly.

obviously voiceless. The task now is to modify this breathing until you can hear that it is accompanied by the droning. The sound you are aiming at is similar to the sound children sometimes use when they want to make someone jump. The voiced **h**, once produced, can easily be combined with **g, j** etc., and practice will soon smooth the sound down until you do not seem to be trying to give your listeners a series of heart-attacks.

Examples for practice आघात: **āghātaḥ** 'blow'; झटिति **jhaṭiti** 'at once'; बाढं **bāḍham** 'certainly'; धातु **dhātu** 'element'; बोधति **bodhati** 'he awakes'; भाग: **bhāgaḥ** 'portion'; बिभेद **bibheda** 'he split'.

Nasals ṅ, ñ, ṇ, n, m

Velar **ṅ** and palatal **ñ** are used almost entirely with stops of their own class, e.g. अङ्गं **aṅgam** 'limb'; पञ्च **pañca** 'five'. **Aṅga** sounds rather like English 'anger'—or 'hunger' without the *h*; **pañca** is rather like 'puncher'. Between **ṇ** and **n** a distinction of retroflex and dental is regularly made by paṇḍits, although in Hindī this distinction—unlike that between retroflex and dental *stops*—has been lost, except as a (learned) spelling pronunciation.

Examples for practice तृणं **tṛṇam** 'grass'; जन: **janaḥ** 'people'; मति **mati** 'thought'.

A note on handwriting

In practising the nāgarī letters, the most important general principle for the acquisition of good handwriting is to give the letters 'body' by keeping the distinctive portion of each full and uncramped. Too often, beginners produce a few tiny curls and loops in an acreage of white. The secret is to divide the vertical bar not into two parts but into three, so that the distinctive portion of letters such as ज and त occupy at least the lower two-thirds, and letters such as प, म and ध at least the upper two-thirds:

Semi-vowels

Four sounds are classified as semi-vowels. They and the vowels associated with them are given places in four of the five series:

palatal	य ya	corresponding to the vowels	i ī
retroflex	र ra	,,	ṛ ṝ
dental	ऌ la	,,	ḷ
labial	व va	,,	u ū

y is often pronounced, nowadays at least, more lightly and unobtrusively than the English *y* in 'yes'. **r** is usually a tapped sound similar to an Italian *r*. It was described as being alveolar (against the arch of the gums) rather than fully retroflex. (However, for convenience of grammatical statement, all members of the 'retroflex' group are treated as truly retroflex.) Speakers of Southern or BBC English should be careful always to give **r** its full value, and should guard against letting it colour their pronunciation of a preceding vowel: distinguish **karma** 'deed', which approximately rhymes with an American's pronunciation of 'firmer', from **kāma** 'desire', which approximately rhymes with an Englishman's 'farmer'. **l** is dental, and so even more like a French than an English *l*. It does not have the 'dark' quality which in varying degrees an English *l* may have. In origin, **v** was a true labial, i.e. a bilabial like the English *w*, and it would be just as appropriate to transliterate it by **w** as by **v**. In most of India it is pronounced now as a labio-dental, that is to say with the upper teeth and the lower lips, and this seems to have been so from an early period. The best method is to try to produce a '*w* sound' but using the upper teeth instead of the upper lip. If you employ a full-blooded labio-dental fricative like the English *v*, it will sound odd when **v** is combined with another consonant, e.g. in the word **svastika**.

In combination with र **r**, the signs for **u** and **ū** are written in a rather different form, beside instead of below the consonant:

रु **ru** रू **rū**: e.g. रूपं **rūpam** 'form'

The (rare) combination of consonant र **r** with vocalic ऋ **ṛ** is made with the aid of the conjunct form of र **r** described below:

र्ऋं **rṛ**: e.g. निर्ऋण **nir-ṛṇa** 'debtless'

Examples for practice छाया **chāyā** 'shade'; रीति **rīti** 'style'; लय: **layaḥ** 'dissolution'; वीर: **vīraḥ** 'hero'.

Sibilants

Three of the five series include voiceless sibilants:

palatal	श	**śa**
retroflex	ष	**ṣa**
dental	स	**sa**

Dental **s** is like an English *s*. The other two sibilants are confounded in modern popular pronunciation: they are similar to an English *sh* as in 'ship'. You may like to make your own distinction between the two on the basis that one is palatal and the other retroflex.

Note carefully that there is no voiced sibilant, i.e. no *z* of any kind, in Sanskrit: **s** is *always* to be pronounced as the *ss* in 'hiss' (so, for instance, in **tasya** 'of him'), *never* as the *s* in 'his'.

Examples for practice आशा **āśā** 'hope'; दोष: **doṣaḥ** 'fault'; रस: **rasaḥ** 'flavour'.

Voiced h

ह ha

As mentioned above, **h** was in classical times a voiced aspirate sound. Nowadays, however, it has lost its voicing and corresponds to an English *h*, although the other voiced aspirates (the five stops) are a fully preserved feature of most modern Indo-Aryan languages. The reason for the loss of voicing in this one case is no doubt connected with the fact that this sound, unlike the other five, is not in phonemic contrast with voiceless and other counterparts (**dh** has to be distinguished from **th** and also from **ḍ**, and so on). The voiceless visarga appears only at the end of a syllable, exactly where **h** does not, and at any rate visarga disappeared completely from Middle Indo-Aryan onwards.

The vowels **ṛ** and **ṝ** are usually written within rather than below this consonant: ह्ऋ **hṛ**, ह्ॠ **hṝ**.

Examples for practice हत **hata** 'killed'; इह **iha** 'here'; बाहु **bāhu** 'forearm'; हृत **hṛta** 'taken'.

Conjunct consonants

In the foregoing description of the alphabet, words in which one consonant immediately follows another have been avoided as far as possible. The only two printed in nāgarī were अङ्गं **aṅgam** and पञ्च **pañca**. The use of the virāma stroke to cancel the inherent **a** of ङ **ṅa** and ञ **ña** is, however, a device contrary to the principles of the script, to be used only in the direst emergencies.[1]

---

[1] In the representation of the early Middle Indo-Aryan dialects for which the brāhmī script is often thought originally to have been designed, the problem of consonant clusters was not particularly acute. The phonology of the dialects limited these to doublings and combinations with class nasals, both of which might be dealt with by

The proper way to represent clusters of two or more consonants (even when the cluster is divided between two words) is to combine them into a single sign whose constituent elements are more or less easily discernible. In this way **aṅgam** and **pañca** should have been represented by अङ्गं and पञ्च. The general principles for combining consonants are given below.

Those consonants from which a vertical bar can easily be separated lose this bar as the initial consonant of the group, and conjoin horizontally:

ग्घ = ग्घ ġgha; घ्य = घ्य ghya; तस्य = तस्य tsya; न्म = न्म nma

Where (*a*) the vertical bar does not exist or cannot easily be detached, or (*b*) the distinctive portion of the following consonant does not provide a convenient point of anchorage, the letters are conjoined vertically, the initial consonant being on top. In this case the letters are reduced in size to preserve symmetry:

(*a*) ङ्ग = ङ्ग ṅga; द्ग = द्ग dga; ट्ठ = ट्ठ ṭṭha; ह्ल = ह्ल hla; क्ल = क्ल kla

(*b*) ञ्च = ञ्च ñca; घ्न = घ्न ghna; त्न = त्न tna; प्त = प्त pta; ष्ट = ष्ट ṣṭa

Minor modifications

A straight line is substituted for the distinctive portion of त **ta** and the loop of क **ka** in some frequent combinations:

त्त = त्त **tta**; क्त = क्त **kta**; (for **tra** and **kra** see below)

special means. The writing of Hindī, however, which has borrowed many words direct from Sanskrit as well as from foreign sources, demands an equally wide range of conjuncts—and this poses a considerable problem in the construction of Hindī typewriters, soluble only with some sacrifice of typographical elegance.

For convenience, स may be substituted for श śa in forming various combinations:

श्च = श्च śca; श्ल = श्ल śla; श्+उ = शु or शु śu

The letter य ya, although frequently the second member of a conjunct, is never written below another. Instead, an open form च or ृ is used:

क्य = क्य kya; ट्य = ट्य ṭya; ड्य = ड्य ḍya

(There is a similar open form for म ma: e.g. ण्म ṇma; द्म dma.)

Combinations with र ra

The forms रु ru and रू rū have been noted above. The isolate form र ra is never used in consonant combinations. As the initial member of a cluster, a semi-circle ॔ is substituted and placed at the extreme top right of the syllable:

र्त = र्त rta; र्य = र्य rya; र्खीं = खीं rkhīṃ

At the middle or end of a cluster, a short diagonal ॒ is substituted:

प्र = प्र pra; त्र = त्र tra; क्र = क्र or क्र kra; श्र्य = श्र्य śrya

The combinations kṣa and jña

Two signs representing conjunct consonants cannot be resolved into constituent parts.

क्ष or क्ष kṣa is the equivalent of the roman x—e.g. लक्ष्मी Lakṣmī, the goddess of prosperity, occasionally transliterated as 'Laxmi'. In some parts of India क्ष kṣa is pronounced as kkha or ccha.

ज्ञ jña: the pronunciation of this varies widely. In some places, for instance, it is like gya, in others dnya. The palatal series is derived from original velar sounds (cf. jan 'to be born' with Greek génos). The point about jñ is that it is a palatalisation so to speak en bloc of an original gn. Thus

jñā 'to know' is connected with Latin *co-gno-scere* and English 'know'. Perhaps the most appropriate of the modern pronunciations to adopt is therefore **gnya**, which (by adding *y* to *gn*) does crudely represent a palatalisation.

A list of conjunct consonants is given at the end of this chapter.

Doubling of consonants

Where the same consonant is written twice, it should be held longer in pronunciation. This happens in English, but usually only between words (or at least morphemes)—cf. the *s*+*s* sound in 'less soap', the *t*+*t* in 'hat-trick' or the *n*+*n* in 'greenness'. Doubled *aspirates* are not written as such: rather, the first appears in unaspirated form. Thus, while ग **g** doubles to ग्ग **gg**, घ **gh** doubles to ग्घ **ggh**.

Miscellaneous
Other signs

Manuscripts were written continuously, and neither paragraphs nor chapters needed to begin on a fresh line. The only marks of sentence punctuation are a single bar **।** (called a **danda**) and a double bar **॥**. Their primary function is to mark respectively the halfway point and the end of a stanza of verse. In prose passages the single bar is used to mark off sentences and the double bar usually to mark off paragraphs.

A small circle above the line indicates an abbreviation. Thus आघात: °तम् °तेन āghātaḥ -tam -tena should be read as āghātaḥ āghātam āghātena. Similarly, शकु° stands, in context, for the name Śakuntalā.

The avagraha ('separation') ऽ is nowadays restricted to marking the disappearance of an initial short **a**. Thus सो ऽवग्रह: **so ˌvagrahaḥ** 'that separation'.

Numerals

The numerical signs are very simple, since we owe our

modern zero-based system to India (by way of the Arabs). The shapes of the numerals vary with the shapes of the letters. For the nāgarī script they are:

१ २ ३ ४ ५ ६ ७ ८ ९ ०
1 2 3 4 5 6 7 8 9 0

१९८४ 1984   १०६६ 1066

The figure 2 after a word (sometimes found in books printed in India) implies that the word is to be repeated:

अहो२ aho aho 'oh, oh!'

Names of the letters

Letters are designated either by their own sound alone or, more explicitly, with the addition of the suffix kāra ('making'). The inherent short a is added to the consonants:

ई or ईकार ī or īkāra 'long *i*'; ग or गकार ga or gakāra 'the letter *g*'.

The letter र r, however, has a special name: रेफ repha 'tearing').

Transliteration

The letters and diacritic marks chosen to represent Sanskrit sounds in the roman alphabet are, of course, purely a matter of convention, but a convention by now so firmly established that it has not been deviated from here even to choose the one significant (but less common) variant, namely ç for ś, even though this would be less confusing than having three kinds of s and more immediately recognisable as a palatal letter.

This and the representation of anusvāra by ṁ instead of ṃ are probably the only two deviations still to be met with in specialist works. However, there are certain nineteenth-century devices still on occasion retained for the benefit of the general reader. They are:

ṛi, ṛī for ऋ ṛ, ॠ ṝ; ch for च c, and chh for छ ch; sh for ष ṣ (or even for श ś)

A further practice, now thoroughly discredited, whereby palatal letters are represented by italicised velars and retroflex by italicised dentals (e.g. *k*a for च ca, *dh*a for ढ ḍha), has unfortunately also to be mentioned, since it was followed in the *Sacred Books of the East* series and by Macdonell in his dictionary (though not in his grammar).

Prosody

Sanskrit verse is quantitative: it is based, that is to say, (as in Latin and Greek) on a regular arrangement of long and short syllables and not, as in English, of stressed and unstressed syllables. To distinguish long and short syllables more clearly from long and short *vowels* the former may be referred to as 'heavy' and 'light' (corresponding to the Sanskrit terms गुरु guru and लघु laghu).

A syllable is heavy if its vowel is long, or if its vowel, though short, is followed (even in another word) by two or more consonants. Thus पश्यामि ग्रामौ paśyāmi grāmau 'I see two villages' contains five heavy syllables (− − − − −).

A syllable is light if its vowel is short and not followed by more than one consonant. अथ पचति atha pacati 'next he cooks' contains five light syllables (∪ ∪ ∪ ∪ ∪). (थ th is, of course, only a single consonant.) Anusvāra and visarga are never followed by a vowel, and a syllable containing either of them is always heavy. ततः कूपं गच्छति tataḥ kūpaṃ gacchati 'then he goes to the well' scans ∪ − − − − ∪ ∪.

In ancient times Sanskrit was characterised by a tonic, or pitch, accent: one syllable in a word was pronounced with a higher musical pitch than the others. This is an Indo-European feature preserved also in ancient Greek, in which language parallel words usually have a corresponding accent (cf. श्रुतस् śrutás 'heard' with *klutós*). In Greek the accent, although retained, changed from one of musical pitch to one of stress. In Sanskrit the pitch accent, which was kept alive for some centuries after Pāṇini, finally disappeared and was replaced (as in Latin) by a regularly positioned stress accent bearing no relation at all to the original Indo-European accent. There are various graphical systems for representing the ancient accent in Vedic works, and it is only in certain methods of reciting the Vedas that any attempt is made nowadays to reproduce the pitch accent in pronunciation.

The position of the modern stress accent is much as in Latin, the principal difference being that it may go one syllable further back. Thus the stress falls on the penultimate syllable if that is heavy, failing which it falls on the antepenultimate if the latter is heavy. If both penultimate and antepenultimate are light, it falls on the fourth syllable from the end. Thus आघात: āghā́taḥ, आघातेन āghā́téna, शकुन्तला Śakúntalā, कामयते kā́mayate, गमयति gámayati.

However, there is a tendency for all heavy syllables to receive a heavier stress than any of the light syllables. The key to reciting Sanskrit is to dwell exaggeratedly on every heavy syllable (and, in particular, to draw out long vowels to a great length) while passing lightly and rapidly over all light syllables.

List of conjunct consonants

(For reference only: most of the combinations listed are easily recognisable.)

क्क k-ka, क्ख k-kha, क्च k-ca, क्ण k-ṇa, क्त k-ta, क्त्य k-t-ya, क्त्र k-t-ra, क्त्र्य k-t-r-ya, क्त्व k-t-va, क्न k-na, क्न्य k-n-ya, क्म k-ma, क्य k-ya, क्र or क्र k-ra, क्र्य or क्र्य k-r-ya, क्ल k-la, क्व k-va,

क्व्य k-v-ya, क्ष or क्ष k-ṣa, क्ष्म k-ṣ-ma, क्ष्य k-ṣ-ya, क्ष्व k-ṣ-va.—
ख्य kh-ya, ख्र kh-ra.—ग्य g-ya, ग्र g-ra, ग्र्य g-r-ya.—घ्न gh-na,
घ्न्य gh-n-ya, घ्म gh-ma, घ्य gh-ya, घ्र gh-ra.—ङ्क ṅ-ka, ङ्क्त ṅ-k-ta,
ङ्क्त्य ṅ-k-t-ya, ङ्क्य ṅ-k-ya, ङ्क्ष ṅ-k-ṣa, ङ्क्ष्व ṅ-k-ṣ-va, ङ्ख ṅ-kha,
ङ्ख्य ṅ-kh-ya, ङ्ग ṅ-ga, ङ्ग्य ṅ-g-ya, ङ्घ ṅ-gha, ङ्घ्य ṅ-gh-ya, ङ्घ्र ṅ-gh-ra,
ङ्ङ ṅ-ṅa, ङ्न ṅ-na, ङ्म ṅ-ma, ङ्य ṅ-ya.

च्च c-ca, च्छ c-cha, च्छ्र c-ch-ra, च्ञ c-ña, च्म c-ma, च्य c-ya.—
छ्य ch-ya, छ्र ch-ra.—ज्ज j-ja, ज्झ j-jha, ज्ञ or ज्ञ j-ña, ज्ञ्य j-ñ-ya,
ज्म j-ma, ज्य j-ya, ज्र j-ra, ज्व j-va.—ञ्च ñ-ca, ञ्च्म ñ-c-ma, ञ्च्य ñ-c-
ya, ञ्छ ñ-cha, ञ्ज ñ-ja, ञ्ज्य ñ-j-ya.

ट्ट ṭ-ṭa, ट्य ṭ-ya.—ठ्य ṭh-ya, ठ्र ṭh-ra.—ड्ग ḍ-ga, ड्ग्य ḍ-g-ya,
ड्घ ḍ-gha, ड्घ्र ḍ-gh-ra, ड्ढ ḍ-ḍha, ड्म ḍ-ma, ड्य ḍ-ya.—ढ्य ḍh-ya,
ढ्र ḍh-ra.—एट ṇ-ṭa, एठ ṇ-ṭha, एड ṇ-ḍa, एड्य ṇ-ḍ-ya, एड्र ṇ-ḍ-ra,
एड्र्य ṇ-ḍ-r-ya, एढ ṇḍha, ण्ण or एण ṇ-ṇa, एम ṇ-ma, एय ṇ-ya,
एव ṇ-va.

त्क t-ka, त्क्र t-k-ra, त्त t-ta, त्त्य t-t-ya, त्त्र t-t-ra, त्त्व t-t-va,
त्थ t-tha, त्न t-na, त्न्य t-n-ya, त्प t-pa, त्प्र t-p-ra, त्म t-ma,
त्म्य t-m-ya, त्य t-ya, त्र or त्र t-ra, त्र्य t-r-ya, त्स t-sa, त्स t-sa,
त्स्न t-s-na, त्स्न्य t-s-n-ya.—थ्य th-ya.—द्ग d-ga, द्ग्र d-g-ra, द्घ d-gha,
द्घ्र d-gh-ra, द्द d-da, द्द्य d-d-ya, द्ध d-dha, द्ध्य d-dh-ya, द्न d-na,
द्ब d-ba, द्भ d-bha, द्भ्य d-bh-ya, द्म d-ma, द्य d-ya, द्र d-ra,
द्र्य d-r-ya, द्व d-va, द्व्य d-v-ya.—ध्न dh-na, ध्न्य dh-n-ya, ध्म dh-ma,
ध्य dh-ya, ध्र dh-ra, ध्र्य dh-r-ya, ध्व dh-va.—न्त n-ta, न्त्य n-t-ya,
न्त्र n-t-ra, न्द n-da, न्द्र n-d-ra, न्ध n-dha, न्ध्र n-dh-ra, न्न n-na,
न्प n-pa, न्प्र n-p-ra, न्म n-ma, न्य n-ya, न्र n-ra, न्स n-sa.

प्त p-ta, प्त्य p-t-ya, प्न p-na, प्प p-pa, प्म p-ma, प्य p-ya, प्र p-ra,
प्ल p-la, प्व p-va, प्स p-sa, प्स्व p-s-va,—ब्घ b-gha, ब्ज b-ja,
ब्द b-da, ब्ध b-dha, ब्न b-na, ब्ब b-ba, ब्भ b-bha, ब्भ्य b-bh-ya,
ब्य b-ya, ब्र b-ra, ब्व b-va.—भ्न bh-na, भ्य bh-ya, भ्र bh-ra,
भ्व bh-va.—म्न m-na, म्प m-pa, म्प्र m-p-ra, म्ब m-ba, म्भ m-bha,
म्म m-ma, म्य m-ya, म्र m-ra, म्ल m-la, म्व m-va.

य्य y-ya, य्व y-va.—ल्क l-ka, ल्प l-pa, ल्म l-ma, ल्य l-ya, ल्ल l-la, ल्व l-va, ल्ह l-ha.—व्न v-na, व्य v-ya, व्र v-ra, व्व v-va.

श्च ś-ca, श्च्य ś-c-ya, श्न ś-na, श्य ś-ya, श्र ś-ra, श्र्य ś-r-ya, श्ल ś-la, श्व ś-va, श्व्य ś-v-ya, श्श ś-śa.—ष्ट ṣ-ṭa, ष्ट्य ṣ-ṭ-ya, ष्ट्र ṣ-ṭ-ra, ष्ट्र्य ṣ-ṭ-r-ya, ष्ट्व ṣ-ṭ-va, ष्ठ ṣ-ṭha, ष्ण ṣ-ṇa, ष्ण्य ṣ-ṇ-ya, ष्प ṣ-pa, ष्प्र ṣ-p-ra, ष्म ṣ-ma, ष्य ṣ-ya, ष्व ṣ-va.—स्क s-ka, स्ख s-kha, स्त s-ta, स्त्य s-t-ya, स्त्र s-t-ra, स्त्व s-t-va, स्थ s-tha, स्न s-na, स्न्य s-n-ya, स्प s-pa, स्फ s-pha, स्म s-ma, स्म्य s-m-ya, स्य s-ya, स्र s-ra, स्व s-va, स्स s-sa.

ह्ण h-ṇa, ह्न h-na, ह्म h-ma, ह्य h-ya, ह्र h-ra, ह्ल h-la, ह्व h-va.

Exercise 1a

(Answers will be found at the beginning of the key in nāgarī to the English–Sanskrit exercises.)

Transcribe into the nāgarī script the following words, some of which may be familiar to you already:

> mahārāja, Sītā, Rāvaṇa, maithuna, devanāgarī, himālaya, Śiva, Kālidāsa, guru, Aśoka, saṃsāra, upaniṣad, Śakuntalā, caitya, piṇḍa, manusmṛti, Viṣṇu, Kauṭilya, saṃskāra, anusvāra, śakti, Aśvaghoṣa, Vātsyāyana, vedānta, brahman, cakra, Candragupta, kāmasūtra, mantra, visargaḥ, nirvāṇa, dharmaśāstra, Bhāratavarṣa, yakṣa, vijñānavādin

Transcribe the following sentences, remembering that in the nāgarī script a word ending in a consonant (ḥ and ṃ apart) will be joined with the next word:

1 ko niyogo ɔnuṣṭhīyatām   2 evaṃ nv etat   3 anantara-karaṇīyam idānīm ājñāpayatv āryaḥ   4 atha kataraṃ punar ṛtuṃ samāśritya gāsyāmi   5 nanu prathamam evāryeṇājñaptam abhijñānaśakuntalaṃ nāmāpūrvaṃ nāṭakam abhinīyatām iti   6 ita itaḥ priyasakhyau

7 sakhi Śakuntale tvatto ∍pi tātakaṇvasyāśramavṛkṣa-
kāḥ priyā iti tarkayāmi yena navamālikākusumapari-
pelavāpi tvam eteṣv ālavālapūraṇeṣu niyuktā

Exercise 1b

(Answers will be found at the beginning of the key in roman
to the English–Sanskrit exercises.)

महायान । योग । महाभारत । रामायण । पुराण । जाति । भीम ।
पाणिनि । साधु । काशी । कैलास । विहार । मीमांसा । अग्नि ।
आत्मन् । पण्डित । क्षत्रिय । वैश्य । शूद्र । चण्डाल । ऋग्वेद । मुद्रा ।
कर्म । जगन्नाथ । गङ्गा । संस्कृत । प्राकृत । अर्धमागधी । सन्धि ।
अश्वमेध । बोधिसत्त्व । अवग्रह । इन्द्र । कृष्ण । अर्जुन । भगवद्गीता ।
पञ्चतन्त्र ॥

सख्यनुसूचे न केवलं तातस्य नियोगो ममापि सहोदरस्नेह एतेषु ।१।
उदकं लम्भिता एते ग्रीष्मकालकुसुमदायिन आश्रमवृक्षकाः ।२।
इदानीमतिक्रान्तकुसुमसमयानपि वृक्षकान्सिञ्चामः ।३।
अतिपिनद्धेनैतेन वल्कलेन प्रियंवदया दृढं पीडितास्मि ।४।
तच्छिथिलय तावदेनत् ।५।
अच तावत्पयोधरविस्तारायितारमात्मनो यौवनारम्भमुपालभस्व
।६।
सख्यावेष वातेरितपल्लवाङ्गुलीभिः किमपि व्याहरतीव मां चूतवृक्षकः
॥७॥

Chapter 2

Roots and verb classes

Descriptions of Sanskrit verbs are based upon the verbal root (Sanskrit धातु dhātu 'element'). Just as in English we might analyse the forms 'bear, bearing, borne, burden' as having a common element 'b-r', so the Indian grammarians described the forms भरति bharati, बभार babhāra, भ्रियते bhriyate, भृत bhṛta as being derived from the verbal root भृ bhṛ. The verbal roots are not words in their own right but convenient grammatical fictions.

Roots are divided into ten classes according to the way in which their present tense is formed. These ten classes are analogous to the four conjugations of Latin or French, but it is essential to grasp that this classification refers solely to the method of forming the present tense and its derivatives: it has no relevance in forming, for example, the aorist or the past participle.

Verbs of classes I, IV, VI and X differ from each other only in the relationship that their present stem bears to the root; in all these classes the present stem, once formed, is thereupon conjugated according to the 'thematic paradigm' (see grammatical section, p. 290). The remaining classes are called 'athematic' because the personal endings are added without a connecting or 'thematic' vowel. Thus भृ bhṛ, which is exceptional in that it may be conjugated *either* in class I *or* in class III (reduplicated class), in the latter instance adds the third person singular ending ति ti directly to the reduplicated stem बिभर् bibhar: बिभर्ति bibhar-ti 'he bears'; but to the class I present stem भर् bhar thematic **a** is added before the personal ending: भरति bhar-a-ti 'he bears'.

Vowel gradation: guṇa and vṛddhi

The present stem भर् bhar is derived from the root भृ bhṛ by a regular process of 'vowel gradation'. The three forms भृ bhṛ, भर् bhar and भार् bhār, found in भृत bhṛta (past participle) 'borne', भरति bharati (present) 'he bears' and बभार babhāra (perfect) 'he bore', exemplify a characteristic pattern of vowel alternation in Sanskrit words. The Indian grammarians described this phenomenon by saying that अर् ar and आर् ār were two successively strengthened grades of the vowel ऋ ṛ. To the first grade, अर् ar, they gave the name गुण guṇa; to the second, आर् ār, the name वृद्धि vṛddhi. The Sanskrit vowels are arranged in this analysis as follows:

normal grade	a, ā	i, ī	u, ū	ṛ	ḷ
guṇa	a, ā	e/ay	o/av	ar	al
vṛddhi	ā	ai/āy	au/āv	ār	āl

From the point of view of the comparative philologist, the truly 'normal' grade is the middle grade, guṇa, and failure to appreciate this landed Indian grammarians in some complications. If we compare the verbs स्रवति sravati 'flows', घोषति ghoṣati 'proclaims' and स्वपति svapati (or स्वपिति svapiti) 'sleeps' with their past participles सुत sruta, घुष्ट ghuṣṭa and सुप्त supta, we may detect the general principle that the formation of the past participle involves elimination of the element a—srav/sru, ghoṣ/ghuṣ, svap/sup (historically **e** and **o** may be taken to represent **ay** and **av**, and

y, r, l, v to represent consonantal alternants of the vowels **i, r̥, l̥, u**). If, however, we take the reduced form as shown in the past participle as our starting-point (which in principle is what the Indian grammarians did), we shall on the analogy of स्रवति sravati and घोषति ghoṣati predict *sopati instead of the correct स्वपति svapati. For this reason the root of verbs such as the last is formed according to the middle grade (thus root स्वप् svap 'sleep' as against स्रु sru and घुष् ghuṣ), and the appearance of reduced forms such as सुप् sup is accounted for by a special process called संप्रसारण samprasāraṇa ('vocalisation [of the semi-vowel]'). Other verbs such as गम् gam 'go' and मन् man 'think' are also quoted in what is essentially their middle grade: this is because the Indo-European vowels m̥ and n̥ (the sonant nasals) were replaced in Sanskrit by a short **a** (the past participles are गत gata, from *gm̥ta, and मत mata, from *mn̥ta), so that a reduced form of the root might be insufficiently distinctive.

The foregoing will help to explain why **a**, which is essentially a guṇa vowel, appears in the table also as a normal-grade vowel whose guṇa equivalent is identical. From the point of view of Sanskrit, स्वप् svap, गम् gam and मन् man are normal-grade roots which when strengthened to the guṇa grade appear without change as स्वप svap, गम gam and मन man.

Classes I, IV and VI

The present stems of these classes are formed according to the following basic principles:

Class I

The root is strengthened to the guṇa grade: शुच् śuc, शोचति śocati 'he grieves'.

Roots containing **a** therefore remain unchanged: वद् vad, वदति vadati 'he says'.

If they immediately precede the thematic a, the guṇa vowels e and o appear as ay and av: जि ji, जयति jayati 'he wins'.

Roots containing a long vowel followed by a consonant, or a short vowel followed by two consonants, remain unchanged: जीव् jīv, जीवति jīvati 'he lives'. (*Note*: This is a general limitation upon the operation of guṇa, and it applies in other formations as well.)

Important irregular formations are गम् gam, गच्छति gac-chati 'he goes' and स्था sthā, तिष्ठति tiṣṭhati 'he stands'.

Class IV

The suffix ya is added to the root, which usually remains unstrengthened: नृत् nṛt, नृत्यति nṛtyati 'he dances'.

Class VI

The root remains both unstrengthened and without suffix. (Historically, it remains unstrengthened because the tonic accent fell not on the stem, as in Class I, but on the thematic a.) लिख् likh, लिखति likháti 'he writes'; प्रछ् prach, पृच्छति pṛccháti (by samprasāraṇa) 'he asks'.

Conjugation of the present indicative

The Sanskrit verb distinguishes, without the aid of pronouns, not only first, second and third persons but also three numbers: singular, dual and plural. Dual terminations are also found in Greek, but rarely, and applied only to things naturally paired together. In Sanskrit the use of the dual is obligatory, both in nouns and in verbs, wherever two people or things are in question. The plural is restricted in application to three or more.

The present indicative of the verb नी nī 'lead' is:

SINGULAR	DUAL	PLURAL
1st person		
नयामि nayāmi I lead	नयाव: nayāvaḥ we two lead	नयाम: nayāmaḥ we lead
2nd person		
नयसि nayasi you (*sg.*) lead	नयथ: nayathaḥ you two lead	नयथ nayatha you (*pl.*) lead
3rd person		
नयति nayati he leads	नयत: nayataḥ the two of them lead	नयन्ति nayanti they lead

The order in which you learn this paradigm is a matter of taste. Traditionally in Sanskrit the third person (which is called the first) is taken as representative of the tense, and the order of recitation would be **nayati, nayataḥ, nayanti, nayasi**, etc. However, Westerners usually adopt the European order (as in Latin) **nayāmi, nayasi, nayati, nayāvaḥ**, etc.

The English distinction between simple present and continuous present does not exist in Sanskrit. नयति **nayati** means both 'he leads' and 'he is leading'. In addition, the present indicative may express an immediate intention or proposal: पृच्छामि **pṛcchāmi** 'I'll ask', गच्छाम: **gacchāmaḥ** 'let's go'.

Prefixes

Verbs may undergo the addition of various prefixes, which may modify, sometimes considerably and sometimes not at all, the basic meaning:

विशति	viśati	he enters
प्रविशति	praviśati	he enters
उपविशति	upaviśati	he sits down

गच्छति	gacchati	he goes
आगच्छति	āgacchati	he comes
अवगच्छति	avagacchati	he understands

Negation is expressed by the word **न na**:

न वदति na vadati he does not say, he is not saying

Sandhi

In English a word that we spell only in one way may be pronounced differently according to its position in a sentence.
Thus the definite article 'the' is pronounced with a neutral
vowel (ðə) before consonants, 'the man, the hill', and with
a short *i* vowel (ðĭ) before vowels, 'the owl, the end'. Moreover, in separating this word out in order to talk about it,
we may use another, a lengthened vowel, and say 'the definite
article ðī'. We have examples like the English non-standard
'doam be stupid'. Here the word 'don't', having lost its final
t, changes its *n* to *m*, which is more like the following *b* (put
more technically, the *alveolar* nasal *n* is replaced by the
bilabial nasal *m* before the *bilabial* stop *b*). A different sort of
example involves not a separate word but a 'morpheme', for
example 'plural *s*': so, the plural of 'cat' is 'cats', but the
plural of 'dog' is 'dogz', although in standard spelling of the
latter the same letter, *s*, is used—the general rule is that voiceless *s* is added to voiceless consonants ('cats', 'pups') and
voiced *z* to voiced consonants and vowels ('dogs', 'toes'),
except that if the word itself ends in a sibilant the suffix takes
the form '-iz' ('bases', 'phrases'). Similar sound changes
occurred in Latin words, as the spelling of their English
derivatives will indicate—compare for instance '*in*duce' and
'*con*duce' with '*im*press' and '*com*press'.

The reason underlying such variations is one of euphony or
ease of utterance, the fact that what is a convenient sound in
one environment may not be at all convenient in another.
The phenomenon is referred to (very often even in talking

about languages other than Sanskrit) by the term sandhi, a Sanskrit word meaning 'juncture'. What we are concerned with at present, as in the first two examples above, is *external* sandhi, i.e. the changes in the appearance of complete words when they come together, or make a juncture, in a sentence. In Sanskrit these changes were particularly widespread and striking, which is why the word sandhi has become generally current among phoneticians. They were fully analysed by the ancient grammarians and are extensively reflected in the orthography. This is not necessarily a good thing. Writing 'thǝ' and 'thi' or 'cats' and 'dogz' in English would obscure the fact that a single word or morpheme is in question—though it would be marginally helpful to foreigners in learning to pronounce the language. Beginners in Sanskrit, being more concerned with reading and writing than with pronunciation, will find the operation of the rules of sandhi a considerable obstacle in the earliest stages of learning the language, but one that is fairly quickly surmounted because met with at every turn.

Use of the sandhi grids

The approach to the problem adopted in this book is primarily a practical one. Instead of attempting to master in one go all the phonetic principles involved in euphonic combination, you are encouraged to make use of the chart between pp. 33 and 34, where all the relevant combinations of final and initial sounds are set out in tabular form. In addition, certain preliminary remarks to aid you in using the tables are here offered.

When sandhi is made between two words, the first may end in a vowel or a consonant and the second may begin with a vowel or a consonant. Four main classes of sandhi are thus distinguished.

1 *Vowel+vowel*

When two vowels come together they coalesce, often into a single vowel. The body of the vowel grid represents the

combination of the two vowels. Thus तत्र tatra followed by
इव iva is written as तत्रेव tatreva 'as if there'. Most of the
features of vowel sandhi will make sense if you remember
that historically the Sanskrit diphthongs **e, o** represent **ay, av**
(or **ăi, ău**) and the diphthongs **ai, au** represent **āy, āv** (or **āi,
āu**). Hiatus is not permitted, in the sense that when the original
vowels come together the appropriate rule of sandhi must be
applied; but *secondary* hiatus is permitted, in that the resultant
sandhi may contain two distinct vowels. So वने vane+इव iva
results in वन इव vana iva 'as if in the forest' (by way of
vanayiva, with elision of the **y**), and this remains and does *not*
further combine into **vanèva*.

2 *Vowel+consonant*

The simplest of all possibilities. The words remain unchanged,
with one very minor exception: if the vowel is short and the
following consonant is छ **ch**, this **ch** changes to च्छ **cch**: so न
छिनत्ति na cchinatti 'he does not cut'. If the vowel is long,
the change is optional (except after the words आ **ā** and मा **mā**,
when it is again obligatory): सा छिनत्ति sā chinatti or
सा छिनत्ति sā cchinatti 'she cuts'.

3 *Consonant+consonant*

Here, the body of the consonant grid represents the form that
the last letter of the first word assumes before the following
consonant. In Sanskrit a word may end only in a vowel or in
k, ṭ, t, p, ṅ, n, m, r or **ḥ** (on these last two, see below),
which is why the grid is not even more complicated than it is.
In the body of the grid a bracketed sound indicates a change
in the form of the following initial: thus तत् tat+शरीरम्
śarīram becomes तच्छरीरम् tac charīram.

4 *Consonant+vowel*

The possibilities of this are represented by the penultimate
horizontal column in the consonant grid.

CONSONANTS

(Bracketed letters indicate the form taken by a following initial)

Permitted finals — the form taken by a following initial:

Initial letters:	k	ṭ	t	p	ṅ	n	m	ḥ/r *(Except āḥ/aḥ)*	āḥ	aḥ
k/kh	k	ṭ	t	p	ṅ	n	ṃ	ḥ	āḥ	aḥ
g/gh	g	ḍ	d	b	ṅ	n	ṃ	r	ā	o
c/ch	k	ṭ	c	p	ṅ	ṃś	ṃ	ś	āś	aś
j/jh	g	ḍ	j	b	ṅ	ñ	ṃ	r	ā	o
ṭ/ṭh	k	ṭ	ṭ	p	ṅ	ṃṣ	ṃ	ṣ	āṣ	aṣ
ḍ/ḍh	g	ḍ	ḍ	b	ṅ	ṇ	ṃ	r	ā	o
t/th	k	ṭ	t	p	ṅ	ṃs	ṃ	s	ās	as
d/dh	g	ḍ	d	b	ṅ	n	ṃ	r	ā	o
p/ph	k	ṭ	t	p	ṅ	n	ṃ	ḥ	āḥ	aḥ
b/bh	g	ḍ	d	b	ṅ	n	ṃ	r	ā	o
nasals (n/m)	g·ṅ	ḍ·ṇ	n	m	ṅ	n	ṃ	r	ā	o
y/v	g	ḍ	d	b	ṅ	n	ṃ	r	ā	o
r	g	ḍ	d	b	ṅ	n	ṃ	zero[1]	ā	o
l	g	ḍ	l	b	ṅ	l̐[2]	ṃ	r	ā	o
ś	k	ṭ	c(ch)	p	ṅ	ñ(ś/ch)	ṃ	ḥ	āḥ	aḥ
s/ṣ	k	ṭ	t	p	ṅ	n	ṃ	ḥ	āḥ	aḥ
h	g(gh)	ḍ(ḍh)	d(dh)	b(bh)	ṅ	n	ṃ	r	ā	o
vowels	g	ḍ	d	b	ṅ/ṅṅ[3]	n/nn[3]	m	r	ā	a[4]
zero	k	ṭ	t	p	ṅ	n	m	ḥ	āḥ	aḥ

[1] ḥ or r disappears, and if a/i/u precedes, this lengthens to ā/ī/ū.

[2] e.g. tān+labhasva = ताँल्लभस्व tāl labhasva.

[3] The doubling occurs when the preceding vowel is short.

[4] Except that aḥ+a = o ऽ.

Note: Various alternative sandhis are permissible, but none has been noted, except in the case of **n**+**ś**.

VOWELS

(*A space is left between two elements where such a space would occur in the nāgarī script.*)

- - - - - - Final vowels - - - - - -

Initial vowels ↓ \ Final →	a	i	u	ṛ	e	ai	o	au
a	ā	ya	va	ra	e	ā a	o	āva
ā	ā	yā	vā	rā	a ā	ā ā	a ā	āvā
i / ī	e	ī	vi	rī	a i	ā i	a i	āvī
u / ū	o	yu	ū	ru	a u	ā u	a u	āvu
ṛ	ar	yṛ	vṛ	ṝ	a ṛ	ā ṛ	a ṛ	āvṛ
e	ai	ye	ve	re	a e	ā e	a e	āve
ai	ai	yai	vai	rai	a ai	ā ai	a ai	āvai
o	au	yo	vo	ro	a o	ā o	a o	āvo
au	au	yau	vau	rau	a au	ā au	a au	āvau

Initial vowels: a, ā, i, ī, u, ū, ṛ, e, ai, o, au

SANDHI GRIDS

5 Zero

There is one further possibility. One word instead of being followed by another may occur at the end of a phrase or sentence, i.e. 'before zero'. In this position the basic form of the word remains without change. To put the matter the other way round, the form that a word assumes by itself or at the end of a sentence has been selected as the basic form: so रमणीयं वनम् ramaṇīyaṃ vanam 'the forest is pleasant'. There is, unfortunately, one exception to this rule:

Sandhi of final r or ḥ

(If the following account seems discouragingly complicated, remember that it is only provided as background explanation; what is important at this stage is simply knowing how to use the sandhi grid.) Visarga (ḥ) is the last letter of many Sanskrit words as they appear at the end of a sentence. It may represent one of two original (Indo-European) sounds, s and r. Thus, from s, अश्वः aśvaḥ (cf. *equus*) 'horse'; अस्थाः asthāḥ (cf. *éstēs*) 'you stood'; गतिः gatiḥ (cf. *básis*) 'going'. But, from original r, मातः mātaḥ (cf. *māter*) 'O mother'; द्वाः dvāḥ (cf. the English cognate) 'door'; चतुः catuḥ (cf. *quattuor*) 'four'.

The sandhi of these words is complicated by two factors: first, by whether the visarga originates from s or from r; secondly, by the vowel that precedes the visarga. We can eliminate the first factor, and so reduce the confusion, by taking r as the basic letter in the comparatively few cases where ḥ derives from r and reserving ḥ for the cases where it represents original s (so aśvaḥ, asthāḥ, gatiḥ; but mātar, dvār, catur). (In practice, however, final r may be reserved for instances of ar or ār alone, since its sandhi when preceded by any other vowel is identical with the sandhi of final ḥ, and therefore a distinction in these cases could be made only after an etymological inquiry, and not always even then.)

After vowels other than a or ā, ḥ and r have the same

sandhi (see grid). Broadly, **r** appears before a word beginning with a voiced sound, **s** or some other unvoiced sound before a word beginning with an unvoiced sound.

Furthermore, this is the sandhi of final **r** even after **a** and **ā** (**mātar, dvār**). But after **ā**, final **ḥ** is lost before voiced sounds, and words ending in **aḥ** change **aḥ** to **o** before voiced consonants. Before all vowels except short **a**, **aḥ** becomes **a**: thus अश्वः+इव **aśvaḥ+iva** becomes अश्व इव **aśva iva** 'like a horse'. In combination with an initial **a**, **aḥ** becomes **o**: thus अश्वः+अस्ति **aśvaḥ+asti** becomes अश्वोस्ति **aśvosti** 'there is a horse'. In modern printing this last sandhi is generally represented as अश्वो ऽस्ति **aśvo ऽsti**, with the avagraha (ऽ) representing the disappearance of an initial short **a**.

Here are some further examples of the operation of sandhi rules:

अपि **api**+अवगच्छसि **avagacchasi** = अप्यवगच्छसि **apy avagacchasi** do you understand?

ननु **nanu**+उपविशामः **upaviśāmaḥ** = ननूपविशामः **nanūpaviśāmaḥ** well, we are sitting down

उभौ **ubhau**+आगच्छतः **āgacchataḥ** = उभावागच्छतः **ubhāv āgacchataḥ** both are coming

कथम् **katham**+स्मरति **smarati** = कथं स्मरति **katham smarati** what, he remembers?

तत् **tat**+जयति **jayati** = तज्जयति **taj jayati** he is winning that

द्विट् **dviṭ**+हसति **hasati** = द्विड्ढसति **dviḍ ḍhasati** the enemy laughs

तान् **tān**+तु **tu** = तांस्तु **tāṃs tu** them however

नरः **naraḥ**+रक्षति **rakṣati** = नरो रक्षति **naro rakṣati** the man protects

पुनर् **punar**+रक्षति **rakṣati** = पुना रक्षति **punā rakṣati** again he protects

गायन् **gāyan**+आगच्छति **āgacchati** = गायन्नागच्छति **gāyann āgacchati** singing he comes

It will be observed in the above examples that frequently the nāgarī script cannot show where the first word ends and the second begins. Spellings such as अप्य् अवगच्छसि **apy avagacchasi** are never found, except in one or two texts intended for beginners. In transcription, on the other hand, the words can usually be separated out. But they still cannot be so where two vowels coalesce into a single vowel, and in such a case, furthermore, there may be considerable ambiguity as to the original vowels: ā, for instance, might represent $a+a$, $a+ā$, $ā+a$ or $ā+ā$. In the system of transcription used in this book, these difficulties are overcome by the use of the signs › and », which for convenience may be thought of as marks of elision. The former stands in the place of an original short vowel and the latter of an original long vowel. They always stand in place of the first of the two original vowels, except that › is used like the avagraha in the nāgarī script after e and o and also after ā. A circumflex over the sandhi vowel indicates that it is not the same as the original second vowel. The following table of possibilities should make things clear:

		a	ā	i	ī	2nd vowel u	ū	e	ai	o	au
	a	› â	› ā	› ê	› ê̆	› ô	› ō	› aî	› ai	› aû	› au
1st vowel	ā	ā ›	» ā	» ê	» ê̆	» ô	» ō	» aî	» ai	» aû	» au
	i			› î	› ī̆						
	ī			» î	» ī̆						
	u					› û	› ū				
	ū					» û	» ū				

Instead of a circumflex, a macron is used over e and o to distinguish instances where the second original vowel was long. So न na+इच्छति icchati = नेच्छति n› êcchati 'he does not want', but न na+ईक्षते īkṣate = नेक्षते n» ēkṣate 'he does not see'.

Note that › always represents a and » ā except in the union of two like simple vowels (namely, ĭ+ĭ, ŭ+ŭ, r̆+r̆, the last being very rare).

In the early lessons, where Sanskrit is given both in nāgarī and in transliteration, the sandhis of the nāgarī text are usually resolved *completely* in the transliterated version. When this is done, the transliteration is put within brackets to show that it is an analysis and not an equivalent: e.g. तन्नेच्छति (tat na icchati) for tan nᵣ êcchati 'he doesn't want that'. No account is taken, however, of a mere change of final m to anusvāra.

Notes on certain words

1 च ca. This is the Sanskrit for 'and'. It is the same word as Latin *-que* and Greek *te*, and like them it is *enclitic*, i.e. cannot stand as the first word in its sentence or clause. In fact, it always follows the word it connects: instead of 'eggs and bacon' one says 'eggs bacon ca'.

शोचति माद्यति च   śocati mādyati ca   he grieves and rejoices

When it connects a whole phrase it may (unlike *-que*) be placed at the very end of the phrase rather than after the first word:

जीवति पुत्रं पश्यति च   jīvati putram paśyati ca

alternatively:

जीवति पुत्रं च पश्यति   jīvati putram ca paśyati   he is living and sees (his) son

When a whole series of items is listed ca, like 'and', may be used with the final item alone ('eggs, bacon, sausage tomato ca'). On the other hand, ca may be attached to the first item as well as to the subsequent item or items ('eggs ca bacon ca'). This is like the English 'both . . . and', but the usage is commoner in Vedic than in Classical Sanskrit.

2 इव iva. This enclitic word introduces comparisons. When

used with a verb it may be translated literally as 'as it were', and expresses the notion of 'to seem':

वदति   vadati   he is speaking

वदतीव   (vadati iva)   [he is speaking as it were:] he seems
   to be speaking

3 किम् kim, *and interrogative sentences*. Used as a pronoun, **kim** means 'what?':

किं वदति   kim vadati?   what is he saying?

It may also mean 'why?':

किं शोचसि   kim śocasi?   why do you grieve?

Finally, both **kim** and अपि **api** may be used at the beginning of a sentence to mark a question (note that, used in this sense, the word **api** is *not* enclitic):

किं तत्र गच्छति   kim tatra gacchati?   is he going there?
   (*or* why is he going there?)

अपि जयति   api jayati?   is he winning?

Of the two particles **api** is the stronger and usually marks a definite request for information. As in English, questions may also lack any interrogative particle, context or tone of voice (**kāku**) indicating that the sentence is not a plain statement.

4 इति iti. Originally this word meant 'thus'. But in classical Sanskrit it is almost wholly confined to the special function of marking off a preceding word or phrase (or even paragraph) as being a quotation of some sort. It is the Sanskrit equivalent of inverted commas:

आगच्छाम इति वदन्ति   (āgacchāmaḥ iti vadanti)   'we
   are coming', they say

There is no system of indirect speech in Sanskrit, and so the above might equally well be translated: 'they say that they are coming'.

The phrase isolated by **iti** need by no means consist of words actually spoken; it frequently expresses an attitude of mind, the grounds upon which something is done, and so in the right context may represent 'because', 'in order that', etc. Most frequently this 'iti clause' stands at the beginning of its sentence:

पुनर्वदतीति तिष्ठन्ति (punar vadati iti tiṣṭhanti) they stop to hear him speak further—*lit.* 'he is speaking again', *so-thinking* they halt

The uses of **iti** are discussed at greater length in Chapter 14.

Vocabulary

Verbs of class I

अवगम् ava+gam (अवगच्छति avagacchati) understand
आगम् ā+gam (आगच्छति āgacchati) come
आनी ā+nī (आनयति ānayati) bring
गम् gam (गच्छति gacchati) go
गै gai (गायति gāyati) sing
जि ji (जयति jayati) win, conquer
जीव् jīv (जीवति jīvati) live, be alive
दृश् dṛś (पश्यति paśyati[1]) see, look (at)
नी nī (नयति nayati) lead, take (with one)
भ्रम् bhram (भ्रमति bhramati) wander, be confused
वद् vad (वदति vadati) say, speak
वस् vas (वसति vasati) live (*i.e.* dwell)
शुच् śuc (शोचति śocati) grieve

[1] This form is *suppletive*, i.e. originally taken from another root, in the same way that in English 'went' is suppletive of the verb 'go'.

स्था sthā (तिष्ठति tiṣṭhati) stand, halt
स्मृ smṛ (स्मरति smarati) remember

Verbs of class IV

नृत् nṛt (नृत्यति nṛtyati) dance
मद् mad (माद्यति mādyati) rejoice

Verbs of class VI

इष् iṣ (इच्छति icchati) want, wish
उपविश् upa+viś (उपविशति upaviśati) sit down
प्रछ् prach (पृच्छति pṛcchati) ask
प्रविश् pra+viś (प्रविशति praviśati) enter, go in(to),
  come in(to)
लिख likh (लिखति likhati) write

Adverbs and particles

अत्र atra here; to here
अद्य adya today
अधुना adhunā now
अपि api also, too, even (*placed after word qualified*)
इतः itaḥ from here; in this direction, this way
एवम् evam thus, so
कथम् katham how?; (*also, introducing an exclamatory
  sentence*) 'what, . . .?'
क्व kva where?
तत्र tatra there; to there
न na not
पुनर् punar again; (*as an enclitic*) however, but
पुनरपि punar api yet again, again, once more

(For च ca, किम् kim, इव iva, इति iti, see text of Chapter 2.)

Exercise 2a

With the help of the sandhi grid, arrange the following sequences of separate words into continuous utterances. Two keys are provided: one in transliteration with punctuation of vowel sandhi (p. 345), the other as the sentences would appear in a normal nāgarī text (p. 356).

For those who like to know what they are writing, the words mean, in the order of sentence 1, 'stealthily; in the darkness; the master's; two horses; the villains; with knives; at last; release; from the reins; in fact'.

1 svairam ; tamasi ; īśvarasya ; aśvau ; durjanāḥ ; śastraiḥ ; cirāt ; muñcanti ; raśmibhyaḥ ; eva. 2 aśvau ; īśvarasya ; eva ; svairam ; śastraiḥ ; raśmibhyaḥ ; muñcanti ; cirāt ; durjanāḥ ; tamasi. 3 svairam ; eva ; īśvarasya ; muñcanti ; aśvau ; śastraiḥ ; durjanāḥ ; cirāt ; tamasi ; raśmibhyaḥ 4 muñcanti ; eva ; tamasi ; aśvau ; śastraiḥ ; īśvarasya ; cirāt ; raśmibhyaḥ ; durjanāḥ ; svairam. 5 raśmibhyaḥ ; tamasi ; śastraiḥ ; muñcanti ; cirāt ; eva ; svairam ; īśvarasya ; aśvau ; durjanāḥ. 6 śastraiḥ ; tamasi ; raśmibhyaḥ ; svairam ; durjanāḥ ; īśvarasya ; cirāt ; aśvau ; muñcanti ; eva. 7 tamasi ; durjanāḥ ; raśmibhyaḥ ; cirāt ; īśvarasya ; aśvau ; svairam ; muñcanti ; śastraiḥ ; eva. 8 muñcanti ; durjanāḥ ; eva ; raśmibhyaḥ ; aśvau ; īśvarasya ; cirāt ; svairam ; śastraiḥ ; tamasi.

Exercise 2b

Translate into English the following sentences. Comparison with the transliterated version (p. 314) will sometimes help to solve difficulties.

गच्छामि ।१। अच न प्रविशामः ।२। पुनरपि लिखति ।३। अधुना क्व वसथ ।४। एवमिच्छसि ।५। क्व पुनस्तिष्ठन्ति ।६।

कथमित आगच्छति । ७ । अच किमानबतः । ८ । पश्यामि लिखामि च । ९ । भमतीव । १० । नृत्यथो गायथश्च । ११ । स्मरन्ति च शोचन्ति च । १२ । अच प्रविशाव इति वदतः । १३ । अधुनापि कथं नागच्छति । १४ । जयामीति माब्यामि । १५ । न जीवन्तीति शोचामः ॥ १६ ॥

Exercise 2c

Translate the following sentences into Sanskrit. Model word order on the Sanskrit–English sentences (adverbs are normally placed before verbs).

1 You are wandering.   2 Now we understand.   3 There too she dances.   4 The two of you live here?   5 What, are they winning?   6 Let us two sit down.   7 The two of them do not say so.   8 Are you asking yet again?   9 What shall I write here?   10 Do you not see?   11 You (*pl.*) seem to be singing.   12 They come and go.   13 Now she both lives and grieves.   14 He sees and seems to speak.   15 'What do you (*pl.*) want?' they ask.   16 We go because they are coming.   17 However we do not rejoice.   18 So also do the two of us remember—What do you remember?—That he is not coming today.

Chapter 3

Some nominal and pronominal paradigms

STEM FORM	SINGULAR			DUAL	PLURAL	
	Nom.	Voc.	Acc.	Nom./Voc./Acc.	Nom./Voc.	Acc.
Nouns						
अश्व horse aśva *masc.*	अश्वः aśvaḥ	अश्व aśva	अश्वम् aśvam	अश्वौ aśvau	अश्वाः aśvāḥ	अश्वान् aśvān
फल fruit phala *neuter*	फलम् phalam	फल phala	फलम् phalam	फले phale	फलानि phalāni	
Pronouns[1]						
1st per.						
मत् अस्मत् mat/asmat	अहम् aham I		माम् mām me	आवाम् āvām	वयम् vayam we	अस्मान् asmān us
2nd per.						
त्वत् युष्मत् tvat/yuṣmat	त्वम् tvam you		त्वाम् tvām	युवाम् yuvām	यूयम् yūyam	युष्मान् yuṣmān
3rd per.						
तत् tat *masc.*	स सः sa/saḥ he		तम् tam him	तौ tau	ते te they	तान् tān them
तत् tat *neuter*		तत् tat it		ते te	तानि tāni	

[1] Though some do have productive stem forms (cf. Chapter 10), personal and demonstrative pronouns are referred to in this book by means of the nominative singular masculine: **aham, tvam, saḥ,** etc.

STEM FORM	SINGULAR			DUAL	PLURAL	
	Nom.	*Voc.*	*Acc.*	*Nom./Voc./Acc.*	*Nom./Voc.*	*Acc.*

Interrog.
—who? | व: | | कम् | | कौ | के | | कान्
—*masc.* | kaḥ who? | | kam whom? | | kau | ke | | kān

किम् what? | | | किम् | | के | | कानि
kim *neuter* | | | kim | | ke | | kāni

(Vocative forms of the pronouns do not occur.)

The nominative and accusative cases are used to express the subject and object respectively of finite verbs.

आचार्यः शिष्यं पश्यति ācāryaḥ śiṣyam paśyati teacher sees pupil

आचार्यं शिष्यः पश्यति ācāryam śiṣyaḥ paśyati pupil sees teacher

There is no definite or indefinite article in Sanskrit: in one context ācāryaḥ is to be translated 'the teacher', in another 'a teacher'. (Where the difference of meaning is crucial, 'the' is sometimes represented by saḥ 'that': चित्रमेतत् citram etat 'this is a picture', तदेतच्चित्रम् (tat etat citram) 'this is the picture'.)

The accusative is also used to express the goal with verbs of motion: नगरं गच्छति nagaram gacchati 'he goes to the city'. Verbs such as nī 'lead' may take this accusative in addition to that of the direct object: नगरं त्वां नयामि nagaram tvām nayāmi 'I'll take you to the city'.

The verb vad 'say, speak' may optionally take an accusative of the person addressed as well as an accusative of that which is said.

As was seen in Chapter 2, the finite verb forms in themselves distinguish person and number. The use of the nominative of the personal pronouns is therefore optional with finite verbs and is normally dispensed with unless at least a slight degree of emphasis is called for: प्रविशामि **praviśāmi** 'I'll go in' as opposed to अहमपि प्रविशामि **aham api praviśāmi** 'I too will go in'.

The vocative is the case of address. It is most frequently placed at the beginning of the sentence, and regularly precedes even connecting particles.

बाल किं वदसि **bāla kim vadasi** what do you say, child?

वयस्य तत्किं शोचसि **vayasya, tat kim śocasi?** then why, friend, do you grieve?

In a phrase such as 'the large cat' we often call 'large' an adjective and 'cat' a noun. More formally, both might be called nouns: 'large' a noun adjective and 'cat' a noun substantive. To preserve this wider sense of the word 'noun' in talking about Sanskrit is not mere pedantry, for many nouns may be used both adjectivally and substantivally, and the classification of nouns by inflexional type is independent of whether they are substantives or adjectives. In this book the terms 'noun' and 'nominal' are to be interpreted in their wider sense.

Adjectives ending in **a** inflect in the masculine like **aśvaḥ**, in the neuter like **phalam**. An adjective accords in number, gender and case with the substantive it qualifies:

रमणीयानि वनानि शोभनं जलं च पश्यामि

ramaṇīyāni vanāni śobhanam jalam ca paśyāmi I see pleasant forests and shining water

Pronouns no less than nouns may be used both adjectivally and substantivally. Thus the pronoun **saḥ** means both 'that' and 'he/it' (i.e. 'that one'). Similarly, the interrogative pronoun may be used alone or qualifying a substantive:

तं शिष्यमिच्छन्ति **tam śiṣyam icchanti** they want that pupil

न तं पश्यामि na taṃ paśyāmi I don't see him

तदिच्छसि (tat icchasi?) do you want it/that?

को नगरं गच्छति (kaḥ nagaram gacchati?) who is going to the city?

कः शिष्य एवं वदति (kaḥ śiṣyaḥ evam vadati?) which pupil says so?

Irregularities of external sandhi

The vowels ī, ū and e when at the end of a *dual* inflexion (whether nominal, pronominal or verbal) are not subject to the operation of sandhi but remain unchanged before vowels:

ते फले इच्छामः te phale icchāmaḥ we want those two fruits

The nominative singular masculine of the pronoun **tat** has really two forms, **sa** and **saḥ** (cf. Greek *ho* with the *hós* in *ê d'hós*). **sa** is used before all consonants. **saḥ** is used in all other circumstances, namely at the end of a sentence and before vowels, but by the normal operation of sandhi it thereby becomes **sa** before all vowels except short **a**:

स गजः । स शिष्यः । स आचार्यः । सो ऽश्वः । अश्वः सः । sa gajaḥ / sa śiṣyaḥ / sa ācāryaḥ / so ⟩śvaḥ / aśvaḥ saḥ

Nominal sentences

There is an important type of sentence in Sanskrit which contains no verb. Such sentences, consisting of a juxtaposition of subject and non-verbal predicate, are a feature of many Indo-European languages. In English the type is almost lost, and when used it has a literary flavour, as in 'happy the man who. . .'. In Greek there are sentences like *sophòs ho philósophos* 'the philosopher is wise'; in a song of Edith Piaf occurs '*balayées les amours*' 'loves are swept away'. Regularly in such an English sentence the subject is *not* placed first. A twentieth-century poet, T. S. Eliot, can write 'dark the Sun and Moon, and the Almanach de Gotha', but 'the Sun and Moon dark' would hardly have been possible. This fact distinguishes such a sentence from one simply involving an ellipse of the verb 'to be': we *may* say 'John is intelligent, Peter stupid'.

In Sanskrit adjectives used predicatively agree in number, gender and case with their substantive, just as when used attributively. As a phrase, शीघ्रावश्वौ (śīghrau aśvau) means 'the two swift horses'; as a complete statement, it means 'the two horses are swift'.

रमणीयो बालः (ramaṇīyaḥ bālaḥ)   the child is pleasant

The predicate may, however, be another substantive, and then agreement of number or gender is not necessary:

स्वल्पं सुखं क्रोधः svalpaṃ sukhaṃ krodhaḥ   anger is a small pleasure

If the subject is a pronoun and the predicate a substantive, the pronoun usually reflects the number and gender of the predicate:

सूर्यः सः   sūryaḥ saḥ   that is the sun

The predicate may also be adverbial. Thus it may consist of an adverb, or of a substantive in some other case such as the locative.

एवं सर्वदा सुखानि evaṃ sarvadā sukhāni   joys are ever thus
क्व देवदत्तः kva Devadattaḥ?   where is Devadatta?
उद्याने देवदत्तः udyāne Devadattaḥ   Devadatta is in the garden

Word order

Many of the relationships that English normally expresses by

means of word order (subject–verb, verb–object, etc.) are
expressed in Sanskrit by means of inflexions—e.g. दुर्लभमभिल-
षति मनोरथ: **durlabham** (*object*) **abhilaṣati** (*verb*) **manorathaḥ** (*subject*) 'desire hankers-after the inaccessible'; to put
these three words in some other order would make no difference to what is hankering after what. As a result, word order
plays a less crucial role in Sanskrit than in English grammar,
and more frequently than in English two or more different
arrangements of the same words are possible without any
strongly felt difference of effect. But this is not to say that if
one were to shake up a sentence of even the most unpreten-
tious Sanskrit prose and spill out the words in some random
new order, that order would always have been equally acceptable to the writer. Word order is important to the rhythm and
emphasis of a Sanskrit sentence. One might suggest that its
role is sometimes analogous to that of stress and intonation in
spoken English, but a detailed investigation of this would
depend upon more adequate accounts both of Sanskrit word
order and of the role of stress/intonation patterns in English
than at present exist. The following generalisations (which
anticipate some grammatical forms to be explained in later
chapters) should be measured against sentences actually
encountered, and particularly against the original sentences
occurring in Chapter 6 onwards. Further remarks will be made
later, for example in connection with imperatives and relative
clauses.

Words that form a natural group are normally placed
together. In particular, adjectives and dependent genitives are
placed with (most often before) their substantives.

Small unemphatic words should not be placed last (unless
they are actual enclitics forming one unit with what immediately precedes). Sentences usually end with a verb or a substantive.

The initial position is the position of greatest emphasis:
पश्यति त्वामाचार्य: **paśyati tvām ācāryaḥ** 'the teacher sees

(/can see) you'; प्रलपत्येष वैधेयः (pralapati eṣa(ḥ) vaidheyaḥ) 'this fool is (just) babbling'. In lively discourse, and especially in nominal sentences or those whose predicate is an intransitive verb, the subject unless emphasised is enclitic; it does not occupy the initial position. It need not actually stand last. Especially if it is a pronoun, it may be inserted into the middle of a predicate of two or more words:

> चिचमेतत् citram etat   this is a picture
>
> तदेतच्चिचम् (tat etat citram)   this is the picture
>
> विनय एष चन्द्रगुप्तस्य (vinayaḥ eṣa(ḥ) Candraguptasya) this is Candragupta's good breeding
>
> द्वितीयमिदमाश्वासजननम् dvitīyam idam āśvāsa-jananam   this is a further ground-for-optimism
>
> बलवद्त्रभवती परिचस्ता (balavat atrabhavatī pari-trastā   the lady is extremely frightened

Examples of emphatic subjects coming first are:

> द्वयमपि प्रियं नः dvayam api priyaṃ naḥ   both things alike are welcome to us
>
> सौहार्दमेवं पश्यति sauhārdam evaṃ paśyati (it is) friendship (which) sees (things) so

There is another rhythm, found more particularly in longer sentences, which is more like the prevailing rhythm of English sentences, where a subject is first announced and then talked about. Where this happens, the subject is frequently marked either by the 'anaphoric' pronoun saḥ or by the addition of some particle: रामस्तावत् (Rāmaḥ tāvat) 'as for Rāma, he...', रामो ऽपि (Rāmaḥ api) 'and Rāma for his part'.

iva

The enclitic particle of comparison **iva** is employed much more commonly with nouns than (as in the previous chapter) with verbs. Where two substantives are compared, they will be in the same case. The word may be translated by English 'like', 'as if', etc.:

आचार्य इव शिष्यो मां पृच्छति (ācāryaḥ iva śiṣyaḥ mām pṛcchati) the pupil is questioning me like a teacher

आचार्यमिव मां शिष्यः पृच्छति ācāryam iva māṃ śiṣyaḥ pṛcchati the pupil is questioning me as if I were a teacher

When an adjective appears as the standard of comparison, the word 'as' may appear twice in English:

अहमिव शून्यमरण्यम् aham iva śūnyam araṇyam the forest is (as) desolate as I

An adjective may also be introduced with **iva** attached to it:

विस्मित इव पश्यति (vismitaḥ iva paśyati) he gazes as if astonished

Where **iva** is used with the predicate of a nominal sentence, either 'is like' or 'seems' may be appropriate:

विस्मित इव पण्डितः (vismitaḥ iva paṇḍitaḥ) the scholar seems astonished

जलमिव सुखम् jalam iva sukham happiness is like water

पण्डित इव स शिष्यः (paṇḍitaḥ iva sa śiṣyaḥ) that pupil seems a scholar (/is like a scholar)

Co-ordinative compounds (dvandva)

Sanskrit inherited from Indo-European a considerable facility in the formation of compound nouns, and subsequently extended the facility even further. English also forms compounds of two members fairly freely, but principally of the determinative type, particularly the dependent determinative ('hand-made', 'wife-beater', etc). In this chapter attention is confined to one class of compounds, co-ordinatives, which from the point of view of English are the most peculiar (we may find a faint echo of them in a word such as 'bitter-sweet' or the compound numerals such as 'sixty-seven').

In English we may wonder whether a phrase such as 'magazine stand' should be classified as a compound at all. In Sanskrit there is a simple criterion which is almost universally valid. All members of a compound except the last appear in their stem form. The stem form of a noun is the form lacking any case termination. **aśva**, **phala** and **ramaṇīya** are stem forms. Nouns are usually quoted in their stem forms in dictionaries: when quoted in this book, however, substantives in **a** usually have visarga or anusvāra added to them as an aid to remembering whether they are masculine or neuter.

To form a co-ordinative compound (called in Sanskrit द्वन्द्व **dvandva** 'couple') two or more stems are put together with a relationship between them such as would be expressed by the English word 'and': आचार्यशिष्य **ācāryaśiṣya** 'teacher and pupil'. The gender of the compound is that of its final member, and the number is that of the sum of the elements;[1] an appropriate inflexion is added:

आचार्यशिष्यावागच्छत: (**ācāryaśiṣyau āgacchataḥ**)
teacher and pupil are coming

The same notion may, of course, be expressed without the use of a compound, by means of the particle **ca**:

आचार्यश्च शिष्यश्चागच्छत: (**ācāryaḥ ca śiṣyaḥ ca āgacchataḥ**)

Stem forms are ambiguous as between singular, dual and plural. **ācāryaśiṣya** may therefore also mean 'teachers and

---

[1] A different type of dvandva (of restricted application) in which the termination is neuter singular has deliberately not been introduced here.

pupils', 'teacher and pupils' or 'teachers and pupil'. In all these instances the inflexions are inevitably plural (signifying three or more).

Any number of stems may be put together in a dvandva. Again, if more than two stems are involved, the final inflexion must necessarily be plural:

अश्वगजबालनरा नृत्यन्ति (aśva;gaja;bāla;narāḥ nṛ-tyanti) horses, elephants, children and men are dancing

Because of the importance of correct analysis of compounds for the understanding of Sanskrit, a system of punctuating transliterated Sanskrit so as to make plain their grammatical structure is used throughout this book. In this system of punctuation, semicolons (as in the above example) indicate dvandva relationship between members.

Vocabulary

Substantives—masculine

अश्व: aśvaḥ horse
आचार्य: ācāryaḥ teacher
क्रोध: krodhaḥ anger
गज: gajaḥ elephant
चन्द्र: candraḥ moon
जन: janaḥ person, people
नर: naraḥ man

पण्डित: paṇḍitaḥ scholar, pandit
पर्वत: parvataḥ mountain
बाल: bālaḥ child, boy
ब्राह्मण: brāhmaṇaḥ brahmin
शिष्य: śiṣyaḥ pupil
सूर्य: sūryaḥ sun

Substantives—neuter[1]

क्षेत्रं kṣetram field
जलं jalam water

दु:खं duḥkham pain, unhappiness, sorrow

---

[1] *Note*: The anusvāra added to neuter **a** stems simply indicates gender: the basic form of the nominative/accusative singular ending should be thought of as **m**, which remains before vowels or zero and converts to anusvāra only before consonants.

फलं phalam fruit,
  reward, advantage
भोजनं bhojanam food
वचनं vacanam word,
  speech

वनं vanam forest
सुखं sukham pleasure,
  happiness

Adjectives

रमणीय ramaṇīya
  pleasant
विस्मित vismita
  astonished

शीघ्र śīghra swift, fast
शोभन śobhana shining,
  bright, beautiful
स्वल्प svalpa small, scant

(*Note*: अत्र atra, as well as meaning 'here', may be translated
by 'in this (matter), on this (point)'.)

Exercise 3a

Translate into English:

आचार्यं शिष्या आनयन्ति ।१। अश्वमश्वानिच्छसि ।२। अहं सूर्यचन्द्रौ
पश्यामि ।३। सुखं को नेच्छति ।४। स्वल्पं भोजनम् ।५। जलमश्वान्तरो
नयति ।६। कस्त्वमिति मां पृच्छतः ।७। कं पर्वतं पण्डितो गच्छति
।८। अत्र क्रोधो न वसतीति वनं प्रविश्रतः ।९। शीघ्रं वचनं
नावगच्छामः ।१०। आचार्यं पर्वत इव स गजः ।११। कं पुनः
पृच्छामि ।१२। किं शिष्या यूयम् ।१३। जलं नरबालाः प्रविशन्ति
।१४। रमणीयमधुना तत्फलमिति विस्मिता वदन्ति ।१५
कथमत्रापि बालाः ।१६। दुःखान्यपि फलमानयन्ति ।१७। बाला
अत्र किं सुखं पश्येति शिष्यानाचार्यो वदति ॥१८॥

Exercise 3b

Translate into Sanskrit (using dvandva compounds where
possible):

1 We want water and food.   2 The two of them see a swift
horse.   3 Scholars, what do you want?   4 Anger conquers

you as if (you were) a child. 5 Which two teachers do you see? 6 The moon is as bright as the sun today. 7 Is he pleasant? 8 Teacher, what brahmin is coming this way? 9 What is the advantage in this? 10 Children, where is that teacher? 11 Do you (*pl.*) not remember even pleasant words? 12 We see scant advantage. 13 Are the teachers astonished? 14 The two boys see fields, mountains and forests. 15 Why do you (*pl.*) say that he does not want happiness? 16 They are taking the elephant to the field. 17 But where the food (is), you do not tell me. [*Use* **iti**.] 18 That man is speaking to the astonished people like a brahmin.

Chapter 4

The past participle

The past participle is the most important of the nominal formations from the verbal root (nominal forms of the verb being those which function not as finite verbs but as substantives or adjectives). Its sense corresponds to that of the English past participle in the latter's more adjectival use; it thus in general signifies completed action and, except in the case of necessarily intransitive verbs, passive voice. So लिखित likhita 'written', स्मृत smṛta 'remembered', गत gata 'gone', मग्न magna 'sunk', 'sunken'.

The past participle is formed by adding to the root one of three suffixes: (a) -ta, (b) -ita, (c) -na. Very few roots form their past participle in more than one of these three ways. In all cases the root remains unstrengthened (without guṇa or vṛddhi).

(a) -ta. Before this suffix, the root usually appears in its very weakest form (cf. the remarks on samprasāraṇa in Chapter 2). Thus उप्त upta (from वप् vap) 'sown' and हत hata (हन् han) 'killed'. The past participle of roots ending in ā or ai may end in ita or īta (and might therefore be mentioned under (b) below): गीत gīta (गै gai) 'sung', स्थित sthita (स्था sthā) 'standing' (in the sense of 'remaining standing'). Important irregular forms are हित hita (धा dhā) 'put' and दत्त datta

(दा dā) 'given'. The operation of internal sandhi often produces a considerable change of appearance: दृष्ट dṛṣṭa (दृश् dṛś) 'seen', पृष्ट pṛṣṭa (प्रछ् prach, with samprasāraṇa) 'asked', लब्ध labdha (लभ् labh) 'taken', ऊढ ūḍha (वह् vah, with samprasāraṇa and lengthening of the resulting u) 'carried'.

(b) -ita. Here the same suffix -ta is added to the root with insertion of the connecting vowel i. The root is not strengthened, neither in general is it reduced by samprasāraṇa or other processes; so पतित patita (पत् pat) 'fallen'. Among exceptional reduced forms are उदित udita (वद् vad) 'spoken' and, with long ī, गृहीत gṛhīta (ग्रह् grah) 'seized'.

(Class X verbs and other verbs with stems ending in -aya substitute -ita for this suffix: कथयति kathayati 'tells'; कथित kathita 'told'. Otherwise -ita is substituted only for the final a of a derivative stem: कण्डूयति kaṇḍūyati 'scratches'; कण्डूयित kaṇḍūyita 'scratched'.)

(c) -na. This suffix is taken by many roots ending in ā/ai, ī, ū, ṝ, d and j. *dn becomes nn and *jn becomes gn. *ṝn generally becomes īrṇ, but after a labial consonant ūrṇ. ā/ai becomes sometimes ā and sometimes ī. So भिन्न bhinna (भिद् bhid) 'split', तीर्ण tīrṇa (तॄ tṝ) 'crossed', पूर्ण pūrṇa (पॄ pṝ) 'filled', ग्लान glāna (ग्लै glai) 'tired', हीन hīna (हा hā) 'left'.

No rule can predict the form that the past participle of a particular verb will take. To ascertain it you should therefore in future consult the list of verbs on pp. 298–310. But the following is a list in order of the past participles of verbs quoted in the vocabularies of Chapters 2 and 4: अवगत avagata, आगत āgata, आनीत ānīta, गत gata, गीत gīta, जित jita, जीवित jīvita, दृष्ट dṛṣṭa, नीत nīta, भ्रान्त bhrānta, उदित udita, उषित uṣita, (past participle of śuc not found), स्थित sthita, स्मृत smṛta, नृत्त nṛtta, मत्त matta,

दृष्ट iṣṭa, उपविष्ट upaviṣṭa, पृष्ट pṛṣṭa, प्रविष्ट praviṣṭa, लिखित likhita, कृत kṛta, त्यक्त tyakta, विस्मृत vismṛta.

The verb कृ kṛ 'do' forms a present stem of Class VIII, which inflects quite differently from the stems so far learnt (thus करोति karoti 'he does', कुर्वन्ति kurvanti 'they do'). Do not feel free therefore to use the *present* stem of any verb unless it is stated to belong to class I, IV, VI or X (the 'thematic' classes).

Use of the past participle

Past participles may be used in all the ways in which other adjectives are used (in fact, in the previous exercise विस्मित vismita 'astonished', like its English counterpart, is actually a participle).

इष्टं फलं न पश्यामि। iṣṭaṃ phalaṃ na paśyāmi I do not see the desired reward

जितो राक्षस:। (jitaḥ Rākṣasaḥ) Rākṣasa is beaten

शिष्यानुपविष्ट: पृच्छति। śiṣyān upaviṣṭaḥ pṛcchati seated, he questions the pupils

In particular, the use of the enclitic particle अपि api 'even' with participles is noteworthy. It has a concessive force and may be translated by 'though' (with or without a finite verb):

इष्टा अपि पण्डिता नागच्छन्ति। (iṣṭāḥ api paṇḍitāḥ na āgacchanti) [even desired:] though wanted, the paṇḍits do not come: though we want the paṇḍits, they do not come

इष्टानपि पण्डितान्न पश्याम:। iṣṭān api paṇḍitān na paśyāmaḥ the paṇḍits, though wanted, we do not see: though we want the paṇḍits, we do not see them

Instrumental case

In addition to nominative, vocative and accusative, Sanskrit nouns distinguish instrumental, dative, ablative, genitive and locative cases. From now on, the paradigms in the grammatical section of the book should be consulted. However, the following are the instrumental forms of the words quoted in Chapter 3:

अश्वेन aśvena, अश्वाभ्याम् aśvābhyām, अश्वै: aśvaiḥ; फलेन phalena, फलाभ्याम् phalābhyām, फलै: phalaiḥ; मया mayā, आवाभ्याम् āvābhyām, अस्माभि: asmābhiḥ; त्वया tvayā, युवाभ्याम् yuvābhyām, युष्माभि: yuṣmābhiḥ; तेन tena, ताभ्याम् tābhyām, तै: taiḥ (*m.* and *n.*); केन kena, काभ्याम् kābhyām, कै: kaiḥ (*m.* and *n.*).

The instrumental case has both an instrumental and a comitative sense: it expresses both main senses of the English 'with'. It also denotes the agent in a passive construction. Among possible translations of its significance are therefore 'with', 'by means of', 'because of', 'through', 'together with', 'by'.

जलेनाश्वान्सिञ्चति। (jalena aśvān siñcati) he sprinkles the horses with water

सुखं योगेन गच्छति। sukham yogena gacchati he [goes to:] attains happiness by means of yoga

बालैरागच्छति। (bālaiḥ āgacchati) he is coming with the children

जितो राक्षसश्चाणक्येन। (jitaḥ Rākṣasaḥ Cāṇakyena) Rākṣasa is beaten by Cāṇakya

saha

The comitative sense of the instrumental is, however, usually reinforced by the addition of the preposition सह saha 'together with', which like most Sanskrit prepositions usually *follows* the substantive it governs:

बालै: सहागच्छति। (bālaiḥ saha āgacchati) he is coming with the children

Past passive sentences

The example given earlier, **jito Rākṣasaś Cāṇakyena** 'Rākṣasa is beaten by Cāṇakya', might with very little alteration of sense also be translated as 'Cāṇakya has beaten Rākṣasa'. But furthermore, since Sanskrit does not normally distinguish perfect from preterite, it might be translated as 'Cāṇakya beat Rākṣasa'. We thus have in Sanskrit a way of expressing past active statements in which the subject is represented by the instrumental case, the object by the nominative case and the verb by a past participle agreeing with the latter.[1]

In Sanskrit this is one among several ways of expressing past statements. Other possibilities include the use of a finite past tense (imperfect, aorist or perfect—often, in the later language, without distinction of meaning) and the use of the past active participle (see Chapter 9). In this and the immediately following exercises it is the past participle construction that is to be practised. In translating into Sanskrit you will find it convenient to recast the sentence mentally in English first:

though tired, the friends seized the very first opportunity
by the friends, though tired, the very first opportunity
   (was) seized
परिश्रान्तैरपि वयस्यैः प्रथम एवावसरो गृहीतः ।
(pariśrāntaiḥ api vayasyaiḥ prathamaḥ eva avasaraḥ
   gṛhītaḥ)

---

[1] This type of construction was so well favoured that it became the regular way of expressing such statements in some of the languages descended from Sanskrit. Thus the Hindi sentence राम ने काम किया *Rāmne kām kiyā* 'Rām did the work' represents the Sanskrit रामेण कर्म कृतम् *Rāmeṇa karma kṛtam.* From this results the apparently curious phenomenon in Hindi that in the past tense the subject of a transitive verb takes a special suffix, and the verb agrees in number and gender with the object.

When a verb is intransitive, an impersonal passive construction might theoretically be used: thus तेन गतम् tena gatam 'by him (it was) gone'; 'he went'. But this is far less common than the use of such a participle in an intransitive sense, with the subject in the nominative case:

ते च वयस्यैः सह नगरं गताः। te ca vayasyaiḥ saha naga-
   raṃ gatāḥ and they are gone/have gone/went with their friends to the city

There are, however, a number of past participles that may have both an active and a passive sense. Thus पीत pīta, like 'drunk' in English, can be applied both to the drink and to the drinker (though in Sanskrit there is no necessary implication of intoxication). Similarly, प्रविष्ट praviṣṭa 'entered' or 'having entered', विस्मृत vismṛta 'forgotten' or 'having forgotten'. Thus with an active construction:

रामो ऽपि नगरं प्रविष्टः (Rāmaḥ api nagaram praviṣṭaḥ)

and with a passive construction:

रामेणापि नगरं प्रविष्टम् (Rāmeṇa api nagaram praviṣ-
   ṭam)

the meaning of both versions being 'and Rāma entered the city'.

Omission of pronouns

It is not uncommon to find in Sanskrit sentences such as हन्त न गतः hanta, na gataḥ 'oh, he hasn't gone!'. Here, the pronominal subject 'he' is completely omitted and can only be inferred from the masculine singular form of the predicate gataḥ. This is parallel to the already mentioned omission of the personal pronouns with finite verbs (न गच्छति na gacchati 'he is not going' etc.) but is of more limited scope. First and second person subjects cannot normally be omitted (unless replaced by the appropriate form of the verb **as** 'be'—see Chapter 5), since they are not distinguished by any special form of the past participle.

The 'logical subject' of past passive sentences, in other words the agent expressed by the instrumental case, is also often omitted. But this omission is of a different order, since the Sanskrit sentence is grammatically complete without any expressed agent. While **jito Rākṣasaś Cāṇakyena** means 'Cāṇakya beat Rākṣasa', there is nothing lacking in the simple **jito Rākṣasaḥ** 'Rākṣasa got beaten'. Hence Sanskrit may not bother to express an agent whose presence is grammatically necessary in English: one person may ask किं दृष्टं तदुद्यानम् (**kim dṛṣṭam tat udyānam?**), meaning 'have (you) seen that garden?', and another may reply दृष्टम् **dṛṣṭam**, meaning '(I) have seen it'. In the following exercises English pronouns are bracketed where they are not expressed or directly implied in the Sanskrit version.

(The term 'logical subject' points to the parallel between the nominative subject of present active sentences and the instrumental agent of past passive sentences. It is a blanket term useful in discussing sentences that attribute past or present behaviour to animate beings. But it cannot be pressed too far, for the term 'subject' is also used to cover the nominative subject of intransitive presents and nominal sentences, and the nominative of past passive sentences is itself often comparable to this latter type of 'subject'.)

eva

एव **eva** is an enclitic particle which serves to emphasise the immediately preceding word. It may thus correspond to the emphatic inflection of the voice which we represent in print, if at all, by the use of italics:

स्वल्पान्येवेच्छामः । (**svalpāni eva icchāmaḥ**) we want the *small* ones

(The degree of emphasis would often be better represented by the use of a stress mark such as ' ('we want the smáll ones'), and such a mark is occasionally used in this book where the use of italics would be particularly distorting to the sense.)

This type of emphasis may also be represented in English by a relative clause construction (as regularly in French—'*c'est moi qui l'ai fait*', '*I did it*').

एतानेव गुणानिच्छाम: । etān eva guṇān icchāmaḥ these are the qualities we want *or* it is these qualities we want

देवेनैवैतदिष्टम् । (devena eva etat iṣṭam) it was His Majesty who wanted this

eva may also be translated by a specific word such as 'really', 'actually', 'in fact', 'quite', 'very', 'just', 'only'. अद्भुत एव (adbhutaḥ eva) 'really extraordinary'; बाल एवैष: (bālaḥ eva eṣaḥ) 'he is just a child'; स एव जन: (saḥ eva janaḥ) 'that very person'. The use with the demonstrative saḥ, as in the last example, is particularly noteworthy and may be represented in English by the word 'same': तदेव चेत्रम् (tat eva kṣetram) 'that very field': 'the same field'.

eva is particularly used to mark the predicate of a nominal sentence:

एष एव स ब्राह्मण: । (eṣaḥ eva saḥ brāhmaṇaḥ) [that brahmin is *this* one] here is the brahmin

eṣaḥ

एष: eṣaḥ 'this' is a compounded form of the demonstrative pronoun saḥ 'that'. Its inflexion follows that of saḥ precisely, except that by internal sandhi the nominative singular masculine saḥ/sa and nominative singular feminine sā become एष:/एष eṣaḥ/eṣa and एषा eṣā respectively. The distribution of the forms eṣaḥ/eṣa is the same as that of saḥ/sa.

Whereas **saḥ** is an unemphatic pronoun used to qualify what is not immediately present to the speaker, **eṣaḥ** is a deictic pronoun normally referring to what is close at hand. When it qualifies an already defined substantive, it may be represented in English by 'here', 'here is/are', 'see', etc.

एष स ब्राह्मण: । (eṣaḥ saḥ brāhmaṇaḥ) here is the brahmin

एष रामो बालानानयति । (eṣaḥ Rāmaḥ bālān ānayati) see, Rāma is bringing the children *or* here is Rāma, bringing the children

The most striking example of this usage is in conjunction with a first or second person verb:

एष उद्यानं प्रविशामि । (eṣaḥ udyānam praviśāmi) see, I am going into the garden

vā

वा **vā** is yet another enclitic particle. It has the meaning 'or' and follows what it 'disjoins' as **ca** follows what it joins. 'Either . . . or . . .' is represented by . . . **vā** . . . **vā**.

आचार्येण वा शिष्यैर्वा गज एष आनीत: । (ācāryeṇa vā śiṣyaiḥ vā gajaḥ eṣaḥ ānītaḥ) either the teacher or the pupils brought this elephant here

kṛtam, alam and *kim*

कृतम् **kṛtam** 'done (with)' and अलम् **alam** 'enough (of)' are used with a substantive in the instrumental to express a negative exhortation, 'cease from' (the exhortation occasionally being addressed to oneself):

अलं शोकेन । (**alam śokena**) enough of sadness: do not be sad

कृतं कुतूहलेन । (kṛtam kutūhalena) have done with curiosity: I/you must not be curious

किम् kim? 'what (with)?' is used in a similar fashion:

किमुद्यानेन रमणीयेन । kim udyānena ramaṇīyena? what is the point of an attractive garden?

Adverbs of manner

Sanskrit adjectives do not have a termination exclusively reserved for adverbial usage. Instead, the accusative singular neuter (acting as an 'internal accusative') may do duty.

शीघ्रं चलति । (śīghram calati) [he moves a swift (moving):] he moves swiftly

Adverbs of manner are also frequently represented by substantives in the instrumental case. विषादेन viṣādena 'with dejection': 'dejectedly'. वचनै: vacanaiḥ 'by words': 'verbally'.

Internal sandhi

The rules of external sandhi, as covered by the sandhi grids, describe juncture phenomena between complete words within a sentence. Internal sandhi concerns the juncture of morphemes within a single word. External sandhi is the more regular and invariable because it is comparatively *ad hoc*: in principle, any Sanskrit word may find itself next to any other Sanskrit word. The rules of internal sandhi are both less invariable and, from the learner's point of view, less overwhelmingly important, because they describe a previously established set of forms, the forms which inflected words do in fact have, and which are due to other factors as well as to the operation of internal sandhi. (Similarly in English, while we may by rules of internal sandhi predict both 'cats' and 'dogz', that 'children' is the plural of 'child' is merely an historically determined fact about the language.)

The principles of internal sandhi are therefore best absorbed by observation of actual nominal and verbal formations. There are many features in common with external sandhi, but broadly speaking, instead of assimilation of the first sound to the second, the assimilation is two-way and a greater variety of combination is permitted. Instead of reducing to **k/ṭ/t/p**, stops preserve both aspiration and voicing, and the palatal series is also retained. Before vowels, semi-vowels and nasals, all these stops remain unchanged. The **t** of the past participle may assimilate the voicing and aspiration of a root final sound: so बुध् **budh** 'awake', बुद्ध **buddha** (for *budh-ta*) 'awakened'. Before vowels and **y**, the diphthongs revert to **ay/āy/av/āv**: so **ne+ati = nayati** (cf. Lesson 2).

Retroflexion of s and n

Included within the scope of internal sandhi are two important rules which are really about possible sequences of sound within a Sanskrit word. (Minor exceptions to both rules occur, but these are not important for the beginner.) The first rule is that **ṣ** is found instead of **s** immediately after **k, r** or any vowel except **a** or **ā**, provided that it is neither final nor followed by **r.** This happens even if there is an anusvāra or visarga between the preceding vowel and the **s.** The rule will appear plainer in tabular form:

k, r, i, ī, u, ū, ṛ, ṝ, e, ai, o or au	in spite of an intervening ṃ or ḥ	changes s to ṣ	unless final or followed by r

Thus eṣa/eṣaḥ in comparison with sa/saḥ. If the following sound is, in fact, t, th or n, this also becomes retroflex. Thus, in comparison with the root sthā 'stand', tiṣṭhati (for *tisthati) 'he stands'.

The second rule is at once more important and more difficult to apply, for the reason that it is capable of operating over a much longer phonetic sequence (though only within a single word). First the rule in tabular form:

r ṛ ṝ r or ṣ	in spite of any combination of velars (k, kh, ġ, ġh, ṅ), labials (p, ph, b, bh, m and v) or y, h, ṃ (ḥ cannot occur)	changes n to ṇ	if followed by vowels, m, y, v, or n (which also becomes ṇ)

The point is this. The pronunciation of the retroflex sounds ṛ, ṝ, r, ṣ (but *not* of ṭ, ṭh, ḍ, ḍh or ṇ) is such that the tongue does not release the retroflex position even after the sound has been made. This retroflex position continues (within a single word) until there occurs either a retroflex sound of the releasing type (ṭ, ṭh, ḍ, ḍh, ṇ) or a sound that requires the use of the tongue in another position (c, ch, j, jh, ñ, ś, t, th, d, dh, l, s). But if n, an easily assimilable sound, occurs while the tongue is in the retroflex position, it is realised as a retroflex ṇ (thus causing release of the retroflex position)—unless, indeed, it is the last sound in the word or is followed by some less easily assimilable sound such as t, which guards the dental quality of both. Under the same circumstances nn becomes ṇṇ.

An illustration of both the above rules occurs in the past participle of सद् sad 'sit' when combined with the prefix नि ni 'down'. The past participle of sad is सन्न sanna. *nisanna becomes by the first rule *niṣanna, which in turn becomes by the second rule निषण्ण niṣaṇṇa 'seated'.

The rules do not apply between separate words or (with rare and unimportant exceptions) between the elements of a nominal compound: thus नरनगराणि nara;nagarāṇi, not *nara;nagarāṇi. After a verbal prefix the rules do operate, but with many exceptions. Generally speaking, n and s are retroflected only if they are the first sound in the following stem (a restriction already naturally applicable to s), and not always even then. Thus, as quoted above, निषण्ण niṣaṇṇa, but as an exception विसर्पति visarpati (from विसृप् vi+sṛp) 'glides'. From नम् nam, प्रणमति praṇamati 'salutes'. But from निन्द् nind, either परिणिन्दति pariṇindati or परिनिन्दति parinindati 'censures'. The vocabularies will show whether or not retroflexion occurs after a prefix. As they will also show, particular lexical items do not always exhibit the expected retroflexion of s: e.g. कुसुमं kusumaṃ 'flower', not *kuṣumaṃ. The most important sphere of application of both rules is in the addition of suffixes: e.g. guru+su = गुरुषु guruṣu, locative plural of guru 'heavy'. The terminations so far encountered containing an n liable to retroflexion are the neuter plural -āni and the instrumental singular -ena.

It is not easy at first always to remember to make n retroflex. If after several exercises you find this is still causing trouble, you should make a special check of each exercise to determine whether the rule has been fully applied.

Absence of external sandhi

When some pause of sense occurs within a sentence, the rules of sandhi are not necessarily observed (in prose). Thus, in particular, sandhi does not occur after interjections and is optional after initial vocatives. If you abstain from making sandhi in the latter circumstances, it is wiser to show that this is deliberate by inserting a dash or a comma.

Vocabulary

अवसर: **avasaraḥ** opportunity, occasion

उद्यानं **udyānam** garden, park

कुतूहलं **kutūhalam** curiosity, interest

गृहं **gṛham** house (*m. in pl.*)

जीवितं **jīvitam**[1] life

दर्शनं **darśanam** sight, spectacle

देव: **devaḥ** god; His Majesty; Your Majesty

नगरं **nagaram** city, town

पुत्र: **putraḥ** son

प्रयत्न: **prayatnaḥ** effort, attempt

वयस्य: **vayasyaḥ** friend (*lit.* of same age)

विषाद: **viṣādaḥ** despair, dejection

संदेह: **saṃdehaḥ** doubt

अद्भुत **adbhuta** extraordinary, marvellous

जीवित **jīvita**[1] alive

दूर **dūra** far off; *adv.* (**dūram**) a long way

परिश्रान्त **pariśrānta**[1] exhausted, tired

प्रथम **prathama** first, previous; *adv.* (**prathamam**) already

प्रिय **priya** dear, beloved

मदीय **madīya** my (*possessive adj.*)

कृ **kṛ** (VIII करोति **karoti**) do, make

त्यज् **tyaj** (I त्यजति **tyajati**)

abandon, leave, give up

विस्मृ **vi+smṛ** (I विस्मरति **vismarati**) forget

अलम् **alam** enough; +*instr.* enough of, do not, etc.

एव **eva** in fact, actually, quite, only, (the) very

एष **eṣaḥ** *pron.* this

वा **vā** or

सह **saha**+*instr.* (together) with

हे **he** (*before vocatives*) O

---

[1] In origin a past participle.

Exercise 4a

Translate into English:

पुत्रैः सह गृहं त्यजति ।१। एतदुद्यानम्—प्रविशामः ।२। आचार्येण
च शिष्येष्वाद्भुतः प्रयत्नः कृतः ।३। प्रियो मदीयो वयस्य इति
जीवितमनेन त्यक्तम् ।४। क एष गृहमागच्छति ।५। रमणीयेन
दर्शनेन किं न माद्यसि ।६। दृष्टमवगतं च ।७। अत्रैते नराः
किमिच्छन्तीति कुतूहलेन गृहं प्रविशति ।८। दूरमेव नगरं वयं
च परिश्रान्ता भ्रमामः ।९। इच्छथैवैतन्न वा ।१०। कृतं वचनैर्गतो
ऽवसर इति विषादेन वदतः ।११। पुत्राः स एवैषो ऽवसरः ।१२।
एते वयं नगरमागताः । १३। विस्मृतो वयस्याभ्यां प्रथमो विषादः
।१४। हे पण्डित त्वमस्यं क्व नयसीति पृष्टो ऽपि वचनं न वदति
।१५। किं प्रयत्नेन—नैव त्वां पश्यति देवः ॥ १६ ॥

Exercise 4b

Translate into Sanskrit:

1 Your Majesty is tired: let us sit down here.   2 The people
did not forget these words.   3 This is quite beautiful.   4 He
remembers (his) son although he has gone to the forest. [*Translate for both meanings of the second* 'he'.]   5 We came only
today.   6 Your Majesty, these two children have even now not
left the garden.   7 Here he stands with (his) friends.   8 What
is extraordinary in this? I have *already* seen this man.   9 See,
His Majesty Candragupta has actually arrived.   10 We have
seen the garden with interest.   11 (He) has gone either to the
forest or to the park.   12 Friends, we have been brought
a long way by this horse.   13 An end of doubt: here come the
two pupils alive.   14 Even today it is with pleasure that we
remember that extraordinary sight.   15 Despair has conquered them.   16 Although astonished by this sight, they are
not giving up the attempt.

Chapter 5

PARADIGMS: m. and n. of **kānta, aham, tvam, saḥ, eṣaḥ** and **ayam**; present indicative of **as** 'be'

Sanskrit grammarians discussed the cases of the noun in terms of inflexional morphemes modifying the nominal stem. In addition to the vocative (**saṃbuddhi**, not regarded as on a par with the other cases), those so far introduced have been the nominative (**prathamā** 'first (inflexion)'), the accusative (**dvitīyā** 'second') and the instrumental (**tṛtīyā** 'third'). The order of the cases in Sanskrit was principally determined by the wish to group like endings together. The following is a brief sketch (by no means a full account) of the chief uses of the remaining cases.

Dative (*caturthī* 'fourth') : 'to, for'

Of all the cases the dative has the smallest scope. In Middle Indo-Aryan dialects it was lost, merged into the genitive. Even in Sanskrit itself the tendency of the genitive to usurp the traditional functions of the dative is very noticeable. The dative may be used to denote the indirect object after verbs of giving, telling, etc.

दत्तं मया ब्राह्मणेभ्यो द्रविणम् । (dattam mayā brāhmaṇebhyaḥ draviṇam)   I have given the brahmins wealth

But in such a sentence the genitive **brāhmaṇānām** may be substituted for the dative.

However, the dative in Classical Sanskrit does have one function not shared by any other case, that of denoting purpose or result. The best translation in English is often by means of an infinitive:

लण्ड्रं गच्छामि नृपस्य दर्शनाय। **Laṇḍraṃ gacchāmi nṛpasya darśanāya** I'm going to London [for the seeing of:] to see the king

अङ्गानां भङ्गायारूढो बालैः प्राकारः। **aṅgānāṃ bhaṅgāya ārūḍhaḥ bālaiḥ prākāraḥ** the children climbed the wall [for the breaking of:] only to break their limbs

Especially noteworthy is the use of such a dative as a predicate in itself:

सर्वमतिमात्रं दोषाय। **sarvam atimātraṃ doṣāya** all (that is) excessive [is for a fault:] becomes reprehensible

Ablative (*pañcamī* 'fifth'): 'from'

The ablative expresses the relationship 'from':

नगरात्क्षेत्राणि गच्छति। **nagarāt kṣetrāṇi gacchati** he goes from the city to the fields

When a causal relationship is implied, translations such as 'because of' may be used: क्रोधात् **krodhāt** 'from anger', 'out of anger', 'because of anger', 'through anger'.

The ablative of comparison will be mentioned later.

Genitive (*ṣaṣṭhī* 'sixth'): 'of, 's/s' '

The genitive is the case with the widest range of uses. It most often qualifies another substantive, and has a possessive sense of some kind:

नृपस्य क्रोधं नावगच्छामः। (nṛpasya krodham na avagacchāmaḥ) we do not understand the king's anger/the anger of the king

Where the substantive embodies a verbal notion, the relationship may be either subjective or objective, just as the word 'its' in English is subjective in the phrase 'its consumption of electricity' and objective in 'its consumption by the community'. **nṛpasya** in the preceding example is subjective (the king is angry); in **नृपस्य दर्शनम्** nṛpasya darśanam when this means 'sight of the king' it is objective (I see the king).

The use of the genitive as an alternative to the dative after verbs of giving, telling, etc. has been mentioned. Furthermore, it is the genitive and *not* the dative which should be used in relation to adjectives to express 'point of view', conveyed in English by 'to' or 'for'.

मित्राणामेव प्रियमेतद्दर्शनम्। (mitrāṇām eva priyam etat darśanam) to friends, this is a welcome sight

तत्स्थाने ऽस्य वृषलो देवश्चन्द्रगुप्तः। (tat sthāne asya 'Vṛṣalaḥ' devaḥ Candraguptaḥ) then appropriately is His Majesty Candragupta (just) 'Vṛṣala' to him

श्रुतम्—न पुनः पर्याप्तं हृदयस्य। (śrutam — na punaḥ paryāptam hṛdayasya) (I) have heard, yet (it is) not sufficient for (my) heart

Similarly, past participles such as **विदित** vidita 'known' take a genitive (instead of an instrumental of the agent) when used adjectivally:

अपि विदितमेतद्देवस्य। (api viditam etat devasya?) is this known to Your Majesty?

But:

अपि विदितो देवेन तेषामभिप्रायः । (api viditaḥ devena
teṣām abhiprāyaḥ?)   did Your Majesty (get to) know
their intentions?

The possessive adjective मदीय madīya 'my, mine' was
given in the previous chapter. There are various others—e.g.
मामक māmaka (same meaning), युष्मदीय yuṣmadīya
'belonging to (all of) you', etc. More commonly, however,
the genitive of the appropriate pronoun is used instead of the
possessive adjective:

मम गृहम्   mama gṛham   [the house of me:] my house
मम चेचाणि   mama kṣetrāṇi   my fields
तव पुत्रः   tava putrāḥ   your sons (*addressing one person*)
युष्माकं पुत्रः   (yuṣmākam putrāḥ)   your sons (*addressing
    several persons*)
कस्य पुष्पाणि   kasya puṣpāṇi?   whose flowers?
तस्य हस्तौ   tasya hastau   his hands

The unemphatic forms of the first and second person pronouns (मे me, नौ nau, etc.) may also be used. Like the ordinary
forms, they may either precede or follow their substantive,
but as enclitics they may not stand first in the sentence.

इमे नो गृहाः ।   (ime naḥ gṛhāḥ)   here is our house (*the
    plural of* gṛha *often has a singular sense*)

Generally speaking, neither possessive adjectives nor the
genitives of pronouns may be used to refer to the subject or
'logical subject' of a sentence. If necessary, the reflexive
adjective स्व sva 'my own, your own, his own, their own,
etc.' or the genitive singular of the reflexive word आत्मन्
ātman 'self' may be employed, but it is usually omitted unless
exceptional emphasis is intended. [sva is often compounded
with its substantive, while as a separate word ātmanaḥ is
more normal.]

पुचात्रक्षति **putrān rakṣati** he protects his sons

तस्य पुचात्रक्षति **tasya putrān rakṣati** he protects his [*i.e.* the other's] sons

खानेव पुचात्रक्षसि **svān eva putrān rakṣasi** you protect your *own* sons

Because the omission of the reflexive possessive is standard, it is from now on *not* normally indicated in the exercises by any bracketing of the English word: 'he protects his sons', not 'he protects (his) sons'.

Locative (*saptamī* 'seventh'): 'at, in, on, among; into, onto'

The locative expresses such notions as station or circumstance:

चरति वने किं चित् **carati vane kiṃ cit** something is moving in the forest

फलके बाला उपविष्टा: **(phalake bālāḥ upaviṣṭāḥ)** the children are seated on the table

मिचाणां दर्शने न किं चिद्वदति **(mitrāṇām darśane na kiṃ cit vadati)** [at the sight of:] on seeing his friends he says nothing

It also expresses the end result of motion:

जले बालं क्षिपति **jale bālaṃ kṣipati** he throws the child into the water

It can bear the sense 'in the matter of':

अपापो ऽहं पर्वतेश्वरे **(apāpaḥ aham Parvateśvare)** I am guiltless [in the matter of:] towards Parvateśvara

In particular, it is used to denote the object of feelings (English 'towards', 'for'):

अवगच्छामि ते तस्मिन्सौहार्दम्। **avagacchāmi te tasmin sauhārdam** I understand your fondness for him

It thus occurs after a verb such as स्निह् snih 'feel affection (for)':

किं नु खलु बाले ऽस्मिन्नौरस इव पुत्रे स्निह्यति मे हृदयम् ।
(kim nu khalu bāle asmin aurase iva putre snihyati me hṛdayam?) now why indeed does my heart feel affection for this child as for a son of my own loins?

The use of the locative in expressing circumstance leads to the 'locative absolute' construction (Lesson 11).

Expressions of time

Many of the cases are used in expressing statements of time. The following is an indication of the main usages:

(*a*) Accusative, 'time *during* which':

त्रीन्दिवसान्भ्रमन्ति ।   trīn divasān bhramanti   they wander for three days

(*b*) Instrumental, 'time *within* which':

ते ऽपि त्रिभिर्दिवसैर्नगरं प्राप्ताः ।   (te api tribhiḥ divasaiḥ nagaram prāptāḥ)   and they reached the city in three days

(*c*) Ablative (sometimes genitive), 'time *after* which':

ते ऽपि त्रिभ्यो दिवसेभ्यः प्राप्ताः ।   (te api tribhyaḥ diva-sebhyaḥ prāptāḥ)   and they arrived after three days
चिरस्य कालस्य प्राप्तो ऽसि ।   (cirasya kālasya prāptaḥ asi   you have arrived after a long time/at long last

(*d*) Locative, 'time *at* which':

ते ऽपि तृतीये दिवसे नगरं प्राप्ताः ।   (te api tṛtīye divase

nagaram prāptāḥ)   and they reached the city on the
third day

ayam

The irregularity of the declension of the pronoun **ayam** is
partly due to the fact that it derives from two stems: one **a**
(cf. the adverbs अत्र **atra** and अतः **ataḥ**), the other **i** (cf. इह
iha and इतः **itaḥ**).

Two pronouns are conventionally translated by the English
'that': सः **saḥ** and असौ **asau** (Lesson 13); and two by the
English 'this': अयम् **ayam** and एषः **eṣaḥ**. Traditionally,
the distinctions are that **saḥ** is used of what is not present to
the speaker, **asau** of what is remote from him (though possibly
visible), **ayam** of what is present and **eṣaḥ** of what is near at
hand. Thus **asau** is the 'stronger' of the two which mean
'that', **eṣaḥ** the 'stronger' of the two which mean 'this'.

It is evident that even if these distinctions were adhered to
there would be considerable overlap within each pair (and
also that **ayam** in particular might represent 'that' as well as
'this'), In practice, the distinctions are somewhat blurred and,
at any rate, not always easy to apply. A different distinction
is that, used in reference to discourse, **eṣaḥ** means 'what
precedes', **ayam** 'what follows'.

श्रुत्वैतदिदं वदति ।   (śrutvā etat idam vadati)   hearing
this, he says the following

This rule also is not universally observed, but it is true enough
to be worth remembering.

In the oblique cases other than the accusative (and in practice to some extent in all cases), **ayam** may be used simply
as an unemphatic third person pronoun. In this sense it is
usually enclitic.

क्रोधमेषां नावगच्छामि ।   (krodham eṣām na avagacchāmi)   I don't understand their anger

Pronominal adjectives

Certain common adjectives in **a** follow wholly or in part the pronominal rather than the nominal declension. **anya** 'other' does so wholly: its neuter singular nominative/accusative is अन्यत् **anyat** (cf. the *d* of Latin *aliud*). सर्व **sarva** 'all', एक **eka** 'one' and स्व **sva** 'own' are also wholly pronominal, except that their neuter singular nominative/accusative is सर्वम् **sarvam**, एकम् **ekam**, स्वम् **svam**.

> सर्वेषां नृपाणामयं मार्गः।   **sarveṣāṃ nṛpāṇām ayaṃ mārgaḥ**   this is the path for all kings
>
> एकस्मिन्नेव देशे सर्वे बालाः।   (**ekasmin eva deśe sarve bālāḥ**)   the children are all in a single place

In conjunction with an interrogative, अन्य **anya** may be translated by 'else':

> अन्यः क आगच्छति।   (**anyaḥ kaḥ āgacchati?**)   who else is coming?

kaś cit and *ko ˈpi*

The addition of an indefinite particle, usually either चित् **cit** or अपि **api,** turns the interrogative pronoun ('who?', 'what?') into an indefinite pronoun ('someone', 'anyone', 'some', 'any', 'a little', 'a few'). The addition of न **na** ('not anyone' etc.) gives the Sanskrit for 'no one', 'nothing', etc.

> केन जलं पीतम्।   **kena jalaṃ pītam?**   who has drunk the water?
>
> केनापि जलं पीतम् / केनचिज्जलं पीतम्।   (**kena api jalam pītam/kena cit jalam pītam**)   someone/somebody has drunk the water
>
> केनापि जलं न पीतम्।   (**kena api jalam na pītam**)   no one/nobody has drunk the water

उद्याने न कश्चिच्चरति । (udyāne na kaḥ cit carati) no one is walking in the park

तव किंचिज्जलं भवति । न किंचिदेव । (tava kim cit jalam bhavati?—na kim cit eva) have you any/a little water?—none at all

Interrogative adverbs are used in the same way:

कलहंसकं न क्वचित्पश्यामि । Kalahaṃsakaṃ na kva cit paśyāmi I don't see Kalahaṃsaka anywhere

कृतः कथमपि घटः । kṛtaḥ kathamapi ghataḥ somehow (he) made the pot

कथमपि kathamapi (or कथंचित् kathaṃcit) has by extension the sense 'scarcely', 'with difficulty':

चन्द्रं कथमपि पश्यामि । candram kathamapi paśyāmi I can only just see the moon

as 'be'

The verb as 'be', a very common irregular verb, is an athematic of class II (Lesson 12). The six first and second person forms of the present indicative provide an alternative to (and are, in fact, much more frequent than) the use of pronominal subjects in nominal and past participial sentences. So अतिकातरो ऽसि (atikātaraḥ asi) as well as अतिकातरस्त्वम् (atikātaraḥ tvam) 'you are over-timid', and गतो ऽस्मि (gataḥ asmi) as well as गतो ऽहम् (gataḥ aham) 'I went'. Similarly, धन्यौ स्वः dhanyau svaḥ 'the two of us are lucky', प्राप्तौ स्थः prāptau sthaḥ 'the two of you have arrived', etc. These forms are normally enclitic.

The third person forms (अस्ति asti, स्तः staḥ, सन्ति santi), on the other hand, are seldom if ever used as a copula but have existential force ('there is', 'there are') and most frequently stand as the first word.

अस्ति पर्वतेषु नगरम् । asti parvateṣu nagaram there
   is in the mountains a city

अतः परमपि प्रियमस्ति । ataḥ param api priyam asti?
   is there (any) blessing beyond this?

अस्त्येतत् । (asti etat) this *is* —*i.e.* this is true, that is so

bhū 'be'

This verb, a regular verb of class I, may mean in its non-
copulative uses either 'exist' (like **as**) or 'come into existence',
'arise':

भवन्ति चात्र श्लोकाः । (bhavanti ca atra ślokāḥ) and
   on this point there are stanzas

क्रोधाद्भवति संमोहः । (krodhāt bhavati saṃmohaḥ)
   from anger arises delusion

As a copulative verb it provides a less frequent alternative
to a nominal sentence, more particularly in general statements.

दर्शनमेवास्य रमणीयं भवति परिश्रान्तानाम् । (darśanam
   eva asya ramaṇīyam bhavati pariśrāntānām) the
   very sight of it is delightful to the exhausted

'To have'

The notion of the English 'have' in the sense of 'possess' is
generally expressed by means of the genitive case: i.e. instead
of 'John has a hat', one says 'of John there is a hat'. However,
even in this existential sense the verb **as** or **bhū** is sometimes
omitted.

तव पुत्राणां धनं न भवति । tava putrāṇāṃ dhanaṃ na
   bhavati your sons have no money

अस्ति चास्माकमन्यदपि मित्रम् । (asti ca asmākam anyat
   api mitram) and we have another friend too

श्रुतम् । असंतोषस्तु हृदयस्य । (śrutam—asaṃtoṣaḥ tu
hṛdayasya) (I) have heard, but [(there is) dissatisfaction for my heart:] my heart has/feels no satisfaction
(*Compare the use of* **vartate** [Lesson 9].)

'To feel'

As the above example suggests, there are various ways in which
the notion 'to feel (an emotion *etc.*)' might be represented
in Sanskrit. It may, however, be worth pointing out that the
equivalent of इव **iva** in first person statements is often 'feel'
('seem' being inappropriate):

अशरण इवास्मि । (aśaraṇaḥ iva asmi)   I feel helpless

The absolutive

Of an ancient verbal action noun in **-tu** (cf. the Latin supine)
two cases survive in Classical Sanskrit: the accusative,
supplying the Sanskrit infinitive (नेतुम् **netum** 'to lead', with
strengthening of the root), and the instrumental, supplying
the absolutive (or 'gerund', or 'indeclinable participle')—नीत्वा
nītvā 'after leading, by leading', with weak grade of the root.

The absolutive in **-tvā** is not difficult to form. With very
few exceptions it may be obtained by substituting **tvā** for
the **-ta** or **-na** of the past participle (with internal sandhi as
appropriate). So उक्त्वा **uktvā** 'after saying', दृष्ट्वा **dṛṣṭvā**
'after seeing', लब्ध्वा **labdhvā** 'after taking', पतित्वा **patitvā**
'after falling', तीर्त्वा **tīrtvā** 'after crossing'.

The absolutive in **-tvā** may *not* be used when a verb is
compounded with a prefix or prefixes. In such a case the
suffix **-ya** (probably itself the instrumental of an old action
noun in **-i**) is added to the verb, which usually appears in its
weaker form. In internal sandhi, fortunately, **y** is without

effect on the preceding sound. Roots ending in a short vowel add -tya instead of -ya, and those roots ending in -an/-am which shorten to -a in the past participle may *optionally* do so (again shortening to -a). So संदृश्य saṃdṛśya 'after seeing', प्रत्युच्य pratyucya 'after replying', विजित्य vijitya 'after conquering', आगम्य āgamya or आगत्य āgatya 'after coming'.

(A minor exception to both the above formations is provided by derivative verbs in -ayati. They form their past participle in -ita but their simple absolutive in -ayitvā. In the compounded absolutive, they substitute -ya for -ayati in general but -ayya if the vowel of the stem is unstrengthened. So गमयित्वा gamayitvā 'after causing to go', आगमय्य āgamayya 'after causing to come', प्रवेश्य praveśya 'after causing to enter'. See pp. 102-5.)

The sense of the absolutive is generally that of action preceding the action of the main verb. Its closest equivalent is often therefore in primer English the perfect participle ('having led') and in ordinary English the present participle ('leading').

गृहं त्यक्त्वा वने परिभ्रमति gṛham tyaktvā vane paribhramati leaving his home, he wanders about in the forest

This might alternatively be translated as 'he leaves his home and wanders. . .'. In English both versions are possible. In Sanskrit a sequence of events is almost invariably represented by the use of absolutives rather than by clauses connected with च ca.

उद्यानं प्रविश्य कुमारं दृष्ट्वा प्रतिच्छन्दकमाच्छादयति udyānam praviśya kumāram dṛṣṭvā praticchandakam ācchādayati he enters the garden, sees the young man, and hides the picture

पुत्रमाह्य पृच्छामि putram āhūya pṛcchāmi I'll call my son and ask him

The subject of the action expressed by the absolutive is not necessarily the grammatical subject of the sentence. Rather it is the logical subject, which in passive sentences will be in the instrumental case and in some other sentences in yet some other case:

तेनापि श्लोकमवगम्य प्रतिवचनमुक्तम् (tena api ślokam ava-gamya prativacanam uktam) and he understood the stanza and spoke a reply

नृपाणां तु कुमारं दृष्ट्वात्यन्तं कुतूहलं भवति (nṛpāṇām tu kumāram dṛṣṭvā atyantam kutūhalam bhavati) [but of the kings, having seen the young man, an intense curiosity arises:] but the kings, on seeing the young man, feel an intense curiosity

Sometimes the logical subject itself remains unexpressed:

कथमचिरेणैव निर्माय लिखितः श्लोकः (katham acireṇa eva nirmāya likhitaḥ ślokaḥ) [what, after composing within a very short while, a stanza has been written:] why, he has (/you/they have) rapidly composed and written out a stanza

हन्त भोः शकुन्तलां विसृज्य लब्धमिदानीं स्वास्थ्यम् । hanta bhoḥ—Śakuntalām visṛjya labdham idānīm svāsthyam Oh, in bidding farewell to Śakuntalā (I have) now found ease

khalu

खलु khalu, like एव eva, is an enclitic particle of emphasis. But whereas eva is an affirmative particle stressing what is new, khalu is a confirmatory particle tending to stress what is already implicitly known. In consequence, whereas eva often marks out a predicate, khalu may equally well qualify the subject (or perhaps spread its emphasis more evenly over the whole statement). The subject is then usually placed first

in the sentence. For convenience, **khalu** is represented in
the exercises by 'indeed', 'assuredly', 'of course', 'after all',
'certainly'.

दारुणः खल्वसि। (dāruṇaḥ khalu asi) you are indeed
cruel

कापालिकः खल्वेषः। (kāpālikaḥ khalu eṣaḥ) this man
is assuredly a monster

अनुत्सेकः खलु विक्रमालंकारः। (anutsekaḥ khalu vikrama-
alaṃkāraḥ) modesty, after all, is valour's ornament

External sandhi

Now that a wider range of forms is occurring in the exercises,
attention is drawn to two disconcerting rules of external
sandhi: (a) final **n** preceded by a short vowel is doubled when
the next word begins with a vowel (thus when **n** closes a word,
the final syllable can never be light) and (b) **t** combines with
a following **ś** to make **cch**.

Vocabulary

आवेगः āvegaḥ alarm

उपायः upāyaḥ method,
means, way

कुमारः kumāraḥ (well-
born) young-man; prince;
Your/His Highness

क्षणः kṣaṇaḥ instant of
time, second, moment

देशः deśaḥ place; country

पादः pādaḥ foot

पुष्पं puṣpam flower

पुस्तकं pustakam book

प्रतिच्छन्दकं praticchandakam portrait, picture

प्रतिवचनं prativacanam
answer, reply

मार्गः mārgaḥ road

मित्रं mitram (N.B. gender)
friend

मुहूर्त muhūrta m./n.
short while, 'minute'

हृदयं hṛdayam heart,
mind

(**Kalahaṃsaka**, **Mādhava** and **Rāma** are proper names.)

अयम् ayam (*pron.*) this
अन्ध andha blind
अन्य anya (*pron.*) other
एक eka (*pron.*) one
कश्चित् कोऽपि kaś cit/ko ᾽pi
  (*see text of chapter*)

काण kāṇa one-eyed
पाप pāpa evil, bad; *m.*
  villain
सर्व sarva (*pron.*) all,
  every; *n. sg.* everything;
  m. sg. everyone

अभिलिख् abhi+likh (VI अभिलिखति abhilikhati) draw
  (picture)
अस् as (II अस्ति asti) be, exist
ग्रह् grah (IX गृह्णाति gṛhṇāti) seize, take
पत् pat (I पतति patati) fall
प्रभू pra+bhū (I प्रभवति prabhavati) arise; prevail, have
  power
भू bhū (I भवति bhavati) become, be
श्रु śru (V शृणोति śṛṇoti) hear, listen

अपि api and (*sentence connective, placed after subject*)
इदानीम् idānīm now
इह iha here; in this world

खलु khalu indeed *etc.*
तु tu (*enclitic*) but, however
हा hā ah! oh!

Exercise 5a

Translate into English:

इमौ खः ।१। प्रतिवचनं मे श्रुत्वा किमन्यदिच्छन्ति ।२। नास्त्येव
ते पुस्तकम् ।३। वयस्य हृदयमिवासि मम ।४। अस्मिन्नुद्याने
मुहूर्तमुपविश्वावः ।५। क्षेत्रेषु सर्वे भ्रमन्ति ।६। देव अन्यस्मान्न-
गराद्ब्राह्मणः कश्चिदागतः ।७। कमुपायं पश्यसि मम पुत्राणां
दर्शनाय ।८। क्रोधमस्य दृष्ट्वावेग इव नो हृदये ।९। अयं
कुमारस्तिष्ठति ।१०। कथं क्षणमेवोपविश्य दृष्टे मया पुनरपि मिचे

। ११। अन्यः को ऽपि मार्गो न भवति । १२। दुःखायैव मिथ्या-
णामिदानीं रामस्य दर्शनम् । १३। अन्येभ्यो ऽपि देवेनैतत्कृतम्
। १४। गृहं प्रविश्य क्व क्रीदानीं स पाप इति सर्वान्पृच्छति । १५।
अन्धानां देशे काण एव प्रभवति । १६। कलहंसक केनैतन्माधवस्य
प्रतिच्छन्दकमभिलिखितम् ॥ १७ ॥

Exercise 5b

Translate into Sanskrit:

1 You are blind indeed. 2 From this house he was led to the
woods. 3 And they went to the park and seized the villains.
4 The anger of these two is extraordinary. 5 You have been
seen, (my) sons. 6 But we have friends in Candanadāsa's
house. 7 I ask because I'm tired. 8 We have seen this on
all the country's roads. 9 Your Majesty, I am that same
prince. 10 He falls at the blind (man)'s feet. 11 By some
means I saw (them) all. 12 This reply of the prince (will
make) for anger. 13 But hearing this they sit in the road.
14 Kalahaṃsaka, we have no interest in books. 15 In just one
garden there are a few flowers. 16 Even after seeing everything Your Highness says nothing. 17 What, have you *doubt*
about it [atra]? 18 Oh Makaranda, oh Kalahaṃsaka, your
friend has gone. 19 But the prince stayed in another place
and heard the villain's whole reply. 20 What advantage does
this (man) see in anger?

Chapter 6

PARADIGMS: f. of **kānta**; f. of **saḥ, ayam** and other pronouns

Feminine gender

In addition to the masculine and neuter genders so far presented, Sanskrit has a feminine gender. Feminine substantives
in -ā decline like the feminine of the adjective **kānta**. There
are no masculine or neuter substantives that end in this -ā,
and no feminine substantives in -a. The majority of adjectives
(among them all past participles) that end in -a form their
feminine in -ā. A substantial minority, however, form their
feminine in -ī and inflect like **nadī** 'river' (among this group
are most adjectives formed by vṛddhi derivation). A certain
number of adjectives have the option of either formation: so
pāpā or **pāpī** (the latter is the more archaic form), feminine of
pāpa 'wicked'. Adjectives in -a with feminines in -ī are so
indicated in the vocabulary, but the use of forms in -ī is not
required in this chapter.

There is, of course, concord of adjectives, including pronominal adjectives, with feminine substantives:

vayasya, iyaṃ sā vārttā   friend, this is that news

Determinative compounds

Present-day English shows a considerable fondness for
forming determinatives. If the food we buy nowadays cannot

be urged on us as either 'home-baked' or 'farm-fresh', it is at

least quite likely to be 'oven-ready'. A determinative compound is one in which the final element, whether adjective or substantive, is merely further defined by what precedes it:

1 black:bird, girl:friend   new:found, ice:cold
2 door-stop   man-eating
3 sword-fight   hand-written
4 dining-room   accident-prone
5 book-learning   trouble-free
6 status-symbol   class-conscious
7 side-door   home-made

Each of the above examples is a limited exemplification of its final element. A blackbird is a bird, but of a particular kind; a dining-room is a room, but for a particular purpose. Similarly, the adjectives (including past participles) in the second column mean: cold to a particular degree, free from a particular thing, and so on.

If we compare determinative with other compounds, the point will become even clearer. Twenty; eight is not a particular kind of eight. Bare: foot is not a particular kind of foot (in fact, the compounded word is not even a substantive). Richard the Lion-heart was not a heart. And an over-head railway is not a 'head railway' of a special sort. (Our use of the underscore is explained on p. 118.)

In analysing in English the meaning of determinatives, we can usually make use of a preposition, chosen according to the sense of the compound. 'Home-made' no doubt means made *in* the home or *at* home (cf. home-baked); but 'hand-made' must mean made *by* hand or *with* one's hands. In Sanskrit it is broadly possible to express the relationship between the elements of any particular determinative (**tat-puruṣa**) compound in terms of one of the seven cases. The above English examples are set out according to this analysis. Compounds analysed as involving nominative relationship will be discussed below. Those involving relationship in any oblique case (accusative to locative) are known as *dependent* determinatives.

Dependent determinatives

In the punctuation of compounds in this book, dependent determinative relationship is represented by a hyphen. Occasionally, when a more precise analysis is desired, a number from 2 to 7 is superscribed, representing the particular case. So **pakṣa-dvāram** 'side-door', with locative (**saptamī** 'seventh case') relationship.

Assignment to a particular oblique case may sometimes be arbitrary, and irrelevant to understanding of the compound. 'Book-learning' has been taken to be learning *from* books, but it might be thought of as learning *in* books (locative) or perhaps *by means of* books (instrumental). As an example of accusative case relationship, 'door-stop' may not be thought entirely convincing (it is here treated as 'a stop (which stops) a door', but perhaps it is simply 'a stop *for* a door' or 'the stop *of* a door'). The point is, of course, that the accusative case essentially relates nouns to verbs. The corresponding relationship between substantives is expressed by the objective genitive. In a sense **nṛpa-darśanam** 'king-seeing' contains an accusative relationship, but expressed by separate words it would appear as **nṛpasya/nṛpayor/nṛpāṇām darśanam** 'sight of the king/kings'. (A subjective genitive relationship may also be expressed by a determinative compound: in the appropriate context **nṛpa-darśanam** could also mean 'sight *by* the king' etc.)

The last example will serve to remind you of the principle that stem forms are indeterminate between singular, dual and plural. There is a similar indeterminacy in English, as the example 'book-learning' will have suggested. In the same way a 'garage-owner' may own one or many garages. A phrase such as 'child welfare' (the welfare of children) shows that determinative relationship in English may exist between words not joined by a hyphen.

Although such compounds are frequent in English, they are by no means substitutable in all circumstances for more analytical turns of phrase. In general they denote characteristic rather than *ad hoc* relationships. A 'hand-held' camera is such by virtue of its design or at least some deliberate policy of its user. We do not say 'He brandished the hand-held book' instead of 'He brandished the book held in his hand'. In Classical Sanskrit there is no such inhibition. Wherever nouns are connected among themselves by oblique case relationships, compounds are formed extensively. In fact, a long sentence composed entirely of short words each with its own case termination would have seemed unnecessarily clumsy.

saṃvadaty ubhayor Mālatī-niveditaḥ śarīr_⟩-ākāraḥ
 [the appearance-of-body reported-by-Mālatī fits for both] they are both as Mālatī described them

kāla-jñā devī—kāry_⟩-ôparodhaṃ me pariharati Her Majesty is ['occasion-knowing'] tactful—she avoids interruption-of-my-business

The compound kāla-jña illustrates the fact that a number of forms are found at the end of determinative compounds which would never be used as words by themselves. In particular, many verbal roots are so used, predominantly with an active participial sense. If the root ends in a consonant, it is inflected according to the consonant declension (to be described later). Furthermore, roots ending in i, u or ṛ add a euphonic t. But roots in ā and certain others are simplified so as to end in a, and are inflected like kānta (thus kāla-jña, from jñā know).

dṛś see	sarva-dṛś all-seeing	
kṛ make	vighna-kṛt obstacle-making, interfering	
ji conquer	satya-jit conquering by truth	
sthā stand	mārga-stha standing (/being) in the road	
jan be born	jala-ja born in the water	

Very frequent also in such compounds is the root extended

by the suffix **a**. So side by side exist **jala-ruh**[7] (consonant-stem) and **jala-ruha**[7] (inflected like **kānta**) growing in the water.

Occasionally compounds are found in which the first member appears in an inflected instead of a stem form, and this is not uncommon when the final member cannot be used as an independent word. So **agre-ga** 'going in front' from **agram** 'front' and the root **gam**. From the same root **hṛdayaṃ-gama** 'going to the heart'. An example of a case termination (here dative singular) before a word which also occurs independently is the grammatical term **parasmai-padam** 'word for another, active voice'. In such instances, one of the most important criteria for the existence of a compound rather than two separate words is lacking, but others remain: in Vedic, specialised meaning or unity of accent; in Classical Sanskrit, specialised meaning or the ability to occur as part of a longer compound.

The word **arthaḥ** 'purpose' is used adverbially at the end of compounds, usually in the accusative case, **artham**, to mean 'for the sake of': **udakɔ-ârtham** 'for the sake of water', 'for water', 'to get water'; **kim-artham** 'for the sake of what', 'for what purpose', 'why?'.

The first member of a dependent determinative must be a nominal or pronominal substantive, or a substantivally used adjective (e.g. **priya** m. and **priyā** f. 'loved one'—or the first of these two forms, **priya**, used with neuter significance, 'benefit, service'). This does not apply to the other class of determinative compounds.

Descriptive determinatives

For this type of determinative there is a special name in Sanskrit, **karmadhāraya**. The notion that it expresses nominative relationship between the two members should not be pressed too far, for where the final member is an adjective it is not usually possible to achieve even an approximate representation of the sense of the compound merely by assigning the same case ending to the first member as to the second. The point is rather that in descriptives the first element stands in an attributive relationship (represented in the punctuation by a colon) to the second. Where the second element is a noun, the relationship is adjectival, the first element being either an adjective or a substantive used 'adjectivally', that is to say in apposition. Where the second element is an adjective, the relationship is adverbial, and the first element is either an adverbially used adjective (or sometimes an actual adverb) or an adverbially used substantive. Karmadhārayas may thus conveniently be discussed under four main headings.

1 *Adjective+substantive* (black:bird). What is true of such compounds in English originally applied in Sanskrit too. They were used principally where the compound had a conventional significance transcending the separate meanings of its parts. In the same way that 'blackbird' in English does not mean just any bird that is black, so the equivalent Sanskrit compound **kṛṣṇa:śakuni** meant, in fact, a crow. Even in the classical period it remains true that an adjective qualifying a substantive preserves its own inflexion in the vast majority of cases, in preference to being compounded in its stem form with the latter. However, there was a continuous whittling away at this principle. It was often violated in verse for reasons of metrical convenience. Common adjectives of unemphatic meaning such as **mahā** 'great' and **sva** '(my *etc.*) own' may be used fairly freely, and so may common collocations such as **priya: vayasyaḥ** 'dear friend'. In later Sanskrit prose words like **sarva** 'all' and **anya** 'other' are compounded in karmadhārayas with increasing frequency. In the exercises you should not yourself form karmadhārayas of adjective plus substantive unless directed to do so. (But this does *not* apply to karmadhārayas forming part of a longer compound: see Chapter 7.)

An adjective has only one stem form for all three genders, deriving from that of the masculine–neuter. So **priya:sakhī** 'dear [female] friend', not **priyāsakhī**, which could only be either two separate words or a dependent compound meaning 'friend of (my) sweetheart'.

2 *Substantive+substantive* (girl:friend). In these compounds
the substantives are in appositional relationship: so **rāja:ṛṣi**
'king-seer'. In particular, titles are compounded: **amātya:**
Bhūrivasu 'Minister Bhūrivasu', **bhaṭṭ:Ôdbhaṭaḥ** 'Dr
Udbhaṭa'. Other types are **strī:janaḥ** 'womenfolk', **dhvani:**
śabdaḥ 'the word "dhvani"'. Where proper names are
involved, the expected order is sometimes reversed: thus
Rāma:bhadraḥ 'dear Rāma', **Sītā:devī** 'Queen Sītā'.

One particular type of karmadhāraya made from two substantives is of great importance in literary style. It may be
called the karmadhāraya of comparison. According to Sanskrit
literary critics, it embodies the figure of speech called **rūpa-**
kam 'metaphor' (as opposed to **upamā** 'simile'), in which
one makes a comparison by stating directly that something is
something else. So if we take the word **padmam** 'lotus' and
qualify it by the word **pādaḥ** 'foot', we have the compound
pāda:padmam 'foot lotus, a lotus consisting of a foot'. This
means, in effect, 'a lotus-like foot', and such compounds are
often so translated, though strictly speaking such translations
would exemplify **upamā** and not **rūpakam**. The more
literal way to translate these compounds is by means of the
preposition 'of', also useful in translating other types of
appositional karmadhāraya, e.g. **Kāñcī:puram** 'the city of
Kāñcī': so 'the lotus of (your) foot'; **smita:jyotsnā** 'the moonlight of (her) smile'; **nara:puṃgavaḥ** 'a bull of a man', etc.:

> **katham, idānīm unmād‹:ôparāga eva Mādhav‹:ên-**
> **dum āskandati** what, does the eclipse of insanity now
> attack the moon of Mādhava? (*i.e.* does insanity engulf
> him, like an eclipse engulfing the moon?)

3 *adjective/adverb+adjective* (new:found). So from **udagra**
'intense' and **ramaṇīya** 'lovely', **udagra:ramaṇīya** 'intensely lovely'. A past participle as a final member is particularly common: **nava:baddha** 'new-bound, newly bound';
madhur‹:ôkta 'spoken sweetly'.

The first member may be an actual adverb: **punar:ukta**
'spoken again, repeated'; **anyathā:vādin** 'speaking otherwise'; **bahiḥ:śruta** 'heard outside'; **atra:stha** 'standing here'.

Certain past participles may be qualified adverbially by words which in a verbal sentence would stand in a predicative relationship. So corresponding to the sentence **sa śrānta āgacchati** 'he arrives tired' is the compound **śrānt:āgata** 'arriving tired'. In particular, substantives, adjectives or adverbs which would appear as the complement of the verb **bhū** 'be' may qualify its past participle **bhūta** 'having become, being': so **nimitta:bhūta** 'being the cause', **sukumāra:bhūta** 'being delicate', **evaṃ:bhūta** 'being so'. **bhūta** need not always be translated into English, serving merely to smooth or clarify the construction in Sanskrit, e.g.:

> **mad-anuja-maraṇa-nimitta:bhūtāyāḥ pāpāyā Bāla-candrikāyāḥ** of the wicked Bālacandrikā, cause of my brother's death . . .

(Occasionally an instance occurs of an adverb predicatively qualifying a *substantive*: **alam anyathā:saṃbhāvanayā** 'enough of supposing otherwise'.)

4 *substantive+adjective* (ice:cold). A substantive adverbially qualifying an adjective typically implies a comparison: **hima: śiśira** 'ice-cold, cold as ice'; **prāṇa:priya** 'dear as life'.

As karmadhārayas, these compounds have such a meaning. Ambiguity arises, however, because they may often be interpreted as dependent determinatives with, for instance, instrumental or ablative relationship: so **hima-śiśira** might mean 'cold because of the ice'. The same author may write in one place **priyaṅgu:śyāma** 'dark *as* the black vine', and in another **kādambinī-śyāmala** '(skies) dark *with* rainclouds'.

Prepositions

The relationships expressed by the Sanskrit case terminations are expressed in English by a number of prepositions: 'to', 'with', 'for', 'from', 'in', etc. The existence of six oblique cases, each used in a variety of circumstances, means that the use of prepositions is a comparatively unimportant feature of Sanskrit. In the Vedic language (as in other Indo-European

languages) the particles used as verbal prefixes are also found
functioning as prepositions, usually placed *after* the noun they
govern. But in Classical Sanskrit only two of these remain
really important, **ā** and **prati**. **ā** governs the ablative and
usually means 'up to': **ā samudrāt** 'up to the ocean'. It is the
only preposition regularly placed *before* its noun (the others
would more appropriately be called *post*positions). **prati**
means firstly 'towards, against' and, by extension, 'with
regard to': **vanaṃ prati** 'towards the forest', **devasyⱦ
âsvāsthyaṃ prati** 'with respect to Your Majesty's illness'.

anu (with accusative) 'after' also occurs. Related to the
verbal prefix **sam** is the preposition **saha** referred to in
Lesson 4.

In addition, there are a number of prepositions of adverbial
and nominal origin, for instance **vinā** (usually with instrumental) 'without', **paścāt** (with ablative or genitive) 'behind'.
These shade into the use, with the genitive, of a number of
nouns of somewhat blunted meaning, e.g. **madhye** 'in the
middle of, among': **eka eva mama putrāṇāṃ madhye**
'one alone among my sons'. Instead of the genitive, a determinative compound may be formed:

tan-madhyāt kim idam ekam? is this one [from
among:] of them?
jāla-mārgeṇa paśyāmaḥ let us watch [by way of:]
through the window

Occasionally such compounding occurs even with actual
prepositions: e.g. **rathⱦ-ôpari** instead of **rathasyⱦ ôpari**
'upon the chariot'.

Verbal action nouns in *a*

It is well worth noticing the more important types of nominal
stem formation from the Sanskrit root, not in order to form
such stems for oneself but in order to make sense of the relationship between various individual items of vocabulary. One

of the most important is the addition of **a** to the root to form a masculine substantive. Normally the root appears in guṇa grade, and the predominant meaning is of an abstract 'action' noun: so from the root **krudh** 'be angry', **krodhaḥ** 'anger'. Similarly, but with some development of meaning, from **diś** 'point', **deśaḥ** 'point, place, country'.

The verbal root and the derived noun may have a prefix: **sam+dih** 'smear, confuse', **saṃdehaḥ** 'confusion, doubt'; **upa+i** 'approach', **upāyaḥ** 'approach, means'.

Vṛddhi instead of guṇa is quite often found, but only where the resulting vowel is ā: **vi+sad** 'be dejected', **viṣādaḥ** 'dejection'; **bhṛ** 'bear', **bhāraḥ** 'burden'. The longer grade is particularly found after a prefix: thus from **ru** 'roar', **ravaḥ** 'roar' but **saṃrāvaḥ** 'uproar'.

A point to be noted particularly is that (for historical reasons) roots ending in a palatal stop usually change that stop to the corresponding velar: **vij** 'start, tremble', **āvegaḥ/saṃvegaḥ** 'agitation'; **śuc** 'grieve', **śokaḥ** 'grief'.

Among examples of the formation in the vocabulary of Exercise 6 are:

> **anu+śī** lie alongside, **anuśayaḥ** consequence, regret
> **abhi+laṣ** crave, **abhilāṣaḥ** craving
> **ā+rabh** begin, **ārambhaḥ** beginning
> **pari+has** laugh, **parihāsaḥ** laughter
> **prati+sidh** forbid, **pratiṣedhaḥ** prohibition
> **pra+viś** enter, **praveśaḥ** entry
> **vi+ava+hṛ** deal with, **vyavahāraḥ** dealings, usage

Ambiguities of external sandhi

Sometimes the operation of different sandhi rules can lead to a single result, so that the final form is ambiguous. The following are the ambiguities most likely to cause difficulty:

1 **nn** may represent **t+n** or **n+n**.

> *Example*: **asmānna** ← **asmāt+na** or **asmān+na**

Furthermore, if the vowel preceding the **nn** is short, this may represent the sandhi of final **n** before a vowel.

Example: **paśyannāste** ← **paśyan+āste, paśyan+nāste** *or* **paśyat+nāste**

2 **a** before a vowel other than **a** may represent **aḥ** *or* **e**.

Example: **aśva eva** ← **aśvaḥ+eva** *or* **aśve eva**

(Theoretically the **a** might also represent a final **o**, but this is rare.)

3 **ā** before a voiced consonant may represent **āḥ** *or* simple **ā**.

Example: **kanyā nayati** ← **kanyāḥ nayati** *or* **kanyā nayati**

4 **cch** may represent **t+ś** *or* **t+ch**.

Example: **asmācchalāt** ← **asmāt+śalāt** *or* **asmāt+chalāt**

5 **ggh** etc. may represent a stop followed by **h** *or* by **gh** etc.

Example: **asmāddhṛtāt** ← **asmāt+hṛtāt** *or* **asmāt+dhṛtāt**

6 Long vowel followed by **r** may represent long/short vowel with **ḥ** *or* itself alone.

Example: **śucī rakṣati** ← **śuciḥ rakṣati, śucīḥ+rakṣati** *or* **śucī+rakṣati**

The sandhi of two vowels is also a source of ambiguity, but here a learner is less likely to assume one particular resolution of the sandhi. The possibilities implicit in the sandhi vowels **ā, ī, ū, e, ai, o, au** are set out in the table on p. 36.

Vocabulary

akṣaraṃ syllable, written character

anarthaḥ reverse, disaster

anuśayaḥ repentance, regret

abhijña conversant with (*gen.*)

abhilāṣaḥ craving, passion for (*loc.*)

amātyaḥ minister

ambā (*irreg. voc.* **amba**) mother (*either one's own or as a title of respect*)

avasthā state, condition

asphuṭa unclear, illegible

āgamanaṃ coming, arrival

ārambhaḥ beginning

ārya noble, honourable; *f.* noble lady

āśaṅkā apprehension

āśā hope

āśramaḥ hermitage

īdṛśa (*f.* **ī**) of this kind, such

uddeśaḥ region, part, place

uparāgaḥ eclipse

ubha both (*only dual*)

katama (*pr. adj.*) which?

kanyā girl, daughter

kaṣṭa grievous, harsh; **kaṣṭam** alas

kāryaṃ task

kālaḥ time

kulaṃ family

kuśalaṃ welfare

Kusumapuraṃ *name of city*

Kaumudī-mahotsavaḥ Full Moon Festival

caritaṃ conduct, deeds

cintā worry

tāpasaḥ ascetic

Duḥṣantaḥ *pr. n.*

dvayaṃ couple, pair (*one way of expressing* two)

niyata constrained; **niyatam** necessarily

niyojyaḥ servant

nirvāṇaṃ bliss

netraṃ eye

°pathaḥ (*usually ifc.*) path

parihāsaḥ joke

puraṃ city

pauraḥ citizen; **paura:janaḥ** citizens, townsfolk

Pauravaḥ descendant of Puru

prajā subject (of king)

pratiṣedhaḥ prohibition, cancellation

prathita widely known

pradeśaḥ place

prayojanaṃ purpose

pravātaṃ breeze

praveśaḥ entry, entering

priyā beloved (woman)

bhadra good; *f. voc.* madam

maṇḍapa *m./n.* pavilion, bower

mahā:rājaḥ great king

mah»:ôtsavaḥ [great] festival, holiday

Mādhavyaḥ *pr. n.*

Mārīcaḥ *pr. n.*

mudrā seal

mūḍha deluded, idiotic; *m.* idiot

mṛgaḥ deer

Lakṣmaṇaḥ *pr. n.*

latā creeper

lokaḥ world

vārttā news

Vāsavaḥ (*epithet of*) Indra

vistīrṇa extensive

vṛttāntaḥ news, happening

Vṛṣalaḥ *pr. n.*

vyavahāraḥ usage

vyasanaṃ vice, vicious failing

vrataṃ vow

Śakuntalā *pr. n.*

Śoṇottarā *pr. n.*

śravaṇaṃ hearing

śrotriyaḥ learned (brahmin), scholar

samvegaḥ agitation

satya true; **satyam** truly

subhaga delightful

sevā attendance (upon some-one), servitude

sthānam place, occasion; **sthāne** in place, appropriate

ā+pat (I āpatati) befall, happen

upa+gam (I upagacchati) go to, reach

pari+grah (IX parigṛhṇāti) accept

pari+bhuj (VII paribhunakti; *p.p.* paribhukta) enjoy

pra+nam (I praṇamati) make obeisance to (*dat./gen./loc./ acc.*)

prati+sidh (I pratiṣedhati) restrain, forbid

labh (I *ātm.* labhate; *p.p.* labdha) take, gain, win

vi+pra+labh (vipralabhate) mislead, deceive

aho oh

ittham thus, so

iha here

kim-artham for what purpose, why?

kutaḥ? from where?

tat (*first word in sentence, frequent connecting particle*) so, then

tarhi (*usually enclitic*) in that case

nanu surely (*often in objection to a previous remark*)

prati (*+acc.*) to, towards; with regard to

Note: The abbreviations *ibc.* and *ifc.* signify respectively 'in the beginning (i.e. as first half) of a compound' and '*in fine compositi*, as second half of a compound'.

Exercise 6a

Translate into English:

श्रोणोत्तरे किमागमनप्रयोजनम् ।१। कष्टम् — अनर्थद्वयमापतितम् ।२। महाराज अपि कुशलं कुमारलक्ष्मणस्य ।३। कुतः पुनरियं वार्त्ता ।४। सत्यमित्यंभूत एवासि ।५। अमात्य विक्षीर्णः कुसुमपुरवृत्तान्तः ।६। त्वमार्याभिः पुत्र इव गृहीतः ।७। कतमस्मिन्प्रदेशे मारीचाश्रमः ।८। अम्ब कासि — किमर्थमहं त्वया प्रतिषिद्धः ।९। नन्वनुशयस्थानमेतत् ।१०। सैवेयम् ।११। उभा-

भ्यामपि वां वासवनियोज्यो दुःषन्तः प्रणमति ।१२। कष्टा खलु
सेवा ।१३। न खलु वृषलस्य श्रवणपथमुपगतो ऽयं मया छतः
कौमुदीमहोत्सवप्रतिषेधः ।१४। किं तवानया चिन्तया ।१५।
माधव्य अप्यस्ति ते शकुन्तलादर्शनं प्रति कुतूहलम् ।१६। श्रोचिय-
लिखितान्यचराणि प्रयत्नलिखितान्यपि नियतमस्फुटानि भवन्ति
॥ १७ ॥

Exercise 6b

Words joined together by points (·) should be translated by
a single compound.

1 This is a deer·of·the·hermitage.   2 A beginning·in·the·task
has been made.   3 Here stands Minister·Rākṣasa.   4 Idiot,
this is no time·for·jokes.   5 In that case whose is this seal?
6 You are indeed conversant with the usages·of·the·world.
7 Then did the townsfolk not accept [our·word:] what we
said?   8 Oh, this part·of·the·wood is delightful·for·its·breeze.
9 Do not be apprehensive.   10 (I) have gained a bliss·for·the·
eyes.   11 How (is it that) you do not see Rāma's condition?
12 Sārṅgarava, such agitation [of you:] on your part from·
entering·the·city is indeed appropriate.   13 Descendants of
Puru have this family·vow.   14 Madam, Duḥṣanta's·conduct
is widely known among his subjects.   15 Then have done
now with the vice·of·hope.   16 I do not of course *truly* have
a passion for the ascetic's·daughter.   17 But with regard to
the eclipse·of·the·moon, someone has misled you [*f.*].   18 I'll
stay for a while just here in the bower·of·creepers enjoyed·by·
(my)·beloved.

Chapter 7

<small>PARADIGMS:</small> Unchangeable consonant stems (**suhṛd, manas,** *etc.*); **nadī**

Nominal stems ending in consonants

The largest class of nouns in Sanskrit is the 'thematic **a**' class, the members of which are inflected like **aśvaḥ** or **phalam**. But historically speaking, thematic **a** is a formational suffix added either to a root or to an existing stem. Nominal stems ending in a consonant in general represent an earlier stage of Indo-European word formation. They may consist of a plain root used in a nominal sense (so from **yudh** 'fight', **yudh** f. 'battle'—and, more important in Classical Sanskrit, the use of a root form at the end of a determinative, as described in Chapter 6); or of the root extended by some consonantal suffix (so from **sad** 'sit', **sadas** n. and **sadman** n. 'seat'). There are two main reasons why the inflexion of consonant stems is more complicated than that of thematic **a** stems. One is that variations may occur in the basic form of the stem in inflexion, due ultimately to an ancient shift of accent. Stems exhibiting this variation are not introduced until Chapter 8. The other reason is that direct contact between the final consonant of the stem and the case terminations causes a number of internal sandhi changes. As opposed to a single stem in thematic **a**, we have in fact a series of related stems in **c, j, t, th, d, dh, p, bh, ś, ṣ, h, as, is, us**, etc.

The basic terminations of consonant stem nouns are exhibited in the declension of the stem **suhṛd** 'friend'. Before a *vowel* the stem final remains unchanged (except that s after i etc. becomes ṣ by internal sandhi—cf. Chapter 4); in the nominative singular or before a termination beginning with a *consonant*, it must be reduced to one of the 'permitted finals' and the rules of *external* sandhi thereafter applied (with consequent voicing before bh, lack of voice before su). This reduction is according to the following scheme (a number of sounds not actually occurring as nominal stem finals are included for completeness):

k, kh, ġ, ġh ; c, *j, *ś, *h *become* k
ṭ, ṭh, ḍ, ḍh ; ch, *j, jh ; *ś, ṣ, *h *become* ṭ
t, th, d, dh ; *h *become* t
p, ph, b, bh *become* p
ṅ, ñ *become* ṅ
n, m *remain*
s *becomes* ḥ, r *remains*
ṇ, y, l, v *do not occur*

The asterisked sounds (j ś h) are those treated differently in different words: where ambiguity exists, the nominative singular form is added in brackets after the stem form in the vocabulary. In a number of words, for historical reasons, a final aspirate throws its aspiration back upon a preceding stop: ġo-duh 'cow-milking', nom. sg. ġo-dhuk.

Feminine consonant stems are inflected like the masculine (though changeable masculine stems may often form corresponding feminines in ī). Among the unchangeable stems, neuters are rare—except for stems in s, which are rarely masculine or feminine (unless at the end of an exocentric compound). Neuter stems have no termination in the nominative, vocative or accusative singular; add ī for au in the dual; and i for aḥ in the plural, with n infixed before a final stop or sibilant and assimilated as appropriate to the class nasal or to anusvāra. The nominative singular of masculine/feminine nouns in as is with lengthened a: āḥ.

In addition to learning the paradigm suhṛd, you should study carefully the examples listed after it of stems ending in other consonants.

Feminines in *ī*

The suffix ī, inflected as in **nadī**, is important as forming a large number of derivative feminine stems—in particular, as mentioned above and in Chapter 6, the feminine of changeable consonant stems and of many stems in **a**.

Causatives

In addition to a simple present tense formed according to one (occasionally more than one) of the ten classes, and to perfect and aorist tenses, to be described later, a verbal root may form some five other finite tense systems, all inflected as if they were thematic presents like **nayati/nayate**. They are: future (**neṣyati** 'will lead'), passive (**nīyate** 'is led'), causative (**nāyayati** 'causes to lead, makes (someone) lead, has (someone) lead/led'), desiderative (**ninīṣati** 'wants to lead') and intensive (**nenīyate** 'leads forcibly'). From the point of view of their formation, all these five are on a more or less equal footing; but since the last three are felt to involve a more fundamental modification of the meaning of the verb and may make formations from their stems (e.g. a past participle) outside the thematic **a** paradigm, they are usually classed together as derivative or secondary conjugations.

Of these three the causative is by far the most important. It may be regarded as having evolved out of the tenth verb class through specialisation of form and meaning. The principal features of its formation are the suffix **aya** and a strengthening of the root. The syllable before **aya** should usually be heavy. Therefore guṇa of the root is almost always employed where this produces a heavy syllable: so from **dṛś, darśayati** 'causes to see, shows'. If the root when strengthened to guṇa grade is still light, vṛddhi is usually employed: **kṛ, kārayati** 'causes to do'; **bhū, bhāvayati** 'causes to be'. But a few causatives with light first syllable are found: **gam, gamayati** 'causes to go'; **tvar, tvarayati** 'causes to hurry'. Among exceptional forms with neither guṇa nor vṛddhi (but still with heavy first syllable) are **duṣ, dūṣayati** 'spoils' and **pṝ, pūrayati** 'fills'.

Most verbs ending in **ā** and some others, including **ṛ** 'go', **adhi+i** 'study' and optionally **ruh** 'rise', take the suffix **p**: **sthā, sthāpayati** 'establishes'; **ṛ, arpayati** 'transfers'; **ruh, rohayati** or **ropayati** 'raises'. An important anomalous form (evidently denominative in origin) is **ghātayati** 'has killed, puts to death' functioning as the causative of **han** 'kill'.

Causatives exist in English, though they are not a morphologically prominent feature of the language. 'Fell' is the causative of 'fall'—'he fells the tree': so 'lay' of 'lie', 'raise' of 'rise'. More frequently, what is expressed by the Sanskrit causative we express by transitive use of otherwise intransitive verbs:

vṛkṣo rohati a tree grows   **artho vardhate** wealth grows, increases

vṛkṣaṃ ropayati he grows a tree   **arthaṃ vardhayati** he increases his wealth

The frequency of causative forms in Sanskrit means that often what we express by pairs of unrelated words in English is directly expressed in Sanskrit by a causative formation: **jan** 'be born', **janayati** 'begets'; **vi+dru** 'run away', **vidrāvayati** 'puts to flight, chases away'. In the same way the French causative *faire voir* 'make to see' or the Sanskrit equivalent **darśayati** may be translated by the English 'show'.

Where, as in the earlier examples, a causative is formed from an intransitive verb, the original subject becomes the object. Where a causative is formed from an already transitive verb, the displaced subject may either join the existing object as a further object in the accusative case or be treated as an agent in the instrumental case:

dāso harati bhāram   a servant carries the luggage

hārayati bhāraṃ dāsam   he has a servant carry the luggage

hārayati bhāraṃ dāsena   he has the luggage carried by a servant

Choice of one or the other is a matter of usage. Construction with the instrumental may be taken as the general rule. But some verbs, notably **kṛ** 'do' and **hṛ** 'carry', are found with either construction. A number of others are regularly found with a double accusative: among these are **smārayati** (**smṛ** 'remember') 'reminds', **āśayati** (**aś** 'eat') 'feeds', **pāyayati** 'makes to drink', **adhyāpayati** 'teaches', **bodhayati** (**budh** 'learn') 'informs', **lambhayati** (irreg. from **labh**) 'causes to take'; and some other verbs with similar meanings.

The formation of absolutives and past participles from the causative stem has already been mentioned (Chapters 4 and 5). In the past participle **ita** is simply substituted for **aya**. A point to note in connection with the past participle is that causatives construed with two accusatives often make the 'secondary' object into the subject of the passive voice, leaving a 'retained accusative' as in English:

> **udakaṃ lambhitā ete vṛkṣāḥ**   these trees have been [caused to take:] given water
>
> **samanantaraṃ garbhᵥ-aîkādaśe varṣe kṣātreṇa kalpenᵥ ôpanīya trayī-vidyām adhyāpitau**   thereafter in the eleventh year from [the womb:] conception, after being initiated according to the kṣatriya rite, (the two of them) were [caused to study:] taught the Science of the Three (Vedas)

Some roots form causatives without causative meaning: so from **dhṛ** 'hold', **dhārayati** 'he holds'. This might be considered a class X verb if the forms **dharati** etc. were not also theoretically possible. Outside the present, formations are often made from the simple root: past participle **dhṛta** is commoner than **dhārita**. Much the same is true of **pṝ**, **pūrayati** 'fills', p.p. **pūrṇa**. With some other verbs, although the simple present is not uncommon, causative forms often seem to occur without any obvious distinction of sense: e.g. **yunakti** or **yojayati** (**yuj**) 'joins'; **muñcati** or **mocayati** (**muc**) 'releases'; **niṣedhati** or **niṣedhayati** (**ni+sidh**) 'prevents'.

Some causatives with well-established meanings behave like simple verbs in their constructions. So **darśayati** 'shows', in addition to the construction with two accusatives, often takes a genitive of reference: **indrāyudhaṃ na kasya cid dar-śayati** 'he does not show the rainbow to anyone'. Similarly, **nivedayati** '[causes to know:] informs', like other verbs meaning 'tell', may take a dative (or genitive) of the indirect object, while **arpayati** 'transfers, hands over' may behave like any verb of giving: **ābharaṇaṃ sūtasyᵒ ârpayati** 'he hands over his insignia to his driver'.

Class X verbs

The present stem of verbs belonging to class X is formed with the addition of the suffix **aya**: so from the root **spṛh** 'desire', **spṛhayati** 'he desires'. But, as has just been described, the suffix **aya** in conjunction with a strengthening of the root is used to form causatives, while another suffix, **ya,** frequently preceded by a short **a,** is used in the formation of denominative verbs (see Lesson 9). And, in fact, all but a handful of the verbs classified by the grammarians under class X may be looked on either as causatives (but lacking obvious causative significance) or as denominatives (but receiving the old tonic accent upon the first **á**, instead of upon the **yá** as do regular denominatives):

> **chad, chādayati** covers
> **varṇ, varṇayati** depicts, describes (*really from* **varṇaḥ** colour, appearance: *the root* **varṇ** *is artificially contrived*)
> **kath, kathayati** relates, tells (*really from* **katham** how?—*i.e.* says how, relates circumstances)

Karmadhārayas with inseparable prefixes

Just as the second member of a *dependent* determinative may be a form that cannot occur in isolation, so the first member of a *descriptive* may be a prefix incapable of independent use. Under this heading might logically be included all verbal nouns beginning with prefixes. Thus, as a compound of **gamanaṃ** 'going', **nirgamanaṃ** 'outgoing'. But where corresponding verbal forms occur or are possible (thus **nirgacchati** 'goes out'), this analysis is unnecessary.

Occasionally, however, verbal prefixes are compounded with nouns where no corresponding verbal form exists: so **adhi:pati** 'over:lord', **ati:dūra** 'extremely far', **prati: nayanam** 'encountering eye', **prati:śabdah** '[responding sound:] echo', **ā:śyāmala** 'darkish'.

More frequent are a number of prefixes never compounded with finite verbs:

su (laudatory particle) 'well, very'—**su:kṛta** 'done well', **su:pakva** 'well cooked, very ripe', **su:bhadra** 'very good', **su:janah** 'nice person', **su:vicārah** 'proper thought'.

dus (pejorative particle) 'ill, badly'—**dur:ukta** 'ill spoken', **duś:ceṣṭā** 'misconduct', **dur:gandhah** 'bad smell, stench'. Like other prefixes ending in **s**, **dus** conforms to internal sandhi, and thus has **ṣ** instead of **ḥ** before **k/kh** and **p/ph**: **duṣ:kṛta** 'ill done'. (Sandhi before other sounds follows the usual pattern.)

Corresponding to the verbal prefix **sam**, occurs occasionally **sa** or **saha** 'together': **saha:maraṇam** 'dying together', **sa:brahmacārin** 'fellow-student'.

The most important karmadhāraya prefix is the negative particle **a** (before consonants) or **an** (before vowels). Unlike other 'non-verbal' prefixes, it may be compounded freely not only with ordinary adjectives and substantives and with past participles but also with other participles and with absolutives and gerundives: **a:kṛta** 'unmade, undone', **an:ukta** 'unspoken', **a:dharmah** 'unrighteousness', **an:ati˘dūra** 'not particularly far', **an:āgacchant** 'not coming'. The negation not infrequently qualifies a whole compound: **a:guṇa˘jña** 'not recognising merit', **a:loka˘sāmānya** 'not common in the world', **a:kāla˘kṣep›˘ârha** 'not brooking delay'.

Especially noteworthy is the use with the absolutive. The best translation is usually 'without': **a:dṛṣṭvā** 'not having seen, without seeing'. Note that the addition of **a/an**, unlike that of a verbal prefix, does not in itself entail the use of the compounded (**ya**) form of the absolutive.

uttaram a:dattv» aîva prasthitā she set off without giving any reply

pūrva

A curious anomaly in the formation of karmadhāraya compounds is that the word **pūrva** 'previous' used adverbially may be placed after the word it qualifies; so **pūrva:kṛta** or **kṛta:pūrva** 'previously done, already done'.

 kim atrabhavatī mayā pariṇīta:pūrvā? Did I previously marry this lady?

Compounds of more than two members

Determinative compounds are based upon a relationship between a prior element and a final element. In a sense therefore a determinative, considered in itself, cannot possibly consist of more than two parts. However, either of these parts may in turn on closer analysis be found to consist of a compound expression, itself resolvable into its constituent parts. In English 'waste paper basket' is a dependent: a basket not 'for paper' but 'for waste paper'. But the prior element is itself a compound, a descriptive determinative 'paper which is waste', subordinated to a larger whole. We may represent the subordination by brackets: (waste:paper)-basket. Thus in Sanskrit:

Mālatī-mukham Mālatī's face
(Mālatī-mukh·)-âvalokanam gazing on Mālatī's face

From a different starting-point, **mukh·-âvalokanam** 'gazing on a face', we may arrive at a compound with the same form but a different meaning:

Mālatī-(mukh·-âvalokanam) Mālatī's gazing on a face

The fact that this latter is a far less natural interpretation illustrates an important point about Sanskrit compounds: they build up as they go along. As each element is added to the compound, it should form by itself a complete final element, to which all that precedes will stand in the relation of prior element:

Mālatī-mukha
(Mālatī-mukh·)-âvalokana

> **[(Mālatī-mukh‹)-âvalokana]-vihasta**   clumsy from gazing on Mālatī's face

This is not an absolute rule. But it represents the first interpretation that will occur to the reader's mind. If therefore two or more elements are to be added *en bloc*, i.e. 'bracketed', they must form a natural group: in other words, the first of the added elements must group itself more naturally with what follows than with what precedes, as in the following:

> **(sāyaṃtana:snāna)-(saviśeṣa:śītala)**   completely cool from the evening bathe

Since it merely represents the normal rhythm of a Sanskrit compound, it is not necessary to indicate by successive bracketings the progressive expansion of the prior element of a compound. Where, on the other hand, a subordinated group is added as the *final* element (for the moment) of the compound, this may be most simply indicated by some sign for subordination, such as ˘, above the relationship sign within the group. The above thus becomes:

> **sāyaṃtana:snāna-saviśeṣa˘śītala**

Slightly more complex is the following:

> **pratyagra:sāyaṃtana˘snāna-saviśeṣa˘śītala**   completely cool from the recent evening bathe

This is a compound built up in three stages:

> **pratyagra**   recent
> **pratyagra:sāyaṃtana˘snāna**   recent evening-bathe
> **pratyagra:sāyaṃtana˘snāna-saviśeṣa˘śītala**

The first three words in this compound illustrate two points. First, as remarked in Chapter 6, there is no restriction on the use of karmadhāraya compounds as part of a longer compound, provided that the finally completed compound is not in itself a karmadhāraya (the rule boils down to this: in general, if you can avoid a karmadhāraya simply by putting an inflexion on an adjective, or on a compound functioning as an adjective, do so). Secondly, where two adjectives qualify the same substantive within a compound, it is more likely that the second is in a closer relationship with the substantive and thus forms a subordinate unit with it than that the two adjectives are linked in a co-ordinative relationship. So in English 'startled: old ̆:woman' means an old woman who is startled, not a woman who is startled and old.

Like karmadhārayas, dvandva compounds occur very frequently as a subordinate part of a longer compound:

Pārā ̣:Sindhu-saṃbhedam avagāhya nagarīm eva pravisāvaḥ let us bathe at the confluence of the (rivers) Pārā and Sindhu, and go into the city

aho samāna:vayo ̆:rūpa-ramaṇīyaṃ sauhārdam atrabhavatīnām how delightful [for the similar age-and-looks:] for its equality in youth and looks is the friendship of you (young) ladies

Within a subordinate group a further subordinate (or 'double-bracketed') group may sometimes be detected. This is even less frequent than one-degree subordination. Subordination in general is more frequent in bahuvrīhi compounds (see Chapter 8) than in determinatives. Here is an example of such a compound, one that can actually be analysed as including *three* degrees of subordination. The point is that such compounds are possible because the way the elements group together is natural and immediately evident to anyone who knows Sanskrit.

virājat ̣:katipaya ̆:komala ̆:danta ̆:kutmal ̆:âgra with (a few (tender (tips of budlike teeth))) gleaming out

If you find any difficulty in grasping the logic of subordinate groupings, remember the analogy with algebra, and 'first solve what is within brackets'—i.e. determine the meaning of words linked by the sign ̆ before relating them to the rest of the compound.

In theory, any word standing outside a compound may form a grammatical relationship only with the compound as a whole, not simply with some prior portion of it. In practice, in Classical Sanskrit this rule is sometimes violated if the alternative of incorporating the extra word into the compound is inconvenient or not sufficiently clear. Typically one may find that a word or phrase in the genitive qualifies the first element or elements of a following compound:

tasya kāmʋ-ônmattasya citra:vadha-vārttā-preṣaṇena (please me) by sending news of the [variegated death:] death by torture of that love-crazed (one)

Here the genitive **-unmattasya** qualifies **citra:vadha** not **-preṣaṇena**.

The use of long compounds

A single compound inserted into a Sanskrit sentence may serve the purpose of a whole clause or even of a separate sentence in English. The following sentence:

itaḥ pradeśād apakramya Mādhavʋ-âpakāraṃ praty abhiniviṣṭā bhavāmi   I'll withdraw from this place and become intent upon the ruin of Mādhava

may be augmented by a compound qualifying **pradeśāt**:

ito Mālatī-vivāha-parikarma-satvara:pratīhāra-śata-saṃkulāt pradeśād apakramya *etc.*   I'll withdraw from this place, (which is) crowded with hundreds of porters busy on preparations for Mālatī's wedding, and work for Mādhava's ruin

But the announcement of withdrawal in the word **apakramya** occurs late in the sentence. We would therefore be more faithful to one aspect of the original, the order of ideas, by translating:

This place is crowded with porters busy on preparations for Mālatī's wedding: I'll withdraw and *etc.*

or even

> Preparations for Mālatī's wedding have brought hundreds of porters flooding into here *etc.*

On the other hand, if we always adhere religiously to the order of the original, this may involve us in destroying its structure, and the latter may sometimes be the more important. This is the dilemma of all translators faced with the more elaborate styles of Sanskrit, and there is no general solution: each case must be judged on its merits.

The construction of long compounds is exploited to good effect in both literary and academic prose, making possible the handling of a vast mass of detail without any obscuring of the main thread of narrative or argument. Beginners in writing Sanskrit prose, however, often misguidedly attempt large numbers of exceptionally long compounds. These are difficult to handle successfully, and the translation of ordinary English prose offers little scope for them. A practical limit to aim at is the compound of three, four or, very occasionally, five members. Page after page of elegant, perspicuous Sanskrit may be read containing no compound longer than this.

gata

The past participle **gata** 'gone to' is often used at the end of a compound to mean '[being] in', without any sense of prior motion. Thus **citra-gatā nārī** 'the woman in the picture'; **kara-tala-gatā ‹kṣamālā** 'the rosary in (his) hand'.

> **Sugāṅga:prāsāda-gatena deven› âham āryasya pāda-mūlaṃ preṣitaḥ** His Majesty was in the Sugāṅga Palace when he sent me to Your Honour['s feet]

(It would be wrong to translate this as 'having gone to the palace, His Majesty *etc.*' For the latter sense one should rather use the absolutive **gatvā**.)

gata may also be translated by 'referring to, about', or it may represent the locative used with verbs of feeling: **putra-gataḥ snehaḥ** 'affection towards a son, love of a son'.

Vocabulary

atyanta excessive, extreme

atyāhitaṃ calamity

a:darśanaṃ lack of sight, not seeing

Avalokitā *pr. n.*

a:vinayaḥ lack of breeding, discourtesy

astraṃ missile, weapon

a:sthāne not in place, inappropriate

ābharaṇaṃ ornament

āryaḥ Your Honour; *voc.* sir

āharaṇaṃ (act of) fetching

udvigna distressed

Urvaśī *pr. n.*

ṛtvij (ṛtvik) m. priest

auṣadhaṃ medicine

kathā story; talk, speaking

kṣīra-vṛkṣaḥ fig-tree

kṣudra mean, common, low

gātraṃ limb

ghātakaḥ executioner

Candraguptaḥ *pr. n.*

cira long (*of time*); **ciraṃ** for a long time

cūrṇaṃ powder

chāyā shade

tātaḥ (one's own) father

tīraṃ bank

darbhaḥ (*and pl.*) a type of (sacrificial) grass

dūre far away

devī goddess; (the) Queen, Her (/Your) Majesty

nirvṛta content, happy

puruṣaḥ man

pūrva previous; *in karmadhāraya* previously, before, once, already

prakāraḥ manner, way

pratīkāraḥ remedy

prabhāvaḥ power

bhagavatī Her Reverence

bhayaṃ fear, danger

bhavatī you (*polite form of address to woman*)

madanaḥ (sexual) love

madanₐ-ôdyānaṃ park of (temple to the god of) Love

miśra mixed

yatnaḥ effort

yoga-cūrṇaṃ magic powder

Rākṣasaḥ *pr. n.*

Rāmāyaṇaṃ *name of an epic poem*

vaṇij (vaṇik) m. businessman, trader

vatsala affectionate, loving

vadhya condemned to death

vibhāgaḥ part, portion

vivādaḥ disagreement, dispute

vṛkṣaḥ tree

vedanā ache, pain

vedī (sacrificial) altar

vaidyaḥ doctor

vyakta evident, clear; **vyaktam** clearly

śarīraṃ body

śiras *n.* head

saṃstaraṇaṃ (act of) strewing

sakhī [female] friend

samidh *f.* firewood

sarasī lake

sahya bearable

Sītā *pr. n.*

suhṛd *m.* friend

saujanyaṃ kindness

snehaḥ affection, love

sparśaḥ touch

sva *pron. adj.* (one's) own

svāgatam (*lit.* 'well come') welcome to (*dat.*)

anu + grah (IX anugṛhṇāti) favour

apa+hṛ (I apaharati)   carry off
ava+tṝ (I avatarati)   descend; *caus.* (avatārayati)   remove
ā+śri (I āśrayati/āśrayate)   resort to (*acc.*)
upa+ram (I uparamate)   cease, die
upa+hṛ (I upaharati)   offer
kath (X kathayati)   tell, relate
kḷp (I kalpate)   be suitable; *caus.* (kalpayati)   arrange, prepare
kṣud (I kṣodati *p.p.* kṣuṇṇa)   trample, tread
dṛś *caus.* (darśayati)   show
dhṛ *caus.* (dhārayati)   hold, carry, wear
ni+yuj (VII niyuṅkte)   engage (someone) upon (*loc.*)
pā (I pibati)   drink; *caus.* (pāyayati)   make to drink
prati+pāl (X pratipālayati)   wait for
prati+budh *caus.* (pratibodhayati)   wake (someone)
prati+i *caus.* (pratyāyayati)   make confident
pra+yuj (VII prayuṅkte)   employ
pra+sthā (I pratiṣṭhate)   set out
pra+iṣ *caus.* (preṣayati)   despatch, send
lajj (VI lajjate)   be embarrassed; *caus.* (lajjayati)   embarrass
vi+krī (IX vikrīṇīte)   sell to (*loc.*)
vi+cint (X vicintayati)   consider, think of
vi+dru (I vidravati)   run away; *caus.* (vidrāvayati)   disperse,
  chase away
vi+dhā (III vidadhāti)   arrange, manage
vi+yuj (VII viyuṅkte)   disjoin, deprive of (*instr.*)
vṛdh (I vardhate)   grow; *caus.* (vardhayati)   increase

aye   ah!
tena hi   therefore
tāvat (*enclitic, lit.* meanwhile)
  and yāvat (*usually first word,*
  lit. during which time) *are*

used to express a present inten-
tion, and may be represented by
just in English (as in I'll just
buy a newspaper)

Exercise 7a

अये इयं देवी ।१। प्रतिबोधित एवास्मि केनापि ।२। इदममा-
त्यराजसगृहम् ।३। अहो वत्सलेन सुहृदा वियुक्ताः स्मः ।४।
सुविचिन्तितं भगवत्या ।५। आर्ये अपि सह्या शिरोवेदना ।६।
लज्जयति मामत्यन्तसौजन्यमेषाम् ।७। तेन हीमां चीरवृच्छा-
यामाश्रयामः ।८। चिरमदर्शनेनार्यस्य वयमुद्विग्नाः ।९। स्वागतं
देव्यै ।१०। अलमस्मद्विनयाग्रहणया ।११। अमात्य कल्पितमनेन

योगचूर्णमिश्रमौषधं चन्द्रगुप्ताय ।७२। अये उर्वशीगाच्चस्यशर्शादिव
निवृतं मे शरीरम ।७३। आर्ये किमत्याहितं सीतादेव्याः ।७४।
यावदिमान्वेदीसंस्तरणार्थं दर्भानृत्लिग्भ्य उपहरामि ।७५। कथि-
तमवलोकितया मदनोद्यानं गतो माधव इति ।७६। कष्टम्
उभयोरप्यस्थाने यत्नः ।७७। नायं कथाविभागो ऽस्माभिरन्येन
वा श्रुतपूर्वः ।७८। वयमपि तावज्ज्वलन्त्यौ सखीगतं किंचित्पृच्छामः
।७९। अमात्य इदमाभरणं कुमारेण स्वशरीरादवतार्य प्रेषितम्
॥ २० ॥

Exercise 7b

1 I am Ātreyī. 2 You increase my curiosity. 3 This is the
bank·of·the·lake. 4 I will just wait for these (girls) [having
resorted·to:] in the shade. 5 This is a road trodden·by·
common·people. 6 Clearly these [n.] too were sold to us by
a trader employed·by·Cāṇakya. 7 Oh, (you) have shown
love·for·(your)·friend. 8 The danger is at (your) head, the
remedy·for·it far away. 9 Dear [use **sakhī**] Madayantikā,
welcome. You [**bhavatī**] have favoured our·house. 10 It is
this dispute which makes me confident. 11 The two of us set
out [for·the·fetching·of:] to·fetch·firewood. 12 Why did you
two ladies check me? 13 That is well·managed on the
occasion·of·the·entry·of·Kalahaṃsaka·and·Makaranda.   14
What, (was) this ornament once·worn by (my) father? 15 I
have in fact engaged her·dear·friend Buddharakṣitā on the
matter [**tatra**]. 16 Are *these* the two·men·in·the·Rāmāyaṇa·
story? 17 This dear·friend Siddhārthaka chased the execu-
tioners away and carried me off from the [place·of·the·con-
demned:] execution ground. 18 Quite different [**anya**] is
this [un·trodden:] unhackneyed way·of·speaking by [*use gen.*]
Her Reverence. 19 This must be [*use* **khalu**] the power·of·
the·Vāruṇa·weapons·employed·by·Prince·Lava. 20 That doctor indeed was made to drink the same medicine, and at once
died. [*Express* at once *by linking the two verbs with* **ca . . . ca.**]

Chapter 8

PARADIGMS: Consonant stems in **an** (**rājan, ātman, nāman**)

Changeable consonant stems

Indo-European vowel gradation was based on the position of
the accent: guṇa or vṛddhi occurred in an accented syllable,
zero grade in an unaccented syllable. From Vedic texts, in
which the ancient accentuation is preserved, we know that
this distinction is broadly true of Sanskrit itself. It applies to
gradations of the root not only in derivative formations (from
i 'go', **éti** 'he goes', **itá** 'gone', **áyanam** 'path') but also within
the inflexion of a single tense: e.g. **émi** 'I go', **imáḥ** 'we go'.
In nominal inflexion we should expect the root to undergo
similar changes, but only the traces of such a system remain,
even in Vedic. An interesting example, mentioned in Chapter
5, is the infinitive (**nétum** 'to lead') in comparison with the
absolutive (**nītvá** 'after leading'): in origin these are the
accusative and instrumental singular respectively of an obsolete verbal action noun. Similarly, in Vedic, from **kṣam**
'earth' occur nominative plural **kṣámaḥ** and ablative singular
kṣmáḥ. But most nouns have standardised one grade of the
root throughout their inflexion. For instance, from **vac** (or **uc**)
'speak' the noun **vāc** 'speech' has standardised vṛddhi grade
throughout (cf. Latin *vōx, vōcis*). So the nominative plural is
vácaḥ and the ablative singular **vācáḥ**, with no distinction
of grade despite the fact that the shift of accent is preserved.
And since the ancient system of accents was lost early in the

Classical period and is not marked in Classical texts, it is
reasonable to say that in Classical Sanskrit the ablative and
genitive singular, and the nominative, vocative and accusative
plural of **vāc** are identical in form.

Nevertheless vowel gradation remains an important feature
of nominal inflexion, for although gradation of the root is
almost entirely lost, gradation of the *suffix* is preserved in many
types of declension. In this chapter attention is confined to
the declension of stems ending in the suffix **an.** [Latin has
a corresponding declension, but has standardised the strong
grade in one type (*sermō, sermōnis*) and a weaker grade in
another (*nōmen, nōminis*).]

Strong cases of the noun (those in which the accent stood
originally not on the termination but on the stem) are nominative, vocative and accusative singular, nominative, vocative
and accusative dual, and nominative and vocative (not accusative) plural for the masculine; and nominative, vocative and
accusative plural only for the neuter. Feminines hardly occur,
the feminine of changeable stems being formed by the addition
of the suffix **ī.** The other cases are the weak cases. Of these,
however, there is a subdivision in many types of declension
between 'weakest' and 'middle' cases. The weakest cases are
those whose termination begins with a vowel (**-aḥ, -i,** etc.);
the middle cases are those whose termination begins with
a consonant (**-bhiḥ, -su,** etc.) and also the nominative, vocative and accusative neuter singular, which has no termination.

Stems in **an,** such as **rājan** 'king' **nāman** 'name', are in
fact among those which distinguish these three grades, strong,
middle and weakest. Here the difference between middle and
weakest is straightforward, and historically easily explained.
The suffix **an** reduces to **n** in the weak grade, and this **n**
remains before a vowel but appears as **a** (representing **n̥*
'syllabic *n*') in the middle cases: so **nāmnā** instrumental
singular of **nāman,** but **nāmabhiḥ** (for **nāmn̥bhiḥ*) instrumental plural. The **n** is assimilated where appropriate to the
class of the preceding consonant: so **rājñā** 'by the king'.

Except in the vocative singular the strong stem appears not
in the guṇa grade **an** but in the vṛddhi grade **ān: rājānau** 'the

two kings'. In the nominative singular masculine the final **n** is lost: **rājā** (cf. Latin *sermō*).

In the locative singular and in the nominative, vocative and accusative dual neuter, **an** may optionally replace **n**: **rājñi** or **rājani** 'in the king', **nāmnī** or **nāmani** 'the two names'. In stems ending in **-man** or **-van** preceded by a consonant, **man/van** necessarily replaces *mn/vn* (for ease of pronunciation) in all the weakest cases: so **ātmanā, karmaṇā**.

An important practical point about nouns with changeable stems (and some consolation for the greater difficulties of inflexion) is that in the masculine plural they distinguish the nominative from the accusative. **suhṛdaḥ** (as well as being ablative and genitive singular) may be either nominative or accusative plural; **rājānaḥ** can only be nominative (or vocative)—and **rājñaḥ**, if plural, can only be accusative.

Exocentric compounds : bahuvrīhi

If a nominal compound functions neither as an aggregate in some sense of its parts (co-ordinative) nor as a hyponym, 'special instance', of one of its parts (determinative—in Classical Sanskrit that part is, in fact, always the *final* element, if we except rarities like **dṛṣṭa:pūrva**), then it must function as the qualifier of some substantival notion outside itself, whether the latter is expressed or left unexpressed. For this reason the term 'exocentric' is used to describe the third main class of nominal compounds. The class is extremely various: in principle, any meaningful collocation of words may be isolated and used as a descriptive tag. This is, in fact, our practice in English: we talk of a *ne'er-do-well* husband, *ban-the-bomb* marchers, the *two-car* family. The English practice helps to explain the way in which such compounds may have arisen in the Indo-European period, namely as survivals of an earlier stage of the language in which nouns had lacked inflexion, and relationships could be expressed by simple juxtaposition, much as in English: to give an example based on Sanskrit, **aśva mukha** 'horse's face'. When a system of inflexions arose, such collocations, where used with their primary value, could easily be superseded: so **aśvasya mukham**. Therefore compounds with determinative sense survived only if well established or of specialised meaning. Used, on the other hand, with exocentric value, **aśvamukha** 'horse face' could not be replaced by two inflected words and would thus survive as an adjective: **aśvamukhaḥ** 'the horse-faced (man)'.

There are very few instances of exocentric compounds in Sanskrit simply based on some random phrase (one example would be **ahaṃpūrva** 'wanting to be first' based on the phrase **aham pūrvaḥ** 'I'm first!'). The commonest type is that exemplified in the preceding paragraph, the compound based on two nouns standing in determinative relationship. This is termed in Sanskrit a **bahuvrīhi** compound (literally 'much-riced', an example of the class). In the system of punctuation here adopted, exocentric value is denoted by an underscore, and this is placed beneath the mark of the relationship between the elements. So based on the *dependent* determinative **aśva-mukham** 'horse's face' is the exocentric compound **aśva‿mukha** 'horse-faced'. In fact, however, the vast majority of bahuvrīhis are based on *descriptive* (karmadhāraya) relationship. Examples are **ugra‿mukha** 'grim-faced', **tri‿śīrṣa** 'three-headed', **kṛṣṇa‿varṇa** 'black-coloured'.

In general, as these examples indicate, the type of compound in English which represents the bahuvrīhi most closely is that formed with the possessive suffix '-ed'. Truly parallel English bahuvrīhis are few, but a useful one to remember is 'bare‿foot'. Like the determinative 'tooth-brush', it illustrates the fact that stem forms do not distinguish singular from plural: a bare-foot man is one whose *feet* are bare.

All bahuvrīhis are essentially adjectival. The compound on which a bahuvrīhi is based is reduced to a stem form, and then inflected to agree with a substantive expressed or understood. The stem form must in the first place be a masculine stem form. Thus a feminine substantive in **ā** at the end of a bahuvrīhi has its final vowel reduced to short **a**: e.g. from **svalp»:êcchā** 'small desire', **svalp»‿êccha** 'having small desire'. But although in theory almost any noun might be used at the end

of a bahuvrīhi, in practice restraint is observed so as to avoid
awkward terminations. For instance, a polysyllabic feminine
in ī is hardly to be found at the end of a bahuvrīhi (cf. Chapter 10). Among bahuvrīhis ending in consonants, a notable
type (paralleled in Greek) is that formed from neuters in -as:
e.g. from su:manas 'good mind', su:manas 'well-disposed',
nom. sg. m. or f. su:manāḥ (cf. Gk. *eumenḗs*).

The adjective **mahānt** 'great' (Chapter 10) when used as the
first member of a karmadhāraya or bahuvrīhi compound takes
the form **mahā: mahā:puruṣaḥ** 'great man', **mahā:bala** 'of
great strength'.

The term bahuvrīhi is often translated 'possessive compound', and this certainly reflects the prevailing sense of these
compounds in Sanskrit. In perhaps nine cases out of ten the
sense can be represented by putting the word 'having' before
the determinative meaning of the compound: 'having three
heads' and so forth. However, the sophisticated exploitation
of bahuvrīhis is a striking feature of Classical Sanskrit, and
the simple notion of 'possession' can be unhelpful or positively
misleading in their interpretation, particularly in the many
instances where a past participle forms the first element in
the compound. Sanskrit commentators have standardised
a more adequate analysis by means of a relative clause, the full
neatness and usefulness of which will be more obvious later
when the construction of Sanskrit relative clauses is explained
(cf. Chapter 11, p. 175). For the present, the analysis is introduced in a translated version. Let us begin by labelling the
first element in the compound A and the second element B.
The compound then means

of/by/in *etc.*	whom/which	B (*sg./du./pl.*)	is/are	A (*or of etc.* ·A)

or simply whose

By this analysis the compounds already encountered might
become 'whose face is grim', 'whose heads are three', 'of which
the colour is black', 'whose feet are bare', 'whose desires are
few', 'whose disposition is good'. Where there is dependent
determinative relationship, a preposition or 'apostrophe *s*'

needs to be attached to A: 'whose face is a horse's', 'of whom there is the face of a horse'. As in the last example, the formula may be varied by substituting 'there is/there are'. This works very well for the normal possessive bahuvrīhis—'of whom there are three heads' etc.—but is not always appropriate elsewhere: the Sanskrit version of the formula usefully blurs this distinction.

Bahuvrīhis based on various special types of karmadhārayas occur. The prefixes **su** and **dus** are perhaps even commoner in bahuvrīhis than in simple karmadhārayas. **su:manas** has been mentioned; similarly, **dur:ātman** 'evil-natured'. The negative prefix **a** is probably rather less common in bahuvrīhi than in karmadhāraya sense (the alternative being the use of the prefix **nis**—see Chapter 9): examples are **a:nimitta** 'for which there is no cause' and **a:viśrāma** 'from which there is no respite, ceaseless'. An example of **sa** converted from karmadhāraya to bahuvrīhi sense is found in **sa:piṇḍa** 'having the ancestral offering in common', but **sa** usually has a different sense in exocentric compounds (see Chapter 9).

The prefixes **su** ('easily') and **dus** ('with difficulty') are used with verbal action nouns to give a 'gerundive' sense: e.g. **dur:jaya** 'difficult to conquer', **su:bodha** 'easy to understand'. The noun is normally in guṇa grade, even in the case of a medial **a**: thus **su:labha** 'easily got', **dur:labha** 'hard to get', even though **labhaḥ** does not occur as an independent word, the form being **lābhaḥ** 'acquisition'.

Corresponding to the karmadhāraya of comparison is a bahuvrīhi in which the same elements appear in reverse order: **vadana:paṅkajam** 'the lotus of (her) face', but **paṅkaja:vadanā** 'the lotus-faced (girl)'. (This latter was classed by critics as simile rather than as metaphor.)

The first element of the bahuvrīhi may be an adverb instead of an adjective. Examples are **sarvato:mukha** '[whose face is in all directions:] facing all ways', and **tathā:vidha** or **evaṃ:vidha** (from **vidhā** 'form, sort') '[whose sort is thus:] of such a kind'.

When the first element of the bahuvrīhi is a past participle, an ambiguity exists which makes correct analysis important.

dṛṣṭ:ârtha 'whose purpose is seen, having a visible purpose' is easily understood. dṛṣṭa:kaṣṭa, however, is used to mean not 'whose calamity is seen' but *by whom* calamity has been seen', i.e. '(one) who has experienced calamity'. Similarly, kṛta:śrama means 'by whom exertions have been made', vidita:vārtta 'by whom news has been learnt'. A past participle like datta 'given' introduces a further ambiguity: datt:ādara may mean either *by whom* respect is given' or '*to whom* respect is given'.

Besides the mainly literal translations mentioned above, the use of bahuvrīhis may correspond to various kinds of idiom in English.

The 'having' of the 'possessive' translation may be replaced by a preposition such as 'of' or 'with', as in:

ramaṇīya:darśanaḥ   (a man) *of* attractive appearance
bahu:svara   (a word) *of* many syllables
ālakṣya:danta:mukulāḥ a:nimitta:hāsaiḥ   (children) *with* their buds of teeth just visible through causeless chuckles
ek:ânvayo ›yam asmākam   he is *of* one family with us

In apposition to the subject, a bahuvrīhi may often be translated by an absolute phrase in English:

ubhe vismayād urasi nihita:haste parasparam āloka-yataḥ   the two (girls) look at each other in astonishment, *their hands placed on their breasts*

The addition of api results in a concessive clause:

avasita:pratijñā:bhāro ›pi Vṛṣal-âpekṣayā śastram dhārayāmi [though one by whom the burden of the promise has been fulfilled, through regard for Vṛṣala I bear the sword:] though I have discharged the burden of my promise, I bear the sword (of office) out of regard for Vṛṣala

van:aûkaso ›pi vayaṃ loka-jñā eva   though our home is the forest, we do know the world

The difference between Sanskrit and English idiom is most

strikingly illustrated in the many sentences in which a bahuvrīhi forms the predicate to a nominal sentence. The way of
translating these will vary, but as a general rule the most
naturally corresponding English sentence will make the final
element of the bahuvrīhi into the subject, and the subject of
the Sanskrit into a word dependent on it:

> **diṣṭyā jīvita:vatsā ›smi** thank God *my* children are
> alive

> **mṛga-pracāra-sūcita:śvāpadam araṇyam** the forest
> is one·in·which·the·beasts·are·indicated·by·the·movements
> ·of·the·deer:] the game in the forest has been tracked by
> the movements of the deer

> **nanv iyam saṃnihita:vetr›-āsan» aîva dvāra-
> prakoṣṭha-śālā** [why, this hall of the entrance-court
> is in fact one·in·which·a·seat·of·cane·is·present:] why,
> there is already a canework couch here in the hall of the
> forecourt

In questions the neuter singular interrogative **kim** may be
used as a stem form:

> **kim:vyāpāro bhagavān Marīcaḥ?** [the revered son of
> Marīci is one whose occupation is what?:] how is the
> revered son of Marīci occupied?

> **teṣāṃ Daśarath›-ātmajānāṃ kiṃ:nāmadheyāny
> apatyāni?** what are the names of the offspring of those
> sons of Daśaratha?

Where a past participle is used, a simple English perfect
may be the obvious translation:

> **pratyāpanna:cetano vayasyaḥ** [(my) friend is one·by·
> whom·consciousness·is·regained:] my friend has regained
> consciousness

> **labdh›:âvakāśā me manorathāḥ** [my desires are ones·
> for·which·scope·has·been·obtained:] I have won the scope
> for my desires

It has already been pointed out that karmadhārayas are not
freely formed as complete compounds. One reason for this will

now be clear, namely the ambiguities of interpretation which would arise: **hataputraḥ** is not used in the sense of 'a slain son' because it is needed in the sense of '(he) whose son is slain' or '(he) who has slain a son'. Conversely, although bahuvrīhis as the earlier part of some longer compound are not impossible, they are not particularly common in simple prose style. The rule of thumb in translating from Sanskrit is therefore: expect **hataputra** as a complete word to be a bahuvrīhi, but as a stem form to be a karmadhāraya—thus **hata:putra-darśanam** 'the sight of (his) slain son [/sons]'.

'Called'

To express the idiom 'a man called Devadatta' the word **nāman** may be used in either of two ways: adverbially in the accusative, e.g. **nāma** 'by name':

> **Devadatto nāma puruṣaḥ**   a man, Devadatta by name

or else at the end of a bahuvrīhi compound (feminine in ī):

> **Devadatta:nāmā puruṣaḥ**   a man whose name is Devadatta
>
> **Madayantikā:nāmnī kanyakā**   a girl called Madayantikā

ātman

This is a masculine substantive meaning 'self'. It is also used, in the masculine *singular*, as a reflexive pronoun for all three numbers, genders and persons:

> **ātmānaṃ praśaṃsatha**   you are praising [the self:] yourselves
>
> **ātmany eṣā doṣaṃ na paśyati**   she sees no fault in herself

In the genitive, **ātmanaḥ**, it is thus a frequent alternative to the reflexive adjective **sva**:

> **ātmano gṛham idānīṃ praviśāmi**   I'll now enter my own house

Often a phrase qualifies **ātman** which in English would qualify the subject:

> **purā kila . . . Sītā:devī prāpta:prasava-vedanam ātmānam ati:duḥkha-saṃvegād Gaṅgā-pravāhe nikṣiptavatī** Once, it seems, Queen Sītā, when the pangs of childbirth were upon her, cast herself in the extremity of her suffering into the Ganges' stream

Neither **ātman** nor **sva** is restricted to referring to the nominative subject: they may refer to any appropriate substantive or pronoun in the vicinity: hence a phrase such as **asya sva:bhṛtyaḥ** 'this man's own servant'. In the following example, the first **sva** refers to **amuṣya**, the second to **mahī-patiḥ**:

> **sva:bhavanᵥ-ôpanayanam apy amuṣya sva:māhāt-mya-prakāśanāya mahī-patir anvamaṃsta** and [for the displaying of:] to display his generosity, the king permitted [the carrying to his own' home of that one:] him to be carried to his own home

svayam

The stem **sva** provides an indeclinable form **svayam**. This represents the notions 'personally' or 'of one's own accord' (the instrumental **ātmanā** is sometimes used in the same way) It may therefore correspond to the emphatic use of the English reflexive: **svayam āgacchati** 'he is coming himself (/in person)'. In combination with a past participle an agentive sense is uppermost: **svayam adhigata** 'acquired by oneself'.

Predicative accusatives

In sentences such as 'he likes his curry hot', 'they drink their martinis dry' much of the burden of statement is carried by an adjective ('hot', 'dry') syntactically dependent upon a subordinate element ('curry', 'martinis') in a sentence that might already appear to be structurally complete. Such an adjective is 'predicative' in rather the same way as is the adjectival complement of a nominal sentence: the sentences are, in fact, closely similar in meaning to 'the curry he likes *is hot*', 'the martinis they drink *are dry*'. In Sanskrit, too, the object of a verb may be qualified by such a predicate. The verb **avagam** 'understand, perceive, *etc.*' may be used to illustrate possible equivalents of the construction in English:

> **mūrkham tvām avagacchāmi**
> (*a*) I think you a fool
> (*b*) I perceive you *to be* a fool
> (*c*) I recognise you *as* a fool (/*for* a fool)
> (*d*) I realise *that* you are a fool

There is no 'accusative and infinitive' construction of the Latin kind in Sanskrit, but an 'accusative and accusative' construction as illustrated by the above is not uncommon and may be an alternative to the use of an '**iti** clause'. Thus the above might also have been expressed by **mūrkhas tvam ity avagacchāmi.**

> **tat kim khalv idānīm pūrṇam ātmano manoratham n᾽ âbhinandāmi?**   [so do I not now rejoice in my own desire (as) fulfilled:] may I not now rejoice that my desire is fulfilled?

Here again, **pūrṇam ātmano manoratham** might conceivably be replaced by **pūrṇo me manoratha iti.**

Particularly noteworthy is the predicative use with a verb such as **iṣ** 'want' of a present participle (Chapter 10):

> **bhadra Bhāsvaraka, na mām dūrī᾽bhavantam[1] icchati kumāraḥ** good Bhāsvaraka, His Highness does not want me [being far away:] to be far away

Verbal action nouns in *ana*

The suffix **ana** added to the verbal root (normally strengthened to guṇa grade) is sometimes used to form nouns with adjectival or agentive force: thus from **śubh** 'shine', **śobhana**

[1] For the tilde ˜ in compounds of **kṛ** and **bhū** see Chapter 12.

'brilliant'; from **nand** 'rejoice', **nandana** 'gladdening'. But its far more frequent function is to provide neuter action nouns. So from **dṛś** 'see', **darśanam** '(act of) seeing'; from **ā+gam** 'come', **āgamanam** '(act of) coming, arrival'. There is thus an overlap of meaning with the masculine action nouns in **a** already described, and sometimes both formations are found from the same root in much the same sense, e.g. **uparodhaḥ** or **uparodhanam** '(act of) blocking'. A more concrete meaning is also not uncommon with this formation: **bhojanam**, from **bhuj** 'enjoy, eat', means 'thing eaten, food' more often than it means 'act of eating'; **vacanam** usually means 'thing spoken, word' rather than 'act of speaking' (cf. in English the two senses of the word 'utterance' and the frequent ambiguity of words ending in '-ation', so that, for instance, 'formation' can equally well mean 'act of forming' and 'thing formed').

The first **a** of the suffix coalesces with the vowel of roots ending in **ā**: **sthānam** 'place', **jñānam** 'knowledge', etc. The roots **labh** and **rabh** insert a nasal: **vipralambhanam** 'deception'. Lengthening of a medial **a** is little found, except to some extent in distinguishing a causative significance: **maraṇam** 'dying', **māraṇam** 'killing'. More generally, however (and especially in later Sanskrit), derivative stems both causative and denominative make use of a related feminine suffix **anā**: **gaṇanā** 'counting', **prārthanā** 'solicitation', **vijñāpanā** 'requesting'.

saṃvṛtta

The past participle of **saṃvṛt** 'happen' is frequently used to express the 'change of state' equivalent (in past time) of a nominal sentence. It thus represents English 'became' or 'has become'.

> **eṣo ɔsmi kārya-vaśād Āyodhyakas tadānīṃˇtanaś ca saṃvṛttaḥ** behold, through (theatrical) need I have become (/turned into) an inhabitant of Ayodhyā and a man of the period

Often **jāta,** the past participle of **jan** 'be born, arise', is used in the same way:

niḥsahā ›si jātā   you [*f.*] have become exhausted

'Palace', 'temple'

Sanskrit usually designates types of buildings more analytically than English. There is no single word that exclusively denotes either the residence of a king or the place where a god is worshipped. Therefore the notion 'palace' may be represented by an indefinite number of phrases meaning 'king's house', e.g. **nṛpa-bhavanam.** (The word **prāsādaḥ** normally denotes a fine building and may therefore be used by itself to mean 'palace' if the context makes it plain who the owner is.) Similarly, 'temple' is expressed by the phrase 'house of god', e.g. **deva-kulam.** Where a specific deity is named, the inclusion of a word such as **devaḥ** or **devatā** is, of course, not necessary: **Śiv›-āyatanam** 'temple of Śiva'.

Vocabulary

aṅgurīyaka   *m./n.* ring (for finger)

ati:bībhatsa   extremely repulsive, foul

atrabhavatī   this lady

anukūla   favourable

anvayaḥ   succession, lineage, family

aparādhaḥ   offence

apavārita   hidden

abhiyukta   diligent

araṇyam   forest

arthaḥ   meaning, matter; purpose, object

avasānam   termination, end, conclusion

avasita   terminated, over

ātman *m.*   self

āmodaḥ   scent

āyatanam   abode

āsakta   fastened, fixed, occupied

autsukyam   eagerness

kaṭaka *m./n.*   (royal) camp

karman *n.*   deed, work

kaṣāya   astringent, sharp (of scent)

Kāma:devaḥ   the god of Love

kusumam   flower

kesaram   hair, filament

kautukam   curiosity

krauryam   cruelty

ǵamanam   going

ǵuṇaḥ   merit, quality, worth

caryā   movement, riding (in vehicle)

cittam   thought, mind

jāpyam   (muttered) prayer

tādṛśa (*f. ī*) (of) such (a kind)
dakṣiṇāpathaḥ southern region (of India), the Deccan
Dāruvarman *m., pr. n.*
divasaḥ day
dur‗bodha difficult to understand
dur:vipākaḥ cruel turn (of fortune)
daivam fate, chance, fortune
doṣaḥ fault, inconvenience
dharmaḥ religious law, duty, piety
nāmadheyam appellation, name
nāman *n.* name
nṛśaṃsa injurious; *m.* monster
Padmapuram *name of a city*
pariṇāmaḥ evolution, outcome
parinirvāṇam complete extinction
parivṛta surrounded, having a retinue
pariṣad *f.* assembly, audience
parīta encompassed, overcome
pādapaḥ tree
puṇḍarīkam lotus
pratigrahaḥ present (*to a brahmin from a king*)
prabandhaḥ (literary) work

bahumānaḥ respect for (*loc.*)
manas *n.* mind
manda sluggish, slack
mahānt (*stem form in compound* mahā) great
mukham face
mudrā authorising seal/stamp, 'pass'
rathaḥ chariot
rājan *m.* king
vatsaḥ dear child
vṛttāntaḥ news; event, scene (of activity)
veśman *n.* residence
vaikhānasaḥ hermit, anchorite
vaitālikaḥ royal bard
vaimanasyaṃ despondency
vairaṃ hostility
vyañjanaṃ sign, insignia, disguise
śaṅkā suspicion, fear
śāpaḥ curse
śītala cool
°sad *ifc.* dweller (in)
sadṛśa (*f. ī*) similar, suitable, worthy
saṃdhyā twilight, evening
siddha achieved
sundara (*f. ī*) beautiful
stambhaḥ pillar

aṅk (X aṅkayati) brand, stamp
adhi+gam (I adhigacchati) find; realise, perceive
anu+kamp (I anukampate) sympathise with, take pity on
abhi+as (IV abhyasyati) practise; *p.p.* abhyasta familiar (to one through practice)
ava+nam (I avanamati, *p.p.* avanata) bow down, bend down
ut+śvas (II ucchvasiti) bloom, blossom
upa+śru (V upaśṛṇoti) hear of, learn of
jan *caus.* (janayati) beget, produce, arouse
nis+diś (VI nirdiśati) designate, specify
nis+kram (I niṣkrāmati) go out of (*abl.*)
pari+īkṣ (I parīkṣate) examine, scrutinise
pari+aṭ (I paryaṭati) wander about

prati+vas (I prativasati) dwell, live (in)
prati+abhi+jñā (IX pratyabhijānāti) recognise
bandh (IX badhnāti, *p.p.* baddha) bind, fix; enter into (friendship *or* hate)
vās (X vāsayati) perfume
vid (II vetti, *p.p.* vidita) know, learn, discover
sam+vṛt (I samvartate) happen, become (*see chapter*)

adhastāt+*gen.* beneath
itaḥ from here; over here
kiṃ tu (*first in sentence*) but
tadā then, at that time
nanu why! well!

bho bhoḥ ho there!
svayam (*emphatic pron.*) myself *etc.*, personally
hanta ah! alas!
hi (*enclitic*) for (*as conj.*)

Exercise 8a

हन्त सिद्धार्थौ स्वः । १ । कृतं रामसदृशं कर्म । २ । अस्ति दक्षि-
णापथे पद्मपुरं नाम नगरम् । ३ । वयस्य इतः स्वभावपवारित-
शरीरौ तिष्ठावः । ४ । रमणीयः खलु दिवसावसानवृत्तान्तो
राजवेश्मनि । ५ । किमर्थमगृहीतमुद्रः कटकान्निष्क्रामसि । ६ ।
वत्स अलमात्मापराधशङ्कया । ७ । भो भोः किंप्रयोजनो ऽयमश्वः
परिवृतः पर्यटति । ८ । कां पुनरत्रभवतीमवगच्छामि । ९ । कुमार
नायमत्यन्तदुर्बोधो ऽर्थः । १० । किंत्वमात्यराचसख्यानके बड्डवैरो
न चन्द्रगुप्ते । ११ । तदेष स्वयं परीक्षितगुणान्ब्राह्मणान्प्रेषयामि
। १२ । हा कष्टम् अतिबीभत्सकर्मा नृशंसो ऽस्मि संवृत्तः । १३ ।
कथम् कृतमहापराधो ऽपि भगवतीभ्यामनुकम्पितो रामः । १४ ।
यावदिदानीमवसितसंध्याजांघ्यं महाराजं पश्यामि । १५ । स तदैव
देव्याः सीतायास्तादृशं दैवदुर्विपाकमुपश्रुत्य वैखानसः संवृत्तः
। १६ । अफलमनिष्टफलं वा दारुवर्मणः प्रयत्नमधिगच्छामि । १७ ।
सुन्दरि अपरिनिर्वाणो दिवसः । १८ । शकुन्तलादर्शनादेव
मन्दौत्सुक्को ऽस्मि नगरगमनं प्रति ॥ १९ ॥

Exercise 8b

1 This is a present from the king. 2 I went, my·curiosity·
aroused·by·Avalokitā, to the temple·of·Kāmadeva. 3 This

signet ring is stamped·with·the·minister's·name. 4 We do not find a work with·the·qualities·specified·by·the·audience. 5 Why, you [*pl.*] too are exhausted by this work·of·piety. 6 'See, I [*m.*] have become Kāmandakī.' 'And I Avalokitā.' 7 Vṛṣala, these inconveniences happen to [**bhū**+*gen.*] kings (who are) themselves not·diligent. 8 Then why are you standing [**sthita**] with·the·lotus·of·your·face·bent·down? 9 For there lives a dear·friend [of me:] of mine, [having·the·dis-guise·of:] disguised·as·a·royal·bard, called Stanakalaśa. 10 Did (my) friend [*m.*] learn her·family·and·name? 11 Dearest, even the cruelty practised [**prayukta**] by me upon you has come [*use* **saṃvṛt**] to·have·a·favourable·outcome. So now I want [myself recognised:] to be recognised by you. 12 Though my mind·is·concerned·with·[**gata**]·Urvaśī, I have the same respect for Her Majesty. 13 But we are forest·dwellers, to·whom·riding·in·a·chariot·is·un·familiar. 14 So let us (both) just sit beneath this very kāñcanāra·tree, [by·which·is·per-fumed:] which·perfumes·the·garden·with·a·sharp·cool·scent·from·the·filaments·of·blossomed·flowers.

Translate the following as nominal sentences with bahuvrīhis for predicate:

15 She has learnt·the·news·of·Sītā. 16 Oh, His Majesty's mind·is·occupied·with·other·(things). 17 What·is·the·name· of this vow of Her Majesty's? 18 And that curse [has·as·its· conclusion:] is ended·by·the·sight·of·the·ring. 19 Though (he is) overcome·with·despondency, the·sight·of His Majesty is· pleasant [**priya**].

Chapter 9

Stems in short i and short u

Substantives in **i** and **u** occur in all three genders, corresponding in inflexion to the adjectives **śuci** and **mṛdu**. In these stems, however, a fair number of alternative forms are possible.

1 For clarity, the distinctively feminine endings **yai/yāḥ/yām**, **vai/vāḥ/vām** of the singular have been listed in the paradigms. These endings have really spread by analogy from the **ī** declension, and it is not uncommon for feminines in the dative, ablative, genitive and locative singular, whether adjective or substantive, to decline like the masculine (reverting, in other words, to their original inflexion): so **tan-matau** or **tan-matyām** 'in his opinion'.

2 The special neuter forms with infix **n** (sg. **ne/naḥ/ni**; du. **noḥ**) are optional in adjectives but *not* in substantives. Therefore neuter adjectives may be declined like the masculine in all cases but the nominative, vocative and accusative: **śucino vāriṇaḥ** or **śucer vāriṇaḥ** (but *not* *vāreḥ*) 'from the clean water'.

3 The vocative singular of neuters may take guṇa like the masculine–feminine: **vāri** or **vāre**, **madhu** or **madho**.

4 Adjectives in **u** may also form their feminine by adding the suffix **ī**: **laghu** f. or **laghvī** f. 'light'. (Feminines in lengthened **ū** are also occasionally found.)

Substantives in **i** occur freely at the end of bahuvrīhi compounds: so from **buddhi** f. 'intelligence', **mugdha꞉buddheḥ** '(this is the argument) of a simple-minded (person)'—a terse comment on another scholar's views.

Stems in *vant* and *mant*

Corresponding in sense to English compounds such as 'white-winged', formed with the possessive suffix '-ed', are bahu-vrīhis such as **sita꞉pakṣa** 'of whom there are white wings', formed without any suffix. The English suffix may also be added to a single word: so 'winged', in the sense of 'possessing wings'. In these latter circumstances Sanskrit, like English, must make use of a suffix. One of the most widely used is the suffix **vant**: so **pakṣavant** 'of whom there are wings, winged'. It combines very freely with stems in **a** or **ā**, but care should be exercised in attaching it to a consonant stem, since it normally follows the rules of *internal* sandhi (e.g. **payasvant** 'juicy').

The suffix **mant** (also with internal sandhi) normally replaces **vant** after stems ending in **i, ī, u, ū, ṛ, o** and **iṣ, uṣ,** and sometimes after stops: **dhīmant** 'having wit, wise'; **Garutmant** '[the Winged One:] the divine bird Garuḍa'.

The inflexion of these stems is straightforward: the strong stem ends in **ant,** the weak in **at**; the feminine ends in **atī**; and the nominative singular masculine in **ān.** In forming compounds the stem form is **at.**

Ātmanepada

The forms of the present indicative so far learnt are those of the active voice or **parasmaipada** ('word for another'). But in Sanskrit, finite tenses (and the participles attached to them) show a second set of forms, those of the **ātmanepada** ('word for oneself'). The distinction is not made in such nominal

formations as the past participle, absolute, etc. The ātmanepada corresponds to the middle voice of Greek, and its underlying implication is that the action or state expressed by the
verb affects the subject. Thus **yajati** 'sacrifices' is used of the
officiating priest (or in earlier times of the Fire God who carries
the oblation), while **yajate** 'sacrifices' is used of the one for
whose benefit the sacrifice is being made. But except in a few
instances like this, the underlying implication is so blurred that
it is not worth pursuing. It must rather be taken as a fact of
the language that some verbs are found only in the parasmaipada, a few only in the ātmanepada, and some show both sets
of forms with little evident distinction of meaning. (Sometimes
there are differences within a single verb, for example between
ātmanepada in the present system and parasmaipada in the
perfect.) The form of the present indicative quoted in the
vocabulary will show whether a verb is to be inflected in
the parasmaipada (termination **ti**) or the ātmanepada (termination **te**).

vartate

It is, however, worth noting that verbs regularly conjugated
in the ātmanepada are more usually intransitive in sense. One
important such verb is **vṛt** (I **vartate**), literally 'turn, revolve'
('turn' in transitive sense is expressed by the causative **varta-
yati**). It is common in such meanings as 'proceed, be current'
and thus often translates 'be, exist' in an 'active' as opposed
to a stative sense, particularly where the subject is an abstract
noun.

> **hanta, bībhatsam agrato vartate** [Oh, repulsiveness is
> going on in front:] What ghastliness is before me!
> **atīva me kautukaṃ vartate** [there is curiosity in me
> excessively:] I am feeling intensely curious
> **kā velā vartate?** what time is it?

Past active participle

The possessive suffix **vant**, in addition to its regular use with substantives, may be added to past participles. Its effect is to convert a passive sense into an active: so **likhita** 'written', **likhitavant** 'having written'. In itself, however, such a description gives a misleading impression of the scope of the formation, for in practice (apart from its occurrence in locative absolutes) it is usually confined to a particular function—that of providing an active alternative to past passive sentences by standing in the nominative as a predicate to a nominative subject. So instead of **tena likhito lekhaḥ** '[by him (is) written the letter:] he has written the letter', we may have **sa lekhaṃ likhitavān** '[he (is) having written the letter:] he has written the letter'. When the subject is first or second person, it is usually expressed by the appropriate form of **as** 'be' (occasionally by the pronoun):

Menakā kila sakhyās te janma-pratiṣṭh» êti sakhī: janād asmi śrutavān I heard from (her) friends that Menakā was the mother of your friend's wife (*the first* **sakhī** = wife of a friend, **janma-pratiṣṭhā** *lit.* birth-foundation)

The participle naturally agrees with the subject in number and gender:

atha tāḥ . . . mām aṅgulī-vilāsen» ākhyātavatyaḥ then they (*f.*) announced me with a playful movement of their fingers

The chief effect of this construction is to enable the subject of past statements to be put into the nominative rather than the instrumental case. The formation is unnecessary with past participles which do not bear a passive sense, and is not usually found in such cases. Occasionally, however, a form such as **(sā) āgatavatī** 'she came' for **(sā) āgatā** does occur. The subject of a past active participle is normally personal, and masculine or feminine in gender.

Exocentric compounds : prepositional compounds

In addition to the ubiquitous determinative-based bahuvrīhis, there exists a rather smaller class of exocentric compounds in Sanskrit in which the first member stands in the relationship of a governing preposition to the second member. These compounds are exceptional in that the relationship between the elements is neither co-ordinative nor determinative: in punctuating them, this relationship has therefore been left unmarked, and only the underscore, denoting exocentric value, is employed.

Typical examples are: **ati_mātra** 'exceeding the proper measure', from **ati** 'beyond' and **mātrā** f. 'measure'; **prati_loma** 'against the nap, *à rebours*'; **upari_martya** 'above mortals, superhuman'. An English example would be 'over_head' as in 'over_head railway'.

The prepositions thus have a different value from when they are used with determinative relationship. This may be illustrated by examples of the prefixes **ati** 'beyond' and **ut** 'up, high', which in prepositional compounds carries the significance 'eschewing':

(*a*) karmadhāraya (substantive or adjective):

> **ati:bhāraḥ** excessive load   **ut:svanaḥ** high sound
> **ati:bībhatsa** excessively repulsive   **uc:caṇḍa** highly violent

(*b*) determinative-based bahuvrīhi:

> **ati:bala** having excessive strength   **ut:karṇa** having the ears (pricked) up

(*c*) prepositional compound:

> **ati_bodhisattva** surpassing the bodhisattvas   **un_nidra** renouncing sleep, wakeful

sa and *nis*

Particularly common is a pair of prefixes of opposed meaning, **sa** 'with, having' and **nis** 'without, lacking'. [Since these prefixes do not occur as independent prepositions, it would be possible to treat them as contracting a karmadhāraya relationship like **su, dus** and **a**: the present treatment is adopted because it is convenient to distinguish, for example, **sa_rūpa** 'having form' from the more indisputably karma-dhāraya value of **sa:rūpa** 'having the same form', and because **nis** is not normally an alternative to **a** in forming simple karmadhārayas.] So **nir_āśa** 'without hope, hopeless'; **sa_viṣa** 'with poison, having poison' (e.g. **sa_viṣam auṣa-dham** 'poisoned medicine').

sa is so common a prefix that it is worth distinguishing various shades of meaning and possible translations:

1 'Accompanied by':

    sa_putra āgataḥ 'he has come with his son' (This is a com-mon alternative to saying **putreṇa saha.**)

2 'And':

This is the previous usage extended to cases where we would probably use co-ordination in English: **sa_śaras cāpaḥ** '[bow with arrow:] bow and arrow'.

    ataḥ khalu me sa_bāhya:karaṇo >ntar:ātmā prasīdati
    [from this of course:] so that is why my soul within and my external senses are at peace

3 'Possessing, containing, having':

Here the sense is close to that of the suffix **vant**. Both **bala-vant** and **sa_bala** may be translated 'possessing strength, strong'. When a distinction can be drawn, it is that **sa** marks a temporary, **vant** a more permanent characteristic: so **sa_putra** means 'having a son with one' as opposed to 'alone'; **putravant** means 'having a son' as opposed to 'childless'. Compounds with **sa** are particularly common in the neuter singular as adverbs of manner: e.g. **sa_kopam** 'with anger, angrily'.

Compounds with *yathā*

Conveniently classed with prepositional compounds, although strictly distinguishable from them, are compounds whose first member is a relative adverb, most often **yathā** 'as': so **yathā_ɔrtha** 'as (is) the meaning, corresponding to the meaning'; **yathā_ɔrha** 'as deserved'; **yathɔ_ôkta** 'as stated', **yathā_nirdiṣṭa** 'as specified'.

The term *avyayībhāva*

These latter particularly, and prepositional compounds in general, are most frequently employed in the neuter singular as adverbs. (The śame usage is found in English, as in 'the aeroplane passed overhead', in contrast with the non-compound form 'the aeroplane passed over our heads'.) When so used, the class has a special name in Sanskrit, **avyayībhāva** 'conversion to indeclinable'. Thus **ā_mūlam** 'down to the root, radically', **anu_Mālinī-tīram** 'along the bank of the Mālinī'. Particularly noteworthy is the distributive use of the preposition **prati**: from **kriyā** 'action', **prati_kriyam** 'action for action'; from **dinaṃ** 'day', **prati_dinam** 'day by day, daily'.

Polite forms of address

In Sanskrit it is not positively impolite to address someone in the second person singular, but more specifically polite forms of address are also common. These usually involve a substantive construed with a third person verb form and having a literal meaning something like 'Your Honour' (cf. Spanish *usted*). Much the commonest, so common that its force is very little different from that of the second person pronoun, is **bhavant** 'you'. (The various translations here attached are merely matters of convenience.) This is usually considered to have originated from a contraction of **bhagavant** 'Your Reverence' and is inflected like any other stem ending in the suffix **vant**: it is thus to be distinguished from **bhavant** 'being', present participle of **bhū** ' be', of which the nominative singular masculine is **bhavan** with short **a**.

> **sulabh» aîva Buddharakṣitā-priyasakhī bhavataḥ**
> Buddharakṣitā's dear friend [is really easily-won by Your Honour:] is easy enough for you to win (*one young man talking to another*)

In talking of someone in his absence, the compound form **tatrabhavant** 'His Honour [there]' may be used; similarly, **atrabhavant** 'His Honour [here]', usually of someone actually present, whether addressed directly or not.

The feminine forms of these pronouns are **bhavatī, tatrabhavatī, atrabhavatī**.

Sometimes as a mark of respect the plural of the second person or of **bhavant** (**yūyam, bhavantaḥ**) is used in addressing one person. Among other possible forms of polite address are:

> **āryaḥ** [the noble one:] Your/His Excellency; *f.* **āryā**
> **āyuṣmant** [the long-lived one:] Sire *etc.*—*used particularly but not exclusively of kings and monks*
> **bhagavant** [the blessed one:] Your/His Reverence—*used of religious people and gods*: *thus* **bhagavad-gītā** Song of the Blessed One (*i.e.* Krishna); *f.* **bhagavatī.**
> **mahābhāgaḥ** [the fortunate one:] noble sir, the noble gentleman *used especially by women in addressing or referring to men of good birth*

These forms (from **āryaḥ** onwards) are also used freely in the vocative. In addition, the vocative form **bhadra** 'my good fellow, my dear man' is often used in addressing men of comparatively low social status.

janaḥ

The word **janaḥ** 'person, people' is used at the end of a determinative compound to imply indefiniteness or plurality: **kāmi:janaḥ** 'a lover, some lovers, lovers in general'. As part of a longer compound it thus helps to suggest a plural: **suhṛd-vacana-saṃmūḍha** 'bewildered by the word of his friend', **suhṛj:jana-vacana-saṃmūḍha** 'bewildered by the words of his (various) friends'. A respectful vagueness rather than plurality may be implied: **guru:janaḥ** 'elders, tutor, guardian'; **mātṛ:janaḥ** '(my) mother'.

diṣṭyā

The form **diṣṭyā**, literally 'by good luck', is used to express strong pleasure:

> **sakhe Śakaṭadāsa, diṣṭyā dṛṣṭo ›si** Śakaṭadāsa my friend, thank heaven I see you

In particular, it is used with the verb **vṛdh** 'grow, prosper' to express congratulations, the reason for the congratulations being expressed in the instrumental:

> **bhadre Madayantike, diṣṭyā vardhase bhrātur Mālatī-lābhena** dear Madayantikā, you are congratulated (I congratulate you) on your brother's winning of Mālatī

[The causative of **vṛdh** thus has the same construction as the English 'congratulate' and is used where the simple verb cannot be (as it can in the previous example): **tāṃ diṣṭyā vardhitavān asi** 'you congratulated her'.]

Denominative verbs

Denominative verbs are verbs formed from nouns: thus in English 'bowdlerise' from the proper name 'Bowdler'; 'hand' ('he hands') from the substantive 'hand'; 'blacken' from the adjective 'black'. Where verbs and nouns exist side by side, we may hesitate (unless we have historical information) as to which has priority—what, for instance, of 'a brush' and 'he brushes'? A practical distinction exists in Sanskrit, in that the grammarians assigned *roots* to all verbs which they did not regard as denominative.

The most usual type of denominative in Sanskrit is made by the addition of the suffix **ya** to the noun stem (the third person singular present thus ends in **yati**). The significance of the formation varies with the noun. From **tapas** 'religious austerity' is formed **tapasyati** 'he practises austerities'; from **namas** 'homage', **namasyati** 'he pays homage'. It may be noted that the roots **tap** 'be hot' and **nam** 'bend' (both class I verbs), from which the above nouns in turn derive, have 'suffer pain, practise austerities' and 'bow, pay homage' among their meanings. Thus **tapati** and **namati** are more 'primitive' non-denominative alternatives to the specialised denominatives **tapasyati** and **namasyati**. Stems in **a** do not lose the vowel before the suffix: so from **deva**, **devayati** 'he cultivates the gods, is pious'.

Stems in **a** also form denominatives with lengthened **ā**. These latter are usually intransitive and conjugated in the ātmanepada, and may correspond to a transitive form in **ayati**: so from **śithila** 'slack', **śithilayati** 'slackens (*trans.*), makes loose' and **śithilāyate** 'slackens (*intrans.*), becomes loose'.

More rarely, another type of denominative is found which lacks the **ya** suffix: thus from **ut:kaṇṭha** '[having the neck raised:] eager', **utkaṇṭhate** 'longs for, is in love with'.

Examples of denominative verbs which, because of their accent, are classed as class X verbs have been given in Chapter 7. Another such example is **mantr** (X **mantráyate**) 'takes counsel', which is really based on **mantraḥ** 'counsel', the latter deriving in turn from the root **man** 'think'. The absolutives of **mantr** are **mantrayitvā** and **-mantrya**.

Vṛddhi derivatives

Secondary nominal formations from existing nominal stems are made in a wide variety of ways in Sanskrit: thus from **rūpam** 'beauty', **rūpavant** (or **rūpin**—see Chapter 10) 'beautiful', **rūpavattara** 'more beautiful', etc. One of the most characteristic types of formation involves a strengthening to vṛddhi grade of the first syllable of the stem and the addition of a suffix, most usually **a** or **ya**. Stems ending in **a** or **ā** lose their final vowel before either suffix (so that one **a** may merely be exchanged for another). The general sense of the formation is something like 'belonging or appertaining to, deriving from', etc. From **puram** 'city', **paura** 'urban'; as a masculine substantive, **paurah** 'citizen'. From **puruṣaḥ** 'man', **pauruṣa** 'manly'; as a neuter substantive, **pauruṣam** 'manliness'. From a consonant stem, **tapas** 'religious austerity', **tāpasaḥ** 'one who practises austerities, an ascetic'. From a feminine substantive **Yamunā** 'the river Yamunā (Jumna)', **Yāmuna** (*f.* **Yāmunī**) 'relating to the Yamunā'. Similarly, from **vidyā** 'learning', **vaidya** 'learned', **vaidyaḥ** 'physician'. Where sandhi has reduced the prefix **vi** to **vy** in the original noun, it is expanded by vṛddhi to **vaiy**: thus **vyākaraṇam** 'analysis, grammar', **vaiyākaraṇaḥ** 'grammarian'.

Two types of formation are especially noteworthy:

1 Many patronymics ('son or descendant of') are formed with vṛddhi and the suffix **a**: **Saubhadraḥ** 'son of Subhadrā'; **Mārīcaḥ** '(Kaśyapa) son of Marīci'; **Daivodāsa** 'descended from Divodāsa'. Stems ending in **u** usually make guṇa of this vowel as well as vṛddhi of the initial syllable: **Pauravaḥ** 'descendant of Puru'. The feminine of these forms is always in **ī**: **Draupadī** 'daughter of Drupada'. Instead of patronymic value, the forms may sometimes bear the sense of 'king' or 'leader': **Śaibyaḥ** 'king of the Śibis'; **Vāsavaḥ** '(the god Indra) chief of the Vasus'. And there are yet other kinds of relationship which may be similarly expressed—thus **Śaivaḥ** 'follower of the god Śiva'.

2 From adjectives and substantives, neuter abstract substantives are often formed by vṛddhi and the suffix **ya**. So **adhika** 'superior', **ādhikyam** 'superiority'; **sadṛśa** 'like, similar', **sādṛśyam** 'likeness, similarity'; **vi:manas** 'despondent', **vaimanasyam** 'despondency'; **sujanaḥ** 'good person', **saujanyam** 'benevolence, kindness'; **paṇḍitaḥ** 'scholar', **pāṇḍityam** 'learning, scholarship'.

Although both types of formation (and especially the latter) are fairly productive, the above remarks are intended merely to be explanatory: vṛddhi derivatives are listed in the vocabulary as required.

Vocabulary

agni *m.* fire

aṅguli *f. or* **aṅgulī** finger

añjali *m.* the hands joined together (*in salutation or for alms*)

atikrānta [gone beyond:] past, bygone

atidāruṇa dreadful

atyudāra proud, noble

anu_rūpa conformable, suitable, proper

anvita accompanied by, full of

aparāgaḥ disaffection

a:pūrva unprecedented, strange

arthaḥ meaning

avagrahaḥ obstacle, restraint

a:viṣayaḥ [non-sphere:] matter beyond the scope (of)

ākhyā appellation, name

ātapaḥ heat (*esp.* of sun)

ātma-jā [born of oneself:] daughter

āyuṣmant long-lived (*see chapter*)

āśrama-padaṃ site of hermitage, hermitage

āsanna near; *ifc.* beside

ugra fierce

utsuka eager; **utsukaṃ** eagerness

upakāraḥ help, aiding (of)

upajāpaḥ instigation to rebellion, 'overtures'

upapanna suitable, possible

ṛṣi *m.* seer

Kaṇvaḥ *pr. n.*

gāthā verse (*esp. in the āryā metre*)

guru heavy; *m.* teacher, elder, senior, guardian

cetas *n.* mind, heart

-jña *ifc.* knowing, aware of, recognising

tatrabhavant His Honour *etc.* (*see chapter*)

tatrabhavatī that lady *etc.* (*see chapter*)

tapas *n.* (religious) austerity

dāruṇa cruel

dhī~mant wise

nir_utsuka without eagerness

patnī wife; **dharma-patnī** lawful wife

para~vant [having another:] under another's control; beside oneself, overwhelmed

paryāpta sufficient

pārthivaḥ king, ruler

Puṇḍarīkaḥ *pr. n.*

prakṛti *f.* nature, disposition; *pl.* subjects (of king)

praṇidhi *m.* (secret) agent

pratijñā promise

prahṛṣṭa delighted

bakulaṃ bakula-tree blossom

bahumānaḥ respect

brahman *n.* (religious) chastity

bhagavant reverend (sir) (*see chapter*)

bhadra good; *m. voc.* my good fellow

bhavanaṃ house, residence

bhavant you (*see chapter*)

Bhūrivasu *m., pr. n.*

mandāraḥ, mandāra:vṛkṣa-
  kaḥ coral-tree
mahiman *m.* greatness
Mah»:êndraḥ [the great] Indra
mālā garland
mṛgayā hunting, the chase
yath»_ôkta as stated, as described
rathyā [carriage-]road, street
ramaṇīya attractive
lajjā shame, embarrassment
lekhaḥ letter, epistle
valaya *m. n.* bracelet; circle,
  enclosure
vikramaḥ valour
vighnaḥ obstacle, hindrance
vibhūti *f.* splendour, wealth;
  pl. riches
vivasvant *m.* [the Shining
  One:] the sun
viṣam poison;   viṣa-kanyā
  poison-girl
Viṣṇuśarman *m., pr. n.*
vismayaḥ astonishment
velā time (of day)

Vaideha belonging to (the
  country of) Videha
vyasanam weak spot, weak-
  ness
vyāpāraḥ occupation
śatru *m.* enemy
śāśvata (*f.* ī) perpetual
sakhe *voc.* of sakhi *m.* friend
sacivaḥ counsellor, minister
saṃdarśanam sight, beholding (of)
saṃnihita present (*as opp.* absent)
samāgamaḥ meeting with,
  union
sambhāvya credible
sammardaḥ crush, encoun-
  ter, throng
sādhu good; *n.* sādhu bravo!
sutā daughter
Saudhātaki *m., pr. n.*
hetu *m.* motive, ground for
  (*loc.*)
homaḥ oblation, sacrifice

anu+sthā (I anutiṣṭhati, *p.p.* anuṣṭhita) carry out, perform, act
anu+smṛ (I anusmarati) remember
abhi+dhā (III abhidadhāti, *p.p.* abhihita) say, speak
abhi+vad *caus.* (abhivādayate) greet
ā+diś (VI ādiśati) order, proclaim
ā+śaṅk (I āśaṅkate) fear, doubt, be afraid
utkaṇṭhate *denom.* long for, be in love with (*gen.*)
upa+labh (I upalabhate) acquire, ascertain, discover
upa+sthā (I upatiṣṭhate) stand near, be at hand
kath (X kathayati) say, tell, relate
kṣam (I kṣamate) be patient, endure
gam *caus.* (gamayati) spend (time)
tarj *caus.* (tarjayati) threaten, scold
dah (I dahati) burn
ni+kṣip (VI nikṣipati) throw, cast into (*loc.*); place, deposit
ni+vid *caus.* (nivedayati) report, inform someone (*dat./gen.*) of
  something (*acc.*)
ni+vṛt (I nivartate) go back, return
pari+vṛdh *caus.* (parivardhayati) cause to grow, tend (plants)
prati+budh (IV pratibudhyate) wake up (*intrans.*)

pra+sthā *caus.* (prasthāpayati)   despatch
man (IV manyate)   think, suppose
vac (II vakti, *p.p.* ukta)   tell, say
vṛt (I vartate)   exist *etc.* (*see chapter*)
vṛdh (I vardhate)   increase, prosper; +diṣṭyā: *see chapter*
sam+car (I saṃcarate)   walk, stroll
sam+diś (VI saṃdiśati)   command
sam+ṛ *caus.* (samarpayati)   hand over to (*dat./gen.*)
sam+mantr (X sammantrayati)   take counsel, consult
smṛ *caus.* (smārayati)   cause to remember, remind
han *caus.* (ghātayati)   cause to be killed, have killed

atha   now (*as unemphatic introductory particle*)
kaccid (*interrogative particle introducing tentative enquiry*)   perhaps?
kim iti   with what in mind? why?
tataḥ   thereupon, then
nāma (*often used as an emphatic particle*)   indeed *etc.*
nis *ibc.*   without, lacking (*see chapter*)
prāk   previously, before
prāyeṇa   generally
bahuśaḥ   often
yathā *ibc.*, *see chapter*
sa *ibc.*, *see chapter*
samprati   now
hi   assuredly

Exercise 9a

किमुक्तवानसि ।१। संप्रति निवर्तामहे वयम् ।२। कृताञ्जलिः
प्रणमति ।३। सर्वानभिवादये वः ।४। सखे पुण्डरीक नैतद्-
नुरूपं भवतः ।५। यावदुपस्थितां होमवेलां गुरवे निवेदयामि
।६। कच्चिदहमिव विस्मृतवांस्त्वमपि ।७। परवन्तो वयं
विस्मयेन ।८। आर्ये अपि श्रचोर्व्यसनमुपलब्धम् ।९। तत्किमि-
त्याशङ्कासे ।१०। अहमधुना यथादिष्टमनुतिष्ठामि ।११। भगवन्
न खलु कच्चिदविषयो नाम धीमताम् ।१२। शकुन्तला सखीम-
दुह्या तर्जयति ।१३। साधु सखे भूरिवसो साधु ।१४। किमयं
प्रतिबुद्धो ऽभिहितवान् ।१५। अथ सा तत्रभवती किमाख्यस्य
राजर्षेः पत्नी ।१६। भद्र अथामिप्रवेश्ये सुहृदस्ति को हेतुः ।१७।

परवती खलु तच्चभवती न च संनिहितगुरुजना । १८ । दिष्ट्या
धर्मपत्नीसमागमेन पुच्चमुखसंदर्श्नेन चायुष्मान्वर्धते । १९ ।
तत्किमयमार्येण सलेखः पुरुषः कुसुमपुरं प्रस्थापितः । २० । तच्-
भवान्कख्वः शाश्वते ब्रह्मणि वर्तते इयं च वः सखी तख्यात्मजेति
कथमेतत् । २१ । ममापि कण्वसुतामनुस्मृत्य मृगयां प्रति
निवृत्सुकं चेतः । २२ । अपि चन्द्रगुप्तदोषा अतिक्रान्तपार्थिवगु-
णान्स्मारयन्ति प्रकृती । २३ । एतामसंभाव्यां ब्राह्मणस्य प्रतिज्ञां
श्रुत्वा ससचिवो राजा प्रहृष्टमना विस्मयान्वितः सबहुमानं तस्मै
विष्णुशर्मणे कुमारान्तमर्पितवान् ॥ २४ ॥

Exercise 9b

Use the past active participle where appropriate. 'You' when
preceded by an asterisk is to be translated by **bhavant**.

1 Is (your) austerity without·hindrance? 2 Friend Makaranda,
are *you in love with Madayantikā? 3 But where did Mālatī
see Mādhava before? 4 Lady, a shame·less Lakṣmaṇa herewith [**eṣaḥ**] salutes (you). 5 What do *you [*pl.*] say? 6
Mālatī has·a·noble·nature. 7 The riches of Minister·Bhūri-
vasu are indeed attractive. 8 There is a dreadful throng·of·
people. 9 I told *you the story·[**vṛttāntaḥ**]·of·(my)·first·sight
of Śakuntalā. 10 Reverend Arundhatī, I Sīradhvaja (King)
of Videha greet (you). 11 Are Candragupta's·subjects
responding to [**kṣam**] our·overtures? 12 He thinks me
actually not·present. 13 A rather [**ko 'pi**] strange ground·
for·respect towards [*loc.*] (one's) elders, Saudhātaki! 14 This
(man), employed·by·Rākṣasa, had Parvateśvara killed by
a poison·girl. 15 (She) casts the garland·of·bakulas into
Mādhava's joined hands. 16 (I) congratulate *you on your
greatness·in·valour, sufficient·for·the·aiding·of·Mahendra. 17
Thereupon there enters, her·occupation·as·described, together
with two [female] friends, Śakuntalā. 18 Truly [**nanu**]
friend, we [two] often walk along [*instr.*] the very street·beside·

the·minister's·residence—so this is possible. 19 To Candra-gupta's·subjects assuredly it is Cāṇakya's·faults which are grounds·for·disaffection. 20 Friend, the sun burns without· restraint, as cruel as fate. 21 Bravo, Vṛṣala, bravo! You have commanded (this) after consulting with my own [eva] heart. 22 Ah! the meaning·of·the·verse is 'I am one·who·has·[jña]· news·of·Kusumapura, and *your·agent'. 23 See, we two have entered Prajāpati's hermitage, its·coral·trees·tended·by·Aditi. 24 This time when·the·heat·is·fierce that lady generally spends with·her·friends on the banks·of·the·Mālinī with·[vant]· (their)·enclosures·of·creepers.

Chapter 10

PARADIGMS: Stems in ī and ū, strī; stems in in; present participles in ant, mahānt; imperative (para. and ātm.) of nī

Stems in *ī* and *ū*

Polysyllabic stems in ī such as **nadī** were introduced in Chapter 7. The declension of the few polysyllables in ū is exactly parallel, with the important exception that they add ḥ in the nominative singular. Quite different from these, and parallel to each other, are the monosyllabic stems in ī and ū: these in effect are like consonant stems, with ī/ū changing to iy/uv before vowels (though they have the option of the special feminine endings ai, āḥ and ām).

It will be noted that the word **strī** 'woman' behaves more like a polysyllabic than a monosyllabic stem: it is to be treated as one, and probably was one in origin.

It has already been mentioned that nouns like **nadī** are rare at the end of an exocentric compound. Sometimes the difficulty is surmounted by the addition of the adjectival suffix **ka**: so **sa_patnī˜ka** 'with one's wife', **pravṛtta:bībhatsaˑ kiṃvadantī˜ka** '(citizens) among whom foul rumours are current'. Exocentric compounds based on ī/ū monosyllables and determinatives formed with verbal roots in ī and ū do occur, and are most usually inflected like the plain monosyllables (alternative forms being possible, but neuter forms of any kind being little found). Examples are **su:dhī** 'of good intelligence', **padma-bhū** 'sprung from a lotus'.

Stems in *in*

The inflexion of stems in **in** presents little difficulty. They are essentially single-stem, but the final **n** drops before consonants and in the nominative (vocative) and accusative neuter singular. The nominative singular masculine ends in **ī**, and the nominative, vocative and accusative neuter plural in **īni**; the feminine adds **ī**—thus **dhaninī**.

The suffix **in** is a common alternative to the suffix **vant** after stems in **a** or **ā**, the final vowel being dropped. Thus **balavant** or **balin** 'possessing strength, strong'; **śikhāvant** or **śikhin** 'crested'. With the same meaning, but rare, are the suffixes **vin** (in particular, after a number of nouns in **as**) and **min**. Two common examples of the former are **tapasvin** 'practising austerities, ascetic' (also 'pitiable') and **manasvin** 'possessed of intelligence'. The substantive **svāmin** 'owner, master' derives from **sva** 'own' and the suffix **min**.

in as a verbal suffix

The same suffix may also be added, with strengthening of the root, to verbs: so from the root **pat**, **pātin** 'flying, falling'. [In this instance at least, it might seem that the suffix can be regarded as added to the verbal action noun **pātaḥ** 'flight, fall', and certainly the distinction between the 'primary' formation described here and the 'secondary' formation described above is not absolute. But there are limiting cases of difference of form: thus from **bhuj** 'enjoy', the velar consonant of **bhogaḥ** 'enjoyment' contrasts with the palatal of **bhojin** 'enjoying'.] In this formation the root syllable is almost invariably heavy, medial **a** being lengthened where necessary to **ā**. Roots ending in **ā** take a connecting **y**: thus **sthāyin** 'remaining, stable'.

The formation has an active verbal meaning, close to that of the present participle. Where it differs from this latter is in tending towards a more general, characterising sense: e.g. **nagara-gāmī mārgaḥ** 'the road going to the city'. The difference is conveniently illustrated by the phrase **Candragupt-ânuyāyinā rāja-lokeṇ ânugamyamānaḥ** 'being attended (on this occasion—*present participle*) by the princes that (would normally—*adjective in* **in**) attend Candragupta'.

Here are examples from the verbs **chid** 'cut out', **anu+kṛ** 'imitate', **hṛ** 'carry', **śaṃs** 'proclaim':

> **vimarśa-cchedi vacanam** [the speech is doubt-removing:] (her) words are such as to remove all doubt
>
> **sakhe, kv› êdānīm upaviṣṭaḥ priyāyāḥ kiṃ cid anukāriṇīṣu latāsu dṛṣṭiṃ vinodayāmi?** Friend, where shall I now [being seated, distract:] sit and distract my gaze among vines that somewhat imitate my beloved?
>
> **kiṃ Kaṇva-saṃdeśa-hāriṇaḥ sa_strī̃kās tapasvinaḥ?** ascetics with women, bringing a message from Kaṇva (you say)?
>
> **aye, dakṣiṇena priyā-caraṇa-̈nikṣepa-śaṃsī nūpura-śabdaḥ** ah, a sound of anklets to the right, proclaiming my beloved's tread

While it may not always be easy to distinguish the meaning of this formation from that of the present participle, certain clear-cut distinctions of a formal nature do exist. The present participle may govern an accusative and may not normally stand at the end of a compound (in these respects it resembles a finite verb form). The verbal noun in **in,** on the other hand, with rare exceptions cannot govern an accusative and (as the above examples illustrate) is commoner at the end of a compound than as an isolated form.

Present participle

Two participles are attached to the present stem (and other thematic **a** paradigms), one in **ant** (parasmaipada) and one in **amāna** (ātmanepada): so **nayant** 'leading', **vartamāna** 'going on, current, contemporary'.

The declension of participles in **ant** differs from that of stems in **vant/mant** in only two particulars: the nominative singular masculine ends in **an** (not *$*\bar{a}n$), and the feminine (and the neuter dual form) is **antī** (not *$*at\bar{\imath}$). (Remember that by sandhi a final **an** becomes **ann** before vowels.)

[On the formation of athematic participles (Chapter 12 onwards) the following points should be noted. The feminine (and neuter dual) is in **atī** (this is also an option for class VI verbs and futures). The strong stem is like the third person plural parasmaipada without the final **i**, and in reduplicated verbs is therefore simply **at**: note that as a further consequence the nominative singular *masculine* (as well as neuter) in these verbs ends in **t** not **n**, e.g. **dadat** '(he) giving'. For athematics, the ātmanepāda termination is **āna** not **amāna**.]

It was pointed out in Chapter 5 that where the English participle in '-ing' represents an action prior to that of the main verb its usual Sanskrit equivalent is the absolutive. The Sanskrit present participle is therefore normally reserved for actions or states which can be seen as contemporaneous with those of the main verb:

> **purā kila Karāl»-āyatane Mālatīm upaharann Aghoraghaṇṭaḥ kṛpāṇa‿pāṇir Mādhavena vyāpāditaḥ**
> some time ago, it seems, while (engaged in) sacrificing Mālatī in the temple of Karālā, Aghoraghaṇṭa knife in hand was slain by Mādhava

Beyond simple contemporaneity, a casual or (with the addition of **api**) a concessive force may be implied. One particular implication, that of responsibility, 'doing B by virtue of doing A', deserves special mention. It may usually be turned in English by the translation 'in/by (doing *etc.*)':

> **ātmanā kṛto ›yaṃ doṣaḥ Saṃjīvakaṃ Piṅgalaka-sakāśam ānayatā** it is (I) myself, in bringing Saṃjīvaka to Piṅgalaka, who have done this mischief
> **evam atidurmanāyamānaḥ pīḍayati māṃ vatsaḥ** the dear child tortures me by being so miserable

The verb **as** 'be' forms a present participle **sant**, feminine **satī**, which may function as an adjective meaning 'real, true, good, virtuous' (hence 'suttee'). As a participle it is sometimes added pleonastically to predicative adjectives, particularly compounds: e.g. **prasanna‿manasā satā Mādhavena** 'by Mādhava, being of tranquil mind'.

mahānt

The adjective **mahānt** 'great' is irregular in having a strong stem in **ānt** (the middle and weak stem is **mahat**). The feminine is **mahatī**, the nominative singular masculine **mahān**. The stem form for karmadhāraya and bahuvrīhi compounds is **mahā**.

enam

enam is an enclitic pronoun, occurring only in the accusative (**enam, enām, enat**; **enau, ene**; **enān, enāḥ, enāni**), the instrumental singular (**enena, enayā**) and the genitive/locative dual (**enayoḥ**). (Of these the commonest forms are **enam** and **enām**.) It is used as an unemphatic third person pronoun ('him', 'her'), not usually adjectival, and normally referring to persons. Oblique cases other than the accusative may be supplied by the pronoun **ayam** (see Chapter 5).

Stem forms in composition

It may be useful to summarise here the ways in which the form of a stem as it appears in a compound may differ from the form in which the word is quoted in a dictionary (apart from the normal operation of the rules of external sandhi). Of nouns in general it need only be pointed out that consonant stems show their middle form: so **ātman** becomes **ātma**; **dhanin, dhani**; and **bhagavant, bhagavat** (this last being at any rate the form in which such stems are often quoted). The use of pronouns in composition is somewhat restricted. The first person forms **mat** and **asmat**, second person **tvat** and **yuṣmat** (dual forms are hardly found), and the demonstrative **tat** are used freely, except as the final member of the compound. The relative **yat** is also used freely, but only as the first member. Of the interrogative pronoun **kaḥ**, the (primarily neuter) form **kim** occurs quite often: not, of course, in the animate sense of 'who(m)', but capable of qualifying a substantive of any gender—as in **kim:vyāpāra** 'of whom the occupation (**vyāpāraḥ** *m.*) is what?' The pronouns **ayam**, **enam** and **asau** do not have productive stem forms.

Certain words change to forms from different, though related, stems when used in composition. So, at the end of a compound, **ahan** 'day', **rājan** 'king', **rātri** 'night' and **sakhi** 'friend' become a stems: **aha**, **rāja**, **rātra** and **sakha**. **mahānt** 'great' when forming the prior member of a karmadhāraya or, in consequence, a bahuvrīhi compound regularly changes to **mahā**: the stem form **mahat**, even in the substantival sense of 'great man', is not very much used. Two of the changes mentioned are illustrated in the karmadhāraya **mahā:rājaḥ** 'great king'.

The imperative

One way of expressing a command or wish in Sanskrit is by means of the imperative mood, which is a part of the present stem: so **gaccha** 'go!', **paritrāyasva naḥ** 'save us!'. The imperative is in effect confined to the second and third persons. The first person forms given in grammars to complete the paradigms are really survivals of the old subjunctive mood, and at any rate are not particularly common; first person expressions like 'let's go' are usually put in the indicative—thus **gacchāvaḥ**.

In moderately urgent second person commands, the verb, as is natural, tends to stand first (after any vocative), unless special emphasis is put on some other item in the sentence:

> **sūta, preray> âśvān**   driver, start the horses
> **masī-bhājanam pattram c> ôpanaya**   bring inkpot and paper

But if an absolutive is also used, chronological sequence should be preserved:

> **vayasya, upasṛtya Lavaṅgikā-sthāne tiṣṭha**   go up and stand in Lavaṅgikā's place, friend

If less urgent instructions or a wish are in question, the verb may stand elsewhere, often (and particularly in the latter case) at the end:

sakhe Virādhagupta, tvam anenꜱ aîvꜱ āhituṇḍika-cchadmanā punaḥ Kusumapuram eva gaccha Virādhagupta my friend, you are to go back again to Kusumapura in this same disguise of a snake-charmer

vatsa, ciraṃ pṛthivīṃ pālaya my child, long may you protect the earth

When an imperative is genuinely 'third person', the same various principles apply:

ārye, tiṣṭhatu tāvad ājñā-niyogaḥ good (wife), for the moment [let the entrusting of orders stand:] never mind what orders I have for you

atrabhavatī tāvad ā prasavād asmad-gṛhe tiṣṭhatu this lady, then, should remain in our house till her confinement

But where the third person is used as a polite form of address, it is particularly common for the imperative to stand as penultimate word followed by the quasi-pronoun:

bho bhos tapasvinaḥ, tapo-vana-saṃnihita:sattva-rakṣaṇāya sajjībhavantu bhavantaḥ ho there ascetics, prepare [for the defending of:] to defend the creatures about the ascetic grove

The second person imperative of **bhū** does not usually stand first word. So **sthiro bhava** 'be firm'. The second person forms of **as** are rare, but the third person forms are freely used and, of course, are necessary as copula where indicative forms could be dispensed with:

viditam astu deva-pādānām be it known to Your Majesty['s feet] . . .

The use of the imperative in an **iti** clause is a device allowing the representation of 'indirect command' in the widest sense.

Translation by means of the English infinitive is usually appropriate:

> **nanv idānīm eva mayā tatra Kalahaṃsakaḥ preṣitaḥ 'pracchannam upagamya Nandaṃ-āvāsa-pravṛttim upalabhasv›' êti** why, I have just now sent Kalahaṃsaka there, [(saying) 'after approaching stealthily find out events in Nandana's house':] to find out discreetly what has been happening in Nandana's house

To express a prohibition the negative particle to be used with the imperative is **mā**, e.g. **mā gaccha** 'don't go'. This, however, is rare, the more elegant alternative (as mentioned in Chapter 15) being the use of **mā** with the unaugmented form of the aorist or occasionally of the imperfect. Even this is not especially frequent. The usual way of expressing a prohibition if it implies 'cease to' is simply **alam** or some other particle with the instrumental: **alaṃ śokena** 'do not grieve (any more)'. But in other circumstances, probably commonest is the use of the gerundive (Chapter 12):

> **Vṛṣala, sa_viṣam auṣadham—na pātavyam** Vṛṣala, the medicine's poisoned—don't drink it

Abstract nouns

Mention was made in the previous chapter of the formation of neuter abstract nouns (i.e. substantives) by means of vṛddhi, e.g. **pāṇḍityam** 'learning'. Another device to achieve the same effect, and a simpler one to apply, is the use of the suffixes **tvam** (neuter) and **tā** (feminine, this latter normally restricted to occurrence after a stem ending in a short vowel, usually **a**): so **paṇḍitatvam** and **paṇḍitatā** 'learning', or more explicitly 'being a paṇḍit'. These suffixes may be added not merely to simple words but also to whole compounds: e.g. **ramaṇīya‿darśana˜tā** 'the state of having an attractive appearance'. [The use of the sign ˜ indicates that the suffix is to be added to the compound as a whole. The following example will illustrate the potential difference of meaning: **niṣ_pāṇḍitya** means '(who is) without scholarship'; **niṣ_paṇḍitatva** would be a very improbable formation with the same meaning; but **niṣ_paṇḍita˜tva** means 'the state of being without a paṇḍit', as in the sentence **lajjayati grāma-nivāsino niṣ_paṇḍita˜ tvam** 'being without a paṇḍit embarrasses those living in the village'.]

Most of the uses of abstract nouns possible in English are possible also in Sanskrit. In particular (and in contrast to Latin and Greek), their use as the subject of an active verb does not imply any vivid personification of the abstract concept:

> **ata eva māṃ prayojana-śuśrūṣā mukharayati** that is why the desire to learn [**śuśrūṣā**] of (your) motives is making me [talkative:] so persistent

Often an abstract noun is the subject of a nominal sentence:

> **rājñāṃ tu carit₊:ârtha˜tā ›pi duḥkh›:ôttar» aîva** but for kings, [even the state of being one whose aims are effected has as a consequence unhappiness:] even success is attended with unhappiness

The difference between Sanskrit and English idiom lies in the thoroughness with which Sanskrit exploits the various possible uses of abstract nouns, and particularly in the potential length of abstract compounds. The following sentence easily permits of literal translation:

> **sa c› Auśanasyāṃ daṇḍa-nītau catuḥṣaṣṭy₊:aṅge jyotiḥ-śāstre ca paraṃ prāvīṇyam upagataḥ** and he has attained a high proficiency in the political science of Uśanas and the [sixty-four-limbed:] sixty-four branches of astronomy

But what in this particular sentence is unremarkable represents a regular Sanskrit idiom whereby almost any verb of motion (and some others implying acquisition etc.) may be construed with the accusative of almost any abstract noun to express what we most usually represent in English by 'become':

so, in the above, 'he has become highly proficient'. Another example, showing better the scope of the idiom, is:

tad idānīṃ rāj›-ârtha˘tām āpadyate   that now [arrives at king-property-ness:] becomes the property of the king

Hence the common idiom for 'he dies', **pañcatvaṃ gacchati** 'he becomes five', i.e. 'is resolved into the five elements'.

Furthermore, the causative of these verbs, and any other verb of appropriate sense such as **nī** 'lead', can be used in the sense of producing a certain condition in someone or something, i.e. 'making A [into] B':

> **loke gurutvaṃ viparītatāṃ ca**
> **sva:ceṣṭitāny eva naraṃ nayanti**
>
> in (this) world it is his own actions which [lead a man to important-ness and opposite-ness:] make a man important or the reverse

In English we know without thinking about it that the phrase 'the greenness of the grass' is related to the phrase 'green grass'. In Sanskrit it is often advisable to keep the point more explicitly in mind. To take an example of extreme simplicity, a commentary discussing an author's use of the term **vyavahāra** 'litigation' in the plural says **tasy› âneka: vidha˘tvaṃ darśayati bahuvacanena** 'he shows by the plural the several-sortedness of it'. We may, if we wish, translate this as 'he indicates by the plural its manifoldness'. But we shall remind ourselves more plainly what we are talking about, besides being fairer to the simplicity of the original, if we say 'he indicates by the plural that it is of several sorts'. Often at any rate literal translation is impossible:

> **n› âsty eva dhvaniḥ, prasiddha:prasthāna-vyatire-kiṇaḥ kāvya-prakārasya kāvyatva-hāneḥ** [*dhvani* (*a technical term of literary criticism*) just does not exist, from the abandonment of [/deficiency in] poetry-ness of a type of poetry distinct from established ways:] there is no such thing as *dhvani*, for a kind of poetry which transgressed the recognised norms would cease to be poetry

It would be quite mistaken to suppose, on the basis of such usages, that the 'thought' of Sanskrit writers is somehow more 'abstract' than our own. It would be truer to say that their style is nominal rather than verbal. In coming to grips with academic prose, students tend to be vague and ill at ease about the meaning of sentences until the purely syntactical nature of this difference sinks in. And, as was implied above, even in translating quite simple nominal phrases the possibility of 'denominalisation' in English should always be kept in mind.

In brief, the difference between English and Sanskrit usage is that English noun clauses ('that the grass is green') and noun phrases with a verbal component such as an infinitive ('for the grass to be green') tend to be replaced in Sanskrit by a straight abstract noun ('the greenness of the grass'). Normally, when both subjective and objective genitives are involved, only the objective genitive is compounded with the abstract— e.g. **bālānāṃ kusumᵥ-âvacayaḥ** 'children's flower-picking': 'for children to pick flowers'.

Furthermore, the use of the abstract noun in various oblique cases corresponds to English adverbial clauses and phrases of various kinds. Commonest is the ablative of cause:

suhṛt-sampādita˜tvāt sādhutaraːphalo me manora-thaḥ [from being brought about by (my) friend:] because (you my) friend brought it about, my desire (has been) better rewarded

No doubt because its ablative is not distinct in form from its genitive, the suffix **tā** is less usual here than **tvaṃ** or a vṛddhi derivative. But it is common enough in the instrumental, another case which is used to express cause ('by (reason of)'):

asau punar abhiniviṣṭayā dṛśā Mālatī-mukhᵥ-âvalo-kana-vihasta˜tayā viṣamaːviracitᵢːaîkaᵣbhāgāṃ tām eva bahu manyamānā 'mahān ayaṃ prasāda' iti gṛhītavatī but she with an intent glance, highly esteeming that same (garland) of·which·one·portion· was·worked·unevenly [by clumsiness through gazing:]

because·(I)·had·been·clumsy·through·gazing·on·Mālatī's· face, accepted it (with the words) ['this is a great favour':] 'thank you very much indeed'

The dative is normally used with another type of abstract noun, the verbal action noun, to express purpose. Examples of this, such as **nṛpa-darśanāya** 'in order to see the king', have already been encountered. The locative expresses circumstance of one kind or another: **kula-kṣaye** 'on the destruction of the family: when/if the family is destroyed', **prayojaṇṁ-ôtpattau** 'if/when/as the need arises'. The addition of **api** gives concessive force: **kula-kṣaye ᵓpi** '[even on destruction of the family:] despite destruction of the family: though the family is/were to be destroyed'.

Exclamations

The English 'what (a) . . .', though it has direct Sanskrit equivalents such as **kīdṛśa,** is more usually represented by the particle **aho** 'oh!' followed by a substantive in the nominative case:

> **aho saṃvaraṇam** what duplícity!
> **aho rāga-parivāhiṇī gītiḥ** [oh the song overflowing with passion/'musical mood':] what an impassioned sóng!

Where the whole emphasis would be put on an adjective qualifying the substantive, the phrase is often turned round and the adjective becomes an abstract noun: in other words, 'oh the blúe sky!' becomes 'oh the sky's blúeness!' Similarly in English, according to the particular emphasis intended, we may say either 'what a blue ský!' or 'how blúe the sky is!' The normal suffix here is **tā,** or a vṛddhi derivative, rather than **tvam**:

> **aho vaidagdhyam** [oh the cleverness:] how cléver (she is)!
> **aho sukha-pratyarthi˜tā daivasya** [oh the·being·hostile·to·happiness of fate:] how hóstile fate is to happiness!

Sentences containing 'how' are slightly ambiguous in English because they can be stressed more than one way. For this reason, an acute accent has been added to mark the main sentence stress: this falls somewhere on the word or phrase which appears as a nominative substantive in the Sanskrit:

aho vyabhrā diśaḥ what a cloudless ský! *or* how cloudless the ský is!

aho diśāṃ vyabhratā how cloúdless the sky is!

aho cĕṣṭā-pratirūpikā kāmi:jana-manovṛttiḥ how like to the deed (itself) is a lover's imaginátion!

'Containing'

The word garbhaḥ 'womb, foetus' occurs at the end of a bahuvrīhi compound with the sense 'having inside, containing': e.g. dhana:garbhaṃ bhāṇḍam 'box containing money'; or, as a sentence, 'the box has money in it'.

Verbal nouns in *ti*

The suffix ti may be added to the weak grade of a root to form a feminine substantive. Thus gati (cf. Greek *básis*) 'going, procedure, course'. The formation is less productive than those in a and ana, and less 'action-oriented', tending towards a more general sense. The ti is normally treated exactly like the ta of the past participle (and is seldom found with verbs that form their past participles in ita or na). Other examples are bhakti 'devotion', dṛṣṭi 'sight, faculty of sight', mati 'thought', siddhi 'achievement', vṛddhi 'growth'. A number of roots ending in d, although forming a past participle in na, do take this suffix: thus utpatti, from ut+pad, 'arising'.

Vocabulary

añcalaḥ border (of dress)	an:adhyayanaṃ [non-study-
atiśaya surpassing	ing:] holiday from lessons

apathya-kārin [doing what is unwholesome (to king):] traitor
apavādin decrying
a:pramādin [not negligent:] vigilant
abhiyogaḥ intentness, pre-occupation
avayavaḥ portion, particle
asuraḥ demon
ādeśaḥ command
āyudham weapon
āveśaḥ attack (of emotion)
utsarpin high-soaring
utsāhaḥ enthusiasm
upagrahaḥ conciliation, winning over
uparodhanam besieging (of)
upādhyāyaḥ teacher
eka *pron. adj.* one, alone
enam *see chapter*
kalakalaḥ disturbance, noise
kārin doing
kāryam affair, business
kīdṛśa (*f.* ī) of what kind? of what kind! what (a)!
kṣitipati *m.* king
kṣipra:kārin [swift-acting:] precipitate
:garbha *see chapter*
gṛham quarters, chamber
gṛha-janaḥ family (*more particularly* wife)
cakravartin *m.* emperor
Candanadāsaḥ *pr. n.*
chidram hole, chink
tapasvin *m.* ascetic
tīkṣṇa sharp, severe
tīkṣṇa:rasaḥ [sharp liquid:] poison
tīkṣṇa:rasa-dāyin [poison-giving:] poisoner
tīrtham ford, sacred bathing place
taikṣṇyam sharpness
trikālam [the three times:] past, present and future

daṇḍaḥ stick; punishment
darśanīya attractive
darśin seeing, that see
diś (dik) *f.* cardinal point, region (of sky); *pl.* sky, skies
duḥ:śīla irritable
dur:ātman vile
dṛḍha firm
Nandanaḥ *pr. n.*
nir_daya pitiless
nṛpaḥ king
nyāyya regular, right
pakṣa-pātin on the side of, partial to
paṅkti *f.* row, line
Pañcavaṭī *name of a place*
paṭaḥ cloth, robe
pati *m.* lord (of)
parijanaḥ attendant, servant
pipīlikā ant
pauraḥ citizen
pratijñā promise, assertion
pratividhānam precaution, countermeasure against (*gen.*)
pratyavāyaḥ reverse, annoyance
pratyāsanna near, at hand, about
pratyutpanna prompt, ready
pratyutpanna:mati ready-witted
prabhūta numerous
prārthanā longing
baṭu *m.* young brahmin (student); fellow (*used contemptuously*)
balam force, strength; *sg. or pl.* (military) forces
balāt forcibly
bahu many
bhaktam food
bhakti *f.* devotion, loyalty
bhāvin future, imminent
bhitti *f.* wall
bhīru fearful
madhura sweet

mati *f.* thought, wit
Madayantikā *pr. n.*
Manmathaḥ (name of the god of) Love
mahārghya valuable
Mādhavyaḥ *pr. n.*
muni *m.* sage
mlecchaḥ barbarian
rakṣas *n.* devil
vayas *n.* youth, age
Vasiṣṭhaḥ *pr. n.*
vidhā kind, sort; -vidha such as
vimardaḥ conflict
vivekaḥ discrimination
vihārin roaming
vyagra engrossed, intent
śayanam repose, sleeping; śayana-gṛham bed-chamber
śarad *f.* autumn
śiṣṭa learned; śiṣṭ-ânadhya-yanam holiday in honour of learned (guests)
śūnya empty, devoid (of)
śokaḥ grief

śobhā brilliance, beauty
śreṣṭhin *m.* eminent business-man, merchant
sakhī [female] friend; wife of one's friend
samayaḥ occasion, season
samādhi *m.* concentration [religious] meditation
sambandhaḥ union
sambhṛta assembled, prepared; augmented
sarpaḥ snake
salilam water
sahabhū inherent, natural
sāṃnidhyaṃ presence
sᵻ_âvadhāna careful
siddhi *f.* accomplishment, success
suraḥ god
suhṛttamaḥ close friend
strī woman
svāmin *m.* master
svīkaraṇam marrying
svairam gently

anu+gam (I anugacchati) follow, attend
anu+bhū (I anubhavati) experience, undergo
anu+rudh (IV anurudhyate) adhere to, comply with (*acc.*)
ava+lok (X avalokayati) see
ākulayati *denom.* confuse, disturb
ā+kṛṣ (I ākarṣati) drag, draw
ā+pad (IV āpadyate, *p.p.* āpanna) attain, come to
ut+pad *caus.* (utpādayati) cause to arise, cause
ut+veṣṭ *caus.* (udveṣṭayati) unwrap, open (letter)
khel (I khelati) play
cint (X cintayati) reflect, think things over
tvar (I tvarate) hurry; *caus.* tvarayati
dah *caus.* (dāhayati) make burn, cause to be fired
dṛś *caus.* (darśayati) cause to see, show
ni+grah (IX nigṛhṇāti) repress, restrain
nis+gam (I nirgacchati) go away, retire from (*abl.*)
pari+tuṣ *caus.* (paritoṣayati) make satisfied, tip, reward
pari+trai (I paritrāyate) rescue, save
pari+pāl (X paripālayati) guard, preserve, keep intact

pari+bhraṃś (IV **paribhraśyate**, *p.p.* **paribhraṣṭa**) fall, drip, slip

pari+hṛ (I **pariharati**) avoid, shun, resist

prati+as (IV **pratyasyati**) cast aside

pra+sthā (I **pratiṣṭhate**) set forth

bhañj (VII **bhanakti**, *p.p.* **bhagna**) break, shatter

mudrayati *denom.* stamp, seal

vand (I **vandate**) venerate, worship

vi+jñā *caus.* (**vijñāpayati**) say politely, request, entreat, beg

vi+sṛj *caus.* (**visarjayati**) release, dismiss

vīj (X **vījayate**) fan

sam+stambh (IX **saṃstabhnāti**, *absol.* **saṃstabhya**) make firm, sustain, compose

ataḥ from this

aho bata oh alas!

kila apparently, it seems that

~tā, ~tvam *abstract noun suffixes; see chapter*

bhoḥ (*in calling*) oh! ho! (*irreg. sandhi* **bho** *before vowels and voiced consonants*)

sāmpratam now, at once

Exercise 10a

पश्य माधवस्यावस्थाम् ।१। महति विषादे वर्तते ते सखीजनः ।२। इदं तत्प्रत्युत्पन्नमतित्वं स्त्रीणाम् ।३। अहो दर्शनीयान्य- क्षराणि ।४। मुहूर्तमुपविश्रत ।५। भोः श्रेष्ठिन् चन्दनदास एवमपथ्यकारिषु तीक्ष्णदण्डो राजा ।६। अनुभवतु राजापथ्य- कारित्वस्य फलम् ।७। प्रत्यासन्नः किल मृगयाविहारी पार्थिवो दुःषन्तः ।८। गच्छतां भवन्तौ ।९। भोस्तपस्विन् चिन्तयन्नपि न खलु स्वीकरणमभवत्याः स्मरामि ।१०। सखे माधव दृढप्रतिज्ञो भव ।११। अहो निर्दयता दुरात्मनां पौराणाम्— अहो रामस्य राज्ञः क्षिप्रकारिता ।१२। भगवन्नथ कृतस्ते कुसुमायुधस्य सतप्तेत्क्ष्णमेतत् ।१३। ननु भवत्यः पटाञ्चलैर्वत्सौ वीजयध्वम् ।१४। भग्नोत्साहः कृतो ऽस्मि मृगयापवादिना माधव्येन ।१५। अहो बत कीदृशीं वयोऽवस्थामापन्नो ऽस्मि ।१६। अथ ग्रिष्टानध्ययनमिति खेलतां बटूनामयं कलकलः

।१७। स्वैरं स्वैरं गच्छन्तु भवत्यः ।१८। परिचायतां सुहृदं महाराजः । १९। तच्चभवतः कुलपतेरसांनिध्याद्रक्षांसि सत्त्रपोवि-घ्नमुत्पादयन्ति ।२०। भद्र अनया मुद्रया मुद्रयैनम् ।२१। शत्रुप्रयुक्तानां च तीक्ष्णरसदायिनां प्रतिविधानं प्रत्यप्रमादिनः परीक्षितभक्तयः क्षितिपतिप्रत्यासन्ना नियुक्ताः पुरुषाः । २२। सम्प्रति मद्यन्तिकासंबन्धेन नन्दोपग्रहात्प्रत्यक्षशङ्काः खलु वयम्। २३। भाविनमेनं चक्रवर्तिनमवगच्छतु भवान् । २४। मया तावत्सुहृत्-मख्य चन्दनदासस्य गृहे गृहजनं निक्षिप्य नगरान्निर्गच्छता न्याय्य-मनुष्ठितम् । २५। देवि संस्तभ्यात्मानमनुरुध्यस्व भगवतो वसिष्ठस्या-देशमिति विज्ञापयामि ॥ २६ ॥

Exercise 10b

1 Look, Your Excellencies. 2 What valuable jéwels! 3 She stands gazing. 4 This lady must hurry. 5 Sages that·see· past·present·and·future have proclaimed [ā+diś] a conflict· (between)·gods·and·demons (to be) imminent. 6 Being a king has·many·annoyances. 7 [It is from this:] That is why (men) such·as·*you are great. 8 May you have success·in·your· affairs. 9 Keeping the seal intact, open (it) and show (me). 10 How devoid·of·discriminátion is the barbarian! 11 Restrain [*dual*] your attack·of·grief and follow me. 12 It is preoccupation·with·affairs, dear child, that is disturbing us, and not [**na punar**] the irritability towards pupils natural·in·a· teacher. 13 Though I am resisting [**pari+hṛ**], love·of· Pañcavaṭī seems to draw me forcibly. 14 How sweet is the sight of these (girls)! 15 Citralekhā, get Urvaśī to hurry. 16 The gods (do) have this fearfulness·of·the·meditations·of· others. 17 The longing of great (men) is of course [high· soaring:] for higher things. 18 At once let our·forces set forth to·besiege·Kusumapura. 19 (Being) partial·to·*your· merits, I have forgotten the merits·of·(my)·master. 20 Priyaṃvadaka, we have no interest in snakes. So tip him and dismiss him. 21 (It) slipped from your friend's wife at the

ford·of·Sacī as she was worshipping the water. 22 Be careful, dear child. 23 Because (my) mind is engrossed·in·affairs and (my) agents numerous, (I had) forgotten. 24 Noble Jājali, you too go back with·the·servants: Bhāgurāyaṇa alone shall attend me. 25 How surpassingly·lóvely the skies are, their·wealth·of·beauty·augmented·by·the·autumn·season. 26 Then, seeing a line of ants emerging from a [eka] hole·in·the·wall carrying·[*use* ġrhīta]·particles·of·food, (he) grasping·the·fact [ġrhīt:ârtha] that [iti] the chamber had·men·in·it, caused that same bed·chamber to be fired.

Chapter 11

Stems in ṛ

In origin the inflexion of stems in ṛ is parallel with that of consonant stems in **an**. They exhibit a strong stem with vṛddhi or guṇa grade (**kartāram, pitaram**: cf. **rājānam**); a weakest grade with the stem in consonant form (**kartrā**: cf. **rājñā**); and a middle grade with the stem in vocalic form (**kartṛbhiḥ**: cf. **rājabhiḥ** $<*rājṇbhiḥ$).

These stems are nevertheless classified as vowel stems rather than consonant stems, for two reasons: **r** has a distinctive vocalic alternant (**ṛ**), whereas **n** does not (since $*ṇ$ became **a**); and some terminations have been acquired through the analogy of other vowel stems. Thus by analogy with **kāntān, śucīn**, etc., an accusative plural in **ṝn** (f. **-ṝḥ**); and by analogy with **kāntānām** etc. a genitive plural in **-ṝṇām**. (These formations create the long alternant of syllabic ṛ, which is not part of inherited Indo-European phonology.)

As with **an** stems, the nominative singular takes vṛddhi and loses its final consonant: **kartā, pitā**. An unusual feature is the genitive singular in **uḥ** (or **ur**). Guṇa grade of the locative singular, an alternative form for stems in **an**, is here obligatory: **kartari**.

Stems in ṛ fall into two main classes, agent nouns and nouns of relationship. Agent nouns end in **tṛ** (thought the **t** is sometimes changed by internal sandhi) and are added to a guṇa grade of the root, often with connecting **i**. [The description of the infinitive in Chapter 13 may be taken as a guide to the formation of this stem, with substitution of **tṛ** for **tum**.] The suffix of agent nouns is always inflected with vṛddhi in the strong grade: **netāram** 'leader' acc. (cf. Latin *amātōrem*). A derived feminine is made with the suffix **ī**: **netrī** 'she who leads'. Neuter forms on the analogy of the neuter of **śuci** etc. are theoretically possible but not very common.

Nouns of relationship normally take guṇa in the strong grade, and may be feminine as well as masculine (in which case the accusative plural ends in **ṝḥ**); **naptṛ** 'grandson', **bhartṛ** 'husband' and **svasṛ** 'sister' are exceptional in taking vṛddhi. Thus **pitaram**, **mātaram**, but **svasāram** (cf. Latin *patrem*, *mātrem*, but *sorōrem*). The dual form **pitarau** means 'parents'. The suffix **ka** may be employed when one of these nouns occurs at the end of a bahuvrīhi compound: **mṛta:bhartṛ̃kā** 'she whose husband is dead'.

Like the present participle active, the agent noun does not normally stand at the end of a determinative compound. But, as might be expected, whereas the present participle construes with an accusative, the agent noun construes with an objective genitive: **varṇ̣:āśramāṇām rakṣitā** 'protector of (all) classes and conditions (of men)'.

The agent noun in **tṛ** is not so prominent a feature of Sanskrit as are nouns in '-er' of English. Other suffixes also denote the agent. For instance, 'leader' may be expressed by **nāyakaḥ** as well as by **netṛ**. 'Potter' ('pot-maker') may be translated by **kumbha-kāraḥ** or possibly **kumbha-kṛt**, but not by **kumbha-kartṛ**. Noun phrases will often be represented by a compound ending in the suffix **in**, e.g. **upatyakā-ιraṇya-vāsinaḥ** 'dwellers in the forests of the foot hills'. There is, however, one distinctive usage of the agent noun which is worth noting. It may have potential force—'someone to do something'. Thus **netā jana upaiṣyati** 'a person will come [as guide:] to guide (you)', or the following:

tvādṛśam punaḥ pratipakṣ,-ôddharaṇe saṃbhāvyaṭ
śaktim abhiyoktāram āsādya kṣipram enaṃ pari-

tyajya tvām ev> āśrayante However, having found (someone) like yourself, with enough power to destroy the enemy, [such as to attack:] to be their champion, they (will) quickly abandon him and flock to you

[*Periphrastic future.* Allied to this potential sense is the use of the agent noun to form a comparatively rare tense known as the periphrastic future. Mention of it is included briefly here, since it will not be introduced into any of the exercises. The agent noun is used predicatively to refer to future time, with the verb **as** in the first and second persons, without in the third person: **kartāsmi** 'I am to do', **kartā** 'he/she is to do'. Three features distinguish the tense formally from a straight-forward deployment of the agent noun. Feminine and (in so far as they occur) neuter subjects do not affect the masculine form of the verb; the ending **-tā** remains unchanged in the first and second persons, even in the dual and plural (**kartā smaḥ** 'we are to do'; and a direct object appears in the accusative, not in the genitive (**kumbhaṃ bāle kartārau** 'the two girls are to make a pot').

The tense is used especially for events fixed for a particular future time: often, in fact, the verb is accompanied by an adverb of time. Thus **śva āgantā** 'he is to come tomorrow'.]

The suffix *tra*

Allied to the agent suffix **tr̥** is the neuter suffix **tra** denoting the instrument used by the agent. Thus **pātr̥** 'drinker', **pātram** '[that which is a drinker's (when he drinks):] drinking-vessel'. Similarly, **astram** '[instrument of throwing:] missile', **gātram** '[instrument of movement:] limb', **śastram** '[instrument of cutting:] knife'—this last to be carefully distinguished from **śāstram** '[instrument of instruction:] treatise'.

The suffix occurs in other Indo-European languages. Thus Greek *árotron*, Latin *arātrum* 'plough', beside *arotér*, *arātor* 'ploughman'.

The passive

In origin the passive may be regarded as a specialisation of the ātmanepada of class IV verbs. It is formed with weak grade of the root, the suffix **ya** and the thematic ātmanepada endings. [Secondary differentiation occurred, in that passives retained the accent on the suffix, while class IV verbs shifted the accent to the root. But this distinction being inoperative in Classical Sanskrit, forms such as **manyate** may be interpreted according to context either as ātmanepada ('thinks') or as passive ('is thought').] The passive is a present system, comprising a present indicative, imperfect, imperative and optative, and a participle in **māna**. [In the future, the perfect, and to some extent the aorist, ātmanepada forms may be used with passive significance.]

With the following exceptions, the root generally remains unchanged before the suffix **ya**:

Final **i** and **u** lengthen: **ci, cīyate** 'is heaped'; **śru, śrūyate** 'is heard'.

Final **ṛ** becomes **ri** after a single consonant, **ar** after two: **kṛ, kriyate** 'is done', but **smṛ, smaryate** 'is remembered'.

Final **ṝ** becomes **īr** generally, but **ūr** after a labial: **kṝ, kīryate** 'is scattered'; **pṝ, pūryate** 'is filled'.

Roots liable to samprasāraṇa display it here: **vac, ucyate** 'is told'; **grah, gṛhyate** 'is taken'.

Roots liable to lose an 'infixed' nasal do so: **bhañj, bhaj-yate** 'is broken', but **nand, nandyate** 'is rejoiced in'.

Roots ending in **ā** or **ai** most often convert to **ī**: **sthā, sthīyate** 'it is stood'. But among several exceptions is **jñā, jñāyate** 'is known'.

When a passive is formed not directly from a root but from a derived stem, the derived stem loses any suffix it may have before adding the suffix **ya**. Thus class X verbs and causatives change **ayati** to **yate**: **coryate** 'is stolen'; **nāyyate** 'is made to lead'; **sthāpyate** 'is made to stand'.

The passive is used, as one would expect, when the agent of action is unknown or indefinite:

tat ko nu khalv evaṃ niṣidhyate then who can it be (whom I hear) being thus checked?

vatse, uparudhyate me tapovaṃ-ânuṣṭhānam dear child, my duties in the ascetic grove are being hindered (*to specify* by you *would strike a jarring note*)

But the fondness for passive constructions so prominent in past statements may be observed to a lesser extent in the present also, so that the natural English translation is often by means of the active voice:

niyatam anayā saṃkalpa-nirmitaḥ priya-samāgamo ›nubhūyate assuredly she is experiencing an imagined union with her beloved

Priyaṃvade, kasy› êdam uśīr›-ânulepanaṃ mṛṇāla-vanti ca nalinī-dalāni nīyante? Priyaṃvadā, to whom are (you) taking the uśīra ointment and the lotus leaves complete with fibres?

The notion of 'logical subject' (to which, for instance, an absolutive refers) is, of course, applicable here as in past statements:

kim ity avijñāya, vayasya, vaiklavyam avalambyate? why without knowing (for certain), friend, [is despondency adopted:] do you grow despondent?

Even commoner than the passive indicative is the passive imperative (usually third person forms only):

anubhūyatāṃ tarhi narapati-kopaḥ experience, then, the king's anger

Raivataka, senāpatis tāvad āhūyatām Raivataka, summon the general, will you?

The imperative, and more particularly the passive imperative, is often best represented in English by 'must', 'should', etc., and may be used in ways the English imperative is not, for instance in a question:

tat kim anyad anuṣṭhīyatām then what else [must be performed:] do you wish done?

The Sanskrit passive may be used impersonally in the third person singular:

purastād avagamyata eva [from there on, it is quite understood:] I can imagine the rest

datta:pūrv» êty āśaṅkyate that she has already been given (in marriage) [it is worried:] is what worries (us)

The neuter demonstrative **idam** is often added with deictic force to an impersonal passive: **idam gamyate** [this is being gone:] 'see, (we) are going'.

In the imperative this impersonal passive is extremely common. Probably the most frequent Sanskrit for 'listen!' is **śrūyatām** ['let it be heard']. Similarly, **āsyatām** or **upaviśyatām** 'be seated'.

ayi bhinn»ːârtham abhidhīyatām ah, speak plainly

sukham sthīyatām remain at your ease

Śārṅgarava, jñāyatām punaḥ kim etad iti Śārṅgarava, find out again what it is

Locative absolute

Analogous to the ablative absolute of Latin (or nominative absolute of English), there is in Sanskrit a locative absolute. So **kāle śubhe prāpte** 'an auspicious time having arrived'. The phrase consists of a small nominal sentence put into the locative, the natural case to express an attendant circumstance. The predicate may be a participle (present or past), an adjective or a predicatively used substantive, and in any of these cases the present participle **sant** of the verb **as** 'be' is sometimes added pleonastically. The force of the construction may usually be represented in English by a temporal clause introduced by 'when' or, where a present participle marks contemporaneous action, by 'as' or 'while': **tasmin dahyamāne** 'as it was burning'. An impersonal passive is not uncommon: **tathā ›nuṣṭhite** '[it having been performed thus:] this done'. According to context there may be a causal or conditional implication as well as the temporal, while the addition of **api** adds a concessive force: **aparādhe kṛte ›pi** 'though an offence be committed'; **evam ukte ›pi** 'despite this being said'. The past active participle may be used in the locative absolute construction: **evam abhihitavati pārthive** 'the king having spoken thus'.

The locative absolute is not as prominent a construction in Sanskrit as its counterpart in Latin. As has already been pointed out, English absolutes are often to be represented by bahuvrīhis—e.g. **śoka-saṃvigna:mānasaḥ** 'his mind overwhelmed with grief'. The locative absolute is better avoided when either of its elements is easily relatable grammatically to the rest of the sentence: one says **vayasyaṃ dṛṣṭvā** 'after seeing (his) friend' rather than **dṛṣṭe vayasye**, if the subject of 'see' is also the subject of the main sentence. We are left with instances like:

> **bhoḥ śreṣṭhin, Candragupte rājany a:parigrahaś
> chalānām** oh merchant, now that Candragupta is
> king, there is no welcome for errors
> **a:gṛhīte Rākṣase, kim utkhātaṃ Nanda-vaṃśasya?**
> with Rākṣasa not taken, what [has been uprooted:]
> uprooting has there been of the Nanda dynasty?

Another factor which militates against the frequency of locative absolutes as such is the possibility of using an abstract noun of circumstance in the locative. Thus the previous example might be rewritten as **Rākṣasasy› âgrahaṇe**, or even **Rākṣasasy› âgṛhītatve.**

[There also occurs occasionally a genitive absolute. It is used mostly with a present participle, sometimes with a verbal adjective in **-in**. A typical example would be **paśyatas tasya** 'while he looked on', the implication usually being 'looked on powerless and disregarded'. And there are borderline examples which might be classified as genitive absolutes but where the genitive can equally be seen as having some other function.]

The relative pronoun

The relative clause in Sanskrit is less frequent than its English counterpart. The reason is evident enough. In English an adjectival relative clause provides a more substantial qualification of a noun than a single adjective can. In Sanskrit the possibility of compound adjectives, whether determinative or bahuvrīhi, enables very lengthy and elaborate qualification without resort to a relative clause. The use of the Sanskrit relative clause, therefore, tends to be confined to the expression of restrictive clauses (the kind written without commas in English) or, rather less commonly, of 'afterthoughts'.

As in other languages, the relative pronoun agrees with its antecedent in number, gender and (in so far as the fact is manifested) person but appears in the case appropriate to its own clause. Two features more special to Sanskrit are striking: the relative clause almost never appears within the main clause but either before it or after it; and the relative pronoun may be placed anywhere within its own clause, occasionally even as last word.

When the relative clause is placed before the main clause, its sense is prevailingly restrictive and the relative pronoun is normally picked up in the main clause by a demonstrative pronoun (most often **saḥ**) as correlative, usually standing at or near the beginning of the main clause. Often, as is natural, the antecedent (if expressed at all other than by the demonstrative pronoun) appears *within* the relative clause, usually immediately after the relative pronoun, and therefore in the same case as the latter.

Putting these points together, one would rearrange an English sentence such as 'I have asked the upholsterer who came to look at the sofa yesterday for his estimate' rather on the following lines: 'to look at the sofa which upholsterer came yesterday, him I have asked for his estimate'.

    yeṣāṃ prasādād idam āsīt, ta eva na santi those by whose grace this was (so), are no (more)

    sarvathā Cāṇakya;Candraguptayoḥ puṣkalāt kāraṇād yo viśleṣa utpadyate, sa ātyantiko bhavati at all events, that estrangement between Cāṇakya and Candragupta which arises from a strong cause, will be lasting

tad atra yat sāmpratam, tatra bhavān eva pramāṇam
so what is proper in this matter, in that *you* are the judge

In the following example a relative clause has been used purely to add restrictive force to a word:

'etad āryaṃ pṛcchāmi'—'kumāra ya āryas taṃ pṛccha. vayam idānīm an:āryāḥ saṃvṛttāḥ' 'I ask (your) honourable (self) this—' 'Your Highness, ask one who *is* honourable. [We:] I am now become without honour'

The addition of **kaś cit** to the relative gives an indefinite sense—'whoever, whatever':

yaḥ kaś cid garbha-dohado ›syā bhavati, so ›vaśyam acirān mānayitavyaḥ any [longing of the womb:] pregnant fancy that she gets, [necessarily after not long must be honoured:] (you) must be sure to satisfy at once

When the relative clause follows the main clause, this may be a mere reversal of the above pattern (but with the antecedent remaining within the main clause):

tayā gavā kiṃ kriyate, yā na dogdhrī, na garbhiṇī? what is (to be) done with a cow which is neither a yielder of milk nor productive of calves?

(Note that in general statements in English the antecedent of a restrictive clause may be qualified equally well by 'the'/ 'that' or by 'a', the last having the sense of 'any'.)

When the main clause stands first, the correlative pronoun is often **eṣaḥ** or **ayam** instead of **saḥ**. And if the main clause consists of no more than a word or two, the correlative is sometimes omitted:

kriyate yad eṣā kathayati (we) are doing what she says

If the antecedent is indefinite or negative, it is naturally not qualified by a demonstrative pronoun:

Vijayasena, apy asti Vindhyaketor apatyaṃ yatr› āsya paritoṣasya phalaṃ darśayāmi? Vijayasena, has Vindhyaketu (any) offspring towards whom [**yatra** =

yasmin] I (may) show [fruit:] a token of [this:] my satisfaction?

In this following position, on the other hand, the relative clause may also be added to an already complete sentence as an additional statement. Here especially there is no need for a preceding demonstrative, and the force of the relative is roughly that of 'and' plus a demonstrative pronoun, or of 'one who/which'.

ath› êdam ārabhyate mitrabhedam nāma prathamam tantram, yasy› âyam ādyah ślokah now here begins the first chapter, called Separation of Friends, of which [= and of it] the following is the initial stanza

asty atra nagaryām mahā:śmaśāna-pradeśe Karālā nāma Cāmundā ... yā kila vividha:jīv›-ôpahāra: priy» êti sāhasikānām pravādah there is in the city in the area of the great burning-ground (an image of) the Fierce Goddess, named Karālā—one who, it seems, is fond of the sacrifice of living creatures of various kinds: so (runs) the report of adventurous (people)

Another very common variety of following relative clause also deserves mention. It is one which gives the reason for the preceding statement. It may be paraphrased by 'for' or 'in that' with a pronoun, and its natural equivalent in English is often an infinitive:

aho a:sādhu!darśī tatrabhavān Kanvo, ya imām valkala-dhārane niyunkte oh, His Honour Kanva is not right-seeing [who puts her:] to put her to wearing a bark-dress

krta:punya eva Nandano, yah priyām īdrśīm kāmayisyate Nandana's really lucky [who will love:] to be going to love such a sweetheart

vayam ev› âtra nanu śocyā, ye Nanda-kula-vināśe ›pi jīvitum icchāmah *we* rather are the ones to be pitied, who even on the destruction of the house of Nanda seek to live (on) (*Note the abstract noun as an alternative to a locative absolute such as* **vinaste ›pi Nanda-kule.**)

Analysis of bahuvrīhis

An example may now be given of the way analysis of bahuvrīhis can be made in Sanskrit glosses, taking advantage of the fact that relative clauses may precede their antecedent and that the relative pronoun may stand at the end of its clause. The two parts of the compound are resolved into a nominal sentence or phrase; the relative pronoun indicates the case-relationship with the substantive that is being qualified; and finally the demonstrative recalls the inflexional termination of the original compound. So **vidita:vārttebhyaḥ paurebhyaḥ** 'from the citizens who had learnt the news' becomes

> **viditā vārttā yais tebhyaḥ paurebhyaḥ**   by whom the news was learnt, from those citizens

Pronouns and pronominal adverbs

Now that a fair number of adverbial and other pronominal forms have been encountered in the exercises, it is worth drawing attention to relationships between them.

The list overleaf, and particularly the fourth column, is intended to be illustrative, not exhaustive. It could be extended either vertically or horizontally. Most pronominal adjectives have at least some adverbial forms—thus **anyatra** 'elsewhere', **ekadā** 'at one time', **sarvathā** 'in every way'.

Attributively used adverbs

The adverbs of 'place where and place from where' listed in the second and third lines of the above table have an obvious affinity of meaning with the locative and ablative cases of the corresponding pronouns—'where?' means 'at, in *or* on what (place)?'; 'from where?' means 'from what (place)?' In fact, to talk of adverbs of *place* in Sanskrit is somewhat misleading, since their reference may be as wide as that of the corresponding pronominal cases, extending to people and things as well as places. Thus a common meaning of **tatra** at the beginning of a sentence is 'among those (people or things just

INTERROGATIVE	RELATIVE	Normal correlative	Other demonstratives
kaḥ? who?	yaḥ who	saḥ he, that	ayam this, asau that
kva? } where? kutra? } [to] where?	yatra where	tatra there	atra, iha here
kutaḥ? from where?	yataḥ from where	tataḥ from there	itaḥ from here; in this direction
,, for what reason?	,, because	therefore	ataḥ hence, for this reason
kadā? when?	yadā when	tadā then	idānīm, adhunā now
katham? how?	yathā as	tathā} so, thus evam}	ittham, evam in this way
kīdṛśa? of what kind?	yādṛśa of which kind	tādṛśa of that kind, such (a)	īdṛśa of this kind, such (a)
kiyant? how much?	yāvant as much as	tāvant so much	iyant this much
kiyacciram? } for how kiyantaṃ kālam? } long?	yāvat as long as, while	tāvat for so long	iyacciram } for this long iyantaṃ kālam }
	yadi } if cet }	tat etc. then	
	yady api} even if, kāmam } granted that	tathā ɔpi} even so, punar } nevertheless	

mentioned)': e.g. **tatra ken› âpy uktam** '[among them someone:] one of them said'.

Similarly, by a common idiom these adverbs may be used as attributive adjectives qualifying substantives in the locative or (apparently rather less frequently) the ablative case. So **atra vane** does not mean 'here in the forest' but is synonymous with **asmin vane** 'in this forest'. Other examples of the usage are:

tatra kāle   at that time
atr› ântare   at this juncture
kutaś cid vyañjanāt   from some indication
atra or **atra vastuni**   in this matter
iha or **iha loke**   in this world

The suffix *taḥ*

It will be noticed that this suffix is used to form all the adverbs with ablative sense. In fact, it may also be added to the first and second person pronouns as a commoner alternative to the theoretical ablative forms: one usually says **mattaḥ** rather than **mat** for 'from me' and so on.

The sense of the suffix is not always strictly ablative: **itaḥ** as well as meaning 'from here' is common in the sense of 'over here' or 'in this direction'. Unlike other adverbial suffixes, **taḥ** is combined with a wide range of nouns as well as pronouns and converts them to adverbs with some such sense as well as pronouns and converts them to adverbs with some such sense as 'in accordance with' or 'in respect of'. The suffix often alternates not only with the ablative case but also with other cases, particularly the instrumental:

saṃkṣepaḥ abridgement   **saṃkṣepeṇa, saṃkṣepāt** or **saṃkṣepataḥ** in brief
vistaraḥ expansion   **vistareṇa, vistarāt** or **vista- rataḥ** in detail
prasaṅgaḥ occasion   **prasaṅgena, prasaṅgāt** or **prasaṅgataḥ** incidentally, in passing
api jñāyante nāma˜taḥ?   do (you) know them by name?

**tau ca bhagavatā Vālmīkinā dhātrī-karma vastu˜taḥ
parigṛhya poṣitau parirakṣitau ca** and the revered
Vālmīki, adopting [as to substance:] in effect the role of
a foster-mother, reared and looked after the two of them

Numerals

Complicated numerals are too infrequent in ordinary texts to
justify the devoting of much space to them in an elementary
primer. It is, however, worth committing to memory the list
of numerals at the back of the book. From 1 to 4 the cardinal
numerals agree with the substantive they qualify in number,
gender and case; from 5 to 19, in number and case, but with
only one form for all genders; from 20 onwards, in case only.
Thus **tisṛbhir nadībhiḥ** 'with three rivers', **ṣoḍaśabhir
nadībhiḥ** 'with sixteen rivers', **śatena nadībhiḥ** 'with
a hundred rivers'. From 20 onwards the numbers are, in fact,
collective nouns, and alternatively therefore the qualified substantive may be put in the genitive plural: **śatena nadīnām**
'with a hundred [of] rivers'. Or, again, a determinative compound may be made: **nadī-śatena** 'with [a river-century:] a
hundred rivers'.

Compounds with collective nouns ('pair', 'triad', etc.) may
also be used to express the smallest numbers. A dual form is
very often avoided by using one of the many words for 'pair':
go-dvayam, go-yugam, go-mithunam, etc. '[cow-pair:]
two cows'.

All the numerals may be compounded attributively in their
stem form: **dvi:pāda** 'two-footed', **śata:mukha** 'having
a hundred mouths', **daśa:kumāra-caritam** 'the story of
the ten princes'.

Concord

The principle that a predicate should agree with its subject is
modified in Sanskrit when the subject consists of a number of
co-ordinated items. In such cases there is a tendency for the
predicate to agree with the nearest item. This happens regularly when the verb precedes the subject.

tataḥ praviśaty Arundhatī Kausalyā kañcukī ca
then enter Arundhatī, Kausalyā and the chamberlain
(*not* **praviśanti**)

tad idaṃ tāvad gṛhyatām ābharaṇam dhanuś ca   so
just take this decoration and (this) bow (*not* **gṛhyetām**)

**prabhavati prāyaśaḥ kumārīṇām janayitā daivam
ca**   (what) generally governs girls (is) their father and
their fate (*not* **prabhavataḥ**)

Nominative with *iti*

Where in English we would quote a word such as a proper
name and isolate it between inverted commas, a Sanskrit word
may be isolated by **iti** and it is then normally put in the nominative case: so **'Rāma' iti viśrutaḥ** 'known as "Rāma" '.

'aśva' iti paśu-samāmnāye sāṃgrāmike ca paṭhyate
'horse' is mentioned in the list of sacrifical animals, and
in the military (list)

mātra

The word **mātrā** 'measure' is used at the end of a bahuvrīhi
compound in the sense of 'sharing the size of' both literally
(**aṅguṣṭha-mātra** 'thumb-sized', **khadyota‿mātra** 'no
bigger than a firefly') and in the sense of 'fully measured by,
being nothing more than', and so 'mere' or 'merely', 'only'.
In this sense it may form a neuter substantive: **jala‿mātram**
'only water', **pravāda‿mātram** 'mere talk'.

Especially striking is the combination of this **mātra** with
a past participle to express 'as soon as': thus **dṛṣṭa‿mātra**
'no more than seen, as soon as seen'.

**praviṣṭa‿mātreṇ› aîva śayana-gṛham durātmanā
Cāṇakya:hataken› âvalokitam**   the very moment he
entered, the evil and accursed Cāṇakya examined the
sleeping quarters

Vocabulary

aṅgaṃ limb (*the four 'limbs' of an army are elephants, chariots, cavalry and infantry*)

adhikāraḥ authority, office

adhiṣṭhātṛ *m.* superintending, at the head of

antevāsin [resident] disciple

apanodanaṃ driving away

abhidhānaṃ statement; appellation, name

abhiprāyaḥ intention, inclination

abhivyakta manifest, visible

abhīśu *m.* rein, bridle

artho-ótsargaḥ expenditure [of money]

ardhaḥ half (portion)

alaṃkaraṇaṃ ornament

ātmajaḥ son

ānuyātrikaḥ escort to (*gen.*)

iṣṭa:janaḥ the loved one

ucita suitable, appropriate

utsavaḥ festival

kalatraṃ (*NB gender*) wife

kalikā bud

Kuśaḥ *pr. n.*

garbhaḥ womb

catur (*stem form*) four

Candraketu *m., pr. n.*

candrikā moonlight

cāpa *m.n.* bow

citta-vṛtti *f.* [activity of mind:] mental process, thought

cūtaḥ mango tree

Jānakī *pr. n.*

tarkaḥ conjecture

trayaṃ triad (of) (*at end of cpd. expresses 'three'*)

dārāḥ *m. pl.* (*NB number and gender*) wife

divya celestial

dīpikā lamp

duṣkara difficult [to do]

duhitṛ *f.* daughter

dvitīya second, another

dhūrtaḥ rogue

dhairyaṃ firmness

nibandhanaṃ bond

paṇāyitṛ *m.* hawker

para *pron. adj.* other, another

Parvateśvaraḥ *pr. n.*

pāṇi *m.* hand

paunaruktaṃ redundancy

pracalita in motion

prabhu *m.* master

pramādaḥ mishap

pravṛtti *f.* news

prasādaḥ favour

prāṇāḥ *m. pl.* [breaths:] life

prārthayitṛ *m.* suitor

Priyaṃvadakaḥ *pr. n.*

bhaṅgaḥ breaking; plucking (of buds); dispersal (of crowd)

bhāgaḥ division, portion, tithe

bhrātṛ *m.* brother

madhu *m.* (season **or** first month of) spring

Mandārikā *pr. n.*

mahānt great, vast, numerous

mahā:māṃsaṃ human flesh

mātṛ *f.* mother

-mātra mere, only (*see chapter*)

mānuṣaḥ human being, mortal

māmakīna my

Mālatī *pr. n.*

mūrkha foolish; *m.* fool

medhya fit for sacrifice, sacrificial

yamaja twin[-born]

yātrā procession

yādṛśa (*f.* ī) *relative adj.* of which kind, such as, just as

rakṣitṛ *m.* guard

ratnaṃ jewel

rājyaṃ kingdom

rāśi *m.* heap

lajjā-kara (*f.* ī) embarrassing

Lavaḥ *pr. n.*
lābhaḥ profit
vane-caraḥ forest dweller
vallabhaḥ sweetheart
Vasuṃdharā *pr. n.*
vastu *n.* thing, matter, subject-matter
Vāmadevaḥ *pr. n.*
Vālmīki *m. pr. n.*
vikretṛ *m.* vendor
vicitra variegated, various
viśeṣaṇa:padaṃ [distinguishing word:] epithet
Vairodhakaḥ *pr. n.*

Vaihīnari *m., pr. n.*
śataṃ a hundred
śāstraṃ treatise, law-book
ślāghya laudable, virtuous
saṃvyavahāraḥ transaction
saṃkulaṃ throng
saṃpradāyaḥ tradition
-saṃbhava *ifc.* arising from, offspring of
sahasraṃ a thousand
sādhanaṃ army
suvarṇaḥ gold; gold piece
snigdha affectionate
hastaḥ hand

ati+sṛj (VI atisṛjati) bestow
anu+pra+hi (V anuprahiṇoti) send (someone after something), despatch
anu+mantr (X anumantrayate) consecrate with mantras, bless
anu+i (II anveti) follow, attend
anu+iṣ (I anveṣate) look for, search
abhi+nand (I abhinandati) rejoice in, prize; greet with enthusiasm
ava+āp (V avāpnoti) obtain, acquire
ava+īkṣ (avekṣate) watch, watch over
ā+rabh (I ārabhate) undertake, begin
ās (II āste) sit, stay, remain; joṣam ās remain silent
ā+hve (I āhvayati *pass.* āhūyate) summon, call
īh (I īhate) long, for, desire
upa+kḷp *caus.* (upakalpayati) equip; assign
upa+nī (I upanayati) bring
krī (IX krīṇāti) buy
jñā (IX jānāti) know, learn, find out
dā (III dadāti) give
nis+vap (I nirvapati) sprinkle, offer, donate
ni+vṛ *caus.* (nivārayati) ward off, drive off
ni+sidh (I niṣedhati) prohibit, cancel
pari+tyaj (I parityajati) leave, abandon
pari+rakṣ (I parirakṣati) protect, save, spare
pra+ci (V pracinoti) accumulate (*the pass. corresponds to the English intrans.*)
prati+śru (V pratiśṛṇoti) promise
rakṣ (I rakṣati) protect
vi+ghaṭ (I vighaṭate, *p.p.* vighaṭita) become separated
vi+muc (VI vimuñcati) release, loose
vi+śram (IV viśrāmyati) rest, cease, take a rest

vi+sṛj (VI visṛjati)   discharge, release
vi+īkṣ (I vīkṣate)   discern, spy
vi+ava+hṛ (I vyavaharati)   act, behave towards (*loc.*)
sam+ṛ *caus.* (samarpayati)   hand over
sam+bhū *caus.* (sambhāvayati)   conceive, imagine
stu (II stauti)   praise

an:antaram [without interval:] immediately
ayi   ha!
ekadā   at one time, once
kiṃ ca   moreover
cirasya   after a long time
tathā   in that way, thus, so
prasaṅgataḥ   in passing

madhyāt   from the middle of,
from among
mṛṣā   vainly
vihāya   ['having left behind':]
beyond (*acc.*)
sarvathā   in every way, alto-
gether, totally

Exercise 11a

कथम् इयं सा कण्वदुहिता शकुन्तला ।१। वत्से यदहमीहे
तदस्तु ते ।२। हे धूर्ते लेखो नीयते न च ज्ञायते कस्येति ।३।
प्रिये मालति इयं वीक्ष्यसे ।४। विश्रम्यतां परिजनेन ।५।
मन्दारिके यद्च वस्तुन्येष ते वल्लभः कथयति अपि तथा तत् ।६।
दैवेनैवं निषिद्धे ऽपि मधूत्सवे चूतकलिकाभङ्गमारभसे ।७।
परिरच्यन्तामस्य प्राणाः ।८। भो राजन् किमिदं जोषमास्ख्ते
।९। तदनुष्ठीयतामात्मनो ऽभिप्रायः ।१०। किं चातिष्ठः
पर्वतेश्वरभ्राचे वैरोधकाय पूर्वप्रतिश्रुतो राज्यार्धः ।११। कथं
शकुन्तलेत्यस्य मातुराख्या ।१२। कः स महापुरुषो येनैतन्मानुष-
माचदुष्करं महत्कर्मानुष्ठितम् ।१३। प्रियंवदक ज्ञायतां का
वेला वर्तत इति ।१४। आर्य वैहीनरे दीयतामाभ्यां वैतालि-
काभ्यां सुवर्णशतसहस्रम् ।१५। वृषल किमयमस्थान एव महान-
र्थोत्सर्गः क्रियते ।१६। भोः श्रेष्ठिन् अपि प्रचीयन्ते संव्यवहाराणां
लाभाः ।१७। भगवति वसुंधरे श्लाघ्यां दुहितरमवेक्षस्व जानकीम्
।१८। कथं निवार्यमाणो ऽपि स्थित एव ।१९। भगवन्वाल्मीकि
उपनीचेतामिमौ सीतागर्भसंभवौ रामभद्रस्य कुशलवौ ।२०।

याद्दृशो ऽयं ताद्दृशौ तावपि । २१ । विश्वष्टश्च वामदेवानुमन्त्रितो
मेध्यो ऽश्वः । उपकल्पिताश्च यथाशास्त्रं तस्य रक्षितारः । तेषा-
मधिष्ठाता लक्ष्मणात्मजयन्द्रकेतुर्वाप्रदिव्यास्त्रसंप्रदायचतुरङ्गसा-
धनान्वितो ऽनुग्रहितः । २२ । हन्त हन्त सर्वथा नृशंसो ऽस्मि
यच्चिरस्य दृष्टान्प्रियसुहृदः प्रियान्द्वारान्न स्निग्धं पश्यामि । २३ ।
अथ तस्मादरण्यात्परित्यज्य निवृत्ते लक्ष्मणे सीतायाः किं वृत्त-
मिति काचिद्दस्ति प्रवृत्तिः । २४ । अस्ति तावदेकदा प्रसङ्गतः
कथित एव मया माधवाभिधानः कुमारो यस्त्वमिव मामकीनस्य
मनसो द्वितीयं निबन्धनम ॥ २५ ॥

Exercise 11b

Translate all present actives (except in 14, 18 and 24) and all
imperatives by means of the passive.

1 Give him an answer.   2 We are twin brothers.   3 Masters
do not summon (those) holding·[**vant**]·office without·a·pur-
pose.   4 Stop right here.   5 Give (me) one [from among:] of
those three·ornaments which (I) bought.   6 Loose the reins.
7 Why speak of 'firmness'?   8 Hurry, my good fellows, hurry.
9 The moonlight (being) visible, what point in a redundancy·of·
lamps?   10 Lātavya, call Urvaśī.   11 Oh, this is the decoration which I removed from my·own·person and sent to Rākṣasa.   12 Ha, dear child [*f.*]! (You) are thus praising yourself.
13 Reward the vendor and accept it.   14 Your Excellency,
have (you) anyone who is going to Kusumapura or coming
from there?   15 Have him come in.   16 Why vainly [search
with conjecture:] speculate?   17 'Minister' is now an embarrassing epithet.   18 Alas, I am quite deluded to behave
towards this forest-dweller (in a way [*n. sg.*]) appropriate·to·
my·friend·Makaranda.   19 Hand over Rākṣasa's family—
enjoy for a long time (to come) the·king's·favour with·its·
various·advantages.   20 Protect, at the cost of [*simply use
instr.*] another's·wife, your own wife and your life.   21 This
is the son·of·Kāmandakī's·friend, Mādhava, (here) to hawk

human flesh. 22 (As) escort to the disciples by whose hand (he) has sent that book to Bharata's·hermitage, (he) has sent our·brother bow·in·hand [**cāpa͜pāṇi**] to·drive·away·mishap. 23 And she having immediately become separated (from me) by the throng of numerous [**mahānt**] townsfolk in·motion· upon·the·dispersal·of·the·procession, I came (here). 24 Fool, these ascetics donate a quite different tithe, one which is prized beyond even heaps·of·jewels. 25 Thus, imagining· [*use* *p.p.*]·by·his·own·inclinations·the·thoughts·of·the·loved· one, the suitor is deceived.

Chapter 12

PARADIGMS: Present of classes II, V and VIII

Athematic presents

The four present classes so far dealt with (I, IV, VI and X) are the thematic classes: they differ from each other only in the way in which the stem is formed from the root, for the stem thus formed always ends in (or: is linked to the endings by) the thematic vowel **a**. The other six classes are comparable with the nominal consonant stems, and their inflexion is of far greater difficulty and variety mainly because the stem is in direct contact (collision may sometimes seem a better word) with the personal endings. One may distinguish practically between the lesser complications of those classes where the stem ends in a suffix (V, VIII, IX) and the greater complications of those where the final letter of the stem is also the final letter of the actual root (II, III, VII).

In class II, the root class, the stem consists simply of the root itself. This generally strengthens to guṇa in the strong grade and remains unchanged in the weak grade. In this and all other athematic classes, the strong grade appears in the whole of the singular parasmaipada both present and imperfect, in the third person singular parasmaipada of the imperative, and in all first person forms of the imperative, while two noteworthy features of the personal terminations of athematic verbs are the absence of **n** in the third person plural ātmanepada present, imperfect and imperative, and the addition of the suffix **dhi** (after consonants) or **hi** (after vowels) in the second person singular imperative parasmaipada.

The conjugation of the commonest class II root, **as** 'be', has already been introduced. The inflexion of **i** 'go' is typical of a root ending in a vowel: among sandhi changes one may note retroflexion of **s** (**eṣi** 'you go') and consonantalisation of **i** (**yanti** 'they go'). The inflexion of **dviṣ** 'hate' illustrates some of the sandhis of final **ṣ**: thus **ṣ**+**s** = **kṣ**, **ṣ**+**dh** = **ḍḍh**.

The strong grade of **han** 'kill' is **han**: so **hanti** 'he kills', which looks misleadingly like a plural form. The weak grade is also stated as **han**, but it appears as **ha** before **t/th** and as **ghn** before **a**: **hatha** 'you kill'; **ghnanti** 'they kill'. The second person singular imperative is **jahi**.

Some roots retain strong grade throughout: **śī**, **śete** 'he lies'. Some, though classed as root verbs, add the suffix **i** before some terminations: **rud, roditi** 'he weeps'. **brū** 'speak' adds **ī** in the strong forms before a consonant: **bravītu** 'let him speak'.

Class V verbs add the suffix **nu** before the terminations, and this strengthens to **no** in the strong grade. The root **śru** 'hear' forms a present stem **śṛṇu/śṛṇo** (on the basis of a more primitive form of the root, **śṛ**): **śṛṇoṣi** 'you hear'. Roots ending in a *vowel* (*a*) do not take the suffix **hi** in the second person singular imperative, (*b*) may optionally reduce **nu** to **n** before **v** and **m**: **śṛṇu** 'listen'; **śṛṇumaḥ** or **śṛṇmaḥ** 'we hear'. Roots ending in a *consonant* (*a*) must add **hi** in the imperative, (*b*) must change **nu** to **nuv** before vowels: **āpnuhi** 'obtain'; **āpnuvanti** 'they obtain'.

Class VIII verbs add the suffix **u**, strengthening to **o**. Of the eight verbs in this class, seven have roots ending in **n** and behave in the same way as class V roots ending in vowels, as described above: **tan, tanoti** 'he extends'; **tanuvaḥ** or **tanvaḥ** 'we two extend'. The eighth verb is the common **kṛ** 'do'. The strong stem is **karo**, the weak **kuru**, but this latter *must* appear as **kur** before **v, m** and **y**. The second person singular imperative parasmaipada is **kuru**.

The formation of the present participles of athematics is mentioned in Chapter 10. Remember that the ātmanepada

participle is in **-āna**, not **-amāna**. The present participle of
ās 'stay' is anomalous, **āsīna**.

Gerundives

The gerundive (sometimes called the future passive participle)
is a verbal adjective with passive sense expressing such notions
as obligation or necessity—'(requiring) to be done' etc. It may
be formed in a number of alternative ways, by the addition to
the root of any of three suffixes: **ya, anīya, tavya**.

The gerundive in **ya** is the most ancient of the three and
shows the greatest variety of formation. In general, the following are the changes undergone by the root before this suffix.
Final **ā** becomes **e**: **dā, deya** 'to be given'. Final **i/ī** strengthens
to **e**: **nī, neya** 'to be led'. Final **u/ū** strengthens to **av** or to
āv: **śru, śravya** or **śrāvya** 'to be heard'. Final **ṛ/ṝ** strengthens
to **ār**: **kṛ, kārya** 'to be done'. Followed by a single consonant,
medial **i/u** becomes **e/o**, medial **ṛ** is unchanged, medial **a**
sometimes remains and sometimes strengthens to **ā**: **śuc,
śocya** 'to be mourned for'; **bhid, bhedya** 'to be split'; **dṛś,
dṛśya** 'to be seen'; **gam, gamya** 'to be gone to'; but **vac,
vācya** 'to be spoken'.

As well as exceptions to the above, there are a number of
alternative forms: most notably, final **i/u/ṛ** may remain unstrengthened and add a connecting **t**: so **śrutya** besides
śravya and **śrāvya**, **kṛtya** besides **kārya**.

Derivative stems drop **aya** before adding **ya**: **varṇya** 'to be
described'. Gerundives in **ya** from causatives are, however,
little found, since they would not usually be distinguishable
from the gerundive of the simple verb.

The suffix **anīya** is an adjectival extension of the suffix
ana, which is most commonly used to form neuter action
nouns (see Chapter 8). The root almost always appears in the
guṇa grade, being strengthened to the same extent as in
forming class I presents: **kṛ, karaṇīya** 'to be done'; **nind,
nindanīya** 'blameworthy'. Derivative stems again drop **aya**.
A number of causative forms are found, e.g. **bhāvanīya** 'to be
caused to be'.

The suffix **tavya** is an adjectival extension of another suffix, this time of the obsolete verbal noun in **tu** on which the infinitive and the absolutive are based. This type of gerundive may in fact be formed by substituting **tavya** for the **tum** of the infinitive, and so the remarks in Chapter 13 (p. 203) on the formation of the infinitive should now be studied and the list of principal parts of verbs consulted. A point to note particularly is that, as in the infinitive, derivative stems retain the suffix **ay**: from **vid** 'know', **veditavya** 'to be known' but **vedayitavya** 'to be made known'. Causatives form gerundives of this type freely.

As was mentioned in Chapter 8, the prefixes **su** and **dus** (as also **īṣat** 'slightly') combine not with a gerundive but with a verbal noun in **a**: **dur:jaya** 'difficult to conquer' etc.

Gerundives may be used predicatively in sentences expressing obligation or necessity: **ahaṃ bhavadbhir draṣṭavyaḥ** 'I am to be seen by you'. As with past participles, a passive is often best translated by an active, and so the above may be represented by 'you must see me'. In English, in fact, it is often appropriate to translate a gerundive as an imperative, and so we may also say '(come and) see me'.

While there is a considerable overlap between the three types of gerundive, certain differences of usage can be distinguished. The types in **ya** and **anīya**, and particularly the former, tend to have a wider, more characterising sense: thus **a:nirvarṇyam khalu para-kalatram** 'one ought not of course to gaze upon the wife of a stranger'—whereas 'don't look at her' would probably be expressed by **na draṣṭavyā**. These forms are thus far more likely than the **tavya** form to be used as simple adjectives—e.g. **ślāghya** 'praiseworthy', **śocanīya** 'lamentable'. They are particularly used after verbs with prefixes; they may also combine with the negative prefix **a**, and even appear to a limited extent at the end of determinative compounds: e.g. **anantara:karaṇīya** 'to be done immediately'. The implication of necessity may be entirely lost in the more general notion of potentiality: 'such as to be', and therefore 'capable of being'. The meaning then comes close to that of the past participle but is normally to be distinguished by the absence of any factual implication: **dṛṣṭa** '(actually) seen', but **dṛśya** 'visible' and **prayatna-prekṣaṇīya** 'to be discerned with difficulty'.

> **ari-balaṃ ca vihata;vidhvastaṃ strī;bāla-hārya: śastraṃ vartate**   and the enemy's forces, broken and shattered, are in a state where their weapons [are takeable:] could be taken by women or children

The gerundive in **tavya,** on the other hand, while it can be used in both general and particular statements and with prefixed and unprefixed verbs, seldom loses the notion of necessity and is normally used as the predicate of a sentence rather than as an attributive adjective. (It may appear as the predicate of a locative absolute: thus **durga-saṃskāra ārabdhavye** '(at a time) when fortifications ought to be undertaken'.) It should not be used at the end of a nominal compound or in combination with the prefix **a.**

A strictly passive sense is more universally prevalent in gerundives than in past participles, even for verbs normally intransitive. Thus **gamya, gamanīya** and **gantavya** may all mean '(requiring) to be gone *to*'. However, a gerundive construction can be given to an essentially intransitive verb by means of the impersonal passive:

> **nanu Lavaṅgike, Kāmandakyā ›pi na khalv ataḥ param . . . jīvitavyam**   why Lavaṅgikā, Kāmandakī too shall certainly not live any longer (*lit.* it is not to be lived by Kāmandakī *etc.*)

Particularly noteworthy, as defying literal translation into English, is the frequent impersonal use of the gerundive of **bhū** 'be'. The complement of the verb like the logical subject itself must be put in the instrumental case:

> **tad bhagavati Godāvari, tvayā tatra s›_āvadhānayā bhavitavyam**   So venerable Godāvarī, you must be watchful in the matter
> **viśrāntena bhavatā mam› ânyasminn an:āyāse karmaṇi sahāyena bhavitavyam**   when rested, you

must be my companion in another task, which is not
a strenuous one

This particular gerundive is often used to mark an inference:

**vyaktam   āhituṇḍika-cchadmanā   Virādhagupten»
ânena bhavitavyam** this (person) must obviously be
Virādhagupta disguised as a snake-charmer
**aye dhīra;praśāntaḥ svaraḥ—tat tapasvibhir bhavi-
tavyam** such strong, calm tones! It must then be
ascetics (I can hear)

Similarly, in an inference about a past event, **evam anayā
praṣṭavyam** '[thus:] this is what she must have asked'.

kṛ and compounds of kṛ and bhū

The verb **kṛ** may be translated by 'do' or 'make' in English:
kiṃ kurmaḥ? 'what shall we do?'; **kumbhaṃ karoti** 'he is
making a pot'. With an abstract noun in the accusative it has
the effect of creating a more complex verb: **vandanāṃ karoti**
'makes salutation, salutes'; **āśvāsana-mātraṃ karoti** 'makes
mere consolation, merely consoles'. Like 'make' in English,
it may also be used with an accusative and a predicative adjective to give causative sense: **tvām a:kāmaṃ karomi** 'I'll
[make you one·whose·desires·are·not:] frustrate you'.

tat kim atra vipīne priyā-vārtt»-āharaṃ karomi?
what then in this forest shall I make a carrier of news to
my beloved?

In this sense of 'turn into', however, there is an alternative
construction. One may compound the predicative adjective
with the verb by changing the **a** of the adjective's stem to **ī**
and adding it directly to the front of **kṛ**: so **tvām a:kāmaṃ
karomi** might appear instead as **tvām akāmīkaromi** (if we
wish to preserve the punctuation we may write **a:kāmī˜
karomi**). The rule is that nouns change final **a, ā, i** or **in** to
ī and final **u** to **ū** (as in **laghu** 'light', **laghūkṛ** 'lighten'),
while most other stems would appear without change; but the

formation is far commoner with nouns in **a** than with any others. Substantives are as freely used as adjectives in this construction, e.g. **aṅgī˜karoti** 'turns into a limb, sub-ordinates'.

The same construction is found with the verb **bhū** in the sense of 'become', e.g. **aṅgī˜bhūta** 'become a limb, sub-ordinated'. This is distinct in meaning from the karmadhāraya **aṅga:bhūta** 'being a limb, subordinate'.

In this way we have pairs of transitive and intransitive denominative verbs. Mention was made in Chapter 9 of the denominative pair **śithilayati** 'slackens (*trans.*)' and **śithilāyate** 'slackens (*intrans.*)'. With the same meanings we may form **śithilī˜karoti** and **śithilī˜bhavati**.

This construction forms a small exception to the general principle in Sanskrit that nouns may compound with each other but not with finite verbs (and even this construction occurs most commonly of all in non-finite forms, in particular in the past participle).

In a similar way there are a number of adverbs and other non-verbal forms which may be combined with **kṛ** and **bhū** (and to a limited extent also with **dhā** 'put' and **as** 'be'). So from the Vedic adverb **āvis** 'openly', **āviṣ˜kṛ** 'reveal', **āvir˜bhū** 'become apparent'. Similarly, from **tiras** 'secretly', **tiras˜kṛ** 'conceal', **tiro˜bhū** 'vanish'. It is **kṛ** which com-bines with the widest variety of such forms. Among other examples one might mention **alaṃkaroti** 'ornaments', **namaskaroti** 'pays homage to', **satkaroti** 'does honour to'.

In all such compounds the absolutive used should be the compound form in **ya**.

Relative adverbs

The tendency of pronominal adverbs to act as extensions of the case system was mentioned in the previous chapter—e.g. **atra vane = asmin vane** 'in this forest'. Relative adverbs used in this way are simple extensions therefore of the relative pronoun. This is often true of **yatra** 'where, in which' and **yataḥ** 'from where, from which'. Thus **tad etat**

Prācetas-**âdhyuṣitam araṇyaṃ, yatra kila devī pari-tyaktā** 'this is the forest inhabited by Prācetasa, in which [*or* where], I believe, Her Majesty was abandoned'. One may substitute **yasmin** for **yatra** in the above sentence without affecting the meaning.

In their characteristic use, however, relative adverbs have simply a more limited scope than the relative pronoun, in that the correlative adverb plays the same role in the main clause as the relative adverb in the relative clause (as when relative and correlative pronoun are in the same case): so **yadā . . . tadā** 'at which time, . . . at that time', **yathā . . . tathā** 'in which way . . . in that way', etc. Thus the relative clause and the main clause share a common feature: in 'where the rain falls, there the plants grow', the falling of the rain and the growing of plants are given a common location; if one substituted 'when . . . then', they would be given a common time.

The general feature of adverbial relative clauses are those already described for other relative clauses. The correlative adverb will correspond in function to its relative, but there may be a choice of forms. For instance, the correlative of **yathā** 'as' may equally well be either **tathā** or **evam** 'so, thus':

kim nu khalu yathā vayam asyām, evam iyam apy asmān prati syāt?   could she for her part possibly [be:] feel towards us as we (do) towards her?

'kim tu katham asmābhir upagantavya iti sampra-dhārayāmi'—**'yath» aîva gurus tath» ôpasadanena'** 'but I am wondering in what way we ought to approach him'—'with the same respectful salutation as (one would) one's preceptor'

A particular use of **yathā** is in inferences—'from the way that':

yath» ôn_mukham ālokayati, tathā vyaktaṃ 'pravās»-ôtsuka:manasā mayā na dṛṣṭ»' êty āha   from the way he gazes up, he is obviously saying, 'with my mind eager for the journey, I didn't see her'

The most usual correlative of **yadā** 'when' is **tadā** 'then', but others such as **tataḥ** 'thereupon' and **atha** 'hereat' are also found. Even if **tadā** itself is used, the relation of the two clauses is often one of sequence rather than of strict contemporaneity. Temporal clauses in narrative tend to be rather long, and for the usual reason that short clauses may be expressed in other ways in Sanskrit. Because it is not necessary for a relative pronoun or adverb to stand at the beginning of its clause, it is quite possible for the writer or speaker to be well launched on his sentence before deciding to subordinate it as a relative clause:

> **tataḥ 'kutas tavꞌ âyaṃ mahān dhanꞌ-āgama?' iti pṛc-chyamāno yadā vākya-bhedam ākulam akathayat, tadā Cāṇakya:hatakꞌ-ādeśād vicitreṇa vadhena vyāpāditaḥ** then, when on being asked 'where did your great accession of wealth (come) from?' he told a confused variety of stories, he was by order of the accursed Cāṇakya [killed by a variegated death:] put to death by torture

The word **yāvat** 'while' deserves comment. It is in origin the adverbially used neuter singular of the relative pronoun **yāvant** 'as much . . . as', whose use is illustrated by

> **yāvān artha udapāne sarvataḥ saṃplutꞌːôdake, tāvān sarveṣu vedeṣu brāhmaṇasya vijānataḥ**

> As much point as (there is) in a water-tank when it has water flooding all round it, so much (is there) in all the Vedas for a brahmin who discerns [*gen. sg. pres. part. of* **vijñā**]

yāvat thus means in origin 'for all the time that, for as long as', and this is the meaning which it has in forming 'prepositional' compounds similar to those made with **yathā** described in Chapter 9, where it may represent the same notion as the English 'throughout': e.g. **yāvad_rājyam** 'throughout the reign', **yāvad_adhyayanam** 'throughout the (period of) study'. As a conjunction **yāvat** may mean 'during all or some of the time that' and thus correspond to 'while':

> **yāvat prāṇimi, tāvad asya . . . madana-saṃtāpasya pratikriyāṃ kriyamāṇām icchāmi** I want a remedy to be contrived for this love-torment while I am (still) breathing
>
> **Vijaye, muhūrtaṃ nibhṛta:pada-saṃcārā bhava, yāvad asya parāṅ:mukhasyı aîva pāṇibhyām nayane niruṇadhmi** Vijayā, keep your footsteps quiet for a moment, while I cover his eyes with my hands as he is looking the other way
>
> **upaśleṣaya rathaṃ yāvad ārohāmi** bring up the chariot while I get in

In the last two examples the idea of purpose is present, and the notion of 'while' shades into that of 'until', which is another meaning of **yāvat**. In this latter sense it is often but not necessarily construed with the future tense:

> **pratīkṣasva kāni cid dināni, yāvad iyam . . . prakṛtāv eva sthāsyati** wait a few days, until she [shall abide in her actual nature:] comes to her senses
>
> **tat sarvathā ısmāt sthānād anyat sthānam āśrayāmi yāvad asya mayā vijñātaṃ cikīrṣitam** so at all events I'll go from this place to another, until I have found out his intentions [*p.p. in the sense of a (future) perfect*]

'Until, up to' is also the usual meaning of **yāvat** when it is a preposition governing (and following) a noun in the accusative: e.g. **sūryı-ôdayaṃ yāvat** 'until sunrise'. This contrasts with the meaning 'throughout' which it usually has in prepositional compounds. (However, the difference will normally also be conveyed by the presence, on the one hand, of a word more naturally implying duration, such as 'life', or, on the other, of one more naturally implying an event, such as 'arrival'.)

Finally, **yāvat** with a negative may be translated 'before'

(although there are other ways of expressing this notion, such
as the use of **prāk** or **pūrvam** with the ablative of an abstract
noun):

> . . . na yāvad āyāti, tāvat tvaritam anena taru-
> gahanem âpasarpata ` [while he is not coming:] before
> he comes, escape quickly through this wood

The following example combines **yāvat** 'while' and **yāvat+
na** 'before':

> yāvad eva sa_cetanā ›smi, yāvad eva ca na parisphu-
> ṭam anena vibhāvyate me madana-duśceṣṭita-
> lāghavam etat, tāvad ev› âsmāt pradeśād apasarp-
> aṇam śreyaḥ it is better to escape from this place
> while I am still conscious, and [while by him is not clearly
> detected:] before he clearly detects in me this disrespect
> (arising) from the mischievous workings of passion

The adverbial suffix *vat*

The possessive suffix **vant** is used adverbially ·in the neuter
singular with the special sense of expressing a comparison:
thus **brāhmaṇa˜vat** 'like a brahmin'. There is nothing in
the form to indicate the grammatical role played by the subject of the comparison in the rest of the sentence, and so
according to context **brāhmaṇa˜vat** may be the equivalent
of **brāhmaṇa iva, brāhmaṇam iva**, etc. In the following
example the context shows that **pitṛ˜vat** is the equivalent of
pitṝn iva:

> Kāśī-pati;Maithiḷ›;Âṅga�=rājāṃś ca suhṛn-niveditān
> pitṛ˜vad apaśyat and he (the prince) looked on the
> kings of Kāśī, Mithilā and the Aṅgas, presented by his
> friends, as his fathers

viśeṣaḥ

viśeṣaḥ literally means 'distinction, difference, particularity',
and is is often used in this literal sense. At the end of a

determinative compound (analysable as either dependent or
descriptive) it may also be used idiomatically to express the
notion 'a particular . . ., a special . . .'. Thus **brāhmaṇa-
viśeṣaḥ** '[a particularity of brahmin, a specialty that is a
brahmin:] a particular brahmin'; **strī-viśeṣaḥ** 'a particular
woman'; **ratna-viśeṣaḥ** 'a special jewel, a particularly excellent jewel'. Less frequently, **viśeṣa** may be used with this same
meaning as the prior member of the compound.

Vocabulary

Agastyaḥ *pr. n.*
apadeśaḥ pretence, pretext
a:parikleśaḥ lack of vexation
apsaras *f.* nymph (of heaven)
a:vighna unhindered
aśokaḥ aśoka-tree
ākula confused; **ākulī~bhū**
grow confused; *p.p.* in confusion
āyus *n.* life
ārta oppressed
āsanam sitting, seat
udghātin having elevations,
bumpy
kathitam thing spoken, talk,
conversation
kaṣṭa~tara more grievous
kāla-haraṇam delay; **kāla-
haraṇam kṛ** (to) delay
kiyant how much?
kṣudh *f.* hunger
tantram administration
tapasvin ascetic; poor, wretched
tapo-vanam ascetics' grove
devatā divinity, god
dhanam wealth
dhyānam meditation, meditating
nayanam eye
patatrin bird
panthan *m., irreg. noun* (p. 283)
road, path, way

para other; *m.* enemy, (hostile) stranger
parikleśaḥ vexation
parigrahaḥ occupation, occupying
parityāgaḥ giving up, sacrificing; liberality
paścāt:tāpaḥ [after-pain:] remorse
piṇḍapātin *m.* mendicant
pracchāyam shade
pratyākhyānam rejection
prayogaḥ performance (of play)
prasādaḥ graciousness, favour;
free gift; **prasādī~kṛ** bestow
[as free gift]
prārabdham thing undertaken, enterprise
prāvīṇyam proficiency
bharataḥ actor, player
bhūmi *f.* ground; fit object
(for); **parityāga-bhūmi** object of liberality, suitable recipient (of)
maṅgalam welfare, auspicious
omen, good luck
manda slow, slack; **mandī~
bhū** slacken
manyu *m.* passion, anger
maraṇam death
maru *m.* desert
Mānasam *name of a lake*
mohaḥ delusion

raśmi *m.* rein, bridle

rahas *n.* solitude, secrecy; **rahasi** in secret

ripu *m.* enemy

lavaḥ fragment; **lavaśo lavaśaḥ** piece by piece

lobhaḥ greed

viklava bewildered, distressed

vinīta disciplined, modest

viśeṣaḥ distinction; *ifc. see chapter*; **viśeṣa˜taḥ** in particular

viśrambhaḥ confidence; **viśrambha-kathā/kathitam** confidential *or* intimate conversation

vṛṣṭi *f.* rain

vegaḥ haste, speed

vetasaḥ cane, reed

veṣaḥ dress, attire

vyasanam vice; weakness; misfortune, misery

śālaḥ sal tree

Śrīparvataḥ *name of a mountain*

saṃyamanam restraint, tightening

saṃjñā signal

sambandhin *m.* relative [by marriage]

sahadharmacārin *m.* lawful husband

sahadharmacāriṇī lawful wife

sāmājikaḥ spectator

sāra *m. n.* substance; property

su:caritam good deed

su:nayana fair-eyed

sthalī [dry] land

sthira firm; **sthirī˜kṛ** make firm, sustain; **sthirī˜bhū** be-[come] firm

svī˜kṛ make one's own, appropriate

ati+kram (I atikrāmati) transgress, go against

apa+nī (I apanayati) remove, take away

ava+gam *caus.* (avagamayati) procure

ākarṇayati *denom.* (ger. ākarṇanīya) give ear, listen to

ā+dā (III ādatte) take, take hold of, bring

āp (V āpnoti) obtain, get

ut+pat (I utpatati) fly up

ut+ās (II udāste) sit idle

upa+ā+labh (I upālabhate) reproach, blame

upa+ās (II upāste) sit by, wait upon, honour

ceṣṭ (I ceṣṭati) move, act, behave (towards), treat (*loc.*)

taḍ (X tāḍayati, *pass.* tāḍyate) strike, beat

ni+kṛt (VI nikṛntati) cut up, shred

parā+pat (I parāpatati) approach, arrive

prati+ā+diś (VI pratyādiśati) reject; put to shame (by example)

pra+dru (I pradravati) run (*p.p. intrans.*)

pra+āp *caus.* (prāpayati) cause to reach, convey

brū (II bravīti) say, tell

vah (I vahati, *p.p.* ūḍha) carry, take, marry

sam+yam (I saṃyacchati) restrain, arrest

sam+ā+sad *caus.* (samāsādayati) approach, attain, meet

sam+upa+diś (VI samupadiśati) point out, show

a:samyak wrongly
āvir~bhū become manifest, reveal oneself
āviṣ~kṛ make manifest, reveal
itas tataḥ hither and thither
tiro~bhū become hidden, vanish
tūṣṇīm·ās stay silent

tūṣṇīṃ bhū be[come] silent
nanu *may be translated as* 'rather' *in rejoinders*
bahiḥ outside
bhavatu [let it be:] right!
yatra, yathā, yadā, yāvat *see chapter*
~vat like (*see chapter*)

Exercise 12a

भद्र भद्र न प्रवेष्टव्यम् ।१। भवतु शृणोमि तावदासां विश्रम्भ-
कथितानि ।२। तूष्णीं भव यावदाकर्णयामि ।३। अमात्य
तथापि प्रारब्धमपरित्याज्यमेव ।४। तदच्च शालप्रच्छाये मुद्ग-
तेमासनपरिग्रहं करोतु तातः ।५। समुपदिश तमुद्देशं यचास्ते स
पिण्डपाती ।६। हृदय स्थिरीभव । किमपि ते कष्टतरमाकर्ण-
नीयम् ।७। किमन्यद्ब्रवीतु ।८। इयं चोर्वशी यावदायुस्तव
सहधर्मचारिणी भवतु ।९। तबावच्छ्रीपर्वतमुपनीय लवश्रो
लवश्र एनां निक्षत्य दुःखमरणां करोमि ।१०। अस्ति नः
सुचरितश्रवणलोभादन्यदपि प्रष्टव्यम् ।११। तत्किमिलुदासते
भरताः ।१२। तच चैवमनुष्ठेयं यथा वदामि ।१३। ननु भव-
तीभ्यामेव शकुन्तला स्थिरीकर्तव्या ।१४। गृहीतगृहसारमेनं
सपुत्रकलत्रं संयम्य रक्ष तावद्यावन्मया वृषलाय कथ्यते ।१५।
संप्रत्यगस्त्याश्रमस्य पन्थानं ब्रूहि ।१६। विनीतवेषप्रवेश्यानि
तपोवनानि ।१७। मरुस्थलां यथा वृष्टि: क्षुधार्ते भोजनं तथा
।१८। उद्धातिनी भूमिरिति रश्मिसंयमनाद्रथस्य मन्दीभूतो
वेग: ।१९। चक्रवर्तिनं पुत्रमाप्नुहि ।२०। तत्कियन्तं कालमक्षा-
भिरेवं संभृतबलैरपि शत्रुव्यसनमवेक्षमाणैरुदासितव्यम् ।२१।
यदेवाङ्गुरीयकदर्शनादनुस्मृतं देवेन सत्यमूढपूर्वां रहसि मया
तच्चभवती शकुन्तला मोहात्मत्याद्दिष्टेति तदैव पश्चात्तापमुपगतो
देव: ।२२। महाधनलाब्दहुपत्नीकानानेन भवितव्यम् ।२३। अमात्य

ईदृग्रस्वाभरणविशेषस्य विशेषतः कुमारेण स्वगात्राद्वतार्य
प्रसादीकृतस्य किमयं परित्यागभूमिः । २४। यावच संबन्धिनो
न परापतर्न्ति तावद्त्सया माळत्या नगरदेवतागृहमविघ्नमङ्गळाय
गन्तव्यम् ॥ २५ ॥

Exercise 12b

For convenience, gerundives in **tavya** are represented by
'must' and those in **ya** and **anīya** by 'should'.

1 What do you say? 2 With this letter (I) must defeat
Rākṣasa. 3 (You) must remain right there until the arrival·of·
Makaranda·and·Madayantikā. 4 Let the two of us just listen.
5 Alas, (my) enemies have made even my heart their own.
6 Stay, Your Majesty [**āyuṣmant**], in this aśoka-tree's·shade,
while I announce you to Indra's·sire. 7 His·Excellency's·
instructions are that I should safeguard Rākṣasa's life. 8 So
let it be as it must [be]. 9 The *whole* administration is in
confusion. 10 Why do *you stay silent? 11 So one should·
not·blame Rākṣasa in this matter. 12 Good Bhāsvaraka, take
him outside and beat him till he talks. 13 Listen to this
wonderful (thing). 14 Śakuntalā must be in this very bower·
of·reed·and·creeper. 15 So now you should not [make:] feel
anger towards your lawful husband. 16 I'll go to the very
spot where that fair·eyed (girl) vanished before [*loc.*] my eyes.
17 The dear child has revealed proficiency·in·speaking. 18 In
that case let us wait upon their honours here the spectators
by [*abl.*] an actual [**eva**] performance·of·it. 19 *You too,
like His Highness, are one·whose·words·(I)·should·not·go·
against. 20 I behaved wrongly in delaying after I had met my
beloved. 21 Alas! See how [*use* **eṣaḥ**], sitting idle like·a·
stranger in our friend's·misfortunes, we are put to shame by
this (man). 22 Oh merchant! You must rather [**nanu**] ask
us 'and how does that lack·of·vexation reveal itself?' 23 Before
these birds fly up from the lake, eager·for·Mānasa, (I) must
procure news·of·(my)·beloved from them. 24 Then, they
having run hither and thither in [*abl.*] a pretence·of·fear

on·receiving·the·signal [*use* **gṛhīta** *in bahuvrīhi*], you must take Śakaṭadāsa away from the execution-ground and convey him to Rākṣasa. 25 As soon as [**yad» aîva . . . tad» aîva**] Menakā came to Dākṣāyaṇī from the nymphs'·pool [**tīrtham**] bringing Śakuntalā distressed·by·(her)·rejection, I learnt·what· had·happened [**vṛttānta** *in bahuvrīhi*] from meditating—that, as a result of [*abl.*] Durvāsas' curse, this poor (girl) had been rejected by her lawful husband.

Chapter 13

PARADIGMS: Presents of classes III, VII and IX; **asau**

Reduplication

Reduplication (as a grammatical phenomenon in Sanskrit) is the prefixing to the root of some initial part of that root in either identical or altered form. Thus from the roots **tud** 'strike' and **kṛ** 'do', the first person plural parasmaipada perfect forms **tutudima** 'we struck' and **cakṛma** 'we did'. Reduplication is a feature of class III presents, of the perfect tense, of some aorists, and of desiderative and intensive formations. The principles of reduplication differ somewhat in each of these formations, but for convenience the following rules may be taken as a norm on the basis of which any variations will be described:

Only the first syllable of the root, i.e. the vowel and what precedes it, is reduplicated: **yuj, yuyuj; dih, didih.**

Of an initial consonant group only the first consonant is repeated: **kruś, cukruś.** But when the group consists of **s** followed by a stop (or by an unvoiced sound—the rule may be stated either way, since **s** is never followed by either a sibilant or a voiced stop), it is the stop which is reduplicated. Thus **stu, tuṣṭu** (with retroflexion by internal sandhi); whereas **sru, susru** follows the general rule.

Long vowels are shortened, and diphthongs represented by **i** or **u** as appropriate: **nī, ninī; dā, dadā; jīv, jijīv; sev,**

siṣev. However, roots ending in **e/ai/o** (often given as ending in **ā** in Western grammars) reduplicate with **a**: **mlai, mamlai.**

Aspirated consonants reduplicate in unaspirated form: **bhid, bibhid.**

Velars are represented by corresponding palatals, and **h** by **j**: **kram, cakram; khan, cakhan; gup, jugup; hu, juhu.**

Roots beginning with a vowel follow the same general pattern of reduplication, but internal sandhi produces considerable changes of appearance. For instance, in the weak reduplicated form of **iṣ, iiṣ** becomes **īṣ**; but in the strong reduplicated form, **ieṣ** becomes **iyeṣ.**

The most important variation of the above principles is that the vowel of the reduplicated syllable is in some circumstances strengthened and in others replaced by **a** or by **i**. The vowels **ṛ/ṝ** never reduplicate without change.

Presents of classes III, VII and IX

The present stem of class III verbs is formed by reduplication of the root: **hu** 'offer (sacrifice)', **juhoti** 'he sacrifices', **juhumah** 'we sacrifice'. The rules of reduplication are in general those described above. **ṛ/ṝ** reduplicates as **i**: **bhṛ** 'carry', **bibharti.**

The chief peculiarity of these reduplicated stems is that in the indicative and imperative parasmaipada the third person plural termination is **ati atu**, not *anti *antu*: **juhvati** 'they sacrifice'. [In the imperfect there is a special third person plural termination **uḥ**.]

Among the more important stems of this class are **dhā** 'put' and **dā** 'give'. Their weak stems reduce to **dadh** and **dat**, and **dadh** becomes **dhat** before **t/th**: **dadhāti** 'he puts', **dadhati** 'they put', **dadhmah** 'we put', **dhattha** 'you put'. The imperative second person singular parasmaipada is **dhehi/dehi**. A noteworthy compound of **dhā** is **śrad-dhā** 'put trust in, believe' (cf. Latin *credo*): **śraddhatte** 'he believes', etc.

The roots **mā** 'measure' and **hā** 'go forth' have weak stems **mimī/jihī** which reduce to **mim/jih** before vowels.

The distinguishing 'suffix' of class VII verbs is the nasal **n** infixed after the vowel of the root and strengthening to **na** in the strong forms. Thus from **yuj** 'join', **yuñj** and **yunaj**: **yunakti** 'he joins', **yuñjanti** 'they join'. One or two roots, such as **bhañj** 'break', are quoted in a form already incorporating the nasal: this is because the nasal remains in various forms outside the present stem—e.g. **bhañjanam** 'a breaking'.

Class IX verbs add a suffix which has the strong form **nā** and the weak forms **nī** before consonants and **n** before vowels: **krī** 'buy', **krīṇāti** 'he buys', **krīṇīmaḥ** 'we buy', **krīṇanti** 'they buy'. Roots in **ū** shorten to **u**: **pū**, **punāti** 'purifies'. The infix nasal found in various forms of roots such as **bandh** 'tie' is dropped: **badhnāti** 'he ties'. Two of the commonest roots of this class are **jñā** 'know' and **grah** 'seize, take': they shorten to **jā** and **gṛh** respectively—**jānāti** 'knows', **gṛhṇāti** 'takes'.

A peculiar termination **āna** for the second person singular parasmaipada imperative is found in verbs of this class whose roots end in a consonant: so **gṛhāṇa** 'take (it)'.

The infinitive

The infinitive is formed by adding the suffix **tum** to the root strengthened to guṇa grade: **nī**, **netum** 'to lead'; **budh**, **boddhum** 'to learn'; **jīv**, **jīvitum** 'to live'; **gam**, **gantum** 'to go'. In a fair number of verbs, most of them ending in a consonant, the suffix is added with connecting **i**: **car**, **caritum** 'to move'; **bhū**, **bhavitum** 'to be'. Generally, but by no means invariably, it is verbs which add **ita** in the past participle which add **itum** in the infinitive. Quite frequently, infinitives of both forms are found: thus **nayitum** beside **netum**. Derivative stems retain the suffix **ay**: **cārayitum** 'to cause to move'.

Strengthening to guṇa is not invariable: thus **likh**, **likhitum** (as well as **lekhitum**) 'to write'. Several verbs containing **ṛ** strengthen this to **ra**: the commonest of them is **dṛś**, **draṣṭum** 'to see'. The infinitive of **grah** 'take' is **grahītum**.

The Sanskrit infinitive has a more limited range of uses than the English infinitive: various ways of representing the English

infinitive have, in fact, been encountered in previous chapters.
The nominalisation of verbal notions may be accomplished in
Sanskrit by means of various nominal suffixes, or (though much
less frequently) by means of relative clauses. Apart from
being employed like the English infinitive to express purpose,
the infinitive is generally restricted to 'prolative' use after
a number of verbs and adjectives with meanings like 'want
to, (be) able to, begin to, (be) ready to', etc.: thus **śrotum
icchāmi** 'I want to hear'. (However, in implying a request,
such a turn of phrase does not have the abruptness of the
English expression, and so 'I should like to' would usually be
a more appropriate translation.) Similarly, **śrotum śaknoti**
'he can hear'; **śrotum samarthaḥ** '(he is) capable of hearing'.
jñā with an infinitive means 'have enough knowledge to, know
how to'.

alam with an infinitive usually means 'has the capacity to':

**bhuvam adhipatir bāl-âvastho py alam pari-
rakṣitum**
a ruler, though a child in years, is capable of
guarding the earth

The verb **arh,** literally 'be worthy to', may express the
notion 'should, ought'. It is frequently used in particular as
a polite way of conveying a request or instruction:

śanaiḥ śanair ārodhum arhati devaḥ   Your Majesty
should ascend very gently: be careful as you ascend,
Your Majesty

The second main use of the infinitive is to express purpose
('in order to'). It has the same sense as a verbal noun in the
dative or in composition with **artham** but is especially used
with verbs of motion or where a verbal noun is not readily
available.

tad eṣa Vṛṣalas tvāṃ draṣṭum āgacchati   here then
is Vṛṣala coming to see you
paścāt kopayitum āyuṣmantaṃ tathā kṛtavān asmi
thereafter to make you angry, sire, I acted thus

An infinitive may be used with words such as **avasaraḥ** and **samayaḥ** 'opportunity to, (right) time to':

> **avasaraḥ khalv ayam ātmānaṃ darśayitum**   this is certainly the moment to reveal myself

Sometimes an infinitive comes near to functioning as the subject of a sentence, when it is an extension of an impersonal passive—e.g. **ālikhituṃ vismṛtam asmābhiḥ** 'we forgot to draw'. Similar and quite frequent is the use with **yukta** 'right, proper', **ayukta** 'wrong', etc. (The finite verb form **yujyate** 'is proper' may be used in the same way.) The construction may be with a genitive of reference, or with a predicative instrumental, as in the impersonal gerundive:

> **na yuktam anayos tatra gantum**   it is not right for the two of them to go there
> **nir_udyogair asmābhir avasthātum ayuktam**   it is wrong for us to remain without exertion

There is no special passive form of the infinitive. It may, however, bear a passive sense when used in a passive context, e.g. **hantuṃ nīyate** 'is taken to be killed'. In particular, the passives of **ārabh** 'begin' and **śak** 'be able' are used where we use a passive infinitive in English: **kartum ārabhyate** 'is beginning to be done'; **kartuṃ śakyate** 'can be done'. The adjective **śakya** 'possible, able to be' is frequent in this passive sense, used either personally or impersonally:

> **śakyaḥ khalv eṣa . . . prajñayā nivārayitum**   he can of course be checked by guile
> **adhunā śakyam anena maraṇam apy anubhavitum**   it is now possible for him to suffer even death

The infinitive suffix appears exceptionally in its stem form **tu** with the nouns **kāmaḥ** 'desire' and (less often) **manas** 'mind' to form bahuvrīhi compounds: **apahnotu_kāma** 'having a desire to conceal, anxious to conceal'; **kartu_manas** 'having a mind to do, intending to do'; **kim asi vaktu_kāmaḥ?** 'what are you wanting to say?'

Future tense

The future tense is formed by adding the suffix **sya,** or **iṣya** (which is the preceding suffix with connecting **i**), to the root strengthened to guṇa grade, the resulting stem being inflected in the thematic **a** class. Thus **nī, neṣyati** 'will lead'; **bhū, bhaviṣyati** 'will be'. There is a general correspondence as to the strengthening of the root and the addition of the connecting vowel between this formation and that of the infinitive: so **drakṣyati** 'will see', **grahīṣyati** 'will take', **likhiṣyati** 'will write'. The most important difference is that all roots ending in **ṛ** must add the connecting vowel: so **kartum** 'to do', but **kariṣyati** 'will do'.

The sense of the future corresponds to that of English 'shall' and 'will', more particularly in the 'uncoloured' usages of these words. If the distinction between 'shall' and 'will' is crucial, it must be represented in some other way in Sanskrit; but a sentence such as **acirād asya pariśramasya phalam anurūpam adhigamiṣyasi** may be translated equally well as 'you shall soon receive' or 'you will soon receive, a suitable recompense for this exertion'.

> **ardharātra-samaye Candraguptasya Nanda-bha-vana-praveśo bhaviṣyati** Candragupta's entry into the Nanda palace will happen at midnight
>
> **nᵊ êdam vismariṣyāmi** I shan't/won't forget this
>
> **ramaṇīyaṃ hi vatsa:Makarandam avalokayiṣyati Madayantikā** Madayantikā will see dear Makaranda (looking) most attractive

Many instances have already been given of the present tense used to announce an immediate intention. If the future tense used in the same way has any difference of force, it is perhaps in making the statement of intention a shade more deliberate: **pṛcchāmi** 'I'll ask (him)', **prakṣyāmi** 'what I'll do is ask (him)'.

> **evaṃ rājā ᵊham iti parijñānaṃ bhavet. bhavatu, atithi-samācāram avalambiṣye** (if I act) like that,

there might be the realisation that I am the king. Well then, I will adopt the behaviour of a (normal) guest

The future may express a prediction about an already existing state of affairs ('it will turn out to be the case that'), as also in English—'that will be the postman'.

jñāsyati Candanadāsasya vṛttāntam (this man) will (be sure to) know what has happened to Candanadāsa

The prediction may also be about a past event, and here, as in the English use of the future perfect, a generalisation may be implied: 'he won't have done anything foolish' implies '—because in general he would not do anything foolish'. Thus 'would' or 'would have' are sometimes possible English translations of the Sanskrit future.

eṣa . . . ratho dṛśyate—na khalu so ꞌkṛtꞌârtho nivartiṣyate look, I can see the chariot! He won't have/wouldn't have returned [/wouldn't return] unsuccessful

na hy an:ātma⁀sadṛśeṣu Rākṣasaḥ kalatraṃ nyāsī̃ kariṣyati Rākṣasa certainly won't have/wouldn't have entrusted [/wouldn't entrust] his wife to those [not worthy of:] less worthy than himself

Relative adverbs continued

Examples have been given in Chapters 11 and 12 of subordinate clauses having a nominal or adverbial feature in common with a main clause. In any language there also arises the need to make the whole notion of one clause a subordinate part of the notion of another. One might alternatively talk of subordinating the *verbal* notion of one clause. These two concepts are not in fact equivalent, but languages have some tendency to treat them as such. For instance, in the English 'his acquiescence has been unhappy', 'unhappy' may qualify the verbal notion of acquiescence ('acquiescence in an unhappy spirit') or the implicit total notion ('that he should have acquiesced is to be regretted'). We may use devices such as intonation and pause to distinguish the two: 'he has acquiesced unhappily' as against 'he has acquiesced, unhappily'.

As should already be clear (e.g. from the discussion of the use of abstract nouns in Chapter 10), Sanskrit deals with such relationships principally by means of nominal constructions. But where finite constructions are used, they are achieved by extending the sense of the relative pronouns and adverbs. (Certain subordinating conjunctions exist, notably **cet** 'if', which are not formally related to the relative base **ya-**, but they may usually be treated as the equivalent of some relative adverb—the major exception being, of course, **iti**.) As a result of this extension of usage, certain ambiguities arise. This is not surprising, for even in English, where subordinate clauses are far more important, there is a similar situation—cf. the two possible interpretations of the phrase 'the fact that we must not forget', or the mere comma (or slight change of intonation) which distinguishes 'he said nothing which annoyed me' from 'he said nothing, which annoyed me'.

In what follows, a number of the more important extensions of usage will be described. The translations of the examples given should usually make the usage plain. The (perhaps rather elaborate) theoretical framework has been introduced to help account for some ambiguities.

First, there is the simple case in which a following ('connecting') relative has as its antecedent the whole of the preceding statement:

. . . **ācakranda rāja-kanyā, yena tat sakalam eva kanyā-ṇtaḥpuram . . . ākulībabhūva** the princess screamed—[by which (screaming) that whole girls' quarters was thrown into confusion:] which threw the whole of the girls' quarters into confusion

bakula-māle upakāriṇy asi, yataḥ svāgatam bhavatyāḥ bakula garland, you are my ally—[as a result of which:] and therefore, welcome to you

katham iyam bhagavatyāḥ . . . ādyā śiṣyā Saudāmanī?—yataḥ sarvam adhunā samgacchate what, is this Her Reverence's earliest pupil Saudāmanī? [as a result of which:] in that case everything now fits

This use of **yataḥ** to mean 'therefore' (introducing an effect) contrasts sharply with its use to mean 'for' (introducing a cause) as described below.

Where the total notion of the clause is subordinate to another statement, it is introduced most neutrally by the neuter singular form **yat**. (In traditional terms, **yat** may be said to represent the 'internal accusative' of the subordinate verb.)

> **yan mithaḥ:samavāyād imāṃ madīyāṃ duhitaram bhavān upayeme, tan mayā prītimatā yuvayor anujñātam** that you, sir, married this my daughter by mutual union, I gladly assent to for you both
>
> **eken> âbhisaṃdhinā pratyarpayāmi . . . yad idam aham eva yathā_sthānaṃ niveśayāmi** I'll hand (it) over on one condition—that I should be the one to put it in place

When a noun clause is the object of a verb meaning 'say', 'know', etc., the regular construction is, of course, with **iti**. But where the noun clause follows the main clause, a frequent alternative is to introduce it with **yathā**. (One might compare the use of 'how' for 'that' in sentences like 'he told me how a man had come to see him'.) In fact, in such cases **iti** is frequently added pleonastically at the end of the clause (in the second of the following examples it is not pleonastic, being needed for the sub-subordinate clause):

> **vatsa, ucyatāṃ Bhāgurāyaṇo yathā 'tvaritaṃ saṃbhāvay> aînam' iti** child, let Bhāgurāyaṇa be told to find him at once
>
> **idaṃ tāvat prasiddham eva, yathā Nandanāya Mālatīṃ prārthayamānaṃ Bhūrivasur nṛpam uktavān 'prabhavati nija:kanyakā:janasya Mahā:rāja' iti** Now it is entirely established that Bhūrivasu told the king when the latter was seeking Mālatī for Nandana, 'Your Majesty has power over his own daughter'

The subordinate clause may be related as reason to the main clause. The implied correlative of **yat** is then **tat** in its

sense of 'then, so', and its force may be represented literally
in English by 'inasmuch as':

> **kim atyāhitaṃ Mādhavasya, yad aniṣṭaṃ vyavasito
> ›si?**   is there (some) disaster to Mādhava, that you have
> (this) dreadful resolve?

This has the same force as the use of the personal relative
pronoun described in Chapter 11 (p. 174), but the latter is, of
course, more restricted in its scope, since it can be used only
when there is some identifiable common element in the two
clauses. In the three examples given in Chapter 11, on the
other, hand, **yat** might be substituted without change of
meaning.

As well as **yat,** other forms of the relative are used. These
forms are somewhat illogical and represent the attraction of
the relative into the case of the antecedent. Thus **yena** really
means **tena yat** 'in view of the (fact) that'.

> **aho mahā:prabhāvo rājā Duhṣantaḥ, yena praviṣṭa:
> mātra ev› âtrabhavati nir_upaplavāni naḥ kāryāṇi
> saṃvṛttāni**   how great is the power of King Duḥṣanta,
> in that from the moment His Honour entered, our rites
> have become unmolested

[Note that, without the locative absolute phrase, **yena** might
have been interpreted personally—'he by whose agency'.]

> **na yathāvad dṛṣṭam, yat kāraṇam bhavān a:pra-
> dhānaḥ**   (you) did not see it properly, for the reason that
> you are not one in authority
>
> **abhimatā vā bhavanam atithayaḥ samprāptāḥ, yata
> eṣa pāka-viśeṣ›-ārambhaḥ?**   or have honoured guests
> come to the house, that there is this embarking upon
> special cooking?
>
> **na khalv anyathā vastu-vṛttam, yataḥ śrāvak›-
> âvasthāyām asmat;Saudāmanī-samakṣam anayor
> vṛtt› êyaṃ pratijñā**   the facts are not really [other-
> wise:] at variance (with what has been said), for when
> they were students the two of them made this promise
> before Saudāmanī and myself

The meaning of 'inasmuch as' shades into that of 'for' (in which sense the emphatic particle **hi** is common) and finally into that of 'because':

> yato ›yaṃ cirān nirvṛto mam› ôpayogaṃ na jānāti, ten› âdhunā mam› āhāra-dāne ›pi mand›‿ādaraḥ because this man, satisfied for (so) long, does not recognise my utility, he is now careless even in providing fodder for me

When the subordinate clause is related as a result to the main clause, it may be introduced by **yathā**. This again is a case of attraction into the form of the correlative: **tathā . . . yathā** means 'in such a way that (as a result)':

> bhos tathā ›ham utpatitā yathā sakala eṣa giri;- nagara;grāma;sarid;araṇya-vyatikaraś cakṣuṣā parikṣipyate oh, I have flown up so (high) that this whole expanse of mountains, cities, villages, rivers and forests is encompassed by my eye

> upoḍha‿rāgeṇa vilola‿tārakaṃ
> tathā gṛhītaṃ śaśinā niśā-mukham
> yathā samastaṃ timir›:âṃśukaṃ tayā
> puro ›pi rāgād galitaṃ na lakṣitam

The moon, with passion [/redness] increased, has seized the tremulous-eyed [/winking-starred] face [/forepart] of the night in such a way that she has not noticed all the garment of her darkness slip away even in front [/in the east] because of (her answering) passion [/redness]

Other relatives and correlatives are possible in result clauses. Thus:

> īdṛśas te nirmāṇa-bhāgaḥ pariṇato, yena lajjayā svacchandam ākranditum api na śakyate your [allotment of creation:] destiny in life has turned out to be such that for very shame one cannot even weep as one would wish

However, Sanskrit usually expresses consequence by sub-ordinating the reason rather than the result: 'he was so miserly he never spent a shilling' would become 'by him being miserly not a shilling was spent'.

aho, Rākṣasam prati me vitarka-bāhulyād ākulā buddhir na niścayam adhigacchati [oh, confused from the multitude of doubts about Rākṣasa, my mind attains no certainty:] I am in such a storm of doubt about Rākṣasa, I cannot make up my mind

evam nirbhinna:hṛday>⁼āvegaḥ śiśu:janen> âpy anu-kampito >smi [thus with the agitation of my heart betrayed, I am pitied even by children:] I betrayed my distress so clearly that even a child takes pity on me

atibhūmim ayam gato na śakyate nivartayitùm [having gone to excess, this one cannot be turned back:] he has gone too far to be turned back

The use of **yathā** in expressing result is commonest in a particular idiom with verbs like **kṛ** 'act' and **vidhā** 'arrange', to express 'act in such a way that', 'see to it that':

yathā svāmī jāgarti tathā mayā kartavyam I must see to it that my master wakes up

yathā >ham bhavadbhyām sah> ākāśa-vartmanā yāmi, sa upāyo vidhīyatām [so that I go with you two by the way of air, let that expedient be arranged:] find a way for me to accompany the two of you in your flight

Similarly with **niṣidh** 'forbid' (note how the common sub-ject is placed with the first verb rather than with the main verb):

yathā ca sainikās tapo-vanam n> ôparundhanti dūrāt pariharanti ca, tathā niṣeddhavyāḥ [and so that the soldiers do not molest the ascetic grove and avoid it from afar, thus (they) are to be checked:] and you must restrain the soldiers from molesting the ascetic grove and have them keep well clear of it

The notion expressed by a noun clause may be a possibility rather than a fact (and even so—as in the example **ekeṇ› âbhisaṃdhinā** . . . above—the verb may remain in the present indicative):

yac ca 'śṛgālo ›yam' iti matvā mam› ôpary avajñā kriyate, tad apy ayuktam   and that (he) should feel (/for him to feel) contempt for me thinking 'he is (just) a jackal', that also (would be) wrong

Here we might most naturally say 'if he should feel'. And the usual word for 'if', **yadi**, is in fact in origin merely **yat** with a strengthening particle. A correlative is often lacking (regularly so when the conditional follows the main clause). When expressed, it is probably most usually **tat**, but other correlatives are often found, such as **tataḥ, tadā, tarhi.**

ārye, yadi nepathya-vidhānam adhyavasitam, tad ih› āgamyatām   lady, if arrangements backstage are completed, come here
iha devam upatiṣṭhatu, yadi na doṣaḥ   let him attend Your Majesty here, if there is no [fault:] objection

The alternative word for 'if', **cet,** must not stand as the first word in its clause:

na ced anya:kāry›-âtipātaḥ, praviśy› âtra gṛhyatām atithi-satkāraḥ   if (it means) no neglect of other duties, enter here and accept (our) hospitality

Other words, such as **atha,** are also found:

atha kautukam,˳āvedayāmi   if (you feel) curiosity, I'll tell you

With **api** added, we have **yadi api** 'even if, though'. Similar in sense is **kāmam** 'granted that, though'. The correlative may be **tathā ›pi, punar, tu** 'even so, yet'.

kāmaṃ khalu sarvasy› âpi kula-vidyā bahumatā, na punar asmākaṃ nāṭyam prati mithyā gauravam   though of course everyone thinks highly of his own

hereditary learning, our regard for the drama is not misplaced

yady apy ete na paśyanti, lobh>-ôpahata:cetasaḥ,
kula-kṣaya-kṛtaṃ doṣaṃ mitra-drohe ca pātakam—
kathaṃ na jñeyam asmābhiḥ pāpād asmān nivartitum,
kula-kṣaya-kṛtaṃ doṣaṃ prapaśyadbhir, Janārdana?

> Even if these men, their understanding killed by greed, do
> not see
> The sin caused by the ruin of a family and the crime in the
> injuring of a friend,
> How should we not know (enough) to turn back from this
> wickedness,
> We, Krishna, who can see such sin?

asau

The pronoun **asau** 'that, he' is less common than the other
demonstrative pronouns. It is used specifically of what is not
near at hand, but anything to which it refers may also be
referred to, if absent by the pronoun **saḥ** and if present by the
pronoun **ayam**. To give stronger deictic force ('thére is, look
at that') the combination **ayam asau** may be used:

> **ayam asau mahā:nadyor vyatikaraḥ**   thére is the con-
> fluence of the two great rivers

Used of what is absent, **asau** offers a perhaps slightly more
emphatic alternative to **saḥ**:

> **Vṛṣala Rākṣasaḥ khalv asau**   Vṛṣala, he (/the man you
> are talking about) is Rākṣasa, don't forget
> **hṛt:âdhikāraḥ kva sāṃpratam asau baṭuḥ?**   where
> is that fellow, now that he has lost his job?

ādi = 'etc.'

ādi m. and less frequently some other word such as **prabhṛti**
f., literally meaning 'beginning', may be used at the end of

a bahuvrīhi compound with the sense 'of which the beginning is X', and therefore 'beginning with X/[consisting of] X, *etc.*/ such as X'

> **Indr›:ādayaḥ surāḥ** the gods Indra, *etc.*, Indra and the other gods
> **śrotr›:ādīn› îndriyāṇi** the senses such as hearing
> **Viśvāvasu:prabhṛtayas trayo bhrātaraḥ** Viśvāvasu and his two (younger) brothers

Note the possibility of the translatión 'X *and*', particularly in the last of the above examples.

Such compounds are often used without the substantive they qualify being expressed. If the omitted substantive has a rather general reference, there is a tendency for the compound itself to be put into the singular:

> **mṛto ›sau Saṃjīvako, ›smābhiś c› âgny:ādinā satkṛtaḥ** that Saṃjīvaka is dead, and we have [honoured him with fire etc.:] given him a cremation ceremony and so forth
> **na hy etābhyām atidīpta:prajñā¦medhābhyām asmad:ādeḥ sah›:âdhyayana-yogo ›sti** for (anyone) like us, there is no managing common lessons with those two, whose understanding and intellect are exceptionally brilliant

The neuter singular form **prabhṛti** comes to be used adverbially with the ablative or with a form ending in the suffix **taḥ** in the sense of 'from X onwards, since': **cirāt prabhṛti** 'since a long time', **tataḥ prabhṛti** 'from that (point) on'.

ājñāpayati and *vijñāpayati*

The causatives of **ājñā** and **vijñā** (of which the past participles have the anomalous alternative forms **ājñapta** and **vijñapta**) may often be translated 'order' and 'request' respectively. More widely, they may both mean 'say', the first with the implication that the speaker is someone (such as a king or guru) whose word is not to be questioned, the second with the reverse implication that the speaker is someone (such as a counsellor or pupil) who should show deference to the person addressed. A form such as **vijñāpayāmi** 'I beg to state' may, of course, simply indicate politeness between equals.

Vocabulary

atithi *m.* guest

anucaraḥ companion, attendant

anutāpaḥ remorse

antaram interval

anveṣin searching, in search of

apatyam offspring

aparāddha (*p.p.*) *and* **aparādhin** offending, guilty

abhiyogaḥ attack

amṛtam nectar, ambrosia

ājñā command, order

ādi *m.* beginning; **-ādi** *see chapter*

āpta trustworthy

iṣu *m.* arrow

upapanna equipped with, possessed of

upasaṃgrahaḥ embracing; collecting; looking after

etāvant this much

kanyakā girl

kāmaḥ wish, desire, love; **°tu-kāma** wanting to, anxious to (*see chapter*)

kāyasthaḥ scribe, letter-writer

kāraṇam reason

kāvyam [that which derives from a **kavi** 'poet, creative writer':] literature

kumārakaḥ young man, son

kṛta-vedin conscious of [things done for one:] debt: grateful, obliged

koṣaḥ treasury, resources, wealth

kriyā doing; rite

kṣatriyaḥ [member of] warrior [caste]

guhya [to be concealed:] secret

Gautamī *pr. n.*

gauravam high esteem, duty of respect [towards an elder]

ghaṭaḥ pot

cakṣus *n.* eye

jāta *p.p.* born; **jāta-karman** *n.* birth-ceremony

jñātṛ knower, person to know/ understand

tīkṣṇa:rasa-daḥ poisoner

tuccha trifling

dāsī slave girl, servant girl

Devarātaḥ *pr. n.*

dauhitraḥ daughter's son, grandson

dhurā pole, yoke, burden

Nandaḥ *pr. n.*

nṛpati *m.* king

payas *n.* water

para far, ultimate, supreme

parigrahaḥ acquisition, possession

paritoṣaḥ satisfaction

puṇya auspicious, holy

purātana (*f.* ī) former

pṛthvī, pṛthivī earth

pracchādanam concealment

pratikūla contrary, hostile

pramāṇaṃ measure, size

prākṛta (f. ā/ī) of the people, vulgar, common

priyaṃ benefit, service

bādhā molestation, damage

brahmacārin m. student; sa:- brahmacārin m. fellow-student

bhārika burdensome

bhūṣaṇaṃ ornament

bhraṃśaḥ fall, decline; sthā-na-bhraṃśaḥ fall from position, loss of place

mati~mant possessing wit, sensible

madhya-stha [mid-stand-ing:] neutral

manorathaḥ desire

mantrin m. minister

yukta proper, right

rahasya secret

rāja-kāryaṃ, rājya-kāryaṃ [business of king/kingdom:] state affairs, state administration

rāmaṇīyakaṃ loveliness, delightful aspect

lakṣaṇaṃ characteristic, (auspicious) mark

Lopāmudrā pr. n.

-vacanāt [from the speech of:] in the name of

varāka (f. ī) wretched, poor

varṇaḥ colour, appearance

vāc f. speech, words

vādin speaking, talking

vāsin living in, dweller

vijñāpanā request

vidhi m. injunction [esp. for performance of religious rite];

vidhi~vat according to [the injunction of] ritual

vivakṣita (desiderative p.p.) wished to be said, meant

vihāraḥ (Buddhist) monastery/ convent

vedin knowing, conscious of, appreciative of

vyapadeśaḥ designation, name

vyayaḥ loss; expense, extravagance

vyāghraḥ tiger

Śakaṭadāsaḥ pr. n.

śaṭha cunning

Śatakratu m. (name of) Indra

Śākuntaleya born of Śakuntalā

śāsanaṃ command

śuddhāntaḥ women's apartments, household

śūla m. n. stake; śūlam ā+ ruh caus. [cause to mount the stake:] impale

śṛgālaḥ jackal

śrotṛ m. listener, someone to listen

śrauta derived from scripture, scriptural

śvapākaḥ outcast

saṃcayaḥ collection, quantity

satkāraḥ hospitality

samartha capable, able

sācivyaṃ being minister, post of minister

Siddhārthakaḥ pr. n.

secanaṃ (act of) sprinkling, watering

Somarātaḥ pr. n.

sainikaḥ soldier

ati+śī (II atiśete) surpass, triumph over

anu+jñā (IX anujānāti) allow, give someone leave to (dat. of verbal noun)

abhi+druh (IV abhidruhyati) do violence to

abhi+vṛt (I abhivartate) approach, go towards, make for

arh (I arhati) be worthy; 'should' (see chapter)

ava+jñā (IX avajānāti) despise
ā+khyā (II ākhyāti) declare, tell
ā+dr̥ (IV ādriyate) heed, respect, defer to, refer to
ā+ruh *caus.* (āropayati) cause to mount, raise onto
ut+ghuṣ (I udghoṣati) cry out
ut+hā (III ujjihīte) start up; depart
upa+bhuj (VII upabhuṅkte) enjoy, consume, spend
upa+rudh (VII uparuṇaddhi) besiege, invade
ut+laṅgh *caus.* (ullaṅghayati) transgress, violate
kam *caus.* kāmayate desire, be in love with
kup *caus.* kopayati anger
duṣ *caus.* (dūṣayati) spoil, defile
pari+ci (V paricinoti) become acquainted with, recognise
pīḍ (X pīḍayati) squeeze
pū (IX punāti, punīte) purify
pr̥̄ (*caus.* pūrayati, *p.p.* pūrṇa) fill, fulfil
pra+khyā *caus.* (prakhyāpayati) publish, proclaim
prati+nand (I pratinandati) receive gladly, welcome
prati+vi+dhā (III pratividadhāti) prepare against, take precautions
pra+bhā (II prabhāti) shine forth, dawn
pra+yat (I prayatate) strive, exert oneself
pra+yuj (VII prayuṅkte) employ; perform (on stage)
man *caus.* (mānayati) esteem, honour
mr̥ṣ *caus.* (marṣayati) overlook, excuse
vi+ā+pr̥̄ *caus.* (vyāpārayati) set to work, employ
śak (V śaknoti) be able, can
śam *caus.* (śamayati) quieten, appease
śrad+dhā (III śraddhatte) trust, believe
sat+kr̥ (VIII satkaroti) receive with hospitality, entertain
sam+dhā (III saṃdhatte) bring together; aim (arrow)
sam+ā+sañj (I samāsajati) attach something to (*loc.*), impose upon
spr̥ś (VI spr̥śati) touch

ati: (*karmadhāraya prefix*) too, over-, extremely, very
aticirāt after very long
anyatra elsewhere
asau that, he
itaretara (*stem form*) mutual, of/to *etc.* each other
kaccit? I hope that . . . ?
kāmam admittedly; granted that

cirāt at long last
cet (*enclitic*) if
prabhr̥ti+*abl.* starting with, from . . . onward, ever since
prādur+bhū become manifest, arise
yat satyam [what is true:] truth to tell, in truth
yady evam [if so:] in that case
yataḥ, yadi, *etc.*: *see chapter*

Exercise 13a

देहि मे प्रतिवचनम् ।१। त्वया सह गौतमी गमिष्यति ।२।
कथं शून्या द्वामी प्रदेशाः ।३। एष तमिमुं संदधे ।४। यदि
रहस्यं तदा तिष्ठतु । यदि न रहस्यं तर्हि कथ्यताम् ।५।
अहमथ्यमुं वृत्तान्तं भगवत्यै लोपामुद्रायै निवेदयामि ।६। स
खलु मूर्खस्तं युष्माभिरतिष्ठं प्रभूतमर्थराशिमवाप्य महता
व्ययेनोपभोक्तुमारब्धवान् ।७। दिष्ट्या सुप्रभातमद्य यदयं देवो
दृष्टः ।८। किं चिदाख्यातुकामास्मि ।९। उपालप्स्ते तावदेनम्
।१०। भद्र सिद्धार्थक काममपर्याप्तमिदमस्य प्रियस्य तथापि
गृह्यताम् ।११। अयमसौ राजाद्नया राजापथ्यकारी कायस्थः
शकटदासः शूलमारोपयितुं नीयते ।१२। न्यास्थः खल्वेतत्
।१३। पुष्पाश्रमदर्शनेनात्मानं पुनीमहे तावत् ।१४। भद्रे न
तत्परिहार्यं—यतो विवक्षितमनुक्तमनुतापं जनयति ।१५। नाय-
मवसरो मम शतक्रतुं द्रष्टुम् ।१६। सखे न तावदेनां पश्यसि
येन त्वमेवंवादी ।१७। अथ एतास्तपस्विकन्याः स्वप्रमाणानुरूपैः
सेचनघटैर्बालपादपेभ्यः पयो दातुमित एवाभिवर्तन्ते ।१८। न
चेन्मुनिकुमारको ऽयं तत्को ऽस्य व्यपदेशः ।१९। मतिमांश्चा-
णक्यस्तुच्छे प्रयोजने किमिति चन्द्रगुप्तं कोपयिष्यति । न च
कृतवेदी चन्द्रगुप्त एतावता गौरवमुल्लङ्घयिष्यति ।२०। तेन हि
विज्ञाप्यतां मद्वचनादुपाध्यायः सोमरातः - अमूनाश्रमवासिनः
श्रौतेन विधिना सत्कृत्य स्वयमेव प्रवेशयितुमर्हसीति ।२१।
स्वतव्यं तु सौजन्यमस्य नृपतेर्यद्परादधिनोरध्यनपराञ्जयोरिव नौ
कृतप्रसादं चेष्टितवान् ।२२। हे व्यसनसब्रह्मचारिन् यदि न गुह्यं
नातिभारिकं वा ततः श्रोतुमिच्छामि ते प्राणपरित्यागकारणम्
।२३। आर्य वैहीनरे अद्य प्रभृत्यनादृत्य चाणक्यं चन्द्रगुप्तः
स्वयमेव राजकार्याणि करिष्यतीति गृहीतार्थाः क्रियन्तां प्रकृतयः
।२४। वयमप्याश्रमबाधा यथा न भवति तथा प्रयतिष्यामहे

। २५ । क्रिमिदानीं चन्द्रगुप्तः खराज्यकार्यधुरामन्यच्च मन्त्रिणात्मनि
वा समासज्य खयं प्रतिविधातुमसमर्थः । २६ । यत्सत्यं काव्यवि-
शेषवेदिन्यां परिषदि प्रयुञ्जानस्य ममापि सुमहान्परितोषः प्रादु-
र्भवति । २७ । चन्द्रगुप्तशरीरमभिद्रोग्धुमनेन व्यापारिता दारुव-
र्मादय इति नगरे प्रख्याप्य घटकटदासः शूलमारोपितः । २८ ।
स खलु कस्मिंश्चिदपि जीवति नन्दान्वयावयवे वृषलस्य साचिव्यं
ग्राहयितुं न शक्यते । २९ । इदमत्र रामणीयकं यदमात्यभूरिव-
सुदेवरातयोश्चिरात्पूर्णो ऽयमितरेतरापत्यसंबन्धामृतमनोरथः
॥ ३० ॥

Exercise 13b

(In this exercise translate 'should' where appropriate by **arh**.)

1 Vijayā, do *you recognise this ornament? 2 That fellow is
certainly cunning. 3 Lavaṅgikā has managed·well, since
Mādhava's·attendant Kalahaṃsaka is in love with that servant·
girl·of·the·convent, Mandārikā. 4 But where will *you
(ladies) wait for me? 5 Why, quite without·giving an answer
he has started to dance. 6 What, are soldiers in·search·of·me
invading the ascetic grove? 7 Granted that this is to be
prized, yet we are neutral about it [atra]. 8 After not very
long the minister will restore [use ā+ruh caus.] us to (our)
former state. 9 It is not right to despise even a common
man. 10 King Candragupta, it is already known to you that
we lived for a certain interval·of·time with [loc.] Malayaketu.
11 Oh Viṣṇugupta, you should not touch me (who am) defiled·
by·the·touch·of·an·outcaste. 12 My dear child, I hope you
have greeted [abhi+nand] this son born of Śakuntalā whose·
birth·ceremony·and·other·rites·were·performed by us according to ritual? 13 Then give me leave to go. 14 *We* are not
able to triumph with words over Your Excellency's words.
15 If Your Excellency thus sees the time·for·attack, why delay?
16 Come in, my dear fellow: you will get someone to listen
and to understand. 17 'Just now (he) has directed his

daughter to (show) hospitality·to·guests and gone to Soma-
tīrtha to appease a fate hostile to her'—'In that case she is the
one I will see.' 18 Why do you ask, friend, un·believing(ly)?
19 Is the earth without·warriors, that (you) cry out in this way?
20 I should like to employ you, my dear fellow, on a certain
task that·must·be·performed·by·a·trustworthy·person. 21 If
the grandson·of·the·sage proves to be [**bhū**] possessed·of·those·
marks, you will welcome her and introduce her into your
household. 22 Do you then not pity the poor (girl) whose·
life·is·departing? 23 Loss·of·place will not oppress one·with-
out·possessions. 24 (We) have established Śakaṭadāsa with
a great quantity·of·wealth to·look·after the poisoners·and·so·
forth employed·by·us to do violence to Candragupta's·person,
and to·instigate·(his)·subjects·to·rebellion. 25 Mādhavya my
friend, you have·not·obtained·the·reward·of·your·eyes, since
you have not seen the ultimate of things to see [**draṣṭavya**].
26 Oh merchant Candanadāsa, a king so severe·in·punishment
towards traitors will not overlook *your concealment·of·
Rākṣasa's·wife. 27 Since those tigers·and·others, deceived·by·
mere·appearance, without·knowing (him to be) a jackal regard
that one (as) king—see [*pl.*] to it that he is recognised. 28
Your Majesty, who else anxious·to·live would have violated
Your Majesty's command? 29 Though (your) master's·
merits cannot be forgotten, Your Excellency should honour
my·request.

Chapter 14

Imperfect tense

Like the imperative, the imperfect is part of the present stem of the verb. It shares its two most prominent characteristics with the aorist tense (Chapter 15): the stem is prefixed by an augment, and the terminations are the 'secondary terminations'.

The augment consists of the vowel **a**: **nayati** 'he leads', **anayat** 'he led'; **karoti** 'he does', **akarot** 'he did'. When the stem begins with a vowel, the combination with **a** always results in vṛddhi, even in the case of **i/ī/u/ū/ṛ**: thus **icchati** 'he wants', **aicchat** 'he wanted'. When a verb is compounded with a prefix, the augment is always placed *after* any such prefix, immediately before the verb: **samudatiṣṭhat** 'he rose up', from **sam+ut+sthā**.

The personal endings of the present tense (e.g. **-ti**) are called 'primary', and those of the imperfect and aorist (e.g. **-t**) are called 'secondary'. The terminology is in fact misguided, since from an historical point of view the 'primary' endings are derived from the 'secondary'. Thus on the basis of a primitive **nayat** (surviving in Vedic as a form of the 'injunctive' mood), the imperfect **anayat** is differentiated by the addition of the augment and the present **nayati** by the addition of a suffix **i** (while the imperative **nayatu** is differentiated by the addition of another suffix, **u**). The relationship of primary and secondary endings is not always so transparent, and there is no alternative to committing the paradigms to memory, but it is perhaps also worth pointing out that the third person plural form **anayan** is reduced (because Sanskrit words cannot normally end in more than one consonant) from an original *anayant.

In the imperfect, as in the present, of athematic verbs, the three parasmaipada singular forms are strong, the rest weak. Those verbs which take -ati not -anti in the third person plural parasmaipada present (class III verbs and some other reduplicated stems) take -uḥ not -an in the corresponding imperfect form. Final ā disappears before this suffix, but i/ī/u/ū/ṛ take guṇa: **ajuhavuḥ** 'they sacrificed'. In a few further verbs of class II this ending is an optional alternative.

The imperfect is used as a simple past narrative tense—'he did', 'he went', etc. It is frequent in certain styles of Sanskrit, but since its sense may also be represented by the past participle and the past active participle (and to some extent by the aorist or perfect) there are other kinds of Sanskrit in which it occurs rarely. The examples of the imperfect in Exercise 14 are taken mainly from Classical prose romances. The imperfect tense is so named because it is parallel in *formation* with the imperfect of various other Indo-European languages, notably Greek. But it is important to realise that in sense it normally has no progressive or durative implication ('he was doing', 'he used to do', etc.). Such implications tend, even in past time, to be expressed in Sanskrit by the present tense (sometimes with the addition of the particle **sma**):

> **atha sā yadā vāyu-preritair vṛkṣa-śākhā-ʾgraiḥ spṛśyate, tadā śabdaṃ karoti, anyathā tūṣṇīm āste** now when the tips of the tree-branches, stirred by the wind, touched that (drum), it would make a noise, (while) otherwise it would remain silent

(Conversely, it should be mentioned, the use of the present as an ordinary past narrative tense—'historic present'—is not characteristic of good Classical writers.)

An exception to the general significance of the imperfect is provided by the imperfect of **as** 'be', which normally has a stative sense (except in a phrase such as **tūṣṇīm āsīt** 'fell silent'):

Ṛṣyaśṛṅg›-āśrame guru:janas tad» āsīt (his) elders were at that time in Ṛṣyaśṛṅga's hermitage

priy›:ārāmā hi sarvathā Vaidehy āsīt the Princess of Videha was always fond of the woodland

Sometimes, by combining with a past participle, this verb can convey a pluperfect sense:

atha tāmbūla-karaṅka-vāhinī madīyā Taralikā nāma may» aîva saha gatā snātum āsīt now my betel-box carrier, called Taralikā [was having gone:] had gone to bathe with me

Imperfect forms may be made from the future stem, giving a tense known as the conditional: thus from **kariṣyati** 'he will do', **akariṣyat** (lit. 'he was going to do') 'he would have done'. The use of this tense is mentioned below.

The optative

From the paradigms it will be seen that the optative links the secondary endings to the present stem by means of a suffix **ī** or **yā**, which in the case of thematic verbs becomes **e** (from **a +** **ī**). Before either form of the suffix the stem of athematic verbs appears in its weak form.

While a prescriptive usage ('he shall do') is common in law-books and similar texts, the prevalent sense of the optative in Classical literary texts is potential, to express what 'may' or 'might' be the case now or in the future (or even occasionally in the past). In plain statements **kadācit** 'perhaps' is often added:

atha vā mayi gate nṛśaṃso hanyād enām but no, with me gone the monster may kill her

kumāra, anyeṣāṃ bhūmipālānāṃ kadācid amātya-vyasanam a:vyasanaṃ syāt, na punaś Candragup-

tasya Your Highness, for other rulers a deficiency in ministers might perhaps be no deficiency, but not for Candragupta

ārāma-prāsāda-vedikāyāṃ krīḍadbhiḥ pārāvataiḥ pātitaṃ bhavet it [may be having been dropped:] may have been dropped by the pigeons while playing in the balcony of the pleasure-pavilion

kv› êdānīm ātmānaṃ vinodayeyam where can I now distract myself?

api khalu svapna eṣa syāt? could this indeed be a dream?

The combination **api nāma** is frequent with the optative, and may express anything from speculation or anxious hope to a wish, even an impossible wish ('if only'):

tad api nāma Rāma:bhadraḥ punar idaṃ vanam alaṃkuryāt? might dear Rāma, then, (be going to) grace this forest again?

api nām› âhaṃ Purūravā bhaveyam if only I (a woman) could become Purūravas!

Remote conditions

The optative is used to express remote hypotheses in relation to the future ('if he were to do') or the present '(if he were doing'). The construction does not in itself distinguish clearly between 'if this were to happen, this would be so' and 'if this were to happen, this *might* be so'.

tad yadi kadācic Candraguptaś Cāṇakyam ati:jita-kāśinam a:sahamānaḥ sācivyād avaropayet, tataḥ . . . amātya:Rākṣasaś Candraguptena saha saṃda-dhīta so if by any chance Candragupta, not enduring Cāṇakya('s being so) extremely arrogant, were to dismiss him from his ministerial post, Minister Rākṣasa might come to terms with Candragupta

One of the optatives may be replaced by a present indicative, as in the following beautiful verse of Kālidāsa:

> anadhigata:manorathasya pūrvaṃ
> śataguṇit» êva gatā mama triyāmā
> yadi tu tava samāgame tath» aîva
> prasarati subhru, tataḥ kṛtī bhaveyam

[Earlier with my desire unobtained:] before I won my desire,
The night passed for me as if multiplied by a hundred:
But if it could stretch like that [upon your union:] when I am
   with you,
I should be satisfied, my fair one

As in any language the conditional clause may be implied (or conveyed by an adverbial word or phrase) rather than directly expressed:

> vyaktaṃ n» âsti—katham anyathā Vāsanty api tāṃ
> na paśyet? obviously she does not (really) exist. Other-
> wise how would Vāsantī not [be seeing:] be able to see
> her too?
> sādhu, sādhu! anena ratha-vegena pūrva:prasthitaṃ
> Vainateyam apy āsādayeyam, kiṃ punas tam
> apakāriṇam . Maghonaḥ bravo, bravo! With this
> speed of the chariot I could even overtake [Vinatā's son:]
> Garuḍa [previously set out:] after giving him a start, let
> alone that offender against Indra

Conversely, there is an idiom whereby the main clause is suppressed and a tentative supposition is expressed by **yadi** with the optative:

> . . . pārāśarī Divākaramitra:nāmā giri-nadīm
> āśritya prativasati—sa yadi vinded vārttām   a wan-
> dering mendicant called Divākaramitra is living (in those
> parts) by a mountain stream—it is possible that he might
> possess some information

The conditional tense may be used (in both the subordinate and the main clause) to express a past unfulfilled condition. To quote Kālidāsa again:

**yadi surabhim avāpsyas tan-mukh̬-ôcchvāsa-
gandham,
tava ratir abhaviṣyat puṇḍarīke kim asmin?**

If (O bee) you had discovered the sweet fragrance of her breath,
Would you (after that) have found pleasure in this lotus?

But for various reasons the conditional is not a very common
tense. Despite its origin, it is not needed in reported statements
to express a non-conditional, 'future in the past' sense ('he
said he would do it') since a direct construction with **iti** is
available in such circumstances. Secondly, sentences of the
type 'he wouldn't have done it without asking' are expressed
by the future (Chapter 13). Thirdly, even in its special function of expressing past unfulfilled conditions it may be
replaced by the optative:

**Vṛṣala, Rākṣasaḥ khalv asau—vikramya gṛhya-
māṇaḥ svayaṃ vā vinaśyed yuṣmad-balāni vā
vināśayet** Vṛṣala, the person (you are speaking of) is
Rākṣasa after all: [being seized:] if we had seized him by
force either he would have died himself or else he would
have destroyed your forces

Comparatives and superlatives

The normal comparative suffix is **tara,** and the normal superlative suffix is **tama**: **mṛdu** 'soft', **mṛdutara** 'softer',
mṛdutama 'softest'. These suffixes are freely attached to
adjectives, and are also found with past participles (**utpīḍita-
tara** 'particularly squeezed') and occasionally substantives
(**suhṛttama** 'very close friend').

Stems in **-yāṃs** (usually **-īyāṃs**) also in principle have
comparative force and are paired with superlative forms in
-iṣṭha. They are primary derivatives of ancient formation,
added always to monosyllabic stems, and do not necessarily
correspond directly to any adjective in the positive degree.
What correspondence there is will be in meaning and/or in

ultimate derivation from the same root rather than in form. Thus **kṣodīyāṃs** 'meaner, inferior' and **kṣodiṣṭha** 'meanest' are derived directly from the root **kṣud** 'trample'; and the simple adjective **kṣudra** 'mean' is a separate formation from the same root; while **kanīyāṃs** 'smaller' and **kaniṣṭha** 'smallest' are related only in meaning to **alpa** 'small'. Some other examples of these stems are:

guru heavy, important	**garīyāṃs**	**gariṣṭha**
vṛddha old	**jyāyāṃs** elder	**jyeṣṭha**
antika near	**nedīyāṃs**	**nediṣṭha**
paṭu sharp	**paṭīyāṃs**	**paṭiṣṭha**
priya dear	**preyāṃs**	**preṣṭha**
balin strong	**balīyāṃs**	**baliṣṭha**
bahu much	**bhūyāṃs**	**bhūyiṣṭha**
mahānt great	**mahīyāṃs**	**mahiṣṭha**
(*cf.* **śrī** splendour)	**śreyāṃs** better	**śreṣṭha**

It should be noted that while some of the forms listed above are frequent, they do not exclude the use of the suffixes **tara** and **tama**: thus 'dearer' may be represented by **priyatara** as well as by **preyāṃs**.

The other term of the comparison is represented by the ablative (or by a form in **-taḥ**):

sv›:ârthāt satāṃ gurutarā praṇayi-kriy» aîva more important to the virtuous than their own interests is carrying out the request of a petitioner

It is not, in fact, necessary for the adjective to be in the comparative degree for the use of this ablative of comparison. 'Dearer even than life' may be represented simply by **prāṇe-bhyo ›pi priyaḥ**. Similarly:

vajrād api kaṭhorāṇi, mṛdūni kusumād api lok›-ôttarāṇāṃ cetāṃsi ko hi vijñātum arhati?

harder even than adamant, softer even than a flower— who can aspire to understand the minds of those who are above the world?

On the other hand, in Sanskrit (unlike English) the comparative adjective by itself need not have overtly comparative force but may be simply a more emphatic equivalent of the positive: **balīyāms**, rather than meaning 'stronger', often just means 'notably strong, particularly strong'. As a result, the comparative force is expressed much more by the ablative of comparison than by the adjective, with the exception of a few adjectives of almost invariably comparative significance such as **jyāyāms** 'elder' and **bhūyāms** 'more'. One should, in fact, beware of translating **balīyāms** as 'stronger' unless the context makes it quite plain that a comparison is intended.

Similar to the ablative of comparison is the ablative after an adjective such as **anya** 'other (than)' or after a verb such as **pari+hā** (*passive*) 'be inferior to':

> **na tarhi prāg:avasthāyāḥ parihīyase**   in that case you are [not inferior to your previous state:] no worse off than you were before

Occasionally, an analytical construction with a negative is found replacing the ablative of comparison. This is the regular construction with the word **varam** 'a preferable thing, the lesser of evils'.

> **varaṃ vandhyā bhāryā na cᵒ âvidvān putraḥ**   [a barren wife is the preferable thing and not:] better a barren wife than an ignorant son
>
> **'sarvathā ɔmātya:Rākṣasa eva praśasyataraḥ'**—' **"na bhavān" iti vākyaśeṣaḥ'**   'at all events it is Minister Rākṣasa who is more to be admired—'["not you" is the rest of the sentence:] than I am, you mean?'

Just as comparatives do not always have comparative force, so superlatives need not imply literal supremacy: **mṛdutama** may mean simply 'pre-eminently soft', 'very soft', rather than '(the) softest (of all)'. The field of comparison may be expressed either by the genitive (**sodaryāṇāṃ ṣaṇṇāṃ jyeṣṭhaḥ** 'eldest of the six [co-uterine] brothers') or by the locative (**buddhimatsu narāḥ śreṣṭhāḥ** 'men are supreme among sentient beings').

Once again, a superlative form is not necessary to express superlative force:

vihageṣu paṇḍit» aîṣā jātiḥ [among birds this is the clever species:] this is the cleverest species of bird

Constructions with *iti*

The uses of the particle **iti** may now be considered in greater detail than was practicable when the word was first introduced into the exercises.

iti is in origin an adverb meaning 'thus, in this way'. But its use in this wider sense is almost entirely lost in Classical Sanskrit. Instead, its function is to indicate that the preceding utterance is a quotation or is in some sense being treated as a quotation. (Unfortunately, there is no corresponding formal indication of where the quotation begins: more often than not it begins with the beginning of the sentence, but ambiguities can occur.) Although in principle (with rare exceptions in verse) **iti** is placed immediately after the quotation, it is not necessarily enclitic. After a long quotation, **iti** may be the first word in a new paragraph or a new stanza of verse. Or it may even refer to the words of another speaker.

iti śrutvā devaḥ pramāṇam having heard (what I have told you), Your Majesty is the judge (of what to do)
vatsa, ity ev› âham pariplavamāna:hṛdayaḥ pra-mugdho ›smi my dear (brother), from just such (thoughts as you have voiced) my heart is trembling and I am faint

The construction with **iti** may represent both direct and indirect discourse in English. In the latter case various appropriate changes must be made: according to circumstance, 'I' and 'you' may be represented by 'he' etc., 'is' by 'was', 'here' by 'there', 'now' by 'then', and so forth.

For greater clarity, the words of the **iti** clause in all the Sanskrit examples which follow have been isolated by inverted commas.

aye 'Candraguptād aparaktān puruṣān jānām›' îty upakṣiptam anena oh, he has hinted ['I know men disloyal to Candragupta':] that he knows men disloyal to Candragupta

tato bhagavaty Arundhatī 'n› âhaṃ vadhū-virahitām Ayodhyāṃ gamiṣyāṃ›' îty āha thereupon the revered Arundhatī said ['I will not go ...':] that she would not go to an Ayodhyā bereft of its bride

abhūc ca ghoṣanā 'śvaḥ kām›-ôtsava' iti and there was a proclamation ['tomorrow (there will be) a Love Festival':] that the next day was to be a Love Festival

However, the principle that the words of the **iti** clause should represent the original form of the quotation is not invariable. Occasionally in practice a first or second person form belonging in the main sentence intrudes into the **iti** clause to avoid a clumsy third person periphrasis. Theoretically, this can lead to ambuiguity, but context or common sense will normally make the meaning plain.

bhartṛdārike, 'tvam asvastha:śarīr›' êti parijanād upalabhya mahādevī prāptā mistress, the Queen has arrived, having heard from her attendants [' *"you"* are unwell':] that you are unwell (*The words actually addressed to the Queen would have been* 'the Princess is unwell'.)

A verb of telling, being told, etc. need not be expressed after **iti**. From its original meaning of 'in this way' it can naturally imply 'with these words'—becoming in effect the equivalent of **ity uktvā**. Thus a speech may conclude with **iti pādayoḥ papāta** 'with these words (she) fell at (the other's) feet', or **iti kiṃ cid asmayata** 'so (saying) she smiled slightly', '—she said, with a slight smile'. This use is especially common in the stage-directions of plays. A line of dialogue will be followed, for example, by **iti Mādhavam āliṅgati** '[so saying] she embraces Mādhava'.

The usage permits great flexibility of construction, since the **iti** clause may represent not actual dialogue but the substance of what is said:

'eṣā ku:matir na kalyāṇ›' îti nivārayantyāṃ mayi

vana-vāsāya kopāt prasthitā [upon my restraining
(her) by saying 'this ill notion is not beneficial':] when I
remonstrated that no good would come of such wrongheadedness, she went off in a temper to live in the forest

'mahān ayaṃ prasāda' iti gṛhītavatī she accepted
(it) [with the words 'this is a great favour':] with grateful
thanks

'pitā te Cāṇakyena ghātita' iti rahasi trāsayitvā
Bhāgurāyaṇeṇ, âpavāhitaḥ Parvataka-putro Mala-
yaketuḥ after secretly frightening him by claiming that
Cāṇakya had had his father murdered, Bhāgurāyaṇa
helped Parvataka's son Malayaketu to escape (*Note here
how the second person in the Sanskrit avoids the ambiguities
of the English third person forms.*)

That **iti** clauses, as well as combining with verbs meaning
'tell' or 'hear' ('be told'), may be used with verbs of knowing,
thinking, supposing, etc. needs little illustration:

'tat-sahacāriṇībhiḥ sakhī te hṛt,' êti me hṛdayam
āśaṅkate my heart suspects that your friend's wife
was carried off by the companions of that (goddess)

But just as **iti** can be used without a verb of saying actually
expressed to mean 'with these words', so it can be used without a verb of thinking actually expressed to mean 'with these
thoughts, with this in mind'. **iti** thus becomes the equivalent
of **iti matvā**, and represents English 'because' or 'since'
where these have the sense of 'on the grounds that'.

'prāṇa-parityāgeṇ, âpi rakṣaṇīyāḥ suhṛd-asava' iti
kathayāmi I speak out because a friend's life must be
saved even at the cost of sacrificing (one's own) life

'kaṭhora:garbh,' êti n, ānītā ,si (we) did not bring
you (with us) because (you were) late in pregnancy

ahaṃ tvayā tasminn avasare nir_dayaṃ nighnaty api
'str,' îty avajñātā on that occasion though I struck
(you) fiercely, you despised me [thinking '(she is) a
woman':] as a woman

As well as expressing statements and suppositions, **iti** clauses are used to some extent to represent situations—'the possibility that', 'the fact that'. The first of the following examples, where a finite verb occurs and where a relative construction with **yat** might perhaps have been used, is less typical than the others:

> **'tatrabhavān Kaṇvaḥ śāśvate brahmaṇi vartate, iyaṃ ca vaḥ sakhī tasyɔ ātmaj»' êti katham etat?** how is it that His Honour Kaṇva lives in perpetual chastity and (yet) this friend of yours is his daughter?

> **bhagavan, 'prāg abhipreta-siddhiḥ, paścād darśanam' ity apūrvaḥ khalu vo ɔnugrahaḥ** revered one, for the fulfilment of (our) wishes to be first and the audience (with you) to come afterwards (constitutes) a quite unprecedented kindness on your part

> **athavā 'kāmam a:satyasandha' iti param ayaśo, na punaḥ śatru-vañcanā-paribhūtiḥ** but in fact to be wilfully false to one's word is a greater disgrace than to be beaten by an enemy's tricks

iti clauses have so far been considered from the point of view of their relation to the main sentence. The examples quoted have been of clauses of statement. But **iti** clauses may also take the form of commands or questions. Where these may best be represented by direct speech in English, they require no special mention. Elsewhere they correspond broadly to the syntactical categories of indirect command and indirect question, and may be treated from that point of view.

Clauses of command

Indirect command in English is generally expressed by an accusative and infinitive construction—'I told him to do it'.

> **tatrabhavatā Kaṇvena vayam ājñāpitāḥ 'Śakuntalā-hetor vanaspatibhyaḥ kusumāny āharaɔ' êti** His Honour Kaṇva has ordered us ['bring blossoms . . .':] to bring blossoms from the trees for Śakuntalā

As well as by an imperative, the command may be expressed in Sanskrit by other means such as a gerundive:

'rakṣaṇīyā Rākṣasasya prāṇā' ity āryʾ-ādeśaḥ His Excellency's orders are ['Rākṣasa's life should be protected':] to protect Rākṣasa's life'

By the use of **iti** in its **ity uktvā** or **iti matvā** sense, the equivalent of a clause of purpose may be obtained.

nanv idānīm eva mayā tatra Kalahaṃsakaḥ preṣitaḥ 'pracchannam upagamya Nandanʾ-āvāsa-pravṛttim upalabhasvʾ' êti why, I have just now sent Kalahaṃsaka there [with the words 'approaching stealthily find out . . .':] to find out discreetly what has been happening in Nandana's house

'mā bhūd āśrama-pīḍʾ' êti parimeya:puraḥsarau (the two of them travelled) with a limited entourage [with the thought 'let there not be affliction of the hermitage':] lest they should trouble the hermitage

Interrogative clauses

These, of course, often occur with verbs meaning 'enquire' or 'speculate':

tad yāvad gṛhiṇīm āhūya pṛcchāmi 'asti kim api prātarāśo na vʾ' êti so I'll just call my wife and ask ['is there breakfast at all or not?':] whether she has any breakfast for me or not

kiṃ tu 'katham asmābhir upagantavya' iti sampradhārayāmi but I am wondering how we should approach him

Indirect questions also occur with verbs of knowing or stating, and here it is interesting to note another modification of the principle that the words of an **iti** clause represent a direct quotation: what is known or stated is the *answer* to the question. There is, in fact, no direct speech equivalent of the indirect interrogative in 'he said who had come', unless it is a statement of the form 'such-and-such a person has come'.

ārye, yady evaṃ tat kathaya sarvataḥ 'ka eṣa vṛttānta' iti   Lady, if so then tell (us) exactly what this is
that has been happening

na tv evaṃ vidmaḥ 'kataro ›yam āyuṣmatoḥ Kuśa;
Lavayor' iti   but we do not know [the following,] which
of the two princes Kuśa and Lava he is

Not infrequently, the **iti** is omitted, so that the interrogative
pronoun has the function in itself of introducing an indirect
question:

paśyasi kā vārttā   you see what the news is

na jāne kim idam valkalānāṃ sadṛśam, utāho
jaṭānāṃ samucitam   I do not know if this is in keeping
with the bark garment (of an ascetic), or in accord with
his matted locks

jñāyatāṃ bhoḥ kim etat   ho there, find out what that is

Sometimes a relative pronoun serves to introduce the same
kind of clause:

brūhi yad upalabdham   tell me what (you) have discovered

tad etat kārtsnyena yo ›yam, yā c› êyam, yathā c›
âsya śravaṇa-śikharaṃ samārūḍhā, tat sarvam
āveditam   so (I) have told it all completely—who he is,
what that (spray of blossoms) is, and how it [attained:]
came to be placed at the tip of his ear

Once again, **iti** may be used in its **ity uktvā** and **iti matvā**
senses: thus 'kiṃ kim' iti sahas» ôpasṛtya 'rushing up
[with the words "what (is it), what (is it)?":] to find out what
was happening'; 'kuto ›yam' ity uparūḍha:kutūhalā 'with
her curiosity mounting as to where it came from'.

Word repetition

Word repetition in Sanskrit may be employed for emphasis
(intensive or iterative use). Thus **sādhu sādhu** 'bravo, bravo!';
hato hataś Caṇḍavarmā 'Candravarman is murdered,

murdered!'; **pacati pacati** 'he cooks and cooks, he's always cooking' (an example given by Sanskrit grammarians); **maṇḍaṃ maṇḍam** 'very slowly'; **punaḥ punaḥ** 'again and again'.

Repetition may also have a distributive sense ('each various one'). This is typical of pronouns. Thus **svān svān bālān ānayanti** 'they bring their various children'; **tat tat kāraṇam utpādya** 'producing [this and that reason:] various reasons'. Similarly with relatives: **yo yaḥ** (alternative to **yaḥ kaś cit**) 'whichever person, whosoever'; **yathā yathā . . . tathā tathā** 'in proportion as, the more that'.

Vocabulary

adhyavasāyaḥ resolution

an:adhyavasāyaḥ irresolution, hesitation

anilaḥ wind, breeze

an:iṣṭa undesired, unpleasant

anurāgaḥ passion, love

antaḥ end

antaḥpuram women's quarters (of palace), harem

antarita hidden, concealed

apadeśaḥ pretext

apara other, different

apasarpaṇam getting away, escape

abhilāṣin desirous, anxious

arthin having an object, wanting, petitioning

a:śeṣa [without remainder:] complete, whole, all

a:śobhana unpleasant, awful

ahamahamikā rivalry

ādaraḥ care, trouble; **ādaraṃ kṛ** take care (to)

ādhoraṇaḥ elephant-driver

āpanna:sattva [to whom a living creature has occurred:] pregnant

ārti f. affliction, distress

ārdra moist, tender

ārya-putraḥ [son of] nobleman; *voc.* noble sir

indriyam (organ or faculty of) sense

uttama uppermost, supreme, top

unmāthaḥ shaking, disturbance; **manmath›-ônmāthaḥ** pangs of love

upakāraḥ help, service

upanyāsaḥ mention, allusion

upasthānam (religious) attendance

ekākin alone

Aikṣvāka descended from King Ikṣvāku

kātara timid, nervous

kānanam forest

kārmukam bow

kiṃvadantī rumour

kusum›:āyudhaḥ [the flower-weaponed:] god of love

kūlam bank, shore

kṛpālu compassionate

kolāhalaḥ clamour

khedaḥ exhaustion

gaṇikā courtesan

gandhaḥ smell, scent
garīyāṃs important, considerable; worthy/worthier of respect
gahanam dense place
gir f. speech, voice, tone
guṇaḥ merit; strand, string
ghrāṇam smelling, (sense of) smell
candana m. n. sandal, sandal-wood tree
cūtaḥ mango tree
jaraṭha old, decrepit
jālapādaḥ goose
jyāyāṃs older, elder
taru m. tree; taru-gahanam thicket of trees, wood
tāmbūlam betel
dakṣiṇa right, on the right hand
dur:nimittam ill omen
dṛṣṭi f. gaze
drohaḥ injury, hostility
dvandvam pair; dvandva-saṃprahāraḥ single combat, duel
dvār f. door
dharma-vit learned in the sacred law
nava:yauvanam [fresh] youth
nikhila entire
nipuṇa clever, sharp
nirbhara excessive, full
nivedaka announcing, indicating
pañca five
paṭu sharp; paṭīyāṃs sharper
pati m. lord; husband
padam step
paravaśa in another's power, helpless
parimalaḥ perfume
pāṭhaḥ recitation, reading; part (in play)
pātram vessel, receptacle; worthy recipient; actor; pāt-ra-vargaḥ cast (of play)

potakaḥ young animal/plant; cūta-potakaḥ young mango· tree
pratikriyā remedy, remedying
pradhāna principal, important
prastāvaḥ prelude
prāsādaḥ mansion; terrace; [upstairs] room
bāṇaḥ arrow
bisam lotus fibre
Bharataḥ pr. n.
bhājanam receptacle, box
bhāryā wife
bhūyāṃs more, further
matta in rut, rutting
madaḥ intoxication
madhukaraḥ, madhukarī bee, honey-bee
mūrchā faint, swoon; ma-dana-mūrchā amorous swoon
mūlam root, basis, foundation
mṛgatṛṣṇikā mirage
raṃhas n. speed
rūpam form; beauty
laghu light; brief
locanam eye
vargaḥ group
vigrahaḥ separation; body
viṭapa m. n. branch, bush, thicket
vitarkaḥ conjecture, doubt
vipinam forest
vilakṣa disconcerted, ashamed
vihvala tottering, unsteady
vīthikā row, grove
śastram knife, sword
saṃskāraḥ preparation, adornment
sa_phala [having fruit:] ful-filled
saṃprahāraḥ fighting, combat
sammūḍha confused
saras n. lake
sārathi m. driver of chariot

su:ratam love-making
surabhi fragrant
su:labha easily got, natural
skhalanam failure, lapse
svapnaḥ dream
svāminī mistress

svedaḥ sweat
Hari *m.*, *pr. n.*
harṣaḥ joy, delight
hastin *m.* elephant
hita beneficial; well-disposed,
    good (friend)

ati+vah *caus.* (ativāhayati) spend (time)
adhi+ruh (I adhirohati) ascend, mount
anu+bandh (IX anubadhnāti) pursue, importune
anu+lip (VI anulimpati) anoint
anu+vṛt (I anuvartate) go after, attend upon
apa+yā (II apayāti) go away, depart
abhi+ghrā (I abhijighrati) smell
abhi+bhū (I abhibhavati) overpower
abhi+syand (I abhiṣyandate) flow
ava+gam (I avagacchati) understand; suppose, consider
ava+dhṛ *caus.* (avadhārayati) determine, resolve
ava+lamb (I avalambate) cling to, hold on to
ā+gam *caus.* (āgamayati) acquire
ā+ghrā (I ājighrati) smell
ā+car (I ācarati) conduct oneself, act, do
ā+śvas *caus.* (āśvāsayati) cause to breathe freely, comfort
ut+cal (I uccalati) move away; rise
ut+sthā (I uttiṣṭhati) stand up, get up
ut+as (IV udasyati) throw up, throw out, push out
upa+kṛ (VIII upakaroti) furnish, provide
upa+kṣip (VI upakṣipati) hint at
upa+jan (IV upajāyate, *p.p.* upajāta) come into being, be roused
upa+sthā *caus.* (upasthāpayati) cause to be near, fetch, bring up
upa+i (II upaiti) approach, come to
klp (I kalpate) be suitable, conduce to, turn to (*dat.*)
tṛp *caus.* (tarpayati) satisfy
nigaḍayati (*denom.*) fetter, bind
ni+śam *caus.* (niśāmayati) perceive, observe
pari+trai (II paritrāti) rescue, protect
prati+dṛś (I pratipaśyati) see
prati+ni+vṛt (I pratinivartate) return
prati+pad (IV pratipadyate) assent, admit
pra+budh *caus.* (prabodhayati) inform, admonish
pra+svap (II prasvapiti) fall asleep
pra+hi (V prahiṇoti) despatch, send
bhid (VII bhinatti) split, separate
vi+kas (I vikasati) burst, blossom, bloom
vi+car (I vicarati) move about, roam
vi+car *caus.* (vicārayati) deliberate, ponder

vi + lok *,caus.* (vilokayati)   look at, watch
vi + sṛp (I visarpati)   be diffused, spread
sam + jan (IV saṃjāyate, *p.p.* saṃjāta)   come into being, be aroused
sam + ā + car (I samācarati)   conduct oneself, act, do
spand (I spandate)   quiver
syand (I syandate)   flow, move rapidly

agrataḥ in front of (*gen.*)	nu khalu (*enclitic stressing interrogative* now (who *etc.*) I wonder?
ati: (*karmadhāraya prefix*) extreme(ly)	
api nāma if only	sakāśam to [the presence of]
kadācit perhaps	yathā yathā . . . tathā tathā in proportion as, the more that
jhaṭiti suddenly	

Exercise 14a

प्रियंवदक ज्ञायतां को ऽस्मद्दर्शनार्थी द्वारि तिष्ठति । १ । क्व नु
खलु गता स्यात् । २ । आसीत्ताद‍ृशो मुनिरस्मिन्नाश्रमे । ३ ।
आयुष्मन् श्रूयतां यदर्थमस्मि हरिणा त्वत्सकाशं प्रेषितः । ४ ।
एवमुक्तो ऽप्यहमेनं प्राबोधयं पुनः पुनः । ५ । चिरात्प्रभृत्यार्यः
परित्यक्तोचितशरीरसंस्कार इति पीड्यते मे हृदयम् । ६ । विषय-
हर्षमूलस्य कोलाहलो लोकस्योद्जिह्ीत । ७ । तदुच्यतां पाचवर्गः
स्वेषु स्वेषु पाठेष्वसंमूढैर्भवितव्यमिति । ८ । सखे चिन्तय तावत्के-
नापदेशेन पुनराश्रमपदं गच्छामः । ९ । अपि नाम दुरात्मनश्चा-
णक्याच्चन्द्रगुप्तो भिद्येत । १० । अयमसौ मम ज्यायानार्यः कृशो
नाम भरताश्रमात्प्रतिनिवृत्तः । ११ । सुरतखेदप्रसुप्तयोस्तयोः
स्वप्ने बिसगुणनिगडितपादो जरठः कश्चिज्जालपादः प्रत्यदृश्यत ।
प्रत्यबुध्येतां चोभौ । १२ । तदन्विष्टतां यदि काचिदापन्नसत्त्वा
तस्य भार्या स्यात् । १३ । आर्यपुत्र नायं विश्रब्धकथायाः अवस-
रस्ततो लघुतरमेवाभिधीयसे । १४ । कथमीदृशेन सह वत्सस्य
चन्द्रकेतोर्द्वन्द्वसंप्रहारमनुजानीयाम् । १५ । इत्यवधार्यापसर्पणाभि-
लाषिण्यहमभवम् । १६ । कस्मिन्प्रयोजने ममायं प्रणिधिः प्रहित
इति प्रभूतत्वात्प्रयोजनानां न खल्ववधारयामि । १७ । यदि

कश्चिदस्त्युपायः पतिद्रोहप्रतिक्रियायै दर्शयासुम । मतिर्हि ते
पटीयसी । १८ । अनयैव च कथया तया सह तस्मिन्नेव प्रासादे
तथैव प्रतिषिद्धाशेषपरिजनप्रवेशा दिवसमत्यवाहयम । १९ ।
तदुपायचिन्त्यतां यथा सफलप्रार्थनो भवेयम । २० । श्रुत्वा चैत-
त्तमेव मत्तहस्तिनमुदस्ताधोरणो राजपुत्रो ऽधिरुह्य रंहसोत्तमेन
राजभवनमभ्यवर्तत । २१ । उपलब्धवानस्मि प्रणिधिभ्यो यथा तस्य
म्लेच्छराजबलस्य मध्यात्प्रधानतमाः पञ्च राजानः परया सुहृत्तया
राक्षसमनुवर्तन्त इति । २२ । यदि पुनरियं किंवदन्ती महाराजं
प्रति स्यन्देत्तत्कष्टं स्यात् । २३ । इत्यवधार्यान्वेष्टुमादरमकरवम ।
अन्वेषमाणश्च यथा यथा नापश्यं तं तथा तथा सुहृत्स्नेहकातरेण
मनसा   तत्तद्ग्रोभनमाशङ्कमानस्तरुगहनानि   चन्द्रनवीथिका
लतामण्डपान्सरःकूलानि च वीक्षमाणो निपुणमितस्ततो दत्तदृष्टिः
सुचिरं व्यचरम । २४ । एकास्मिंश्च प्रदेशे झटिति वनानिलेनोपनीतं
निर्भरविकसिते ऽपि कानने ऽभिभूतान्यकुसुमपरिमलं विसर्पन्त-
मतिसुरभितयानुलिम्पन्तमिव तर्पयन्तमिव पूरयन्तमिव घ्राणेन्द्रि-
यमहमहमिकया   मधुकरकुलैरनुबध्यमानमनाघ्रातपूर्वममानुष-
लोकोचितं कुसुमगन्धमभ्यजिघ्रम ॥ २५ ॥

Exercise 14b

Translate past tenses by the imperfect except in sentence 23.

1 Lātavya, do *you know whose arrow this is? 2 Ah you fool!
Are *you more·learned·in·the·sacred·law than our preceptor?
3 And I observed in that hermitage in the shade of a young·
mango-tree an ascetic of·melancholy·appearance. 4 The
writing might be spoiled, friend, by the sweat·from·(my)·
fingers. 5 What then is this great hesitation at every step?
6 And so saying she drew it (**pattrikā** the letter) from the
betel-box and showed it (to me). 7 The allusion to (such)
considerable love·and·service is indeed opportune [**avasare**].
8 Raivataka, tell our·driver to bring up the chariot complete·

with·[sa_]·bow·and·arrows. 9 He may even, perhaps, ashamed·of·his·lapse·from·self-control, do something dreadful [aniṣṭa]. 10 Now [yāvat] I heard that it was Mālatī who was the cause·of^ his ^pangs·of·love. 11 And she became mistress·of^ his ^entire·harem. 12 Tell (me) what further benefit I (can) provide for you. 13 After speaking thus he fell silent, his·gaze·fixed·on·my·face (to see) what I [f.] would say. 14 Whereabouts then in this forest may I acquire news· of·my·beloved? 15 He forsooth [kila], (feeling) compassion- ate, comforted those people in a tender tone and asked the courtesan the reason·for·her·distress. 16 Your Highness, Śakaṭadāsa will never ever [na kadācid api] admit in front of minister·Rākṣasa that he wrote it. 17 Why my dear Bhāgurāyaṇa, minister·Rākṣasa is the dearest and best (of friends) to us. 18 *You [f.] having departed, I stayed alone for a little while [muhūrtam iva], and my·doubts·aroused as to what he was now doing I returned and with·my·body· concealed·in·the·thickets watched the place. 19 If only this prelude does not, like a mirage, turn in the end to disappoint- ment. 20 Come to me (who am) Purūravas, returned from attendance·upon·the·Sun, and tell me what (I) must protect *you[f.pl.] from. 21 While speaking thus I [f.] managed, with limbs unsteady·from·the·exhaustion·of·my·amorous·swoon to get up by holding on to hér. And (when I had) risen, my right eye quivered, indicating·an·ill-omen. And my·anxieties· roused, I thought, 'here is something untoward [apara] hinted at by fate'. 22 If (you) consider Rākṣasa worthier of respect than we are, then give him this sword of ours. 23 To start with [tāvat] friend, I should like to hear what the poisoners·and·others employed·by·me have done since Can- dragupta's entry·into·the·city. 24 Yet if the descendant of Ikṣvāku King Rāma were to see you such (as you are), then his heart would flow with tenderness. 25 Just as I [f.] was pondering in this way, the love natural·to·youth, by·which· distinctions·of·merit·and·demerit·are·not·pondered (but which is) solely·partial·to·beauty made me as helpless as the intoxica- tion·of·the·season·of·blossoms does the honey-bee.

Chapter 15

PARADIGMS Perfect and aorist tenses; **ahan**

Perfect tense

The perfect tense is formed by reduplication of the root and the addition of a special set of personal endings. As in athematic present stems, the three parasmaipada singular forms are strong, involving guṇa or sometimes vṛddhi of the root, while the other forms are weak. Thus from **dṛś** 'see', **dadarśa** 'he saw', **dadṛśuḥ** 'they saw'.

The vowel of the reduplication is **i/u** for roots containing **ǐ/ǔ**, **a** for other roots. Initial **a** reduplicates to **ā**: as 'be', **āsa**, **āsuḥ**. Initial **i** reduplicates to **ī** (from **i+i**) in the weak forms, **iye** (**i+e**) in the strong: **iṣ** 'want', **iyeṣa**, **īṣuḥ**. **yaj** 'sacrifice', **vac** 'speak', and a number of other roots liable to samprasāraṇa, reduplicate with samprasāraṇa of the semi-vowel: **iyāja**, **ījuḥ** (**i+ij-**); **uvāca**, **ūcuḥ** (**u+uc-**); similarly, from **svap** 'sleep', **suṣvāpa**, **suṣupuḥ**.

The strong grade is normally guṇa. In the third person singular it is vṛddhi in the case of roots ending in a vowel or in **a** followed by a single consonant—in other words, where guṇa would produce a prosodically light syllable. Thus **dṛś**, **dadarśa**, but **kṛ**, **cakāra**; **nī**, **nināya**; **pat**, **papāta**. This vṛddhi is optional in the first person singular, and such verbs may therefore distinguish the first from the third person singular, whereas these forms are necessarily identical in other verbs. Thus **cakara** 'I did,' **cakāra** 'I did/he did'; **ninaya** 'I led', **nināya** 'I led/ he led'; **papata** 'I fell', **papāta** 'I fell/he fell'. Roots ending in **-ā** make a first and third person form in **-au**: **sthā** 'stand', **tasthau** 'I stood/he stood'.

The terminations **-itha, -iva, -ima, -iṣe, -ivahe, -imahe** contain a connecting **i** which is omitted in a few verbs ending in **r** or **u**, including **kr** 'do' and **śru** 'hear': thus **śuśruma** 'we heard'. In the second person singular form **-itha**, the **i** is omitted in a number of other verbs as well, and is optional in yet others, including those ending in **-ā**.

The form of weak stem which requires most comment is that of roots with medial **a**. Sometimes this **a** is eliminated: **gam** 'go', **jagāma, jagmuh**; **han** 'kill', **jaghāna, jaghnuh**. Similarly, by a process of internal sandhi the root **sad** 'sit' gives **sasāda, seduh** (from *sasduh*). But the analogy of this last form is followed by other roots with medial **a** if the initial consonant reduplicates unchanged: **pat** 'fall, fly', **papāta, petuh** (the expected form **paptuh** does occur in Vedic); **tan** 'stretch', **tatāna, tenuh**.

The root **bhū** 'be' is irregular in reduplicating with **a** and in failing to strengthen to guṇa or vṛddhi: **babhūva, babhūvuh**.

The root **vid** 'know' forms a perfect without reduplication which has a present sense: **veda** 'he knows', **viduh** 'they know'.

The root **ah** 'say' is very defective. It occurs only in the perfect and only in the third person forms **āha, āhatuh, āhuh**, and the second person forms **āttha** and **āhathuh**. It may have a present as well as a past sense—'he says/he said'.

The ātmanepada forms of the perfect may have a passive as well as a middle sense—**ninye** 'was led', **jagrhe** 'was seized', etc.

The ātmanepada participle in **-āna** attached to the perfect stem scarcely occurs at all in Classical Sanskrit; and the parasmaipada participle in **-vāṃs** is rare, with the exception of **vidvāṃs**, which is formed from the non-reduplicated perfect of **vid** referred to above and is used as an adjective meaning 'wise, learned'.

Perfect forms may be made from causative and other derivative verbs by means of the periphrastic perfect. This arose from the combination of the accusative of an abstract noun (not otherwise used) with the perfect of the verb kṛ: darśayāṃ cakāra '[he did a showing:] he showed'. In the parasmaipada, however, kṛ is normally replaced in Classical Sanskrit by the perfect of **as** (very occasionally of **bhū**): darśayām āsa 'he showed', darśayām āsuḥ 'they showed'. This formation is also utilised by one or two simple verbs which do not form an ordinary perfect: e.g. īkṣ 'look', īkṣāṃ cakre 'he looked'.

Despite its name (and its Indo-European origins) the perfect is not used in Classical Sanskrit to express any stative or perfective sense. It is a tense of historical narrative, which according to the grammarians should not be used to describe events within the personal experience of the speaker. In consequence the first and second person forms are not at all common and the tense as a whole is not much used in dialogue. Its frequent use is a characteristic of narrative poetry, both epic and Classical, as in the extract given in Exercise 15a from the *Kumārasaṃbhava* of Kālidāsa.

Aorist tense

The aorist and imperfect tenses are specialisations of a single past tense characterised by the augment and the 'secondary' endings. From the point of view of its formation, the imperfect might be looked on as an 'aorist of the present stem'. An aorist is an aorist, and not an imperfect, if no corresponding present forms exist. Thus ayāt 'he went', from yā 'go', and atudat 'he struck', from tud 'strike', are imperfect forms because they correspond to the presents yāti 'he goes' (class II) and tudati 'he strikes' (class VI). But adhāt 'he put' and agamat 'he went' are aorist forms derived directly from the root, since dhā 'put' and gam 'go' form presents of a different kind, dadhāti (class III) and gacchati (class I), with corresponding imperfect forms adadhāt and agacchat. These remarks concern formation: in *meaning* an imperfect form (such as ayāt) should differ from an aorist form (such as

adhāt), although the distinction becomes of little importance in Classical Sanskrit.

Some forms of aorist, the sigmatic aorists, are characterised by the addition of some variety of suffixal **s**. These aorists are more sharply differentiated from an imperfect, since no present stem employs such a suffix. There are seven main varieties of aorist, three non-sigmatic and four sigmatic. The endings of two of the non-sigmatic and one of the sigmatic aorists are thematic, i.e. precisely similar to those of the imperfect of **nī**. The other types of aorist have athematic endings comparable with the imperfect of athematic verbs but without the same pattern of strong and weak forms. In all athematic types the third person plural parasmaipada ending is **-uḥ** (as in the imperfect of class III and some class II verbs). In all athematic types of the sigmatic aorist, the second and third person singular parasmaipada forms end in **īḥ** and **īt** respectively.

Non-sigmatic aorists

1 *root aorist* (small class: athematic endings; parasmaipada only). This type of aorist is confined in the Classical period to a number of roots ending in **ā** and to **bhū**. [The class was originally much larger, and other isolated forms of it survive—notably to supply the second and third person singular ātmanepada in the sigmatic aorist of some verbs: thus from **kṛ** 'do', **akārṣīḥ**, **akārṣīt** parasmaipada, but **akṛthāḥ**, **akṛta** ātmanepada.] The third person plural ending **an** in **abhūvan** is anomalous.

2 **a** *-aorist* (thematic endings; weak grade of root). The class is not particularly large, and ātmanepada forms are uncommon. The class includes two reduplicated forms: **pat** 'fall', **apaptat**; and **vac** 'speak', **avocat** (*a-va-uc-at*).

3 *Reduplicated aorist* (thematic endings; root syllable light, reduplicated syllable heavy; sense normally causative). This form is analogous to the periphrastic perfect. It provides the ordinary aorist of one or two verbs: thus **dru** 'run', **adudruvat**

'he ran'. But, while formed directly from the root, it normally supplies the aorist of causative and class X verbs: **nī, nāyayati** 'he causes to lead', **anīnayat** 'he caused to lead'; **cur, corayati** 'he steals', **acūcurat** 'he stole'. Vowels other than **u** reduplicate as **i**. The reduplicated **i** or **u** lengthens to **ī/ū** if the reduplicated syllable would otherwise be light. The root syllable does not appear in guṇa grade unless it can continue to be prosodically light (and not invariably even then—cf. **adudruvat**).

grah	seize	**ajigrahat**	he caused to be seized
jan	be born	**ajījanat**	he begat
dṛś	see	**adīdṛśat**	he showed
muc	free	**amūmucat**	he caused to be freed
ji	conquer	**ajījayat**	he caused to be conquered
mṛ	die	**amīmarat**	he put to death

If the root syllable even in its reduced grade remains heavy, the reduplicated syllable is light. But even in such verbs a special shortening of the root often occurs, to preserve the normal rhythm of 'heavy-light'. Thus from **dīp** 'shine', either **adidīpat** or **adīdipat** 'caused to shine, kindled'.

Sigmatic aorists

4 **s**-*aorist* (suffix **s**; athematic endings; vṛddhi in parasmaipada, guṇa or weak grade in ātmanepada). All roots take vṛddhi throughout the parasmaipada; in the ātmanepada, roots ending in **ĭ** or **ŭ** take guṇa, others remain unstrengthened. The paradigm of **dah** illustrates complications caused by internal sandhi.

5 **iṣ**-*aorist* (suffix **iṣ**; athematic endings; vṛddhi or guṇa in parasmaipada, guṇa in ātmanepada). This is the suffix **s** added with connecting **i**. The basic grade is guṇa, but in the parasmaipada final **ĭ/ŭ/ṛ̆** is strengthened to vṛddhi (thus ensuring a heavy syllable before the suffix), and medial **a** is sometimes strengthened to **ā** and sometimes remains unchanged.

6 **siṣ**-*aorist* (small class: suffix **siṣ**; athematic endings; parasmaipada only). This aorist (inflected like the **iṣ** aorist) is formed only from a number of roots ending in -**ā** and from **nam** 'bow', **yam** 'hold' and **ram** 'take pleasure'.

7 **sa**-*aorist* (small class: suffix **s** with thematic endings; weak grade). This aorist is confined to a number of roots containing **i/u/ṛ** and ending in some consonant which by internal sandhi combines with the **s** of the suffix to make **kṣ**. In the ātmane-pada, three of the terminations are athematic—**i**, **āthām** and **ātām**.

8 *Aorist passive.* There is a formation, independent of the types of aorist listed above, which conveys the sense of a third person singular aorist passive: e.g. **akāri** 'was done', **adarśi** 'was seen', etc. The augment is prefixed to the root, and a suffix, **i**, is added. Medial **i/u/ṛ** take guṇa; otherwise vṛddhi is normal. A **y** is inserted after roots ending in **ā**: thus **ajñāyi** 'was known'.

The aorist tense, like the imperfect, expresses simple past statements. In particular, it is supposedly the most appropriate tense where the speaker is describing a recent event. But this function was usurped at an early stage by participial constructions, and the aorist became a learned formation little used in simple Sanskrit. In the Classical literature it takes its place beside the imperfect and the perfect as a narrative tense. Despite its complicated variety of forms, the aorist is easy to spot because of the augment and the secondary terminations; the best way to acquire familiarity with it is to read extensively in a work which makes use of it (e.g. the *Daśakumāracarita* of Daṇḍin).

Injunctive

In the Vedic language unaugmented forms of the aorist or imperfect are often used with imperative or subjunctive force and are then described as 'injunctive' forms. This usage has disappeared in Classical Sanskrit, with the following exception. The particle **mā** may be used with the unaugmented forms of the aorist, or very occasionally the imperfect, to express prohibition. Thus **mā bhaiṣṭa** 'do not fear', **m» aîvaṃ maṃsthāḥ** 'do not suppose so', **mā bhūt** 'let it not be', **mā ›dhyavasyaḥ sāhasam** 'do not resolve (anything) rash'.

Precative

The precative, or benedictive, is a kind of aorist optative. In Classical Sanskrit it is used only in the parasmaipada. It is formed by the addition of the suffix **yās** to the unstrengthened root, which appears as before the passive suffix **ya**. It is used to express wishes and prayers:

> **a:virahitau dampatī bhūyāstām** may husband and wife be unseparated
>
> **kriyād aghānāṃ Maghavā vighātam** may Indra cause elimination of evils

ahan 'day'

The neuter substantive **ahan** 'day' has **ahar** as its middle stem. The form **ahar** is thus nominative, vocative and accusative singular, and also the normal stem form as the prior member of a compound; it has, however, the further irregularity of appearing before the voiced middle case endings as **aho** (as if it were from *ahas*)—thus instrumental, dative and ablative dual **ahobhyām** etc. As the last member of a compound it appears as a (masculine) short **a** stem in one of two forms, **aha** or **ahna**.

antaram

Among the meanings of the word **antaram** is 'interval, difference'. At the end of a determinative compound, as well as meaning literally 'a difference of', it can signify 'a different —, another —': thus **varṇ-ântaram** 'a difference of colour' or 'a different colour'.

> **likhit-ântaram asy₂ ānīyatām** bring another [thing written of him:] example of his writing

śastrapāṇi, aśrumukha

There are a few bahuvrīhis in which the second member expresses the location of the first. Thus **śastra-pāṇi** 'sword-handed', i.e. '[having a hand in which there is a sword:] whose hand holds a sword'; **aśru-mukha** 'tear-faced', i.e. '[having tears on the face:] tearful-faced'. Grammarians analysed such compounds by putting the second member in the locative case: e.g. **gaḍu-kaṇṭha** 'goitre-necked', **gaḍuḥ kaṇṭhe yasya** 'on whose neck there is a goitre'. Similarly, 'in whose hand there is a sword' etc.

Sanskrit metre

Mention was made in Chapter 1 of the quantitative nature of Sanskrit verse and of the rules for distinguishing light and heavy syllables. A general description of Classical Sanskrit metre is given here, and individual details of the commoner metres will be found in the grammatical section at the back of the book. The subject is often omitted from standard Sanskrit grammars, which is a pity, since Sanskrit poetry cannot be fully appreciated by those who are metrically deaf. Much of a poet's creative effort is obviously lost upon the reader for whom a poem might just as well have been written in prose. The need, of course, is not simply to understand metrical structure analytically but to be able to feel the rhythm of the verse without conscious effort as it is read or recited. (A practical advantage of this ability, and a test of it, is that one may, through simply noticing that a line does not scan, be alerted to some of the small misprints which plague many editions of Sanskrit texts.) While learning to master the rhythms of Sanskrit verse, there is no harm in exaggerating to any degree that is helpful the natural tendency in Sanskrit recitation to prolong and stress the heavy syllables.

The anuṣṭubh metre

This is the bread-and-butter metre of Sanskrit verse, comparable in function and importance with the Latin hexameter or the English iambic pentameter. As well as being frequently used in Classical poetry, it is the staple metre of Sanskrit epic and of the many didactic works composed in verse. It is a simple, easily handled metre, since the pattern of light and heavy syllables is not fixed throughout the line.

As with other Sanskrit metres, a normal anuṣṭubh stanza is divisible into four quarters, called pādas. The word **pāda** literally means 'foot', and the latter word is therefore better avoided where possible in discussing Sanskrit versification, although in the case of the anuṣṭubh each pāda falls naturally for purposes of analysis into two groups of four syllables which might well be termed 'feet' in the English sense. The last group in each half-verse, i.e. the last group in the second and fourth pādas, consists of a double iambus: $\cup - \cup -$. Any of the preceding four syllables may in principle be either light or heavy. If we represent such a syllable of indeterminate quantity by o, the pattern of the second or fourth pāda is therefore o o o o $\cup - \cup -$. In the first and third pādas the pattern of the last two syllables is reversed, which gives o o o o $\cup - - \cup$.

An anuṣṭubh stanza thus consists of two half-verses of sixteen syllables each and has the following basic rhythm (with the sign ´ indicating a rhythmically prominent syllable):

$$\text{o o o o } \cup \stackrel{\prime}{-} \stackrel{\prime}{-} \cup \,/\, \text{o o o o } \cup \stackrel{\prime}{-} \cup \stackrel{\prime}{-} \,|$$
$$\text{o o o o } \cup \stackrel{\prime}{-} \stackrel{\prime}{-} \cup \,/\, \text{o o o o } \cup \stackrel{\prime}{-} \cup \stackrel{\prime}{-} \,\|$$

The syncopation at the end of the first and third pādas gives a feeling of suspense which is resolved at the end of each half-verse.

There should be a caesura (a break between words—or sometimes a break between two members of a long compound) at the end of each pāda. But the break between the second

and third pādas, i.e. at the half-verse, is stronger than that
between first and second or third and fourth. Thus the break
at the half-verse is treated for purposes of sandhi as the end
of a sentence, whereas sandhi is obligatory at all points within
the half-verse.

The scheme given above is subject to the following qualifications:

1 The final syllable of the second and fourth pādas (as in
other metres) and also of the first and third pādas may, in
fact, be either heavy or light. (It was given as above merely to
emphasise the underlying rhythm.)

2 No pāda may begin o ⌣ ⌣ o (i.e. either the second or the
third syllable must always be heavy).

3 The second or fourth pāda must not end ⌣ – ⌣ – ⌣ o (i.e. in
three iambi).

4 The above pattern for the first or third pāda is the **pathyā**
(regular) form. The less common **vipulā** (permitted) forms
are given at the back of the book.

The first stanza of Exercise 15 scans as follows:

– – – ⌣ ⌣ – – – – – ⌣ ⌣ ⌣ – ⌣ –

e vaṃ vā di ni de var ṣau / pār śve pi tu ra dho mu khī|

– – – ⌣ ⌣ – – – – ⌣ ⌣ ⌣ – ⌣ –

lī lā ka ma la pat trā ṇi / ga ṇa yā mā sa pār va tī||

Even (samacatuṣpadī) metres

In addition to the anuṣṭubh, Classical literature employs a wide
range of more elaborate metres, some of the commoner of which
are listed at the back of the book (pp. 310 ff.). In most of these,
each pāda is identical and consists of a fixed pattern of light
and heavy syllables normally between eleven and twenty-one
in number. Thus the fourteen-syllabled Vasantatilakā metre,
which has the pattern – – ⌣ – ⌣ ⌣ ⌣ – ⌣ ⌣ – ⌣ – – (if such a long
'unstructured' string seems daunting at first sight, it may be

helpful, purely as an aid to learning, to think of it as made up
of – ⌣́ ⌣ ⌣́ ⌣ ⌣ ⌣ ⌣́ ⌣ ⌣ ⌣́ ⌣ ⌣́ –):

> preyān manoratha-sahasra-vṛtaḥ sa eṣa,
> supta;pramatta;janam etad amātya-veśma |
> prauḍhaṃ tamaḥ—kuru kṛtajñatay» aîva bhadram,
> utkṣipta;mūka;maṇi-nūpuram ehi yāmaḥ ||

(*A girl is persuaded to elope:*) Here is that lover wooed in
a thousand dreams. Here is the minister's house where the
people are asleep or inattentive. The darkness is thick.
Simply from gratitude [do good:] treat your lover well.
With jewelled anklets raised and muffled, come, let us be off.

Similarly, the nineteen-syllabled Śārdūlavikrīḍita, – – – ⌣ ⌣
– ⌣ – ⌣ ⌣ ⌣ – / – – ⌣ – – – ⌣ – (or ⌣́ – ⌣́ ⌣ ⌣ ⌣́ ⌣ ⌣́ ⌣ ⌣ ⌣ ⌣́ /
– ⌣́ ⌣ ⌣́ ⌣́ ⌣ –):

> manda:kvāṇita;veṇur ahni śithile vyāvartayan go-
>   kulaṃ
> barh»-āpīḍakam uttamāṅga-racitaṃ go-dhūli-dhūm-
>   raṃ dadhat |
> mlāyantyā vana-mālayā parigataḥ śrānto ›pi ramy»:
>   ākṛtir
> gopa-strī-nayan»-ôtsavo vitaratu śreyāṃsi vaḥ Keśa-
>   vaḥ ||

(*A benediction:*) Sounding his flute gently, driving the cattle
back [the day being slack:] as the day declines, wearing
[placed] on his head a crest of peacock feathers grey with
the dust from the cows, encircled with a fading garland of
wild flowers, though tired attractive to look at, a feast for
the eyes of the cowherd girls, may Kṛṣṇa bestow blessings
upon you

Many metres, particularly the longer ones, contain one or
more fixed caesuras within the pāda. Thus in the Śārdūlavikrīḍita there is always a break after the twelfth syllable, so
that the final seven syllables form a separate rhythmical unit.
The final syllable of the pāda in any of these metres is supposed
to be heavy. A light syllable may, however, be substituted

at the end of the half-verse or verse, since it is compensated for by the following pause. A light syllable at the end of the first or third pāda is not normal, but it is permissible in some metres, notably the Vasantatilakā.

The way to master any of these metres is simply to fix its rhythm in one's head. This may be achieved pleasantly enough by committing stanzas of Sanskrit poetry to memory. But for those who do not find it too arid, another possibility with practical advantages, which, of course, does not preclude the other method, is to memorise a Sanskrit definition of each metre. Such definitions can embody in a single pāda of the appropriate metre a statement of its metrical pattern, including any caesuras, and its name. The last is especially useful since it is all too easy to recognise a particular metre without remembering what it is called. (The name of a metre always fits somewhere into its metrical pattern, and may perhaps sometimes have been a phrase taken from an early example of the type.)

Sanskrit prosodists refer to a heavy syllable as **ġuru** 'heavy', or simply **ġ** or **ġa**; and to a light syllable as **laġhu** 'light', or simply **l** or **la**. They proceed to an economical analysis by similarly assigning a letter to each possible group of three syllables:

y	∪ – –	bh	– ∪ ∪	m	– – –	ġ –
r	– ∪ –	j	∪ – ∪	n	∪ ∪ ∪	l ∪
t	– – ∪	s	∪ ∪ –			

(The value of these letters can be learnt by memorising them in the following pattern:

yamātārājabhānasalaġāḥ

where each letter initiates its own pattern—**yamātā, mātārā, tārāja, rājabhā**, etc.)

Thus the definition of the Vasantatilakā, as given by Kedāra in his *Vrttaratnākara*, is:

uktā Vasantatilakā ta ;bha ;jā ja ;ġau ġaḥ   the Vasantatilakā is described as **t, bh** and **j**, (then) **j** and **ġ**, (then) **ġ**
—i.e. – – ∪, – ∪ ∪, ∪ – ∪, ∪ – ∪, –, –

The group of three syllables is, of course, in no sense
a rhythmical unit, and the pāda is analysed continuously without reference to any caesura (**yati**). Caesuras are mentioned
separately by a numerical grouping—e.g. the Śārdūlavikrīḍita
is said to consist of twelve syllables plus seven. Symbolic
numbers rather than the ordinary numerals are mostly used for
this purpose (these symbolic numbers are found in other
contexts in Sanskrit, for instance in verses giving dates). For
the ordinary numeral there is substituted some noun frequently
associated with that particular number (as if we were to say
'sin' for 'seven' in English because there are seven deadly
sins). Thus **yuga** 'age of the world' means 'four'; **sūrya** 'sun'
means 'twelve' (with reference to the signs of the zodiac);
aśva 'horse' means 'seven' (because there were seven horses
of the sun). Kedāra's definition of the Śārdūlavikrīḍita is:

> **sūry**ə**aśvair yadi māt sa**ː**jau sa**ː**ta**ː**ta**ː**gāḥ, Śārdūla-**
> **vikrīḍitam** if, with twelve (syllables) plus seven,
> (there is) after **m** both **s** and **j**, (and then) **s, t, t** and **g**,
> (we have) the Śārdūlavikrīḍita

(The ablative to express 'after' is a grammarian's usage mentioned below.)

Semi-even (*ardhasamacatuṣpadī*) metres

There exists a number of metres which are not absolutely
identical in each pāda, although each half-verse corresponds
exactly. The commonest of these comprise a small family
group in which the second or fourth pāda differs from the
first or third simply by the insertion of an extra heavy syllable.
Of these metres the Puṣpitāgrā is the most frequently occurring.

The Āryā metre

This metre, which was adopted into Sanskrit from more
popular sources, differs fundamentally in structure from all
the preceding. It is divided into feet (here the English term
is appropriate and difficult to avoid), each of four **mātrā**s in
length. A **mātrā** 'mora' is a unit of prosodic length equivalent

to a light syllable. Each foot (except the sixth) may therefore consist of ∪ ∪ ∪ ∪, – –, – ∪ ∪ or ∪ ∪ –; and the second, fourth and sixth may further take the form ∪ – ∪. A stanza is normally made up of two lines of seven and a half feet each, with the sixth foot of the second line consisting of a single light syllable. In its Classical Sanskrit use, the metre usually contains a caesura after the third foot in each line.

In this metre the rhythmical ictus often falls upon a light syllable, and it can be difficult when reading some Āryā stanzas to keep a proper grip on the rhythm and at the same time avoid an unnatural manner of recitation. The following example, however, flows smoothly.

> gacchati puraḥ śarīram, dhāvati paścād a:saṃsthi-
> tam cetaḥ |
> cīnāṃśukam iva ketoḥ prati_vātaṃ nīyamānasya ‖

(as I think of the girl I have just parted from) my body moves forward, but my unsteady mind runs back, like the silk of a banner being carried into the wind

The Kumāra-saṃbhava of Kālidāsa

Kālidāsa, in almost every estimation the greatest of Sanskrit poets, wrote both plays and poems. Among the latter are two examples of the **mahā:kāvya** or major narrative poem, **Raghu-vaṃśa** 'The race of Raghu' and **Kumāra-saṃbhava** 'The birth of Kumāra'. Kumāra (lit. 'the Prince') is another name of Skanda or Kārttikeya, god of war and son of the mighty god Śiva. Cantos I to VIII of the poem (all that are regarded as genuinely the work of Kālidāsa) describe the events leading up to his birth, but stop short of the birth itself. The gods need a powerful general to defeat the demon Tāraka, and such a general will be born only from the union of Śiva with Pārvatī, the daughter of the mountain-god Himālaya. However, Śiva is a practising ascetic and has no thought of marriage. Kāma, the god of love, attempts to inflame Śiva's feelings and is reduced to ashes for his pains; but Pārvatī finally wins Śiva's love by becoming an ascetic herself and practising the severest austerities. Canto VI describes how Śiva sends the Seven Sages (accompanied by Arundhatī, wife of one of them) to ask Himālaya for his daughter's hand in marriage. The extract given in Exercise 15 begins just after the Sage Aṅgiras has conveyed this request.

Each canto of a mahākāvya is normally written in a single metre, with the exception of one or more closing verses. The metre used is either the anuṣṭubh or one of the shorter of the other metres, Indravajrā, Vaṃśastha, Viyoginī, etc. (but never the Āryā). The longer metres such as the Śārdūlavikrīḍita do not lend themselves to use in continuous narrative; and even with the shorter metres actually employed, the stanzaic structure, with each stanza a polished and self-contained unit, is one of the more striking features of such poetry. The concluding stanza or stanzas of each canto are written in a different and normally somewhat more elaborate metre: this is illustrated by the present extract, which extends to the end of the canto and closes with a Puṣpitāgrā stanza.

The extract has been chosen because it is a simple passage which illustrates both the anuṣṭubh metre and the perfect tense, but in its slight way it does also suggest some of the qualities of Kālidāsa's genius: his luminous and unerringly exact use of language, the mark of the great poet everywhere, and his ability to view human life and activity (here, the giving of a daughter in marriage) under a transfiguring sense of divine order—an ability sometimes superficially seen as a tendency to treat the gods in secular and sensual terms.

Here, as a preliminary guide to the general sense of the passage, is a comparatively free translation of it:

84 When the divine sage had spoken,
   Pārvatī, at her father's side,
   Keeping her face bent down began to count
   The petals of the lotus she was playing with.

85 The Mountain, though he had all he could wish for,
   Looked enquiringly at Menā.
   For where his daughter is concerned
   A man's eyes are his wife.

86 And Menā gave her assent
   To all that her husband longed for.
   The wishes of a devoted wife
   Are never at odds with those of her husband.

87 Determining inwardly
   The way he should reply,
   When the speech was over
   He took hold of his daughter, adorned for the happy
     occasion.

88 'Come, dearest child,
   You are destined as alms for the Most High.
   The Sages themselves are here to sue for you.
   My life as a householder has found its fulfilment.'

89 Having said this much to his child
   The Mountain spoke to the Sages:
   'The bride of the Three-eyed God
   Herewith salutes you all.'

90 Joyfully the sages acknowledged
   The noble generosity of these words,
   And bestowed upon Ambā
   Blessings that would immediately be fulfilled.

91 She, in her anxiety to do them homage,
   Displaced the golden ornaments at her ears,
   And as she showed her confusion
   Arundhatī took her upon her lap,

92 And the mother, whose face was full of tears,
   Made anxious by love for her daughter,
   She reassured about the merits of that bridegroom,
   Who had no other to make prior claims on him.

93 When Śiva's father-in-law
   Had consulted them upon the wedding-date,
   And they had answered it should be three days hence,
   The sages departed.

94 After taking their leave of Himālaya
They returned to the Trident-holder,
Announced the success of their mission,
And, dismissed by him, flew up to heaven.

95 And the Lord of Creatures passed those days with
　　difficulty,
Longing for union with the Mountain's daughter.
When even our Lord is not immune from such feelings,
What ordinary, helpless man can escape the torments?

In stanza 87 'adorned for the happy occasion' refers to the
occasion of the Sages' visit; but by a literary resonance it hints
also at the coming occasion of the wedding. In stanza 92 the
compound **ananyapūrva,** as well as meaning (as Mallinātha
takes it) 'not having another more senior wife', is a pun meaning 'having none other than Pārvatī herself as a previous wife'—
a reference to the fact that Śiva's earlier wife Satī was a
previous incarnation of Pārvatī. (I am indebted to Dr. Wendy
O'Flaherty for both these observations.)

Mallinātha's commentary

The extract from the Kumāra-saṃbhava is accompanied by
a commentary upon it by the medieval scholar Mallinātha,
the author of standard commentaries on Kālidāsa's two other
main non-dramatic works, as well as on the mahākāvyas of
other Sanskrit poets. His work is an excellent example of the
more literal type of Sanskrit commentary, which expounds
the original text by means of a continuous close verbal paraphrase. It is an interesting reflection of the structure of the
Classical language and the difficulties of Classical literary
style that such a word-for-word paraphrase should be worth
making. The style of such commentaries should be mastered,
since when they are by good scholars they are an extremely
important aid in the interpretation of Classical texts. It should
also be noted that many major works by writers on philo-
sophical and other subjects are, formally speaking, commentaries upon earlier texts (or even upon some more succinctly

expressed version of the writer's own views) and exhibit certain peculiarities of style deriving from this fact. The following remarks, although concerned primarily with the present extract from Mallinātha, should be of some help in the interpretation of commentaries in general.

The basis of the commentatorial style is oral exposition, and the simplest starting-point in understanding Mallinātha is to imagine him as a teacher sitting with a manuscript of the original text in front of him. He reads out or recites from memory—inevitably the latter, had he been expounding Pāṇini or the Vedas—the portion of the original, normally one stanza, which he is about to explain. (This is indicated in the written text of the commentary by the first word of the original followed by **iti**: thus in Exercise 15 **evam iti** means 'the portion beginning with the word **evam**', i.e. stanza 84.) He then goes back and takes the words one at a time or in small phrases, selecting them in the order most convenient for exposition and resolving sandhi as necessary.

As he takes up each word or phrase, he follows it with a literal equivalent, unless he considers it too obvious for helpful paraphrase. This habit of making paraphrase (or 'gloss') the rule rather than the exception is a useful one. It may seem pointless at times: on stanza 92 it is hardly likely to help anyone to be told that **duhitṛ-snehena** means **putrikā-premṇā**. But this is a small price to pay for the advantage of having a check on the interpretation of passages which are not so obvious as they seem at first sight.

The commentary is often unobtrusively helpful in analysing compounds by resolving them into separate words. When this is done the compound is frequently not quoted in its original form in the commentary. Thus in 88 **gṛhamedhi-phalam** 'reward of a householder' occurs only as **gṛhamedhinaḥ phalam** (with **gṛhamedhinaḥ** glossed as **gṛhasthasya**). When the original form of the compound *is* quoted, it tends to appear after the analysis: e.g. 92 **tasyāḥ** . . . **mātaram tan-mātaram.** This forms an exception to the general principle that the paraphrase is placed after the original. (In the transliterated version of Exercise 15 any direct gloss is placed in parentheses, and a colon is placed between the gloss and the original—i.e. normally immediately before the gloss, sometimes immediately after.) The practice serves to 're-establish' an original form after analysis and is commoner with less straightforward compounds such as bahuvrīhis: e.g. 92 (aśrūṇi mukhe yasyās tām:) aśrumukhīm. Even in such cases the original compound may be replaced by a phrase like tath» ôktaḥ '(being one) so described': thus in 85 gṛhiṇī:netrāḥ 'having a wife as one's eye' appears as gṛhiṇy eva netram . . . yeṣāṃ te tath» ôktāḥ 'of whom the eye is in fact the wife—those such' (the particle eva serving, as frequently, to distinguish the predicate).

The formula yathā tathā is used to indicate adverbial value. Thus if śīghram has the meaning 'swiftly', this may be made clear by the gloss śīghraṃ yathā tathā 'in such a way as to be swift'.

While bahuvrīhi compounds are regularly analysed by means of relative clauses, the analysis of other formations is generally by means of an iti clause, with the relative pronoun replaced by ayam (or, in the nominative case, omitted): e.g. balam asy» âst› îti balī 'the word balin means ["this has strength":] "that which has strength" '; pacyata iti pākaḥ 'the word pāka means ["it is cooked":] "that which is cooked" '.

As in the above examples (balī, pākaḥ), a formation to be analysed is normally mentioned in the nominative case. The formation is thereafter 'picked up', and if necessary returned to the appropriate oblique case, by means of the pronoun saḥ. The discussion of an:anya‡pūrvasya in stanza 92 illustrates the use of saḥ and also of the relative clause and the iti clause:

1 anyā pūrvaṃ yasy› âsti so ›nya:pūrvaḥ 'anya:pūrva means "one who has another (woman) as a prior (claim)" '.

2 sa na bhavat› îty an:anya‡pūrvaḥ 'an:anya‡pūrva means "one who is not anya:pūrva" '.

3 tasya an:anya‡pūrvasya 'this latter formation when placed in the genitive singular provides (the word contained in the text, namely) an:anya‡pūrvasya'.

The present participle of **as, sant,** is often inserted in the course of exegesis and serves to distinguish attributive words from the substantive they qualify: so in stanza 84 **adhomukhī satī** '(Pārvatī counted the petals) being downward-gazing (as she did so)'. The phrase **tathā hi** 'for thus' indicates that the following portion of the text is an explanation or amplification of the preceding.

The syntactical structure of the original text provides a framework for the commentary, but syntactical continuity is frequently interrupted by the insertion of explanatory remarks (such asides being natural in a spoken exposition.) One type of insertion, that occasioned by detailed grammatical analysis, has already been touched upon. In the same way the word-for-word gloss may be interrupted by a freer paraphrase of the preceding words, followed by **ity arthaḥ** 'such is the meaning', 'in other words . . .', or **iti bhāvaḥ** 'such is the essence or implication', 'i.e. . . ., that is . . .'. **iti yāvat** 'which is as much as to say', 'in fact' is especially used where something is glossed in terms of a simpler or more precise concept which might not have occurred to the reader. Where something is to be supplied in the original, this is indicated by **iti śeṣaḥ** 'such is the remainder', 'understand . . .'.

Quotations and opinions from other authors are indicated by **iti** plus the name of the writer or the work. The use made of Pāṇini's rules in explaining grammatical forms is discussed below. Lexicons are also appealed to. The oldest and most reliable of these is the Amarakoṣa by Amara or Amarasiṃha (written in verse, for ease of memorisation). Lexicons make continual use of the locative case in a technical meaning of 'in the sense of'. Thus **udāro dātṛ ;mahatoḥ**, quoted under stanza 90, means '(the word) **udāra** (occurs) in (the sense of) **dātṛ** or **mahānt**'.

The use of punctuation and sandhi in commentary style is naturally different from their use in a normal text. The daṇḍa may be used at any 'pause for breath' and separates the asides from the mainstream of the commentary. The following policy on sandhi has been adopted in editing the present extract: no sandhi has been made between the words of the text quoted directly in the commentary and the surrounding words of Mallinātha himself, and similarly none before **iti** where this marks a quotation by Mallinātha from any other author.

Pāṇinian grammar

When Mallinātha considers a form worthy of grammatical analysis, he explains it by quoting the relevant rules of Pāṇini's grammar. For the non-specialist, in fact, the operation of the Pāṇinian system can be studied more enjoyably in a literary commentator such as Mallinātha, where its application to the normal forms of the language can be observed, than in the commentaries upon Pāṇini himself, which are frequently concerned with *recherché* forms and complex theoretical considerations. A brief explanation of the references to Pāṇini in Exercise 15 may help to give a first faint inkling of how his grammar works.

Pāṇini's sūtras, or aphoristic rules, are formed with the greatest possible succinctness. They are arranged in such a way that they frequently depend for their understanding upon the statements made in the sūtras immediately preceding, and have indeed in principle to be interpreted in the light of all the other sūtras in the grammar. The suffixes which combine with word bases to form actual words are abstractions just as the verbal roots are. Thus the causative–denominative suffix is treated as having the basic form **i**, which by the operation of various sūtras changes to **ay** and combines with the inflexional endings. Systematic use is made of anubandhas, 'indicatory letters' attached to these suffixes. Thus the past participle suffix is known as **kta,** the **k** indicating that the preceding stem appears in its weak form. The causative–denominative is similarly known as **ṇi**: the **ṇ** permits the vṛddhi of a root such as **kṛ** in **kārayati,** while other sūtras ensure other grades of the root where necessary. The **ṇ** also serves to distinguish **ṇi** from other **i** suffixes, such as **śi** the neuter plural ending (**kāntāni, manāṃsi,** etc.) or the Vedic **ki** as in **papi** 'drinking'. The compound-final suffix **ṭac** referred to in sūtra 5.4.91 is one of a host of **a** suffixes: the **ṭ** indicates that the feminine is in ī, and the c that the accent is on the final. These artificial words are inflected like ordinary stems of the language, so that ṇi is a substantive in short i (gen. ṇeḥ, loc. ṇau) and ṭac is a consonant stem. But ṭac illustrates the fact that certain sounds may occur in final position in made-up words that are not so found in the natural words of the language.

The cases are used in technical senses: the ablative to signify 'after', the locative 'before', the genitive 'for, in place of', while the substitute which is put 'in place' is expressed in the nominative. It is as if one were to say 'after *child* for *s* (there is) *ren*' to express the irregular plural of *child*; or 'for *soft* (there is) *sof* before *en*' to indicate that the *t* of *soften* is not pronounced. To describe the sandhi of *the* mentioned in Chapter 2, we may (if we select *ðí* as the basic form) say 'for *ðí* (there is) *ə* before consonants'. It is not necessary to say in full '(there is) *ðə*', since (with certain qualifications) it is a principle of interpreting Pāṇinian rules that a single-letter substitute is to be treated as replacing only the final letter of the original.

The first sūtra which Mallinātha quotes, Pāṇini 7.3.43, illustrates this last point. It concerns the fact that the causative of **ruh** 'ascend' may take the form **ropayati** as well as the regular **rohayati**. It runs **ruhaḥ po ʼnyatarasyām**. From an earlier sūtra (7.3.36) the word **ṇau** 'before ṇi' is to be supplied. **ruhaḥ** is the genitive of **ruh**. **anyatarasyām** means 'optionally'. The sūtra therefore means 'before the causative suffix, for (the final h of) **ruh**, p is substituted optionally'.

The discussion of the word **try:ahaḥ** 'period of three days' in stanza 93 is more complex. It may be observed in passing that such compounds, which correspond to the English 'a fortnight', 'a twelvemonth', are best looked on as having exocentric value—'that (period) in which there are fourteen nights/twelve months'. But Sanskrit grammarians include them in a special class called **dvigu** 'numerical compound', which is treated as a sub-variety of tatpuruṣa.

Mallinātha begins by quoting 2.1.51 **taddhit:ârth›; ôttarapada;samāhāre ca. samān›:âdhikaraṇena** must be supplied from 2.1.49, which states that certain words may combine 'with (another word) having the same case relationship' to form a compound. This is a way of saying that they may be prefixed with adjectival or appositional value to another word so as to form a descriptive determinative. **dik ;saṃkhye** must be supplied from 2.1.50, which deals with the fact that '(words denoting) either region or number' combine in the same type of compound to express various proper names. The present sūtra thus says that words expressing region or number may compound with a word having the same case relationship 'in the following further circumstances **(ca)**: to express the sense of a **taddhita** (secondary suffix), or when there is a further member (added to the compound), or to express collective sense'. The first two possibilities will not be discussed since they are not relevant here. In **tryahaḥ** we have the numeral **tri** 'three' combining with **ahan** 'day' to express the sense 'collection consisting of three days'. The locative **samāhāre** does not here have its sense of 'before' but its other technical sense of 'in the sense of' as used in lexicons.

The following sūtra, 2.1.52, not quoted by Mallinātha, says **saṃkhyā ;pūrvo dviguḥ**, i.e. 'the name **dvigu** is given to a compound (of one of these three kinds) when the first member is a numeral'. (This explains why Pāṇini did not make 2.1.50 and 2.1.51 a single sūtra: the name dvigu does *not* apply to a compound like **sapta:rṣayaḥ** (nom. pl.) 'the Seven Sages', the Sanskrit name for the Great Bear.)

Although the word **ahan** 'day' is a consonant stem, **tryahaḥ** is an a-stem. Mallinātha quotes 5.4.91 **rāj ;ahaḥ ;sakhibhyaṣ ṭac.** This is governed by 5.4.68 **samās ;-ântāḥ** 'the following suffixes (down to the end of Book 5, in fact) are compound-final'. The sūtra thus means 'after the words **rājan**, **ahan** and **sakhi** there occurs as a compound-final suffix **ṭac**'.

Mallinātha does not bother to quote 6.4.145 **ahnaṣ ṭa ;khor eva**, which shows how to apply this last rule. The words **lopaḥ** 'elision', i.e. 'zero-substitution', and **ṭeḥ** 'in place of ṭi' are to be supplied. **ṭi** is a technical term meaning 'the final vowel of a word plus the following consonant if any'. The sūtra therefore means 'zero is substituted for the final vowel and consonant of **ahan,** but only before a suffix with indicatory ṭ or **kha**'. Thus **ahan**+**ṭac** becomes **ah**+**ṭac**, i.e. **aha**.

Mallinātha refers to, without actually quoting, 2.4.1 **dvigur ekavacanam** 'dvigu compounds are singular'; and finally justifies the masculine gender of **tryahaḥ** (though Kālidāsa only uses the ambiguous ablative form **tryahāt**) by 2.4.29 **rātr›;āhn›;āhāḥ puṃsi.** From 2.4.26 **dvandva;tatpuruṣayoḥ** is supplied: 'the words **rātra, ahna** and **aha** (used at the end of a co-ordinative or determinative compound) occur in the masculine'.

To summarise the above:

tri+**ahan** means 'group of three days' by 2.1.51
the compound takes the suffix **ṭac** by 5.4.91
ahan+**ṭac** becomes **aha** by 6.4.145
the compound is a dvigu by 2.1.52
and therefore singular by 2.4.1
and masculine by 2.4.29.

Sūtra 5.2.80 **utka unmanāḥ** is interesting as an example of **nipātaḥ,** a formation listed ready-made by Pāṇini without justification in terms of its components. **utka** 'eager' is listed among formations made with the suffix **kan,** but is anomalous both because **kan** is added not to a nominal stem but to the prefix **ut** and because its meaning, which refers to a mental state, is not fully explicable from its elements. Pāṇini thus lists it as a special form and gives its meaning. The word **nipātaḥ** is better known in the sense of 'particle', a meaning it acquires because particles exist ready-made without undergoing grammatical formation.

Quotations from literary critics

Besides citing grammarians and lexicographers, Mallinātha quotes from many other sources, including popular sayings and works on right conduct (dharma-śāstra) or political science (nīti-śāstra), and in particular from many literary critics. He seldom gives the name of the work he is quoting from, and sometimes when he does so the attribution is wrong. It may be assumed that his quotations are normally made from memory.

Sanskrit literary criticism as it is known from about the ninth century onward is the development of an earlier alaṃkāra-śāstra 'Science of Embellishment' in combination with certain elements of nāṭya-śāstra 'Theatrical Science'. The term alaṃkāra 'ornament, embellishment' is wider than the English 'figure of speech' and somewhat different in scope. It includes almost all the usages by means of which a poet's language departs from the most colourless possible presentation of facts and ideas, and covers devices of sound such as assonance and rhyme as well as devices of sense such as simile and metaphor. In addition to the alaṃkāras proper, various possible 'Qualities' (guṇas) are enumerated. Mallinātha observes that stanza 94 illustrates the Quality known as Conciseness (saṃkṣepa) and quotes a rather tautologous definition of this Quality from a work called the Pratāparudrīya. An examination of the stanza will indeed show that Kālidāsa's telescoping of the narrative at this point is sufficiently marked and deliberate to be considered a literary device.

Although Mallinātha does not bother to point the fact out, the second half of stanza 85 (like the second half of 86, which is parallel) illustrates a common rhetorical figure known as arthāntaranyāsa 'Substantiation' or 'Corroboration'. In its most typical form, as here, it consists of a general reflection provoked by the particular facts of the situation that is being described, and is frequently signalled by the presence of a word such as **prāyeṇa** 'generally'. The figure thus has the flavour of 'moral-drawing', There is a similar flavour to the second half of stanza 95, but here, as Mallinātha points out, the precise figure involved is arthāpatti 'Strong Presumption', i.e. reasoning *a fortiori*.

From nāṭya-śāstra literary critics adopted the theory of rasa (lit. 'flavour, taste'), which in its most developed form is a subtle theory of the nature of aesthetic experience. Its basis is the division of the spectator's experience of a play into

a number of 'flavours' (at first eight, later usually nine)—
comic, horrific, etc. To each of these rasas corresponds a basic
human emotion (**sthāyi:bhāva** 'Stable or Dominant State'),
which will normally be represented in one or more of the
characters of the drama. Around the basic emotion various
minor emotions come fleetingly into play—the thirty-three
Transitory or Subordinate States, called either **vyabhicāri:**
bhāva or **samcāri:bhāva.** Thus in the Amorous or Romantic
rasa (**śṛṅgāra**) the hero and heroine feel the sthāyibhāva of
Love (**rati**) and the vyabhicāribhāvas of Impatience, Disappointment, Contentedness and so on. Mallinātha points out
that stanza 84 illustrates the vyabhicāribhāva of Dissimulation (**avahittha** or **avahitthā**). In fact, this stanza is the one
most quoted in textbooks as an example of this particular
State.

Vocabulary

aṅkaḥ hook; curve of the body,
lap

Aṅgiras *m., pr. n.*

aṅgī˘kṛ make a part, subordinate; adopt, accept, promise

adri *m.* rock, mountain

adho:mukha (*f.* ī) down-
faced, with face bent down

antaram interval, difference;
-**antaram** *ifc.* a different,
another

anyatarasyām (*gram.*) optionally

apara *pron. adj.* other

apūpaḥ cake: *see* **daṇḍāpū-**
pikā

apeta departed; free from (*abl.*)

abhīpsita desired; **abhīpsi-**
tam thing desired, desire

Amaraḥ, Amarasiṃhaḥ *pr.
n., author of the lexicon*
Amara-kośaḥ

Ambā, Ambikā *pr. n., the
wife of Śiva*

arth-ântara-nyāsaḥ (*lit.
crit.*) Substantiation

arth-āpatti *f.* (*lit. crit.*) Strong
Presumption

alaṃkāraḥ ornament; (*lit.
crit.*) embellishment, literary
figure

a:vaśa powerless, helpless

avahittham, avahitthā dissimulation

aśru *n.* tear; **aśru:mukha**
'tear-faced', tearful-faced

ahan *n. irreg.* day

-**ahaḥ,** -**ahnaḥ** (*ifc. for* **ahan**)
day

ākāraḥ form, appearance,
(facial) expression

ākāśam ether, sky

āpatanam occurrence, (sudden) appearance, arising

āpatti *f.* happening, occurrence

āśis *f. irreg.* prayer, benediction

āśīrvādaḥ blessing, benison

āsakti *f.* adherence, intentness (on)

itara *pron. adj.* other

iṣṭaṃ thing wished, wish

īpsita desired, wished for

utka eager, longing for

uttara following, subsequent, further; **uttaraṃ** answer

udāra noble, generous

un:manas eager, longing

eka-vacanaṃ (*gram.*) singular (number)

kanakaṃ gold

kamala *m. n.* lotus

karaṇaṃ doing, performing

kavi *m.* poet, creative writer

kāraṇaṃ instrument, means

kuṭumbaṃ household, family

kuṭumbin *m.* householder, family man

kuṇḍalaṃ earring, ear-ornament

kṛcchraṃ hardship; **kṛcchrāt** with difficulty

kaimutika deriving from the notion **kim uta** 'let alone'; **kaimutika:nyāyāt** [from the principle of 'let alone':] *a fortiori*

khaṃ hole; vacuum; sky, heaven

gaḥ the letter **g**; (*in prosody*) heavy syllable

gaṇanā counting

gārhasthyaṃ being a householder

giri *m.* mountain

gṛhamedhin [performer of domestic sacrifices:] householder

gṛha-sthaḥ one who is in a house, householder

gṛhiṇī housewife, wife

gopanaṃ concealment, hiding

caturtha (*f.* ī) fourth

cīraṃ strip of bark (worn by ascetic)

jaḥ the letter **j**; (*in prosody*) the syllables ∪ – ∪

jāmbūnada (*f.* ī) golden

jijñāsā desire to know, wish to determine

jñānaṃ knowledge, perceiving

ṭac (*gram.*) the suffix **a**

tat:kṣaṇaṃ at that moment, thereupon

taddhitaḥ [*i.e.* **tat-hitaḥ** 'suitable for that'] (*gram.*) secondary suffix

tanayā daughter

tāraka causing to cross over, rescuing, liberating

tithi *m.f.* lunar day (*esp. as auspicious* date *for ceremony*)

tri three

tri:locanaḥ the Three-eyed (god), Śiva

Tryambakaḥ *name of Śiva*

try:ahaḥ [period of] three days

daṇḍāpūpikā the stick-and-cake principle ('if a mouse eats a stick he'll certainly eat a cake'), reasoning *a fortiori*

dalaṃ petal

dātṛ giver, granting

dānaṃ gift, bestowal

dvigu *m.* [from **dvi:gu** 'worth two cows'] (*gram.*) numerical compound

naḥ the letter **n**; (*in prosody*) the syllables ∪ ∪ ∪

namas-kāraḥ making obeisance

nipātaḥ (*gram.*) ready-made form (laid down without grammatical analysis)

niścayaḥ determination, resolve

nyāyaḥ rule, principle; propriety

paḥ, pa-kāraḥ the letter p

pattram feather; leaf, petal

padam word, member of a compound

para:tantra under another's control, not in control (of)

pariṇayaḥ marriage

:paryanta [having as an end:] ending with, up to

Paśupati *m. name of Śiva*

pākaḥ cooking; ripeness, fulfilment

Pārvatī *pr. n. wife of Śiva*

pārśvam flank, side

pitṛ *m.* father

pum:liṅga having masculine gender

pumvant (*gram.*) masculine

pums *m.* (*irreg.*) man, male, masculine

putrī, putrikā daughter

puraskṛta placed in front, before the eyes

puṣpitāgrā (*in prosody*) name of a metre

pṛthag:janaḥ separate person, ordinary person

praṇāmaḥ salutation

pratyayaḥ (*gram.*) suffix

:pradhāna having as one's authority

preman *m. n.* affection

bandhu *m.* kinsman

buddhi *f.* intelligence, mind

bhartṛ *m.* husband

bhāvaḥ state of being; essence, meaning; emotional state, emotion

bhikṣā alms

bhīta afraid

mahīdharaḥ mountain

mṛtyum-jayaḥ Conqueror of Death

Menā *pr. n. Pārvatī's mother*

ya-kāraḥ the letter y; (*in prosody*) the syllables ◡ – –

yācitṛ *m.* suer, petitioner

yukti *f.* argument

yugam pair; *ifc.* two

yuj joined, even (in number); **a:yuj** uneven, odd

yogya suitable

raḥ the letter r; (*in prosody*) the syllables – ◡ –

rātraḥ *at the end of compound for* **rātri** *f.* night

ruh the root **ruh**

rephaḥ = **raḥ**

lakṣaṇam mark, characteristic; definition

liṅgam mark, sign; phallus; (*gram.*) gender

līlā play, sport

vacas *n.* word, words, speech

vatamsaḥ/vatamsakaḥ ornament, *esp.* earring

vadhū *f.* woman, bride

varaḥ suitor

valkala *m. n.* bark (of tree)

vaśaḥ power; **-vaśāt** from the power of, because of

vasanam dress

vākyam utterance

vikāraḥ transformation; mental disturbance; *ifc.* made out of

vipratipanna perplexed, uncertain; **a:vipratipanna** not uncertain, entirely fixed

vibhu powerful, *esp. as an epithet of Śiva*

vilambaḥ delay

vivāhaḥ wedding

vi:śoka free from sorrow, at ease

viśv-ātman *m.* Soul of the Universe, Supreme Godhead

viṣayaḥ dominion, sphere, field of action

vistaraḥ expansion, prolixity

vṛttam metre

vṛtti *f.* behaviour, conduct; (*gram.*) synthetic expression (*by compounding, as opp. analytic expression by separate words*)

vaivāhika (*f.* ī) (suitable) for a wedding

voḍhṛ bridegroom

vyabhicāraḥ deviation, swerving

vyabhicārin liable to deviate, swerving; **a:vyabhicārin** unswerving

vyājaḥ fraud, pretence

Śivaḥ *pr. n.*

śūlin Trident-bearer, *epithet of Śiva*

śeṣaḥ remainder, portion to be supplied

śailaḥ mountain

ślokaḥ stanza

saṃketaḥ agreement, assignation; **saṃketa-sthānam** place of assignation

saṃkṣipta abbreviated, in concise form

saṃkṣepaḥ conciseness

saṃcārin going together, transitory; **saṃcārī bhāvaḥ** (*lit. crit.*) Subsidiary Emotional State

samarthanam establishment, confirmation

samāsaḥ (*gram.*) compound

samāhāraḥ group, collection

sampūrṇa fulfilled

sarva-nāman *n.*(*gram.*) [name for anything:] pronoun

sāpatnyam the state of being the sharer of a husband (sapatnī)

siddha accomplished

sūtram aphorism, aphoristic rule

stambaḥ clump of grass

-stha standing, being at/in *etc.*

Smara-haraḥ the Destroyer of Love, *epithet of Śiva*

Haraḥ *name of Śiva*

Himavant *m.*, **Himālayaḥ** the mountain (range) Himālaya

---

anu+yuj (VII **anuyuṅkte**) question, examine

alam+kṛ (VIII **alaṃkaroti**) adorn, embellish

ah (*defective verb, perf.* **āha**) say, speak

ā+pat (I **āpatati**) occur, befall, appear suddenly, present oneself

ā+prach (VI **āpṛcchati**) take leave of, say goodbye

ā+mantr (X **āmantrayate**) salute; take leave of

ā+ruh *caus.* (**āropayati**) cause to mount, raise onto

ut+īkṣ (I **udīkṣate**) look at

ut+yā (II **udyāti**) rise up

upa+īkṣ (I **upekṣate**) overlook, disregard

edh *caus.* (**edhayati**) cause to prosper, bless

gaṇ (X **gaṇayati**) count

gup (*denom. pres.* **gopāyati**) guard; hide

car (I **carati**) move, go, depart

cal (I **calati**) stir, move, go away

jñā *caus.* (**jñāpayati**) inform, announce

nam (I **namati**) bow, salute

nis+ci (V **niścinoti**) ascertain, settle, fix upon

nis+pad (IV niṣpadyate) come forth, be brought about; *p.p.*
  niṣpanna completed

pac (I pacati) cook, ripen; *pass.* pacyate be cooked, ripen

pari+kīrt (X parikīrtayati) proclaim, declare

pari+kḷp *caus.* (parikalpayati) fix, destine for (*dat.*)

pra+āp (V prāpnoti) reach, go to; obtain, win

bhī (III bibheti) fear; *p.p.* bhīta afraid

yā (II yāti) go

yā *caus.* (yāpayati) spend (time)

lajj (VI lajjate) be shy, blush, show confusion

vi+kṛ (VIII vikaroti) alter, change, distort, cause mental disturbance (vikāraḥ) to

vid (VI vindati) find; *pass.* vidyate is found, exists

vi+pra+kṛ (VIII viprakaroti) injure, torment

vi+mṛś (VI vimṛśati) perceive, reflect, deliberate

sam+vṛdh *caus.* (saṃvardhayati) congratulate

sam+stu (II saṃstauti) praise

sam+khyā (II saṃkhyāti) count, reckon up

sah (I sahate; *irreg. inf.* soḍhum) withstand, endure, bear

sūc (X sūcayati) point out, indicate

sraṃs (I sraṃsate; *p.p.* srasta) drop, slip

upari after (*abl.*)	world
ūrdhvam after (*abl.*)	puraḥ in front, immediate
ehi (*imperv. of* ā+i) come	yasmāt inasmuch as, since
paratra elsewhere, in the next	

Exercise 15

Note: The transliterated version of this exercise should be of
particular help in solving difficulties.

एवंवादिनि देवर्षौ पार्श्वे पितुरधोमुखी ।

लीलाकमलपत्त्राणि गणयामास पार्वती ॥ ८४ ॥

एवमिति ॥ देवर्षौ अङ्गिरसि एवंवादिनि सति पार्वती पितुः
पार्श्वे अधोमुखी सती । लज्जयेति शेषः । लीलाकमलपत्त्राणि
गणयामास सञ्चख्यौ । लज्जावशात्कमलदलगणनाव्याजेन हर्षं
जुगोपेत्यर्थः । अनेनावहित्थाख्यः संचारी भाव उक्तः । तदुक्तम्—
अवहित्था तु लज्जादेर्हर्षाद्याकारगोपनमिति ॥

शैलः संपूर्णकामो ऽपि मेनामुखमुदैक्षत ।

प्राचेण गृहिणीनैचाः कन्यार्थेषु कुटुम्बिनः ॥ ८५ ॥

शैल इति ॥ शैलः हिमवान् संपूर्णकामो ऽपि । दातुं कृतनिश्चयो ऽपीत्यर्थः । मेनामुखमुदैक्षत । उचितोत्तरजिज्ञासयेति भावः । तथा हि । प्राचेण कुटुम्बिनः गृहस्थाः कन्यार्थेषु कन्याप्रयोजनेषु गृहिणीव नैचं कार्यज्ञानकारणं येषां ते तथोक्ताः । कलत्र-प्रधानवृत्तय इत्यर्थः ॥

मेने मेनापि तत्सर्वं पत्युः कार्यमभीप्सितम् ।

भवन्त्यव्यभिचारिण्यो भर्तुरिष्टे पतिव्रताः ॥ ८६ ॥

मेन इति ॥ मेनापि पत्युः हिमालयस्य तत्सर्वमभीप्सितं कार्यं मेने अङ्गीचकार । तथा हि । पतिरिव व्रतं यासां ताः भर्तुरिष्टे अभीप्सिते न विद्यते व्यभिचारो यासां ताः अव्यभिचारिण्यो भवन्ति । भर्तृचित्ताभिप्रायज्ञा भवन्तीति भावः ॥

इदमत्रोत्तरं न्याय्यमिति बुद्ध्वा विमृश्य सः ।

आदद्दे वचसामन्ते मङ्गलालंकृतां सुताम् ॥ ८७ ।

इदमिति ॥ सः हिमवान् वचसामन्ते मुनिवाक्यावसाने अत्र मुनिवाक्ये इदम् उत्तरश्लोके वक्ष्यमाणं दानमेव न्याय्यम् न्याया-दनपेतम् उत्तरमिति बुद्ध्वा चित्तेन विमृश्य विचिन्त्य मङ्गलं यथा तथालंकृतां मङ्गलालंकृतां सुतामाद्दे हस्ताभ्यां जग्राह ॥

एहि विश्वात्मने वत्से भिक्षासि परिकल्पिता ।

अर्थिनो मुनयः प्राप्तं गृहमेधिफलं मया ॥ ८८ ॥

एहीति ॥ हे वत्से पुत्रि एहि आगच्छ । त्वं विश्वात्मने शिवाय भिक्षा परिकल्पितासि निश्चितासि । रत्नादि स्तम्बपर्यन्तं सर्वं भिक्षा तपस्विनः इति वचनादिति भावः । अर्थिनः याचितारः मुनयः । मया गृहमेधिनः गृहस्थस्य फलं प्राप्तम् । इह परत्र च तारकत्वात्पात्रे कन्यादानं गार्हस्थ्यस्य फलमित्यर्थः ॥

एतावदुक्त्वा तनयामृषीनाह महीधरः ।
इयं नमति वः सर्वांस्त्रिलोचनवधूरिति ॥ ८९ ॥

एतावदिति ॥ महीधरः हिमवान् तनयाम् एतावत् पूर्वोक्तम्
उक्त्वा ऋषीन् आह । किमिति । इयं त्रिलोचनवधूः त्र्यम्बकपत्नी
वः सर्वान् नमति इति । त्रिलोचनवधूरिति सिद्धवदभिधानेना-
विप्रतिपन्नं दानमिति सूचयति ॥

ईप्सितार्थक्रियोदारं ते ऽभिनन्द्य गिरेर्वचः ।
आशीर्भिरेधयामासुः पुरःपाकाभिरम्बिकाम् ॥ ९० ॥
ईप्सितार्थेति ॥ ते मुनयः ईप्सितार्थक्रियया इष्टार्थकरणेन उदारं
महत् । उदारो दातृमहतोः इत्यमरः । गिरेः हिमवतः वचः
वचनम् अभिनन्द्य साध्विति संस्तुत्य । अम्बिकाम् अम्बाम् ।
पचत इति पाकः फलम् । पुरःपाकाभिः पुरस्कृतफलाभिः
आशीर्भिः आशीर्वादैः एधयामासुः संवर्धयामासुः ॥

तां प्रणामादरस्रस्तजाम्बूनदवतंसकाम् ।
अङ्कमारोपयामास लज्जमानामरुन्धती ॥ ९१ ॥
तामिति ॥ प्रणामादरेण नमस्कारासक्त्या स्रस्ते जाम्बूनदे सुवर्ण-
विकारे वतंसके कनककुण्डले यस्याःतां लज्जमानां ताम् अम्बि-
काम् अरुन्धती अङ्कमारोपयामास । रुहः पो ऽन्यतरस्याम् इति
पकारः ॥

तन्मातरं चाश्रुमुखीं दुहितृस्नेहविक्लवाम् ।
वरेणान्यपूर्वेण विशोकामकरोन्मुनैः ॥ ९२ ॥
तदिति ॥ दुहितृस्नेहेन पुत्रिकाप्रेम्णा विक्लवां वियोच्यत इति
भीताम् । अत एवाश्रूणि मुखे यस्याःतां अश्रुमुखीं तस्याः
अम्बिकायाः मातरं तन्मातरं मेनां च । अन्या पूर्वं यस्याःति सो
ऽन्यपूर्वः । सर्वनाम्नो वृत्तिविषये पुंवद्भावः इति पूर्वपदस्य पुंवद्भावः ।
स न भवतीत्यनन्यपूर्वस्तस्य अनन्यपूर्वेण । सापत्नदुःखमकुर्वत

इत्यर्थः । वरस्य वोढुः गुणैः मृत्युंजयत्वादिभिः विश्शोकां निर्दुः-
खाम् अकरोत् ॥

वैवाहिकीं तिथिं पृष्टास्तत्क्षणं हरबन्धुना ।
ते च्यहादूर्ध्वमाख्याय चेरुश्चीरपरिग्रहाः ॥ ७३ ॥

वैवाहिकीमिति ॥ चीरपरिग्रहाः वल्कलमाचवसनाः ते तपस्विनः
तत्क्षणम् तस्मिन्नेव क्षणे हरबन्धुना हिमवता वैवाहिकीं विवाह-
योग्यां तिथिं पृष्टाः केत्यनुयुक्ताः सन्तः । चयाणामह्नां समाहार-
स्त्र्यहः । तद्वितार्थोत्तरपदसमाहारे च इति समासः । राजाहः-
सखिभ्यष्टच् इति टच्प्रत्ययः । द्विगुलादेकवचनम् । राचाह्नाहाः
पुंसि इति पुंलिङ्गता । तस्मात् त्र्यहात् ऊर्ध्वम् उपरि आख्याय
चतुर्थे ऽहनि विवाहः इत्युक्ता चेरुः चलिताः ॥

ते हिमालयमामन्त्र्य पुनः प्राप्य च शूलिनम् ।
सिद्धं चास्मै निवेद्यार्थं तद्दिष्टाः खमुदययुः ॥ ७४ ॥

त इति ॥ ते मुनयः हिमालयमामन्त्र्य साधु याम इत्यापृच्छ्य
पुनः शूलिनम् हरं संकेतस्थानस्थं प्राप्य च । सिद्धम् निष्पन्नम्
अर्थम् प्रयोजनम् अस्मै निवेद्य ज्ञापयित्वा च । तद्दिष्टाः तेन
शूलिना विस्सृष्टाः खम् आकाशं प्रति उदययुः उत्पेतुः । अच
संक्षिप्तार्थाभिधानात्संक्षेपो नाम गुण उक्तः । तदुक्तम्—संक्षिप्त-
र्थाभिधानं यत्संक्षेपः परिकीर्तितः इति ॥

भगवान्पशुपतिस्त्र्यहमाचविलम्बमपि सोढुं न श्शशाक तदौत्सुक्या-
दित्याह

पशुपतिरपि तान्यहानि कृच्छ्राद्
अगमयद्द्रिसुतासमागमोत्कः ।
कमपरमवशं न विप्रकुर्युर्
विभुमपि तं यदमी स्पृशन्ति भावाः ॥ ७५ ॥

पशुपतिरिति ॥ उत्कं मनो यस्य सः उत्कः । उत्क उन्मनाः
इति निपातः । अद्रिसुतासमागमोत्कः पार्वतीपरिणयोत्सुक:
पशुपतिरपि तानि । चीणीति ग्रेषः । अहानि छच्छादगमयत्
अयापयत् । कविराह — अमी भावाः औत्सुक्यादयः संचारिणः
अवश्यम् इन्द्रियपरतन्त्वम् अपरम् पृथग्जनं कं न विप्रकुर्युः न
विकारं नयेयुः । यत् यस्मात् विभुम् समर्थम् । जितेन्द्रियमिति
यावत् । तम् स्वरहरम् अपि सुश्रन्ति । विकुर्वन्तीत्यर्थः । अत्र
विभुविकारसमर्थनादर्थादितरजनविकारः कैमुतिकन्यायादापत-
तीत्यर्थापत्तिरलंकारः । तथा च सूत्रम् — दण्डापूपिकया-
थान्तरापतनमर्थापत्तिः इति । अर्थान्तरन्यास इति के चित्
तदुपेक्षणीयम् । युक्तिसु विस्तरभयान्नोच्यते । पुष्पिताग्रा वृत्तम्
— अयुजि नयुगरेफतो यकारो युजि च नजौ जरगाश्च
पुष्पिताग्रा इति लक्षणात् ॥

Appendix 1

Further Sanskrit Study

ANYONE who has mastered the present volume is adequately equipped to read simple Classical Sanskrit. Those whose interest lies particularly in Indian religious thought may well wish to begin with the best loved of all Hindu religious texts, the *Bhagavad Gītā*, written in eighteen short cantos of easy, straightforward verse. Innumerable texts and translations of this work exist. For the student, the most scrupulously faithful translation is probably that by F. Edgerton (Harper Torchbooks). Other distinguished scholars who have translated the work include R. C. Zaehner (*Hindu Scriptures*, Everyman; also *The Bhagavad Gītā* with commentary and text in transcription, Oxford University Press) and S. Radhakrishnan (Allen & Unwin, including text in transcription). The pocket edition with a text in nāgarī by Annie Besant (Theosophical Publishing House) is cheap and convenient, though the accompanying translation is unreliable.

In secular literature a good starting-point is the *Pañcatantra*, a witty and sophisticated collection of animal fables (the ultimate source of La Fontaine), written in fluent, racy Sanskrit. Many versions of this work have survived, and these were collated by Edgerton, who produced a recension as near as he thought it was possible to get to the original. His translation of this has been reprinted recently (Allen & Unwin), but not unfortunately the Sanskrit text (American Oriental Series, Volume 2, New Haven, 1924), which should, however, be obtainable from specialist libraries.

An especially attractive and accessible branch of Classical Sanskrit literature is the drama. The prose dialogue is straightforward (many sentences are likely to seem familiar to the student of this book!). Certain characters speak in Prakrit, but almost all editions include a Sanskrit translation (**chāyā**) of these passages. The stanzas of verse interspersed among the prose are more elaborate in style but should not prove too difficult with the help of a translation and notes such as have been provided for most standard Sanskrit plays by M. R. Kale: Kale's student editions are very useful and workmanlike, and are usually in print in India—though regrettably these reprints often bristle with grotesque printing errors. The best known of all Sanskrit plays is the *Śakuntalā* of Kālidāsa. Other masterpieces include the *Mṛcchakaṭikā* ('Toy Cart') of Śūdraka, the *Mudrārākṣasa* '(The Signet Ring and Rākṣasa') of Viśākhadatta and the *Uttararāmacarita* ('The Later Story of Rāma') of Bhavabhūti—the last, although a moving and beautiful work, being of the four perhaps the least immediately attractive to Western taste in its style and feeling.

Sanskrit dictionaries

A. A. Macdonell's *A Sanskrit Dictionary for Students* (Oxford University Press, 382 pp.) is much the most convenient in the early stages of study. The author lists in the preface the Sanskrit works for which the dictionary is specifically a vocabulary. In reading other works or for more scholarly use, M. Monier-Williams' *A Sanskrit-English Dictionary* (Oxford University Press, 1333 pp.), effectively a translation and condensation of the great *Sanskrit-Wörterbuch* of Böhtlingk and Roth, is indispensable. Unfortunately, it suffers the irritating drawback of being arranged not in strict alphabetical order but according to verbal roots. All present dictionaries are grossly out of date: Sanskrit studies will be revolutionised when the vast work at present under preparation in Poona finally sees the light of day.

Sanskrit grammars

A. A. Macdonell's *A Sanskrit Grammar for Students* (Oxford University Press) is again the most convenient work available and, despite some inaccuracies and omissions, is a model of clarity and conciseness. The standard Sanskrit grammar in English is still that of W. D. Whitney (2nd edition 1889, reprinted by Oxford University Press), but this is now very out of date, the presentation of Vedic and Classical material is confusingly intertwined and the treatment of syntax is sketchy in the extreme. The really standard work is in German, the monumental *Altindische Grammatik* of Wackernagel and Debrunner (Göttingen, 1896–1957); but special mention should be made of a French work, the *Grammaire sanscrite* of Louis Renou (Paris, 2nd edition 1961), which, while of a more manageable size than Wackernagel, treats of Classical Sanskrit in considerable detail and is full of valuable observations on syntax.

Vedic studies

Students primarily interested in comparative Indo-European philology may like to turn to the Vedic language at an early stage in their studies, and here yet again the path is smoothed by A. A. Macdonell. His *Vedic Reader for Students* (Oxford University Press) contains a selection of Vedic hymns transliterated, analysed and translated, with very full notes on points of linguistic interest and a complete vocabulary at the back of the book. The Vedic hymns, which are not without their attraction from the literary point of view, are thus made easily accessible to the non-specialist. Macdonell's *Vedic Grammar for Students* is arranged to correspond paragraph for paragraph with his Sanskrit Grammar mentioned above, so facilitating the comparison of Vedic grammar with Classical.

Appendix 2

Grammatical Paradigms

(For use in conjunction with the foregoing chapters, where further irregularities and alternative forms may be mentioned.)

NOUNS

It will be noticed that in all nouns each of the following groups has a single form:

- (i) Nominative, vocative and accusative dual
- (ii) Instrumental, dative and ablative dual
- (iii) Genitive and locative dual
- (iv) Dative and ablative plural
- (v) Nominative and vocative dual or plural
- (vi) Nominative and accusative *neuter*, any number

1 Vowel stems

Stems in **a/ā**: **kānta** 'beloved'

		Masculine	*Neuter*	*Feminine*
Nominative singular		**kāntaḥ**	**kāntam**	**kāntā**
Accusative	,,	**kāntam**	**kāntam**	**kāntām**
Instrumental	,,	**kāntena**	**kāntena**	**kāntayā**
Dative	,,	**kāntāya**	**kāntāya**	**kāntāyai**
Ablative	,,	**kāntāt**	**kāntāt**	**kāntāyāḥ**
Genitive	,,	**kāntasya**	**kāntasya**	**kāntāyāḥ**
Locative	,,	**kānte**	**kānte**	**kāntāyām**
Vocative	,,	**kānta**	**kānta**	**kānte**

		Masculine	Neuter	Feminine
N. V. A.	dual	kāntau	kānte	kānte
I. D. Ab.	,,	kāntābhyām	kāntābhyām	kāntābhyām
G. L.	,,	kāntayoḥ	kāntayoḥ	kāntayoḥ
N. V.	plural	kāntāḥ	kāntāni	kāntāḥ
A.	,,	kāntān	kāntāni	kāntāḥ
I.	,,	kāntaiḥ	kāntaiḥ	kāntābhiḥ
D. Ab.	,,	kāntebhyaḥ	kāntebhyaḥ	kāntābhyaḥ
G.	,,	kāntānām	kāntānām	kāntānām
L.	,,	kānteṣu	kānteṣu	kāntāsu

Stems in ī *and* ū: nadī f. 'river', vadhū f. 'woman', strī f. 'woman', dhī f. 'thought', bhū f. 'earth'

	Polysyllabic		Irregular	Monosyllabic	
N. sg.	nadī	vadhūḥ	strī	dhīḥ	bhūḥ
A.	nadīm	vadhūm	strīm/ striyam	dhiyam	bhuvam
I.	nadyā	vadhvā	striyā	dhiyā	bhuvā
D.	nadyai	vadhvai	striyai	dhiye	bhuve
Ab. G.	nadyāḥ	vadhvāḥ	striyāḥ	dhiyaḥ	bhuvaḥ
L.	nadyām	vadhvām	striyām	dhiyi	bhuvi
V.	nadi	vadhu	stri	dhīḥ	bhūḥ
N. V. A. du.	nadyau	vadhvau	striyau	dhiyau	bhuvau
I. D. Ab.	nadībhyām	vadhūbhyām	strībhyām	dhībhyām	bhūbhyām
G. L.	nadyoḥ	vadhvoḥ	striyoḥ	dhiyoḥ	bhuvoḥ
N. V. pl.	nadyaḥ	vadhvaḥ	striyaḥ	dhiyaḥ	bhuvaḥ
A.	nadīḥ	vadhūḥ	strīḥ/ striyaḥ	dhiyaḥ	bhuvaḥ
I.	nadībhiḥ	vadhūbhiḥ	strībhiḥ	dhībhiḥ	bhūbhiḥ
D. Ab.	nadībhyaḥ	vadhūbhyaḥ	strībhyaḥ	dhībhyaḥ	bhūbhyaḥ
G.	nadīnām	vadhūnām	strīṇām	dhiyām	bhuvām
L.	nadīṣu	vadhūṣu	strīṣu	dhīṣu	bhūṣu

Stems in i *and* u: śuci 'clean', mṛdu 'soft'

	m.	n.	f.	m.	n.	f.
N. sg.	śuciḥ	śuci	śuciḥ	mṛduḥ	mṛdu	mṛduḥ
A.	śucim	śuci	śucim	mṛdum	mṛdu	mṛdum
I.	śucinā	śucinā	śucyā	mṛdunā	mṛdunā	mṛdvā
D.	śucaye	śucine	śucyai	mṛdave	mṛdune	mṛdvai
Ab. G.	śuceḥ	śucinaḥ	śucyāḥ	mṛdoḥ	mṛdunaḥ	mṛdvāḥ
L.	śucau	śucini	śucyām	mṛdau	mṛduni	mṛdvām
V.	śuce	śuci	śuce	mṛdo	mṛdu	mṛdo

	m.	n.	f.	m.	n.	f.
N. V. A.						
du.	śucī	śucinī	śucī	mṛdū	mṛdunī	mṛdū
I .A. Ab.	śuci-	śuci-	śuci-	mṛdu-	mṛdu-	mṛdu-
	bhyām	bhyām	bhyām	bhyām	bhyām	bhyām
G. L.	śucyoḥ	śucinoḥ	śucyoḥ	mṛdvoḥ	mṛdunoḥ	mṛdvoḥ
N. V. pl.	śucayaḥ	śucīni	śucayaḥ	mṛdavaḥ	mṛdūni	mṛdavaḥ
A.	śucīn	śucīni	śucīḥ	mṛdūn	mṛdūni	mṛdūḥ
I.	śucibhiḥ	śucibhiḥ	śucibhiḥ	mṛdubhiḥ	mṛdubhiḥ	mṛdubhiḥ
D. Ab.	śuci-	śuci-	śuci-	mṛdu-	mṛdu-	mṛdu-
	bhyaḥ	bhyaḥ	bhyaḥ	bhyaḥ	bhyaḥ	bhyaḥ
G.	śucīnām	śucīnām	śucīnām	mṛdūnām	mṛdūnām	mṛdūnām
L.	śuciṣu	śuciṣu	śuciṣu	mṛduṣu	mṛduṣu	mṛduṣu

Stems in ṛ: kartṛ m. 'maker', pitṛ m. 'father', svasṛ f. 'sister', mātṛ f. 'mother'

	Masculine		*Feminine*	
N. sg.	kartā	pitā	svasā	mātā
A.	kartāram	pitaram	svasāram	mātaram
I.	kartrā	pitrā	svasrā	mātrā
D.	kartre	pitre	svasre	mātre
Ab. G.	kartuḥ	pituḥ	svasuḥ	mātuḥ
L.	kartari	pitari	svasari	mātari
V.	kartar	pitar	svasar	mātar
N. V. A. du.	kartārau	pitarau	svasārau	mātarau
I. D. Ab.	kartṛbhyām	pitṛbhyām	svasṛbhyām	mātṛbhyām
G. L.	kartroḥ	pitroḥ	svasroḥ	mātroḥ
N. V. pl.	kartāraḥ	pitaraḥ	svasāraḥ	mātaraḥ
A.	kartṝn	pitṝn	svasṝḥ	mātṝḥ
I.	kartṛbhiḥ	pitṛbhiḥ	svasṛbhiḥ	mātṛbhiḥ
D. Ab.	kartṛbhyaḥ	pitṛbhyaḥ	svasṛbhyaḥ	mātṛbhyaḥ
G.	kartṝṇām	pitṝṇām	svasṝṇām	mātṝṇām
L.	kartṛṣu	pitṛṣu	svasṛṣu	mātṛṣu

Note: The feminine of kartṛ is kartrī.

2 Consonant stems

Unchangeable stems: suhṛd m. 'friend', go-duh m. f. 'cow-milker', manas n. 'mind', sumanas m. f. 'benevolent'

N. sg.	suhṛt	godhuk	manaḥ	sumanāḥ
A.	suhṛdam	goduham	manaḥ	sumanasam
I.	suhṛdā	goduhā	manasā	sumanasā
D.	suhṛde	goduhe	manase	sumanase
Ab. G.	suhṛdaḥ	goduhaḥ	manasaḥ	sumanasaḥ
L.	suhṛdi	goduhi	manasi	sumanasi
V.	suhṛt	godhuk	manaḥ	sumanaḥ
N. V. A. du.	suhṛdau	goduhau	manasī	sumanasau
I. D. Ab.	suhṛdbhyām	godhugbhyām	manobhyām	sumanobhyām
G. L.	suhṛdoḥ	goduhoḥ	manasoḥ	sumanasoḥ

N. V. A. pl.	suhṛdaḥ	goduhaḥ	manāṃsi	sumanasaḥ
I.	suhṛdbhiḥ	godhugbhiḥ	manobhiḥ	sumanobhiḥ
D. Ab.	suhṛdbhyaḥ	godhugbhyaḥ	manobhyaḥ	sumanobhyaḥ
G.	suhṛdām	goduhām	manasām	sumanasām
L.	suhṛtsu	godhukṣu	manaḥsu	sumanaḥsu

The neuter of **sumanas** is inflected like **manas**. The following are examples of stems ending in other consonants:

Stem	N. sg.	N. pl.	I. pl.	L. pl.
suyudh *m.* good fighter	suyut	suyudhaḥ	suyudbhiḥ	suyutsu
kakubh *f.* region	kakup	kakubhaḥ	kakubbhiḥ	kakupsu
vāc *f.* speech	vāk	vācaḥ	vāgbhiḥ	vākṣu
vaṇij *m.* business-man	vaṇik	vaṇijaḥ	vaṇigbhiḥ	vaṇikṣu
parivrāj *m.* medicant	parivrāṭ	parivrājaḥ	parivrāḍbhiḥ	parivrāṭsu
diś *f.* direction	dik	diśaḥ	digbhiḥ	dikṣu
viś *m.* settler	viṭ	viśaḥ	viḍbhiḥ	viṭsu
dviṣ *m.* enemy	dviṭ	dviṣaḥ	dviḍbhiḥ	dviṭsu
madhulih *m.* bee	madhuliṭ	madhulihaḥ	madhuliḍbhiḥ	madhuliṭsu

Stems in **ir/ur** (both rare) lengthen to **īr/ūr** before consonants and in the nominative singular. Stems in **is/us** become **iṣ/uṣ** or **ir/ur** according to sandhi, and also lengthen the vowel in the nominative, vocative and accusative neuter plural.

gir *f.* speech	gīḥ	giraḥ	gīrbhiḥ	gīrṣu
dhur *f.* yoke	dhūḥ	dhuraḥ	dhūrbhiḥ	dhūrṣu
barhis *n.* sacred grass	barhiḥ	barhīṃṣi	barhirbhiḥ	barhiḥṣu
cakṣus *n.* eye	cakṣuḥ	cakṣūṃṣi	cakṣurbhiḥ	cakṣuḥṣu
āśis[1] *f.* benediction	āśīḥ	āśiṣaḥ	āśīrbhiḥ	āśīḥṣu

Stems in **in**: dhanin m. n. (dhaninī f.) 'rich'

	SINGULAR		DUAL		PLURAL	
	m.	*n.*	*m.*	*n.*	*m.*	*n.*
N.	dhanī	dhani	dhaninau	dhaninī	dhaninaḥ	dhanīni
A.	dhaninam	dhani	„	„	dhaninaḥ	dhanīni
I.	dhaninā		dhanibhyām		dhanibhiḥ	
D.	dhanine		„		dhanibhyaḥ	
Ab.	dhaninaḥ		„		„	
G.	dhaninaḥ		dhaninoḥ		dhaninām	
L.	dhanini		„		dhaniṣu	
V.	dhanin	dhani/dhanin	(*as N.*)		(*as N.*)	

[1] Although an **is** stem, this noun lengthens its **i** in the same circumstances as a stem in **ir**.

Stems in **an**: **rājan** m. 'king', **ātman** m. 'self', **nāman** n. 'name', **panthan** m. 'road' (irreg.) **ahan** n. 'day' (irreg.)

N. Sg.	rājā	ātmā	nāma	panthāḥ	ahar
A.	rājānam	ātmānam	nāma	panthānam	ahar
I.	rājñā	ātmanā	nāmnā	pathā	ahnā
D.	rājñe	ātmane	nāmne	pathe	ahne
Ab. G.	rājñaḥ	ātmanaḥ	nāmnaḥ	pathaḥ	ahnaḥ
L.	rājñi/	ātmani	nāmni/	pathi	ahni/
	rājani		nāmani		ahani
V.	rājan	ātman	nāma/	panthāḥ	ahar
			nāman		
N. V. A.	rājānau	ātmānau	nāmnī/	panthānau	ahnī/ahanī
du.			nāmanī		
I. D. Ab.	rāja-	ātma-	nāmabhyām	pathibhyām	ahobhyām
	bhyām	bhyām			
G. L.	rājñoḥ	ātmanoḥ	nāmnoḥ	pathoḥ	ahnoḥ
N. V. pl.	rājānaḥ	ātmānaḥ	nāmāni	panthānaḥ	ahāni
A.	rājñaḥ	ātmanaḥ	nāmāni	pathaḥ	ahāni
I.	rājabhiḥ	ātmabhiḥ	nāmabhiḥ	pathibhiḥ	ahobhiḥ
D. Ab.	rāja-	ātma-	nāmabhyaḥ	pathibhyaḥ	ahobhyaḥ
	bhyaḥ	bhyaḥ			
G.	rājñām	ātmanām	nāmnām	pathām	ahnām
L.	rājasu	ātmasu	nāmasu	pathiṣu	ahaḥsu

Stems in **ant** *and* **at**: **dhanavant** 'rich', **nayant** 'leading', **dadhat** 'putting'

	m.	*n.*	*m.*	*n.*	*m.*	*n.*
N. Sg.	dhanavān	dhana-	nayan	nayat	dadhat	dadhat
		vat				
A.	dhana-	„	nayantam	„	dadhatam	„
	vantam					
I.	dhanavatā		nayatā		dadhatā	
D.	dhanavate		nayate		dadhate	
Ab. G.	dhanavataḥ		nayataḥ		dadhataḥ	
L.	dhanavati		nayati		dadhati	
V.	dhanavan	dhana-	nayan	nayat	dadhat	dadhat
		vat				
N. V. A.	dhana-	dhana-	nayantau	nayantī	dadhatau	dadhatī
du.	vantau	vatī				
I. D. Ab.	dhanavadbhyām		nayadbhyām		dadhadbhyām	
G. L.	dhanavatoḥ		nayatoḥ		dadhatoḥ	
N. V. pl.	dhana-	dhana-	nayantaḥ	nayanti	dadhataḥ	dadhanti
	vantaḥ	vanti				
A.	dhana-	„	nayataḥ	„	dadhataḥ	„
	vataḥ					
I.	dhanavadbhiḥ		nayadbhiḥ		dadhadbhiḥ	
D. Ab.	dhanavadbhyaḥ		nayadbhyaḥ		dadhadbhyaḥ	
G.	dhanavatām		nayatām		dadhatām	
L.	dhanavatsu		nayatsu		dadhatsu	

Stems in **yāṃs**: **śreyāṃs** m. n. (**śreyasī** f.) 'better'

	SINGULAR		DUAL		PLURAL	
	m.	*n.*	*m.*	*n.*	*m.*	*n.*
N.	śreyān	śreyaḥ	śreyāṃsau	śreyasī	śreyāṃsaḥ	śreyāṃsi
A.	śreyāṃsam	śreyaḥ	,,	,,	śreyasaḥ	śreyāṃsi
I.		śreyasā		śreyobhyām		śreyobhiḥ
D.		śreyase		,,		śreyobhyaḥ
Ab.		śreyasaḥ		,,		,,
G.		śreyasaḥ		śreyasoḥ		śreyasām
L.		śreyasi		,,		śreyaḥsu
V.	śreyan	śreyaḥ	*as N.*)		(*as N.*)	

Stems in **vāṃs**: **vidvāṃs** m. n. (**viduṣī** f.) 'learned'

	SINGULAR		DUAL		PLURAL	
	m.	*n.*	*m.*	*n.*	*m.*	*n.*
N.	vidvān	vidvat	vidvāṃsau	viduṣī	vidvāṃsaḥ	vidvāṃsi
A.	vidvāṃsam	vidvat	,,	,,	viduṣaḥ	vidvāṃsi
I.		viduṣā		vidvadbhyām		vidvadbhiḥ
D.		viduṣe		,,		vidvadbhyaḥ
Ab.		viduṣaḥ		,,		,,
G.		viduṣaḥ		viduṣoḥ		viduṣām
L.		viduṣi		,,		vidvatsu
V.	vidvan	vidvat	(*as N.*)		(*as N.*)	

Stems in **añc**: **pratyañc** m. n. (**pratīcī** f.) 'western'

	SINGULAR		DUAL		PLURAL	
	m.	*n.*	*m.*	*n.*	*m.*	*n.*
N. V.	pratyaṅ	pratyak	pratyañcau	pratīcī	pratyañcaḥ	pratyañci
A.	pratyañ- cam	pratyak	,,	,,	pratīcaḥ	pratyañci
I.		pratīcā		pratyagbhyām		pratyagbhiḥ
D.		pratīce		,,		pratyagbhyaḥ
Ab.		pratīcaḥ		,,		,,
G.		pratīcaḥ		pratīcoḥ		pratīcām
L.		pratīci		,,		pratyakṣu

In words such as **prāñc** 'eastern', where two a's (**pra+añc**) coalesce, the middle and weak stems are identical: **prāc**. Thus ablative, genitive and locative plural **prāgbhyaḥ**, **prācām**, **prākṣu**.

PRONOUNS

1ST PERSON:	2ND PERSON	3RD PERSON
aham 'I'	tvam 'you'	saḥ 'he, that'
(Enclitic forms in brackets.)		

			m.	n.	f.
N. Sg.	aham	tvam	saḥ	tat	sā
A.	mām (mā)	tvām (tvā)	tam	tat	tām
I.	mayā	tvayā	tena		tayā
D.	mahyam (me)	tubhyam (te)	tasmai		tasyai
Ab.	mat *or* mattaḥ	tvat *or* tvattaḥ	tasmāt		tasyāḥ
G.	mama (me)	tava (te)	tasya		tasyāḥ
L.	mayi	tvayi	tasmin		tasyām
N. A. du.	āvām	yuvām	tau	te	te
I. D. Ab.	āvābhyām	yuvābhyām		tābhyām	
G. L.	āvayoḥ (A. D. G. nau)	yuvayoḥ (A. D. G. vām)		tayoḥ	
N. pl.	vayam	yūyam	te	tāni	tāḥ
A.	asmān (naḥ)	yuṣmān (vaḥ)	tān	tāni	tāḥ
I.	asmābhiḥ	yuṣmābhiḥ	taiḥ		tābhiḥ
D.	asmabhyam (naḥ)	yuṣmabhyam (vaḥ)	tebhyaḥ		tābhyaḥ
Ab.	asmat *or* asmattaḥ	yuṣmat *or* yuṣmattaḥ	tebhyaḥ		tābhyaḥ
G.	asmākam (naḥ)	yuṣmākam (vaḥ)	teṣām		tāsām
L.	asmāsu	yuṣmāsu	teṣu		tāsu

The accusative singular enclitic forms **mā** and **tvā** are seldom used in the Classical language.

The following pronouns follow the inflexion of **saḥ, tat, sā** in any forms not quoted here.

(*a*) **eṣaḥ, etat, eṣā** this

(*b*) **yaḥ, yat, yā** who *relative pronoun*

(*c*) **anyaḥ, anyat, anyā** other

(*d*) **kaḥ, kim, kā** who? *interrogative pronoun*

(*e*) **sarvaḥ, sarvam, sarvā** all

(*f*) **ekaḥ, ekam, ekā** one

(*g*) **svaḥ, svam, svā** own

	ayam 'this'			asau 'that'		
	m.	n.	f.	m.	n.	f.
N. sg.	ayam	idam	iyam	asau	adaḥ	asau
A.	imam	idam	imām	amum	adaḥ	amūm
I.		anena	anayā		amunā	amuyā
D.		asmai	asyai		amuṣmai	amuṣyai

Ab.	asmāt	asyāḥ	amuṣmāt	amuṣyāḥ
G.	asya	asyāḥ	amuṣya	amuṣyāḥ
L.	asmin	asyām	amuṣmin	amuṣyām

N. A. du.	imau ime ime	amū
I. D. Ab.	ābhyām	amūbhyām
G. L.	anayoḥ	amuyoḥ

N. pl.	ime imāni	imāḥ	amī	amūni amūḥ
A.	imān imāni	imāḥ	amūn	amūni amūḥ
I.	ebhiḥ	ābhiḥ	amībhiḥ	amūbhiḥ
D. Ab.	ebhyaḥ	ābhyaḥ	amībhyaḥ	amūbhyaḥ
G.	eṣām	āsām	amīṣām	amūṣām
L.	eṣu	āsu	amīṣu	amūṣu

For the pronoun **enam** 'him' see Chapter 10, p. 151.

NUMERALS

	Cardinals			Ordinals
1	eka	41	eka ;catvāriṃśat	1st prathama
2	dvi	42	dvā ;catvāriṃśat	2nd dvitīya
3	tri	43	tri ;catvāriṃśat	3rd tṛtīya
4	catur	44	catuś ;catvāriṃśat	4th caturtha, turīya, turya
5	pañca	45	pañca ;catvāriṃśat	5th pañcama
6	ṣaṣ	46	ṣaṭ ;catvāriṃśat	6th ṣaṣṭha
7	sapta	47	sapta ;catvāriṃśat	7th saptama
8	aṣṭa	48	aṣṭā ;catvāriṃśat	8th aṣṭama
9	nava	49 {	nava ;catvāriṃśat	9th navama
10	daśa		ūna:pañcāśat	10th daśama
11	ekādaśa	50	pañcāśat	11th–18th as cardinals
12	dvādaśa	60	ṣaṣṭi	19th navadaśa, ūnaviṃśa
13	trayodaśa	70	saptati	20th viṃśa, viṃśatitama
14	caturdaśa	80	aśīti	30th triṃśa, triṃśattama
15	pañcadaśa	82	dvy:aśīti	40th catvāriṃśa, catvāriṃśattama
16	ṣoḍaśa	90	navati	50th pañcāśa, pañcāśattama
17	saptadaśa	96	ṣaṇ ;ṇavati	60th ṣaṣṭitama
18	aṣṭādaśa	100	śatam	61st ekaṣaṣṭa
19 {	navadaśa	102 {	dvy-adhikaṃ śatam	70th saptatitama
	ūna:viṃśati		dvi ;śatam	71st ekasaptata
20	viṃśati	200 {	dve śate	80th aśītitama
23	trayo ;viṃśati		dvi:śatam	81st ekāśīta
30	triṃśat	1000	sahasraṃ	90th navatitama
33	trayas ;triṃśat	100 000	lakṣaṃ	91st ekanavata
40	catvāriṃśat	10 000 000	koṭi	100th śatatama

To form the cardinal numbers not included in the list, the

analogy of 41 to 49 may be followed, though some alternative forms are possible.

For the ordinals 60th, 70th, 80th, 90th by themselves only the forms in **-tama** are allowed. But wherever short forms are permitted, the forms in **-tama** are always a possible alternative: thus 61st **ekaṣaṣṭa** *or* **ekaṣaṣṭitama**.

The sandhi of **ṣaṣ** is as if it were **ṣaṭ**, except that **ṣaṣ+d** = **ṣoḍ** and **ṣaṣ+n** = **ṣaṇṇ**.

The ordinals are all inflected like **kānta**. Their feminine is always in **-ī**, except for **prathamā, dvitīyā, tṛtiyā, turīyā** and **turyā**.

Inflexion of cardinals

The cardinal numbers below 100 are all quoted above in stem form. **viṃsati** and higher numbers ending in **-i** are feminine **i** stems; those ending in **-t** are feminine consonant stems.

The inflexion of **eka** is mentioned under the pronouns. **dvi** inflects like the dual of **kānta**: **dvau, dve, dve; dvābhyām; dvayoḥ.**

	tri *three*			catur *four*		
N. V.	trayaḥ	trīṇi	tisraḥ	catvāraḥ	catvāri	catasraḥ
A.	trīn	trīṇi	tisraḥ	caturaḥ	catvāri	catasraḥ
I.	tribhiḥ		tisṛbhiḥ	caturbhiḥ		catasṛbhiḥ
D. Ab.	tribhyaḥ		tisṛbhyaḥ	caturbhyaḥ		catasṛbhyaḥ
G.	trayāṇām		tisṛṇām	caturṇām		catasṛṇām
L.	triṣu		tisṛṣu	caturṣu		catasṛṣu

	pañca *five*	ṣaṣ *six*	aṣṭa *eight*
N. V. A.	pañca	ṣaṭ	aṣṭa/aṣṭau
I.	pañcabhiḥ	ṣaḍbhiḥ	aṣṭabhiḥ/aṣṭābhiḥ
D. Ab.	pañcabhyaḥ	ṣaḍbhyaḥ	aṣṭabhyaḥ/aṣṭābhyaḥ
G.	pañcānām	ṣaṇṇām	aṣṭānām
L.	pañcasu	ṣaṭsu	aṣṭasu/aṣṭāsu

The numbers 7 and 9 to 19 inflect like **pañca**.

VERBS

General view of the Sanskrit verb

The following scheme (which is not exhaustive) will give some idea of the range of possible formations from the verbal root.

The second column adds parallel formations from the most highly developed secondary stem, the causative. For the particular verb quoted, some forms are theoretical rather than actually found.

1 Finite formations

From the root **nī** 'lead'

From the stem **nāy(aya)** 'cause to lead'

Primary verb

PRESENT
nayati 'he leads'
(Included in the present system:
Imperfect **anayat** 'he led'
Imperative **nayatu** 'let him lead'
Optative **nayet** 'he may lead')

Secondary verb

PRESENT CAUSATIVE
nāyayati 'he causes to lead'
(*Imperfect* **anāyayat** 'he caused to lead'
Imperative **nāyayatu** 'let him cause to lead'
Optative **nāyayet** 'he may cause to lead')

PERFECT
nināya 'he led'

PERIPHRASTIC PERFECT
nāyayām āsa 'he caused to lead'

AORIST

anaiṣīt 'he led'

REDUPLICATED AORIST (an independent formation)
anīnayat 'he caused to lead'

FUTURE
neṣyati 'he will lead'

(*Conditional* **aneṣyat** 'he would have led')

FUTURE CAUSATIVE
nāyayiṣyati 'he will cause to lead'

(**anāyayiṣyat** 'he would have caused to lead')

PASSIVE
nīyate 'he is led'

CAUSATIVE PASSIVE
nāyyate 'he is caused to lead'

Secondary verbs

CAUSATIVE (see above, second column)
nāyayati 'he causes to lead'

Tertiary verb

DESIDERATIVE CAUSATIVE

nināyayiṣati 'he wants to cause to lead'

DESIDERATIVE

niniṣati 'he wants to lead'
(*Adjective* **niniṣu** 'wanting to lead'
Substantive **niniṣā** 'the wish to lead')

nināyayiṣu 'wanting to cause to lead'
nināyayiṣā 'the wish to cause to lead')

INTENSIVE

nenīyate 'he leads forcibly'

Two further independent formations from the root are the AORIST PASSIVE (third person singular only) **anāyi** 'he was led' and the PRECATIVE, or benedictive, an aorist optative, **nīyāt** 'may he lead!'

Parasmaipada or ātmanepada participles, as appropriate, may be formed from the present, the future and all other formations in **-ati/-ate.** The aorist has no participle, and of the perfect participles the parasmaipada is infrequent and the ātmanepada hardly found.

2 Nominal formations

With weak grade

PAST PARTICIPLE

nīta 'led'

nāyita 'caused to lead'

PAST ACTIVE PARTICIPLE

nītavant 'having led'

nāyitavant 'having caused to lead'

ABSOLUTIVE

(uncompounded) **nītvā** 'after leading'

(after prefix) **-nīya**   ,,

nāyayitvā } 'after causing to lead'
-nāyya

With strong grade

INFINITIVE

netum 'to lead'

nāyayitum 'to cause to lead'

AGENT NOUN

netṛ 'leader'

nāyayitṛ 'causer of leading'

GERUNDIVES

(a) **neya** '(requiring) to be led'   **nāyya** '(requiring) to be caused to lead'

(b) **netavya**   ,,   **nāyayitavya**   ,,
(c) **nayanīya**   ,,   **nāyanīya**   ,,

3 Remoter nominal formations

Formations of the following types may be regarded as less integrated into the verbal structure. Often they are lacking in particular roots or have developed some independent meaning. They fall into two broad categories:

(a) Action nouns ('leading, guidance'): **nayanam**; **nayaḥ** 'prudent conduct'; **nīti** f. 'prudent conduct'

(b) Agentives ('that lead'): **-nī**; **-nāyin**; **nāyakaḥ** 'leading actor'; **netram** '[instrument of guidance:] eye' (**nayanam** may also have this sense).

Present paradigms

Thematic paradigm

The inflexions of the present system of class I verbs, as illustrated by **nī,** are shared by classes IV, VI and X, the future, the passive and all derivative verbs in **ati/ate** (which means all derivative verbs except one type of intensive).

nī 'lead'

	PRESENT	IMPERFECT	IMPERATIVE	OPTATIVE
		parasmaipada		
1st sg.	nayāmi	anayam	nayāni	nayeyam
2nd	nayasi	anayaḥ	naya	nayeḥ
3rd	nayati	anayat	nayatu	nayet
1st du.	nayāvaḥ	anayāva	nayāva	nayeva
2nd	nayathaḥ	anayatam	nayatam	nayetam
3rd	nayataḥ	anayatām	nayatām	nayetām
1st pl.	nayāmaḥ	anayāma	nayāma	nayema
2nd	nayatha	anayata	nayata	nayeta
3rd	nayanti	anayan	nayantu	nayeyuḥ
Part.	nayant			

ātmanepada

1st sg.	naye	anaye	nayai	nayeya
2nd	nayase	anayathāḥ	nayasva	nayethāḥ
3rd	nayate	anayata	nayatām	nayeta
1st du.	nayāvahe	anayāvahi	nayāvahai	nayevahi
2nd	nayethe	anayethām	nayethām	nayeyāthām
3rd	nayete	anayetām	nayetām	nayeyātām
1st pl.	nayāmahe	anayāmahi	nayāmahai	nayemahi
2nd	nayadhve	anayadhvam	nayadhvam	nayedhvam
3rd	nayante	anayanta	nayantām	nayeran
Part.	nayamāna			

Class II (*root class*)

dviṣ 'hate'

	PRESENT	IMPERFECT	IMPERATIVE	OPTATIVE

parasmaipada

1st sg.	dveṣmi	adveṣam	dveṣāṇi	dviṣyām
2nd	dvekṣi	adveṭ	dviḍḍhi	dviṣyāḥ
3rd	dveṣṭi	adveṭ	dveṣṭu	dviṣyāt
1st du.	dviṣvaḥ	adviṣva	dveṣāva	dviṣyāva
2nd	dviṣṭhaḥ	adviṣṭam	dviṣṭam	dviṣyātam
3rd	dviṣṭaḥ	adviṣṭām	dviṣṭām	dviṣyātām
1st pl.	dviṣmaḥ	adviṣma	dveṣāma	dviṣyāma
2nd	dviṣṭha	adviṣṭa	dviṣṭa	dviṣyāta
3rd	dviṣanti	adviṣan	dviṣantu	dviṣyuḥ
Part.	dviṣant			

ātmanepada

1st sg.	dviṣe	adviṣi	dveṣai	dviṣīya
2nd	dvikṣe	adviṣṭhāḥ	dvikṣva	dviṣīthāḥ
3rd	dviṣṭe	adviṣṭa	dviṣṭām	dviṣīta
1st du.	dviṣvahe	adviṣvahi	dveṣāvahai	dviṣīvahi
2nd	dviṣāthe	adviṣāthām	dviṣāthām	dviṣīyāthām
3rd	dviṣāte	adviṣātām	dviṣātām	dviṣīyātām
1st pl.	dviṣmahe	adviṣmahi	dveṣāmahai	dviṣīmahi
2nd	dviḍḍhve	adviḍḍhvam	dviḍḍhvam	dviṣīḍhvam
3rd	dviṣate	adviṣata	dviṣatām	dviṣīran
Part.	dviṣāṇa			

as 'be'

	PRESENT	IMPERFECT	IMPERATIVE
	parasmaipada		
1st sg.	asmi	āsam	asāni
2nd	asi	āsīḥ	edhi
3rd	asti	āsīt	astu
1st du.	svaḥ	āsva	asāva
2nd	sthaḥ	āstam	stam
3rd	staḥ	āstām	stām
1st pl.	smaḥ	āsma	asāma
2nd	stha	āsta	sta
3rd	santi	āsan	santu
Opt.	syām, syāḥ *etc.*		
Part.	sant		

ās 'sit, stay'

	PRESENT	IMPERFECT	IMPERATIVE
	ātmanepada		
1st sg.	āse	āsi	āsai
2nd	āsse	āsthāḥ	āssva
3rd	āste	āsta	āstām
1st du.	āsvahe	āsvahi	āsāvahai
2nd	āsāthe	āsāthām	āsāthām
3rd	āsāte	āsātām	āsātām
1st pl.	āsmahe	āsmahi	āsāmahai
2nd	āddhve	āddhvam	āddhvam
3rd	āsate	āsata	āsatām
Opt.	āsīya, āsīthāḥ, *etc.*		
Part.	āsīna (*irreg.*)		

i 'go'

	PRESENT	IMPERFECT	IMPERATIVE
	parasmaipada		
1st sg.	emi	āyam	ayāni
2nd	eṣi	aiḥ	ihi
3rd	eti	ait	etu
1st du.	ivaḥ	aiva	ayāva
2nd	ithaḥ	aitam	itam
3rd	itaḥ	aitām	itām
1st pl.	imaḥ	aima	ayāma
2nd	itha	aita	ita
3rd	yanti	āyan	yantu
Opt.	iyām, iyāḥ, *etc.*		
Part.	yant		

i 'go' (in adhi+i 'study')

	PRESENT	IMPERFECT	IMPERATIVE
		ātmanepada	
1st sg.	iye	aiyi	ayai
2nd	iṣe	aithāḥ	iṣva
3rd	ite	aita	itām
1st du.	ivahe	aivahi	ayāvahai
2nd	iyāthe	aiyāthām	iyāthām
3rd	iyāte	aiyātām	iyātām
1st pl.	imahe	aimahi	ayāmahai
2nd	idhve	aidhvam	idhvam
3rd	iyate	aiyata	iyatām
Opt.	iyīya, iyīthāḥ, *etc.*		
Part.	iyāna		

Class III (reduplicated class)

hu 'sacrifice'

	PRESENT	IMPERFECT	IMPERATIVE	OPTATIVE
		parasmaipada		
1st sg.	juhomi	ajuhavam	juhavāni	juhuyām
2nd	juhoṣi	ajuhoḥ	juhudhi	juhuyāḥ
3rd	juhoti	ajuhot	juhotu	juhuyāt
1st du.	juhuvaḥ	ajuhuva	juhavāva	juhuyāva
2nd	juhuthaḥ	ajuhutam	juhutam	juhuyātam
3rd	juhutaḥ	ajuhutām	juhutām	juhuyātām
1st pl.	juhumaḥ	ajuhuma	juhavāma	juhuyāma
2nd	juhutha	ajuhuta	juhuta	juhuyāta
3rd	juhvati	ajuhavuḥ	juhvatu	juhuyuḥ
Part.	juhvat			

The second person singular imperative **juhudhi** (instead of
*juhuhi) is anomalous.

	ātmanepada			
1st sg.	juhve	ajuhvi	juhavai	juhvīya
2nd	juhuṣe	ajuhuthāḥ	juhuṣva	juhvīthāḥ
3rd	juhute	ajuhuta	juhutām	juhvīta
1st du.	juhuvahe	ajuhuvahi	juhavāvahai	juhvīvahi
2nd	juhvāthe	ajuhvāthām	juhvāthām	juhvīyāthām
3rd	juhvāte	ajuhvātām	juhvātām	juhvīyātām
1st pl.	juhumahe	ajuhumahi	juhavāmahai	juhvīmahi
2nd	juhudhve	ajuhudhvam	juhudhvam	juhvīdhvam
3rd	juhvate	ajuhvata	juhvatām	juhvīran
Part.	juhvāna			

Class V (**nu** *class*)

su 'press'

	PRESENT	IMPERFECT	IMPERATIVE
		parasmaipada	
1st sg.	sunomi	asunavam	sunavāni
2nd	sunoṣi	asunoḥ	sunu
3rd	sunoti	asunot	sunotu
1st du.	sunuvaḥ/sunvaḥ	asunuva/asunva	sunavāva
2nd	sunuthaḥ	asunutam	sunutam
3rd	sunutaḥ	asunutām	sunutām
1st pl.	sunumaḥ/sunmaḥ	asunuma/asunma	sunavāma
2nd	sunutha	asunuta	sunuta
3rd	sunvanti	asunvan	sunvantu
Opt.	sunuyām, *etc.*		
Part.	sunvant		

		ātmanepada	
1st sg.	sunve	asunvi	sunavai
2nd	sunuṣe	asunuthāḥ	sunuṣva
3rd	sunute	asunuta	sunutām
1st du.	sunuvahe/ sunvahe	asunuvahi/ asunvahi	sunavāvahai
2nd	sunvāthe	asunvāthām	sunvāthām
3rd	sunvāte	asunvātām	sunvātām
1st pl.	sunumahe/ sunmahe	asunumahi/ asunmahi	sunavāmahai
2nd	sunudhve	asunudhvam	sunudhvam
3rd	sunvate	asunvata	sunvatām
Opt.	sunvīya, *etc.*		
Part.	sunvāna		

Class VII (*infix nasal class*)

rudh 'obstruct'

	PRESENT	IMPERFECT	IMPERATIVE	OPTATIVE
		parasmaipada		
1st sg.	ruṇadhmi	aruṇadham	ruṇadhāni	rundhyām
2nd	ruṇatsi	aruṇat	runddhi	rundhyāḥ
3rd	ruṇaddhi	aruṇat	ruṇaddhu	rundhyāt
1st du.	rundhvaḥ	arundhva	ruṇadhāva	rundhyāva
2nd	runddhaḥ	arunddham	runddham	rundhyātam
3rd	runddhaḥ	arunddhām	runddhām	rundhyātām
1st pl.	rundhmaḥ	arundhma	ruṇadhāma	rundhyāma
2nd	runddha	arunddha	runddha	rundhyāta
3rd	rundhanti	arundhan	rundhantu	rundhyuḥ
Part.	rundhant			

	PRESENT	IMPERFECT	IMPERATIVE	OPTATIVE
		ātmanepada		
1st sg.	rundhe	arundhi	ruṇadhai	rundhīya
2nd	runtse	arunddhāḥ	runtsva	rundhīthāḥ
3rd	runddhe	arunddha	runddhām	rundhīta
1st du.	rundhvahe	arundhvahi	ruṇadhāvahai	rundhīvahi
2nd	rundhāthe	arundhāthām	rundhāthām	rundhīyāthām
3rd	rundhāte	arundhātām	rundhātām	rundhīyātām
1st pl.	rundhmahe	arundhmahi	ruṇadhāmahai	rundhīmahi
2nd	runddhve	arunddhvam	runddhvam	rundhīdhvam
3rd	rundhate	arundhata	rundhatām	rundhīran
Part.	rundhāna			

Class VIII (u *class*)

kṛ 'do'

	PRESENT	IMPERFECT	IMPERATIVE	OPTATIVE
		parasmaipada		
1st sg.	karomi	akaravam	karavāṇi	kuryām
2nd	karoṣi	akaroḥ	kuru	kuryāḥ
3rd	karoti	akarot	karotu	kuryāt
1st du.	kurvaḥ	akurva	karavāva	kuryāva
2nd	kuruthaḥ	akurutam	kurutam	kuryātam
3rd	kurutaḥ	akurutām	kurutām	kuryātām
1st pl.	kurmaḥ	akurma	karavāma	kuryāma
2nd	kurutha	akuruta	kuruta	kuryāta
3rd	kurvanti	akurvan	kurvantu	kuryuḥ
Part.	kurvant			

		ātmanepada		
1st sg.	kurve	akurvi	karavai	kurvīya
2nd	kuruṣe	akuruthāḥ	kuruṣva	kurvīthāḥ
3rd	kurute	akuruta	kurutām	kurvīta
1st du.	kurvahe	akurvahi	karavāvahai	kurvīvahi
2nd	kurvāthe	akurvāthām	kurvāthām	kurvīyāthām
3rd	kurvāte	akurvātām	kurvātām	kurvīyātām
1st pl.	kurmahe	akurmahi	karavāmahai	kurvīmahi
2nd	kurudhve	akurudhvam	kurudhvam	kurvīdhvam
3rd	kurvate	akurvata	kurvatām	kurvīran
Part.	kurvāṇa			

The other seven verbs of this class inflect like **su**.

Class IX (nā *class*)

krī 'buy'

	PRESENT	IMPERFECT	IMPERATIVE	OPTATIVE
		parasmaipada		
1st sg.	krīṇāmi	akrīṇām	krīṇāni	krīṇīyām
2nd	krīṇāsi	akrīṇāḥ	krīṇīhi	krīṇīyāḥ

3rd	krīṇāti	akrīṇāt	krīṇātu	krīṇīyāt
1st du.	krīṇīvaḥ	akrīṇīva	krīṇāva	krīṇīyāva
2nd	krīṇīthaḥ	akrīṇītam	krīṇītam	krīṇīyātam
3rd	krīṇītaḥ	akrīṇītām	krīṇītām	krīṇīyātām
1st pl.	krīṇīmaḥ	akrīṇīma	krīṇāma	krīṇīyāma
2nd	krīṇītha	akrīṇīta	krīṇīta	krīṇīyāta
3rd	krīṇanti	akrīṇan	krīṇantu	krīṇīyuḥ
Part.	krīṇant			

ātmanepada

1st. sg.	krīṇe	akrīṇi	krīṇai	krīṇīya
2nd	krīṇīṣe	akrīṇīthāḥ	krīṇīṣva	krīṇīthāḥ
3rd	krīṇīte	akrīṇīta	krīṇītām	krīṇīta
1st du.	krīṇīvahe	akrīṇīvahi	krīṇāvahai	krīṇīvahi
2nd	krīṇāthe	akrīṇāthām	krīṇāthām	krīṇīyāthām
3rd	krīṇāte	akrīṇātām	krīṇātām	krīṇīyātām
1st pl.	krīṇīmahe	akrīṇīmahi	krīṇāmahai	krīṇīmahi
2nd	krīṇīdhve	akrīṇīdhvam	krīṇīdhvam	krīṇīdhvam
3rd	krīṇate	akrīṇata	krīṇatām	krīṇīran
Part.	krīṇāna			

Perfect paradigms

	dṛś 'see'	kṛ 'do'	vac 'speak'	pac 'cook'	dhā 'put'
			parasmaipada		
1st sg.	dadarśa	cakara/ cakāra	uvaca/ uvāca	papaca/ papāca	dadhau
2nd	dadarśitha	cakartha	uvaktha/ uvacitha	papaktha/ pecitha	dadhātha/ dadhitha
3rd	dadarśa	cakāra	uvāca	papāca	dadhau
1st du.	dadṛśiva	cakṛva	ūciva	peciva	dadhiva
2nd	dadṛśathuḥ	cakrathuḥ	ūcathuḥ	pecathuḥ	dadhathuḥ
3rd	dadṛśatuḥ	cakratuḥ	ūcatuḥ	pecatuḥ	dadhatuḥ
1st pl.	dadṛśima	cakṛma	ūcima	pecima	dadhima
2nd	dadṛśa	cakra	ūca	peca	dadha
3rd	dadṛśuḥ	cakruḥ	ūcuḥ	pecuḥ	dadhuḥ
Part.	dadṛśivāṃs	cakṛvāṃs	ūcivāṃs	pecivāṃs	dadhivāṃs
			ātmanepada		
1st sg.	dadṛśe	cakre	ūce	pece	dadhe
2nd	dadṛśiṣe	cakṛṣe	ūciṣe	peciṣe	dadhiṣe
3rd	dadṛśe	cakre	ūce	pece	dadhe
1st du.	dadṛśivahe	cakṛvahe	ūcivahe	pecivahe	dadhivahe
2nd	dadṛśāthe	cakrāthe	ūcāthe	pecāthe	dadhāthe
3rd	dadṛśāte	cakrāte	ūcāte	pecāte	dadhāte
1st pl.	dadṛśimahe	cakṛmahe	ūcimahe	pecimahe	dadhimahe
2nd	dadṛśidhve	cakṛdhve	ūcidhve	pecidhve	dadhidhve
3rd	dadṛśire	cakrire	ūcire	pecire	dadhire
Part.	dadṛśāna	cakrāṇa	ūcāna	pecāna	dadhāna

as 'be' (parasmaipada): āsa āsitha āsa; āsiva āsathuḥ āsatuḥ; āsima āsa āsuḥ—no participle.

Aorist paradigms

Non-sigmatic aorists

	ROOT AORIST		a-AORIST	REDUPLICATED AORIST
	dhā 'put'	bhū 'be'	sic 'moisten'	nī (cause to) 'lead'
		parasmaipada		
1st sg.	adhām	abhūvam	asicam	anīnayam
2nd	adhāḥ	abhūḥ	asicaḥ	anīnayaḥ
3rd	adhāt	abhūt	asicat	anīnayat
1st du.	adhāva	abhūva	asicāva	anīnayāva
2nd	adhātam	abhūtam	asicatam	anīnayatam
3rd	adhātām	abhūtām	asicatām	anīnayatām
1st pl.	adhāma	abhūma	asicāma	anīnayāma
2nd	adhāta	abhūta	asicata	anīnayata
3rd	adhuḥ	abhūvan	asican	anīnayan
		ātmanepada		
1st sg.			asice	anīnaye
2nd			asicathāḥ	anīnayathāḥ
3rd			asicata	anīnayata
1st du.			asicāvahi	anīnayāvahi
2nd			asicethām	anīnayethām
3rd			asicetām	anīnayetām
1st pl.			asicāmahi	anīnayāmahi
2nd			asicadhvam	anīnayadhvam
3rd			asicanta	anīnayanta

Sigmatic aorists

	S-AORIST		iṣ-AORIST	siṣ-AORIST	sa-AORIST
	After vowel	After consonant			
	nī 'lead'	dah 'burn'	pū 'purify'	yā 'go'	diś 'point'
			parasmaipada		
1st sg.	anaiṣam	adhākṣam	apāviṣam	ayāsiṣam	adikṣam
2nd	anaiṣīḥ	adhākṣīḥ	apāvīḥ	ayāsīḥ	adikṣaḥ
3rd	anaiṣīt	adhākṣīt	apāvīt	ayāsīt	adikṣat
1st du.	anaiṣva	adhākṣva	apāviṣva	ayāsiṣva	adikṣāva
2nd	anaiṣṭam	adāgdham	apāviṣṭam	ayāsiṣṭam	adikṣatam
3rd	anaiṣṭām	adāgdhām	apāviṣṭām	ayāsiṣṭām	adikṣatām

	s-AORIST		iṣ-AORIST	siṣ-AORIST	sa-AORIST
		parasmaipada			
1st pl.	anaiṣma	adhākṣma	apāviṣma	ayāsiṣma	adikṣāma
2nd	anaiṣṭa	adāgdha	apāviṣṭa	ayāsiṣṭa	adikṣata
3rd	anaiṣuḥ	adhākṣuḥ	apāviṣuḥ	ayāsiṣuḥ	adikṣan

		ātmanepada			
1st sg.	aneṣi	adhakṣi	apaviṣi		adikṣi
2nd	aneṣṭhāḥ	adagdhāḥ	apaviṣṭhāḥ		adikṣathāḥ
3rd	aneṣṭa	adagdha	apaviṣṭa		adikṣata
1st du.	aneṣvahi	adhakṣvahi	apaviṣvahi		adikṣāvahi
2nd	aneṣāthām	adhakṣāthām	apaviṣāthām		adikṣāthām
3rd	aneṣātām	adhakṣātām	apaviṣātām		adikṣātām
1st pl.	aneṣmahi	adhakṣmahi	apaviṣmahi		adikṣāmahi
2nd	aneḍhvam	adhagdhvam	apaviḍhvam		adikṣadhvam
3rd	aneṣata	adhakṣata	apaviṣata		adikṣanta

Precative

bhū 'be' (parasmaipada): bhūyāsam bhūyāḥ bhūyāt ; bhūyāsva
bhūyāstam bhūyāstām ; bhūyāsma bhūyāsta bhūyāsuḥ.

Principal parts of verbs

The following list of verbs (arranged in Sanskrit alphabetical
order) shows the main formations from each root. The less
important verbs and those, such as class X verbs, whose
derivative forms are obvious are omitted. The past participle
is to be taken as a guide to the formation of the PAST ACTIVE
PARTICIPLE and of the uncompounded ABSOLUTIVE in -tvā;
the infinitive to the formation of the AGENT NOUN and of the
GERUNDIVE in tavya. Similarly, the GERUNDIVE in anīya, when
it is found, is based on the verbal noun in ana (here normally
given as anam since it is most often a neuter substantive).
Where parasmaipada and ātmanepada forms both exist, only
the former are mentioned. A blank indicates that the part of
the verb in question is not known to appear in Classical
Sanskrit; and even of those forms given some are rare or
dubious.

	ad 'eat'	as 'be'	āp 'obtain'	ās 'sit'	i 'go'	iṣ 'want'
ROOT	ad 'eat'	as 'be'	āp 'obtain'	ās 'sit'	i 'go'	iṣ 'want'
PRESENT	II atti	II asti	V āpnoti	II āste	II eti	VI icchati
PERFECT		āsa	āpa	āsām cakre	iyāya	iyeṣa
AORIST			āpat			aiṣit
FUTURE	atsyati		āpsyati	āsiṣyate	eṣyati	eṣiṣyati
PASSIVE	adyate		āpyate	āsyate	īyate	iṣyate
CAUSATIVE	ādayati		āpayati		āyayati	eṣayati
PAST PARTICIPLE	jagdha		āpta	āsita	ita	iṣṭa
ABSOLUTIVE in ya			-āpya	-āsya	-itya	-iṣya
INFINITIVE	attum		āptum	āsitum	etum	eṣṭum
GERUNDIVE in ya	adya		āpya			eṣya
NOMINAL in ana	adanam		āpanam	āsanam	ayanam	eṣaṇam
" in in	ādin		āpin		āyin	eṣin

	īkṣ 'see'	kṛ 'do'	kṛṣ 'drag'	kḷp 'be fit'	kram 'stride'	krī 'buy'
ROOT	īkṣ 'see'	kṛ 'do'	kṛṣ 'drag'	kḷp 'be fit'	kram 'stride'	krī 'buy'
PRESENT	I īkṣate	VIII karoti	I karṣati	I kalpate	I krāmati	IX krīṇāti
PERFECT	īkṣām cakre	cakāra	cakarṣa	cakḷpe	cakrāma	
AORIST	aikṣit	akārṣit	akārkṣit	(acīkḷpat)		
FUTURE	īkṣiṣyate	kariṣyati		kalpiṣyate	kramiṣyati	
PASSIVE	īkṣyate	kriyate	kṛṣyate		kramyate	krīyate
CAUSATIVE	īkṣayati	kārayati	karṣayati	kalpayati	kramayati	
PAST PARTICIPLE	īkṣita	kṛta	kṛṣṭa	kḷpta	krānta	krīta
ABSOLUTIVE in ya	-īkṣya	-kṛtya	-kṛṣya		-kramya	-krīya
INFINITIVE	īkṣitum	kartum	kraṣṭum		krāntum	kretum
GERUNDIVE in ya		kārya	kṛṣya		kramya	kreya
NOMINAL in ana	īkṣaṇam	karaṇam	karṣaṇam	kalpanam	kramaṇam	krayaṇam
" in in	īkṣin	kārin	karṣin			-krayin

ROOT	kṣip 'throw'	(ā)khyā 'tell'	gam 'go'	gai 'sing'	grah 'seize'	car 'move'
PRESENT	VI kṣipati	II khyāti	I gacchati	I gāyati	IX gṛhṇāti	I carati
PERFECT	cikṣepa	cakhyau	jagāma	jagau	jagrāha	cacāra
AORIST			agāmat		ajīgrahat	acīcarat
FUTURE	kṣepsyati	khyāsyati	gamiṣyati	gāsyati	grahīṣyati	cariṣyati
PASSIVE	kṣipyate	khyāyate	gamyate	gīyate	gṛhyate	caryate
CAUSATIVE	kṣepayati	khyāpayati	gamayati	gāpayati	grāhayati	cārayati
PAST PARTICIPLE	kṣipta	khyāta	gata	gīta	gṛhīta	carita
ABSOLUTIVE in ya	-kṣipya	-khyāya	-gatya/-gamya	-gīya	-gṛhya	-carya
INFINITIVE	kṣeptum	khyātum	gantum	gātum	grahītum	caritum
GERUNDIVE in ya	kṣepya	-khyeya	gamya	geya	grāhya	
NOMINAL in ana	kṣepaṇam		gamanaṃ		grahaṇaṃ	caraṇaṃ
" in in	-kṣepin		gāmin	gāyin	grāhin	cārin

ROOT	ci 'collect'	chid 'cut'	jan 'be born'	ji 'win'	jīv 'live'	jñā 'know'
PRESENT	V cinoti	VII chinatti	IV jāyate	I jayati	I jīvati	IX jānāti
PERFECT	cikāya	ciccheda	jajñe	jigāya	jijīva	jajñau
AORIST		achidat/achaitsīt	ajaniṣṭa	ajaiṣīt		ajñāsit
FUTURE	ceṣyati	chetsyati	janiṣyati	jeṣyati	jīviṣyati	jñāsyati
PASSIVE	cīyate	chidyate		jīyate	jīvyate	jñāyate
CAUSATIVE	cāyayate	chedayati	janayati		jīvayati	jñāpayati
PAST PARTICIPLE	cita	chinna	jāta	jita	jīvita	jñāta
ABSOLUTIVE in ya	-citya	-chidya		-jitya	-jīvya	-jñāya
INFINITIVE	cetum	chettum		jetum	jīvitum	jñātum
GERUNDIVE in ya	ceya	chedya		jeya		jñeya

	cayanaṃ / -cāyin	chedanaṃ / -chedin	-jāyin		jīvanaṃ / -jīvin	jñānam
NOMINAL in ana / " in in	cayanaṃ / -cāyin	chedanaṃ / -chedin	-jāyin		jīvanaṃ / -jīvin	jñānam
ROOT	tan 'stretch'	tud 'strike'	tṛ 'cross'	tuṣ 'be content'	tyaj 'forsake'	tvar 'hurry'
PRESENT	VIII tanoti	VI tudati	I tarati	IV tuṣyati	I tyajati	I tvarate
PERFECT	tatāna	tutoda	tatāra	tutoṣa	tatyāja	tatvare
AORIST			atārṣīt		atyākṣīt	
FUTURE			tariṣyati		tyakṣyati / tyajiṣyati	
PASSIVE	tanyate	tudyate	tīryate		tyajyate	tvaryate
CAUSATIVE	tānayati	todayati	tārayati	toṣayati	tyājayati	tvarayati
PAST PARTICIPLE	tata	tunna	tīrṇa	tuṣṭa	tyakta	tvarita
ABSOLUTIVE in ya	-tatya / -tāya	-tudya	-tīrya	-tuṣya	-tyajya	
INFINITIVE			taritum		tyaktum	
GERUNDIVE in ya			tārya		tyajya	
NOMINAL in ana			taraṇam	toṣaṇam		
" in in				toṣin	tyāgin	
ROOT	dah 'burn'	dā 'give'	duṣ 'spoil'	diś 'point'	dṛś 'see'	dru 'run'
PRESENT	I dahati	III dadāti	IV duṣyati	VI diśati	I paśyati	I dravati
PERFECT	dadāha	dadau		dideśa	dadarśa	dudrāva
AORIST	adhākṣīt	adāt		adikṣat	adrākṣīt / adarśat	
FUTURE	dhakṣyati	dāsyati		dekṣyati	drakṣyati	
PASSIVE	dahyate	dīyate		diśyate	dṛśyate	
CAUSATIVE	dāhayati	dāpayati	dūṣayati	deśayati	darśayati	drāvayati

PAST PARTICIPLE	druta	dṛṣṭa	duṣṭa	diṣṭa	datta	dagdha
ABSOLUTIVE	-drutya	-dṛśya		-diśya	-dāya	-dahya
INFINITIVE	drotum	draṣṭum		deṣṭum	dātum	dagdhum
GERUNDIVE in ya		dṛśya	dūṣya	deśya	deya	dāhya
NOMINAL in ana	dravaṇam	darśanam	dūṣaṇam		dānam	dahanam
,, in in		-darśin	-dūṣin	deśin	dāyin	dāhin

ROOT	naś 'perish'	nam 'bow'	nand 'be glad'	dhṛ 'hold'	dhā 'put'	druh 'hurt'
PRESENT	IV naśyati	I namati	I nandati	(I dharati)	III dadhāti	IV druhyati
PERFECT	nanāśa	nanāma	nananda	dadhāra	dadhau	dudruhe
AORIST	anaśat	anaṃsīt			adhāt	adruhat
FUTURE	naśiṣyati/naṅkṣyati	naṃsyati		dhariṣyati	dhāsyati	
PASSIVE		namyate	nandyate	dhriyate	dhīyate	
CAUSATIVE	nāśayati	namayati	nandayati	dhārayati	dhāpayati	
PAST PARTICIPLE	naṣṭa	nata	nandita	dhṛta	hita	drugdha
ABSOLUTIVE in ya		-namya	-nandya	-dhṛtya	-dhāya	-druhya
INFINITIVE		namitum/nantum		dhartum	dhātum	drogdhum
GERUNDIVE in ya			-nandya	dhārya	dheya	
NOMINAL in ana	naśanam	namanam	nandana	dhāraṇam	-dhānam	
,, in in			nandin	dhārin	-dhāyin	drohin

ROOT	pā 'drink'	pad 'go'	pac 'cook'	pat 'fall'	nṛt 'dance'	nī 'lead'
PRESENT	I pibati	IV padyate	I pacati	I patati	IV nṛtyati	I nayati
PERFECT	papau	papāda	papāca	papāta	nanarta	nināya
AORIST	apāt	apādi		apaptat		anaiṣīt

FUTURE	neṣyati	nartiṣyati	pakṣyati	patiṣyati	patsyate	pāsyati
PASSIVE	nīyate	nṛtyate	pacyate			pīyate
CAUSATIVE	nāyayati	nartayati	pācayati	pātayati	pādayati	pāyayati
PAST PARTICIPLE	nīta	nṛtta	(pakva)	patita	panna	pīta
ABSOLUTIVE in ya	-nīya			-patya	-padya	-pāya
INFINITIVE	netum	nartitum		patitum	pattum	pātum
GERUNDIVE in ya	neya					peya
NOMINAL in ana	nayanam	nartanam	pacanam	patanam		pānam
" in in	-nāyin	nartin		pātin	-pādin	-pāyin

ROOT	pṛ 'fill'	bandh 'bind'	budh 'wake'	brū 'say'	bhaj 'divide'
PRESENT	III piparti	IX badhnāti	I bodhati/ IV budhyate	II bravīti	I bhajati
PERFECT	pupūre	babandha	bubudhe		babhāja
AORIST			abuddha		abhākṣit
FUTURE		bhantsyati	bhotsyate		bhakṣyati
PASSIVE	pūryate	badhyate	budhyate		bhajyate
CAUSATIVE	pūrayati	bandhayati	bodhayati		bhājayati
PAST PARTICIPLE	pūrṇa/pūrta	baddha	buddha		bhakta
ABSOLUTIVE in ya	-pūrya	-badhya	-budhya		-bhajya
INFINITIVE		bandhum	boddhum		bhaktum
GERUNDIVE in ya		bandhya	bodhya		
NOMINAL in ana	pūraṇam	bandhanam	bodhanam		bhajanam
" in in		bandhin	bodhin		bhajin

ROOT	bhañj 'break'	bhid 'split'	bhī 'fear'	bhuj 'enjoy'	bhū 'be'	bhṛ 'carry'
PRESENT	VII bhanakti	VII bhinatti	III bibheti	VII bhunakti	I bhavati	III bibharti

	bhañj	bhid	bhī	bhuj	bhū	bhṛ
PERFECT	babhañja	bibheda	bibhāya	bubhuje	babhūva	babhāra
AORIST	abhāṅkṣīt		abhaiṣīt	abhaukṣīt	abhūt	abhārṣīt
FUTURE	bhaṅkṣyati	bhetsyati		bhokṣyate	bhaviṣyati	bhariṣyati
PASSIVE	bhajyate	bhidyate	bhiyate	bhujyate	bhūyate	bhriyate
CAUSATIVE	(bhañjayati)	bhedayati	bhāyayati/bhīṣayate	bhojayati	bhāvayati	bhārayati
PAST PARTICIPLE	bhagna	bhinna	bhīta	bhukta	bhūta	bhṛta
ABSOLUTIVE in ya	-bhajya	-bhidya	-bhīya		-bhūya	-bhṛtya
INFINITIVE		bhettum	bhetum	bhoktum	bhavitum	bhartum
GERUNDIVE in ya		bhedya		bhojya	bhāvya	bhārya
NOMINAL in ana	bhañjanam	bhedanam		bhojanam	bhavanam	bharaṇam
,, in in		bhedin		bhojin	bhāvin	bhārin

ROOT	bhram 'wander'	mad 'rejoice'	man 'think'	muc 'let go'	mṛ 'die'	yaj 'sacrifice'
PRESENT	I bhramati/IV bhrāmyati	IV mādyati	IV manyate	VI muñcati	IV mriyate	I yajati
PERFECT	babhrāma		mene	mumoca	mamāra	iyāja
AORIST		amādīt	amaṃsta	amucat		ayākṣīt
FUTURE	bhramiṣyati		maṃsyate	mokṣyati	mariṣyati	yakṣyati
PASSIVE			manyate	mucyate	(mriyate)	ijyate
CAUSATIVE	bhrāmayati	mādayati	mānayati	mocayati	mārayati	yājayati
PAST PARTICIPLE	bhrānta	matta	mata	mukta	mṛta	iṣṭa
ABSOLUTIVE in ya	-bhramya		-manya/-matya	-mucya		
INFINITIVE	bhrāntum		mantum	moktum	martum	yaṣṭum

GERUNDIVE in ya	ijya		mocya			
NOMINAL in ana	yajanaṃ	maraṇaṃ	mocanaṃ	mananaṃ	madana	bhramaṇaṃ
„ in in	yajin	-mārin	-mocin	mānin		
ROOT	rakṣ 'guard'	yudh 'fight'	yuj 'join'	yā 'go'	yam 'reach'	yat 'strive'
PRESENT	I rakṣati	IV yudhyate	VII yunakti	II yāti	I yacchati	I yatate
PERFECT	rarakṣa	yuyodha	yuyoja	yayau	yayāma	
AORIST	arakṣīt	ayuddha	ayujat	ayāsīt		
FUTURE	rakṣiṣyati	yotsyati	yokṣyati	yāsyati	yamiṣyati	yatiṣyati
PASSIVE	rakṣyate	yudhyate	yujyate		yamyate	yatyate
CAUSATIVE	rakṣayati	yodhayati	yojayati	yāpayati	yāmayati	yātayati
PAST PARTICIPLE	rakṣita	yuddha	yukta	yāta	yata	yatta
ABSOLUTIVE in ya	-rakṣya	-yudhya	-yujya	-yāya	-yamya	
INFINITIVE	rakṣitum	yoddhum	yoktum	yātum	yantum/ yamitum	

GERUNDIVE in ya	rakṣya	yodhya	yojya			
NOMINAL in ana	rakṣaṇaṃ	yodhanaṃ	yojanaṃ	yānaṃ	yamanaṃ	-yatanaṃ
„ in in	rakṣin	yodhin		yāyin	yamin	
ROOT	likh 'write'	lamb 'hang'	labh 'grasp'	ruh 'ascend'	rudh 'obstruct'	rabh 'grasp'
PRESENT	VI likhati	I lambate	I labhate	I rohati	VII runad-dhi	I rabhate
PERFECT	lilekha	lalambe	lebhe	ruroha	rurodha	rebhe
AORIST				aruhat/ arukṣat	arudhat/ arautsīt	
FUTURE	likhiṣyati	lambiṣyate	lapsyate	rokṣyati	rotsyati	rapsyate

PASSIVE	rabhyate	rudhyate	ruhyate	labhyate	lambyate	likhyate
CAUSATIVE	rambhayati	rodhayati	rohayati/ropayati	lambhayati	lambhayati	lekhayati
PAST PARTICIPLE	rabdha	ruddha	rūḍha	labdha	lambita	likhita
ABSOLUTIVE in ya	-rabhya	-rudhya	-ruhya	-labhya	-labhya	-likhya
INFINITIVE	rabdhum	roddhum	roḍhum	labdhum	lambitum	likhitum
GERUNDIVE in ya		-rodhya		labhya	labhya	lekhya
NOMINAL in ana	-rambhaṇam	rodhanam	rohaṇam	lambhanam	-lambanam	lekhanam
„ in in	rambhin	rodhin	rohin	lābhin	-lambin	lekhin

ROOT	vac 'speak'	vad 'speak'	vas 'dwell'	vah 'carry'	vid 'know'	viś 'enter'
PRESENT	II vakti	I vadati	I vasati	I vahati	II vetti (pres. perf. veda)	VI viśati
PERFECT	uvāca		uvāsa	uvāha	viveda	viveśa
AORIST	avocat	avādit	avātsīt	avākṣit	avedit	avikṣat
FUTURE	vakṣyati	vadiṣyati	vatsyati	vakṣyati	vetsyati	vekṣyati
PASSIVE	ucyate	udyate	uṣyate	uhyate	vidyate	viśyate
CAUSATIVE	vācayati	vādayati	vāsayati	vāhayati	vedayati	veśayati
PAST PARTICIPLE	ukta	udita	uṣita	ūḍha	vidita	viṣṭa
ABSOLUTIVE in ya	-ucya	-udya	-uṣya	-uhya		-viśya
INFINITIVE	vaktum	vaditum	vastum/vasitum	voḍhum	veditum	veṣṭum
GERUNDIVE in ya	vācya	vadya		vāhya	vedya	veśya
NOMINAL in ana	vacanam	vadanam	vasanam	vahanam	vedanam	
„ in in	vācin	vādin	vāsin	vāhin	vedin	

ROOT	vṛt 'turn'	vṛdh 'in-crease'	śak 'be able'	śī 'lie'	śuc 'grieve'	śram 'be tired'

	vart	vardh	śak	śī	śuc	śram
PRESENT	I vartate	I vardhate	V śaknoti	II śete	I śocati	IV śrāmyati
PERFECT	vavarta	vavardha	śaśāka	śiśye	śuśoca	śaśrāma
AORIST	avṛtat	avṛdhat/avardhiṣṭa	aśakat	aśayiṣṭa	aśucat	
FUTURE	vartsyate/vartiṣyate	vartsyati	śakṣyati	śayiṣyate	śociṣyati	
PASSIVE			śakyate			śramyate
CAUSATIVE	vartayati	vardhayati		śāyayati	śocayati	śrāmayati
PAST PARTICIPLE	vṛtta	vṛddha	śakta	śayita		śrānta
ABSOLUTIVE in ya	-vṛtya			-śayya		-śramya
INFINITIVE	vartitum	vardhitum		śayitum	śocitum	
GERUNDIVE in ya			śakya		śocya	
NOMINAL in ana	vartanam	vardhanam		śayanam	-śocanam	śramaṇa
,, in in	vartin	vardhin		śayin	-śocin	

ROOT	śri 'resort'	śru 'hear'	sañj 'adhere'	sad 'sit'	sah 'endure'	sṛj 'emit'
PRESENT	I śrayati	V śṛṇoti	I sajati	I sīdati	I sahate	VI sṛjati
PERFECT	śiśrāya	śuśrāva	sasañja	sasāda		sasarja
AORIST	aśiśriyat	aśrauṣīt	asāṅkṣīt	asadat		asrākṣīt
FUTURE	śrayiṣyati	śroṣyati		satsyati/sidiṣyati	sahiṣyate	srakṣyati
PASSIVE	śrīyate	śrūyate	sajyate	sadyate	sahyate	sṛjyate
CAUSATIVE		śrāvayati	sañjayati	sādayati	sāhayati	sarjayati
PAST PARTICIPLE	śrita	śruta	sakta	sanna	soḍha	sṛṣṭa
ABSOLUTIVE in ya	-śritya	-śrutya	-sajya	-sadya	-sahya	-sṛjya
INFINITIVE	śrayitum	śrotum	saktum	sattum	soḍhum	sraṣṭum
GERUNDIVE in ya		śrāvya			sahya	

	stu 'praise'	sthā 'stand'	smṛ 'remember'	spṛś 'touch'	svap 'sleep'	han 'strike'
NOMINAL in ana	-śrayaṇam	śravaṇam	sadanam	sañjanam	sahanam	sarjanam
,, in in	-śrayin	śravin	sādin	saṅgin	-sāhin	-sargin
ROOT	stu 'praise'	sthā 'stand'	smṛ 'remember'	spṛś 'touch'	svap 'sleep'	han 'strike'
PRESENT	II stauti	I tiṣṭhati	I smarati	VI spṛśati	II svapiti	II hanti
PERFECT	tuṣṭāva	tasthau	sasmāra	pasparśa	suṣvāpa	jaghāna
AORIST	astāvīt/astauṣīt	asthāt		asprākṣīt	asvāpsīt	(avadhīt)
FUTURE	stoṣyati	sthāsyati	smariṣyati	sprakṣyati	svapsyati	haniṣyati
PASSIVE	stūyate	sthīyate	smaryate	spṛśyate	supyate	hanyate
CAUSATIVE	stāvayati	sthāpayati	smārayati	sparśayati	svāpayati	ghātayati
PAST PARTICIPLE	stuta	sthita	smṛta	spṛṣṭa	supta	hata
ABSOLUTIVE	-stutya	-sthāya	-smṛtya	-spṛśya		-hatya
INFINITIVE	stotum	sthātum	smartum	spraṣṭum	svaptum	hantum
GERUNDIVE in ya	stutya/stavya	stheya	smarya	spṛśya		(vadhya)
NOMINAL in ana	stavanam	sthānam	smaraṇam	sparśanam	svapanam	hananam
,, in in		sthāyin	smārin	sparśin		ghātin

	hā 'leave'	hṛ 'take'	hve 'call'
ROOT	hā 'leave'	hṛ 'take'	hve 'call'
PRESENT	III jahāti	I harati	I hvayati
PERFECT	jahau	jahāra	juhāva
AORIST	ahāt/ahāsit	ahārṣīt	
FUTURE	hāsyati	hariṣyati	
PASSIVE	hīyate	hriyate	hūyate

CAUSATIVE	hāpayati	hārayati	hvāyayati
PAST PARTICIPLE	hīna	hṛta	hūta
ABSOLUTIVE in ya	-hāya	-hṛtya	-hūya
INFINITIVE	hātum	hartum	hvātum
GERUNDIVE in ya	heya	hārya	
NOMINAL in ana	hānam	haraṇam	hvānam
,, in in	hāyin	hārin	

Appendix 3

Classical Metres

1 Anuṣṭubh

Normal form:

    o o o o ᴗ – – o / o o o o ᴗ – ᴗ o (half-verse)

(i) The second or third syllable of each pāda must be heavy.

(ii) The half-verse must not end ᴗ – ᴗ – ᴗ o.

Permitted variant forms of the first or third pāda:

(*a*) o o – ⎫
         ⎬ – ᴗ ᴗ ᴗ o (i.e. the fourth syllable as well as the
   o – ᴗ ⎭   second or third must be heavy)

(*b*) o – ᴗ – – ᴗ ᴗ o

(*c*) o – ᴗ – – / – – o (caesura after fifth syllable)

(*d*) o o o – / – ᴗ – o (caesura after fourth syllable)

2 Samacatuṣpadī metres (in order of length)

(Name; analysis, including caesura; definition, normally taken from Kedāra's *Vṛttaratnākara*.)

Indravajrā – – ᴗ – – ᴗ ᴗ – ᴗ – – (t t j g g)

    syād Indravajrā yadi tau ja ;gau gaḥ

Upendravajrā ᴗ – ᴗ – – ᴗ ᴗ – ᴗ – – (j t j g g)

    Upendravajrā ja ;ta ;jās tato gau

Upajāti Any mixture of Indravajrā and Upendravajrā pādas (i.e. first syllable light or heavy at will)

Rathoddhatā – ∪ – ∪ ∪ ∪ – ∪ – ∪ – (r n r l g)

 rān na;rāv iha Rathoddhatā la;gau

Vaṃśastha ∪ – ∪ – – ∪ ∪ – ∪ – ∪ – (j t j r)

 ja;tau tu Vaṃśastham udīritaṃ ja;rau

Indravaṃśā – – ∪ – – ∪ ∪ – ∪ – ∪ – (t t j r)

 syād Indravaṃśā ta;ta;jai ra-saṃyutaiḥ

Vaṃśamālā Any mixture of Vaṃśastha and Indravaṃśā pādas (i.e. first syllable light or heavy at will)

Vasantatilakā – – ∪ – ∪ ∪ ∪ – ∪ ∪ – ∪ – – (t bh j j g g)

 uktā Vasantatilakā ta;bha;jā ja;gau gaḥ

Mālinī ∪ ∪ ∪ ∪ ∪ ∪ – – / – ∪ – – ∪ – – (n n m y y 8+7)

 na;na;ma;ya;ya-yut» êyaṃ / Mālinī bhogi;lokaiḥ

Śikhariṇī ∪ – – – – – / ∪ ∪ ∪ ∪ ∪ – – ∪ ∪ ∪ – (y m n s bh l
 g 6+11)

 rasai rudraiś chinnā / ya;ma;na;sa;bha;lā gaḥ
 Śikhariṇī

Hariṇī ∪ ∪ ∪ ∪ ∪ – / – – – – / ∪ – ∪ ∪ – ∪ – (n s m r s l g
 6+4+7)

 rasa;yuga;hayair / n;sau m;rau s;lau go / yadā Hariṇī
 tadā

Mandākrāntā – – – – / ∪ ∪ ∪ ∪ ∪ – / – ∪ – – ∪ – – (m bh n t
 t g g 4+6+7)

 Mandākrāntā / jaladhi;ṣaḍ;agair / m;bhau na;tau
 tād gurū cet

Śārdūlavikrīḍitam – – – ∪ ∪ – ∪ – ∪ ∪ ∪ – / – – ∪ – – ∪ –
 (m s j s t t g 12+7)

 sūry»;âśvair yadi māt sa;jau sa;ta;ta;gāh / Śārdūlavikrīḍitam

Sragdharā – – – – ∪ – – / ∪ ∪ ∪ ∪ ∪ ∪ – / – ∪ – – ∪ – –
 (m r bh n y y y 7+7+7)

 m;ra;bh;nair yānāṃ trayeṇa / tri‿muni:yati-yutā /
 Sragdharā kīrtit» êyam

y ∪ – –	bh – ∪ ∪	*Symbolic numbers*
r – ∪ –	j ∪ – ∪	4　**yuga** (age of world); **jaladhi**
t – – ∪	s ∪ ∪ –	(ocean)
m – – –	n ∪ ∪ ∪	6　**rasa** (flavour)
g̣ –	l ∪	7　**loka** (world); **aśva, haya**

7　**loka** (world); **aśva, haya**
　　(horse); **aga** (mountain); **muni**
　　(star of Great Bear)
8　**bhogin** (serpent-demon)
11　**rudra** (god)
12　**sūrya** (sun)

3 Ardhasamacatuṣpadī metres

(The bracketed syllable occurs only in the second and fourth pādas.)

Viyoginī ∪ ∪ – (–) ∪ ∪ – ∪ – ∪ – (s s j g̣+s bh r l g̣)

　　viṣame sa;sa;jā guruḥ, same
　　sa;bha;rā lo ›tha gurur Viyoginī

Mālabhāriṇī ∪ ∪ – (–) ∪ ∪ – ∪ – ∪ – – (s s j g̣ g̣+s bh r y)

　　sa;sa;jāḥ prathame pade gurū cet
　　sa;bha;rā yena ca Mālabhāriṇī syāt

Aparavaktra ∪ ∪ ∪ ∪ (–) ∪ ∪ – ∪ – ∪ – (n n r l g̣+n j j r)

　　a:yuji na;na;ra;lā guruḥ, same
　　tad Aparavaktram idaṃ na;jau ja;rau

Puṣpitāgrā ∪ ∪ ∪ ∪ (–) ∪ ∪ – ∪ – ∪ – – (n n r y+n j j r g̣)

　　a:yuji na-yuga;repha˜to yakāro
　　yuji ca na;jau ja;ra;gāś ca Puṣpitāgrā

(*Note*: Both the first two metres are known by a number of other names.)

4 Āryā

1	2	3	/	4	5	6
	∪ – ∪			∪ – ∪		∪ – ∪
∪ ∪ ∪ ∪	∪ ∪ ∪ ∪	∪ ∪ ∪ ∪		∪ ∪ ∪ ∪	∪ ∪ ∪ ∪	∪/∪ ∪ ∪
– –	– –	– –		– –	– –	– –

7   8
◡◡ ◡◡
–   –   – (half-verse)

In the usual form of the second half-verse a light syllable
replaces the whole of the sixth foot. Such a stanza, made up of
30+27 mātras, constitutes the Āryā proper.

Āryā 30+27
Udgīti 27+30
Upagīti 27+27
Gīti 30+30
Āryāgīti or Skandhaka 32+32 (i.e. the eighth foot is
    extended to – – or ◡◡ –)

Sanskrit–English Exercises: Transcription

Exercise 2b

1 gacchāmi   2 atra na praviśāmaḥ   3 punar api likhati
4 adhunā kva vasatha?   5 evam icchasi?   6 kva punas
tiṣṭhanti?   7 katham, ita āgacchati?   8 atra kim
ānayataḥ?   9 paśyāmi likhāmi ca   10 bhramat› îva
11 nṛtyatho gāyathaś ca   12 smaranti ca śocanti ca
13 'atra praviśāva' iti vadataḥ   14 adhunā ›pi katham
n› āgacchati?   15 jayām› îti mādyāmi   16 na jīvant› îti
śocāmaḥ

Exercise 3a

1 ācāryam śiṣyā ānayanti   2 apy aśvān icchasi?   3
aham sūrya;candrau paśyāmi   4 sukham ko n› êcchati?
5 svalpam bhojanam   6 jalam aśvān naro nayati   7
'kas tvam?' iti mām pṛcchataḥ   8 kam parvatam
paṇḍito gacchati?   9 atra krodho na vasat› îti vanam
praviśataḥ   10 śīghram vacanam n› âvagacchāmaḥ
11 ācārya, parvata iva sa gajaḥ   12 kam punaḥ pṛcchāmi?   13 kim śiṣyā yūyam?   14 jalam nara;bālāḥ
praviśanti   15 'ramaṇīyam adhunā tat phalam' iti
vismitā vadanti   16 katham, atr› âpi bālāḥ?   17 duḥ-
khāny api phalam ānayanti   18 'bālā, atra kim sukham
paśyath›?' êti śiṣyān ācāryo vadati

Exercise 4a

1 putraiḥ saha gṛham tyajati 2 etad udyānam—pravíśāmaḥ 3 ācāryeṇa ca śiṣyaiś c› âdbhutaḥ prayatnaḥ kṛtaḥ 4 priyo madīyo vayasya iti jīvitam etena tyaktam 5 ka eṣa gṛham āgacchati? 6 ramaṇīyena darśanena kiṃ na mādyasi? 7 dṛṣṭam avagatam ca 8 'atr› aîte narāḥ kim icchant›?' îti kutūhalena gṛham praviśati 9 dūram eva nagaram, vayaṃ ca pariśrāntā bhramāmaḥ 10 icchath› aîv› aîtan, na vā? 11 'kṛtaṃ vacanair, gato ›vasara' iti viṣādena vadataḥ 12 putrāḥ, sa ev› aîṣo ›vasaraḥ 13 ete vayaṃ nagaram āgatāḥ 14 vismṛto vayasyābhyāṃ prathamo viṣādaḥ 15 'he paṇḍita, tvam aśvaṃ kva nayas›?' îti pṛṣṭo ›pi vacanam na vadati 16 kiṃ prayatnena?—n› aîva tvāṃ paśyati devaḥ

Exercise 5a

1 imau svaḥ 2 prativacanaṃ me śrutvā kim anyad icchanti? 3 n› âsty eva te pustakam 4 vayasya, hṛdayam iv› âsi mama 5 asminn udyāne muhūrtam upaviśāvaḥ 6 kṣetreṣu sarve bhramanti 7 deva, anyasmān nagarād brāhmaṇaḥ kaścid āgataḥ 8 kam upāyaṃ paśyasi mama putrāṇāṃ darśanāya? 9 krodham asya dṛṣṭv» āvega iva no hṛdaye 10 ayaṃ kumāras tiṣṭhati 11 katham, kṣaṇam ev› ôpaviśya dṛṣṭe mayā punar api mitre 12 anyaḥ ko ›pi mārgo na bhavati 13 duḥkhāy› aîva mitrāṇām idānīṃ Rāmasya darśanam 14 anyebhyo ›pi deven› aîtac chrutam 15 gṛham praviśya 'kva kv› êdānīm sa pāpa?' iti sarvān pṛcchati 16 andhānāṃ deśe kāṇa eva prabhavati 17 Kalahaṃsaka, ken» aîtan Mādhavasya praticchandakam abhilikhitam?

Exercise 6ā

1 Śoṇottare, kim āgamana-prayojanam? 2 kaṣṭam, anartha-dvayam āpatitam 3 mahārāja, api kuśalaṃ kumāra:Lakṣmaṇasya? 4 kutaḥ punar iyaṃ vārttā? 5 satyam ittham:bhūta ev› âsmi 6 amātya, vistīrṇaḥ Kusumapura-vṛttāntaḥ 7 tvam āryābhiḥ putra iva gṛhītaḥ 8 katamasmin pradeśe Mārīc›-âśramaḥ? 9 amba, kā ›si? kim-artham ahaṃ tvayā pratiṣiddhaḥ? 10 nanv anuśaya-sthānam etat 11 s» aîv› êyam 12 ubhābhyām api vāṃ Vāsava-niyojyo Duḥṣantaḥ praṇa-mati 13 kaṣṭā khalu sevā 14 na khalu Vṛṣalasya śravaṇa-patham upagato ›yaṃ mayā kṛtaḥ Kaumudī-mahotsava-pratiṣedhaḥ? 15 kiṃ tav› ânayā cintayā? 16 Mādhavya, apy asti te Śakuntalā-darśanaṃ prati kutūhalam? 17 śrotriya-likhitāny akṣarāṇi prayatna-likhitāny api niyatam asphuṭāni bhavanti

Exercise 7a

1 aye, iyaṃ devī 2 pratibodhita ev› âsmi ken› âpi 3 idam amātya:Rākṣasa-gṛham 4 aho vatsalena su-hṛdā viyuktāḥ smaḥ 5 su:vicintitaṃ bhagavatyā 6 ārya, api sahyā śiro-vedanā? 7 lajjayati mām atyanta: saujanyam eṣām 8 tena h› îmāṃ kṣīra-vṛkṣa-cchā-yām āśrayāmaḥ 9 ciram adarśanen› āryasya vayam udvignāḥ 10 svāgataṃ devyai 11 alam asmad-avinay›-āśaṅkayā 12 amātya, kalpitam anena yoga-cūrṇa-miśram auṣadhaṃ Candraguptāya 13 aye, Urvaśī-gātra-sparśād iva nirvṛtam me śarīram 14 ārye, kim atyāhitaṃ Sītā:devyāḥ? 15 yāvad imān vedī-saṃstaraṇ›-ârtham darbhān ṛtvigbhya upaha-rāmi 16 kathitam Avalokitayā 'Madan›-ôdyānaṃ gato Mādhava' iti 17 kaṣṭam, ubhayor apy asthāne yatnaḥ 18 n› âyaṃ kathā-vibhāgo ›smābhir anyena vā śruta: pūrvaḥ 19 vayam api tāvad bhavatyau sakhī-gataṃ kiṃcit pṛcchāmaḥ 20 amātya, idam ābharaṇaṃ kumāreṇa sva:śarīrād avatārya preṣitam

Exercise 8a

1 hanta, siddh‹:ârthau svaḥ 2 kṛtaṃ Rāma-sadṛśaṃ karma 3 asti dakṣiṇāpathe Padmapuraṃ nāma nagaram 4 vayasya, itaḥ stambh‹-âpavārita:śarīrau tiṣṭhāvaḥ 5 ramaṇīyaḥ khalu divas‹-âvasāna-vṛttānto rāja-veśmani 6 kim-artham a:gṛhīta:mudraḥ kaṭakān niṣkrāmasi? 7 vatsa, alam ātm‹-âparādha-śaṅkayā 8 bho bhoḥ, kiṃ:prayojano ›yam aśvaḥ parivṛtaḥ paryaṭati? 9 kāṃ punar atrabhavatīm avagacchāmi? 10 kumāra, n› âyam atyanta:durbodho ›rthaḥ 11 kiṃ tv amātya:Rākṣasaś Cāṇakye baddha:vairo, na Candragupte 12 tad eṣa svayaṃ parīkṣita:guṇān brāhmaṇān preṣayāmi 13 hā kaṣṭam, atibībhatsa:karmā nṛśaṃso ›smi saṃvṛttaḥ 14 katham, kṛta:mahā? ›parādho ›pi bhagavatībhyām anukampito Rāmaḥ 15 yāvad idānīm avasita:saṃdhyā-jāpyaṃ mahārājaṃ paśyāmi 16 sa tad› aîva devyāḥ Sītāyās tādṛśaṃ daiva-durvipākam upaśrutya vaikhānasaḥ saṃvṛttaḥ 17 a:phalam an:iṣṭa:phalaṃ vā Dāruvarmaṇaḥ prayatnam adhigacchāmi 18 sundari, a:parinirvāṇo divasaḥ 19 Śakuntalā-darśanād eva mand›:autsukyo ›smi nagara-gamanaṃ prati

Exercise 9a

1 kim uktavān asi? 2 samprati nivartāmahe vayam 3 kṛt›:âñjaliḥ praṇamati 4 sarvān abhivādaye vaḥ 5 sakhe Puṇḍarīka, n› aîtad anurūpaṃ bhavataḥ 6 yāvad upasthitāṃ homa-velāṃ gurave nivedayāmi 7 kaccid aham iva vismṛtavāṃs tvam api? 8 paravanto vayaṃ vismayena 9 ārya, api śatror vyasanam upalabdham? 10 tat kim ity āśaṅkase? 11 aham adhunā yath›_ādiṣṭam anutiṣṭhāmi 12 bhagavan, na khalu kaścid a:viṣayo nāma dhīmatām 13 Śakuntalā sakhīm aṅgulyā tarjayati 14 sādhu sakhe Bhūrivaso sādhu 15 kim ayaṃ pratibuddho ›bhihitavān? 16 atha sā tatrabhavatī kim:ākhyasya rāja:ṛṣeḥ patnī? 17 bhad-

ra, ath› âgni-praveśe suhṛdas te ko hetuḥ? 18 para-
vatī khalu tatrabhavatī, na ca saṃnihita:guru'janā
19 diṣṭyā dharma-patnī-samāgamena putra-mukha-
saṃdarśanena c› āyuṣmān vardhate 20 tat kim ayaṃ
āryeṇa sa_lekhaḥ puruṣaḥ Kusumapuraṃ prasthāpi-
taḥ? 21 tatrabhavān Kaṇvaḥ śāśvate brahmaṇi vartate, iyaṃ ca vaḥ sakhī tasy› ātmaj» êti katham etat?
22 mam› âpi Kaṇva-sutāṃ anusmṛtya mṛgayāṃ prati
nir_utsukaṃ cetaḥ 23 api Candragupta-doṣā atikrān-
ta:pārthiva-guṇān smārayanti prakṛtīḥ? 24 etāṃ
a:saṃbhāvyāṃ brāhmaṇasya pratijñāṃ śrutvā sa_sa-
civo rājā prahṛṣṭa:manā vismay›-ânvitaḥ sa_bahu-
mānaṃ tasmai Viṣṇuśarmaṇe kumārān samarpitavān

Exercise 10a

1 paśya Mādhavasy› âvasthāṃ 2 mahati viṣāde vartate
te sakhī:janaḥ 3 idaṃ tat pratyutpanna:mati~tvaṃ
strīṇāṃ 4 aho darśanīyāny akṣarāṇi 5 muhūrtam
upaviśata 6 bhoḥ śreṣṭhin Candanadāsa, evam
apathya-kāriṣu tīkṣṇa:daṇḍo rājā 7 anubhavatu rāj›-
âpathya-kāri~tvasya phalam 8 pratyāsannaḥ kila
mṛgayā-vihārī pārthivo Duḥṣantaḥ 9 gacchatāṃ
bhavantau 10 bhos tapasvin, cintayann api na khalu
svīkaraṇam atrabhavatyāḥ smarāmi 11 sakhe Mādhavya, dṛḍha:pratijño bhava 12 aho nir_daya~tā dur:
ātmanāṃ paurāṇām—aho Rāmasya rājñaḥ kṣipra:
kāri~tā 13 bhagavan Manmatha, kutas te kusum›
:āyudhasya sataḥ taikṣṇyam etat? 14 nanu bhavatyaḥ
paṭ-âñcalair vatsau vījayadhvam 15 bhagn›:ôtsāhaḥ
kṛto ›smi mṛgayā-›pavādinā Mādhavyena 16 aho bata,
kīdṛśīṃ vayo-›vasthām āpanno ›smi 17 adya śiṣṭ›-
ânadhyayanam iti khelatāṃ baṭūnāṃ ayaṃ kalakalaḥ
18 svairaṃ svairaṃ gacchantu bhavatyaḥ 19 pari-
trāyatāṃ suhṛdaṃ Mahārājaḥ 20 tatrabhavataḥ kula-
pater asāṃnidhyād rakṣāṃsi nas tapo-vighnam utpā-
dayanti 21 bhadra, anayā mudrayā mudray› aînam
22 śatru-prayuktānāṃ ca tīkṣṇa:rasa-dāyināṃ prati-

vidhānaṃ praty apramādinaḥ parīkṣita:bhaktayaḥ
kṣitipati-pratyāsannā niyuktāḥ puruṣāḥ 23 saṃprati
Madayantikā-saṃbandhena Nandaṃ-ôpagrahāt praty-
asta:śaṅkāḥ khalu vayam 24 bhāvinam enaṃ cakra-
vartinam avagacchatu bhavān 25 mayā tāvat suhṛtta-
masya Candanadāsasya gṛhe gṛha-janaṃ nikṣipya
nagarān nirgacchatā nyāyyam anuṣṭhitam 26 devi,
saṃstabhy› ātmānam anurudhyasva bhagavato Vasiṣ-
ṭhasy› ādeśam iti vijñāpayāmi

Exercise 11a

1 katham, iyaṃ sā Kaṇva-duhitā Śakuntalā? 2 vatse,
yad aham īhe tad astu te 3 he dhūrta, lekho nīyate, na
ca jñāyate 'kasy›?' êti? 4 priye Mālati, iyaṃ vīkṣyase
5 viśramyatāṃ parijanena 6 Mandārike, yad atra
vastuny eṣa te vallabhaḥ kathayati, api tathā tat?
7 devaṃ› aîvaṃ niṣiddhe ›pi Madh›-ûtsave, cūta-
kalikā-bhaṅgam ārabhase? 8 parirakṣyantām asya
prāṇāḥ 9 bho rājan, kim idaṃ joṣam āsyate? 10 tad
anuṣṭhīyatām ātmano ›bhiprāyaḥ 11 kiṃ c› âtisṛṣṭaḥ
Parvateśvara-bhrātre Vairodhakāya pūrva:pratiśruto
rājy›-ârdhaḥ 12 katham, 'Śakuntal›' êty asya mātur
ākhyā? 13 kaḥ sa mahā:puruṣo yen› aîtan mānuṣa-
mātra-duṣkaraṃ mahat karm› ânuṣṭhitam? 14 Priyaṃvadaka, jñāyatām 'kā velā vartata?' iti 15 ārya
Vaihīnare, dīyatām ābhyāṃ vaitālikābhyāṃ suvarṇa-
śata-sahasram 16 Vṛṣala kim ayam asthāna eva
mahān arth›-ôtsargaḥ kriyate? 17 bhoḥ śreṣṭhin, api
pracīyante saṃvyavahārāṇāṃ lābhāḥ? 18 bhagavati
Vasuṃdhare, ślāghyāṃ duhitaram avekṣasva Jānakīm
19 katham, nivāryamāṇo ›pi sthita eva? 20 bhagavan
Vālmīke, upanīyetām imau Sītā-garbha-saṃbhavau
Rāma:bhadrasya Kuśa;Lavau 21 yādṛśo ›yam, tādṛśau
tāv api 22 visṛṣṭaś ca Vāmadev›-ânumantrito medhyo
›śvaḥ. upakalpitāśca yathā_śāstraṃ tasya rakṣitāraḥ.
teṣām adhiṣṭhātā Lakṣmaṃ›-ātmajaś Candraketur
avāpta:divy›¹âstra-saṃpradāyaś catur:aṅga:sādhan›-

ânvito ›nuprahitaḥ 23 hanta, hanta, sarvathā nṛśaṃso
›smi, yaś cirasya dṛṣṭān priya:suhṛdaḥ priyān dārān
na snigdhaṃ paśyāmi 24 atha tasmād araṇyāt
parityajya nivṛtte Lakṣmaṇe Sītāyāḥ kiṃ vṛttam? iti
kācid asti pravṛttiḥ? 25 asti tāvad ekadā prasaṅgataḥ
kathita eva mayā Mādhav›:âbhidhānaḥ kumāro, yas
tvam iva māmakīnasya manaso dvitīyaṃ nibandhanam

Exercise 12a

1 bhadra, bhadra, na praveṣṭavyam   2 bhavatu, śṛṇomi
tāvad āsāṃ viśrambha-kathitāni 3 tūṣṇīṃ bhava,
yāvad ākarṇayāmi 4 amātya, tathā ›pi prārabdham
a:parityājyam eva   5 tad atra śāla-pracchāye muhūrtam āsana-parigrahaṃ karotu tātaḥ 6 samupadiśa
tam uddeśaṃ yatr› āste sa piṇḍapātī 7 hṛdaya sthirī˜
bhava. kim api te kaṣṭataram ākarṇanīyam 8 kim
anyad bravītu? 9 iyaṃ c› Ôrvaśī yāvad_āyus tava
sahadharmacāriṇī bhavatu 10 tad yāvac Chrīparva-
tam upanīya lavaśo lavaśa enāṃ nikṛtya duḥkha:ma-
raṇāṃ karomi 11 asti naḥ sucarita-śravaṇa-lobhād
anyad api praṣṭavyam 12 tat kim ity udāsate bhara-
tāḥ? 13 tatra c› aîvam anuṣṭheyaṃ yathā vadāmi
14 nanu bhavatībhyām eva Śakuntalā sthirīkartavyā
15 gṛhīta:gṛha˜sāram enaṃ sa_putra;kalatraṃ saṃ-
yamya rakṣa tāvad yāvan mayā Vṛṣalāya kathyate
16 sampraty Agasty›-āśramasya panthānaṃ brūhi
17 vinīta:veṣa-praveśyāni tapo-vanāni 18 maru-sthal-
yāṃ yathā vṛṣṭiḥ, kṣudh» ārte bhojanaṃ tathā 19
udghātinī bhūmir iti raśmi-saṃyamanād rathasya
mandībhūto vegaḥ 20 cakravartinaṃ putram āpnuhi
21 tat kiyantaṃ kālam asmābhir evaṃ sambhṛta:
balair api śatru-vyasanam avekṣamāṇair udāsitav-
yam? 22 yad» aîv› âṅgurīyaka-darśanād anusmṛtaṃ
devena 'satyam ūḍha:pūrvā rahasi mayā tatrabhavatī
Śakuntalā mohāt pratyādiṣṭ»' êti, tad» aîva paścāttā-
pam upagato devaḥ 23 mahā:dhana˜tvād bahu:pat-
nī˜ken› ânena bhavitavyam 24 amātya, īdṛśasy› ābha-

raṇa-viśeṣasya viśeṣataḥ kumāreṇa sva:gātrād avatārya prasādīkṛtasya kim ayaṃ parityāga-bhūmiḥ?
25 yāvac ca saṃbandhino na parāpatanti, tāvad vatsayā
Mālatyā nagara-devatā-gṛham avighna:maṅgalāya
gantavyam

Exercise 13a

1 dehi me prativacanam 2 tvayā saha Gautamī
gamiṣyati 3 kathaṃ, śūnyā iv› āmī pradeśāḥ 4 eṣa
tam iṣuṃ saṃdadhe 5 yadi rahasyaṃ, tadā tiṣṭhatu—
yadi na rahasyaṃ, tarhi kathyatām 6 aham apy amuṃ
vṛttāntaṃ bhagavatyai Lopāmudrāyai nivedayāmi 7
sa khalu mūrkhas taṃ yuṣmābhir atisṛṣṭaṃ prabhū-
tam artha-rāśim avāpya, mahatā vyayen› ôpabhoktum
ārabdhavān 8 diṣṭyā su:prabhātam adya, yad ayaṃ
devo dṛṣṭaḥ 9 kiṃ cid ākhyātu‑kāmā ›smi 10 upā-
lapsye tāvad enam 11 bhadra Siddhārthaka, kāmam
a:paryāptam idam asya priyasya, tathā ›pi gṛhyatām
12 ayam asau rāj›-ājñayā rāj›-âpathya-kārī kāyasthaḥ
Śakaṭadāsaḥ śūlam āropayituṃ nīyate 13 jñāsyathaḥ
khalv etat 14 puṇy›:âśrama-darśanen› ātmānaṃ punī-
mahe tāvat 15 bhadre, na tat parihāryaṃ, yato viva-
kṣitam an:uktam anutāpaṃ janayati 16 n› âyam
avasaro mama Śatakratuṃ draṣṭum 17 sakhe, na
tāvad enāṃ paśyasi, yena tvam evaṃ:vādī 18 aye, etās
tapasvi-kanyakāḥ sva:pramāṇ›-ânurūpaiḥ secana-gha-
ṭair bāla:pādapebhyaḥ payo dātum ita ev› âbhivar-
tante 19 na cen muni-kumārako ›yaṃ, tat ko ›sya
vyapadeśaḥ? 20 matimāṃś Cāṇakyas tucche prayojane kim iti Candraguptaṃ kopayiṣyati? na ca kṛta-
vedī Candragupta etāvatā gauravam ullaṅghayiṣyati
21 tena hi vijñāpyatām mad-vacanād upādhyāyaḥ
Somarātaḥ—'amūn āśrama-vāsinaḥ śrautena vidhinā
satkṛtya svayam eva praveśayitum arhas›' îti 22
smartavyaṃ tu saujanyam asya nṛpater, yad aparā-
dhinor apy an:aparāddhayor iva nau kṛta:prasādaṃ
ceṣṭitavān 23 he vyasana-sabrahmacārin, yadi na

guhyaṃ n› âtibhārikaṃ vā, tataḥ śrotum icchāmi te
prāṇa-parityāga-kāraṇam 24 ārya Vaihīnare, 'adya
prabhṛty an:ādṛtya Cāṇakyaṃ Candraguptaḥ svayam
eva rāja-kāryāṇi kariṣyat›' îti gṛhīt›:ârthāḥ kriyantāṃ
prakṛtayaḥ 25 vayam apy āśrama-bādhā yathā na
bhavati, tathā prayatiṣyāmahe 26 kim idānīṃ Candraguptaḥ sva:rājya-kārya:dhurām anyatra mantriṇy
ātmani vā samāsajya svayaṃ pratividhātum a:samar-
thaḥ? 27 yat satyaṃ, kāvya-viśeṣa-vedinyāṃ pariṣadi
prayuñjānasya mam› âpi su:mahān paritoṣaḥ prādur‾
bhavati 28 'Candragupta-śarīram abhidrogdhum
anena vyāpāritā Dāruvarm›:ādaya' iti nagare pra-
khyāpya Śakaṭadāsaḥ śūlam āropitaḥ 29 sa khalu kasmiṃś cid api jīvati Nand›-ânvay›-âvayave Vṛṣalasya
sācivyaṃ grāhayituṃ na śakyate 30 idam atra rāmaṇīyakam, yad amātya:Bhūrivasu ̓Devarātayoś cirāt
pūrṇo ›yam itaretar›-âpatya-saṃbandh›:âmṛta-mano-
rathaḥ

Exercise 14a

1 Priyaṃvadaka, jñāyatāṃ ko ›smad-darśan›-ârthī
dvāri tiṣṭhati 2 kva nu khalu gatā syāt? 3 āsīt tādṛśo
munir asminn āśrame 4 āyuṣman, śrūyatāṃ yad-
artham asmi Hariṇā tvat-sakāśaṃ preṣitaḥ 5 evam
ukto ›py aham enaṃ prābodhayaṃ punaḥ punaḥ 6
cirāt prabhṛty āryaḥ parityakt›:ôcita ̓śarīra‾saṃskāra
iti pīḍyate me hṛdayam 7 vismaya;harṣa:mūlaś ca
kolāhalo lokasy› ôdajihīta 8 tad ucyatāṃ pātra-
vargaḥ 'sveṣu sveṣu pāṭheṣv asaṃmūḍhair bhavitavyam' iti 9 sakhe, cintaya tāvat ken› âpadeśena
punar āśrama-padaṃ gacchāmaḥ 10 api nāma dur:
ātmanaś Cāṇakyāc Candragupto bhidyeta 11 ayam
asau mama jyāyān āryaḥ Kuśo nāma Bharat›-āśramāt
pratinivṛttaḥ 12 surata-kheda-prasuptayos tu ta-
yoḥ svapne bisa-guṇa-nigaḍita:pādo jaraṭhaḥ kaś
cij jālapādaḥ pratyadṛśyata. pratyabudhyetāṃ c›
ôbhau 13 tad anviṣyatāṃ yadi kā cid āpanna:sattvā

tasya bhāryā syāt 14 āryaputra, n› âyaṃ viśrambha-
kathāyā avasaras, tato laghutaram ev› âbhidhīyase
15 katham īdṛśena saha vatsasya Candraketor dvanda-
saṃprahāram anujānīyām? 16 ity avadhāry› âpasar-
paṇ›-âbhilāsiṇy aham abhavam 17 kasmin prayojane
mam› âyaṃ praṇidhiḥ prahita iti prabhūta⁀tvāt
prayojanānāṃ na khalv avadhārayāmi 18 yadi kaś cid
asty upāyāḥ pati-droha-pratikriyāyai, darśay› âmum—
matir hi te paṭīyasī 19 anay» aîva ca kathayā tayā saha
tasminn eva prāsāde tath» aîva pratiṣiddh›:âśeṣa⁚pari-
jana⁀praveśā divasam atyavāhayam 20 tad upāyaś
cintyatāṃ yathā saphala⁚prārthano bhaveyaṃ 21
śrutvā c› aîtat tam eva matta:hastinam udast›:âdho-
raṇo rāja-putro ›dhiruhya raṃhas» ôttamena rāja-
bhavanam abhyavartata 22 upalabdhavān asmi pra-
ṇidhibhyo yathā tasya mleccha-rāja-balasya madhyāt
pradhānatamāḥ pañca rājānaḥ parayā suhṛt⁀tayā Rākṣasam anuvartanta iti 23 yadi punar iyaṃ kiṃvadantī
mahārājaṃ prati syandet, tat kaṣṭaṃ syāt 24 ity
avadhāry› ânveṣṭum ādaram akaravam. anveṣamāṇaś
ca yathā yathā n› âpaśyaṃ taṃ, tathā tathā suhṛt-
sneha-kātareṇa manasā tat tad aśobhanam āśaṅka-
mānas taru-gahanāni candana-vīthikā latā-maṇḍa-
pān saraḥ-kūlāni ca vīkṣamāṇo nipuṇam itas tato
datta⁚dṛṣṭiḥ su:ciraṃ vyacaram 25 ekasmiṃś ca
pradeśe jhaṭiti vaṃ›-ânilen› ôpanītaṃ nirbhara:vikasite
›pi kānane ›bhibhūt›⁚ânya⁚kusuma⁀parimalaṃ visar-
pantam ati:surabhi⁀tayā ›nulimpantam iva tarpayan-
tam iva pūrayantam iva ghrāṇ›-êndriyam, ahamaha-
mikayā madhukara-kulair anubadhyamānam an:āgh-
rāta:pūrvam a:mānuṣa⁀lok›⁀ôcitaṃ kusuma-gandham
abhyajighram

Exercise 15

evaṃ:vādini deva:rṣau pārśve pitur adhomukhī |
līlā-kamala-pattrāṇi gaṇayām āsa Pārvatī ||84||

evam iti || *deva:ṛṣau* (: Aṅgirasi) *evaṃ:vādini* sati
Pārvatī pituḥ pārśve adhomukhī satī | lajjay» êti śeṣaḥ
| *līlā-kamala-pattrāṇi gaṇayām āsa* (: saṃcakhyau) |
lajjā-vaśāt kamala-dala-gaṇanā:vyājena harṣaṃ jugopı
êty arthaḥ | anenı âvahitth»:ākhyaḥ saṃcārī bhāva
uktaḥ | tad uktam—
'avahitthā tu lajj»:āder harṣ»:ādy-ākāra-gopanam'
iti ||

Śailaḥ sampūrṇa:kāmo ›pi Menā-mukham udaik-
ṣata |
    prāyeṇa gṛhiṇī:netrāḥ kanyā-›rtheṣu kuṭumbinaḥ
||85||

Śaila iti || *Śailaḥ* (: Himavān) *sampūrṇa:kāmo ›pi* |
dātuṃ kṛta:niścayo ›pı îty arthaḥ | *Menā-mukham
udaikṣata* | ucitı:ôttara-jijñāsay» êti bhāvaḥ | tathā hi |
prāyeṇa kuṭumbinaḥ (: gṛhasthāḥ) *kanyā-›rtheṣu*
(: kanyā-prayojaneṣu) *gṛhiṇy* eva *netraṃ* (: kārya-
jñāna-kāraṇam) *yeṣāṃ* te tath» ôktāḥ | kalatra:pra-
dhāna:vṛttaya ity arthaḥ ||

mene Menā ›pi tat sarvaṃ patyuḥ kāryam abhīpsi-
tam |
    bhavanty avyabhicāriṇyo bhartur iṣṭe pati:vratāḥ
||86||

mena iti || *Menā ›pi patyuḥ* (: Himālayasya) *tat sar-
vam abhīpsitaṃ kāryaṃ mene* (: aṅgī˜cakāra) | tathā hi |
patir eva *vrataṃ yāsāṃ tāḥ bhartur iṣṭe* (: abhīpsite)
(na vidyate vyabhicāro yāsāṃ tāḥ:) *avyabhicāriṇyo
bhavanti* | bhartṛ-cittı-âbhiprāya-jñā bhavantı îti
bhāvaḥ ||

'idam atrı ôttaraṃ nyāyyam' iti buddhyā vimṛśya
saḥ |
    ādade vacasām ante maṅgalı-âlaṃkṛtāṃ sutām ||87||

idam iti || *saḥ* (: Himavān) *vacasām ante* (: muni-

vāky›-âvasāne) *atra* (: muni-vakye) *idam* (: uttara:śloke
vakṣyamāṇaṃ dānam eva) *nyāyyam* (: nyāyād an:ape-
tam) *uttaram iti buddhyā* (: cittena) *vimṛśya* (: vicintya)
(maṅgalaṃ yathā tathā ›laṃkṛtāṃ :) *maṅgaḥ-âlaṃ-
kṛtāṃ sutām ādade* (: hastābhyāṃ jagrāha) ‖

'ehi, Viśvātmane, vatse, bhikṣā ›si parikalpitā |
arthino munayaḥ—prāptaṃ gṛhamedhi-phalaṃ
mayā' ‖88‖

eh› îti ‖ he *vatse* (: putri) *ehi* (: āgaccha) | tvaṃ *Viśvāt-
mane* (: Śivāya) *bhikṣā parikalpitā ›si* (: niścitā ›si) |
'ratn›_:ādi stamba_:paryantaṃ sarvaṃ bhikṣā tapasvinaḥ'
iti vacanād iti bhāvaḥ | *arthinaḥ* (: yācitāraḥ) *mu-
nayaḥ* | *mayā gṛhamedhinaḥ* (: gṛhasthasya) *phalaṃ
prāptam* | iha paratra ca tāraka‾tvāt pātre kanyā-
dānaṃ gārhasthyasya phalam ity arthaḥ ‖

etāvad uktvā tanayāṃ ṛṣīn āha mahīdharaḥ |
'iyaṃ namati vaḥ sarvāṃs Trilocana-vadhūr' iti
‖89‖

etāvad iti‖ *mahīdharaḥ* (: Himavān) *tanayām etāvat*
(: pūrv›:ôktam) *uktvā ṛṣīn āha* | kim iti? | '*iyaṃ Trilo-
cana-vadhūḥ* (: Tryambaka-patnī) *vaḥ sarvān namati*'
iti | 'Trilocana-vadhūr' iti siddha‾vad abhidhānen›
'â:vipratipannaṃ dānam' iti sūcayati ‖

īpsit›:ârtha-kriy›-ôdāraṃ te ›bhinandya girer vacaḥ
āśīrbhir edhayām āsuḥ puraḥ_:pākābhir Ambikām
‖90‖

īpsit›:ârth› eti ‖ *te* (: munayaḥ) *īpsit›:ârtha-kriyayā*
(:_iṣṭ›:ârtha-karaṇena) *udāraṃ* (: mahat) | 'udāro
dātṛ_:mahatoḥ' ity Amaraḥ | *gireḥ* (: Himavataḥ)
vacaḥ (: vacanam) *abhinandya* (: 'sādhv' iti saṃstutya) |
Ambikām (: Ambām) | 'pacyata' iti *pākaḥ* (: phalam)
| *puraḥ_:pākābhiḥ* (: puraskṛta_:phalābhiḥ) *āśīrbhiḥ*
(: āśīrvādaiḥ) *edhayām āsuḥ* (: saṃvardhayām āsuḥ) ‖

tāṃ praṇām›-ādara-srasta:jāmbūnada꞉vataṃsa-kam |

aṅkam āropayām āsa lajjamānām Arundhatī ||91||

tām iti || *praṇām›-ādareṇa* (: namaskār›-āsaktyā) *sraste jāmbūnade* (: suvarṇa-vikāre) *vataṃsake* (: kanaka-kuṇḍale) yasyās tāṃ *lajjamānāṃ tām* (: Ambikām) *Arundhatī aṅkam āropayām āsa* | 'ruhaḥ po ›nyatarasyām' iti pakāraḥ ||

tan-mātaraṃ c› âśru-mukhīṃ duhitṛ-sneha-vikla-vām |

varasy› ân:anya꞉pūrvasya vi:śokām akarod guṇaiḥ ||92||

tad iti || *duhitṛ-snehena* (: putrikā-premṇā) *viklavāṃ* (: 'viyokṣyata' iti bhītām) | ata ev› (âśrūṇi mukhe yasyās tām :) *aśrumukhīm* (tasyāḥ (: Ambikāyāḥ) mātaram :) *tan-mātaram* (: Menām) *ca* | (anyā pūrvaṃ yasy› âsti so :) ›nya:pūrvaḥ | 'sarvanāmno vṛtti-viṣaye puṃvad-bhāvaḥ' iti pūrva:padasya puṃvad-bhāvaḥ | ('sa na bhavat›' îty an:anya꞉pūrvas, tasya:) *an:anya꞉pūrvasya* | sāpatnya-duḥkham a:kurvata ity arthaḥ | *varasya* (: voḍhuḥ) *guṇaiḥ* (: mṛtyuṃjaya˜tv›:ādibhiḥ) *vi:śokām* (: nir_duḥkhām) *akarot* ||

vaivāhikīṃ tithiṃ pṛṣṭās tatkṣaṇaṃ Hara-ban-dhunā |

te tryahād ūrdhvam ākhyāya ceruś cīra:parigrahāḥ ||93||

vaivāhikīṃ iti || *cīra:parigrahāḥ* (: valkala-mātra: vasanāḥ) *te* (: tapasvinaḥ) *tatkṣaṇam* (: tasminn eva kṣaṇe) *Hara-bandhunā* (: Himavatā) *vaivāhikīṃ* (: vivāha-yogyāṃ) *tithiṃ pṛṣṭāḥ* (: 'k›?' êty anuyuktāḥ) santaḥ | trayāṇām ahnāṃ samāhāras try:ahaḥ | 'taddhit›:ârth›:ôttarapada:samāhāre ca' iti samāsaḥ | 'rāj›:âhaḥ:sakhibhyaṣ ṭac' iti ṭac:pratyayaḥ | dvigu˜ tvād ekavacanam | 'rātr›:âhn›:âhāḥ puṃsi' iti puṃ:

liṅga˜tā | (tasmāt :) try꞉ahāt ūrdhvam (: upari)
ākhyāya (: 'caturthe ›hani vivāhaḥ' ity uktvā) ceruḥ
(: calitāḥ) ||

te Himālayam āmantrya punaḥ prāpya ca Śūlinam |
siddham c› âsmai nivedy› ârtham tad-visṛṣṭāḥ kham
udyayuḥ ||94||

ta iti || *te* (: munayaḥ) *Himālayam āmantrya* (: 'sādhu,
yāma' ity āpṛcchya) *punaḥ Śūlinam* (: Haram) sam-
keta-sthāna-stham *prāpya ca* | *siddham* (: niṣpannam)
artham (: prayojanam) *asmai nivedya* (: jñāpayitvā) *ca* |
tad-visṛṣṭāḥ (: tena (: Śūlinā) visṛṣṭāḥ) *kham* (: ākāśam)
prati *udyayuḥ* (: utpetuḥ) | atra samkṣipt›꞉ârth›-
âbhidhānāt 'samkṣepo' nāma guṇa uktaḥ | tad uktam—
'samkṣipt›꞉ârth›-âbhidhānam yat, samkṣepaḥ pari-
kīrtitaḥ' iti ||

bhagavān Paśupatis tryaha꞊mātra꞉vilambam api
soḍhum na śaśāka tad-autsukyād ity āha—

Paśupatir api tāny ahāni kṛcchrād
agamayad adri-sutā-samāgam›-ôtkaḥ |
kam aparam avaśam na viprakuryur
vibhum api tam yad amī spṛśanti bhāvāḥ? ||95||

Paśupatir iti || (utkam mano yasya saḥ :) utkaḥ |
'utka unmanāḥ' iti nipātaḥ | *adri-sutā-samāgam›-
ôtkaḥ* (: Pārvatī-pariṇay›-ôtsukaḥ) *Paśupatir api tāni* |
trīṇ› îti śeṣaḥ | *ahāni kṛcchrād agamayat* (: ayāpayat) |
kavir āha—*amī bhāvāḥ* (: autsuky›꞉ādayaḥ samcāriṇaḥ)
avaśam (: indriya-paratantram) *aparam* (: pṛthag꞉
janam) *kam na viprakuryuḥ* (: na vikāram nayeyuḥ)
yat (: yasmāt) *vibhum* (: samartham) | jit›꞉êndriyam iti
yāvat | *tam* (: Smaraharam) *api spṛśanti* | vikurvant›
îty arthaḥ | atra vibhu-vikāra-samarthanād arthād
itara꞉jana-vikāraḥ kaimutika꞉nyāyād āpatat› îty arth›-
āpattir alamkāraḥ | tathā ca sūtram—'daṇḍāpūpikayā

ᵣrthᵣ-ântarᵣ-āpatanam arthᵣ-āpattiḥ' iti | arthāntara-
nyāsa iti ke cit, tad upeksaṇīyam | yuktis tu vistara-
bhayān nᵣ ôcyate | puṣpitāgrā vṛttam—

'a:yuji na-yuga;repha~to yakāro
yuji ca na;jau ja;ra;gāś ca puṣpitāgrā'

iti lakṣaṇāt ||

Sanskrit–English Exercises: Key

Exercise 2b

1 I am going. 2 We aren't going [/Let us not go] in here.
3 He writes yet again. 4 Where are you [*pl.*] living now?
5 Do you so wish? 6 But where are they standing? 7 What,
is he coming this way? 8 What are the two of them bringing
here? 9 I see and write. 10 He seems to be wandering [/to
be confused]. 11 The two of you dance and sing. 12 They
both remember and grieve. 13 'We are coming in here,' the
two of them say. 14 How (is it that) he is not coming even
now. 15 I rejoice that I am winning. 16 We grieve that
they are not [living:] alive.

Exercise 3a

1 The pupils are bringing the teacher. 2 Do you want horses
[/the horses]? 3 I see the sun and moon. 4 Who does not
want happiness? 5 The food is scant. 6 The man takes the
horses to the water. 7 'Who are you?' the two of them ask
me. 8 To what mountain is the scholar going? 9 The two
of them enter the forest because anger does not dwell there
[here *of direct speech often becomes* there *of indirect*]. 10 We
do not understand swift speech. 11 Teacher, that elephant
is like a mountain. 12 But whom shall I ask? 13 Are you
pupils? 14 Men and children are entering the water. 15
'That fruit is now pleasant' they say astonished. 16 What,
children here too? 17 Even sorrows bring reward. 18
'Children, what pleasure do you see in this?' the teacher
says to the pupils.

Exercise 4a

1 He quits the house with his sons.   2 Here is a garden: let us go in.   3 Both teacher and pupils made an extraordinary effort.   4 This man gave up life because his friend was dear [*or possibly* because my friend was dear (to him)].   5 Who (is) this (who) is coming to the house?   6 Why do you not rejoice at the pleasant sight?   7 (I have) seen and understood.   8 In curiosity as to what these [/the] men want here [/there], he goes into the house.   9 The city is far, and we are wandering exhausted.   10 Do you *want* this or not?   11 'Have done with words, the opportunity is gone' the two of them say in despair (/dejectedly).   12 Sons, this is the very opportunity.   13 See, we have come to the city.   14 The two friends have forgotten (their) first despair.   15 Though asked, 'O paṇḍit, where are you taking the horse?' he speaks not a word.   16 What point in effort? His Majesty is not looking at you.

Exercise 5a

1 Here we (both) are.   2 [After hearing:] They have heard my answer—what else do they want?   3 You do not [/do you not] in fact have a book.[/?]   4 Friend, you are like my (own) heart.   5 Let the two of us sit for a while in this garden.   6 They are all wandering in the fields.   7 Your Majesty, a [certain] brahmin has come from another city.   8 What means (can) you see for seeing my sons?   9 When we see his anger, we feel alarm in our heart (/our heart feels alarm).   10 Here stands His Highness.   11 Why, after sitting for just a moment I have seen my two friends once more.   12 There is no other road.   13 The sight of Rāma now actually [is for sorrow:] causes sorrow to his friends.   14 Your Majesty has heard this from others too.   15 He goes into the house and asks everyone 'Where, where is the villain now?' [*The repetition of* kva *is for emphasis*.]   16 In the country of the blind it is the one-eyed man who has power.   17 Kalahaṃsaka, who drew this picture of Mādhava?

Exercise 6a

1 Soṇottarā, what is (your) purpose in coming? 2 Alas, two disasters have befallen (me). 3 Great king, [is there welfare of:] is it well with Prince Lakṣmaṇa? 4 But where is this news from? 5 Truly I am exactly so. 6 Minister, the news from Kusumapura is extensive. 7 You are accepted as a son by the noble ladies [*in fact an honorific plural* = the Queen]. 8 In which place is Mārīca's hermitage? 9 Mother, who are you? Why did you restrain me? 10 Surely this is an occasion for regret. 11 This is the same (woman). 12 To both of you alike Indra's servant Duḥṣanta makes obeisance. 13 Servitude is indeed harsh. 14 Has this cancellation [made] by me of the Full Moon festival not indeed reached Vṛṣala's [path of hearing:] ears? 15 What have you (to do) with this worry? 16 Mādhavya, do you feel curiosity [with regard to seeing:] to see Śakuntalā? 17 [The characters written by a scholar, though written with care, are necessarily illegible:] However painstakingly a scholar writes, he is bound to be illegible.

Exercise 7a

1 Ah, here is Her Majesty. 2 Someone [/something] has woken me. 3 Here is Minister Rākṣasa's house. 4 Oh, we have been deprived of a loving friend. 5 (That was) well thought of by Her Reverence. 6 Sir, is (your) head-ache bearable? 7 Their excessive kindness embarrasses me. 8 Therefore let us [resort to:] shelter in this fig-tree's shade. [*Note that* this *more conveniently qualifies* tree *in English*, shade *in Sanskrit*.] 9 We have been distressed at not seeing Your Honour for a long time. 10 Welcome to Her [/Your] Majesty. 11 Do not fear discourtesy from us. 12 Minister, he prepared a medicine mixed with a magic powder for Candragupta. 13 Ah, my body is (as) happy as if [from the touch of Urvaśī's limbs:] it had been touched by Urvaśī. 14 Noble lady, [is there calamity of:] has some calamity happened to Queen Sītā? 15 I will just offer the priests this

grass for strewing on the altar.   16 Avalokitā has told (me)
that Mādhava is gone to the park of (the) Love (temple).   17
Alas, the effort of both alike (was) misplaced.   18 This portion
of the story has not been heard before by us or (anyone) else.
19 We for our part will just ask you [two ladies] something
concerning your friend.   20 Minister, here is an ornament
which His Highness has removed from his own person and
sent (you).

Exercise 8a

1 Ah, we [two] have achieved our object.   2 A deed worthy of
Rāma has been done.   3 There is in the Deccan a city called
Padmapura.   4 Friend, let us stand over here [with our
bodies] hidden by the pillar.   5 Pleasant indeed is the scene
at the end of the day in the king's palace.   6 Why are you
going out of the camp [with seal unreceived:] without getting
a pass?   7 Dear child, do not fear [offence by (your)self:] that
you have offended.   8 Ho there, for what purpose does this
horse wander around with a retinue?   9 But whom (am) I (to)
understand this lady (to be)?   10 Your Highness, this matter
is not terribly difficult to understand.   11 But Minister
Rākṣasa's hostility is fixed on Cāṇakya, not on Candragupta.
12 So I personally send (you) herewith [eṣa] brahmins of
proven worth. [Or svayam *may be taken with* parīkṣita:
whose worth has been examined by myself.]   13 Alas, I am
become a man of foul deeds, a monster.   14 What, though
he has committed great offence, have the two blessed (god-
desses) taken pity on Rāma?   15 I will just (go and) see the
king, now that his evening prayers are over.   16 He at that
very time, hearing of such a cruel turn of fortune for Queen
Sītā, became an anchorite.   17 I perceive that Dāruvarman's
efforts (were) fruitless or had an unwished-for fruit.   18
Beautiful one, the day is not completely over.   19 From meeting Śakuntalā, my eagerness to go (back) to the city has
slackened.

Exercise 9a

1 What did you say? 2 Now we are going back. 3 He salutes [having made an añjali:] with joined hands. 4 I greet you all. 5 Friend Puṇḍarīka, this is [not proper for:] wrong of you. 6 I will just inform my teacher that the time of sacrifice is at hand. 7 Did you too perhaps forget like me? 8 We are overwhelmed with astonishment. 9 Have (you) discovered a weakness of the enemy, sir? 10 Why then are you afraid? 11 I shall now act as ordered. 12 Reverend sir, there is indeed no matter beyond the scope of the wise. 13. Śakuntalā threatens (/scolds) her friend with (a shaking of) her finger. 14 Bravo, friend Bhūrivasu, bravo! 15 What did he say on waking? 16 Now [that good lady is the wife of a royal seer called what?:] what is the name of the royal seer whose wife that lady is? 17 Now what (was) your friend's motive, good fellow, in entering the fire [i.e. committing suicide]? 18 The lady is of course under another's control, and her guardian is not present. 19 Congratulations to you, sire, on your (re)union with your lawful wife and on beholding the face of your son. 20 Then why did Your Honour despatch this man to Kusumapura with a letter? 21 How is it that His Honour Kaṇva lives in perpetual chastity and (yet) this friend of yours is his daughter? [Note: The answer is that she is an adopted child.] 22 For my part too, when I remember Kaṇva's daughter, my heart is without eagerness for the chase. 23 Do Candragupta's faults cause his subjects to remember the merits of bygone rulers? 24 Hearing this incredible promise by the brahmin, the king in company with his ministers, with delighted mind (and) full of astonishment, respectfully handed his royal sons over to that (same) Viṣṇu-śarman.

Exercise 10a

1 See Mādhava's condition. 2 Your friends are in great distress. 3 This is women's well-known [tat] readiness of wit. 4 What attractive [characters:] hándwriting! 5 Sit down [pl.] for a minute. 6 Oh merchant Candanadāsa, you see

how [**evam**] severe in punishment towards traitors is the king. 7 Let him [experience:] reap the reward of being a traitor to the king. 8 It seems that King Duhṣanta is at hand, roaming in the hunt. 9 Go (both of) you. 10 Oh ascetic! Even when I think it over, I certainly do not remember marrying this lady. 11 Mādhavya my friend, be firm in your assertions. 12 How pítiless (were) the vile citizens! How precípitate King Rāma! 13 Blessed god of Love, from where do you, who are armed with flowers, get this sharpness? 14 Well (all of), you [*f.*] fan the two dear children with the borders of your robes. 15 In decrying hunting Mādhavya has made me [of shattered enthusiasm:] lose my enthusiasm. 16 Oh alas! to what a state of (old) age am I come! 17 This noise is (the sound) of young brahmins playing because today is a holiday in honour of learned (guests). 18 Go very gently, ladies. 19 Save (your) friend, sire. 20 Because the revered lord of our house is not present, devils are causing hindrance to our austerities. 21 Seal it, my dear fellow, with this ring. 22 Men of proven loyalty have been appointed about the king, vigilant in countermeasures against poisoners engaged by the enemy. 23 Now that Nandana is won over by Madayantikā's union, we have indeed cast aside our cares. 24 [You must understand him to be a future emperor:] know that in time to come he will be emperor. 25 Well, I did right to deposit my family in the house of my close friend Candanadāsa [and retire:] before retiring from the city. 26 Your Majesty [*f.*], I beg you to compose yourself and comply with the revered Vasiṣṭha's command.

Exercise 11a

1 What, is this Kaṇva's daughter Śakuntalā? 2 Dear child, may you have what I desire (for you). 3 You rogue. You are taking a letter and you don't known for whom? 4 Dear Mālatī, see you are spied [*or* See, I am searching you out]. 5 Let the servants take a rest. 6 Mandārikā, what your sweetheart here says on this matter—is it so? 7 Though the

Spring Festival has been thus cancelled by His Majesty, do you begin plucking the mango buds? 8 Spare his life. 9 Ho sire! Why do you remain silent like this? 10 Do, then, [your own inclination:] as you will. 11 Moreover (he) bestowed on Parvateśvara's brother Vairodhaka the half of the kingdom previously promised (to Parvateśvara). 12 What, is his mother's name 'Śakuntalā'? 13 Who is the great man who has performed this great deed, difficult for a mere mortal? 14 Priyaṃvadaka, find out what time it is. 15 Noble Vaihī-nari, give these two bards a hundred thousand gold pieces. 16 Vṛṣala, why are you quite inappropriately making this vast expenditure? 17 Ho merchant! Are the profits of your transactions accumulating? 18 Blessed Vasumdharā, watch over your virtuous daughter Jānakī. 19 What, does he just stay, though driven off? 20 Reverend Vālmīki, bring these two offspring of Sītā's womb, Kuśa and Lava, to dear Rāma [or (who are) dear Rāma's (sons)]. 21 Just as he is, so also are the two of them. 22 And a sacrificial horse blessed by Vāmadeva has been released, and (men) assigned in conformity with the law-books to guard it. At their head, Lakṣmaṇa's son Candraketu, who has acquired the tradition of the celestial missiles, has been despatched, attended by a [four-limbed:] full army. 23 Alas, alas, I am a total monster not to look affectionately on the dear wife of a dear friend, seen after (so) long. 24 Is there any news as to [iti] what then happened to (/became of) Sītā when Lakṣmaṇa had returned from that forest after abandoning (her there)? 25 There is then a young man called Mādhava [actually spoken of by me:] whom I did mention once in passing, someone who is another bond such as you (yourself are) to my heart. [*The unusual possessive adjective* **māmakīna** *avoids the ugly sound of* **mama manaso** *or* **man-manaso**. *The speaker is a Buddhist nun who ought to shun all ties of affection.*]

Exercise 12a

1 My good fellow, my good fellow, you mustn't come in. 2 Right—I'll just listen to the confidential talk of these

(girls).   3 Be quiet while I listen.   4 Even so, minister, (you) should certainly not give up the enterprise [*or* one should not give up something one has undertaken].   5 So [let father make an occupying of a seat:] take a seat, father, for a while in the shade of this sal tree. [**atra** *for* **asmin**; *cf. also note on Exercise 8a, no. 8.*]   6 Show (me) the place where that mendicant stays.   7 Be firm, my heart. You have something more grievous to listen to.   8 What else is she [/he] to say?   9 And let Urvaśī here be your [throughout life:] lifelong lawful spouse.   10 So I'll just take her to Śrīparvata, shred her piece by piece and make her have a painful death.   11 In our greed to hear of good deeds, we have (something) else to ask as well.   12 So why do the players sit idle?   13 And there you must do as I tell you.   14 It is rather *you* two (girls) who must sustain Śakuntalā.   15 Seize his household property, arrest him and his son and wife, and hold him while I tell Vṛṣala.   16 Now tell the way to Agastya's hermitage.   17 One should enter ascetic groves in modest attire.   18 Like rain on desert land is food to one oppressed by hunger. [*This is a line of verse—hence the unusual position of* **tathā**.]   19 From (my) tightening the reins because the ground was bumpy, the speed of the chariot has slackened.   20 May you get a son (to be) Emperor.   21 How long, then, must we sit idle like this, though with our forces assembled, watching for a weakness in the enemy?   22 As soon as His Majesty, from seeing the ring, remembered that he really had previously married in secret the Lady Śakuntalā (and) from delusion rejected her, His Majesty became remorseful.   23 Since he has great wealth, he must have many wives.   24 Minister, is this man a suitable recipient for such a special decoration, particularly one that His Highness removed from his own person and bestowed (upon you)?   25 And before the (bridegroom's) relatives arrive, dear Mālatī must go to the city temple (to make an offering) for unhindered good luck.

Exercise 13a

1 Give me an answer.   2 Gautamī will go with you.   3 Why, those places seem deserted!   4 See, I am aiming that arrow.

5 If (it is) a secret, let it be—if it is not a secret, then tell (me).
6 And I for my part will announce that news to the reverend
Lopāmudrā. 7 That fool, of course, on obtaining that large
pile of money that you lavished (on him), began to spend it
with great extravagance. 8 Thank heaven, it has dawned fair
today, in that I see His Majesty here. 9 I [*f.*] want to tell
(you) something. 10 I will just rebuke him. 11 Good
Siddhārthaka, admittedly this is (an) inadequate (reward) for
this service, but take it! 12 There is that letter-writer
Śakaṭadāsa, a traitor to the king, being taken by the king's
order to be impaled. 13 You [*du.*] will certainly learn this.
14 Let us just purify ourselves by seeing a holy hermitage.
15 Dear (young) lady, do not omit it—since what is meant but
unsaid causes remorse. 16 This is not the right moment for
me to see Indra. 17 Well, friend, you [are not a seer of:]
have not seen her, for you to talk in that way. 18 Oh! here
are ascetics' girls making this way, to [give water to:] water
the young trees with watering-pots appropriate to their own
(small) size. 19 If he is not the son of a sage, what is his
name? 20 Why should Cāṇakya, being sensible, anger
[/have angered] Candragupta over a trifling cause? And
Candragupta, conscious of his debt, would not violate [/have
violated] his duty of respect (just) for this much. 21 In that
case beg to tell (my) preceptor Somarāta in my name that he
should entertain those hermitage dwellers [by the scriptural
injunctions to ritual:] with scriptural rite and personally show
them in (to me). 22 But we must remember the kindness of
this king, in treating us though guilty as graciously as if (we
had been) innocent. 23 Ah fellow-student in misery! if (it is)
not secret, nor too burdensome, I should like to hear your
reason for (your intention of) sacrificing your life. 24 Noble
Vaihīnari, let the people be [made aware:] given to understand
that from today onward Candragupta shall conduct state
affairs in person, without reference to Cāṇakya. 25 We for
our part will exert ourselves (to see) that there is no damage
to the hermitage. 26 Is Candragupta now incapable of
imposing the yoke of his state administration upon another
[**anyatra = anyasmin**] minister or upon himself and (thus)

taking precautions for himself? 27 In truth, the greatest
satisfaction arises for myself, performing (as I am) before an
audience that appreciates especial(ly good) literature. 28
Śakaṭadāsa was impaled after proclamation in the city that he
had employed Dāruvarman and others to do violence to
Candragupta's person. 29 He of course while any member at
all of Nanda's family is (still) alive [**jīvati** *loc. sg. pres. part.*]
cannot be brought to accept the post of Vṛṣala's minister.
30 The delightful thing in this is that Ministers Bhūrivasu and
Devarāta's desire for the ambrosia of a union of each other's
offspring is at long last hereby fulfilled.

Exercise 14a

1 Priyaṃvadaka, find out who is standing at the door wanting
to see us. 2 Now where, I wonder, can she have gone?
3 There was (once) such a sage in this hermitage. 4 Sire,
hear for what purpose Hari has sent me to you. 5 Though
addressed in these terms, I admonished him again and again.
6 My heart is grieved that Your Excellency has for (so) long
given up proper adornment of your person. 7 And a clamour
of [which the basis was] astonishment and delight rose up
from the people. 8 So tell the cast to be [not confused:] well
rehearsed in their various parts. 9 Just think, friend, on
what pretext we can go to the hermitage again. 10 If only
Candragupta can be separated from the vile Cāṇakya. 11
There is my noble elder (brother), named Kuśa, returned
from Bharata's hermitage. 12 But when the two of them had
fallen asleep from the exhaustion of lovemaking, they saw
in a dream an old goose, its feet bound with strands of lotus
fibre; and they both woke up. 13 So enquire whether he
may have any wife who is pregnant. 14 Noble sir, this is no
time for intimate conversation—and so I (will) speak to you
quite briefly. 15 How can I allow dear Candraketu (to engage
in) single combat with such a one? 16 So determining, I [*f.*]
became anxious to get away. 17 [From the numerousness of
concerns:] My concerns are so numerous that I cannot at all
determine which concern it was that (I) sent this agent of

mine on. 18 If there exists any means of remedying (your) husband's hostility, reveal it—for you have the sharper mind [*or* a particularly sharp mind]. 19 And I spent the day with her in just such conversation—in just that room and in just that way, forbidding entry to all my servants. 20 Think of some means, then, whereby my desires may be fulfilled. 21 And hearing this, the prince mounted that same rutting elephant after pushing out the driver, and made for the palace at top speed. 22 I have learnt from my agents that out of the forces of the barbarian kings the five most important kings attend upon Rākṣasa with particular affection. 23 But if this rumour should reach the king, it would be disastrous. 24 So determining, I took care to search (for him). And, with my mind (made) nervous by my fondness for my friend, fearing some awful thing or other the more I failed to see him in my search, I roamed a good long time, directing my gaze sharply here and there, scrutinizing the woods, the groves of sandalwood trees, the bowers of vine and the banks of the lakes. 25 And in one place, borne suddenly on the jungle breeze, spreading so as to overpower the perfume of other flowers even in a forest fully in bloom, seeming with its extreme fragrance to anoint and satisfy and enrich the sense of smell, pursued by swarms of bees in rivalry (with each other), I smelt a scent of blossom, such as I had never smelt before, one [not appropriate:] alien to the human world.

Exercise 15

84 The divine sage so speaking, Pārvatī at her father's side, with face bent down, counted the petals on the [play lotus:] lotus she was playing with.

Stanza 84: *The divine sage* (Aṅgiras) *so speaking, Pārvatī at her father's side*, being *with face bent down* (understand 'because of shyness') *counted* (reckoned up) *the petals on her play-lotus*. In other words, out of shyness she hid her delight under the pretence of counting the petals on the lotus. This describes the Subsidiary State (of mind) known as 'Dissimulation': to quote—

'Now Dissimulation is the hiding of the expression of anything such as delight from (a motive) such as shyness'.

85 The Mountain(-god), though with his desires fulfilled, looked at Menā['s face]. Usually in matters (concerning) their daughters, family-men make their wives their eyes.

Stanza 85: *The Mountain* (Himālaya) *though with his desires fulfilled* (in other words, though resolved to bestow (her)) *looked at Menā's face* (i.e. in his wish to determine the right answer). The reason being: *usually family-men* (householders) *in matters concerning their daughters* (in their daughters' concerns) are described as ones whose *eye* (means of perceiving matters) is their *wife*. In other words, their conduct is submitted to the authority of their spouse.

86 And Menā approved the whole matter desired by her husband. [Those devoted to their husband:] Devoted wives are unswerving [in respect of their husband's wish:] in following their husband's wishes.

Stanza 86: *And Menā approved* (accepted) *the whole matter desired by her husband* (Himālaya). The reason being: those women whose *vow* is simply their *husband are unswerving* (ones in whom there exists no swerving) *in respect of their husband's wish* (desire): that is, are aware of the inclination of their husband's mind.

87 He, having deliberated in his mind ['this is the proper answer to this':] what would be the proper answer to this, at the end of the speech took hold of his auspiciously adorned daughter.

Stanza 87: *He* (Himālaya) *at the end of the speech* (at the conclusion of the sage's utterance) *having deliberated* (having reflected) *in his mind* (in his thoughts) *that this* (the bestowal about to be declared in the following stanza) *would be the proper* (not lacking in propriety) *answer to this* (to the sage's utterance), *took hold of* (grasped in his arms) *his auspiciously adorned* (adorned so that there was auspiciousness) *daughter*.

88 'Come, dear child, you are destined as alms for the Supreme Godhead; the Sages are the petitioners—I have won the reward of (being) a householder.'

Stanza 88: O *dear child* (daughter) *come* (approach). *You are destined* (fixed upon) *as alms for the Supreme Godhead* (for Śiva)—i.e. because of the saying that 'the alms given to an ascetic may be anything at all from a gem to a clump of grass'. *The Sages are the petitioners* (are (here) to sue). *I have won the reward of a householder* (of one in (charge of) a house). In other words, because it is liberating in this world and the next, the bestowing of a daughter upon a worthy recipient is the reward of being a householder.

89 Having said this much to his daughter, the Mountain spoke to the Sages, 'Herewith the bride of the Three-Eyed God salutes you all'.

Stanza 89: *The Mountain* (Himālaya) *having said this much* (the foregoing words) *to his daughter, spoke to the Sages*. In what terms?— '*Herewith the bride of the Three-Eyed God* (the wife of Tryambaka) *salutes you all*'. By saying 'the bride of the Three-Eyed God' as if it were an accomplished fact, he indicates that the bestowal is immutably determined.

90 They, applauding the Mountain's words, [generous in effecting the wished-for object:] which generously granted their wishes, blessed Ambikā with benedictions whose fulfilment would be immediate.

Stanza 90: *They* (the Sages), *applauding* (praising with 'bravo!') *the Mountain's* (Himālaya's) *words* (statement), *generous* (noble) *in effecting the wished-for object* (because of performing the desired object). According to Amara '**udāra** is used in the sense of **dātṛ** granting or **mahānt** great, noble'. [*Despite Mallinātha, the former sense is obviously not irrelevant* *here.*] **pākaḥ** *fulfilment* means that which is ripened, i.e. fruit, reward. *With benedictions* (benisons) *whose fulfilment would be immediate* (whose fruit was before the eyes) *they blessed* (congratulated) *Ambikā* (Ambā).

91 Her, when her golden earrings slipped in her anxiety to salute them, as she showed confusion, Arundhatī took upon her lap.

Stanza 91: *Her* (Ambikā), *whose golden* (made out of gold) *earrings* (gold ear-ornaments) *slipped in her anxiety to salute them* (because of intentness upon making obeisance), *as she showed confusion Arundhatī took upon her lap*. The **p** (in **āropayām āsa**) occurs by the rule '(before the causative suffix) for (the final **h** of) **ruh,** there occurs optionally **p**'.

92 And her mother, tearful-faced (and made) distressed by love for her daughter, she set at ease by (describing) the qualities of the suitor who had no other (with) prior (claim on him).

Stanza 92: *And her mother* (the mother (Menā) of her (Ambikā)) because of her *love for her daughter* (affection for her child) *distressed* (afraid that she would be separated), and therefore *tearful-faced* (one on whose face there were tears). **anyapūrva** means 'having another woman as a prior (claim)'. The masculine gender of the prior member of the compound occurs by the rule that 'a pronoun takes the masculine gender [in the sphere of synthetic expression:] when forming part of a compound'. **ananyapūrva** means not being this, and is here used in the genitive. *She set at ease* (without distress) *by the qualities* (such as being the Conqueror of Death) *of the suitor* (bridegroom) *who had no other with prior claim on him*— in other words, who did not occasion the distress caused by sharing a husband.

93 Being asked the date for the wedding thereupon by Hara's (new) kinsman, they the bark-garmented ones declared (it to be) after three days, and departed.

Stanza 93: *They* (the ascetics) *bark-garmented* (dressed only in bark) *thereupon* (at that very instant) *by Hara's kinsman* (Himālaya) being *asked* (questioned as to what was) *the date for the wedding* (suitable for the wedding). **tryahaḥ** means a group of three days. The compound occurs by the rule that '(words denoting a region or number compound with another word having the same case-relationship) also (*a*) to express the sense that would be expressed by a secondary suffix, (*b*) where there is a further member (added to the compound), (*c*) to express collective sense'. The suffix *ṭac* occurs by the rule that '(the compound-final suffix) *ṭac* occurs after the words **rājan, ahan** and **sakhi**'. The singular is because it is a **dvigu** compound. It is masculine in gender by the rule that '(when at the end of a co-ordinative or determinative compound) the words **rātra, ahna** and **aha** occur in the masculine'. Here the word is used in the ablative. *They declared it after* (subsequent to) *three days* (said 'the wedding (shall be) on the fourth day') *and departed* (went away).

94 They, after taking leave of Himālaya and going back to the Trident-bearer and reporting to him that their business was accomplished, dismissed by him rose up to heaven.

Stanza 94: *They* (the Sages) *taking leave* (saying goodbye with the words 'good, let us go') *of Himālaya, and going back to the Trident-bearer* (Hara), who was at the appointed place [*mentioned in fact in stanza 33*], and reporting (announcing) *to him that their business* (mission) *was accomplished* (completed), *dismissed by him* (by the Trident-bearer) *rose up* (flew up) towards *heaven* (the sky). In this (stanza), since there is a stating of matters in a concise form, the quality known as 'Conciseness' is expressed: to quote—

'Conciseness is declared to be [that which is] the stating of matters in a concise form'.

(The poet now) states that the blessed Paśupati could not bear even a delay of merely three days, because of his longing for her:

95 And Paśupati passed those days with difficulty, longing for
union with the Mountain's daughter. What other helpless
(person) would such emotions not torment, in that they affect
even him who is (so) powerful?

Stanza 95: **utka** means 'of whom the mind is **utka** [raised
up, i.e.] eager'. The form is given ready-made by the rule that
'**utka** occurs (in the sense of) one who is **un_manas** longing'.
And longing for union with the Mountain's daughter (eager for
marriage with Pārvatī) *Paśupati passed* (spent) *those* (understand 'three') *days with difficulty*. The poet comments: *such
emotions* (the Subsidiary (States) such as longing) *what other*
(ordinary person) *helpless* (not in control of his senses) *would
they not torment* (cause mental disturbance to), *in that* (since)
even him (the Destroyer of Love) *who is powerful* (is capable—
has conquered his senses, in fact) *they affect* (in other words,
mentally disturb)?

The embellishment here is Strong Presumption, since from
(one) matter, the confirmation of mental disturbance in the
All-powerful one, (another matter) the mental disturbance of
other people [presents itself:] is inferred on the *a fortiori*
principle. As the sūtra states, 'Strong Presumption is the
arising (through inference) of another matter by the stick-and-
cake rule'. Some consider it Substantiation, but this should be
disregarded, though the arguments (for rejection) are not stated
for fear of going on too long.

The metre is Puṣpitāgrā, since this is defined as follows:

'In the odd (lines), after two **n**s and an **r**, a **y**,
And in the even (lines), **n** and **j**, **j**, **r** and **g**—(make) a Puṣpitāgrā.'

English–Sanskrit Exercises: Roman Key

Exercise 1b

mahāyāna, yoga, Mahābhārata, Rāmāyaṇa, purāṇa, jāti, Bhīma, Pāṇini, sādhu, Kāśī, Kailāsa, vihāra, mīmāṃsā, agni, ātman, paṇḍita, kṣatriya, vaiśya, śūdra, caṇḍāla, ṛgveda, mudrā, karma, Jagannātha, Gaṅgā, saṃskṛta, prākṛta, ardhamāgadhī, sandhi, aśvamedha, bodhisattva, avagraha, Indra, Kṛṣṇa, Arjuna, Bhagavadgītā, Pañcatantra

In the following sentences words have been separated where appropriate, but the student is of course not expected to have been able to do this for himself:

1 sakhy Anusūye na kevalaṃ tātasya niyogo, mamāpi sahodarasneha eteṣu 2 udakaṃ lambhitā ete grīṣ-makālakusumadāyina āśramavṛkṣakāḥ 3 idānīm ati-krāntakusumasamayān api vṛkṣakān siñcāmaḥ 4 atipinaddhenaitena valkalena Priyaṃvadayā dṛḍhaṃ pīḍitāsmi 5 tac chithilaya tāvad enat 6 atra tāvat payodharavistārayitāram ātmano yauvanārambham upālabhasva 7 sakhyāv eṣa vāteritapallavāṅgulībhiḥ kim api vyāharatīva māṃ cūtavṛkṣakaḥ

Exercise 2a

1 svairaṃ tamas› īśvarasy› âśvau durjanāḥ śastraiś

cirān muñcanti raśmibhya eva 2 aśvāv īśvarasy› aîva svairaṃ śastrai raśmibhyo muñcanti cirād durjanās tamasi 3 svairam ev› ēśvarasya muñcanty aśvau śastrair durjanāś cirāt tamasi raśmibhyaḥ 4 muñcanty eva tamasy aśvau śastrair īśvarasya cirād raśmibhyo durjanāḥ svairam 5 raśmibhyas tamasi śastrair muñcanti cirād eva svairam īśvarasy› âśvau durjanāḥ 6 śastrais tamasi raśmibhyaḥ svairaṃ durjanā īśvarasya cirād aśvau muñcanty eva 7 tamasi durjanā raśmibhyaś cirād īśvarasy› âśvau svairaṃ muñcanti śastrair eva 8 muñcanti durjanā eva raśmibhyo ›śvāv īśvarasya cirāt svairaṃ śastrais tamasi

Exercise 2c

1 bhramasi 2 adhunā ›vagacchāmaḥ 3 tatr› āpi nṛtyati 4 atra vasathaḥ? 5 katham, jayanti? 6 upaviśāvaḥ 7 evaṃ na vadataḥ 8 kiṃ punar api pṛcchasi? 9 atra kiṃ likhāmi? 10 kiṃ na paśyasi? 11 gāyath› êva 12 gacchanty āgacchanti ca (Note the usual order of this pair in Sanskrit.) 13 adhunā jīvati ca śocati ca 14 paśyati vadat› îva ca 15 ‘kim icchath›?’ êti pṛcchanti 16 āgacchant› îti gacchāmaḥ 17 na punar mādyāmaḥ 18 evam api smarāvaḥ—kiṃ smarathaḥ?—‘adya n› āgacchat›’ îti (Note that the context shows ‘you’ to be dual.)

Exercise 3b

1 jala;bhojane icchāmaḥ [Note the absence of sandhi.] 2 śīghram aśvaṃ paśyataḥ 3 paṇḍitāḥ kim icchatha? 4 tvāṃ bālam iva krodho jayati 5 kāv ācāryau paśyasi? 6 sūrya iv› âdya candraḥ śobhanaḥ 7 api ramaṇīyaḥ saḥ? 8 ācārya, ko brāhmaṇa ita āgacchati? 9 atra kiṃ phalam? 10 bālāḥ, kva sa ācāryaḥ? 11 kiṃ ramaṇīyāny api vacanāni na smaratha? 12 svalpaṃ phalaṃ paśyāmaḥ 13 api vismitā ācāryāḥ? 14 kṣetra; parvata;vanāni bālau paśyataḥ 15 ‘sukhaṃ sa n›

êcchat›' îti kiṃ vadatha? 16 kṣetraṃ gajaṃ nayanti
17 kva punar bhojanam iti māṃ na vadasi 18 vismi-
taṃ janaṃ brāhmaṇa iva sa naro vadati

Exercise 4b

1 pariśrānto devaḥ—atr› ôpaviśāvaḥ 2 na vismṛtāni
janen› aîtāni vacanāni 3 śobhanam ev› aîtat 4 vanaṃ
gato ›pi [or gatam api] putraṃ smarati 5 ady› aîv›
āgatā vayam 6 deva, adhunā ›py etābhyāṃ bālābhyām
udyānaṃ na tyaktam 7 eṣa vayasyaiḥ saha tiṣṭhati
8 atra kim adbhutam?—prathamam eva dṛṣṭo may»
aîṣa naraḥ 9 eṣa āgata eva devaś Candraguptaḥ 10
dṛṣṭaṃ kutūhalen› âsmābhir udyānam 11 vanaṃ v»
ôdyānaṃ vā gataḥ 12 vayasyāḥ, dūram eten› âśvena
vayam ānītāḥ 13 kṛtaṃ saṃdehena—etau jīvitāv
āgacchataḥ śiṣyau 14 ady› âpi sukhen› aîva tad adbhu-
taṃ darśanaṃ smarāmaḥ 15 jitās te viṣādena 16
vismitā apy etena darśanena, prayatnaṃ na tyajanti

Exercise 5b

1 andhaḥ khalv asi 2 asmād gṛhād vanāni sa nītaḥ
3 tair apy udyānaṃ gatvā pāpā gṛhītāḥ 4 adbhuto
›nayoḥ krodhaḥ 5 putrāḥ, dṛṣṭāḥ stha 6 santi tv
asmākaṃ Candanadāsasya gṛhe mitrāṇi 7 pariśrānto
›sm› îti pṛcchāmi 8 sarveṣu deśasya mārgeṣu dṛṣṭam
idam asmābhiḥ 9 deva, sa ev› âsmi kumāraḥ 10
andhasya pādayoḥ patati 11 sarve mayā ken› âpy
upāyena dṛṣṭāḥ 12 krodhāy› aîtat kumārasya prativacanam 13 śrutvā tv etan mārga upaviśanti 14
Kalahaṃsaka, na naḥ kutūhalaṃ pustakeṣu 15 ekas-
minn ev› ôdyāne puṣpāṇi kānicid bhavanti 16 dṛṣṭvā ›pi
sarvaṃ n› aîva kiṃcid vadati kumāraḥ 17 kathaṃ
saṃdeha ev› âtra te? 18 hā Makaranda, hā Kalahaṃsaka, gato vāṃ vayasyaḥ [Note that 'your' must be dual.]
19 kumāreṇa tv anyasmin deśe sthitvā sarvaṃ pāpasya
prativacanaṃ śrutam 20 krodhe kiṃ phalam eṣa
paśyati?

Exercise 6b

1 āśrama-mṛgo ⟩yam 2 kṛtaḥ kāry⟩-ārambhaḥ 3 ayam amātya:Rākṣasas tiṣṭhati 4 mūḍha, n⟩ âyaṃ parihāsa-kālaḥ 5 iyaṃ tarhi kasya mudrā? 6 abhijñaḥ khalv asi loka-vyavahārāṇām 7 tat kiṃ na parigṛhītam asmad-vacanaṃ paura:janena? 8 aho, pravāta-subhago ⟩yaṃ van⟩-ôddeśaḥ 9 alam āśaṅkayā 10 labdhaṃ netra-nirvāṇam 11 kathaṃ na paśyasi Rāmasy⟩ âvasthām? 12 Śārṅgarava, sthāne khalu pura-praveśāt tav⟩ ēdṛśaḥ saṃvegaḥ 13 asty etat kula-vrataṃ Pauravāṇām 14 bhadre, prathitaṃ Duḥṣanta-caritaṃ prajāsu 15 tat kṛtam idānīm āśā:vyasanena 16 na khalu satyam eva tāpasa-kanyāyām abhilāṣo me 17 candr⟩-ôparāgaṃ prati tu, ken⟩ âpi vipralabdhā ⟩si 18 ih⟩ aîva priyā-paribhukte latā-maṇḍape muhūrtaṃ tiṣṭhāmi

Exercise 7b

1 Ātreyy asmi 2 vardhayasi me kutūhalam 3 tad idaṃ sarasī-tīram 4 yāvad etāś chāyām āśritaḥ pratipālayāmi 5 kṣudra:jana-kṣuṇṇa eṣa mārgaḥ 6 vyaktam etāny api Cāṇakya-prayuktena vaṇijā ⟩smāsu vikrītāni 7 aho, darśito mitra-snehaḥ 8 śirasi bhayaṃ dūre tat-pratīkāraḥ 9 sakhi Madayantike, svāgatam. anugṛhītam asmad-gṛhaṃ bhavatyā 10 eṣa vivāda eva māṃ pratyāyayati 11 samid-āharaṇāya prasthitāv āvām [āharaṇ⟩-ârtham would also do. Note samid from samidh by external sandhi.] 12 kim-arthaṃ bhavatībhyāṃ pratiṣiddho ⟩smi? 13 Kalahaṃsaka;Makaranda-praveś⟩-âvasare tat su:vihitam 14 katham, tātena dhṛta:pūrvam idam ābharaṇam? 15 niyukt⟩ aîva mayā tatra tat-priya!sakhī Buddharakṣitā 16 etāv eva Rāmāyaṇa-kathā-puruṣau? 17 anena priya:suhṛdā Siddhārthakena ghātakān vidrāvya vadhya-sthānād apahṛto ⟩smi 18 anya ev⟩ âyam a:kṣuṇṇaḥ kathā-prakāro bhagavatyāḥ 19 kumāra:

Lava-prayukta:Vāruṇ›̈âstra-prabhāvaḥ khalv eṣaḥ
20 sa khalu vaidyas tad ev› auṣadhaṃ pāyitaś c› ôpara-
taś ca

Exercise 8b

1 rājñaḥ pratigraho ›yam 2 gato ›ham Avalokitā-
janita:kautukaḥ Kāmadev›-āyatanam 3 amātya-nām›
-âṅkit›› êyaṃ mudrā 4 pariṣan-nirdiṣṭa:guṇaṃ pra-
bandhaṃ n› âdhigacchāmaḥ 5 nanu yūyam apy anena
dharma-karmaṇā pariśrāntāḥ 6 eṣo ›smi Kāmandakī
saṃvṛttaḥ. aham apy Avalokitā 7 Vṛṣala, svayam
an:abhiyuktānāṃ rājñām ete doṣā bhavanti 8 tat kim
avanata:mukha⸱puṇḍarīkaḥ sthito ›si? 9 tatra hi me
priya:suhṛd vaitālika-vyañjanaḥ Stanakalaśo nāma
prativasati 10 api vayasyena vidite tad-anvaya⸱
nāmanī? 11 priye, krauryam api me tvayi prayuktam
anukūla:pariṇāmaṃ saṃvṛttam. tad aham idānīṃ
tvayā pratyabhijñātam ātmānam icchāmi 12 Urvaśī-
gata:manaso ›pi me sa eva devyāṃ bahumānaḥ 13
kiṃ tv araṇya-sado vayam an:abhyasta:ratha-caryāḥ
14 tad asy› aîva tāvad ucchvasita:kusuma-kesara-
kaṣāya⸱śītal⸱āmoda-vāsit›: ôdyānasya kāñcanāra:pād-
apasy› âdhastād upaviśāvaḥ 15 vidita:Sītā-vṛttānt››
êyam 16 aye, any›-āsakta:citto devaḥ 17 kiṃ:nām-
adheyam etad devyā vratam? 18 sa c› âṅgurīyaka-
darśan››:âvasānaḥ śāpaḥ 19 vaimanasya-parīto ›pi
priya:darśano devaḥ

Exercise 9b

1 api nir_vighnaṃ tapaḥ? 2 vayasya Makaranda,
api bhavān utkaṇṭhate Madayantikāyāḥ? 3 kva
punar Mālatī Mādhavaṃ prāg dṛṣṭavatī? 4 ārye, eṣa
nir_lajjo Lakṣmaṇaḥ praṇamati 5 kiṃ kathayanti
bhavantaḥ? 6 atyudāra:prakṛtir Mālatī 7 ramaṇīyāḥ
khalv amātya:Bhūrivasor vibhūtayaḥ 8 atidāruṇo
jana-saṃmardo vartate 9 Śakuntalāyāḥ prathama:

darśana-vṛttāntaṃ kathitavān asmi bhavate 10 bhagavaty Arundhati, Vaidehaḥ Sīradhvajo ›bhivādaye
11 api kṣamante ›smad-upajāpaṃ Candragupta-
prakṛtayaḥ? 12 a:saṃnihitam eva māṃ manyate
13 apūrvaḥ ko ›pi bahumāna-hetur guruṣu, Saudhātake
14 eṣa Rākṣasa-prayukto viṣa-kanyayā Parvateśvaraṃ
ghātitavān 15 Mādhavasy› âñjalau bakula-mālāṃ
nikṣipati 16 diṣṭyā Mahendr›-ôpakāra-paryāptena
vikrama-mahimnā vardhate bhavān 17 tataḥ praviśati
yath»_ôkta:vyāpārā saha sakhībhyāṃ Śakuntalā 18
vayasya, nanv amātya-bhavan›-āsanna: rathyay» aîva
bahuśaḥ saṃcarāvahe—tad upapannam etat 19
Candragupta-prakṛtīnāṃ hi Cāṇakya-doṣā ev›
âparāga-hetavaḥ 20 vayasya, nir_avagrahaṃ dahati
daivam iva dāruṇo vivasvān 21 sādhu Vṛṣala
sādhu—mam› aîva hṛdayena saha saṃmantrya saṃ-
diṣṭavān asi 22 aye, 'Kusumapura-vṛttānta-jño ›haṃ,
bhavat-praṇidhiś c›' êti gāthā-›rthaḥ 23 etāv Aditi-
parivardhita:mandāra:vṛkṣakaṃ Prajāpater āśrama-
padaṃ praviṣṭau svaḥ 24 imām ugr›:ātapāṃ velāṃ
prāyeṇa latā-valaya˜vatsu Mālinī-tīreṣu sa_sakhī˜janā
tatrabhavatī gamayati

Exercise 10b

1 āryāḥ paśyata 2 aho mahārghyāṇy ābharaṇāni 3
paśyantī tiṣṭhati 4 tvaratām atrabhavatī 5 trikāla-
darśibhir munibhir ādiṣṭaḥ sur›:âsura-vimardo bhāvī
6 bahu:pratyavāyaṃ nṛpatvam 7 ata eva bhavad_vidhā
mahāntaḥ 8 astu te kārya-siddhiḥ 9 mudrāṃ
paripālayann udveṣṭya darśaya 10 aho viveka-śūnya˜tā
mlecchasya 11 nigṛhya śok›-āveśaṃ mām anugac-
chatam 12 vatsa, kāry›-âbhiyoga ev› âsmān ākulayati,
na punar upādhyāya-sahabhūḥ śiṣya:jane duḥśīlatā
13 phariharantam api māṃ Pañcavaṭī-sneho balād
ākarṣat› îva 14 aho madhuram āsāṃ darśanam 15
Citralekhe, tvaray› Ôrvaśīm 16 asty etad anya-
samādhi-bhīru˜tvaṃ devānām 17 utsarpiṇī khalu

mahatām prārthanā 18 sāmpratam eva Kusumapur‹-
ôparodhanāya pratiṣṭhantām asmad-balāni 19 vismṛtā
bhavad-guṇa-pakṣapātinā mayā svāmi-guṇāḥ 20
Priyaṃvadaka, na naḥ kutūhalaṃ sarpeṣu—tat
paritoṣya visarjay‹ aînam 21 Śacī-tīrthe salilaṃ vand-
amānāyās tava sakhyāḥ paribhraṣṭam 22 vatsa,
sāvadhāno bhava 23 kārya-vyagra‾tvān manasaḥ
prabhūtatvāc ca praṇidhīnāṃ vismṛtam 24 ārya
Jājale, tvam api sa_parijano nivartasva—Bhāgurāyaṇa ev‹ aîko mām anugacchatu 25 aho śarat:
samaya-saṃbhṛta:‚śobhā‾-vibhūtīnāṃ diśām ati-
śaya:ramaṇīya‾tā 26 tata ekasmād bhitti-cchidrād
gṛhīta‚bhakt‹‾âvayavānāṃ pipīlikānāṃ niṣkrāmantī-
nāṃ paṅktim avalokya, 'puruṣa‚garbham etad gṛham'
iti gṛhīt‹‚ârthena dāhitaṃ tad eva śayana-gṛham

Exercise 11b

1 dīyatām asmai prativacanam 2 bhrātarāv āvāṃ
yamajau 3 na niṣ_prayojanam adhikāra‾vantaḥ pra-
bhubhir āhūyante 4 atr‹ aîva sthīyatām 5 yat tad
alaṃkaraṇa-trayaṃ kṛtam, tan-madhyād ekaṃ dīyatām 6 vimucyantām abhīṣavaḥ 7 kim ucyate 'dhairyam' iti? 8 bhadrās tvaryatāṃ tvaryatām 9 abhi-
vyaktāyāṃ candrikāyāṃ kiṃ dīpikā-paunaruktena?
10 Lātavya, āhūyatām Urvaśi 11 aye, tad idam ābharaṇam yan mayā sva:śarīrād avatārya Rākṣasāya
preṣitam 12 ayi vatse, evam ātmā stūyate 13 paritoṣya vikretāraṃ gṛhyatām 14 ārya, asti kaścid yaḥ
Kusumapuraṃ gacchati, tata āgacchati vā? 15 prave-
śyatām 16 kiṃ mṛṣā tarkeṇ‹ ânviṣyate? 17 'amātya'
iti lajjā-karam idānīṃ viśeṣaṇa:padam 18 hanta,
mūḍha ev‹ āsmi, yo ›smin vanecare vayasya:Maka-
rand‹-ôcitaṃ vyavaharāmi 19 samarpyatāṃ Rākṣasasya gṛha-janaḥ. anubhūyatāṃ ciraṃ vicitra‚phalo
rāja-prasādaḥ 20 rakṣyatāṃ para-kalatreṇ‹ ātmanaḥ
kalatraṃ jīvitaṃ ca 21 sa eṣa Kāmandakī-suhṛt-
putro mahā:māṃsasya paṇāyitā Mādhavaḥ 22 yeṣāṃ

antevāsināṃ hastena tat pustakaṃ Bharat›-āśramaṃ
preṣitam, teṣām ānuyātrikaś cāpa͜pāṇiḥ pramād›-
âpanodaṃ-ârtham asmad-bhrātā preṣitaḥ 23 anan-
taraṃ ca yātrā-bhaṅga-pracalitasya mahataḥ paura:
janasya saṃkulena vighaṭitāyāṃ tasyām āgato ›smi
24 mūrkha, anyam eva bhāgam ete tapasvino nir-
vapanti, yo ratna-rāśīn api vihāy› âbhinandyate 25
evam ātm›-âbhiprāya-saṃbhāvit͜êṣṭa˙jana˷cittavṛttiḥ
prārthayitā vipralabhyate

Exercise 12b

1 kiṃ bravīṣi? 2 anena lekhena Rākṣaso jetavyaḥ 3
tatr› aîva Makaranda;Madayantik»-āgamanaṃ yāvat
sthātavyam 4 śṛṇuvas tāvat 5 hanta, hṛdayam api
me ripubhiḥ svīkṛtam 6 asyām aśoka-cchāyāyām
āstām āyuṣmān, yāvat tvām aham Indra-gurave nivedayāmi 7 rakṣaṇīyā Rākṣasasya prāṇā ity ārya›-
ādeśaḥ 8 tad yathā bhavitavyaṃ tathā bhavatu 9
sarvam eva tantram ākulībhūtam 10 kiṃ bhavāṃs
tūṣṇīm āste? 11 tad atra vastuny an:upālabhyo
Rākṣasaḥ 12 bhadra Bhāsvaraka, bahir nītvā tāvat
tāḍyatām yāvat kathyate ›nena 13 śṛṇu vicitram idam
14 asminn eva vetasa;latā-maṇḍape bhavitavyaṃ
Śakuntalayā 15 tad idānīṃ sahadharmacāriṇaṃ prati
na tvayā manyuḥ karaṇīyaḥ 16 tam ev› ôddeśaṃ
gacchāmi yatra me nayanayoḥ sā su͜nayanā tiro˜
bhūtā 17 āviṣkṛtaṃ kathā-prāvīṇyaṃ vatsena 18
tena hi tat-prayogād ev› âtrabhavataḥ sāmājikān
upāsmahe 19 kumāra iv› ân:atikramaṇīya͜vacano
bhavān api 20 a:samyak ceṣṭitam priyāṃ samā-
sādya kāla-haraṇaṃ kurvatā mayā 21 kaṣṭam, ete
suhṛd-vyasaneṣu para˜vad udāsīnāḥ pratyādiśyā-
mahe vayam anena 22 bhoḥ śreṣṭhin, sa c› âparikle-
śaḥ katham āvirbhavat› îti nanu praṣṭavyā vayam eva
bhavatā 23 yāvad ete Mānas›-ôtsukāḥ patatriṇaḥ
saraso n› ôtpatanti, tāvad etebhyaḥ priyā-pravṛttir
avagamayitavyā 24 tatas teṣu gṛhīta͜saṃjñeṣu bhay›-

âpadeśād itas tataḥ pradruteṣu Śakaṭadāso vadhya-
sthānād apanīya Rākṣasaṃ prāpayitavyaḥ 25 yad»
aîv› âpsaras-tīrthāt pratyākhyāna-viklavāṃ Śakuntalām ādāya Dākṣāyaṇīm upagatā Menakā, tad» aîva
dhyānād avagata:vṛttānto ›smi 'Durvāsasaḥ śāpād
iyaṃ tapasvinī sahadharmacāriṇā pratyādiṣṭ›' êti

Exercise 13b

1 Vijaye, pratyabhijānāti bhavatī bhūṣaṇam idam?
2 śaṭhaḥ khalv asau baṭuḥ 3 su:vihitaṃ Lavaṅgikayā,
yato Mādhav›-ânucaraḥ Kalahaṃsakas tāṃ vihāra-
dāsīṃ Mandārikāṃ kāmayate 4 kva punar māṃ
bhavatyaḥ pratipālayiṣyanti? 5 katham, a:dattv» aîva
prativacanaṃ nartitum ārabdhaḥ 6 katham, mad-
anveṣiṇaḥ sainikās tapo-vanam abhirundhanti? 7
kāmam etad abhinandanīyaṃ, tathā ›pi vayam atra
madhyasthāḥ 8 n› âticirād amātyo ›smān purātanīm
avasthām āropayiṣyati 9 na yuktaṃ prākṛtam api
puruṣam avajñātum 10 rājan Candragupta, viditam
eva te yathā vayaṃ Malayaketau kiṃ cit kāl›-ântaram
uṣitāḥ 11 bho Viṣṇugupta, na māṃ śvapāka-sparśa-
dūṣitaṃ spraṣṭum arhasi 12 vatsa, kaccid abhinan-
ditas tvayā vidhivad asmābhir anuṣṭhita:jāta-karm›ī
ādi:kriyaḥ putra eṣa Śākuntaleyaḥ? 13 tad anujānīhi
māṃ gamanāya 14 na śaknumo vayam āryasya vācā
vācam atiśayitum 15 yady evam abhiyoga-kālam
āryaḥ paśyati, tat kim āsyate? 16 bhadra, praviśa—
lapsyase śrotāraṃ jñātāraṃ ca 17 'idānīm eva duhitaram atithi-satkārāy› ādiśya, daivam asyāḥ pratikū-
laṃ śamayituṃ Somatīrthaṃ gataḥ'—'yady evaṃ,
tām eva drakṣyāmi' 18 sakhe, kim a:śraddadhānaḥ
pṛcchasi? 19 kim a:kṣatriyā pṛthivī, yad evam
udghuṣyate? 20 bhadra, kasmiṃś cid āpta:jan›-
ânuṣṭheye karmaṇi tvāṃ vyāpārayitum icchāmi 21 sa
cen muni-dauhitras tal:lakṣaṃ-ôpapanno bhavati tataḥ
pratinandya śuddhāntam enāṃ praveśayiṣyasi 22 tat
kim ujjihāna:jīvitāṃ varākīṃ n› ânukampase? 23 na

niṣ_parigrahaṃ sthāna-bhraṃśaḥ pīḍayiṣyati 24 Candragupta-śarīram abhidrogdhum asmat-prayuktānāṃ tīkṣṇa:rasa-d›:ādīnām upasaṃgrah›-ârthaṃ prakṛty-upajāp›-ârthaṃ ca mahatā koṣa-saṃcayena sthāpitaḥ Śakaṭadāsaḥ 25 sakhe Mādhavya, an:avāpta:cakṣuḥ²phalo ›si, yena tvayā draṣṭavyānāṃ paraṃ na dṛṣṭam 26 bhoḥ śreṣṭhin Candanadāsa, evaṃ rāj›-âpathya-kāriṣu tīkṣṇa:daṇḍo rājā na marṣayiṣyati Rākṣasa-kalatra-pracchādanaṃ bhavataḥ 27 yato ›mī vyāghr›:ādayo varṇa_mātra-vipralabdhāḥ śṛgālam a:jñātvā rājānam amuṃ manyante, tad yathā ›yaṃ paricīyate tathā kuruta 28 deva, jīvitu_kāmaḥ ko ›nyo devasya śāsanam ullaṅghayiṣyati? 29 yady api svāmi-guṇā na śakyante vismartuṃ, tathā ›pi mad-vijñāpanāṃ mānayitum arhaty āryaḥ

Exercise 14b

1 Lātavya, api jānīte bhavān kasy› âyaṃ bāṇa iti? 2 aye mūrkha, kiṃ bhavān asmākam upādhyāyād dharma-vit̃taraḥ? 3 nyaśāmayaṃ ca tasminn āśrame kasya cic cūta-potakasya cchāyāyāṃ kam apy udvigna:̣ varṇaṃ tāpasam 4 vayasya, aṅgulī-svedena dūṣyerann akṣarāṇi 5 tat ko ›yaṃ pade pade mahān an: adhyavasāyaḥ? 6 ity uktvā ca sā tāmbūla-bhājanād ākṛṣya tām adarśayat 7 avasare khalv anurāg›;ôpakārayor garīyasor upanyāsaḥ 8 Raivataka, ucyatām asmat-sārathiḥ sa_bāṇa̧kārmukaṃ ratham upasthāpay› êti 9 sa kadācid dhairya-skhalana-vilakṣaḥ kiṃ cid aniṣṭam api samācaret 10 yāvad aśṛṇavaṃ Mālaty ev› âsya manmath›-ônmātha-hetur iti 11 nikhil›:ântaḥpura-svāminī ca tasy› âbhavat 12 ucyatāṃ kiṃ te bhūyaḥ priyam upakaromi 13 ity abhidhāya kim iyaṃ vakṣyat› îti man-mukh›-āsakta:dṛṣṭis tūṣṇīm āsīt 14 tat kuto ›smin vipine priyā-pravṛttim āgamayeyam? 15 sa kila kṛpālus taṃ janam ārdrayā gir› āśvāsy› ārti-kāraṇaṃ tāṃ gaṇikām apṛcchat 16 kumāra, na kadācid api Śakaṭadāso ›mātya:Rākṣasasy›

âgrato 'mayā likhitam' iti pratipatsyate 17 sakhe
Bhāgurāyaṇa, nanv asmākam amātya:Rākṣasaḥ priya-
tamo hitatamaś ca 18 apayātāyāṃ bhavatyāṃ muhūrtam iva sthitv» aîkākī 'kim ayam idānīm ācaraṭ›?' îti
saṃjāta:vitarkaḥ pratinivṛtya viṭap›-ântarita:vigrahas
taṃ pradeśaṃ vyalokayam 19 api nāma mṛgatṛṣṇik»
êva n› âyam ante prastāvo viṣādāya kalpeṭa 20 sūry›-
ôpasthānāt pratinivṛttaṃ Purūravasaṃ mām upetya
kathyatāṃ kuto bhavatyaḥ paritrātavyā iti 21 ity
abhidadhānā madana-mūrchā-kheda-vihvalair aṅgaiḥ
kathaṃ cid avalambya tām ev› ôdatiṣṭham. uccalitā-
yāś ca me durnimitta-nivedakam aspandata dakṣiṇaṃ
locanam. upajāta:śaṅkā c› âcintayam 'idam aparaṃ
kim apy upakṣiptaṃ daiven›' êti 22 yady asmatto
garīyān Rākṣaso ›vagamyate, tadā ›smākam idaṃ
śastraṃ tasmai dīyatām 23 sakhe, Candraguptasy›
aîva tāvan nagara-praveśāt prabhṛti mat-prayuktais
tīkṣṇa:rasa-d›:ādibhiḥ kim anuṣṭhitam iti śrotum icchāmi 24 yadi punar īdṛśaṃ tvām Aikṣvāko rājā Rāmaḥ
paśyet tadā ›sya snehena hṛdayam abhiṣyandeta 25 iti
vicārayantīm eva mām a:vicārita:guṇa;doṣa-viśeṣo
rūp›-aîka:pakṣapātī nava:yaùvana-sulabhaḥ kusum›-
āyudhaḥ kusuma-samaya-mada iva madhukarīṃ para-
vaśām akarot

English–Sanskrit Exercises: Nāgarī Key

Exercise 1a

महाराज । सीता । रावण । मैथुन । देवनागरी । हिमालय । शिव । कालिदास । गुरु । अशोक । संसार । उपनिषद् । शकु-न्तला । चैत्य । पिण्ड । मनुस्मृति । विष्णु । कौटिल्य । संस्कार । अनुस्वार । शक्ति । अश्वघोष । वात्स्यायन । वेदान्त । ब्रह्मन् । चक्र । चन्द्रगुप्त । कामसूत्र । मन्त्र । विसर्गः । निर्वाण । धर्मशास्त्र । भारत-वर्ष । यक्ष । विज्ञानवादिन् ॥

को नियोगो ऽनुष्ठीयताम् । १ । एवं न्वेतत् । २ । अनन्तर-करणीयमिदानीमाज्ञापयत्वार्यः । ३ । अथ कतरं पुनर्श्चेतुं समाश्रित्य गास्यामि । ४ । ननु प्रथममेवार्येणाच्छत्रमभिज्ञान-शकुन्तलं नामापूर्वं नाटकमभिनीयतामिति । ५ । इत इतः प्रियसख्यौ । ६ । सखि शकुन्तले त्वत्तो ऽपि तातकण्वस्याश्रम-वृक्षकाः प्रिया इति तर्कयामि येन नवमालिकाकुसुमपरिपेलवापि त्वमेतेष्वालवालपूरणेषु नियुक्ता । ७ ।

Exercise 2a

खैरं तमसीश्वरस्याश्र्यौ दुर्जनाः ग्रस्तैश्चिरान्मुञ्चन्ति रश्मिभ्य एव । १ । अश्वावीश्वरखैव खैरं ग्रस्तै रश्मिभ्यो मुञ्चन्ति चिराद्दुर्जना-स्तमसि । २ । खैरमेवेश्वरस्य मुञ्चन्त्यश्रौ ग्रस्तैर्दुर्जनाश्चिरात्तमसि

रश्मिभ्यः । ३ । मुञ्चन्त्येव तमस्खस्त्रौ ग्रस्तैरीश्वरस्य चिराद्रश्मि-
भ्यो दुर्जनाः स्वैरम् । ४ । रश्मिभ्यस्तमसि ग्रस्तैर्मुञ्चन्ति चिरादेव
स्वैरमीश्वरस्याश्रौ दुर्जनाः । ५ । ग्रस्तैस्तमसि रश्मिभ्यः स्वैरं
दुर्जना ईश्वरस्य चिराद्खौ मुञ्चन्त्येव । ६ । तमसि दुर्जना रश्मि-
भ्यश्चिरादीश्वरस्याश्रौ स्वैरं मुञ्चन्ति ग्रस्तैरेव । ७ । मुञ्चन्ति दुर्जना
एव रश्मिभ्यो ऽश्रावीश्वरस्य चिरात्स्वैरं ग्रस्तैस्तमसि ॥ ८ ॥

Exercise 2c

भ्रमसि । १ । अधुनावगच्छामः । २ । तच्चापि नृत्यति । ३ । अत्र
वसथ । ४ । कथं जयन्ति । ५ । उपविश्रावः । ६ । एवं न वदतः
। ७ । किं पुनरपि पृच्छसि । ८ । अत्र किं लिखामि । ९ । किं न
पश्यसि । १० । गायथेव । ११ । गच्छन्त्यागच्छन्ति च । १२ । अधुना
जीवति च श्रोचति च । १३ । पश्यति वदतीव च । १४ । किमि-
च्छथेति पृच्छन्ति । १५ । आगच्छन्तीति गच्छामः । १६ । न पुनरागा-
च्छामः । १७ । एवमपि स्वरावः । किं स्वरथ । अत्र नागच्छ-
तीति ॥ १८ ॥

Exercise 3b

जलभोजने इच्छामः । १ । श्रीघ्रमश्वं पश्यतः । २ । पण्डिताः
किमिच्छथ । ३ । त्वां बालमिव क्रोधो जयति । ४ । कावाचार्यौ
पश्यसि । ५ । सूर्यं द्वावाद्य चन्द्रः श्रोभनः । ६ । अपि रमणीयः
सः । ७ । आचार्यं को ब्राह्मण इत आगच्छति । ८ । अत्र किं
फलम् । ९ । बालाः क्व स आचार्यः । १० । किं रमणीयान्यपि
वचनानि न स्मरथ । ११ । स्वल्पं फलं पश्यामः । १२ । अपि
विस्मिता आचार्याः । १३ । क्षेत्रपर्वतवनानि बालौ पश्यतः । १४ ।
सुखं स नेच्छतीति किं वदथ । १५ । क्षेत्रं गजं नयन्ति । १६ । क्व
पुनर्भोजनमिति मां न वदसि । १७ । विस्मितं जनं ब्राह्मण इव
स नरो वदति ॥ १८ ॥

Exercise 4b

परिश्रान्तो देवः — अत्रोपविश्यावः । १ । न विस्मृतानि जननी-
तानि वचनानि । २ । शोभनमेवैतत् । ३ । वनं गतो ऽपि (गतमपि)
पुत्रं स्मरति । ४ । अद्यैवागता वयम् । ५ । देव अधुनाप्येताभ्यां
बालाभ्यामुद्यानं न त्यक्तम् । ६ । एष वयस्यैः सह तिष्ठति । ७ ।
अत्र किमद्भुतम् — प्रथममेव दृष्टो मयैष नरः । ८ । एष आगत
एव देवचन्द्रगुप्तः । ९ । दृष्टं कुतूहलेनास्माभिरुद्यानम् । १० । वनं
वोद्यानं वा गतः । ११ । वयस्याः दूरमेतेनाश्वेन वयमानीताः
। १२ । व्रतं संदेहेन — एतौ जीवितावागच्छतः शिष्यौ । १३ ।
अद्यापि सुखेनैव तद्द्भुतं दर्शनं स्मरामः । १४ । जिताक्षे विषादेन
। १५ । विस्मिता अद्येतेन दर्शनेन प्रयत्नं न त्यजन्ति ॥ १६ ॥

Exercise 5b

अन्धः खल्वसि । १ । अक्ष्णाद्गृहाद्धनानि स नीतः । २ । तैरप्युद्यानं
गत्वा पापा गृहीताः । ३ । अद्भुतो ऽनयोः क्रोधः । ४ । पुत्राः
दृष्टाः स्थ । ५ । सन्ति लक्ष्मांक चन्द्नदासस्य गृहे मित्राणि । ६ ।
परिश्रान्तो ऽस्मीति पृच्छामि । ७ । सर्वेषु देशस्य मार्गेषु दृष्टमि-
दमस्माभिः । ८ । देव स एवासि कुमारः । ९ । अन्धस्य पादयोः
पतति । १० । सर्वे मया केनाप्युपायेन दृष्टाः । ११ । क्रोधायैत-
त्कुमारस्य प्रतिवचनम् । १२ । श्रुत्वा श्वेतत्क्मार्गे उपविशन्ति । १३ ।
कलहंसक न नः कुतूहलं पुस्तकेषु । १४ । एकस्मिन्नेवोद्याने पुष्पाणि
कानिचिद्ध्वन्ति । १५ । दृष्ट्वापि सर्वं नैव किंचिद्वदति कुमारः
। १६ । कथं संदेह एवाच ते । १७ । हा मकरन्द हा कलहंसक
गतो वां वयस्यः । १८ । कुमारेण त्वन्यस्मिन्देशे स्थित्वा सर्वं
पापस्य प्रतिवचनं श्रुतम् । १९ । क्रोधे किं फलमेष पश्यति ॥ २० ॥

Exercise 6b

आश्रममृगो ऽयम् । १ । कृतः कार्यारम्भः । २ । अयममात्यराक्ष-
सस्तिष्ठति । ३ । मूढ नायं परिहासकालः । ४ । इयं तर्हिं कस्य
मुद्रा । ५ । अभिज्ञः खल्वास लोकव्यवहाराणाम् । ६ । तत्किं न
परिगृहीतमस्मद्वचनं पौरजनेन । ७ । अहो प्रवातसुभगो ऽयं
वनोद्देशः । ८ । अलमाशङ्कया । ९ । लब्धं नेत्रनिर्वाणम् । १० ।
कथं न पश्यसि रामस्यावस्थाम् । ११ । शार्ङ्गरव स्थाने खलु
पुरप्रवेशात्तवेदृशः संवेगः । १२ । अस्थ्येतत्कुलव्रतं पौरवाणाम्
। १३ । भद्रे प्रथितं दुःषन्तचरितं प्रजासु । १४ । तत्क्रतमिदानी-
माश्वाव्यसनेन । १५ । न खलु सत्यमेव तापसकन्यायामभिलाषो
मे । १६ । चन्द्रोपरागं प्रति तु केनापि विप्रलब्धासि । १७ ।
इहैव प्रियापरिभुक्ते लतामण्डपे मुहूर्तं तिष्ठामि ॥ १८ ॥

Exercise 7b

आचेष्यसि । १ । वर्धयसि मे कुतूहलम् । २ । तदिदं सरसीतीरम्
। ३ । यावदेतारूकायामाश्रितः प्रतिपालयामि । ४ । क्षुद्र जनक्षुरण
एष मार्गः । ५ । व्यक्तमेतान्यपि चाणक्यप्रयुक्तेन वणिजाख्यासु
विक्रीतानि । ६ । अहो दर्शितो मित्रस्नेहः । ७ । शिरसि भयं
दूरे तत्प्रतीकारः । ८ । सखि मदयन्तिके स्वागतम् । अनुगृहीत-
मस्मद्गृहं भवत्या । ९ । एष विवाद एव मां प्रत्याययति । १० ।
समिदाहरणाय प्रस्थितावावाम् । ११ । किमर्थं भवतीभ्यां प्रति-
षिद्धो ऽस्मि । १२ । कलहंसकमकरन्दप्रवेशावसरे तत्सुविहितम्
। १३ । कथम् तातेन धृतपूर्वमिदमाभरणम् । १४ । नियुक्तैव मया
तत्र तत्प्रियसखी बुद्धरक्षिता । १५ । एतावेव रामायणकथापुरुषौ
। १६ । अनेन प्रियसुहृदा सिद्धार्थकेन घातकान्विद्राव्य वधस्था-
नादपहृतो ऽस्मि । १७ । अन्य एवायमक्षुरणः कथाप्रकारो भगव-
त्याः । १८ । कुमारलवप्रयुक्तवारुणास्त्रप्रभावः खल्वेषः । १९ । स
खलु वैद्यस्तदेवौषधं पायितस्योपरतश्च ॥ २० ॥

Exercise 8b

राज्ञः प्रतिग्रहो ऽयम् ।१। गतो ऽहमवलोकिताजनितकौतुकः कामदेवायतनम् ।२। अमात्यनामाङ्कितेयं मुद्रा ।३। परिषत्नि- र्दिष्टगुणं प्रबन्धं नाधिगच्छामः ।४। ननु यूयमथनेन धर्मकर्मणा परिश्रान्ताः ।५। एषो ऽस्मि कामन्दकी संवृत्तः । अहमथ्यवलो- किता ।६। वृषल स्वयमनभियुक्तानां राज्ञामेते दोषा भवन्ति ।७। तत्किमवनतमुखपुण्डरीकः स्थितो ऽसि ।८। तच्च हि मे प्रियसुहृद्वैतालिकव्यञ्जनः स्तनकलशो नाम प्रतिवसति ।९। अपि वयस्येन विदिते तदन्वयनामनी ।१०। प्रिये कौर्यमपि मे त्वयि प्रयुक्तमनुकूलपरिणामं संवृत्तम् । तदहमिदानीं त्वया प्रत्यभिज्ञा- तमात्मानमिच्छामि ।११। उर्वशीगतमनसो ऽपि मे स एव देव्यां बहुमानः ।१२। किंत्वरणसदो वयमनभ्यस्तरथचर्याः ।१३। तदस्यैव तावदुच्छ्वसितकुसुमकेसरकषायशीतलामोद्वासितोबा- नस्य काञ्चनारपादपस्याधस्तादुपविशावः ।१४। विदितसीतावृ- त्तान्तेयम् ।१५। अये अन्यासक्तचित्तो देवः ।१६। किंनामधेय- मेतद्दैव्या व्रतम् ।१७। स चाङ्गुरीयकदर्शनावसानः शापः ।१८। वैमनस्यपरीतो ऽपि प्रियदर्शनो देवः ॥१९॥

Exercise 9b

अपि निर्विघ्नं तपः ।१। वयस्य मकरन्द अपि भवानुत्कण्ठते मद्यन्तिकायाः ।२। क्व पुनर्मालती माधवं प्रागद्दृष्टवती ।३। आर्ये एष निर्लज्जो लक्ष्मणः प्रणमति ।४। किं कथयन्ति भवन्तः ।५। अत्युदारप्रकृतिर्मालती ।६। रमणीयाः खल्वमात्यभूरिव- सोर्विभूतयः ।७। अतिदारुणो जनसंमर्दो वर्तते ।८। शकुन्त- लायाः प्रथमदर्शनवृत्तान्तं कथितवानस्मि भवते ।९। भगवत्यह- न्वति वैदेहः सीरध्वजो ऽभिवादये ।१०। अपि क्षमन्ते ऽस्मदुप- जापं चन्द्रगुप्तप्रकृतयः ।११। असंनिहितमेव मां मन्यते ।१२।

अपूर्वः को ऽपि बहुमानहेतुर्गुरूषु सौधातके । १३ । एष राक्षस-
प्रयुक्तो विषकन्यया पर्वतेश्वरं घातितवान् । १४ । माधवस्याञ्जलौ
बकुलमालां निक्षिपति । १५ । दिष्ट्या महेन्द्रोपकारपर्याप्तेन विक्रम-
महिम्ना वर्धते भवान् । १६ । ततः प्रविशति यथोक्तव्यापारा
सह सखीभ्यां शकुन्तला । १७ । वयस्य नन्वमात्यभवनासन्नरथ्ययैव
बहुशः संचरावहे । तदुपपन्नमेतत् । १८ । चन्द्रगुप्तप्रकृतीनां हि
चाणक्यदोषा एवापरागहेतवः । १९ । वयस्य निरवग्रहं दहति
दैवमिव दारुणो विवस्वान् । २० । साधु वृषल साधु । ममैव
हृदयेन सह संमन्त्र्य संदिष्टवानसि । २१ । अये कुसुमपुरवृत्तान्तज्ञो
ऽहं भवत्प्रणिधिश्चेति गाथार्थः । २२ । एतावदितिपरिवर्धितमन्द्र-
रवृक्षकं प्रजापतेराश्रमपदं प्रविष्टौ खः । २३ । इमामुद्ग्रातपां वेलां
प्रायेण लतावलयवत्सु मालिनीतीरेषु ससखीजना तत्रभवती
गमयति ॥ २४ ॥

Exercise 10b

आर्याः पश्यत । १ । अहो महाघ्यार्णाभरणानि । २ । पश्यन्ती
तिष्ठति । ३ । त्वरतामत्रभवती । ४ । त्रिकालदर्शिभिर्मुनिभिरादिष्टः
सुरासुरविमर्दो भावी । ५ । बहुप्रत्यवायं नृपत्वम् । ६ । अत एव
भवद्विधा महान्तः । ७ । अस्तु ते कार्यसिद्धिः । ८ । मुद्रां परि-
पालयन्नुद्दिष्टश्च दर्शय । ९ । अहो विवेकशून्यता म्लेच्छस्य । १० ।
निगृह्य शोकावेगं मामनुगच्छतम् । ११ । वत्स कार्याभियोग
एवास्मानाकुलयति न पुनरुपाध्यायसहभूः श्लिष्टजने दुःशीलता
। १२ । परिहरन्तमपि मां पञ्चवटीस्नेहो बलादाकर्षतीव । १३ ।
अहो मधुरमासां दर्शनम् । १४ । चित्रलेखे त्वरयोर्वशीम् । १५ ।
अस्त्वेतदन्यसमाधिभीरूलं देवानाम् । १६ । उत्सर्पिणी खलु महतां
प्रार्थना । १७ । सांप्रतमेव कुसुमपुरोपरोधनाय प्रतिष्ठन्तामस्कन्ध-
लानि । १८ । विस्मृता भवत्रणपक्षपातिना मया स्वामिगुणाः
। १९ । प्रियंवदक न नः कुतूहलं सर्पेषु । तत्परितोष्य विसर्जयैनम्

। २० । शुचीतीर्थे सलिलं वन्दमानायास्तव सख्याः परिभ्रष्टम्
। २१ । वत्स सावधानो भव । २२ । कार्यव्यग्रत्वान्मनसः प्रभूतत्वाच्च
प्रणिधीनां विस्मृतम् । २३ । आर्य जाजले त्वमपि सपरिजनो
निवर्तस्व । भागुरायण एवैको मामनुगच्छतु । २४ । अहो भरत्स-
मयसंभृतप्रोभाविभूतीनां दिशामतिभयंरमणीयता । २५ । तत
एकस्मान्भित्तिच्छिद्राद्गृहीतभक्तावयवानां पिपीलिकानां निष्क्राम-
न्तीनां पङ्क्तिमवलोक्य पुरुषगर्भमेतन्नृहमिति गृहीतार्थेन दाहितं
तदेव शयनगृहम् ॥ २६ ॥

Exercise 11b

दीयतामस्मै प्रतिवचनम् । १ । भ्रातरावावां यमजौ । २ । न
निष्प्रयोजनमधिकारवन्तः प्रभुभिराहूयन्ते । ३ । अत्रैव स्थीयताम्
। ४ । यत्तदलंकरणत्रयं क्रीतं तन्मध्यादेकं दीयताम् । ५ । विसृ-
ज्यन्तामभीशवः । ६ । किमुच्यते धैर्यमिति । ७ । भद्रास्त्वर्यतां
त्वर्यताम् । ८ । अभिव्यक्तायां चन्द्रिकायां किं दीपिकापौनरुक्त्येन
। ९ । लातव्य आहूयतामुर्वशी । १० । अर्चे तदिदमाभरणं यन्मया
स्वशरीरादवतार्य राक्षसाय प्रेषितम् । ११ । अयि वत्से एवमात्मा
स्तूयते । १२ । परितोष्य विक्रेतारं गृह्यताम् । १३ । आर्य अस्ति
कश्चिद्वः कुसुमपुरं गच्छति तत आगच्छति वा । १४ । प्रविश्यताम्
। १५ । किं मृषा तर्केणान्विष्यते । १६ । अमात्य इति लज्जाकर-
मिदानीं विशेषणपदम् । १७ । हन्त मूढ एवास्मि यो ऽस्मिन्ननैचरे
वयस्यमकरन्दोचितं व्यवहरामि । १८ । समर्प्यतां राक्षसस्य गृह-
जनः । अनुभूयतां चिरं विचित्रफलो राजप्रसादः । १९ । रक्ष्यतां
परकलत्रेणात्मनः कलत्रं जीवितं च । २० । स एष कामन्दकीसु-
हृत्पुत्रो महामांसस्य पण्यायिता माधवः । २१ । येषामन्तेवासिनां
हस्तेन तत्पुस्तकं भरताश्रमं प्रेषितं तेषामानुयात्रिकाश्चापपाणिः
प्रमादापनोदनार्थमस्मद्भ्राता प्रेषितः । २२ । अनन्तरं च याचा-
भङ्गप्रचलितस्य महतः पौरजनस्य संकुलेन विघटितायां तस्यामा-

गतो ऽस्मि । २३ । मूर्खे अन्यमेव भागमेते तपस्विनो निर्वपन्ति
यो रत्नराशीनपि विहायाभिनन्द्यते । २४ । एवमाढ्याभिप्रायसंभा-
वितेष्टजनचित्तवृत्तिः प्रार्थयिता विप्रलभ्यते ॥ २५ ॥

Exercise 12b

किं ब्रवीषि । १ । अनेन लेखेन राक्षसो जेतव्यः । २ । तत्रैव
मकरन्दमदयन्तिकागमनं यावत्स्थातव्यम् । ३ । शृणुवस्तावत् । ४ ।
हन्त हृदयमपि मे रिपुभिः स्वीकृतम् । ५ । अक्षाम्यशोकच्छाया-
यामास्तामायुष्मान्यावत्त्वामहमिन्द्रगुरवे निवेदयामि । ६ । रक्ष-
णीया राक्षसस्य प्राणा इत्यार्यादेशः । ७ । तद्यथा भवितव्यं
तथा भवतु । ८ । सर्वमेव तन्ममाकुलीभूतम् । ९ । किं भवांस्तू-
ष्णीमास्ते । १० । तदच वस्तुन्यनुपालब्धो राक्षसः । ११ । भद्र
भास्वरक बहिर्नीला तावत्ताड्यतां यावत्कक्ष्यते ऽनेन । १२ । शृणु
विचित्रमिदम् । १३ । अस्मिन्नेव वेतसलतामण्डपे भवितव्यं शकुन्त-
लया । १४ । तदिदानीं सहधर्मचारिणां प्रति न त्वया मन्युः
करणीयः । १५ । तमेवोद्देशं गच्छामि यत्र मे नयनयोः सा
सुनयना तिरोभूता । १६ । आविष्कृतं कथाप्रावीणं वत्सेन । १७ ।
तेन हि तत्प्रयोगादेवाचभवतः सामाजिकानुपास्महे । १८ । कुमार
द्वानतिक्रमणीयवचनो भवानपि । १९ । असम्यक्चेष्टितं प्रियां
समासाद्य कालहरणं कुर्वता मया । २० । कष्टम् एते सुहृद्व्यासनेषु
परवदुदासीनाः प्रत्यादिष्टास्महे वयमनेन । २१ । भोः श्रेष्ठिन् स
चापरिक्लेशः कथमाविर्भवतीति ननु प्रष्टव्या वयमेव भवता
। २२ । यावदेते मानसोत्सुकाः पतत्रिणः सरसो नोत्पतन्ति तावदे-
तेभ्यः प्रियाप्रवृत्तिरवगमयितव्या । २३ । ततस्तेषु गृहीतसंज्ञेषु
भयापदेश्यादितस्ततः प्रद्रुतेषु घकटदासो वध्यस्थानादपनीय
राक्षसं प्रापयितव्यः । २४ । यदेवापसरस्तीर्थान्प्रत्याख्यानविक्लवां
शकुन्तलामादाय दाक्षायणीमुपगता मेनका तदैव ध्यानादवगत-

वृत्तान्तो ऽस्मि दुर्वासस: शापादियं तपस्विनी सहधर्मचारिणा
प्रत्यादिष्टेति ॥ २५ ॥

Exercise 13b

विजये प्रत्यभिजानाति भवती भूषणमिदम् । १ । शठः खल्वसौ
बटु: ।२। सुविहितं लवङ्गिकया यतो माधवानुचर: कलहंसकस्तां
विहारदासीं मन्दारिकां कामयते ।३। क्व पुनर्मां भवत्य: प्रति-
पालयिष्यन्ति ।४। कथम् अदत्त्वैव प्रतिवचनं नर्तितुमारब्ध: ।५।
कथं मद्न्वेषिण: सैनिकास्तपोवनमभिरुन्धन्ति । ६ । काममेतद्भि-
नन्दनीयं तथापि वयमत्र मध्यस्था: । ७ । नातिचिरादमात्यो
ऽस्मान्पुरातनीमवस्थामारोपयिष्यति । ८ । न युक्तं प्राक्तनमपि
पुरुषमवज्ञातुम् । ९ । राजन् चन्द्रगुप्त विदितमेव ते यथा वयं
मलयकेतौ किंचित्कालान्तरमुषिता: । १० । भो विष्णुगुप्त न मां
स्वपाकस्पर्शदूषितं स्प्रष्टुमर्हसि ।११। वत्स कच्चिदभिनन्दितस्त्वया
विधिवत्स्वाभिरनुष्ठितजातकर्मादिक्रिय: पुत्र एष शाकुन्तलेय:
। १२ । तदनुजानीहि मां गमनाय । १३ । न शक्नुमो वयमार्यस्य
वाचा वाचमतिशयितुम् । १४ । यद्येवमभियोगकालमार्य: पश्यति
तत्किमास्यते । १५ । भद्र प्रविश । लप्स्यसे श्रोतारं ज्ञातारं च
। १६ । इदानीमेव दुहितरमतिथिसत्कारायादिश्य दैवमस्याः
प्रतिकूलं शमयितुं सोमतीर्थं गत: । यद्येवं तामेव द्रक्ष्यामि । १७ ।
सखे किमश्रद्धान: पृच्छसि । १८ । किमक्षत्रिया पृथिवी यदेव-
मुद्घुष्यते । १९ । भद्र कस्मिंश्चिदात्मजनानुष्ठेये कर्मणि त्वां व्यापा-
रयितुमिच्छामि । २० । स चेन्मुनिदौहित्रस्तल्लक्षणोपपन्नो भवति
तत: प्रतिनन्द्य शुद्धान्तमेनां प्रवेशयिष्यसि । २१ । तत्किमुज्झित्हा-
जीवितां वराकीं नानुकम्पसे । २२ । न निष्परिग्रहं स्थानभ्रंश:
पीडयिष्यति । २३ । चन्द्रगुप्तशरीरमभिद्रोग्धुमस्मत्प्रयुक्तानां तीक्ष्ण-
रसदादीनामुपसंग्रहार्थं प्रणिधयुपजापार्थं च महता कोषसंचयेन
स्थापित: शकटदास: । २४ । सखे माधव्य अनवाप्तचक्षु:फलो ऽसि

येन त्वया द्रष्टव्यानां परं न दृष्टम् । २५ । भो: श्रेष्ठिन् चन्दन-
दास एवं राजापथ्यकारिषु तीक्ष्णदण्डो राजा न मर्षयिष्यति
राक्षसकलत्रप्रच्छादनं भवत: । २६ । यतो ऽमी व्याघ्राद्यो वर्ण-
मात्रविप्रलब्धा: शृगालमज्ञात्वा राजानममुं मन्यन्ते तवथायं
परिचीयते तथा कुरुत । २७ । देव जीवितुकाम: को ऽन्यो
देवस्य शासनमुल्लङ्घयिष्यति । २८ । यद्यपि स्वामिगुणा न प्रकल्यन्ते
विस्तरं तथापि मद्विज्ञापनं मानयितुमर्हत्याय: ॥ २९ ॥

Exercise 14b

ज्ञातव्य अपि जानीति भवान्क्षायं बाण ब्रूति । १ । अथे मूर्ख
किं भवानस्माकमुपाध्यायाद्धर्मविचित्तर: । २ । न्यश्चामयं च तस्मि-
न्नाश्रमे कस्य चिच्चूतपोतकस्य च्छायायां कमप्युद्दिग्नवर्णं तापसम्
। ३ । वयस्य अङ्गुलीखेदेन दूष्येरन्नक्षराणि । ४ । तत्को ऽयं पदे
पदे महाननध्यवसाय: । ५ । इत्युक्ता च सा ताम्बूलभाजनादाङ्गुष्ठ
तामदर्शयत् । ६ । अवसरे खल्वनुरागोपकारयोर्गरीयसोरुपन्यास:
। ७ । रैवतक उच्चतामस्मत्सारथि: सबाणकार्मुकं रथमुपस्थापयेति
। ८ । स कदाचिद्वैर्यस्खलनविलक्ष: किंचिदनिष्टमपि समाचरेत्
। ९ । यावच्छृणवं मालत्येवास्य मन्मथोन्माथहेतुरिति । १० ।
निखिलान्त:पुरस्वामिनी च तस्याभवत् । ११ । उच्चतां किं ते
भूय: प्रियमुपकरोमि । १२ । इत्यभिधाय किमियं वच्चतीति
मन्मुखासक्तदृष्टिस्तूष्णीमासीत् । १३ । तत्कुतो ऽस्मिन्विपिने प्रिया-
प्रवृत्तिमागमयेयम् । १४ । स किल कृपालुस्तं जनमाईर्द्याद गिरा-
स्वाख्यातिकारणं तां गणिकामपृच्छत् । १५ । कुमार न कदाचिदपि
शकटदासो ऽमात्यराक्षससखागतो मया लिखितमिति प्रतिपत्त्यते
। १६ । सखे भागुरायण नन्वस्माकममात्यराक्षस: प्रियतमो हित-
तमश्च । १७ । अपयातायां भवत्यां मुहूर्तमिव स्थित्वैकाकी किम-
र्थमिदानीमाचरतीति संजातवितर्क: प्रतिनिवृत्य विटपान्तरितवि-
ग्रहस्तं प्रदेशं व्यलोकयम् । १८ । अपि नाम मृगतृष्णिकेव नायमन्ते

प्रस्तावो विषादाय कल्पेत । १९ । सूर्योपस्थानात्प्रतिनिवृत्तं पुरू-
रवसं मामुपेत्य कथ्यतां कुतो भवत्यः परिचातव्या इति । २० ।
इत्यभिदधाना मदनमूर्छाखेदविह्वलैरङ्गैः कथंचिदवलम्ब्य तामे-
वोदतिष्ठम् । उच्चलितायाश्च मे दुर्निमित्तनिवेदकमस्पन्दत दक्षिणं
लोचनम् । उपजातशङ्का चाचिन्तयम् इदमपरं किमप्युपक्षिप्तं
दैवेनेति । २१ । यदसक्तो गरीयान्राक्षसो ऽवगम्यते तदास्माक-
मिदं शस्त्रं तस्मै दीयताम् । २२ । सखे चन्द्रगुप्तस्यैव तावन्नगर-
प्रवेशात्प्रभृति मत्प्रयुक्तैश्चीच्चारसद्दादिभिः किमनुष्ठितमिति श्रोतु-
मिच्छामि । २३ । यदि पुनरीदृशं स्वामित्वाको राजा रामः
पश्येत्तदास्य स्नेहेन हृदयमभिष्यन्देत । २४ । इति विचारयन्तीमेव
मामविचारितगुणदोषविशेषो रूपैकपक्षपाती नवयौवनसुलभः
कुसुमायुधः कुसुमसमयमद इव मधुकरीं परवशामकरोत ॥ २५ ॥

Vocabulary

1 Sanskrit–English

Alphabetical order

The order of the Sanskrit alphabet is **a, ā, i, ī, u, ū, ṛ, ṝ, ḷ, e, ai, o, au, ṃ, ḥ, k, kh, g, gh, ṅ, c, ch, j, jh, ñ, ṭ, ṭh, ḍ, ḍh, ṇ, t, th, d, dh, n, p, ph, b, bh, m, y, r, l, v, ś, ṣ, s, h.**

The position of anusvāra (ṃ) given above applies where the anusvāra is followed by **y, r, l, v, ś, ṣ, s** or **h.** But in accordance with the usual practice of Sanskrit dictionaries, anusvāra before a stop or nasal is given the alphabetical place of the appropriate class nasal. Thus the word **saṃtoṣaḥ** is treated as if it were **santoṣaḥ.** (The latter spelling, which better represents the pronunciation of the word, is in fact possible, though hardly ever found nowadays in printed texts.) In looking up a word containing anusvāra, therefore, the anusvāra should be converted mentally into a nasal consonant wherever this is possible.

A similar principle applies in the case of visarga (ḥ): **ḥś, ḥṣ** and **ḥs** occupy the position of **śś, ṣṣ** and **ss** respectively. In practice, however, this will cause comparatively little difficulty.

Gender

Substantives ending in **a** are given as ending in **aḥ** if masculine and **am** if neuter. Substantives ending in **ā** or **ī** should be assumed to be feminine. The gender of nouns ending in **-in** and -tṛ is not normally specified, since these may, if appropriate, be treated as adjectival (with feminines in -inī and -trī).

Verbs

While a point has been made of quoting the present tense of all verbs listed, it should be mentioned that present stem formations may sometimes be far less common than the particular form, such as past participle or absolutive, which has led to the inclusion of the verb in the Vocabulary.

अ **a** *negative prefix* not, no, un- *etc.*

अंशुकं **aṃśukaṃ** cloth, garment

अकथयत् **akathayat** *3rd sg. imperf. para. of* **kath**

अकृतार्थ **a:kṛtḥ:ârtha** [whose aim is unachieved:] unsuccessful

अक्षमाला **akṣa-mālā** [garland of Eleocarpus seeds:] rosary

अक्षरं **akṣaraṃ** syllable, written character

अग: **agaḥ** [not moving:] mountain

अगस्त्य: **Agastyaḥ** *pr. n.*

अग्नि **agni** *m.* fire

अग्रं **agraṃ** front, top, tip

अग्रत: **agrataḥ** in front of (*gen.*)

अघं **aghaṃ** evil, impurity

अङ्क **aṅk** (X **aṅkayati**) brand, stamp

अङ्क: **aṅkaḥ** hook; curve of body, lap

अङ्गं **aṅgaṃ** limb, division

अङ्गीकृ **aṅgī˘kṛ** make a part, subordinate; adopt, accept, promise

अङ्गुरीयक aṅgurīyaka *m./n.* ring (for finger)

अङ्गुलि aṅguli *f. or* aṅgulī finger, toe

अङ्गुष्ठ: aṅguṣṭhaḥ thumb, big toe

अचिर a:cira [not long:] soon

अचिरात् acirāt after a short while

अचिरेण acireṇa within a short while

अञ्चल: añcalaḥ border (of dress)

अञ्जलि añjali *m.* joined hands

अत: ataḥ from this, hence, for this reason; **ata eva**
[precisely from this:] that is why

अति ati *prefix* excessive(ly), extreme(ly), too, very *etc.*

अतिक्रम् ati+kram (I atikrāmati) go beyond; transgress, go against

अतिक्रान्त atikrānta past, bygone

अतिचिर ati:cira very long

अतिथि atithi *m.* guest; **atithi-satkāraḥ** honouring of
guests, hospitality

अतिदारुण ati:dāruṇa [very] dreadful

अतिदीप्त ati:dīpta exceptionally brilliant

अतिदु:खसंवेग: ati:duḥkha-ʾsaṃvegaḥ extreme pangs of
pain

अतिपात: atipātaḥ lapse, neglect

अतिभूमि atibhūmi *f.* culmination, excess

अतिमात्र ati_mātra [beyond measure:] excessive

अतिवह् ati+vah *caus.* (ativāhayati) spend (time)

अतिशय atiśaya surpassing

अतिशी ati+śī (II atiśete) surpass, triumph over

अतिसृज् ati+sṛj (VI atisṛjati) bestow, lavish

अतीत atīta [ati+ita gone beyond:] past

अतीव atīva excessively, intensely

अत्यन्त **aty_anta** [beyond limit:] excessive, extreme, intensely, 'terribly'.

अत्याहितं **atyāhitaṃ** calamity, disaster

अत्र **atra** here, in this, on this; on this matter, about this

अत्रभवन्त् **atrabhavant** His Honour here

अत्रभवती **atrabhavatī** Her Honour here, this Lady

अथ **atha** *introductory or connecting particle* now, next, then

अथवा **atha vā** or rather, but no, but

अदर्शनं **a:darśanaṃ** not seeing

अद्भुत **adbhuta** extraordinary

अद्य **adya** today, now

अद्य प्रभृति **adya prabhṛti** from today onward

अद्रि **adri** *m.* rock, mountain

अधस्तात् **adhastāt** beneath (*gen.*)

अधिक **adhika** additional, superior

अधिकरणं **adhikaraṇaṃ** grammatical relationship

अधिकार: **adhikāraḥ** authority, responsibility, office, job

अधिगम् **adhi+gam** (I **adhigacchati**) find, obtain, receive; realise, perceive

अधिपति **adhipati** *m.* overlord, ruler

अधिरुह **adhi+ruh** (I **adhirohati**) ascend, mount

अधिष्ठातृ **adhiṣṭhātṛ** *m.* superintending, at the head of

अधी **adhī** (adhi+i) (II **adhīte**) study; *caus.* (**adhyā-payati**) teach

अधुना **adhunā** now

अधोमुख **adho:mukha** down-faced, with face bent down

अध्ययनं **adhyayanaṃ** studying, study

अध्यवसाय: **adhyavasāyaḥ** resolution

अध्यवसित **adhyavasita** resolved, accomplished, completed

अध्यवसो adhy+ava+so (IV **adhyavasyati**) resolve, decide, accomplish

अध्युषित adhyuṣita (*p.p. of* adhi+vas) inhabited

अनध्ययनं an:adhyayanam freedom from study, (academic) holiday

अनध्यवसाय: an:adhyavasāyaḥ irresolution, hesitation

अनन्तरम् an:antaram [without interval:] immediately

अनपराद्ध an:aparāddha unoffending, innocent

अनर्थ: anarthaḥ reverse, disaster

अनादृत्य an:ādṛtya *absolutive* not heeding, without reference to

अनायास an:āyāsa [in which there is no exertion:] not strenuous

अनिमित्त a:nimitta without cause

अनिल: anilaḥ wind, breeze

अनिष्ट an:iṣṭa undesired, unpleasant, dreadful

अनुकम्प् anu+kamp (I **anukampate**) sympathize with, pity

अनुकारिन् anukārin (anu+kṛ imitate) imitative

अनुकूल anukūla favourable

अनुगम् anu+gam (I **anugacchati**) follow, attend

अनुग्रह् anu+grah (IX **anugṛhṇāti**) favour

अनुग्रह: anugrahaḥ favour, kindness

अनुचर: anucaraḥ companion, attendant

अनुज: anujaḥ [born after:] younger brother

अनुज्ञा anu+jñā (IX **anujānāti**) allow, give leave, assent

अनुताप: anutāpaḥ remorse

अनुत्सेक: an:utsekaḥ [non-arrogance:] modesty

अनुप्रहि anu+pra+hi (V **anuprahiṇoti**) send (someone after something), despatch

अनुबन्ध् anu+bandh (IX **anubadhnāti**) pursue, importune

अनुभू anu+bhū (I **anubhavati**) experience, undergo, 'reap, enjoy'

अनुमन्त्र् anu+mantr (X **anumantrayate**) consecrate with mantras, bless

अनुयायिन् anuyāyin (anu+yā attend) attendant upon

अनुयुज् anu+yuj (VII **anuyuṅkte**) question, examine

अनुराग: anurāgaḥ passion, love

अनुरुध् anu+rudh (IV **anurudhyate**) adhere to, comply with (*acc.*)

अनुरूप anu_rūpa conformable, suitable, proper, appropriate

अनुलिप् anu+lip (VI **anulimpati**) anoint

अनुलेपनं anulepanam ointment

अनुवृत् anu+vṛt (I **anuvartate**) go after, attend upon

अनुशय: anuśayaḥ consequence, repentance, regret

अनुष्ठा anuṣṭhā (anu+sthā) (I **anutiṣṭhati**) carry out, perform, act, do

अनुष्ठानं anuṣṭhānam carrying out, [performance of task:] 'duties'

अनुस्मृ anu+smṛ (I **anusmarati**) remember

अनेक an:eka [not one:] several

अन्त: antaḥ end, boundary, final (syllable of word)

अन्त:पुरं antaḥpuram women's quarters (of palace), harem

अन्तरं antaram interval, juncture, difference; -antaram *ifc.* a different, another

अन्तरात्मन् antar:ātman *m.* soul within, internal feelings

अन्तरित **antarita** (*p.p. of* **antar+i** go between) hidden, concealed

अन्तेवासिन् **antevāsin** [resident] disciple

अन्ध **andha** blind

अन्य **anya** *pron.* other, another, else, different

अन्यतरस्याम् **anyatarasyām** (*gram.*) optionally

अन्यत्र **anyatra** elsewhere, on *etc.* another

अन्यथा **anyathā** otherwise, in other circumstances

अन्वमंस्त **anvamaṃsta** 3rd sg. *ātm.* s-*aorist of* **anu+ man** 'assent, permit'

अन्वय: **anvayaḥ** succession, lineage, family

अन्वित **anvita** attended by, full of

अन्विष् **anviṣ** (**anu+iṣ**) (I **anveṣate**) look for, search for, enquire

अन्वेषिन् **anveṣin** searching for

अपकार: **apakāraḥ** doing harm, injury, ruination

अपकारिन् **apakārin** (*from* **apa kṛ** 'do harm') harming, offending

अपक्रम् **apa+kram** (I **apakrāmati**) go away, withdraw

अपत्यं **apatyaṃ** offspring

अपथ्य **a:pathya** unwholesome

अपथ्यकारिन् **apathya-kārin** doing what is inimical (to king), traitor

अपदेश: **apadeśaḥ** pretence, pretext

अपनी **apa+nī** (I **apanayati**) remove, take away

अपनोदनं **apanodanaṃ** driving away

अपया **apa+yā** (II **apayāti**) go away, depart

अपर **apara** other, different

अपरक्त **aparakta** disaffected, disloyal

अपराग: aparāgaḥ disaffection, disloyalty

अपराद्ध aparāddha having offended, guilty

अपराध: aparādhaḥ offence, guilt

अपराधिन् aparādhin offending, guilty

अपरिक्लेश: a:parikleśaḥ lack of vexation

अपर्याप्त a:paryāpta inadequate

अपवादिन् apavādin decrying

अपवारित apavārita hidden

अपवाहित apavāhita p.p. of caus. of apa+vah 'carry off'

अपश्यत् apaśyat 3rd sg. imperf. para. of dṛś 'see'

अपसर्पणं apasarpaṇam getting away, escape

अपसृप apa+sṛp (I apasarpati) get away, escape

अपहृ apa+hṛ (I apaharati) carry off

अपह्नु apa+hnu (II apahnute) conceal

अपाप a:pāpa without sin, guiltless

अपि api enclitic also, too, as well, alike, and; even,
though, however; gives indefinite sense to interrog. pronouns;
api non-enclitic marks a question

अपि नाम api nāma with opt. could it be that?, if only!

अपूप: apūpaḥ cake: see daṇḍāpūpikā

अपूर्व a:pūrva unprecedented, strange

अपेक्षा apekṣā consideration, regard

अपेत apeta (apa+ita) departed; free from (abl.), lacking

अप्रमादिन् a:pramādin [not negligent:] vigilant

अप्सरस apsaras f. nymph (of heaven)

अभिघ्रा abhi+ghrā (I abhijighrati) smell

अभिज्ञ abhijña knowing, conversant with (gen.)

अभिद्रुह abhi+druh (IV abhidruhyate) do violence to

अभिधा abhi+dhā (III abhidadhāti/abhidhatte) tell,
say, speak

अभिधानं abhidhānam appellation, name; speaking, stating

अभिनन्द् abhi+nand (I abhinandati) rejoice in, greet with enthusiasm, prize

अभिनिविष्ट abhiniviṣṭa concentrated, intent

अभिप्रायः abhiprāyaḥ inclination, will, intention

अभिप्रेतं abhipretam [thing willed:] wish

अभिभू abhi+bhū (I abhibhavati) overpower

अभिमत abhimata respected, honoured

अभियुक्त abhiyukta diligent

अभियोक्तृ abhiyoktṛ attacker

अभियोगः abhiyogaḥ intentness, preoccupation; assault, attack

अभिलष् abhi+laṣ (I abhilaṣati) wish for, crave, hanker after

अभिलाषः abhilāṣaḥ craving, passion for (loc.)

अभिलाषिन् abhilāṣin desirous, anxious

अभिलिख abhi+likh (VI abhilikhati) draw (picture)

अभिवद् abhi+vad caus. (abhivādayate) greet

अभिवृत् abhi+vṛt (I abhivartate) approach, go towards, make for

अभिव्यक्त abhivyakta manifest, visible

अभिष्यन्द् abhiṣyand (abhi+syand) (I abhiṣyandate) flow

अभिसंधि abhisaṃdhi m. agreement, condition

अभिहित abhihita p.p. of abhidhā

अभीप्सित abhīpsita desired; abhīpsitam [thing desired:] desire

अभीशु abhīśu m. rein, bridle

अभूत् abhūt 3rd sg. aorist of bhū

अभ्यस्त **abhyasta** practised, familiar

अभ्रं **abhram** cloud

अमर: **Amaraḥ** *author of the* **Amarakośaḥ**

अमात्य: **amātyaḥ** minister (of king)

अमी अमुम् अमुष्य **amī, amum, amuṣya** *forms of* **asau**

अमृतं **amṛtam** nectar, ambrosia

अम्बा **ambā** mother

अम्बा अम्बिका **Ambā, Ambikā** *pr. n.*

अयम् **ayam** *pron.* this, this one, he; here (is), see, hereby

अयशस् **a:yaśas** *n.* [non-fame:] disgrace

अयि **ayi** ha!, ah!

अयुक्त **a:yukta** [not right:] wrong

अयुज् **a:yuj** uneven, odd

अयोध्या **Ayodhyā** *name of a city* (Oudh)

अये **aye** ah!, oh!

अरण्यं **araṇyam** forest

अरि **ari** *m.* enemy

अरुन्धती **Arundhatī** *pr. n.*

अर्थ: **arthaḥ** matter, business; object, purpose, point, aim, interests; meaning, sense; wealth, property

अर्थम् **-artham** *ifc.* for the sake of, in order to

अर्थान्तरन्यास: **arthᵥ-ântara-nyāsaḥ** (*lit. crit.*) Substantiation

अर्थापत्ति **arthᵥ-āpatti** *f.* (*lit. crit.*) Strong Presumption

अर्थिन् **arthin** having an object, wanting, petitioning

अर्थौत्सर्ग: **arthᵥ-ôtsargaḥ** expenditure of money

अर्ध: **ardhaḥ** half (portion)

अर्धरात्र: **ardharātraḥ** midnight

अर्पयति **arpayati** *caus. of* ṛ

अर्ह् **arh** (I **arhati**) be worthy; be able, 'aspire to'; should, ought

अर्ह **arha** deserving, meriting; proper, deserved

अलंकरणं **alamkaraṇam** ornament

अलंकार: **alamkārah** ornament; (*lit. crit.*) embellishment, literary figure

अलंकृ **alam+kṛ** (VIII **alamkaroti**) adorn, embellish

अलम् **alam** enough; +*instr.* enough of, do not *etc.*; +*inf.* capable of

अल्प **alpa** small

अवकाश: **avakāśah** space, scope

अवगम् **ava+gam** understand, learn, know; suppose, consider

अवगम् **ava+gam** *caus.* (**avagamayati**) procure

अवगाह् **ava+gāh** (I **avagāhate**) plunge into, bathe in (*acc.*)

अवग्रह: **avagrahah** obstacle, restraint; separation (of words)

अवचय: **avacayah** gathering, picking

अवज्ञा **ava+jñā** (IX **avajānāti**) despise

अवज्ञा **avajñā** contempt

अवतृ **ava+tṝ** *caus.* (**avatārayati**) remove

अवधृ **ava+dhṛ** *caus.* (**avadhārayati**) determine, resolve

अवनत **avanata** (*p.p. of* **ava+nam**) bent down

अवयव: **avayavah** portion, particle, member

अवरुह् **ava+ruh** *caus.* (**avaropayati**) cause to descend, dismiss from office

अवलम्ब् **ava+lamb** (I **avalambate**) cling to, hold on to; adopt (position)

अवलोक् **ava+lok** (X **avalokayati**) see, look at

अवलोकनं avalokanam looking at, gazing on

अवलोकिता Avalokitā pr. n.

अवश a:vaśa powerless, helpless

अवश्यम् avaśyam necessarily

अवसर: avasaraḥ opportunity, occasion, right moment, time (for)

अवसरे avasare at the right moment, opportune

अवसानं avasānam termination, end, conclusion

अवसित avasita (p.p. of ava+so) terminated, over, fulfilled

अवस्था ava+sthā stay (in a state), remain

अवस्था avasthā state, condition, period of life

अवहित्थं avahittham, avahitthā dissimulation

अवाप् avāp (ava+āp) (V avāpnoti) obtain, acquire

अविघ्न a:vighna unhindered

अविद्वान् a:vidvān ignorant

अविनय: a:vinayaḥ lack of breeding, discourtesy

अविप्रतिपन्न a:vipratipanna not uncertain, entirely fixed

अविषय: a:viṣayaḥ [non-sphere:] matter beyond the scope (of)

अवेक्ष् avekṣ (ava+īkṣ) (I avekṣate) watch, watch over

अव्यभिचारिन् a:vyabhicārin undeviating, unswerving

अशरण a:śaraṇa without refuge, helpless

अशेष a:śeṣa [without remainder:] complete, whole, all

अशोक: aśokaḥ aśoka tree

अशोभन a:śobhana unpleasant, awful

अश्रु aśru n. tear

अश्रुमुख aśru=mukha tearful-faced

अश्व: aśvaḥ horse

अस् as (II asti) be, exist; may express 'have' etc.

असंतोष: a:saṃtoṣaḥ dissatisfaction

असमर्थ a:samartha incapable

असंभाव्य a:saṃbhāvya incredible

असम्यक् a:samyak wrongly

असु asu *m.* breath; *pl.* life

असुर: asuraḥ demon

असौ asau *pron.* that

अस्त्रं astraṃ missile, weapon

अस्था: asthāḥ *2nd sg. aorist para. of* sthā

अस्थाने a:sthāne not in place, misplaced, inappropriately

अस्फुट a:sphuṭa unclear, illegible

अस्मत् asmat *stem of 1st pl. pron.* vayam

अस्वस्थशरीर a:svastha:śarīra [whose body is not well:] [physically] unwell

अस्वास्थ्यं a:svāsthyaṃ discomfort, illness

अह ah *see* āha

अहन् ahan *n. irreg.* day

अह: अह्: -ahaḥ, -ahnaḥ *ifc. for* ahan

अहमहमिका ahamahamikā rivalry

अहो aho oh!, what a—!; aho bata oh alas!

आ ā+*abl.* up to, until

आकर्णयति ākarṇayati (*denom.*) give ear, listen to

आकार: ākāraḥ form, appearance, (facial) expression

आकाशं ākāśaṃ ether, air, sky

आकुल ākula confused

आकुलयति ākulayati (*denom.*) confuse, disturb

आकुलीभू ākulī˜bhū grow confused

आकुलीभूत ākulī˜bhūta [being] in confusion

आकृति ākṛti *f.* appearance, figure

आकृष ā+kṛṣ (I ākarṣati) drag, draw

आक्रन्द् ā+krand (I ākrandati) cry out, scream, lament

आख्या ā+khyā (II ākhyāti) declare, tell, announce

आख्या ākhyā appellation, name; ːākhya [having as a name:] called, known as

आगम् ā+gam (I āgacchati) come, approach, arrive

आगम् ā+gam caus. (āgamayati) acquire

आगम: āgamaḥ arrival, accession

आगमनं āgamanam coming, arrival

आघ्रा ā+ghrā (I ājighrati) smell

आचक्रन्द् ācakranda 3rd sg. para. perf. of ākrand

आचर् ā+car (I ācarati) conduct oneself, act, do

आचार्य: ācāryaḥ teacher

आच्छद् ā+chad (X ācchādayati) hide, conceal

आज्ञा ājñā command, order

आज्ञा ā+jñā caus. (ājñāpayati) order, say (authoritatively)

आतप: ātapaḥ heat (esp. of sun)

आत्मज: ātma-jaḥ [born of oneself:] son

आत्मजा ātma-jā daughter

आत्मन् ātman m. self, myself etc.

आत्यन्तिक ātyantika (cf. atyanta) perpetual, lasting

आत्रेयी Ātreyī pr. n.

आदर: ādaraḥ care, respect, trouble, anxiety (to do something); ādaram kṛ take care (to)

आदा ā+dā (III ādatte) take, take hold of, bring

आदि ādi m. beginning

आदि ːādi etc.

आदिश् ā+diś (VI ādiśati) order, proclaim, direct

आदृ ā+dṛ (IV ādriyate) heed, respect, defer to, refer to

आदेश: ādeśaḥ command, order, instruction

आद्य ādya initial, first, earliest

आधोरण: ādhoraṇaḥ elephant-driver

आनी ā+nī (I ānayati) bring

आनुयात्रिक: ānuyātrikaḥ escort

आप् āp (V āpnoti) obtain, get

आपत् ā+pat (I āpatati) occur, befall, appear suddenly, present oneself

आपतनं āpatanam occurrence, (sudden) appearance, arising

आपत्ति āpatti f. (from ā+pad) happening, occurrence

आपद् ā+pad (IV āpadyate) attain, come to, happen, occur

आपन्नसत्त्व āpanna:sattva [to whom a living creature has occurred:] pregnant

आपीड: āpīḍaḥ, āpīḍakaḥ chaplet, crest

आप्त āpta trustworthy

आप्रछ् ā+prach (VI āpṛcchati) take leave of, say goodbye

आभरणं ābharaṇam ornament, jewel, decoration, insignia

आमन्त्र् ā+mantr (X āmantrayate) salute; take leave of

आमोद: āmodaḥ scent

आयतनं āyatanam abode, [abode of god:] temple

आया ā+yā (II āyāti) come

आयास: āyāsaḥ effort, exertion

आयुधं āyudham weapon

आयुस् āyus n. life

आयुष्मन्त् āyuṣmant long-lived, (title of respect) sire etc.

आयोध्यक Āyodhyaka inhabiting Ayodhyā

आरभ ā+rabh (I ārabhate) undertake, begin, start

आरम्भ: ārambhaḥ beginning, undertaking

आराम: ārāmaḥ pleasure; pleasure-grove, woodland

आरुह् ā+ruh (I ārohati) ascend, climb, mount, get in(to chariot)

आरुह् ā+ruh *caus.* (āropayati) cause to mount, raise on to; *with* śūlam impale

आर्त ārta afflicted, oppressed

आर्ति ārti *f.* affliction, distress

आर्द्र ārdra moist, tender

आर्य ārya noble, honourable

आर्य: āryaḥ Your/His Excellency/Honour, sir, *etc.*

आर्यपुत्र: ārya-putraḥ [son of] nobleman; *voc.* noble sir

आर्या āryā noble lady, Madam, *etc.*

आलक्ष्य ālakṣya discernible, just visible

आलिख् ā+likh (VI ālikhati) draw (picture)

आलिङ्ग् ā+liṅg (I āliṅgati) embrace

आलोक् ā+lok (X ālokayati) gaze, look at

आवास: āvāsaḥ dwelling, house

आविद् ā+vid *caus.* (āvedayati) make known, tell

आविर्भू āvir~bhū become manifest, reveal oneself

आविष्कृ āviṣ~kṛ make manifest, reveal

आवेग: āvegaḥ alarm, agitation

आवेश: āveśaḥ attack (of emotion)

आशङ्क् ā+śaṅk (I āśaṅkate) fear, doubt, suspect, be afraid

आशङ्का āśaṅkā apprehension, fear

आशा āśā hope

आशिस् āśis *f. irreg.* prayer, benediction

आशीर्वाद: āśīrvādaḥ blessing, benison

आश्रम: āśramaḥ hermitage; *more widely* one of the four stages of life (of which entering a hermitage is the third)

आश्रमपदं āśrama-padam [site of] hermitage

आश्रि ā+śri (I āśrayati/āśrayate) resort to, take shelter with (*acc.*)

आश्रित्य āśritya [having resorted to:] at, in, by

आश्वस ā+śvas *caus.* (āśvāsayati) cause to breathe freely, comfort, console

आश्वास: āśvāsaḥ [breathing freely:] feeling of comfort, optimism

आश्वासनं āśvāsanam comforting, consolation

आस् ās (II āste) sit, stay, remain

आसक्त āsakta fastened, fixed, occupied

आसक्ति āsakti *f.* adherence, intentness (on)

आसद् ā+sad *caus.* (āsādayati) reach, overtake; find, acquire

आसनं āsanam seat, couch

आसन्न āsanna near; *ifc.* beside

आसीत् āsīt *3rd sg. imperf.* of as 'be'

आस्कन्द् ā+skand (I āskandati) leap upon, attack

आह āha (*3rd sg. para. perf.* of ah 'say') says, said

आहर -āhara *ifc.* bringer, carrier

आहरणं āharaṇam bringing, fetching

आहार: āhāraḥ fodder

आहितुण्डिक: āhituṇḍikaḥ snake-charmer

आहूय āhūya *absolutive of* āhve

आहृ ā+hṛ (I āharati) bring, fetch

आह्वे ā+hve (I āhvayati) summon, call

इ i (II eti) go

इच्छा **icchā** wish, desire

इत: **itaḥ** from here, from this; in this direction, this way, over here; **itas tataḥ** hither and thither

इतर **itara** other

इतरेतर **itaretara** mutual, of/to *etc.* each other

इति **iti** [thus:] with these words, with this thought *etc.*; *see Chapters 2, 14 and 15*

इत्थम् **ittham** in this way, so

इत्थंभूत **ittham:bhūta** [being in this way:] such, so·

इदम् **idam** *n. sg. of* **ayam**

इदानीम् **idānīm** now

इन्दु **indu** *m.* moon

इन्द्र: **Indraḥ** the god Indra

इन्द्रायुधं **Indrɔ-āyudham** [Indra's weapon:] rainbow

इन्द्रियं **indriyam** (organ or faculty of) sense

इव **iva** as it were, as if, like, as, such as, *etc.*

इष् **iṣ** (VI **icchati**) want, wish, desire, 'should like'

इषु **iṣu** *m.* arrow

इष्टं **iṣṭam** thing wished, wish

इष्टजन: **iṣṭa:janaḥ** the loved one

इह **iha** here, in this; in this world

ईक्ष् **īkṣ** (I **īkṣate**) look upon, see

ईदृश् **īdṛśa** (*f.* ī) of this kind, such

ईप्सित **īpsita** desired, wished for

ईषत् **īṣat** slightly

ईह् **īh** (I **īhate**) long for, desire

उक्त **ukta** *p.p. of* **vac**

उग्र **ugra** fierce, grim

उचित **ucita** suitable, appropriate, proper, right

उच्चल् **uccal** (ut+cal) (I **uccalati**) move away; rise

उच्छ्वस् **ucchvas** (ut+śvas) (II **ucchvasiti**) breathe, bloom, blossom

उच्छ्वास: **ucchvāsaḥ** breath

उत् **ut** *prefix* up *etc.*

उताहो **utāho** or? (*marking alternative question*)

उत्क **utka** eager, longing for

उत्कण्ठते **utkaṇṭhate** *denom.* long for, be in love with (*gen.*)

उत्क्षिप् **ut+kṣip** (VI **utkṣipati**) throw up, raise

उत्खात **utkhāta** (*p.p. of* ut+khā) dug up, uprooted

उत्तम **uttama** uppermost, supreme, top

उत्तमाङ्गं **uttam**ɔ:**âṅgam** [highest limb:] head

उत्तर **uttara** following, subsequent, further; upper, superior to, above

उत्तरं **uttaram** answer, reply; consequence, prevalent result

उत्पत् **ut+pat** (I **utpatati**) fly up

उत्पत्ति **utpatti** *f.* arising

उत्पद् **ut+pad** (IV **utpadyate**) arise

उत्पद् **ut+pad** *caus.* (**utpādayati**) cause to arise, cause

उत्पीडित **utpīḍita** squeezed

उत्सर्गः **utsargaḥ** pouring out, expenditure

उत्सर्पिन् **utsarpin** (*from* ut+sṛp 'soar up') high-soaring

उत्सव: **utsavaḥ** festival

उत्साह: **utsāhaḥ** enthusiasm

उत्सुक **utsuka** eager

उत्सुकं **utsukam** eagerness

उत्स्था **ut+sthā** (I **uttiṣṭhati**) get up

उदकं **udakam** water

उदग्र **udagra** intense

उदपान **udapāna** *m./n.* well, water-tank

उदय: **udayaḥ** (*from* ut+i) rising

उदस **udas** (ut+as) (IV. **udasyati**) throw up, throw out, push out

उदार **udāra** noble, generous

उदास **udās** (ut+ās) (II **udāste**) sit idle

उदीक्ष **udīkṣ** (ut+īkṣ) (I **udīkṣate**) look at

उद्घातिन् **udghātin** having elevations, bumpy

उद्घुष् **udghuṣ** (ut+ghuṣ) (I **udghoṣati**) cry out

उद्देश: **uddeśaḥ** region, part, place, spot

उद्धरणं **uddharaṇam** (*from* ut+hṛ) tearing out, destruction

उद्धा **uddhā** (ut+hā) (III **ujjihīte**) rise up, start up; depart

उद्या **udyā** (ut+yā) (II **udyāti**) rise up

उद्यानं **udyānam** garden, park

उद्योग: **udyogaḥ** exertion

उद्विग्न **udvigna** distressed, love-sick, melancholy

उद्वेष्ट **udveṣṭ** (ut+veṣṭ) *caus.* (**udveṣṭayati**) unwrap, open (letter)

उन्मत्त **unmatta** insane, crazed

उन्मनस् **un_manas** eager, longing

उन्माथ: **unmāthaḥ** shaking up, pangs

उन्माद: **unmādaḥ** insanity

उन्मुखम् **un_mukham** [with the face] upwards

उपकार: **upakāraḥ** help, aiding (of), service

उपकारिन् **upakārin** helper, ally

उपक्र **upa+kṛ** (VIII **upakaroti**) furnish, provide, help

उपक्लृप **upa+klṛp** *caus.* (**upakalpayati**) equip; assign

उपक्षिप् upa+kṣip (VI upakṣipati) hint at

उपगम् upa+gam (I upagacchati) go to, come to, reach, approach

उपग्रहः upagrahaḥ conciliation, winning over

उपजन् upa+jan (IV upajāyate) come into being, be roused

उपजाप: upajāpaḥ (secret) instigation to rebellion, 'overtures'

उपत्यका upatyakā foothill

उपनयनं upanayanam bringing, carrying

उपनी upa+nī (I upanayati) bring, take, carry, bear; initiate (into adulthood)

उपन्यास: upanyāsaḥ mention, allusion

उपपन्न upapanna suitable, possible; possessed of

उपप्लव: upaplavaḥ affliction, molestation

उपभुज् upa+bhuj (VII upabhuṅkte) enjoy, consume, spend

उपमा upamā simile

उपयेमे upayeme *3rd sg. ātm. perf. of* upa+yam 'marry'

उपयोग: upayogaḥ use, utility

उपरम upa+ram (I uparamate) cease, die

उपराग: uparāgaḥ eclipse

उपरि upari above, on; about, concerning (*gen.*); after (*abl.*)

उपरुध् upa+rudh (VII uparuṇaddhi) besiege, invade, molest, hinder

उपरोध: uparodhaḥ obstruction, interruption

उपरोधनं uparodhanam besieging

उपलभ् upa+labh (I upalabhate) acquire, ascertain, discover, learn

उपविश् upa+viś (VI upaviśati) sit down

उपश्रु upa+śru (V upaśṛṇoti) hear of, learn of

उपश्लिष upa+śliṣ *caus.* (upaśleṣayati) cause to come near, bring near

उपसंग्रह: upasaṃgrahaḥ embracing; collecting; looking after

उपसदनं upasadanam respectful salutation

उपसृ upa+sṛ (I upasarati) go up to, approach

उपस्था upa+sthā (I upatiṣṭhate) stand near, be at hand; (upatiṣṭhati) attend

उपस्था upa+sthā *caus.* (upasthāpayati) cause to be at hand, bring near

उपस्थानं upasthānam attendance

उपहत upahata struck, hurt, killed

उपहार: upahāraḥ offering up, sacrifice

उपहृ upa+hṛ (I upaharati) offer; offer up, sacrifice

उपाध्याय: upādhyāyaḥ teacher, preceptor

उपाय: upāyaḥ means, way, expedient

उपारूढ upārūḍha *p.p. of* upa+ā+ruh 'mount'

उपालम् upa+ā+labh (I upālabhate) reproach, rebuke, blame

उपास् upās (upa+ās) (II upāste) sit by, wait upon, honour

उपे upe (upa+i) (II upaiti) approach, come to

उपेक्ष् upekṣ (upa+īkṣ) (I upekṣate) overlook, disregard

उपोढ upoḍha (*p.p. of* upa+ūh) produced, increased

उभ ubha (*dual only*) both

उरस् uras *n.* chest, bosom, breast

उर्वशी Urvaśī *pr. n.*

उल्लङ्घ् ullaṅgh (ut+laṅgh) *caus.* (ullaṅghayati) transgress, violate

उशीर uśīra *m./n.* a fragrant root

उषित uṣita *p.p. of* vas

ऊढ ūḍha *p.p. of* vah

ऊर्ध्वम् ūrdhvam after (*abl.*)

ऋ ṛ *caus.* (arpayati) transfer, hand over

ऋणं ṛṇam debt

ऋत्विज् ṛtvij (ṛtvik) *m.* priest

ऋषि ṛṣi *m.* seer, sage

एक eka *pron.* one, a, only, alone, single

एकदा ekadā at one time, once

एकवचनं eka-vacanam (*gram.*) singular (number)

एकाकिन् ekākin alone

एकादश ekādaśa (*f.* ī) eleventh

एतत् etat *n. sg. and stem form of* eṣaḥ

एतावन्त् etāvant this much

एध् edh *caus.* (edhayati) cause to prosper, bless

एनम् enam *enclitic pron.* him, her, it, *etc.*

एव eva *enclitic particle of emphasis* in fact, really, actually, exactly, just, only, entirely, quite, (the) very, the same, it is . . . that, *etc.*

एवम् evam in this way, like this, thus, so, you see how

एष: eṣaḥ *pron.* this, this one, he; here (is), see, herewith

एहि ehi (*2nd sg. para. imperv. of* ā+i) come

ऐक्ष्वाक Aikṣvāka (*f.* ī) descended from King Ikṣvāku

ओकस okas *n.* home

औत्सुक्यं autsukyam eagerness, longing

औरस aurasa (*f.* ī) produced from the breast (**uras**), belonging to oneself

औशनस Auśanasa (*f.* ī) originating from Uśanas

औषधं auṣadham medicine

क ka *suffix sometimes added to exocentric compounds*

कः kaḥ *interrog. pron.* who? what? which?; **kaḥ+api/cit** any(one), any(thing), some(one), some(thing), a (certain), a few

कच्चित् kaccit I hope that . . .?

कञ्चुकिन् kañcukin *m.* chamberlain

कटक kaṭaka *m./n.* (royal) camp

कठोर kaṭhora hard, full-grown

कठोरगर्भ kaṭhora:garbha [with foetus full-grown:] late in pregnancy

कण्ठः kaṇṭhaḥ neck, throat

कण्वः Kaṇvaḥ *pr. n.*

कतम katama *pron.* which?

कतर katara *pron.* which (of two)?

कतिपय katipaya a few

कथ् kath (X kathayati) tell, relate, say, mention, speak of

कथम् katham how? in what way? What, . . .? why, . . .!

कथंचित् katham cit, katham api somehow, only just

कथा kathā story, talk, speaking, conversation

कथितं kathitam thing spoken, talk, conversation

कदा kadā when?

कदाचित् kadācit sometimes, perhaps

कनकं kanakam gold

कन्यका kanyakā, kanyā girl, daughter

कम् kam *caus.* (kāmayate) desire, love, be in love with

कमल kamala *m./n.* lotus

कर -kara *ifc.* making, causing

कर: karaḥ hand **kara-talaḥ** palm of the hand

करङ्क: karankaḥ skull, vessel, box

करणं karaṇam doing, performing; sense organ

कराला Karālā *name of a goddess*

कर्ण: karṇaḥ ear

कर्तृ kartṛ *m.* doer, agent

कर्मन् karman *n.* deed, task, [the work of:] 'role'

कलकल: kalakalaḥ disturbance, noise

कलत्रं kalatram wife, spouse

कलहंसक: Kalahamsakaḥ *pr. n.*

कलिका kalikā bud

कल्प: kalpaḥ sacred precept or practice, rite

कल्याण kalyāṇa (*f.* ī) fair, auspicious, beneficial

कवि kavi *m.* poet, (creative) writer

कश्चित् kaś cit *see* kaḥ+cit

कषाय kaṣāya astringent, sharp(-smelling)

कष्ट kaṣṭa grievous, harsh, disastrous, calamitous

कष्टम् kaṣṭam alas!

काकु kāku *f.* tone of voice

काञ्चनार: kāñcanāraḥ mountain ebony

काण kāṇa one-eyed

कातर kātara timid, nervous

कादम्बिनी kādambinī bank of clouds

काननं kānanam forest

कान्त kānta (*p.p. of* kam) beloved

कापालिक: **kāpālikaḥ** (repulsive) Śaiva ascetic

काम: **kāmaḥ** wish, desire, love

काम: **Kāmaḥ, Kāma:devaḥ** the God of Love

कामम् **kāmam** at will, wilfully; admittedly, granted that, though

कामयिष्यते **kāmayiṣyate** *3rd sg. ātm. fut.* of **kam**

कामिन् **kāmin** loving, lover

कायस्थ: **kāyasthaḥ** scribe, letter-writer

कारणं **kāraṇam** reason, cause; instrument, means

कारिन् **kārin** doing, doer

कात्स्न्यं **kārtsnyam** totality; **kārtsnyena** in full

कार्मुकं **kārmukam** bow

कार्यं **kāryam** task, duty, affair, business, matter

काल: **kālaḥ** time, right time, occasion

कालक्षेप: **kāla-kṣepaḥ, kāla-haraṇam** wasting of time, delay

काव्यं **kāvyam** poetry, (creative) literature

काशी **Kāśī** *name of city* (Banaras)

किंवदन्ती **kiṃvadantī** rumour

किंच **kiṃ ca** moreover

किंचित् **kiṃ cit** something; somewhat, slightly

किंतु **kiṃ tu** but

किंनुखलु **kiṃ nu khalu** can it be that?

किम् **kim** (*n. sg. of* **kaḥ**) what?; why?; *may mark a question*; +*instr.* what is the point in? what business (have you *etc.*) with?

किमपि **kim api** something; somewhat, at all

किमिति **kim iti** in what terms?; with what in mind? why?

किमुत **kim uta, kiṃ punar** [what then of:] let alone

कियन्त् **kiyant** how much?

किल **kila** it seems that, apparently, I believe

कीदृश **kīdṛśa** (*f. ī*) of what kind? of what kind! what (a)!

कीर्त् **kīrt** (X **kīrtayati**) declare

कु **ku:** *pejorative prefix* ill

कुटुम्बं **kuṭumbam** household, family

कुटुम्बिन् **kuṭumbin** *m.* householder, family-man

कुट्मल **kuṭmala** *m./n.* bud

कुण्डलं **kuṇḍalam** earring, ear-ornament

कुतः **kutaḥ** from where? from what?; in what direction, whereabouts?

कुतूहलं **kutūhalam** curiosity, interest

कुप् **kup** *caus.* (**kopayati**) make angry, anger

कुमति **ku:mati** *f.* ill thought, wrongheadedness

कुमारः **kumāraḥ** (well-born) young man, son; prince; Your/His Highness

कुमारः **Kumāraḥ** the Prince (*name of Skanda, god of war*)

कुमारकः **kumārakaḥ** young man, son

कुमारी **kumārī** girl, daughter, princess

कुम्भः **kumbhaḥ** pot

कुलं **kulam** family, dynasty, house; herd, swarm (of bees)

कुलविद्या **kula-vidyā** learning that is [in a family:] hereditary

कुशः **Kuśaḥ** *pr. n.*

कुशलं **kuśalam** welfare

कुसुमं **kusumam** flower, blossom

कुसुमपुरं **Kusumapuram** 'flower-city' *name of Pāṭaliputra*

कुसुमायुधः **kusum)-āyudhaḥ** [the flower-weaponed:] God of Love

कूलं **kūlam** bank, shore

कृ **kṛ** (VIII **karoti**)   do, act, see to, conduct (affairs); make, cause, contrive; *forms verbal periphrasis with abstract or action nouns, e.g.* **avajñāṃ kṛ** feel contempt, despise

कृच्छ्रं **kṛcchraṃ** hardship; **kṛcchrāt** with difficulty

कृतम् **kṛtam**+*instr.*   have done with

कृतज्ञ **kṛta-jña, kṛta-vedin** conscious of [things done for one:] debt, grateful, obliged

कृतज्ञता **kṛtajñaˉtā** gratitude

कृतपुण्य **kṛta:puṇya**   [who has done meritorious things (in a previous life):] fortunate, lucky

कृतिन् **kṛtin** [having something done:] satisfied, fulfilled

कृपाणः **kṛpāṇaḥ** sword, (sacrificial) knife; **kṛpāṇa:pāṇi** *cf. Chapter 15, p. 249*

कृपालु **kṛpālu** compassionate

कृष्ण **kṛṣṇa** black

कृष्णशकुनि **kṛṣṇa:śakuni** *m.* [black bird:] crow

कॢप् **kl̥p** (I **kalpate**)   be suitable, conduce to, turn to (*dat.*)

कॢप् **kl̥p** *caus.* (**kalpayati**) arrange, prepare

केतु **ketu** *m.* flag, banner

केशव: **Keśavaḥ** *name of the god Kṛṣṇa*

केसरं **kesaram** hair, filament

कैमुतिकन्यायात् **kaimutika:nyāyāt** [from the principle kim uta 'let alone':] *a fortiori*

कोप: **kopaḥ** anger

कोऽपि **ko ›pi** *see* **kaḥ**+**api**

कोमल **komala** tender

कोलाहल: **kolāhalaḥ** clamour

कोश: **kośaḥ, koṣaḥ** treasury, resources, wealth

कौतुकं **kautukam** curiosity

कौमुदी **kaumudī** moonlight; day of full moon

क्रिया **kriyā** doing, performing, effecting, action; rite

क्री **krī** (IX krīṇāti) buy

क्रीड् **krīḍ** (I krīḍati) play

क्रोध: **krodhaḥ** anger

क्रौर्यं **krauryam** cruelty

क्व **kva** where? in what?

क्वण **kvaṇ** *caus.* (kvǎṇayati) [cause to] sound

क्षण: **kṣaṇaḥ** instant of time, second, moment

क्षत्रिय: **kṣatriyaḥ** [member of] warrior [caste]

क्षम् **kṣam** (I kṣamate) be patient, endure, tolerate

क्षय: **kṣayaḥ** destruction, ruin

क्षात्र **ksātra** (*f.* ī) relating to the kṣatriya caste

क्षितिपति **kṣiti-pati** *m.* [lord of earth:] king

क्षिप् **kṣip** (VI kṣipati) throw; waste (time)

क्षिप्र **kṣipra** swift, quick

क्षिप्रकारिन् **kṣipra:kārin** [swift-acting:] precipitate

क्षीरवृक्ष: **kṣīra-vṛkṣaḥ** fig-tree

क्षुद् **kṣud** (I kṣodati) trample, tread

क्षुद्र **kṣudra** mean, common, low

क्षुध् **kṣudh** *f.* hunger

क्षेत्रं **kṣetram** field

क्षेप: **kṣepaḥ** (*from* kṣip) throwing, wasting

खं **kham** hole; vacuum; sky, heaven

खद्योत: **khadyotaḥ** firefly

खलु **khalu** *confirmatory particle* indeed, of course, after all, certainly, don't forget; **na khalu** certainly not, not at all

खेद: **khedaḥ** exhaustion

खेल् **khel** (I khelati) play

ग -ga *ifc.* going

गः gaḥ the lettter g; (*in prosody*) heavy syllable

गङ्गा Gaṅgā the Ganges

गजः gajaḥ elephant

गडु gaḍu *m.* goitre

गण gaṇ (X gaṇayati) count

गणना gaṇanā counting

गणिका gaṇikā courtesan

गत gata (*p.p. of* gam) gone; *ifc.* gone to, [being] in, concerning, *etc.*

गन्धः gandhaḥ scent, smell, fragrance

गम् gam (I gacchati) go, attain

गम् gam *caus.* (gamayati) spend, pass (time)

गमनं gamanaṃ going

गरीयांस् garīyāṃs important, considerable; worthy/ worthier of respect

गर्भः garbhaḥ womb, foetus; *ifc.* containing

गर्भिन् garbhin [having foetuses:] productive of offspring

गल् gal (I galati) drip, slip away

गहनं gahanaṃ dense place, thicket

गात्रं gātraṃ limb, body, 'person'

गाथा gāthā verse (*esp.* in the āryā metre)

गामिन् gāmin going

गार्हस्थ्यं gārhasthyaṃ being a householder

गिर् gir *f.* speech, voice, tone

गिरि giri *m.* mountain

गीत gīta *p.p. of* gai

गीता gītā, gīti *f.* song

गुणः guṇaḥ merit, quality, worth; strand, string; '-fold', *e.g.* tri:guṇa threefold

गुप् **gup** (*denom. pres.* **gopāyati**) guard; hide

गुरु **guru** heavy, important; *m.* teacher, elder, senior, guardian

गुह्य **guhya** [to be concealed:] secret

गृहं **gṛham** (*m. in pl.*) house, home, household; quarters, chamber

गृहजनः **gṛha-janaḥ** family (*more particularly* wife)

गृहमेधिन् **gṛhamedhin** *m.*, **gṛhasthaḥ** householder

गृहिणी **gṛhiṇī** housewife, wife

गृहीत **gṛhīta** *p.p. of* **grah**

गृहीतार्थ **gṛhīt:ârtha** [by whom the fact has been grasped:] aware

गै **gai** (I **gāyati**) sing

गो **go** *m.* ox; *f.* cow; **go-kulam** herd of cows, cattle

गोपः **gopaḥ** cowherd

गोपनं **gopanam** concealment, hiding

गौतमी **Gautamī** *pr. n.*

गौरवं **gauravam** high esteem, regard, duty of respect [towards an elder]

ग्रह् **grah** (IX **gṛhṇāti**) seize, grasp, take, receive, accept

ग्रहणं **grahaṇam** seizing, taking

ग्रामः **grāmaḥ** village

घटः **ghaṭaḥ** pot

घातकः **ghātakaḥ** executioner

घातयति **ghātayati** *caus. of* **han** 'strike, kill'

घुष् **ghuṣ** (I **ghoṣati**) proclaim

घोषणा **ghoṣaṇā** proclamation

घ्राणं **ghrāṇam** smelling, (sense of) smell

च **ca** *enclitic* and, in addition; ...ca ...ca both ...and ...,
no sooner ... than ...

चक्रवर्तिन् **cakravartin** *m.* emperor

चक्षुस् **cakṣus** *n.* eye

चण्ड **caṇḍa** violent

चतुर् **catur** four

चतुर्थ **caturtha** (*f.* ī) fourth

चतुःषष्टि **catuḥ;ṣaṣṭi** *f.* sixty-four

चन्दन **candana** *m./n.* sandal, sandalwood tree

चन्दनदासः **Candanadāsaḥ** *pr. n.*

चन्द्रः **candraḥ** moon

चन्द्रकेतु **Candraketu** *m. pr. n.*

चन्द्रगुप्तः **Candraguptaḥ** *pr. n.*

चन्द्रिका **candrikā** moonlight

चर् **car** (I **carati**) move, go, depart; behave, act; do, effect

चरणं **caraṇam** *m./n.* foot; **caraṇa-nikṣepaḥ** [putting
down of feet:] tread

चरितं **caritam** conduct, deeds, 'story'

चर्या **caryā** going about, riding (in vehicle)

चल् **cal** (I **calati**) stir, move, go away

चाणक्यः **Cāṇakyaḥ** *pr. n.*

चाप **cāpa** *m./n.* bow

चामुण्डा **Cāmuṇḍā** *name of the goddess Durgā*

चिकीर्षितं **cikīrṣitam** [thing desired to be done:] intention

चित् **cit** *enclitic, gives indefinite sense to interrogative pronouns*

चित्तं **cittam** thought, mind

चित्तवृत्ति **citta-vṛtti** *f.* [activity of mind:] mental process,
thought

चित्र **citra** variegated

चित्रं **citram** picture

चित्रलेखा **Citralekhā** *pr. n.*

चिन्त् **cint** (X **cintayati**) reflect, think (things over), think of

चिन्ता **cintā** thought, worry

चिर **cira** long (*of time*)

चिरम् **ciram** for a long time

चिरस्य **cirasya, cirāt** after a long time

चीनांशुकं **cīn-âmśukam** [Chinese cloth:] silk

चीरं **cīram** strip of bark (worn by ascetic)

चुर् **cur** (X **corayati**) steal

चूत: **cūtaḥ** mango tree

चूर्णं **cūrṇam** powder

चेत् **cet** *enclitic* if

चेतना **cetanā** consciousness

चेतस् **cetas** *n.* mind, heart, intelligence, understanding

चेष्ट् **ceṣṭ** (I **ceṣṭati, ceṣṭate**) move, act, behave (towards), treat (*loc.*)

चेष्टा **ceṣṭā** conduct, action

चेष्टितं **ceṣṭitam** action

छद्मन् **chadman** *n.* disguise

छलं **chalam** fraud, fallacy, error

छाया **chāyā** shade

छिद् **chid** (II **chinatti**) cut, cut out

छिद्रं **chidram** hole, chink

छिन्न **chinna** (*p.p. of* **chid**) cut, divided

छेदिन् **chedin** cutting out, removing

ज: **jaḥ** the letter **j**; (*prosody*) the syllables ◡ – ◡

जटा **jaṭā** matted locks (of ascetic)

जन् **jan** (IV **jāyate**) be born, arise, become

जन् **jan** *caus.* (**janayati**) cause to arise, cause, beget, produce, rouse

जन: **janaḥ** person, people, folk; *ifc. gives plural or indefinite sense*

जननं **jananam** thing producing, 'ground for'

जनयितृ **janayitṛ** *m.* begetter, father

जनार्दन: **Janārdanaḥ** *name of Kṛṣṇa*

जन्मन् **janman** *n.* birth; **janma-pratiṣṭhā** [birth-foundation:] mother

जय: **jayaḥ** conquest

जरठ **jaraṭha** old, decrepit

जलं **jalam** water

जलधि **jaladhi** *m.* ocean; the number four

जागृ **jāgṛ** (II **jāgarti**) be awake, wake up

जाजलि **Jājali** *m., pr. n.*

जात **jāta** (*p.p. of* **jan**) born, become; **jāta-karman** *n.* birth ceremony

जाति **jāti** *f.* birth

जानकी **Jānakī** *pr. n.*

जाप्यं **jāpyam** (muttered) prayer

जाम्बूनद **jāmbūnada** (*f.* ī) golden

जालं **jālam** net, lattice, window

जालपाद: **jālapādaḥ** [web-footed:] goose

जि **ji** (I **jayati**) win, conquer, beat, defeat

जिज्ञासा **jijñāsā** desire to know, wish to determine

जितकाश्रिन् **jita-kāśin** flushed with victory, arrogant

जीव् **jīv** (I **jīvati**) live, be alive

जीव: **jīvaḥ** living creature, soul

जीवित **jīvita** alive

जीवितं **jīvitam** life

जोषमास् **joṣam ās** (II **joṣam āste**) remain silent

ज्ञ -**jña** *ifc.* knowing, aware of, recognising

ज्ञा **jñā** (IX **jānāti**) know, learn, find out, recognise

ज्ञा **jñā** *caus.* (**jñāpayati**) make known, announce

ज्ञातृ **jñātṛ** knower, person to know/understand

ज्ञानं **jñānam** knowledge, perceiving

ज्ञेय **jñeya** *ger. of* **jñā**

ज्यायांस् **jyāyāṃs** older, elder

ज्योतिस् **jyotis** *n.* light; heavenly body; **jyotiḥ-śāstram** astronomy, astrology

ज्योत्स्ना **jyotsnā** moonlight

झटिति **jhaṭiti** suddenly, at once

टच् **ṭac** (*gram.*) the suffix **a**

त: **taḥ** *adverbial suffix* from, in respect of *etc.*

तट: **taṭaḥ** slope, bank

तड् **taḍ** (X **tāḍayati**) strike, beat

तत् **tat** *n. sg. and stem form of* **sah**

तत **tat** *connecting particle* then, so

तत: **tataḥ** from there, from that, thereupon, then, and so, therefore

तत्क्षणम् **tat:kṣaṇam** at that moment, thereupon

तत्र **tatra** there, in/on *etc.* that, among them

तत्रभवन्त् **tatra:bhavant** His Honour [there], that (honourable) man, the revered

तत्रभवती **tatra:bhavatī** Her Honour [there], that (good) lady

तथा **tathā** thus, in such a way, so

तथापि **tathā ›pi** even so, nevertheless, but, yet

तदा **tadā** then, at that time

तदानीम् **tadānīm** (*cf.* **idānīm**) then, at that time; **tadā-nīṃ˜tana** belonging to that time, of that period

तद्धित: **taddhitaḥ** (*gram.*) ['suitable for that':] secondary suffix

तन् **tan** (VIII **tanoti**) extend, stretch

तन **tana** *suffix added to words denoting time*

तनया **tanayā** daughter

तन्त्रं **tantram** framework; administration; chapter of a text-book

तपस् **tapas** *n.* (religious) austerity

तपस्विन् **tapasvin** practiser of austerities, ascetic; wretched, 'poor'

तपोवनं **tapo-vanam** ascetics' grove

तम **tama** *superlative suffix* most, pre-eminently, very

तमस् **tamas** *n.* darkness

तर **tara** *comparative suffix* more, notably, particularly

तरु **taru** *m.* tree; **taru-gahanam** thicket of trees, wood

तर्क: **tarkaḥ** conjecture

तर्ज **tarj** *caus.* (**tarjayati**) threaten, scold

तर्हि **tarhi** in that case, then

तल **tala** *m./n.* palm (of the hand)

तव **tava** of you, your, of yours

ता **tā** *abstract noun suffix* -ness *etc.*

तात: **tātaḥ** (one's own) father

तादृश **tādṛśa** (*f.* **ī**) (of) such (a kind), so

तापस: **tāpasaḥ** ascetic

ताम्बूलं **tāmbūlaṃ** betel

तारक **tāraka** causing to cross over, rescuing, liberating

तारका **tārakā** star; pupil of eye

तावत् **tāvat** (*n. sg. of* **tāvant**) during that time, for so long, meanwhile

तावत् **tāvat** *enclitic* well now, (now) then, to start with, now as for—; + *pres. or imperv.* (I'll) just, (would you) just *etc.*

तावन्त **tāvant** that much, so much

तिथि **tithi** *m. f.* lunar day (*esp. as auspicious date for ceremony*)

तिमिरं **timiraṃ** darkness

तिरोभू **tiro˜bhū** (I **tirobhavati**) become hidden, vanish

तीच्ण **tīkṣṇa** sharp, severe

तीच्णरस: **tīkṣṇa:rasaḥ** [sharp liquid:] poison

तीरं **tīraṃ** bank

तीर्थं **tīrthaṃ** ford, sacred bathing-place, pool

तु **tu** *enclitic* but, yet, now

तुच्छ **tuccha** trifling

तूष्णीमस् **tūṣṇīm as, tūṣṇīṃ bhū** fall silent

तूष्णीमास् **tūṣṇīm ās** remain silent

तृतीय **tṛtīya** third

तृप् **tṛp** *caus.* (**tarpayati**) satisfy

ते **te** (i) *nom. pl. m. etc. of* **saḥ**, (ii) *enclitic dat./gen. sg. of* **tvam**

तेन **tena** therefore, in that case

तैच्णं **taikṣṇyaṃ** sharpness

त्यज् **tyaj** (I **tyajati**) abandon, quit, leave, give up, sacrifice

त्रयं **trayaṃ** triad; *ifc.* three

चयी **trayī** triad, the Three (Vedas)

चस **tras** *caus.* (**trāsayati**) make afraid, frighten

त्रि **tri** three

चिकालं **tri:kālam** (*dvigu cpd.*) [the three times:] past, present and future

चियामा **tri:yāmā** [containing three watches:] night

चिलोचन: **tri:locanaḥ** the three-eyed (god), Śiva

च्यम्बक: **Tryambakaḥ** *name of Śiva*

च्यह: **try:ahaḥ** [period of] three days

त्वं **tvam** *abstract noun suffix* -ness *etc.*

त्वम् **tvam** (*stem forms* **tvat** *and* **yuṣmat**) you

त्वर् **tvar** (I **tvarate**) hurry; *caus.* **tvarayati**

त्वरितम् **tvaritam** hurriedly, quickly, at once

त्वादृश **tvādṛśa** (*f.* ī) like you

द **-da** *ifc.* giving, administering

दक्षिण **dakṣiṇa** right, on the right hand; **dakṣiṇena** on the right, to the right

दक्षिणापथ: **dakṣiṇāpathaḥ** southern region (of India), the Deccan

दण्ड: **daṇḍaḥ** stick; punishment; vertical stroke (as punctuation mark)

दण्डनीति **daṇḍa-nīti** *f.* administration of justice, political science

दण्डापूपिका **daṇḍāpūpikā** [the 'stick-and-cake' principle:] reasoning *a fortiori*

दत्त **datta** *p.p. of* **dā**

दधत् **dadhat** *nom. sg. m. pres. part. para. of* **dhā**

दन्त: **dantaḥ** tooth

दम्पति **dam-pati** *m.* (*Vedic*) lord of the house; *du.* husband and wife

दया **dayā** pity, compassion

दर्भः **darbhaḥ** *sg. and pl.* *a type of* (sacrificial) grass

दर्शनं **darśanam** (act of) seeing, meeting, sight, appearance; sight (of king or god), audience

दर्शनीय **darśanīya** worth seeing, attractive

दर्शयति **darśayati** *caus. of* dṛś

दर्शिन् **darśin** seeing

दलं **dalam** petal, leaf

दश **daśa** ten

दह् **dah** (I dahati) burn

दह् **dah** *caus.* (dāhayati) cause to burn

दा **dā** (III dadāti) give, bestow, direct (gaze)

दाक्षायणी **Dākṣāyaṇī** [daughter of Dakṣa:] Aditi

दातृ **dātṛ** giver, granting

दानं **dānam** gift, bestowal, provision (of)

दायिन् **dāyin** giving, administering

दाराः **dārāḥ** *m. pl.* (*NB number and gender*) wife

दारुण **dāruṇa** cruel

दारुवर्मन् **Dāruvarman** *m.*, *pr. n.*

दासः **dāsaḥ** slave, servant

दासी **dāsī** slave girl, servant girl

दिनं **dinam** day

दिवसः **divasaḥ** day

दिव्य **divya** celestial

दिश् **diś** (dik) *f.* direction, cardinal point, region; *pl.* sky, skies

दिष्ट्या **diṣṭyā** [by good luck:] thank heaven that; +**vṛdh** congratulations!

दीपिका **dīpikā** lamp

दीप्त **dīpta** (**dīp** 'blaze, shine') brilliant

दुःखं **duḥkham** sorrow, unhappiness, pain, distress

दुरात्मन् **dur:ātman** evil-natured, evil, vile

दुर्गं **durgam** [hard to get at:] stronghold, citadel;
   durga-saṃskāraḥ preparation of stronghold, fortification

दुर्निमित्तं **dur:nimittam** ill omen

दुर्बोध **dur:bodha** difficult to understand

दुर्मनस् **dur:manas** in bad spirits, miserable

दुर्मनायते **durmanāyate** *denom.* be miserable

दुर्लभ **dur:labha** hard to obtain, inaccessible

दुर्वासस् **Durvāsas** *m., pr. n.*

दुर्विपाक: **dur:vipākaḥ** cruel turn (of fortune)

दुष्चेष्टितं **duś:ceṣṭitam** mischievous action

दुःशील **duḥ:śīla** bad-tempered, irritable

दुष् **duṣ** *caus.* (**dūṣayati**) spoil, defile

दुष्कर **duṣ:kara** difficult [to do]

दुःषन्त: **Duhṣantaḥ** *pr. n.*

दुस् **dus** *pejorative prefix* ill, bad, evil, mis- *etc.*; difficult to

दुह् **duh** (II **dogdhi**) milk; (**dugdhe**) yield milk

दुहितृ **duhitṛ** *f.* daughter

दूर **dūra** far (off), remote; **dūram** (for) a long way;
   dūrāt from afar; **dūre** at a distance, far away

दूरीभवन्तम् **dūrī˘bhavantam** *acc. sg. m. pres. part. of*
   dūrī˘bhū 'be far away'

दृढ **dṛḍha** firm

दृश् **dṛś** (I **paśyati**) see, look/gaze at/on, watch

दृश् **dṛś** *caus.* (**darśayati**) show, reveal

दृश् **dṛś** *f.* look, glance

दृष्ट **dṛṣṭa** *p.p. of* **dṛś**

दृष्टि dṛṣṭi *f.* look, gaze

देव: devaḥ god; His/Your Majesty

देवता devatā divinity, god

देवतागृहं devatā-gṛham [house of god:] temple

देवपादा: deva-pādāḥ the feet (*NB pl.*) of Your Majesty, *honorific for* Your Majesty

देवरात: Devarātaḥ *pr. n.*

देवी devī goddess; (the) Queen, Her/Your Majesty

देश: deśaḥ place, country

दैवं daivam fate, chance, fortune

दोग्ध्री dogdhrī *f.* of dogdhṛ (doh+tṛ), *agent noun of* duh

दोष: doṣaḥ fault, demerit, blemish, sin, offence, harm

दोहद: dohadaḥ (pregnant) longing

दौहित्र: dauhitraḥ daughter's son, grandson

द्रविणं draviṇam wealth

द्रष्टव्य draṣṭavya *ger. of* dṛś

द्रोह: drohaḥ injury, hostility

द्वन्द्वं dvandvam pair; dvandva-samprahāraḥ single combat, duel

द्वयं dvayam couple, pair; *ifc.* two

द्वार् dvār *f.*, dvāram door; dvāra-prakoṣṭhaḥ forecourt

द्वि dvi two

द्विगु dvigu *m.* (*gram.*) numerical compound

द्वितीय dvitīya second, another, a further

द्विष् dviṣ (II dveṣṭi) hate

द्विष् dviṣ (dviṭ) *m.* enemy

धनं dhanam wealth, money

धनुस्   dhanus   *n.* bow

धन्य   dhanya   lucky

धर्म: dharmaḥ   religious law, duty, piety

धर्मपत्नी   dharma-patnī   lawful wife

धा   dhā (III dadhāti)   put, hold, wear

धातु   dhātu   *m.* (primary) element; (*gram.*) root

धातृ   dhātṛ   creator, supporter

धात्री   dhātrī   nurse, fostermother

धारणं   dhāraṇam (dhṛ)   holding, wearing

धाव्   dhāv (I dhāvati)   run

धी   dhī   *f.* intelligence

धीमन्त्   dhī˜mant   intelligent, wise

धीर   dhīra   steady, firm, resolute, strong

धुरा   dhurā   pole, yoke, burden

धूम्र   dhūmra   smoke-coloured, grey

धूर्त: dhūrtaḥ   rogue

धूलि   dhūli   *f.* dust

धृ   dhṛ   *caus.* (dhārayati, *p.p.* dhārita/dhṛta)   hold, carry, wear

धैर्यं   dhairyam   steadiness, firmness, self-control

ध्यानं   dhyānam   meditation, meditating

ध्वनि   dhvani   *m.* sound; (*lit. crit.*) 'Suggestion'

न   na   not, no, 'fail to'; (*in comparisons*) rather than, than; na kaś cit, na ko ⟩pi [not anyone]: no one, nobody

न: naḥ   the letter **n**; (*prosody*) the syllables ◡ ◡ ◡

नगरं   nagaram, nagarī   city, town

नदी   nadī   river

ननु   nanu   why! well!; (*in objection or qualification*) surely, rather

नन्द: Nandaḥ *pr. n.*

नन्दन: Nandanaḥ *pr. n.*

नम् nam (I **namati**) bow, salute

नमस् namas *n.* homage

नमस्कार: namaskāraḥ making obeisance

नयनं nayanam eye

नर: naraḥ man

नरपति narapati *m.* king

नलिनी nalinī lotus

नव nava new, fresh

नवयौवनं nava:yauvanam [fresh] youth

नाटचं nāṭyam acting, drama

नाम nāma *enclitic* by name; indeed

नामधेयं nāmadheyam appellation, name

नामन् nāman *n.* name; *ifc.* named, called

नारी nārī woman

निकृत् ni+kṛt (VI **nikṛntati**) cut up, shred

निक्षिप् ni+kṣip (VI **nikṣipati**) throw, cast into (*loc.*); place, deposit

निक्षेप: nikṣepaḥ (act of) putting down

निखिल nikhila entire

निगडयति nigaḍayati *denom.* fetter, bind

निग्रह् ni+grah (IX **nigṛhṇāti**) repress, restrain

निघ्नती nighnatī *nom. sg. f. pres. part. para. of* ni+han 'strike'

निज nija one's own

निपात: nipātaḥ (*gram.*) ready-made form, particle

निपुण nipuṇa clever, sharp

निबन्धनं nibandhanam bond

निभृत nibhṛta secret, quiet

निमित्तं **nimittam** sign, omen; cause, motive

नियत **niyata** constrained; **niyatam** necessarily, assuredly

नियुज् **ni+yuj** (VII **niyuṅkte**) engage (someone) upon (*loc.*), appoint, set to (doing)

नियोग: **niyogaḥ** employment, entrusting

नियोज्य: **niyojyaḥ** servant

निरुणध्मि **niruṇadhmi** *1st sg. pres. para. of* **ni+rudh** 'confine, restrain'

निरुत्सुक **nir_utsuka** without eagerness

निर्गम् **nirgam** (**nis+gam**) (I **nirgacchati**) go away, retire from (*abl.*)

निर्दय **nir_daya** pitiless, fierce

निर्दिश् **nirdiś** (**nis+diś**) (VI **nirdiśati**) designate, specify

निर्भर **nirbhara** excessive, full

निर्भिन्न **nirbhinna** blossomed forth, found out, betrayed

निर्मा **nirmā** (**nis+mā**) (II **nirmāti**) create, compose

निर्माणं **nirmāṇam** creation

निर्मित **nirmita** created

निर्वप् **nirvap** (**nis+vap**) (I **nirvapati**) sprinkle, offer, donate

निर्वर्ण **nirvarṇ** (**nis+varṇ**) (X **nirvarṇayati**) gaze upon

निर्वाणं **nirvāṇam** bliss

निर्वृत **nirvṛta** content, happy, satisfied

निवासिन् **nivāsin** living (in), inhabitant

निविद् **ni+vid** *caus.* (**nivedayati**) report, announce, inform someone (*dat./gen.*) of (*acc.*), present someone (*acc.*)

निविश् **ni+viś** *caus.* (**niveśayati**) cause to settle, put in place

निवृ **ni+vṛ** *caus.* (**nivārayati**) ward off, drive off; check, restrain

निवृत् ni+vṛt (I nivartate) go back, turn back, return

निवृत् ni+vṛt *caus.* (nivartayati) turn back (*trans.*)

निवेदक nivedaka announcing, indicating

निशम् ni+śam *caus.* (niśāmayati) perceive, observe

निशा niśā night

निश्चय: niścayaḥ determination, resolve, certainty

निश्चि niści (nis+ci) (V niścinoti) ascertain, settle, fix upon

निषिध् niṣidh (ni+sidh) (I niṣedhati) prohibit, cancel, prevent, check

निष्क्रम् niṣkram (nis+kram) (I niṣkrāmati) go out of (*abl.*), emerge

निष्पन्न niṣpanna (*p.p. of* nis+pad 'be brought about') completed

निस् nis *prefix* without, -less, *etc.*

निःसह niḥsaha weak, exhausted

निहित nihita *p.p. of* ni+dhā 'place'

नी nī (I nayati) lead, guide, take, carry; +*abstract noun* cause a condition in someone

नीति nīti *f.* conduct, policy, political science

नु खलु nu khalu *enclitic, stressing interrogative* now (who *etc.*) I wonder?

नूपुर nūpura *m./n.* (ornamental) anklet

नृत् nṛt (IV nṛtyati) dance

नृप: nṛpaḥ king

नृपति nṛpati *m.* king

नृशंस nṛśaṃsa injurious; *m.* monster

नेतृ netṛ leader

नेत्रं netram eye

नेपथ्यं nepathyam area behind stage

न्याय: nyāyaḥ rule, principle; propriety

न्याय्य nyāyya regular, right, proper

न्यास: nyāsaḥ deposit, pledge

न्यासीकृ nyāsī̄kṛ deposit, entrust

प: paḥ, pakāraḥ the letter **p**

पक्व pakva cooked, ripe

पक्ष: pakṣaḥ wing, 'flank', side

पक्षपातिन् pakṣa-pātin on the side of, partial to

पङ्कजं paṅkajam [mud-born:] lotus

पङ्क्ति paṅkti f. row, line

पच् pac (I pacati) cook, ripen (*trans.*); *pass.* be cooked, ripen (*intrans.*)

पञ्च pañca five

पञ्चम pañcama (*f.* ī) fifth

पञ्चवटी Pañcavatī *name of a place*

पट: paṭaḥ cloth, robe

पटु paṭu sharp; **paṭīyāṃs** sharper

पठ् paṭh (I paṭhati) read (aloud), study; cite, mention

पणायितृ paṇāyitṛ hawker

पण्डित paṇḍita clever, learned; *m.* scholar, paṇḍit

पत् pat (I patati) fall, fly

पत् pat *caus.* (pātayati) cause to fall, drop

पतत्रिन् patatrin bird

पति pati, *m.* lord, king; (*irreg.*) husband

पत्त्रं pattram feather; leaf, petal; leaf for writing, 'paper'

पत्नी patnī wife

पथ: -pathaḥ (*usually ifc.*) path (*cf.* **panthan**)

पथ्य pathya suitable, salutary, regular

पदं **padaṃ** step, footstep, foot; position, site; word, member of nominal compound

पद्मं **padmaṃ** lotus

पद्मपुरं **Padma-puraṃ** *name of city*

पन्थन् **panthan** *m.* (*irreg.*) road, path, way

पयस् **payas** *n.* water, juice

पर **para** *pron. adj.* other, another; *m.* stranger; far, ultimate, supreme, great, particularly marked, (+**na**) greater than

परम् **param** beyond, further than (*abl.*)

परतन्त्र **para‑tantra** under another's control, not in control (of)

परत्र **paratra** elsewhere, in the next world

परवन्त् **paravant** under another's control; beside oneself, overwhelmed

परवश **paravaśa** in another's power, helpless

परस्पर **paraspara** mutual; **parasparam** one another, each other

पराञ् **parāñc** turned the other way

परापत् **parā+pat** (I **parāpatati**) approach, arrive

परिकर्मन् **parikarman** *n.* preparation

परिकीर्त् **pari+kīrt** (X **parikīrtayati**) proclaim, declare

परिकॢप् **pari+kḷp** *caus.* (**parikalpayati**) fix, destine for (*dat.*)

परिक्लेश: **parikleśaḥ** vexation

परिक्षिप् **pari+kṣip** (VI **parikṣipati**) encircle, encompass

परिगम् **pari+gam** (I **parigacchati**) surround, encircle

परिग्रह् **pari+grah** (IX **parigṛhṇāti**) accept, adopt, possess, occupy

परिग्रह: **parigrahaḥ** acceptance, welcome; possession, wrapping round, dress

परिचि **pari+ci** (V **paricinoti**) become acquainted with, recognise

परिजन: **parijanaḥ** attendant, servant

परिज्ञानं **parijñānam** realisation

परिणम् **pariṇam** (**pari+nam**) (I **pariṇamati**) develop, turn out (to be)

परिणय: **pariṇayaḥ** marriage

परिणाम: **pariṇāmaḥ** development, outcome

परिणी **pariṇī** (**pari+nī**) (I **pariṇayati**) marry

परितुष् **pari+tuṣ** *caus.* (**paritoṣayati**) make satisfied, reward, tip

परितोष: **paritoṣaḥ** satisfaction

परित्यज् **pari+tyaj** (I **parityajati**) give up, abandon

परित्याग: **parityāgaḥ** giving up, sacrificing; liberality

परित्रस्त **paritrasta** frightened

परित्रै **pari+trai** (I **paritrāyate**) rescue, save, protect

परिनिर्वाणं **parinirvāṇam** complete extinction

परिपाल् **pari+pāl** (X **paripālayati**) guard, preserve, keep intact

परिप्लु **pari+plu** (I **pariplavate**) float, move restlessly, tremble

परिभुज् **pari+bhuj** (VII **paribhunakti**) enjoy

परिभूति **paribhūti** *f.* humiliation, defeat

परिभ्रंश् **pari+bhraṃś** (IV **paribhraśyate**) fall, drop, slip

परिभ्रम् **pari+bhram** (I **paribhramati**) wander around

परिमल: **parimalaḥ** perfume

परिमेय **parimeya** measurable, limited

परिरक्ष् **pari+rakṣ** (I **parirakṣati**) protect, look after, save, spare

परिवाहिन् parivāhin overflowing

परिवृत parivṛta surrounded, having a retinue

परिवृध् pari+vṛdh *caus.* (parivardhayati) cause to grow, tend (plants)

परिश्रम: pariśramaḥ fatigue, exertion

परिश्रान्त pariśrānta exhausted, tired

परिषद् pariṣad *f.* assembly, audience

परिस्फुट parisphuṭa clear, distinct

परिहा pari+hā *passive* (parihīyate) be deficient, be inferior to (*abl.*)

परिहास: parihāsaḥ joke, laughter

परिहृ pari+hṛ (I pariharati) avoid, shun, omit (to do), resist

परीक्ष parīkṣ (pari+īkṣ) (I parīkṣate) examine, scrutinise; *p.p.* parīkṣita examined, proven

परीत parīta encompassed, overcome

पर्यट् paryaṭ (pari+aṭ) (I paryaṭati) wander about

पर्यन्त: paryantaḥ limit, end; *ifc.* [having as an end:] ending with, up to

पर्याप्त paryāpta sufficient, adequate

पर्वत: parvataḥ mountain

पर्वतेश्वर: Parvateśvaraḥ *pr. n.*

पशु paśu *m.* animal, sacrificial animal

पशुपति Paśupati *m.* [lord of beasts:] *name of Śiva*

पश्चात् paścāt behind, backward; after, afterwards

पश्चात्ताप: paścāt:tāpaḥ [after-pain:] remorse

पश्यति paśyati *present of* dṛś 'see'

पा pā (I pibati) drink; *caus.* (pāyayati) make to drink

पाक: pākaḥ cooking; ripeness, fulfilment

पाठः **pāṭhaḥ** recitation, reading; part (in play)

पाणि **pāṇi** *m.* hand

पाण्डित्यं **pāṇḍityam** learning, scholarship

पातकं **pātakam** [causing to fall:] sin, crime

पातिन् **pātin** falling, flying

पात्रं **pātram** vessel, receptacle; worthy recipient; actor;
  pātra-vargaḥ cast (of play)

पादः **pādaḥ** foot

पादपः **pādapaḥ** [drinking by the foot:] tree

पादमूलं **pāda-mūlam** [foot-root:] feet (*in deferential
reference to person*)

पाप **pāpa** evil, bad, wicked; *m.* villain; *n.* wickedness

पारावतः **pārāvataḥ** pigeon

पाराशरिन् **pārāśarin** wandering mendicant

पार्थिवः **pārthivaḥ** king, ruler

पार्वती **Pārvatī** *pr. n.*, *wife of Śiva*

पार्श्वं **pārśvam** flank, side

पाल् **pāl** (X **pālayati**) protect

पिण्डः **piṇḍaḥ** ball of rice, ritual offering to ancestors

पिण्डपातिन् **piṇḍapātin** *m.* mendicant

पितृ **pitṛ** *m.* father; *du.* parents

पिपीलिका **pipīlikā** ant

पीड् **pīḍ** (X **pīḍayati**) squeeze, oppress, torture, grieve

पीडा **pīḍā** oppression, affliction

पीत **pīta** *p.p. of* **pā** 'drink'

पुंलिङ्ग **puṃ:liṅga** having masculine gender

पुंवन्त् **puṃvant** (*gram.*) masculine

पुंस् **puṃs** *m.* (*irreg.*) man, male, masculine

पुंगवः **puṃgavaḥ** bull

पुण्डरीकं **puṇḍarīkam** lotus

पुण्डरीकः **Puṇḍarīkaḥ** *pr. n.*

पुण्य **puṇya** auspicious, virtuous, holy; *n.* religious merit

पुत्रः **putraḥ** son

पुत्रिका **putrikā, putrī** daughter

पुनर् **punar** again, back (again); *enclitic* however, but, even so, yet, nevertheless

पुनरपि **punar api** yet again, once more

पुनरुक्त **punar:ukta** repeated, redundant

पुर् **pur** *f.* rampart, city

पुरं **puram** city

पुरः **puraḥ** forward, in front, immediate, in the east

पुरस्कृत **puraskṛta** placed in front, before the eyes; honoured

पुरस्तात् **purastāt** forward, from there on

पुरःसरः **puraḥsaraḥ** forerunner, attendant; *pl.* entourage

पुरा **purā** formerly, previously, once

पुरातन **purā˜tana** (*f.* ī) former

पुरुषः **puruṣaḥ** man

पुरूरवस् **Purūravas** *m. pr. n.*

पुष् **puṣ** *caus.* (**poṣayati**) cause to thrive, rear

पुष्कल **puṣkala** abundant, strong

पुष्पं **puṣpam** flower

पुष्पिताग्रा **puṣpitāgrā** (*prosody*) *name of a metre*

पुस्तकं **pustakam** book

पू **pū** (IX **punāti/punīte**) purify

पूरयति **pūrayati** *caus. of* **pṝ**

पूर्ण **pūrṇa** full (*p.p. of* **pṝ**)

पूर्व **pūrva** *pron. adj.* previous, earlier, first, prior, foregoing

पूर्वम् **pūrvam** previously, earlier; before (*abl.*)

पृथक् **pṛthak** separately

पृथग्जनः **pṛthag:janaḥ** separate person, ordinary person

पृथिवी **pṛthivī, pṛthvī** earth

पृष्ट **pṛṣṭa** *p.p. of* **prach**

पॄ **pṝ** *caus.* (**pūrayati**) fill, fulfil, 'enrich'

पोतकः **potakaḥ** young animal/plant

पौनरुक्तं **paunaruktaṃ** redundancy

पौर **paura** urban; *m.* citizen; **paura:janaḥ** townsfolk

पौरव **Paurava** (*f.* ī) descended from Puru

प्रकारः **prakāraḥ** manner, way, type, kind

प्रकाशनं **prakāśanam** displaying

प्रकृति **prakṛti** *f.* nature, disposition; *pl.* subjects (of king), people

प्रकोष्ठ **prakoṣṭhaḥ** courtyard

प्रख्या **pra+khyā** *caus.* (**prakhyāpayati**) publish, proclaim

प्रचलित **pracalita** in motion

प्रचारः **pracāraḥ** roaming, movement

प्रचि **pra+ci** (V **pracinoti**) accumulate (*trans.*); *pass.* **pracīyate** accumulate (*intrans.*)

प्रच्छन्नम् **pracchannam** secretly, stealthily

प्रच्छादनं **pracchādanam** concealment

प्रच्छायं **pracchāyam** shade

प्रछ् **prach** (VI **pṛcchati**) ask, question

प्रजा **prajā** subject (of king)

प्रजापति **Prajāpati** *m., pr. n.*

प्रज्ञा **prajñā** intelligence, understanding, guile

प्रणम् **praṇam** (**pra+nam**) (I **praṇamati**) make obeisance to, salute

प्रणयः **praṇayaḥ** affection, entreaty

प्रणयिन् praṇayin entreating, suppliant, petitioner; pra-
ṇayi-kriyā acting for a petitioner, carrying out a request

प्रणाम: praṇāmaḥ salutation

प्रणिधि praṇidhi *m.* (secret) agent

प्रति prati +*acc.* towards, against, with regard to, about

प्रतिकूल prati_kūla [against the bank:] contrary, hostile

प्रतिक्रिया pratikriyā [action against:] remedy, remedying

प्रतिग्रह: pratigrahaḥ present (*to a brahmin from a king*)

प्रतिच्छन्दकं praticchandakam portrait, picture

प्रतिज्ञा pratijñā promise, assertion

प्रतिदृश् prati+dṛś (I pratipaśyati) see

प्रतिनन्द् prati+nand (I pratinandati) receive gladly,
welcome

प्रतिनिवृत् prati+ni+vṛt (I pratinivartate) return

प्रतिपक्ष: pratipakṣaḥ opposite side, enemy

प्रतिपद् prati+pad (IV pratipadyate) assent, admit

प्रतिपाल् prati+pāl (X pratipālayati) wait for

प्रतिबुध् prati+budh (IV pratibudhyate) wake up
(*intrans.*)

प्रतिबुध् prati+budh *caus.* (pratibodhayati) wake up
(*trans.*)

प्रतिरूपक pratirūpaka (*f.* ikā) corresponding in form,
like

प्रतिवचनं prativacanam answer, reply

प्रतिवस् prati+vas (I prativasati) dwell, live (in)

प्रतिवातम् prati_vātam against the wind, into the wind

प्रतिविधा prati+vi+dhā (III pratividadhāti) prepare
against, take precautions

प्रतिविधानं pratividhānam countermeasure

प्रतिश्रु prati+śru (V pratiśṛṇoti) promise

प्रतिषिध् pratiṣidh (prati+sidh) (I pratiṣedhati), restrain, forbid

प्रतिषेध: pratiṣedhaḥ prohibition, cancellation

प्रतिष्ठा pratiṣṭhā foundation

प्रती pratī (prati+i) *caus.* (pratyāyayati) make confident

प्रतीकार: pratīkāraḥ remedy

प्रतीक्ष् pratīkṣ (prati+īkṣ) (I pratīkṣate) wait (for)

प्रतीहार: pratīhāraḥ door-keeper, porter

प्रत्यग्र pratyagra fresh, recent

प्रत्यभिज्ञा pratyabhi+jñā (IX pratyabhijānāti) recognise

प्रत्यय: pratyayaḥ (*gram.*) suffix

प्रत्यर्थिन् pratyarthin hostile

प्रत्यर्पयति pratyarpayati (*caus. of* prati+ṛ) hand over, give back

प्रत्यवाय: pratyavāyaḥ reverse, annoyance

प्रत्यस् pratyas (prati+as) (IV pratyasyati) cast aside

प्रत्याख्यानं pratyākhyānam rejection

प्रत्यादिश् pratyā+diś (VI pratyādiśati) reject; put to shame (by example)

प्रत्यापन्न pratyāpanna returned

प्रत्यासन्न pratyāsanna near, at hand, about

प्रत्युत्पन्न pratyutpanna prompt, ready

प्रथम prathama first, previously; **prathamam** already

प्रथित prathita widely known

प्रदृश् pra+dṛś (I prapaśyati) see

प्रदेश: pradeśaḥ place, area

प्रद्रु pra+dru (I pradravati) run (*p.p. intrans.*)

प्रधान pradhāna principal, important, (person) in authority; *ifc.* having as one's authority

प्रबन्ध: prabandhaḥ (literary) work

प्रबुध् **pra+budh** *caus.* (**prabodhayati**) wake up; inform, admonish

प्रभा **pra+bhā** (II **prabhāti**) shine forth, dawn

प्रभाव: **prabhāvaḥ** power

प्रभु **prabhu** *m.* master

प्रभू **pra+bhū** (I **prabhavati**) arise; prevail, have power over, govern (*gen.*)

प्रभूत **prabhūta** numerous, abundant, large

प्रभृति **prabhṛti** *f.* beginning; *ifc.* etc. *etc.*

प्रभृति **prabhṛti** +*abl. or ifc.* (ever) since; **cirāt prabhṛti** [since a long time:] for (so) long

प्रमत्त **pramatta** negligent, inattentive

प्रमाणं **pramāṇam** measure, size; standard of authority, 'judge'

प्रमाद: **pramādaḥ** negligence, mishap

प्रमुग्ध **pramugdha** (*p.p. of* **pra+muh**) in a swoon, faint

प्रयत् **pra+yat** (I **prayatate**) strive, exert oneself

प्रयत्न: **prayatnaḥ** effort, attempt

प्रयुज् **pra+yuj** (VII **prayuṅkte**) employ; put into practice; perform (on stage)

प्रयोग: **prayogaḥ** performance (of play)

प्रयोजनं **prayojanam** purpose, motive, need, mission, matter, concern

प्रलप् **pra+lap** (I **pralapati**) talk idly, babble

प्रवातं **pravātam** breeze

प्रवाद: **pravādaḥ** talk, report

प्रवास: **pravāsaḥ** travel abroad, journey

प्रवाह: **pravāhaḥ** stream, current

प्रविश् **pra+viś** (VI **praviśati**) enter, go/come in(to)

प्रविश् **pra+viś** *caus.* (**praveśayati**) cause to come in, show in, introduce into

प्रवृत्त **pravṛtta** commenced, under way, in operation, current

प्रवृत्ति **pravṛtti** *f.* news, events, what has been happening

प्रवेश: **praveśaḥ** entry, entering

प्रशंस् **pra+śaṃs** (I **praśaṃsati**) praise, extol

प्रशस्य **praśasya** praiseworthy, to be admired

प्रशान्त **praśānta** calm

प्रसङ्ग: **prasaṅgaḥ** contingency, occasion: **prasaṅga˜taḥ** in passing

प्रसद् **pra+sad** (I **prasīdati**) become tranquil, be at peace

प्रसन्न **prasanna** tranquil

प्रसव: **prasavaḥ** parturition, childbirth

प्रसाद: **prasādaḥ** favour, grace, graciousness; free gift

प्रसादीकृ **prasādī˜kṛ** bestow (as free gift)

प्रसिद्ध **prasiddha** established, recognised

प्रसुप्त **prasupta** *p.p. of* **pra+svap**

प्रसृ **pra+sṛ** (I **prasarati**) move forward, extend, stretch

प्रस्ताव: **prastāvaḥ** prelude

प्रस्था **pra+sthā** (I **pratiṣṭhate**) set out/off/forth

प्रस्था **pra+sthā** *caus.* (**prasthāpayati**) send off, despatch

प्रस्थानं **prasthānaṃ** departure; system, way

प्रस्वप् **pra+svap** (II **prasvapiti**) fall asleep

प्रहि **pra+hi** (V **prahiṇoti**) despatch, send

प्रहृष्ट **prahṛṣṭa** delighted

प्राक् **prāk** previously, before, first(ly); +*abl.* before

प्राकार: **prākāraḥ** rampart, wall

प्राकृत **prākṛta** (*f.* ā/ī) of the people, vulgar, common

प्राण **prāṇ** (**pra+an**) (II **prāṇiti**) breathe

प्राण: **prāṇaḥ** breath; *pl.* life

प्रातराश: **prātar:aśaḥ** [morning eating:] breakfast

प्रादुर्भू **prādur+bhū** (**prādurbhavati**) become manifest, arise

प्राप् **prāp** (**pra+āp**) (V **prāpnoti**) reach, arrive, go to; obtain, win

प्राप् **pra+āp** *caus.* (**prāpayati**) cause to reach, convey

प्राप्त **prāpta** obtained, arrived, upon one

प्रायश: **prāyaśaḥ, prāyeṇa** generally, usually

प्रारब्धं **prārabdham** [thing undertaken:] enterprise

प्रार्थ **prārth** (**pra+arth**) (X **prārthayate**) long for, seek, sue for

प्रार्थना **prārthanā** longing, desire

प्रार्थयितृ **prārthayitṛ** suitor

प्राबीण्यं **prāviṇyam** proficiency

प्रासाद: **prāsādaḥ** mansion, palace, pavilion; terrace; [upstairs-]room

प्रिय **priya** dear, dearest, beloved, welcome; *ibc. or ifc.* fond of; *m./f.* sweetheart, loved one

प्रियं **priyam** benefit, service, blessing

प्रियंवदक: **Priyaṃvadakaḥ** *pr. n.*

प्रियङ्गु **priyaṅgu** *m./f. a type of creeper*

प्रियसखी **priya:sakhī** [dear] friend

प्रीतिमन्त् **prīti˜mant** full of joy or affection, glad

प्रेक्ष **prekṣ** (**pra+īkṣ**) (I **prekṣate**) see, discern

प्रेमन् **preman** *m./n.* affection

प्रेयांस् **preyāṃs** dearer; *m.* loved one, lover

प्रेर् **prer** (**pra+īr**) *caus.* (**prerayati**) drive on, impel, stir

प्रेष् **preṣ** (**pra+iṣ**) *caus.* (**preṣayati**) despatch, send

प्रेषणं **preṣaṇam** sending

प्रौढ **prauḍha** full-grown

फलं **phalam** fruit, reward, recompense, advantage

फलकं **phalakam** board, bench, table

बकुल: **bakulaḥ** *a type of tree*; **bakulam** bakula-tree blossom

बटु **baṭu** *m.* young brahmin (student); fellow (*contemptuously*)

बत **bata** *enclitic* alas!

बन्ध् **bandh** (IX **badhnāti**) tie, bind, fix; enter into (friendship or hate)

बन्धु **bandhu** *m.* kinsman

बर्ह **barha** *m./n.* (peacock's) tail-feather

बलं **balam** force, strength; *sg./pl.* (military) forces; **balāt** forcibly

बलवन्त् **bala˜vant** possessing strength, strong; **balavat** strongly, extremely

बलिन् **balin** possessing strength, strong

बहि: **bahiḥ** outside

बहु **bahu** much, many; +**man** (**bahu manyate**) think much of, esteem highly

बहुमान: **bahu:mānaḥ** high esteem, respect

बहुवचनं **bahu-vacanam** (*gram.*) plural (number)

बहुश: **bahu˜śaḥ** many times, often

बाण: **bāṇaḥ** arrow

बाधा **bādhā** molestation, damage

बाल **bāla** young; *m.* boy, child; *f.* girl, child

बाहुल्यं **bāhulyam** abundance, multitude

बाह्य **bāhya** external

बिसं **bisaṃ** lotus fibre

बीभत्स **bībhatsa** repulsive, foul; *n.* repulsiveness

बुद्धरक्षिता **Buddharakṣitā** *pr. n.*

बुद्धि **buddhi** *f.* intelligence, mind

बुद्धिमन्त् **buddhi˘mant** possessing intelligence, sentient

बुध् **budh** (I **bodhati/bodhate,** IV **budhyate**) awake, perceive, learn

बोधिसत्त्व: **bodhi:sattvaḥ** [whose essence is enlightenment:] Buddhist saint in the final stage of enlightenment

ब्रह्मचारिन् **brahmacārin** student

ब्रह्मन् **brahman** *n.* spirituality, (religious) chastity

ब्राह्मण: **brāhmaṇaḥ** brahmin

ब्रू **brū** (II **bravīti**) say, tell, speak

भक्तं **bhaktaṃ** food

भक्ति **bhakti** *f.* devotion, loyalty

भगवन्त् **bhagavant** reverend, revered, venerable, blessed; *m.* His Reverence, Reverend Sir; *f.* (**bhagavatī**) Her Reverence

भग्न **bhagna** *p.p. of* **bhañj**

भङ्ग: **bhaṅgaḥ** breaking; plucking (of buds); dispersal (of crowds)

भञ्ज् **bhañj** (VII **bhanakti**) break, shatter

भञ्जनं **bhañjanaṃ** breaking

भट्ट: **bhaṭṭaḥ** lord, master, learned man

भद्र **bhadra** good, dear; *voc.* **bhadra** my good man, **bhadre** dear lady, madam

भयं **bhayaṃ** fear, danger

भरत: **bharataḥ** actor, player

भरत: **Bharataḥ** *pr. n.*

भर्तृ **bhartṛ** *m.* [supporter:] master; husband

भर्तृदारिका **bhartṛ-dārikā** [daughter of (my) master:] mistress

भवती **bhavatī** *f. of* **bhavant**

भवतु **bhavatu** [let it be:] right then!

भवनं **bhavanam** house, home; [house (of king):] palace

भवस्त् **bhavant** *pres. part. of* **bhū**

भवन्त् **bhavant** *m.*, **bhavatī** *f.* you (*politely*), you sir *etc.*

भवेत **bhavet** (*3rd sg. para. opt. of* **bhū**) might be

भाग: **bhāgaḥ** division, portion, allotment, tithe

भागुरायण: **Bhāgurāyaṇaḥ** *pr. n.*

भाजनं **bhājanam** receptacle, box

भाण्डं **bhāṇḍam** box

भार: **bhāraḥ** burden, load, luggage

भारिक **bhārika** burdensome

भार्या **bhāryā** wife

भाव: **bhāvaḥ** state of being; essence, meaning, implication; emotional state, emotion

भाविन **bhāvin** future, imminent

भास्वरक: **Bhāsvarakaḥ** *pr. n.*

भिक्षा **bhikṣā** alms

भित्ति **bhitti** *f.* wall

भिद् **bhid** (VII **bhinatti**) split, separate

भिन्न **bhinna** split, open, different; **bhinn>:ârtha** with open meaning, plain

भीत **bhīta** afraid

भीरु **bhīru** fearful

भू **bhū** (I **bhavati**) become, be; arise, happen; *expresses* 'have, get' *etc.*

भू **bhū** *f.* earth

भूत **bhūt** *3rd sg. injunctive of* **bhū**

भूत **bhūta** having become, being

भूमि **bhūmi** *f.* ground; fit object (for); **parityāga-bhūmi** suitable recipient (of)

भूमिपाल: **bhūmi-pālaḥ** king, ruler

भूयांस् **bhūyāṃs** more, further

भूरिवसु **Bhūrivasu** *m., pr. n.*

भूषणं **bhūṣaṇam** ornament

भृ **bhṛ** (I **bharati**, III **bibharti**) bear, support

भृत्य: **bhṛtyaḥ** servant

भेद: **bhedaḥ** division, separation, variety

भैष्ट **bhaiṣṭa** *2nd pl. para. injunctive of* **bhī** 'fear'

भो: **bhoḥ** oh! ho!; **bho bhoḥ** ho there!

भोग: **bhogaḥ** enjoyment

भोगिन् **bhogin** serpent; the number eight

भोजनं **bhojanam** food

भंश: **bhraṃśaḥ** fall, decline

भ्रम् **bhram** (I **bhramati**) wander, be confused

भ्रातृ **bhrātṛ** *m.* brother

संस्था: **maṃsthāḥ** *2nd sg. ātm. injunctive of* **man**

मकरन्द: **Makarandaḥ** *pr. n.*

मघवन्त् **Maghavant** *m. irreg.* (*gen. sg.* **Maghonaḥ**) *name of Indra*

मङ्गलं **maṅgalam** welfare, good luck, auspicious omen, auspiciousness

मणि **maṇi** *m.* jewel

मण्डप **maṇḍapa** *m./n.* pavilion, bower

मत् **mat** *stem form and abl. sg. of* **aham**

मति **mati** *f.* thought, wit, mind, opinion, notion

मतिमन्त् mati~mant possessing wit, sensible

मत्त matta in rut, rutting

मत्त: mat~taḥ from me

मद् mad (IV mādyati) rejoice, be intoxicated

मद: madaḥ intoxication

मदन: madanaḥ love, passion; god of love

मदयन्तिका Madayantikā pr. n.

मदीय madīya my, mine

मधु madhu m. (season or first month of) spring

मधुकर: madhukaraḥ, madhukarī [honey-maker:] bee, honey-bee

मधुर madhura sweet

मध्य madhya middle; madhyāt from the middle of, from among; madhye in the middle of, among

मध्यस्थ madhya-stha [mid-standing:] neutral

मन् man (IV manyate) think, suppose, regard (as), esteem, approve

मन् man caus. (mānayati) esteem, honour

मनस् manas n. mind, heart, intelligence

मनोरथ: manorathaḥ desire, fancy

मनोवृत्ति mano-vṛtti f. process of mind, fancy, imagination

मन्त् ~mant possessive suffix

मन्त्रिन् mantrin minister

मन्द manda slow, slack, gentle; mand‸:ādara careless

मन्दार: mandāraḥ, mandāra:vṛkṣakaḥ coral tree

मन्दारिका Mandārikā pr. n.

मन्दीभू mandī~bhū become slack, slacken

मन्मथ: manmathaḥ love, god of love

मन्यु manyu m. passion, anger

मरणं maraṇam death, dying

मरीचि Marīci m. name of a sage

मरु maru m. desert

मर्त्य martya mortal, human

मलयकेतु Malayaketu m., pr. n.

मषी maṣī, masī black powder, ink; **masī-bhājanam**
receptacle for ink, ink-pot

महा mahā descriptive stem form of **mahānt**

महादेवी mahā:devī chief queen

महान्त् mahānt great, noble, vast, numerous

महामांसं mahā:māmsam [great flesh:] human flesh

महाराज: mahā:rājaḥ great king, king

महार्घ्य mahārghya valuable

महिमन् mahiman m. greatness

मही mahī earth

महीधर: mahī-dharaḥ [earth-supporter:] mountain

महीपति mahī-pati m. [lord of earth:] king

महेन्द्र: Mah»:êndraḥ [great] Indra

महोत्सव: mah»:ôtsavaḥ [great] festival, holiday

मा mā prohibitive particle (do) not etc.

मांसं māmsam flesh, meat

मातृ mātṛ f. mother

मात्रा mātrā measure, size; **-mātra** having the size of,
mere, only etc.

माधव: Mādhavaḥ pr. n.

माधव्य: Mādhavyaḥ pr. n.

मानयितव्य mānayitavya (ger. of caus. of **man**) requiring
to be honoured

मानसं mānasam [that which is mental:] mind

मानसं Mānasam name of a lake

मानुष: mānuṣaḥ human being, mortal

मामकीन māmakīna my, mine

मारीच: Mārīcaḥ (Kaśyapa) son of Marīci

मार्ग: mārgaḥ road, path, way

मालती Mālatī *pr. n.*

माला mālā garland

मालिनी Mālinī *name of river*

माहात्म्यं māhātmyam greatness of spirit, generosity

मित्रं mitram friend

मिथ: mithaḥ together, mutually

मिथुनं mithunam pair

मिथ्या mithyā wrong(ly), improper(ly)

मिश्र miśra mixed

मुकुलं mukulam bud

मुखं mukham (*f.* ī *when ifc.*) face, mouth, front, forepart

मुखर mukhara talkative

मुखरयति mukharayati *denom.* make talkative

मुखोच्छ्वास: mukh₎-ôcchvāsaḥ breath [of the mouth]

मुग्ध mugdha naïve, simple

मुद्रयति mudrayati *denom.* stamp, seal

मुद्रा mudrā seal, stamp, (signet-)ring, [authorising seal:] 'pass'

मुनि muni *m.* sage

मुहूर्त muhūrta *m./n.* (short) while, 'minute', moment

मूक mūka dumb, silent

मूढ mūḍha deluded, idiotic; *m.* idiot

मूर्ख mūrkha foolish; *m.* fool

मूर्छा mūrchā faint, swoon

मूलं mūlam root, basis, foundation

मृग: mṛgaḥ deer

मृगतृष्णिका **mṛgatṛṣṇikā** [deer-thirst:] mirage

मृगया **mṛgayā** hunting, the chase

मृणालवन्त् **mṛṇāla~vant** possessing lotus-fibres

मृत **mṛta** (*p.p. of* mṛ 'die') dead

मृत्युंजय: **mṛtyuṃ-jayaḥ** Conqueror of Death

मृदु **mṛdu** soft

मृष् **mṛṣ** *caus.* (**marṣayati**) overlook, excuse

मृषा **mṛṣā** vainly

मेधा **medhā** mental power, intellect

मेध्य **medhya** fit for sacrifice, sacrificial

मेनका **Menakā** *pr. n.*

मेना **Menā** *pr. n.*

मेने **mene** *3rd sg. ātm. perf. of* **man**

मैथिल **Maithila** belonging to Mithilā; *m.* king of Mithilā

मोह: **mohaḥ** delusion

म्लेच्छ: **mlecchaḥ** barbarian

म्लै **mlai** (I **mlāyati**) fade, wither

य: **yaḥ, ya-kāraḥ** the letter y; (*prosody*) the syllables ⏑ – –

य: **yaḥ** *rel. pron.* who, which, that; *n. sg.* **yat** that, in that, inasmuch as *etc.* (*Chapters 11 to 13*)

य: कश्चित् **yaḥ kaś cit** whoever

यत: **yataḥ** *rel. adv.* from which, since *etc.*

यति **yati** *f.* (*prosody*) caesura

यत्न: **yatnaḥ** effort

यत्र **yatra** *rel. adv.* in which, where

यत्सत्यम् **yat satyam** [what is true:] truth to tell, in truth

यथा **yathā** *rel. adv.* in the way that, as; so that *etc.*;
yathā yathā ... tathā tathā in proportion as, the more that

यथा   yathā *ibc.*   as, according to, in conformity with

यथावत्   yathāvat   exactly, properly

यदा   yadā *rel. adv.*   when; **yad» aîva** as soon as

यदि   yadi   *rel. adv.*   if, whether; **yady api** even if, though

यम: yamaḥ   twin

यमज   yamaja   twin[-born]

या   yā (II yāti)   go

या   yā *caus.* (yāpayati)   spend (time)

याचितृ   yācitṛ (*from* yāc 'solicit')   suer, petitioner

याचा   yātrā   procession

यादृश   yādṛśa   (*f.* ī) *rel. adj.*   of which kind, such as, just as

याम: yāmaḥ   night watch (of three hours)

यावत्   yāvat   *connective particle* [during which time:] (I'll) just

यावत्   yāvat   +*acc.* until, up to; *ibc.* throughout

यावत्   yāvat   *rel. adv.* for as long as, while, until; **yāvat**+ **na** before

यावन्त   yāvant   *rel. adj.*   as much as

युक्त   yukta   proper, right

युक्ति   yukti   *f.*   argument

युगं   yugam   pair; *ifc.* two

युज्   yuj   joined, even (in number); **a:yuj** uneven, odd

युत   yuta   united, equipped with

युष्मत्   yuṣmat   *pl. stem form and abl. pl. of* tvam

युष्मदीय   yuṣmadīya   belonging to you (*pl.*)

युष्माकम्   yuṣmākam   of you (*pl.*), your, of yours

योग: yogaḥ   use, application, managing; magical art; system of meditation

योग्य   yogya   suitable

र: रेफ: raḥ, rephaḥ   the letter r; (*prosody*) the syllables
– ‿ ‿ –

रंहस् raṃhas *n.* speed

रक्ष् rakṣ (I rakṣati)   protect, save, guard, hold

रक्षणं rakṣaṇam   protection, defending

रक्षस् rakṣas *n.* devil

रक्षितृ rakṣitṛ   protector, guard

रचित racita   placed

रति rati *f.* pleasure, lovemaking, love

रत्नं ratnam   jewel, gem

रथ्या rathyā (rathaḥ carriage) [carriage-]road, street

रमणीय ramaṇīya   pleasant, attractive, lovely, delightful

रम्य ramya   attractive

रश्मि raśmi *m.* rein, bridle

रस: rasaḥ   juice, liquid; flavour, taste

रहस् rahas *n.*   solitude, secrecy; **rahasi** in secret, secretly

रहस्य rahasya   secret

राक्षस: Rākṣasaḥ *pr. n.*

राग: rāgaḥ   passion; redness; musical mood

राजकन्या rāja-kanyā   princess

राजकार्यं rāja-kāryam   [king's business:] state administration

राजन् rājan *m.*   king, prince, chieftain; *voc.* sire

राजपुत्र: rāja-putraḥ   king's son, prince

राजभवनं rāja-bhavanam   palace

राजलोक: rāja-lokaḥ   [company of] kings or princes

राज्यं rājyam   kingdom, state; kingship, reign

रात्र: rātraḥ *at end of cpd. for* **rātri** *f.* night

राम: Rāmaḥ *pr. n.*

रामणीयकं rāmaṇīyakam   loveliness, delightful aspect

रामायणं **Rāmāyaṇam** *name of an epic poem*

राशि **rāśi** *m.* heap

रिपु **ripu** *m.* enemy

रुध् **rudh** (VII **ruṇaddhi**) obstruct

रुह् **ruh** (I **rohati**) rise, grow

रुह् **ruh** *caus.* (**rohayati/ropayati**) raise, grow

रूपं **rūpam** form; beauty, looks

रूपकं **rūpakam** (*lit. crit.*) metaphor

रेफ: **rephaḥ** *see* **raḥ**

रैवतक: **Raivatakaḥ** *pr. n.*

लक्ष् **lakṣ** (X **lakṣayati**) notice

लक्षणं **lakṣaṇam** characteristic, (auspicious) mark; definition

लक्ष्मण: **Lakṣmaṇaḥ** *pr. n.*

लघु **laghu** light; brief

लज्ज् **lajj** (VI **lajjate**) be embarrassed, blush, show confusion

लज्ज् **lajj** *caus.* (**lajjayati**) embarrass

लज्जा **lajjā** shame, embarrassment, shyness

लज्जाकर **lajjā-kara** (*f.* **ī**) embarrassing

लण्ड्र **Laṇḍra** London

लता **latā** creeper, vine

लभ् **labh** (I **labhate**) take, gain, win, get, obtain, find

लभ् **labh** *caus.* (**lambhayati**) cause to take, give

लव: **lavaḥ** fragment; **lavaśo lavaśaḥ** piece by piece

लव: **Lavaḥ** *pr. n.*

लवङ्गिका **Lavaṅgikā** *pr. n.*

लाघवं **lāghavam** lightness, levity, [light treatment of a guru:] disrespect

लातव्य: **Lātavyaḥ** *pr. n.*

लाभ: **lābhaḥ** getting, winning, acquisition; profit

लिख् **likh** (VI **likhati**) write

लिङ्ग **liṅgam** mark, sign; phallus; (*gram.*) gender

लीला **lilā** play, sport

लेख: **lekhaḥ** letter, document

लोक: **lokaḥ** world, people

लोचनं **locanam** eye

लोपामुद्रा **Lopāmudrā** *pr. n.*

लोभ: **lobhaḥ** greed

लोमन् **loman** *n.* hair (on body)

वंश: **vaṃśaḥ** lineage, dynasty, race

वच् **vac** (II **vakti**) tell, say, state, express, declare, speak
of, describe, speak to, address

वचनं **vacanam** saying, statement, speech, word; **-vacanāt**
[from the statement of:] in the name of

वचस् **vacas** *n.* word, words, speech

वज्र **vajra** *m./n.* thunderbolt, diamond, hard substance

वञ्चना **vañcanā** cheating, trick

वणिज् **vaṇij** (**vaṇik**) *m.* businessman, trader

वत् ~**vat** (*n. sg. of* **vant**) like, as, in accordance with

वतंस: **vataṃsaḥ, vataṃsakaḥ** ornament, *esp.* earring

वत्स: **vatsaḥ** calf; dear child

वत्सल **vatsala** affectionate, loving

वद् **vad** (I **vadati**) say, speak, tell

वदनं **vadanam** mouth, face

वध: **vadhaḥ** killing, death

वधू **vadhū** *f.* woman, bride

वध्य **vadhya** [due to be executed:] condemned to death

वनं vanaṃ forest, jungle, wood, grove; **vana-mālā** [jungle-garland:] garland of wild flowers

वनस्पति vanaspati *m.* [lord of the jungle:] (forest) tree

वनेचर: vanecaraḥ forest-dweller

वन्त् ~vant *possessive suffix*

वन्द् vand (I vandate) venerate, worship

वन्ध्य vandhya barren

वयम् vayam (*nom. pl. of* aham) we *etc.*

वयस् vayas *n.* vigour, youth; age (in general)

वयस्य: vayasyaḥ [one of same age:] friend

वरं varaṃ a preferable thing, better

वर: varaḥ suitor

वराक varāka (*f.* ī) wretched, pitiable, 'poor'

वर्ग: vargaḥ group

वर्ण् varṇ (X varṇayati) depict, describe

वर्ण: varṇaḥ colour, appearance; social class

वर्त्मन् vartman *n.* track, path, way

वर्ष: varṣaḥ rain; year

वलय valaya *m./n.* bracelet; circle, enclosure

वल्कल valkala *m./n.* bark (of tree), bark-dress (worn by ascetic)

वल्लभ vallabha beloved; *m.* sweetheart

वश: vaśaḥ power; -vaśāt from the power of, because of

वस् vas (I vasati) dwell, live (in)

वसनं vasanaṃ dress

वसिष्ठ: Vasiṣṭhaḥ *pr. n.*

वसुंधरा Vasuṃdharā *pr. n.*

वस्तु vastu *n.* thing, matter, substance; **vastu-vṛttam** [what has happened in substance:] the facts

वह् vah (I vahati) carry, take, marry

वा **vā** *enclitic* or; . . . **vā** . . . **vā** either . . . or . . .; **na vā** or not; **na** . . . **na vā** not . . . nor

वाक्यं **vākyam** statement, utterance, sentence

वाच् **vāc** *f.* speech, words

वात: **vātaḥ** wind

वादिन् **vādin** speaking, talking

वामदेव: **Vāmadevaḥ** *pr. n.*

वायु **vāyu** *m.* wind

वारि **vāri** *n.* water

वारुण **Vāruṇa** (*f.* ī) deriving from the god Varuṇa

वार्त्ता **vārttā** news

वाल्मीकि **Vālmīki** *m.*, *pr. n.*

वास् **vās** (X **vāsayati**) perfume

वास: **vāsaḥ** dwelling, living

वासव: **Vāsavaḥ** (Indra) chief of the Vasus

वासिन् **vāsin** living in, dweller

वाहिन् **vāhin** carrier

विकस् **vi+kas** (I **vikasati**) burst, blossom, bloom

विकार: **vikāraḥ** transformation; mental disturbance; *ifc.* made out of

विकृ **vi+kṛ** (VIII **vikaroti**) alter, change, distort, mentally disturb

विक्रम: **vikramaḥ** valour

विक्रम्य **vikramya** (*absol. of* **vi+kram**) after attacking, by force

विक्री **vi+krī** (IX **vikrīṇīte**) sell to (*loc.*)

विक्रेतृ **vikretṛ** vendor

विक्लव: **viklava** bewildered, distressed

विग्रह: **vigrahaḥ** separation; body

विघट् **vi+ghaṭ** (I **vighaṭate**) become separated

विघात: **vìghātaḥ** destruction, elimination

विघ्र: **vighnah** obstacle, hindrance

विचर् **vi+car** (I **vicarati**) move about, roam

विचर् **vi+car** *caus.* (**vicārayati**) deliberate, ponder

विचार: **vicārah** pondering, thought

विचिच्र **vicitra** variegated, various, wonderful

विचिन्त **vi+cint** (X **vicintayati**) consider, think of, reflect

विजया **Vijayā** *pr. n.*

विज्ञा **vi+jñā** (IX **vijānāti**) find out, discern, understand, know

विज्ञा **vi+jñā** *caus.* (**vijñāpayati**) say politely, request, beg, beg to say/tell

विज्ञापना **vijñāpanā** request

विटप **viṭapa** *m./n.* branch, bush, thicket

वितर्क: **vitarkah** conjecture, doubt

वितृ **vi+tṝ** (I **vitarati**) grant, bestow

विद् **vid** (II **vetti**) know, learn, discover

विद् **vid** (VI **vindati**) find, acquire, possess; *pass.* **vidyate** is found, exists

विद् **-vid** *ifc.* knowing, learned in

विद्ग्ध **vidagdha** skilful, clever

विद्या **vidyā** learning, science

विद्रु **vi+dru** *caus.* (**vidrāvayati**) chase away, disperse

विद्वांस् **vidvāṃs** (*perf. part. of* **vid**) learned, wise

विधा **vi+dhā** (III **vidadhāti**) arrange, manage, provide for (something)

विधा **vidhā** kind, sort; *ifc.* of the same sort as, such as

विधानं **vidhānam** arrangement

विधि **vidhi** *m.* injunction (*esp. of ritual*); **vidhi~vat** according to [the injunction of] ritual

विध्वंस् **vi+dhvaṃs** (I **vidhvaṃsate**) fall to pieces, shatter

विनय: **vinayaḥ** discipline, good breeding

विनश् **vi+naś** (IV **vinaśyati**) perish, die; *caus.* (**vināś-ayati**) destroy

विनष्ट **vinaṣṭa** *p.p. of* **vi+naś**

विना **vinā** +*instr.* without

विनाश: **vināśaḥ** destruction

विनीत **vinīta** disciplined, well bred, modest

विनुद् **vi+nud** *caus.* (**vinodayati**) divert, distract

विपरीत **viparīta** inverted, reverse, opposite

विपिनं **vipinam** forest

विप्रकृ **vi+pra+kṛ** (VIII **viprakaroti**) injure, torment

विप्रतिपन्न **vipratipanna** perplexed, uncertain

विप्रलभ् **vi+pra+labh** (I **vipralabhate**) mislead, deceive

विभाग: **vibhāgaḥ** part, portion

विभु **vibhu** powerful *esp. as epithet of Śiva*

विभू **vi+bhū** *caus.* (**vibhāvayati**) make manifest; perceive distinctly, detect

विभूति **vibhūti** *f.* splendour, wealth; *pl.* riches

विमनस् **vi:manas** despondent

विमर्द: **vimardaḥ** conflict

विमर्श: **vimarśaḥ** deliberation, doubt

विमुच् **vi+muc** (VI **vimuñcati**) release, loose

विमृश् **vi+mṛś** (VI **vimṛśati**) perceive, reflect, deliberate

वियुज् **vi+yuj** (VII **viyuṅkte**) disjoin, separate, deprive of (*instr.*)

विरच् **vi+rac** (X **viracayati**) construct, fashion, work

विरहित **virahita** separated, bereft

विराज् **vi+rāj** (I **virājati**) gleam, shine out; **virājant** *pres. part.* gleaming out

विलक्ष **vilakṣa** disconcerted, ashamed

विलम्ब: **vilambaḥ** delay

विलास: **vilāsaḥ** coquetry, playful movement

विलोक् **vi+lok** *caus.* (**vilokayati**) look at, watch

विलोल **vilola** unsteady, tremulous

विवक्षित **vivakṣita** (*p.p. of desiderative* **vivakṣati**) wished to be said, meant

विवस्वन्त् **vivasvant** *m.* [the Shining One:] sun

विवाद: **vivādaḥ** disagreement, dispute

विवाह: **vivāhaḥ** wedding

विविध **vi:vidha** of various kinds

विवेक: **vivekaḥ** discrimination

विशेष: **viśeṣaḥ** distinction; *ifc.* a particular —, a special —; **viśeṣa~taḥ** in particular

विशेषणपदं **viśeṣaṇa:padam** [distinguishing word:] epithet

विशोक **vi:śoka** free from sorrow, at ease

विश्रम् **vi+śram** (IV **viśrāmyati**) rest, cease, take a rest

विश्रम्भ: **viśrambhaḥ** confidence; **viśrambha-kathā/ kathitam** confidential or intimate conversation

विश्रान्त **viśrānta** *p.p. of* **vi+śram**

विश्राम: **viśrāmaḥ** rest, respite

विश्रुत **viśruta** widely heard of, known, famous

विश्लेष: **viśleṣaḥ** separation, estrangement

विश्वं **viśvam** the whole world, universe

विश्वात्मन् **viśv›-ātman** *m.* Soul of the Universe, Supreme Godhead

विषं viṣam poison

विषम viṣama uneven

विषय: viṣayaḥ dominion, sphere, field of action

विषाद: viṣādaḥ despair, dejection, disappointment, distress

विष्णुगुप्त: Viṣṇuguptaḥ pr. n.

विष्णुशर्मन् Viṣṇuśarman m., pr. n.

विसृज् vi+sṛj (VI visṛjati) discharge, release, dismiss

विसृज् vi+sṛj caus. (visarjayati) release, dismiss, bid farewell to

विसृप् vi+sṛp (I visarpati) be diffused, spread, glide

विस्तर: vistaraḥ expansion, prolixity; vistara~taḥ at length, in detail

विस्तीर्ण vistīrṇa extensive

विस्मय: vismayaḥ astonishment

विस्मित vismita astonished

विस्मृ vi+smṛ (I vismarati) forget

विहग: vihagaḥ bird

विहत vihata (p.p. of vi+han) struck, broken

विहस्त vi:hasta [with hands awry:] clumsy

विहाय vihāya [having left behind:] beyond (acc.)

विहार: vihāraḥ (Buddhist) monastery/convent

विहारिन् vihārin roaming

विहित vihita p.p. of vi+dhā

विह्वल vihvala tottering, unsteady

वीक्ष् vīkṣ (vi+īkṣ) (I vīkṣate) discern, spy, scrutinize

वीज् vīj (X vījayate) fan

वीथिका vīthikā row, grove

वृक्ष: वृक्षक: vṛkṣaḥ, vṛkṣakaḥ tree

वृत् **vṛt** (I **vartate**) proceed, currently exist, abide, happen; (*of promises etc.*) be entered upon

वृत **vṛta** (*p.p. of* **vṛ**) chosen, preferred, asked in marriage

वृत्त **vṛtta** (*p.p. of* **vṛt**) happened *etc.*

वृत्तं **vṛttam** metre; **vṛtta-ratnākaraḥ** 'Treasury of Metres'

वृत्तान्त: **vṛttāntaḥ** news, what has happened, 'scene', 'story'

वृत्ति **vṛtti** *f.* behaviour, conduct; (*gram.*) synthetic expression (*i.e. by cpds.*)

वृध् **vṛdh** (I **vardhate**) grow; + **diṣṭyā** be congratulated

वृध् **vṛdh** *caus.* (**vardhayati**) increase (*trans.*); + **diṣṭyā** congratulate

वृषल: **Vṛṣalaḥ** *pr. n.*

वृष्टि **vṛṣṭi** *f.* rain

वेग: **vegaḥ** haste, speed

वेणु **veṇu** *m.* bamboo, reed; flute

वेतस: वेत्र **vetasaḥ, vetra** *m./n.* reed, cane

वेद: **vedaḥ** (*from* **vid**) knowledge, sacred knowledge, scripture

वेदना **vedanā** ache, pain, pang

वेदिका **vedikā** balcony

वेदिन् **vedin** knowing, conscious (of), appreciative

वेदी **vedī** (sacrificial) altar

वेला **velā** boundary; shore; time (of day)

वेश्मन् **veśman** *n.* residence, house, *etc.*

वेष: **veṣaḥ** dress, attire

वैक्लव्यं **vaiklavyam** (**viklava**) bewilderment, despondency

वैखानस: **vaikhānasaḥ** hermit, anchorite

वैतालिक: vaitālikaḥ (royal) bard

वैदग्ध्यं vaidagdhyaṃ (vidagdha) cleverness (*esp.* verbal dexterity)

वैदेह Vaideha (*f.* ī) belonging to (the country of) Videha; *m.* King of Videha; *f.* Queen/Princess of Videha

वैद्य vaidya learned; *m.* physician, doctor

वैधेय vaidheya foolish; *m.* fool

वैनतेय: Vainateyaḥ [Vinatā's son:] Garuḍa (King of the Birds)

वैमनस्यं vaimanasyaṃ despondency

वैरं vairaṃ hostility

वैरोधक: Vairodhakaḥ *pr. n.*

वैवाहिक vaivāhika (*f.* ī) (suitable) for a wedding

वैहीनरि Vaihīnari *m., pr. n.*

वोढृ voḍhṛ *m.* bridegroom

व्यक्त vyakta clear, obvious

व्यग्र vyagra engrossed, intent

व्यञ्जनं vyañjanaṃ sign, indication; insignia, disguise

व्यतिकर: vyatikaraḥ (kṝ 'mix') blending together, confluence, 'expanse'

व्यतिरेकिन् vyatirekin differing, distinct

व्यपदेश: vyapadeśaḥ designation, name

व्यभिचार: vyabhicāraḥ deviation, swerving

व्यभिचारिन् vyabhicārin liable to deviate, swerving

व्यभ्र vyːabhra cloudless

व्यय: vyayaḥ loss; expense, extravagance

व्यवसो vyavaso (vi+ava+so) (IV vyavasyati *p.p.* vyavasita) decide, resolve

व्यवहार: vyavahāraḥ dealings, usage; litigation

व्यवह् vyavahṛ (vi+ava+hṛ) (I **vyavaharati**) act, deal with, behave towards (*loc.*)

व्यसनं vyasanam vice, vicious failing, weakness, deficiency; misfortune, misery

व्याघ्र: vyāghraḥ tiger

व्याज: vyājaḥ fraud, pretence

व्यापद् vyā+pad *caus.* (**vyāpādayati**) [cause to perish:] kill, slay

व्यापार: vyāpāraḥ occupation

व्यापृ vyā+pṝ *caus.* (**vyāpārayati**) set to work, employ

व्यावृत् vyā+vṛt *caus.* (**vyāvartayati**) cause to turn back, drive back

व्रतं vratam vow; *ifc.* [having as one's vow:] devoted to

व्रीहि vrīhi *m.* rice

श: ˜śaḥ *distributive suffix*: eka˜śaḥ in ones, singly; lava˜śaḥ in pieces

शंस् śaṃs (I **śaṃsati**) praise, proclaim

शंसिन् śaṃsin proclaiming

शक् śak (V **śaknoti**) be able, 'can'

शकटदास: Śakaṭadāsaḥ *pr. n.*

शकुनि śakuni *m.* bird

शकुन्तला Śakuntalā *pr. n.*

शक्ति śakti *f.* ability, power

शक्य śakya possible, able to be

शङ्का śaṅkā suspicion, fear, anxiety, care

शची Sacī *name of Indra's wife*

शठ śaṭha cunning

शतं śatam a hundred

शतक्रतु Śatakratu *m. name of Indra*

शतगुण **śata:guṇa** hundredfold; **śataguṇayati** *denom.* multiply by a hundred

शत्रु **śatru** *m.* enemy

शनै: **śanaiḥ** quietly, gently; **śanaiḥ śanaiḥ** very gently

शब्द: **śabdaḥ** sound, noise; word

शम् **śam** *caus.* (**śamayati**) quieten, appease

शयनं **śayanam** (**śī** 'lie') repose, sleeping; **śayana-gṛham** sleeping-quarters, bedchamber

शर: **śaraḥ** arrow

शरणं **śaraṇam** shelter, refuge

शरद् **śarad** *f.* autumn

शरीरं **śarīram** body, 'person'

शशिन् **śaśin** *m.* moon

शस्त्रं **śastram** knife, sword, weapon

शाकुन्तलेय **Śākuntaleya** born of Śakuntalā

शाखा **śākhā** branch

शाप: **śāpaḥ** curse

शाङ्र्गरव: **Śārṅgaravaḥ** *pr. n.*

शार्दूल: **śārdūlaḥ** tiger

शाल: **śālaḥ** sal tree

शाला **śālā** hall, apartment

शाश्वत **śāśvata** (*f.* ī) perpetual

शास् **śās** (II **śāsti**) govern, teach

शासनं **śāsanam** command

शास्त्रं **śāstram** (technical) treatise, law-book

शिखर **śikhara** *m./n.* point, tip

शिखा **śikhā** crest

शिथिल **śithila** loose, slack

शिरस **śiras** *n.* head

शिव: **Śivaḥ** *name of a god*

शिशिर śiśira cold

शिशु śiśu *m.* child

शिष्ट śiṣṭa (*p.p. of* śās) learned; śiṣṭ-ânadhyayanaṃ holiday in honour of learned (guests)

शिष्यः śiṣyaḥ [one requiring to be taught:] pupil

शीघ्र śīghra swift, fast

शीतल śītala cool

शीर्ष śīrṣaṃ head

शुच् śuc (I śocati) grieve, mourn

शुचि śuci pure, clean

शुद्धान्तः śuddhāntaḥ women's apartments, household

शुभ śubha auspicious

शुश्रूषा śuśrūṣā (*desiderative of* śru) desire to hear/learn

शून्य śūnya empty, devoid (of), deserted, desolate

शूल śūla *m./n.* stake, spit, lance, trident (*of Śiva*); śūlam āruh *caus.* [cause to mount the stake:] impale

शूलिन् śūlin Trident-bearer (*epithet of Śiva*)

शृगालः śṛgālaḥ jackal

शेषः śeṣaḥ remainder, portion to be supplied

शैलः śailaḥ mountain

शोकः śokaḥ grief, sadness

शोचनीय śocanīya, śocya (*ger. of* śuc) to be mourned for, pitiable, lamentable

शोणोत्तरा Śoṇottarā *pr. n.*

शोभन śobhana shining, bright, beautiful

शोभा śobhā brilliance, beauty

श्मशानं śmaśānaṃ burning ground, cemetery

श्याम śyāma, śyāmala dark

श्रद्धा śrad+dhā (III śraddhatte) put trust in, believe

श्रमः śramaḥ exertion

श्रवणं śravaṇam hearing

श्रवणः śravaṇaḥ ear

श्रान्त śrānta (*p.p. of* śram 'tire') tired

श्रावकः śrāvakaḥ Buddhist disciple, student

श्रीपर्वतः Śrīparvataḥ *name of a mountain*

श्रु śru (V śṛṇoti) hear, listen to

श्रेयांस śreyāṃs better; *n. sg.* śreyas welfare, blessing

श्रेष्ठ śreṣṭha best, supreme

श्रेष्ठिन् śreṣṭhin *m.* eminent businessman, merchant

श्रोतृ śrotṛ listener, someone to listen

श्रोत्रं śrotram (organ *or* act of) hearing

श्रोत्रियः śrotriyaḥ learned (brahmin), scholar

श्रौत śrauta (*f.* ī/ā) deriving from scripture, scriptural

श्लाघ्य ślāghya praiseworthy, virtuous

श्लोकः ślokaḥ stanza

श्वः śvaḥ *adv.* tomorrow

श्वपाकः śvapākaḥ outcaste

श्वापद śvāpada *m./n.* beast of prey, 'big game'

षष् ṣaṣ (ṣaṭ) six

षोडश ṣoḍaśa(n) sixteen

स sa *prefix* co-, fellow-; having (with one), accompanied by, possessing, sharing *etc.*

सः saḥ *pron.* that, the, that one, he *etc.*; saḥ+eva just that, that very, the same

सं सम् sam, sam[1] *verbal prefix* together *etc.*

संयम् sam+yam (I saṃyacchati) restrain, arrest

---

[1] sam is the basic form, but for brevity in the following entries sam+yam is written instead of saṃyam (sam+yam) and so forth.

संयमनं samyamanaṃ restraint, tightening

संयुत samyuta joined

संवद् saṃ+vad (I saṃvadati) accord, fit

संवरणं saṃvaraṇaṃ covering up, duplicity

संविग्न saṃvigna agitated, overwhelmed

संवृत्त saṃvṛtta (*p.p. of* sam+vṛt) become, turned into *etc.*

संवृध् saṃ+vṛdh *caus.* (saṃvardhayati) congratulate

संवेग: saṃvegaḥ agitation

संव्यवहार: saṃvyavahāraḥ transaction

संस्कार: saṃskāraḥ preparation, adornment

संस्तम्भ् sam+stambh (IX saṃstabhnāti) make firm, sustain, compose

संस्तरणं saṃstaraṇaṃ strewing

संस्तु sam+stu (II saṃstauti) praise

संस्थित saṃsthita standing, remaining, steady

सकल sakala whole

सकाशम् sakāśam [to the presence of:] to

सखि sakhi *m.* (*irreg.*) comrade, friend; *voc.* sakhe (my) friend, my dear—*etc.*

सखी sakhī (female) friend, wife of friend; *voc.* sakhi my dear *etc.*

संकल्पनिर्मित saṃkalpa-nirmita [created by conception:] imagined

संकुल saṃkula crowded, thronged; *n.* throng

संकेत: saṃketaḥ agreement, assignation; saṃketa-sthānam place of assignation

संक्षिप्त saṃkṣipta abbreviated, in concise form

संक्षेप: saṃkṣepaḥ abridgement, conciseness

संख्या sam+khyā (II saṃkhyāti) count, reckon up

संख्या saṃkhyā number, numeral

संगम् sam+gam (I saṃgacchate) come together, agree, fit

सचिव: sacivaḥ counsellor, minister

सज्ज sajja prepared, equipped

सज्जीभू sajjī˜bhū (I sajjībhavati) become prepared, prepare

संचय: saṃcayaḥ collection, quantity

संचर् sam+car (I saṃcarate) walk, stroll

संचार: saṃcāraḥ movement

संचारिन् saṃcārin going together, transitory; saṃcāri bhāvaḥ (lit. crit.) Subsidiary Emotional State

संजन् sam+jan (IV saṃjāyate) come into being, be aroused

संज्ञा saṃjñā signal

सत्कार: satkāraḥ honouring, hospitality, entertainment

सत्कृ sat˜kṛ (VIII satkaroti) honour; receive with hospitality, entertain

सत्त्वं sattvam being, essence; creature

सत्य satya true, real; satyam truly, really; satyam truth

सत्यसंध satya˳saṃdha [whose compact is true:] true to one's word

सत्वर sa_tvara full of haste, busy

सद् sad (I sīdati) sit, abide

सद् -sad ifc. dweller (in)

सदृश sadṛśa (f. ī) similar, like, suitable, in keeping with, worthy

सन्त् sant pres. part. of as; true, virtuous

संताप: saṃtāpaḥ burning, torment

संतोष: saṃtoṣaḥ satisfaction

संदर्शनं saṃdarśanam sight, beholding

संदिश् sam+diś (VI saṃdiśati) command

संदेश: saṃdeśaḥ message

संदेह: saṃdehaḥ doubt, confusion

संधा sam+dhā (III saṃdhatte) bring together; agree, come to terms; aim (arrow)

संधा saṃdhā agreement, compact

संध्या saṃdhyā twilight, evening

संनिहित saṃnihita present, [in the area of:] about

सप्त sapta(n) seven

सप्तम saptama seventh

सफल sa_phala [having fruit:] fulfilled

सम sama even, equal

समक्षम् samakṣam visibly, in front of

समनन्तरम् samanantaram immediately after, thereupon

समय: samayaḥ occasion, season, time

समर्थ samartha capable, able

समर्थनं samarthanam establishment, confirmation

समर्पयति samarpayati (caus. of sam+ṛ) hand over

समवाय: samavāyaḥ coming together, union

समस्त samasta combined, all

समागम: samāgamaḥ meeting with, union

समाचर् sam+ā+car (I samācarati) conduct oneself, act, do

समाचार: samācāraḥ conduct, behaviour

समाधि samādhi m. concentration, (religious) meditation

समान samāna similar, same

समाम्नाय: samāmnāyaḥ traditional enumeration, list

समारुह् sam+ā+ruh (I samārohati) ascend, attain

समास: samāsaḥ (*gram.*) compound

समासञ्ज् sam+ā+sañj (I samāsajati) attach to (*loc.*), impose upon

समासद् sam+ā+sad *caus.* (samāsādayati) approach, attain, meet

समाहार: samāhāraḥ group, collection

समिध् samidh *f.* firewood

समुचित samucita suitable, in accord with

समुत्था samutthā (sam+ut+sthā) (I samuttiṣṭhati) rise up

समुद्र: samudraḥ ocean

समुपदिश् sam+upa+diś (VI samupadiśati) point out, show

संपद् saṃ+pad *caus.* (sampādayati) bring about

संपूर्ण sampūrṇa fulfilled

संप्रति samprati now

संप्रदाय: sampradāyaḥ tradition

संप्रधृ sam+pra+dhṛ *caus.* (sampradhārayati) deliberate, wonder

सप्रहार: samprahāraḥ fighting, combat

संप्राप् samprāp (sam+pra+āp) (V samprāpnoti) arrive, come to

संप्लुत sampluta flowed together, flooding

संबन्ध: sambandhaḥ union

संबन्धिन् sambandhin relative (by marriage)

संबुद्धि sambuddhi *f.* calling out; (*gram.*) vocative

संभव -sambhava *ifc.* arising from, offspring of

संभव: sambhavaḥ birth, origin

संभावना sambhāvanā supposing

संभाव्य **sambhāvya** credible, conceivable, adequate

संभू **sam+bhū** (I **sambhavati**) arise, be born

संभू **sam+bhū** *caus.* (**sambhāvayati**) conceive, imagine; meet with, find

संभृत **sambhṛta** assembled, concentrated, augmented

संभेद: **sambhedaḥ** union, confluence

संमन्त्र् **sam+mantr** (X **sammantrayati**) take counsel, consult

संमर्द: **sammardaḥ** crush, encounter, throng

संमूढ **sammūḍha** (*p.p. of* **sam+muh**) bewildered, confused, deluded

संमोह: **sammohaḥ** bewilderment, delusion

सरस् **saras** *n.*, **sarasī** lake

सरित् **sarit** *f.* river

सर्प: **sarpaḥ** snake

सर्व **sarva** *pron.* all, whole, every; *n. sg.* everything, anything (at all); *m. sg.* everyone (in general)

सर्वत: **sarvataḥ** on all sides, in all directions; totally, in full detail

सर्वथा **sarvathā** in every way, totally, at all events, [in all circumstances:] always

सर्वदा **sarvadā** always, ever

सर्वनामन् **sarva-nāman** *n.* (*gram.*) [name for anything:] pronoun

सलिलं **salilam** water

सविशेषम् **sa_viśeṣam** [with particulars:] particularly, completely

सह **sah** (I **sahate**) withstand, endure, bear

सह **saha** + *instr.* together with, with

सहचारिन् **sahacārin** accompanying, companion

सहधर्मचारिन् **sahadharmacārin** *m.* lawful husband; **sahadharmacāriṇī** lawful wife

सहभू **sahabhū** inherent, natural

सहसा **sahasā** vehemently, suddenly

सहस्रं **sahasram** a thousand

सहाध्ययनं **sah∵:âdhyayanam** studying together, common lessons

सहाय: **sahāyaḥ** companion

सह्य **sahya** (*ger. of* **sah**) bearable

सांग्रामिक **sāṃgrāmika** (*f.* **ī**) relating to war (**saṃgrāmaḥ**), military

साचिव्यं **sācivyam** being minister, post of minister

साधनं **sādhanam** army

साधु **sādhu** good, virtuous, right; *adv.* **sādhu** bravo!; **sādhu˜tara** better

सांनिध्यं **sāṃnidhyam** presence

सापत्न्यं **sāpatnyam** the state of being the sharer of a husband (**sapatnī**)

सामाजिक: **sāmājikaḥ** spectator

सामान्य **sāmānya** common, general

सांप्रत **sāṃprata** [relating to now (**samprati**):] timely, proper; *adv.* **sāṃpratam** now, at once

सायम् **sāyam** at evening; **sāyaṃ˜tana** (*f.* **ī**) [relating to] evening

सार **sāra** *m./n.* substance; property

सारथि **sārathi** *m.* driver of chariot

सावधान **s∵_âvadhāna** careful, watchful

साहस **sāhasa** rash, reckless

साहसिक **sāhasika** (*f.* **ī**) reckless, adventurous

सिच् **sic** (VI **siñcati**) sprinkle, moisten

सित **sita** white

सिद्ध **siddha** (*p.p. of* **sidh**) achieved, accomplished

सिद्धार्थकः **Siddhārthakaḥ** *pr. n.*

सिद्धि **siddhi** *f.* achievement, success, fulfilment

सीता **Sītā** *pr. n.*

सीरध्वजः **Sīradhvajaḥ** *pr. n.*

सु **su** *laudatory prefix* well, fair, good, very *etc.*; easily, easy

सुकुमार **su:kumāra** (*f.* ī) delicate

सुखं **sukham** pleasure, happiness; *adv.* **sukham** comfortably, at one's ease

सुचरितं **su:caritam** good deed

सुतः **sutaḥ** son

सुता **sutā** daughter

सुन्दर **sundara** (*f.* ī) beautiful

सुप्त **supta** (*p.p. of* **svap**) asleep

सुभग **subhaga** fortunate, lovely, delightful

सुभ्रू **su:bhrū** fair-browed, fair

सुरः **suraḥ** god

सुरतं **su:ratam** lovemaking

सुरभि **surabhi** fragrant

सुलभ **su:labha** easily got, natural

सुवर्णं **suvarnam** gold; **suvarnaḥ** gold piece

सुहृत्तमः **suhṛt˘tamaḥ** close friend

सुहृत्ता **suhṛt˘tā** being friendly, affection

सुहृद् **suhṛd** *m.* friend

सूच् **sūc** (X **sūcayati**) point out, indicate

सूतः **sūtaḥ** driver of chariot

सूत्रं **sūtram** thread; aphorism, aphoristic rule

सूर्यः **sūryaḥ** sun

सेचनं **secanam** (act of) sprinkling, watering

सेना **senā** army

सेनापति **senā-pati** *m.* [lord of army:] general

सेवा **sevā** attendance (upon someone), servitude

सैनिक: **sainikaḥ** [belonging to army:] soldier

सोढुम् **soḍhum** *inf. of* **sah**

सोदर: **sodaraḥ, sodaryaḥ** [one born of same womb:] brother [of same mother]

सोमतीर्थं **Somatīrtham** *name of pilgrimage place*

सोमरात: **Somarātaḥ** *pr. n.*

सौजन्यं **saujanyam** kindness

सौधातकि **Saudhātaki** *m., pr. n.*

सौहार्दं **sauhārdam** friendship, fondness

स्खलनं **skhalanam** failure, lapse

स्तनकलश: **Stanakalaśaḥ** *pr. n.*

स्तम्ब: **stambaḥ** clump of grass

स्तम्भ: **stambhaḥ** pillar

स्तु **stu** (II **stauti**) praise

स्त्री **strī** *irreg.* woman

स्थ **-stha** standing, being at/in, *etc.*

स्थली **sthalī** dry land

स्था **sthā** (I **tiṣṭhati**) stand, stay, remain, abide, stop, halt

स्था **sthā** *caus.* (**sthāpayati**) cause to stand, establish

स्थानं **sthānam** place, occasion; **sthāne** in place, appropriate(ly)

स्थानभ्रंश: **sthāna-bhraṃśaḥ** fall from position, loss of place

स्थायिन् **sthāyin** lasting, stable

स्थास्यति **sthāsyati** *3rd sg. fut. para. of* **sthā**

स्थित **sthita** (*p.p. of* **sthā**) standing *etc.*

स्थिर **sthira** firm; **sthirī~kṛ** make firm, sustain; **sthirī~**
bhū be[come] firm

स्नानं **snānam** bathing, bathe

स्निग्ध **snigdha** affectionate

स्निह् **snih** (IV **snihyati**) feel affection for (*loc.*)

स्नेहः **snehaḥ** affection, fondness, tenderness, love

स्पन्द् **spand** (I **spandate**) quiver

स्पर्शः **sparśaḥ** touch

स्पृश् **spṛś** (VI **spṛśati**) touch, affect

स्प्रष्टुम् **spraṣṭum** *inf. of* **spṛś**

स्फुट **sphuṭa** clear, distinct

स्मरहरः **Smara-haraḥ** Destroyer of Love (*epithet of Śiva*)

स्मि **smi** (I **smayate**) smile

स्मितं **smitam** smile

स्मृ **smṛ** (I **smarati**) remember (*acc. or gen.*)

स्मृ **smṛ** *caus.* (**smārayati**) cause to remember, remind

स्यन्द् **syand** (I **syandate**) flow, move rapidly

स्यात् **syāt** *3rd sg. opt. of* **as**

संस् **sraṃs** (I **sraṃsate**) drop, slip

स्रु **sru** (I **sravati**) flow

स्व **sva** *pron. adj.* (one's) own

स्वच्छन्दम् **svacchandam** at one's will, as one would
wish

स्वनः **svanaḥ** sound

स्वप् **svap** (II **svapiti**) sleep

स्वप्नः **svapnaḥ** sleep; dream

स्वयम् **svayam** *emphatic pron.* myself *etc.*, by/for myself
etc., personally, of one's own accord

स्वरः **svaraḥ** sound, tone, syllable

स्वल्प **sv:alpa** small, scant

स्वसृ svasṛ *f.* sister

स्वागतम् sv:āgatam welcome to (*dat.*)

स्वामिन् svāmin owner, master; **svāminī** mistress

स्वास्थ्यं svāsthyam comfort, ease

स्वीकरणं svī̈karaṇam [making one's own:] marrying

स्वीकृ svī̈kṛ make one's own, appropriate

स्वेद: svedaḥ sweat

स्वैरम् svairam gently

हत hata *p.p. of* han

हतक hataka *ifc.* accursed

हन् han (II hanti) kill, slay, murder

हन् han *caus.* (ghātayati) get killed, have killed, put to death

हन्त hanta ah! alas!

हय: hayaḥ horse

हर: Haraḥ *name of Śiva*

हरणं haraṇam (*from* hṛ) taking

हरि Hari *m. name of Viṣṇu or Indra*

हर्ष: harṣaḥ joy, delight

हस् has (I hasati) laugh

हस्त hastaḥ hand, arm, trunk (of elephant)

हस्तिन् hastin elephant

हा hā ah! oh!

हानि hāni *f.* abandonment

हारिन् hārin taking, bringing

हार्य hārya *ger. of* hṛ

हास: hāsaḥ laugh, chuckle

हि hi *enclitic particle* for; assuredly, certainly, *etc.*

हित **hita** (*p.p. of* **dhā**) put; beneficial, well-disposed, good (friend)

हिमं **himam** frost, snow, ice

हिमवन्त् **Himavant** *m.*, **Himālayaḥ** the mountain (range) Himālaya

हु **hu** (III **juhoti**) sacrifice

हृ **hṛ** (I **harati**) take, carry, carry off, take away

हृ **hṛ** *caus.* (**hārayati**) cause to carry

हृदयं **hṛdayam** heart, mind

हे **he** (*before vocatives*) O, ah

हेतु **hetu** *m.* motive, ground for (*loc.*), cause; **hetoḥ** for the sake of, for

होम: **homaḥ** oblation, sacrifice

2 English–Sanskrit

THIS is solely a vocabulary to the English–Sanskrit exercises: words which occur only in the Sanskrit–English sections or in the body of the chapters are not included. No exhaustive attempt has been made to indicate the limits within which the Sanskrit word is equivalent to the English. It must be gathered from the context of the sentences themselves that, for instance, **prati+pad** corresponds to 'admit' in its sense of 'confess' and that **smārayati** means 'recall' in the sense of 'bring to another's mind'. Where distinctions are made, the colon is used to mean 'in the sense of'—e.g. 'call (:summon)', 'call in the sense of summon'.

Where an English word (e.g. 'wish') occurs as more than one part of speech, its verbal usage is normally listed first; but the Sanskrit equivalent should at any rate indicate which part of speech is in question. The same applies to forms in -ing such as 'seeing': **darśanam** is the substantive (action noun), **darśin** the adjective (agent noun).

Morphological indications such as verb class are not usually given where these may be found in the special vocabularies or in the verb list.

a/an *usually omit*, **kaś cit, ko >pi, ekaḥ**

abandon **hā, vi+hā**; abandoned **ujjhita** (*p.p. of* **ujjh**)

abide **ās**

able, be — (to) **śak**

about (:concerning) **prati**; about this (:on this matter) **atra**

absent-minded **śūnya-hṛdaya**

abundance **bāhulyaṃ**

accept **grah, pari+grah, prati+grah, aṅgī-kṛ**

acceptance **parigrahaḥ**

acclamation **praśaṃsā-ālāpaḥ**

accompany **anu+vṛt**

accomplished **siddha**

accomplishment (:act of achieving) **siddhi** *f.*; (:technical ability) **śilpaṃ**

accord, of one's own — **svayam**

according to **~vat**

accursed **hatakaḥ** *ifc.*

acknowledge **abhi+upa+i**

acquire **ā+gam** *caus.*

act (:do) **anu+sthā**

act (a play) **naṭ** *caus.*

acting (:doing) **kārin**

acting (in play) **nṛttaṃ**; science of acting **nāṭya-śāstraṃ**

activity **kriyā**

actual *use* **eva**

actually **eva**

address **abhi+dhā**

administration **tantraṃ**

admit **prati+pad**

adored one **priyatamā**

advantage **phalaṃ**

advice **upadeśaḥ**

affair **kāryaṃ**

affection **praṇayaḥ**

after **pareṇa**+*abl.*; *use absol.*; after very long **aticirāt**

after all **khalu**

afterwards **paścāt**

again **punar**; yet again **punar api**

agent **praṇidhiḥ** *m.*

agitation **saṃvegaḥ**

ah! **aye**

aiding **upakāraḥ**

alas! **hanta, kaṣṭam**

alight, set — **ut+dīp** *caus.* (**uddīpayati**)

alive **jīvita**

all **sarva** *pron.*; on all sides **sarvataḥ**; at all **eva**; after all **khalu**

allusion **upanyāsaḥ**

alone **eka**; (:solitary) **ekākin**

already **prathamam, pūrva** *in cpd. with p.p., sometimes just* **eva**

also **api** *enclitic*

altercation **saṃgharṣaḥ**

although **api**

among, from — **madhyāt**+*gen. or ifc.*

amorous swoon **madana-mūrchā**

and **ca** *enclitic,* **ca . . . ca**; *connecting two verbs, usually expressed by absol.*; *connecting sentences, often expressed by* **api** *after new subject*

anger **krodhaḥ, kopaḥ, manyu** *m.*

announce **ni+vid** *caus.*

announcing **nivedanaṃ**

annoyance **pratyavāyaḥ**

another **anya, para**

answer **prativacanam**

ant **pipīlikā**

anxiety **śankā**

anxious to **-kāma**

any **kaś cit, ko ›pi**

anyone **kaś cit, ko ›pi**; (:no matter who) **sarvaḥ**

apart from **antareṇa+**_acc._

appearance **varṇaḥ**

appease (:quieten) **śam** _cause._; (curry favour with) **ā+rādh** _caus._

appeasement **anunayaḥ**

appointment **saṃketaḥ**

apprehension **āśankā**

appropriate, to — **svī˜kṛ**

appropriate **ucita**; appropriate(ly) **sthāne**

approve **abhi+nand**

army (:forces) **balam**

arouse (:bring about) **jan** _caus._; aroused **janita, saṃjāta**

arrival **āgamanam**

arrive **ā+gam, pra+āp**

arrow **bāṇaḥ, śaraḥ**

as (:like) **iva**; _introducing subordinate clause_ **yathā . . . tathā**; _in cpd._ **yathā**

as if _use_ **iva**

as soon as **yad» aîva . . . tad» aîva**

as well (:also) **api**

ascetic **tāpasaḥ, tapasvin**

ascetic grove **tapo-vanam**

ashamed **vilakṣa**

ask (about) **prach** (+ _acc._)

asleep **supta**

assistant in gambling-house **sabhyaḥ**

assume (role) **grah**

assuredly **hi**

astonished **vismita**

astonishment **vismayaḥ**

at _use loc._

at all **eva**

at once **sāmpratam**

attachment **prasakti** _f._

attack (of emotion) **āveśaḥ**; (on enemy) **abhiyogaḥ**

attempt **prayatnaḥ**

attend **anu+gam**

attendance **upasthānam**

attendant **anucaraḥ**

attentive **avahita**

attractive **ramaṇīya**

audience **parisad** _f._

augmented **saṃbhṛta**

aunt (maternal) **mātṛ-ṣvasṛ**

austerity (religious-) **tapas** _n._

autumn **śarad** _f._

avoid **pari+hṛ**

bad news **a:priyam**

bakula (blossom) **bakulam**

banish **nis+vas** _caus._

bank **tīram**

barb **śalya** _m./n._

barbarian **mlecchaḥ**

bard (royal —) **vaitālikaḥ**

battle **samaraḥ**

be **as, bhū**; (be currently) **vṛt**

bearing **dhārin**

beat **taḍ**

beat off **apa+han**

beating **tāḍaḥ**

beautiful **śobhana**

beauty **śobhā, rūpam**

because _use instr. or abl. of abstract noun_; (:with the thought that) **iti**

become **bhū** (_in past_ **saṃvṛtta**), _or use verb of motion with abstract noun_

become an object **viṣayī˜bhū**

bedchamber **śayana-gṛham**

before (:previously) **prāk**; _in cpd. with p.p._ **pūrva**

before (_conj._) **yāvat na . . . tāvat**

begin (:undertake) **sam+ā+rabh**, (:make a start) **upa+kram** beginning **ārambhaḥ**

behalf, on — of -**artham**

behave **ceṣṭ, ā+ceṣṭ; (:deal with) vi+ava+hṛ**

belief **pratyayaḥ**

believe **śrad+dhā**

beloved **priya, vallabha;** beloved wife **praṇayinī**

bend down **ava+nam**

beneath **adhastāt**+*gen.*

benefit **priyam**

besieging **uparodhanam**

beside **āsanna, -samīpe**

bestow **pra+dā** (+*dat.*)

betel **tāmbūlam;** betel-box **tāmbūla-bhājanam**

beyond **vihāya**

bird **patatrin, pakṣin**

birth **janman** *n.*; birth-ceremony **jāta-karman** *n.*

bit **chedaḥ**

blame **upa+ā+labh**

blessing **maṅgalam**

blind **andha**

bliss **nirvāṇam**

blossom **ut+śvas**

blossom **kusumam**

boast **ślāgh (I ślāghate)**

body **śarīram, vigrahaḥ, gātram**

bodyguard, provide a — for **pari+vṛ (V parivṛṇoti)+** *dcc.*

bondage **bandhanam**

book **pustakam**

born of Śakuntalā **Śākuntaleya**

both (*adj.*) **ubha;** both . . . and . . . **ca . . . ca**

bow **cāpa** *m./n.*, **kārmukam**

bower **maṇḍapa** *m./n.*

box **bhāṇḍam**

boy **bālaḥ**

brahmin **brāhmaṇaḥ**

bravo! **sādhu**

breast **uras** *n.*

breeze **pravātam**

bride **vadhū**

bridegroom **varaḥ;** bride and groom **vara;vadhū**

bright **śobhana**

bring **ā+nī, ā+dā;** bring to a pass **avasthāṁ gam** *caus.*

bring up (chariot) **upa+sthā** *caus.*

broken **bhagna**

brother **bhrātṛ**

brother-in-law **śyālaḥ**

burn **dah**

busy **vyagra**

busy oneself on **abhi+yuj** *pass.+loc.*

but **punar** *enclitic,* **tu** *enclitic,* **kiṁ tu;** but then **athavā**

buy **krī**

by *normally use instr.*; by (virtue of doing something) *use pres. part.*

call (:summon) **ā+hve**

called (:named) *use* **nāma** 'by name' *or* ꞉**nāman**

camp **ni+viś**

can *use* **śak;** *sometimes not necessary to translate*

cancellation **pratiṣedhaḥ**

capture **grah**

careful **s꞉_âvadhāna**

carriage **pravahaṇam**

carry off **apa+hṛ**

case, in that — **tarhi, tena hi, yady evam**

cast **ni+kṣip**

cause (to) *use caus.*

cause **hetu** *m.*

ceremony **saṁskāraḥ**

certain, a — **kaścit, ko ꞉pi**

certainly **khalu**

change **pariṇāmaḥ**

character **śīlam**

chariot **rathaḥ**

chase away **vi+dru** *caus.*

check **prati+sidh**

chieftain **rājan** *m.*

child **bālaḥ**; dear child **vatsaḥ**

childless **an:apatya**

circumstances **daśā**

citizen **pauraḥ**

city **nagaram, puram**

clamour **kolāhalaḥ**

clean **śuci**

clearly **vyaktam**

clever **nipuṇa**

clod of earth **loṣṭa** *m./n.*

come **ā+gam, upa+gam, upa+i, ā+yā, sam+ā+ gam**

come! (*imperv.*) **ehi**

come in **pra+viś**

comfort **ā+śvas** *caus.*

command **sam+diś**

command **śāsanam, saṃde- śaḥ, ājñā**

common **prākṛta**

company, in the — of **-sameta**

compassion, feel — day (I **dayate**)

compassionate **kṛpālu**

complacent **subhagammanya**

complete **sam+āp**

complete with **sa_**

conceal **ā+chad** (X **ācchā- dayati**)

concealed **antarita**

concealment **pracchādanam**

conceive **pari+kḷp** *caus.*

concern **cintā**

conclusion **avasānam**

condemned **vadhya**

condition (:state) **avasthā**

conduct **caritam**

confer (on) **prati+pad** *caus.* + *dat.*

confidence, inspiring of — **viś- vasanīya**

confident, make — **prati+i** *caus.*

confirmation **pratipatti** *f.*

conflict **vimardaḥ**

confused **ākula**

confusion, in — **ākulī˜bhūta**

congratulate *use* **diṣṭyā vṛdh** *or its caus.* (*see Chapter* 9)

conjecture **tarkaḥ**

connive at (:overlook) **upa+ īkṣ**

conquer **ji**

conscious of **-vedin**

consciousness **saṃjñā**

consecrated **abhimantrita**

consider **ava+gam, cint** (X **cintayati**)

considerable **garīyāṃs**

contemporary **vartamāna**

contemptuous **avamānin**

contrive [:bring about] **ut+ pad** *caus.*

control, under one's own — **svādhīna**

convent **vihāraḥ**

conversant with **abhijña+**gen.

conversation **saṃlāpaḥ**

convey **pra+āp** *caus.*

cool **śītala**

coral-tree **mandāraḥ**

correctly **samyak**

council **pariṣad** *f.*

counsellor **sacivaḥ**

countermeasures, take — **prati +vi+dhā**

country **deśaḥ**

course **gati** *f.*

course, of — **khalu** *enclitic*

court **rāja-kulam**

courtesan **gaṇikā**

crag **śilā-cayaḥ**

creak **vi+ru** (II **virauti**)

create **nis+mā** (*p.p.* **nirmita**)

creeper **latā**

crime **doṣaḥ**

crowd of people **janapada- samavāyaḥ**

cruel **dāruṇa**

cruelty **krauryam**

cry ā+krand (I ākrandati)

cry out ut+ghuṣ

cunning śaṭha

curiosity kutūhalaṃ, kautu-
kaṃ

curlew krauñcaḥ

curse śāpaḥ

dance nṛt

danger bhayaṃ

dare ut+sah

darkness tamas n.

daughter kanyā, sutā, duhitṛ

day divasaḥ; by day divā

dead mṛta

dear priya, vallabha; dear
child vatsaḥ/vatsā; my dear
X (voc.) use sakhe m./sakhi
f.; my dear fellow bhadra;
dear Rāma Rāma:bhadraḥ

death mṛtyu m.

debtless an:ṛṇa

decayed jīrṇa

deceive vi+pra+labh

declare ā+cakṣ (II ācaṣṭe),
but normally ā+khyā outside
pres. stem

decoration bhūṣaṇaṃ

decrepit jīrṇa

deed karman n.

deer mṛgaḥ

defeat ji

defeat parājayaḥ

defile duṣ caus.

deity devatā

delay kāla-haraṇaṃ kṛ, ās

delight harṣaḥ; (:delightful
event) utsavaḥ

delighted prahṛṣṭa

delightful subhaga

deluded mūḍha

demerit doṣaḥ

demon asuraḥ

denounce apa+diś

depart ut+hā, apa+yā

departure prasthānaṃ

depict abhi+likh

depressed, feel — durmanāyate

descendant of use vṛddhi derivative

describe varṇayati; as described yathₐ_ôkta

desert pari+tyaj

desirable kānta

desire prārthitaṃ, prārthanā

despatch pra+hi (p.p. prahita)

despise ava+jñā

despondency vaimanasyaṃ

destiny vidhi m.

destroying vadhaḥ

destruction vināśaḥ

determination niścayaḥ

devoid śūnya

die upa+ram

different anya pron.

difficult dus:kara; difficult (to
achieve) dur:labha

diligence abhiyogaḥ

diligent abhiyukta

direct ā+diś

direction diś f.; in one —... in
another anyataḥ ... anyataḥ

disaffection aparāgaḥ

disappointment viṣādaḥ

discern sam+vi+jñā, upa+
lakṣ (X upalakṣayati)

disciple antevāsin

discover vid, pari+jñā

discrimination vivekaḥ

disgrace, in — sa_nikāram

disguise vyañjanaṃ

disinclined parāṅmukha

disloyalty aparāgaḥ

dismiss vi+sṛj caus.

dispersal (of crowd) bhaṅgaḥ

dispute vivādaḥ

distance, at a good — from
atidūre+gen.

distinction viśeṣaḥ

distract (pleasurably) **vi+nud** *caus.*

distracted (:crazed) **unmatta**

distress **ārti** *f.*; distress of mind **citta-khedaḥ**

distress, be in — **duḥkham sthā, duḥkham ās**

distressed **viklava**

disturb **ākulayati**

do **kṛ, anu+sthā, ā+car; sam+ā+car**

do violence to **abhi+druh**

doctor **vaidyaḥ**

don **pari+dhā** *ātm.*

donate **nis+vap**

done, have — with **kṛtam+** *instr.*

don't *use* **alam**, *or* **na+**ger.

door **dvāram, kapāṭam**

doubt **saṃdehaḥ, vitarkaḥ**

draw **ā+kṛṣ**

draw near **prati+ā+sad**

dreadful **atidāruṇa, aniṣṭa**

drink **pā**

drink **pānam**

drinking **-pa** *ifc.*

drive *use* **nī** *with abstract noun*

driver **sārathi** *m.*

driving away **apanodanam**

dweller **-sad**

dynasty **vaṃśaḥ**

each other **anyonya**

eager **utsuka**

ear **karṇaḥ**

earlier **pūrva** *pronom.*

earth **pṛthivī, bhū** *f.*

easy **sulabha**

eclipse **uparāgaḥ**

effect **kṛ**

either . . . or . . . **vā . . . vā**

elder **jyāyāṃs**; elder (person) **guru** *m.*

elder brother **jyāyāṃs bhrātṛ, agrajaḥ**

elephant **gajaḥ**

else **anya** *pron.*; somewhere else **anyatra kvᵛ âpi**

embarrassing **lajjā-kara**

embrace **pari+svaj** (I **pari- ṣvajate**)

emerge **nis+kram**

employ **pra+yuj, vi+ā+pṝ** *caus.*

enclosure **valaya** *m./n.*, **vāṭikā**

end **antaḥ**; to what end? **kim:nimittam**; an end of **kṛtam+**instr.

enemy **ripu** *m.*

engage **ni+yuj**

engrossed **vyagra**

enjoin **vi+dhā**

enjoy **pari+bhuj,** (:experi- ence) **anu+bhū**

enough **alam**

enrage **caṇḍī˜kṛ**

enter **pra+viś**

enter upon (vow) **sam+ā+ ruh**

entering **praveśaḥ**

enterprise **ārambhaḥ**

entire **nikhila**

entirely **eva**

entry **praveśaḥ**

epithet **viśeṣaṇa:padam**

escape **apakramaṇam**

escort **ānuyātrikaḥ**

especially **˜tara**

establish **sthā** *caus.*

even **api** *enclitic*

ever **kadācit**

every **sarva** *pron.*

everyone (of a number) **sarve** (*pl.*); (in general) **sarvaḥ** (*sg.*)

everything **sarvam**

evil **pāpa**

evil-natured **dur:ātman**

Excellency, His/Your **āryaḥ**

excessively **ati** *prefix*

execution-ground **vadhya- sthānam**

executioner **ghātakaḥ**

exertion **pariśramaḥ**
exhausted **pariśrānta**
exploits **caritam**
extermination **unmūlanam**
extraordinary **adbhuta**
extremely **ati** *prefix*
eye **netram, nayanam, cakṣus** *n.,* **locanam**

face **mukham, vaktram**
fact, in — **eva**; from the fact
that **yathā . . . tathā**
faint **moham upa+gam**
fair-eyed **su:nayana**
fall **pat, ni+pat**; (to one's lot)
upa+nam
fall silent **tūṣṇīm as**
falling **nipātaḥ**
fame **yaśas** *n.*
familiar **abhyasta**
family **kulam, anvayaḥ, kuṭumbam**; (:members of immediate household) **gṛha-janaḥ**
far away **dūre**
fast to death **an:aśanena
sam+sthā** *ātm.*
fate **daivam**
father **pitṛ**; (one's own) **tātaḥ**
father-in-law **śvaśuraḥ**
fault **doṣaḥ**
favour **anu+grah**
favour **prasādaḥ**
favourable **anukūla**
fearful **trasta**
fearfulness **bhīru˜tvam**
fearing **śaṅkin**
fellow **baṭu** *m.*; good fellow,
dear fellow **bhadraḥ**
festival **mahotsavaḥ**
fetch down (from carriage)
ava+tṛ *caus.*
fetching **āharaṇam**
few, a — *use* **kaścit**
field **kṣetram**
fierce **ugra**
filament **kesaram**

find **adhi+gam**
find out **upa+labh**
finger **aṅguli/aṅgulī** *f.*
fire **agni** *m.,* **analaḥ, vahni** *m.*
fired, cause to be — **dah** *caus.*
firewood **samidh** *f.*
firmness **dhairyam**
first **prathama**
fixed (on) **-āsakta**
flame **jvālā**
flesh **māṃsam**
flow **abhi+syand**
flower **puṣpam, kusumam**
fly up **ut+pat, ut+dī (uḍḍī)**
folk **janaḥ**
follow **anu+gam**
follower **anuyātrikaḥ**
fondness **prīti** *f.*
food **bhojanam, bhaktam**
fool **mūrkhaḥ**
foot **pādaḥ**
for (*prep.*) *use gen.*; for (a period
of time) *use acc.*; for (the sake
of) **-artham** *or use dat.*
for (*conj.*) **hi** *enclitic*
for oneself (:of one's own accord)
svayam
forcibly **balāt**
ford **tīrtham**
forest **vanam,   araṇyam,
vipinam**
forest-dweller **vanecaraḥ**
forget **vi+smṛ**
forgive **kṣam** (*pass.* **kṣamy-
ate**)
form **vapus** *n.*
former **purātana** (*f.* **ī**)
forsooth **kila**
forth, and so — **:ādi**
fortune **bhāgyam**
forward **anu+pra+iṣ** *caus.*
anupreṣayati)
four **catur**
free **muc**
free from **nis** *prefix*
freedom (:scope) **prasaraḥ**

friend **vayasyaḥ, mitraṃ, suhṛd** *m.,* **sakhi** *m.* (*voc.* **sakhe**); (female) friend **sakhī,** (= *pl.*) **sakhī:janaḥ**

friend's wife **sakhī**

friendship **sakhyaṃ**

frivolous **cañcala**

from *use abl.*; from what/where? **kutaḥ**; from someone **kutaś cit**

front, in — of **agrataḥ**+*gen.,* -**samakṣam**

fruit **phalaṃ**

fruitful **sa_phala**

fruitless, make — **viphalī˜kṛ**

fulfil **pṝ** *caus.*

full of -**pūrṇa**

Full Moon Festival **Kaumudī-mahotsavaḥ**

further **bhūyāṃs**

gain **labh**

gale **nabhasvant** *m.*

gallery **vīthikā, śālā**

game **krīḍā**

gaming master **sabhikaḥ**

Gandharva **Gandharvaḥ**; Gandharva rite **Gāndharva vidhi** m.

garden **udyānaṃ**

garland **mālā**

garment **vāsas** *n.*

gaze **dṛś**

gaze **dṛṣṭi** *f.*

gem **ratnaṃ**

generally **prāyeṇa**

get **labh**; get (done) *use caus.*

get up **ut**+**sthā** (**s** *lost between the* **t** *and* **th** — *e.g. p. p.* **utthita**)

girl **kanyā, kanyakā**

give **dā**

give up **tyaj**

giving **dānaṃ**

glory **śrī**

go **gam, yā**

go against **ati**+**kram**

go back **ni**+**vṛt**

go in(to) **pra**+**viś**

god **suraḥ, devaḥ**

God of Love **Manmathaḥ, Kusumāyudhaḥ**

goddess **devī**

going **gamanaṃ**

gold **suvarṇaṃ, heman** *n.*

good **sādhu,** (friend) **hita,** (*in voc.*) **bhadra;** (:prosperity) **śreyas** *n.*

good fellow **bhadraḥ**

good man **su:janaḥ**

good woman (*voc.*) **bhadre**

gotra **gotraṃ**

grandson **dauhitraḥ**

grant **pra**+**yam**

granted that **kāmam**

grasp **grah**

great **mahānt**

greatness **mahiman** *m.*

greet (person) **abhi**+**vad** *caus.* *ātm.*; (thing) **abhi**+**nand**

grief **śokaḥ**

grieve **śuc**

groom *see* bridegroom

ground **bhūmi** *f.*; (:cause) **hetu** *m.*

guard **rakṣ**

guest **atithi** *m.* **abhyāgataḥ**

guide, someone to — **netṛ**

ha! **ayi, hanta, āḥ**

half (portion) **ardhaḥ**

hand, hand over **sam**+**ṛ** *caus.,* **ṛ** *caus.*

hand **hastaḥ, pāṇi** *m.*

hand, at — **āsanna**

handmaid **ājñākarī**

happen: what happens/has happened *etc.* **vṛttāntaḥ**

happiness **sukhaṃ**

hard to attain **dur:adhigama**

hard to win **dur:labha**

harem **antaḥpuram**

harlot **veśyā**

harsh **viṣama**

hate **dviṣ**

have *use gen. with verb meaning 'be'* — *usually* **as**, *sometimes* **bhū** *or* **vṛt**; have (something done) *use caus.*

having *use bahuvrīhi, suffixes* **vant/mant**, **sa**, *etc.*

hawker **paṇāyitṛ**

he, him *etc.* **saḥ**, **ayam**, **enam**, **eṣaḥ**, **asau** *or omit*

head **śiras** *n.*

heap **rāśi** *m.*

hear **śru**

heart **hṛdayam**, **cittam**

heat **ātapaḥ**

heavens, thank — **diṣṭyā**

hell **naraka** *m./n.*

helpful **upakārin**

helpless **paravaśa**

here **atra**, **iha**, *or use* **eṣaḥ**, **ayam**; over here **itaḥ**

hereditary **pitṛ-paryāy>-āgata**

herewith *use* **eṣaḥ**

hermitage **āśramaḥ**, **āśrama-padam**

hero **vīraḥ**

hesitation **an:adhyavasāyaḥ**

high-soaring **utsarpin**

highest(:most excellent) **parārdhya**

Highness, Your/His — **kumāraḥ**

hindrance **vighnaḥ, antarāyaḥ**

hint at **upa+kṣip**

his **tasya** *etc.*; his (own) **sva**

hither and thither **itas tataḥ**

ho, ho there! **bhoḥ**

hold on to **ava+lamb**

hole **chidram**

homage **namas** *n.*

home **gṛham, āvasathaḥ**

honey-bee (female) **madhukarī**

honour (request *etc.*) **man** *caus.*; (:do honour to) **puras+kṛ**, **pūj** (X **pūjayati** *ger.* **pūjya**)

Honour, His/Your — **āryaḥ**; His Honour here **atrabhavant**

honourable **ārya**

hope **ā+śaṃs** (I **āśaṃsate**); I hope **kaccid** (*particle*)

hope **āśā**

horse **aśvaḥ**

hospitality **satkāraḥ**

hostile (:adverse) **pratikūla**

house **gṛham, geham**

household **śuddhāntaḥ, gaṇaḥ**

how? **katham**; *in exclamations use* **aho**

however **punar** *enclitic*

human flesh **mahā:māṃsam**

huntsman **vyādhaḥ**

hurry **tvar** *ātm.*

husband, lawful — **sahadharmacārin**

husband and wife **dampatī** (*du.*)

I **aham**

idiot **mūḍhaḥ**

idle, sit — **ut+ās**

if **yadi**, **cet** *enclitic*; if only! **api nāma**

ignoble **an:ārya**

ignorant **an:abhijña**

ill-disposed to **vimukha**+*gen.*

ill omen **dur:nimittam**

imagine **sam+bhū** *caus.*

immediately **an:antaram**, **sadya eva**; immediately upon **-anantaram eva**

imminent **bhāvin**

impairment **śaithilyam**

important thing **pradhānam**

in *use loc., sometimes adverb in* -tra; (being) in -gata; having (with)in **:garbha**; in . . . ing *often use pres. part.*

inclination **abhiprāyaḥ**

incline **pra+vṛt**

including **urīkṛtya**+*acc.*
inconvenience *use* **doṣaḥ**
increase **vṛdh** *caus.*
indeed **khalu** *enclitic*
indicate **upa**+**diś**
indicating **nivedaka**
inevitably **niyatam**
inferiority **lāghavaṃ**
inflammatory **saṃdīpana**
inform **ni**+**vid** *caus.*+*dat./gen.*
ingratitude **kṛtaghna~tā**
inscrutable **acintya**
instigation to rebellion **upajā-paḥ**
instructed **śikṣita**
instructions **ādeśaḥ**
intact, keep — **pari**+**pāl**
intelligence **buddhi** *f.*
intention **abhiprāyaḥ**
interest **kutūhalaṃ**
interval **antaraṃ**
intimacy **viśrambhaḥ**
intoxication **madaḥ**
introduce (into) **pra**+**viś** *caus.*, **upa**+**nī**+*acc.*
invade **upa**+**rudh**
invite **upa**+**ni**+**mantr** (X **upanimantrayati**)
irritability **duḥśīla~tā**
it **saḥ**, **ayam**, **enam**, **eṣaḥ**, **asau** (*usually in n.*)
its **tasya** *etc.*

jackal **śṛgālaḥ**
jewel **ābharaṇam**
join **ghaṭ** *caus.* (**ghaṭayati**)
joined hands **añjali** *m.*
joke **parihāsaḥ**
juncture **antaraṃ**; at this juncture **atr**‿**āntare**
just **eva** *enclitic* (:merely) ‗**mātra**; (I'll) just ... **tāvat** *enclitic*, **yāvat**

kill **vi**+**ā**+**pad** *caus.*; have (:cause to be) killed **ghātayati**

killing **vināśaḥ**
king **rājan** *m.* (*ifc.* **-rājaḥ**), **nṛpaḥ**
king of Videha **Vaidehaḥ**
kingdom **rājyaṃ**
kinsman **bandhu** *m.*
know **jñā**, **vid**, **ava**+**gam**; know how to **jñā**

lack of *use* **a:/an:**
lady, noble lady **āryā**; this lady **atrabhavatī**; that lady **tatrabhavatī**
lake **sarasī**
lamp **dīpikā**
lapse **skhalanaṃ**
later, some time — **kasya cit kālasya**
laugh **has** (I **hasati**)
Lāvāṇaka, (being) at — **Lāvā-ṇaka** *adj.*
law, sacred — **dharmaḥ**
lay **ā**+**ruh** *caus.*
lead **nī**
learn **vid**, **ava**+**gam**
learned in the sacred law **dhar-ma-vit**
leave **tyaj**, **pari**+**tyaj**
leave, give — **anu**+**jñā**
-less **nis‗**, **a:/an:**
let *use imperv.*, *sometimes indicative*
let alone **kiṃ punar**
let go **muc**
letter **lekhaḥ**, **pattrikā**, **pat-traṃ**
licked **avalīḍha**
life **jīvitaṃ**, **prāṇa** *m. pl.*
like, I should — to **icchāmi**
like *use* **iva**, **~vat**, **sadṛśa** (*f.* **ī**) +*instr.*
limb **aṅgaṃ**
line **paṅkti** *f.*
listen (to) **śru**
listen, someone to — **śrotṛ**
little while **muhūrta** *m./n.*

live (:be alive) **jīv**; (:dwell)
  vas, prati+vas, ni+vas
long **dūra**; (for) a long way
  dūram; for a long time **ciram**
long, after very — **aticirāt**
long, at — last **cirāt**
long-lived **āyuṣmant**
look (at) **dṛś**; look upon **īkṣ**
looking after **upasaṃgrahaḥ**
loose **vi+muc**
lord **pati** m., **adhipati** m.
loss of place **sthāna-bhraṃ-**
  śaḥ
lotus **puṇḍarīkam**
loudly **uccaiḥ**
love (:fondness) **snehaḥ**,
  (:devotion) **anurāgaḥ**, (:pas-
  sion) **manmathaḥ**
Love (god of-) **Manmathaḥ**,
  Kusumāyudhaḥ, **Makara-**
  dhvajaḥ
love, be in — with **utkaṇ-**
  ṭhate, kam caus.
loved one **iṣṭa:janaḥ**
lovely **ramaṇīya, manohara**
low (:mean) **kṣudra**

Madam (voc.) **bhadre**
magnanimous **mah»:ātman**
maidservant **paricārikā**
maintain (fire) **ā+dhā**
Majesty, Her/Your — **devī**
Majesty, His/Your — **devaḥ,**
  āyuṣmant
make **kṛ, ut+pad** caus.
maker **kartṛ**
man **naraḥ, puruṣaḥ**; (:per-
  son) **janaḥ**
manage **vi+dhā**; manage to
  use **katham cit**
mango tree **cūtaḥ**
manœuvre **ceṣṭā**
many **bahu**
mark **lakṣaṇam**
marriage **dāra-karman** n.

marry **vah**
mass **saṃghātaḥ**
master **svāmin** m.
matching **saṃvādaḥ**
mating **yugma-cārin** ('going
  in a pair')
matter **vastu** n.
me **mām** etc.
meaning **arthaḥ**
means **upāyaḥ**
measure **mā** (caus. **māpayati**)
measure **pramāṇam**
medicine **auṣadham**
meditating **dhyānam**
meditation **samādhi** m.
meet **sam+ā+sad** caus.; (:re-
  ceive) **prati+ut+gam**
meeting **samāgamaḥ**
melancholy **udvigna**
memory **smṛti** f.
mendicant **kṣapaṇakaḥ**
mental turmoil **vikāraḥ**
merchant **śreṣṭhin** m.
mere **_-mātra, eva**
merit **guṇaḥ**; of merit **guṇa~**
  vant
milk **kṣīram**
mind **manas** n., **cittam, cetas**
  n., **hṛdayam**
mine, of mine say 'of me, my'
minister **amātyaḥ**
mirage **mṛgatṛṣṇikā**
misconduct **apacāraḥ**
misdeed **akāryam**
misfortune **vyasanam**
mishap **pramādaḥ**
mislead **vi+pra+labh**
mission **prayojanam**
mistress **svāminī, īśvarī**
moment **muhūrta** m./n.
money **dhanam**
monster **nṛśaṃsaḥ**
moon **candraḥ**
moonlight **candrikā**
morning (:of the —) adj.
  pragetana (f. **ī**)

mother **janani, amba** (*voc.*
amba), **matr**

motion, in — **pracalita**

mountain **parvatah, sailah,
acalah**

mouth **vadanam**

murder **vi+a+pad** *caus.*

must *use ger. in* **tavya**

mutual (:of *etc.* each other)
itaretara-

my **madiya,** *or say* 'of me',
or omit

my own **sva;** of my own accord
svayam

myself *reflexive* **atman;** (:me)
use **aham**

name **naman** *n.*, **namadhe-
yam**

natural **sulabha,** (:innate)
sahabhu

nature **prakrti** *f.*, **atman** *m.*

necklace **mala**

negligent **pramatta**

neutral **madhyastha**

never **na kadacit**

news **vrttantah, pravrtti** *f.*

night, by — **ratrau**

no *use* **na** *or* **a:**

noble **arya, atyudara**

noise **sabdah**

normal **ucita**

not **na, a:;** A not B **A na tu B**

nothing **na kim cit**

notice **laks** (X **laksayati**)

now (:at the present time)
adhuna, idanim, samprati;
(*connective*) **atha, yavat, ta-
vat**

numerous **prabhuta, mahant**

nymph **apsaras** *f.*

object (:province) **visayah**

observe **ni+sam** *caus.*

obstacle **vighnah**

obstruct **ni+rudh**

obtain **ava+ap**

obviously **nunam**

occasion **avasarah, sthanam**

occupation **vyaparah**

occupy **adhi+as**

occur **jan**

ocean **sagarah**

of *use gen.,* *vrddhi derivative,*
bahuvrihi cpd. etc.

offend against **apa+radh +
gen.** (*p.p.* **aparaddha**)

office **adhikarah**

often **bahusah**

oh! **ha, aye, bhoh, ayi**

on *use loc.;* on . . . ing *use absol.
or loc. of verbal noun*

once *use* **purva;** once more
punar api

one **eka** *pron.;* (:a person) *use
impersonal construction*

only **eva,** **-matra**

open (letter) **ut+vest** *caus.*

opportune **avasare**

opportunity **avasarah**

oppress **pid**

or **va** *enclitic;* (:nor) **va na**

ornament **abharanam, alam-
karanam, bhusanam**

other **anya, para;** and other(s)
-adi

otherwise **anyatha**

our, of ours *say* 'of us'

out of *use abl.*

outcaste **svapakah**

outcome **parinamah, vijrm-
bhitam**

outside **bahih**

over here **itah**

overcome **parita**

overlook **mrs** *caus.*

overtures (:instigation to rebellion) **upajapah**

own, my/your *etc.* — **sva,
atmanah;** make one's own
svi~kr

paint ā+likh

painter citrakaraḥ

pair yugalam

palace rāja-kulam; Sugāṅga Palace Sugāṅga:prāsādaḥ

pang vedanā; pangs of love manmath₁-ônmāthaḥ

pardon mṛṣ (IV mṛṣyati)

parents pitṛ du.

park udyānam

part uddeśaḥ; for (someone's) part use api

partial pakṣapātin

particle avayavaḥ

partisan pakṣapātin

pass avasthā, daśā

pass over ati+kram

passion abhilāṣaḥ

past atīta

past, present and future trikālam

path -pathaḥ

peak sānu m.

people janaḥ

perceive ava+lok (X avalokayati)

perform (:do) anu+sthā; (a play) pra+yuj

performance prayogaḥ

perfume vas

persistence (:adherence) anubandhaḥ

person janaḥ; (:body) śarīram, deha m./n.

personally svayam eva

petition pra+arth (X prārthayate)

picking avacayaḥ

picture citram

piety dharmaḥ

pity anu+kamp

place ni+kṣip

place deśaḥ, sthānam, pradeśaḥ

place of sacrifice agnihotraśaraṇam

plan saṃkalpaḥ

play a role bhūmikāṃ kṛ ātm.

pleasant ramaṇīya, priya

pleasure sukham

pluck out ut+hṛ

poet kavi m.

point, what — in? kim+instr.

poison viṣam

poisoner tīkṣṇa:rasa-daḥ

ponder vi+car caus.

pool tīrtham

poor, poor fellow (pityingly) tapasvin; poor girl varākī

poor material adravyam

portrait ālekhyam

possessed of -upapanna

possessions parigrahaḥ

possessor of ~mant

possible upapanna

power prabhāvaḥ; have power over pra+bhū+gen.

practise (cruelty) pra+yuj, (austerities) car

praise stu

prayer japaḥ

preceptor upādhyāyaḥ

prelude prastāvaḥ

presence, to the — of -sakāśam; in the — of pratyakṣam+gen.

present saṃnihita

present pratigrahaḥ

present with prati+pad caus. +double acc.

pretence apadeśaḥ

previously pūrva ifc.

prince kumāraḥ

princess rāja-putrī

prisoner bandhana-sthaḥ

prize (:value highly) abhi+nand

proceed ut+cal

procession yātrā

proclaim ut+ghuṣ caus.; (:declare authoritatively) ā+diś

proclamation, after — **pra-khyāpya** (*lit.* 'having proclaimed')

procure **ava+gam** *caus.*

proficiency **prāvīṇyaṃ**

promised **pratiśruta**

proper **yukta**

protect **rakṣ,** **pari+trai,** **pari+pāl;** (someone) to protect (one) **trātṛ**

provide **upa+kṛ**

punishment **daṇḍaḥ**

pupil **śiṣyaḥ, śiṣyā**

purse-proud **artha-matta**

pursue **anu+sṛ**

put to shame **prati+ā+diś**

quality **guṇaḥ**

quantity **saṃcayaḥ**

queen **rājñī,** (*as title*) **devī**

quickly **āśu**

quiet **nibhṛta**

quite **eva** *enclitic*

quiver **spand**

rag **paṭaccaraṃ**

rather **nanu**

reach **anu+pra+āp**

ready **udyata**

realize **ava+gam**

really **satyam**

reason **kāraṇaṃ**

rebuke **upa+ā+labh**

rebuking **upālambhaḥ**

recall **smṛ** *caus.*

receive **grah**

recklessness **asamīkṣya:kāri~tā**

recognise **prati+abhi+jñā,** **pari+ci**

reconciled **prasanna**

redundancy **paunaruktaṃ**

reed **vetasaḥ**

refuse to *use* **na**

regain (consciousness) **upa+labh**

regard (:think) **man**

regard for -**anurodhaḥ;** with regard to **prati+acc.**

rein **abhīśu** *m.*

reject **prati+ā+diś**

rejection **pratyākhyānaṃ,** **pratyādeśaḥ**

rejoice **mad**

release **vi+sṛj**

relent **prasādaṃ kṛ**

religious power **siddhi** *f.*

remain **sthā**

remaining part **śeṣaḥ**

remark **vacanaṃ**

remedy **pratīkāraḥ**

remember **smṛ**

remnant **śeṣaḥ**

remove **apa+nī;** (ornaments etc.) **ava+tṝ** *caus.*

reply **prativacanaṃ**

report **prasiddhi** *f.*

request **vijñāpanā**

rescue **abhi+upa+pad**

rescue **prāṇa-rakṣā**

residence **bhavanaṃ**

resist **pari+hṛ**

resolve **niścayaḥ**

resort to **ā+śri**

respect for **bahumānaḥ+loc.**

respect, worthier of — **garīyāṃs**

respectfully **sa_gauravam**

resplendent **dīpti~mant**

restrain **ni+grah, upa+sam +hṛ**

restraint **avagrahaḥ**

return **prati+ni+vṛt**

reveal **āviṣ~kṛ, pra+kāś** *caus.*

reveal oneself **āvir~bhū**

revered **tatrabhavant;** my revered father **tāta-pādāḥ**

Reverence, Her/Your — **bhagavatī**

reverend **bhagavant** (*f.* **bhagavatī**)

reward **pari+tuṣ** *caus.*

reward **phalaṃ**
rewarding **paritoṣaḥ**
riches **vibhūti** *f. pl.*
riding **caryā**
right *adv.* **eva**
right (:proper) **yukta**; rightly **yuktam**
right (*opp.* left) **dakṣiṇa**; to the right of **dakṣiṇena**+*acc.*
ring **aṅgurīyaka** *m./n.*
rise **ut+cal, ut+sthā**
rite **kriyā, vidhi** *m.,* **maṅgalaṃ**
river **nadī**
road, roadway **mārgaḥ**
rock **śilā**
role **bhūmikā**
rosary **akṣamālā**
roused **upajāta**
royal bard **vaitālikaḥ**
royal seer **rāja:ṛṣi** *m.*
ruined, be — **ava+sad**
ruler **īśvaraḥ**
run **pra+dru**

sacred law **dharmaḥ**
sacrifice **hu**
sacrifice, place of — **agnihotra-śaraṇam**
sacrificial **medhya**
sacrilege **abrahmaṇyaṃ**
safeguard **rakṣ**
sage **muni** *m.*
sake, for the — of **-artham**
salute **pra+nam, vand** (*ger.* **vandya**)
same, the/that — **saḥ+eva**; this same **ayam** *etc.*+**eva**
say **vad, vac, kath, brū, abhi+dhā**
scandal **kaulīnaṃ**
scant **svalpa**
scare **ut+tras** *caus.* (**uttrāsayati**)
scent **āmodaḥ**
scholar **paṇḍitaḥ**

science **śāstraṃ**
scold **upa+ā+labh**
seal **mudrā**
search **anu+iṣ**
search, in — of **anveṣin**
season **samayaḥ**
seated, be — **ni+sad**
second **dvitīya**
secret **rahasyaṃ**
seduce **ā+vṛj** *caus.*
see **dṛś, ava+lok, ā+lok;** see to it that **kṛ+yathā**
see, see how *use* **eṣaḥ** *or* **ayam**
seeing **darśanaṃ**
seeing **darśin**
seem *use* **iva**
seer **ṛṣi** *m.,* great seer **maha:ṛṣi** *m.*
seize **grah**
self, myself *etc.* (*reflexive*) **ātman** *m. sg.*; (*emphatic*)/for oneself *etc.* **svayam**
self-control **dhairyaṃ**
selfsame **eva**
sell **vi+krī**
send **pra+iṣ** *caus.* (**preṣayati**)
senior to **guru**+*gen.*
separated, having become — **vighaṭita**
serpent **viṣadharaḥ, nāgaḥ, phaṇabhṛt** *m.*
servant **parijanaḥ, dāsī**; servant girl **dāsī**
service **upakāraḥ, priyaṃ**
set **sthā** *caus.*
set forth, set out **pra+sthā**
severe (punishment) **tīkṣṇa**; (austerity) **kaṣṭa**
shade **chāyā**
shake **cal** *caus.* (**calayati**)
shame **lajjā**; shame (on) **dhik** (+*acc.*)
shame, put to — **prati+ā+diś**
sharp **niśita**; (:astringent) **kaṣāya**
shoot **vyadh** (*pass.* **vidhyate**)

should *use* arh *or* ger. *in* ya/anīya
show dṛś *caus.*
show prekṣaṇīyakam
shower abhi+vṛṣ (I abhivar-ṣati)
shower (:multitude) nikaraḥ
shut āvṛta
side pakṣaḥ
sides, on all — sarvataḥ
sight darśanam
sign liṅgam, cihnam
signal saṃjñā
signature svahastaḥ
silent, stay — tūṣṇīm ās; fall silent tūṣṇīm as (*in imperf.*)
sin pāpman *m.*
since (*prep.*) prabhṛti+*abl.*; (:because) *use* abl./instr. of abstract noun, *or* yena, yataḥ, yat, iti
sing gai
sir ārya
sire rājan
sister bhaginī, svasṛ
sit (down) upa+viś
skill kauśalam
sky gaganam; skies diś *f. pl.*
slab talam
slender *use* yaṣṭi *f.*
slip pari+bhraṃś
slow, by — stages śanaiḥ śanaiḥ
snake sarpaḥ
snatch hṛ
so (*simple connective*) tat, (:I infer that) tarhi; (:thus) evam, (:to such an extent) evam
sobriquet prasiddhi *f.*
soft mṛdu
sojourn sahavāsaḥ
soldier sainikaḥ
solely kevalam; solely partial eka:pakṣapātin
solitary ekākin

some, someone kaś cit, ko 'pi; someone (to do something) *agent noun*
son putraḥ, dārakaḥ, sutaḥ, putrakaḥ
sorrow viṣādaḥ
sovereignty rājyam
speak vad, vac, abhi+dhā
speaking kathā
specify nis+diś
spectator sāmājikaḥ
speech vāc *f.*
spend (time) gam *caus.*, yā *caus.* (yāpayati)
spoil duṣ *caus.*
spot (:place) uddeśaḥ
stages, by slow — śanaiḥ śanaiḥ
stamp aṅk
stand sthā
standing -stha *ifc.*
start ā+rabh
state avasthā
stay sthā, ās
step padam
still idānīm api
stone śilā
stop sthā
story vṛttāntaḥ
strange (:unprecedented) apūrva; (:marvellous) citra
stranger paraḥ
strategy nīti *f.*
street rathyā
stroll through anu+vi+car+*acc.*
student baṭu
stupid bāliśa
subject prajā, prakṛti *f.*
success siddhi *f.*
such īdṛśa, evam:vidha, īdṛś (īdṛk)
such as -vidha, :ādi
suddenly sahasā
śūdra śūdraḥ
suffering vyathā

sufficient **paryāpta**
suicide **ātma-tyāgaḥ**
suited **anurūpa**
suitor **prārthayitṛ**
summon **ā+hve, sam+ā+hve**
sun **sūryaḥ, vivasvant** m.
support **nibandhanam**
suppress **ni+grah**
suppressing **nigrahaḥ**
surely **khalu**
surmise **tark** (X **tarkayati**)
surpassing (:extreme) **atiśaya**; (:going beyond) **-atirikta**
surround **pari+vṛ**
sweat **svedaḥ**
sweet **madhura**
swift **śīghra, kṣipra**
swoon **mūrchā**
sword · **śastram**
syllable **akṣaram**

take (:convey) **nī**; (:accept, understand) **grah**
take away **apa+nī**
talk **kath**
talking **ālāpaḥ**
task **kāryam, karman** n.
taunt **adhi+kṣip**
teacher **ācāryaḥ, upādhyāyaḥ**
tell **vad, vac, kath**
temple **āyatanam**
tend (plants) **pari+vṛdh** caus.
tender **ārdra**; make tender **vatsalayati**
tenderness **snehaḥ**
that (demon.) **saḥ, asau**; (conj.) **iti, yat, yathā**
the usually omit, **saḥ, asau**
then **tadā, tataḥ**; (:so) **tat**; but then **atha vā**
there **tatra**; from there **tataḥ**
there is **asti**; thére is **ayam asau**
therefore **ataḥ**
thereupon **tataḥ**

thicket **viṭapa** m./n.
think **man, cint**
this **eṣaḥ, ayam, enam**; in/on/about this **atra**; from this **ataḥ**
though **api, yady api**
thoughts **citta-vṛtti** f.
thread **sūtram**
three **-trayam**; three or four **tricatura**
threshold **dvār** f.
throne **siṃhāsanam**
throng **sammardaḥ, saṃkulam**
thus **evam**
tiger **vyāghraḥ**
time **kālaḥ, velā, avasaraḥ**; some time later **kasya cit kālasya**
tip **pari+tuṣ** caus.
tired **pariśrānta**
tithe **bhāgaḥ**
title **śabdaḥ**
to use gen., dat., inf. etc.; (:in the direction of) use acc., **prati, -antikam**; (:in order to) use dat. or **-artham**
today **adya**
together with **saha+instr.**
tone **gir** f.
too **api**
top **śikharam**
touch **spṛś**
touch **sparśaḥ**
towards **prati+acc.**; (— an object of feeling) **prati** or use loc.
town **puram**
townsfolk **paura:janaḥ**
trader **vaṇij** m.
trainer **vinetṛ**
traitor **rāj-âpathya-kārin**
tread **kṣud**
tree **pādapaḥ, vṛkṣakaḥ, vṛkṣaḥ**; young tree **potakaḥ**

tremble **kamp** (I kampate)
triumph over **ati+śī**
trouble **bādh** (I bādhate)
true **satya**
truly **satyam, nanu**
trust **vi+śvas** (I visvasati)+ loc.
trustworthy **āpta**
try **yat**
turmoil, in a — **tumula**
turn (to) **kḷp**+*dat.*
turn away **parā+vṛt** *caus.*
turn back **prati+ni+vṛt**
turn into (:become) *use* **saṃ-vṛtta**; (:convert into) *use* **kṛ** *in compound*
turn round **pari+vṛt** *caus.*
twin **yamaja**
two *use du. or* **-dvayam**
twofold **dvaya** (*f.* dvayī)

ugliness **vairūpyaṃ**
ultimate **para**
un- **a:/an:**
uncalled for **a:kāraṇa**
uncertainty **vikalpaḥ**
understand **ava+gam, grah**
understand, someone to— **jñātṛ**
underway **pravṛtta**
unite **yuj** *caus.*
unshakeable (resolve) **ahārya**
unsteady **vihvala**
until **yāvat**
untoward **apara**
upon *use loc.*
us **asmān** *etc.*
usher in **pra+viś** *caus.*
utterance **bhāratī**

vain **vitatha**
vainly **mṛṣā**
valour **vikramaḥ**
valuable **mahārghya**
vanish **tiras+bhū**
vapour **dhūmaḥ**

various **vicitra**; various-ness **vaicitryaṃ**
vendor **vikretṛ**
verse **gāthā**
very (*adj.*) *use* **eva**
vexation **parikleśaḥ**
victorious, be — **vi+ji** *ātm.*
victory **vijayaḥ**
Videha, of — **Vaideha** (*f.* ī)
vile **dur:ātman**
villain **pāpaḥ**
vine **latā**
violate **ut+laṅgh** *caus.*
violence, do — to **abhi+druh**
violent **pracaṇḍa**
virtuous **sādhu** (*f.* sādhvī)
visible **abhivyakta**
voice **vāc** *f.*
void **śūnya**
vow **vrataṃ, pratijñā**

wait for **prati+pāl**
wait upon **upa+ās**
walk **sam+car** *ātm.*
wall **bhitti** *f.*
wander **bhram**
want **iṣ**
warrior **kṣatriyaḥ**
washed **dhauta**
watch **vi+lok** *caus.*, **dṛś**
water **jalaṃ, salilaṃ**
way **prakāraḥ**; in this way **evam**; this way (:in this direction) **itaḥ**; on the way **antarā**
wayward **dur:vinīta**
wealth **vibhūti** *f.*, **kośaḥ, dyumnaṃ**
weaning **stanya-tyāgaḥ** ('leaving the breast')
weapon **astraṃ**
wear **dhṛ**
wed **upa+yam**
weep **rud**
welcome **prati+nand**; welcome! **svāgatam**

welfare **kuśalam**

well **su** *prefix*

well, as — **api**

wet **klinna**

what? **kaḥ (kim)**; what, . . . ?
katham; what (a)! *use* **aho**;
what (:that which) **yat**; from
what? **kutaḥ**; what of it?
tataḥ kim

when **yadā, yāvat**

where? **kva**; where (*conj.*) **yatra**; where from? **kutaḥ**

whereabouts? **kutaḥ**

which? **kaḥ**; which (*rel. pron.*)
yaḥ

while (:short time) **muhūrta**
m./n.; for a little while **muhūrtam iva**

while (*conj.*) **yāvat**

who/whom? **kaḥ**; who/whom
(*rel. pron.*) **yaḥ**; it is . . . who
use **eva**

whole **sarva, sakala, aśeṣa**

whore **puṃścalī**

whose **kasya** *etc.*, **yasya** *etc.*

why? **kim**, (:for what purpose?) **kim-artham**, (:from
what cause?) **kasmāt**; why!
(*in surprise*) ⟨ **katham**, (*in mild
admonition*) **nanu**

wicked **dur:ātman**

widespread **prathita**

wife **kalatram, dārāḥ** *m. pl.*;
friend's wife **sakhī**

win **ji**

wine **madhu** *n.*

wish **iṣ**

wish **manorathaḥ**

with *use instr.*; (:together with)

saha+*instr.*, sa *in cpd.*; (:pos-
sessing) **⁓vant** *or* **bahuvrīhi**

withdraw **sam+hṛ**

without *use prefixes* **nis** *or* a;
without (doing) a+*absol.*

witness **pratyakṣī⁓kṛ**

witness (to) **-sākṣin**

woman **strī, nārī, yoṣit** *f.*

wonder, I — (*after interrog.*)
nu khalu

wonderful **vicitra**

woo **pra+arth** (X **prar-
thayate**)

wood **vanam, kānanam**

word **vacanam**

work **karman** *n.*; (:literary
work) **prabandhaḥ, pray-
oga-bandhaḥ, kṛti** *f.*

working **vyāpāraḥ**

world **lokaḥ**

worried, be — **śaṅk** (I **śaṅ-
kate**)

worship **vand**

worthier of respect **garīyāṃs**

worthy **ārya**

worthy holder **bhājanam**

wounded . **vraṇita**

wretch **varākaḥ**

write **likh, abhi+likh**

writer **kavi** *m.*

yet **tathā ∤pi, punar** *enclitic*

you **tvam (tvat/yuṣmat)** *etc.*;
*∗*you (*polite form*) **bhavant**
(*f.* **bhavatī**)

young tree **potakaḥ**

younger **kanīyāṃs**

your/yours/of yours *say* 'of you'

youth **nava:yauvanam**

Supplementary English–Sanskrit Exercises

FOR fuller practice in the material covered in each chapter, students are strongly advised at least to read through the exercises, with keys, provided in the body of the book—particularly from Chapter 6 onwards, where all sentences are taken directly from Sanskrit literature.

Up to Exercise 5 the special vocabulary of the corresponding chapter will be found adequate. Thereafter words required will not necessarily be found anywhere except in the general English–Sanskrit vocabulary.

A short drill in grammatical forms is provided from Exercise 6 onwards: much of the point of this will, of course, be lost unless the grammatical paradigms prescribed for each chapter are previously committed to memory. The English equivalents given for the forms are purely conventional—'from the two clean (men)' is merely a more convenient and less abstract way of saying 'give the ablative dual masculine of the adjective śuci'. The cases are represented by 'with' (instrumental), 'to' (dative), 'from' (ablative), 'of' (genitive) 'at/in' (locative), 'O' (vocative). The use of 'stay' (tiṣṭhati etc.) and 'he sees' (paśyati)—'the girls stay, he sees the girls'—is an adaptation of a device used by Sanskrit grammatical commentators to distinguish nominative and accusative case respectively. It need hardly be said that where synonyms exist the grammatically relevant one should be chosen (e.g. in Exercise 7 for 'friend' use suhṛd).

Exercise 1

Transcribe into the nāgarī script the following words, some of which may be familiar to you already:

jātaka, hīnayāna, pūjā, gopī, rāga, guṇa, jaina, Gaṇeśa, kaliyuga, Kālī, hitopadeśa, ahiṃsā, ṛṣi, tapas, mahāt-mā, stūpa, maṇḍala, apsaras, Avalokiteśvara, Cāṇakya, advaita, āraṇyaka, bhakti, śāntiḥ, buddha, brahma-cārin, Vikramāditya, apabhraṃśa, āśrama, Pāṭali-putra, tantrā, Durgā, arthaśāstra, maurya, Harṣa, Takṣaśilā, prajñāpāramitā

Transcribe the following sentences, remembering that in the nāgarī script a word ending in a consonant (ḥ and ṃ apart) will be joined with the next word:

1 sakhi Śakuntale ihaiva muhūrtaṃ tiṣṭha 2 tvayā samīpasthitayā latāsanātha ivāyaṃ cūtavṛkṣakaḥ pra-tibhāti 3 ata eva Priyaṃvadeti tvam ucyase 4 iyaṃ svayaṃvaravadhūḥ sahakārasya tvayā kṛtanāmadheyā vanajyautsnīti navamālikā 5 sakhy Anasūye ramaṇī-yaḥ khalv asya pādapamithunasya vyatikaraḥ saṃ-vṛttaḥ 6 iyaṃ navakusumayauvanā navamālikā, ayam api baddhaphalatayopabhogakṣamaḥ sahakāraḥ 7 jānāsi kiṃnimittaṃ Śakuntalā vanajyautsnīm atimā-traṃ prekṣata iti 8 yathā vanajyautsnī sadṛśena pādapena saṃgatā tathāpi nāmāham apy ātmano ꜚnurūpaṃ varaṃ labheyeti 9 eṣa ātmanas te cittagato manorathaḥ

Exercise 2

(a) With the help of the sandhi grid arrange the following sequences of separate words into continuous utterances (in the order of sentence 1, the words mean 'the-women; indeed; in(to)-this; garden; by-the-ascetics; angrily; from-the-house; (were) brought.'):

1 nāryaḥ. khalu. asmin. udyāne. tapasvibhiḥ. sakopam.

gṛhāt. ānītāḥ   2 asmin. khalu. udyāne. nāryaḥ. tapasvibhiḥ. gṛhāt. sakopam. ānītāḥ   3 ānītāḥ. sakopam.
khalu. nāryaḥ. gṛhāt. udyāne. asmin. tapasvibhiḥ   4
ānītāḥ. asmin. nāryaḥ. udyāne. sakopam. khalu.
tapasvibhiḥ. gṛhāt   5 tapasvibhiḥ. khalu. sakopam.
gṛhāt. nāryaḥ. asmin. udyāne. ānītāḥ   6 sakopam.
khalu. gṛhāt. tapasvibhiḥ. asmin. nāryaḥ. ānītāḥ.
udyāne   7 asmin. ānītāḥ. gṛhāt. khalu. udyāne. nāryaḥ.
sakopam. tapasvibhiḥ   8 udyāne. gṛhāt. asmin.
sakopam. khalu. ānītāḥ. tapasvibhiḥ. nāryaḥ

(b) Translate into Sanskrit:

1 So they are saying   2 The two of them sing.   3 Do you
remember?   4 Why are you [pl.] asking now?   5 Let us see.
6 I won't write.   7 What, is she going?   8 I understand that
they are dancing.   9 Where are the two of you wandering?
10 They are now winning.   11 The two of them are coming
this way.   12 Here the two of us stand.   13 You both see and
understand.   14 'Where are you going?' they seem to ask.
15 But you [pl.] do not understand.   16 We won't sit down
now.   17 What do the two of you want here today?   18 We
don't go in, because they are living there once more.   19
Now the two of them seem to be grieving again.   20 So,
however, do we wish.   21 I ask because I do not remember.

Exercise 3

1 Pupils, where are you taking me?   2 'Does the brahmin
live?' they again ask the two men.   3 The sun and moon
are beautiful.   4 Who wants water?   5 The children do not
see the sun today.   6 Let us two go into the forest.   7 Let us
too go to the mountains.   8 Children, the teacher is writing.
9 What, do you ask me, a brahmin?   10 Those two children
want food.   11 Teacher and pupils stand astonished.   12
Teacher, that field is small.   13 'Where are those scholars
going?' he asks us.   14 Even the brahmins do not remember
it.   15 That too we do not understand.   16 Anger leads men

to unhappiness. 17 Who now remembers those scholars? 18 Like a child, he does not see (any) advantage in this. 19 Are you Makaranda? 20 Child, why do you speak to me so?

Exercise 4

1 This is a pleasant town. 2 Shall I go *there*? 3 Look, he is coming into the house with (his) friends. 4 The children are gone: I will go too. 5 (They) have brought the two scholars, alive. 6 I ask this, dear friend: what have my sons done? 7 You have forgotten the *previous* words. 8 What, are you asking *me*? 9 No more despair. 10 They want either a swift horse or a beautiful (one). 11 But Your Majesty has not seen *my* two sons. 12 Though he has come to the forest, he does not see the pupils. 13 Your Majesty, these (men) are exhausted by the attempt. 14 My friends brought a quite extraordinary person to the house. 15 It was he who made this garden. 16 I did not write this, Your Majesty. 17 Your Majesty, although we had already come here, we did not in fact look at it because (our) friends were tired.

Exercise 5

1 Your Majesty, we are beaten. 2 You [*pl.*] have occasion for anger. 3 We have brought this (man) from the fields. 4 Leaving his home he wanders with his sons in the woods. 5 Dear friend, where are you? 6 We'll go to another house and ask. 7 Your Highness is indeed exhausted. 8 What is this extraordinary alarm of everyone? 9 Nothing (makes) for happiness in this world. 10 Did you see Stanakalaśa in Kusumapura? 11 After being [**bhū**] blind for a while, they now see all. 12 'There is in another country a certain blind prince,' he says to the children. 13 We feel exhausted. 14 Mārīca wants [a sight of you:] to see you. 15 Has His Highness too just one son? 16 From the alarm of (my) two friends I apprehend [**avagam**] something evil. 17 Whose book is this? 18 Oh, (there is) no one here. 19 'Here is the villain,' (he) said, and seized the one-eyed (man). 20 A tree

[**pādapaḥ**] has fallen right on the road. 21 The very letter [**lekhaḥ**] is not mine. 22 What is this? Where has your extraordinary love [**anurāgaḥ**] for me gone? 23 What, even after seeing me have you deserted (me) and gone? 24 This is the determination [**niścayaḥ**] of us *all*.

Exercise 6

Grammatical practice (first memorise prescribed paradigms):
1 from the girls 2 of Ūrmilā 3 with the two noble (ladies)
4 O Sītā 5 in the seals 6 he sees the girl 7 to those *f.*
8 with this seal 9 these two *f.* stay 10 at that *f.*

(Words joined together by points (·) should be translated by a single compound.)

1 Your Majesty, where is this girl from? 2 The noble lady is asking about Ūrmilā. 3 Here is the honourable·Cāṇakya's house. 4 I've forgotten my [thread·of·measure:] tape measure. 5 Vṛṣala, why have (you) summoned us? 6 Ha, he has flown up from the mountain-top to the sky and is showering me with arrows. 7 I have bestowed her upon you. 8 The time·for·advice is of course long·past. 9 It is by my·father's· command that I have come here to·your·presence. 10 (I) have seen this decayed·garden. 11 And I for my part will not grant (you) the seal. 12 Oh, two·men asleep. 13 Madam, is this really the same gold·box? 14 She has defeated me [*f.*], Your Majesty. 15 And I gave this to Siddhārthaka on some occasion·for·rewarding (him). 16 It is still you who have power over this (girl). 17 And the sacrificial horse has been released, consecrated·by·Vāmadeva. 18 The painter has depicted in this gallery Your Honour's exploits (as) indicated· by·us. 19 Good fellow, is it this cancellation·of·the·Full· Moon·festival alone that is Candragupta's reason·for·anger towards Cāṇakya, or [**uta**] is there another (reason) as well? 20 What, have I brought the two of them to this pass through (*abl.*) announcing·bad·news? But then [**athavā**] what else, apart from poison, emerges from a serpent's·mouth?

Exercise 7

Grammatical practice: 1 in a friend 2 with minds 3 of two rivers 4 to Her Majesty 5 the direction stays 6 from friends 7 he sees rivers 8 minds stay 9 to the direction 10 in rivers

1 This is well·known to me. 2 Vetravatī, did you not indeed see Queen Vasumatī on your way [**antarā**]? 3 Vasantasenā's [two] garments are wet. 4 What, did Rākṣasa have my father killed—not Cāṇakya? 5 The time·for·going·home is drawing near. 6 Bābhravya, this (girl) is like [**sadṛśa**] the princess. 7 Your Majesty, I will so announce to the council·of·ministers. 8 You are telling an excessively·confused (story). 9 Pṛthvī· and·Bhāgīrathī have rescued the noble lady. 10 She did not go surely in [*instr.*] that direction? 11 Concerning·oneself· [**vyavahāraḥ**]·with·another's·wife is ig·noble. 12 Now where, I wonder, with a mind disinclined·for·normal·occupation shall I spend this remaining·part·of·the·day? 13 The mere sight of these ladies has honoured me. 14 Sir, is this cancellation·of·the·Full·Moon·Festival actually un·known to His Majesty Candragupta? 15 The word·'abandoned' has aroused our curiosity. 16 You have beaten me (while I am) actually in·the·roadway. 17 What, has Her Majesty gone without at all relenting? 18 I'll just get my followers to camp at a good distance from the ascetic·grove. 19 Has the scandal· of·Śakuntalā's·rejection not come to the [path·of·the·ears:] hearing of these two ladies? 20 By this diligence·in·service· to·me you recall my earlier·pupil Saudāmanī. 21 So I'll just sit for a moment on this broken·stone·slab, natural·in·the· harsh·change·in·(my)·circumstances. 22 (You) whore! My friends have been [*use pres.*] describing your [**tvad-gata**] misconduct. 23 For this is some girl (whom I) conceived [with:] in my own·mind and painted, not one seen·before. 24 Let us [two] go to the bower·of·mādhavī·vines and wait for the time·of·appointment·with·(my)·adored·one.

Exercise 8

Grammatical practice: 1 O king 2 from names 3 the king

stays 4 to the self 5 to the king 6 to two names 7 he
sees two kings 8 of selves 9 in kings 10 the two names
stay

1 Homage to this (man) whose·austerities·are·severe. 2 See,
immediately·upon·the·command of Your Highness, all the
chieftains have turned back. 3 Here comes Candrikā, maidservant to your friend's wife, her·hands·busy·with·picking·
flowers. 4 I'll just conceal myself and remain. 5 This is not
the remedy for this sin. 6 A vapour·drinking śūdra called
Śambūka is practising austerities in this same Janasthāna.
7 So I'll just send Śatrughna [for the extermination of:] to
exterminate this evil·natured son·of·Kumbhīnasī. 8 I can
see (that) appeasement (is) difficult·to·achieve here. 9 When·
I·have·plucked·out·the·barb·of·sorrow, I will tell. 10 Why,
this show has turned into (something) quite different. 11 The
highest blessing in marriage is assuredly mutual·love. 12
Why do you ask me, though you·know·what·has·happened?
13 And it was he who created this extremely·lovely wood
called Caitraratha. 14 Everyone of course sees himself (as)
desirable. 15 I seem to be entering a darkness where·support·
for·(my)·steps·is·not·discerned. 16 From·[gata]·the·Sugāṅga·
palace His Majesty perceived entirely for himself that Kusumapura [did·not·have·underway:] was·not·celebrating·the·Full·
Moon·Festival. 17 Ha! Who (is) this villain (who) has
[become a hindrance to:] intruded upon us? 18 With·my·
freedom·of·manœuvre·obstructed so on all sides by Your
Excellency, [sovereignty is like bondage to me, not like
sovereignty:] I feel more like a prisoner than a king.

Translate the following as nominal sentences with·bahuvrīhis
for predicate:

19 I have completed·my·prayers. 20 Your intention·has·been·
grasped by Vasantaka. 21 What·is·the·name·of her [male]
friend? 22 Your Majesty, in the science·of·acting assuredly
the important·thing·is·performance. 23 Now my exertions^
have become ^fruitful.

Exercise 9

Use the past active participle where indicated. 'You' when preceded by an asterisk is to be translated by **bhavant**.

Grammatical practice: 1 You two hurry 2 to the fire 3 by *you 4 of the two clean (women) 5 of the two clean (things) 6 they hurry 7 of the soft ones 8 he sees *you *pl.* 9 the clean (things) stay 10 *you two hurry

1 Welcome Mitrāvasu! 2 *You are clever. 3 See, we are hurrying. 4 Then what did she say? [*use past active part.*] 5 But the audience has often seen the work of earlier poets. 6 I greet *you [two]. 7 And the king's·daughter is (at present) with [*loc.*] her father-in-law's·family. 8 Bravo, lord·of·Kosala, bravo! 9 Who are *you two [*f.*], and who is this (girl)? 10 With regard to (my) beloved Mālatī, I am become without·hope. 11 Such persistence·in·anger towards one's friends [*f.*] is certainly not right. 12 You have understood correctly, my friend. [*p.a.p.*] 13 Did *you [*pl.*] hear? 14 Here is the house of some good (person), with·its·side·door· un·shut. 15 Friend, (they) seem to be having a conversation. 16 Thank heavens my uncertainty about Śakaṭadāsa is removed. 17 Sire, possessors·of·religious·power of course have·their·welfare·under·their·own·control. 18 But to·what· end have these mass·deaths occurred? 19 Is he (still) living right there?—he didn't go to an ascetic·grove, or again enter upon [**samāruh** *p.a.p.*] a vow? 20 I'll get (it) measured and begin the work. 21 How [**aho**] fraught·with·[**vant**]·obstacles is success·[*pl.*]·in·one's·desires. 22 Bravo, friend—cleverly begun! Now we (can feel) hope in this enterprise, though success·in·it·is·hard·to·attain. 23 Susaṃgatā, how did *you know me (to be) [standing·] here? 24 (I) congratulate husband and wife on (their) son's·victory. 25 Your Reverence [*f.*], here (is) a letter (which) the King, the ruler·of·Padmāvatī, approved· by·a·delighted·Nandana, has written in the presence of Bhūrivasu and sent [*use absol. plus p.p.*] to the long-lived Mādhava. 26 But for one·who·maintains·the·(sacred)·fire [**āhit·agni**] the ceremony (of cremation) is enjoined (to be)

by no other fire. Therefore let us bring fires from the place·of·sacrifice and set ourselves alight. 27 And after (their) weaning, the Goddess·Gaṅgā herself handed the two·sons of that (queen) to the great-seer Prācetasa.[*p.a.p.*] 28 At this juncture a brahmin laid [**āruh** *caus.*] his dead son at the king's·threshold and with·a·beating·of·his·breast proclaimed (an act of) sacrilege.

Exercise 10

Clauses marked as compounds (as in sentence 14) should be translated by means of abstract nouns.

Grammatical practice: 1 go *pl.* 2 in ascetics 3 from a bride 4 of the two leading 5 see the women 6 to an ascetic (while) leading. 7 let great (men) stay 8 hurry, ascetics 9 in the earth 10 singing, the two should go

1 Welcome! Be seated (both of you) over here. 2 Obviously being·childless makes me tender. 3 What, have I offended against the ascetics? 4 So call her and come. 5 All this is the outcome of my recklessness, monster (that I am). 6 May Your [two] Highnesses be victorious. 7 And this (tree) in falling has killed a woman. 8 Oh magnanimous one, I am in distress, thinking myself to be as it were licked·by·the·flames of·the·fires·of·hell. 9 Mother, you too go back now. 10 What inflammatory sýllables. 11 Her Majesty and I [*reverse order*] are partisans of the two of them. 12 Vardhamānaka, turn the carriage round. Maitreya my friend, fetch Vasantasenā down. 13 Dear child, may this utterance of yours be not·vain. 14 Since·gems·are·abundant in a great palace, a matching of ornaments is not improbable [**durlabha**]. 15 Do not think of [**alam alam**] rebuking (her). She is helpful to you. 16 *You should consider yourself similarly [**api**] a worthy·holder·of·the·title·'queen'. 17 Other women too have been driven distracted by the wayward god of love. 18 How várious is the noble·Cāṇakya's·strategy. 19 Let my revered father pardon [Lava's being:] Lava for being·stupid. 20 Shame on me [contemptuous·of:] in·my·contempt·for·the·

good·(that·had)·fallen (to me). 21 Thereupon fearing·the destruction·of·the·whole·serpent·world, the king·of·the·serpents Vāsuki addressed Garutmant. 22 Know Sumati, Mādhavasena's·counsellor, to be my elder brother. 23 Jayasenā, when·the·task·is·accomplished bring confirmation (of the fact) quickly. 24 The accursed·Cāṇakya surely did not discover them to be living there? 25 And I for my part acted quite rightly in placing her respectfully in·Her·Majesty's· hand(s). 26 But my father because·he·was·childless greeted my·birth with a festival surpassing·the·birth·of·a·son. 27 [At the end of me too:] And when I myself die, this (will be) what happens [vṛttāntaḥ] to the glory·of·the·dynasty·of·Puru. 28· Reverend (sir), I have offended against the revered Kaṇva (who is) of·your·gotra, in (first) wedding [absol.] this your hand-maid by the Gandharva rite, (then, when she had been) brought by her kinsmen some time later, rejecting (her) because·my·memory·was·impaired. Afterwards, from seeing· the·ring, I realized her (to have been) previously·married (to me). [The p.p. of avagam may have an active sense.] 29 And (I) introduced him into Kusumapura [bearing·the·signs·of:] disguised·as·a·mendicant immediately upon (my) vow·of· destroying·the·dynasty·of·Nanda, and 'had him make friends with all·the·Nanda·ministers. [make friends sakhyaṃ grah]

Exercise 11

Translate all present actives (except in 8, 13, 16 and 30) and all imperatives by means of the passive.

Grammatical practice: 1 with two makers 2 he sees the sisters 3 of fathers 4 we two are led 5 he sees the mother 6 the sisters stay 7 from a maker 8 let the two mothers be led 9 O sister 10 to the father

1 So give (me) this seal. 2 That royal·seer is [heard:] reputed to be a good man. 3 Homage to Yogācārya, whose first pupil I am. 4 Lava dear child, withdraw your weapon. 5 What, have (my) parents left me and gone to an ascetic·

grove? 6 But *you, where are you going? 7 Why, this is the one in whose [hand:] care your aunt forwarded the letter. 8 With Her Majesty now reconciled, it is solely concern·for· Sāgarikā that troubles me. 9 Who (is) to protect you, (my) son? 10 Swiftly pursue and seize the vile Śakaṭadāsa. 11 Ah, to the right of the enclosure·of·trees (I) seem to hear talking. 12 Susaṃgatā, this is actually just·a·game. 13 Kāṇelīmātṛ, is there any sign you (can) discern? 14 Vasan- taka, meet [pratyudgam] Vasubhūti and usher him in. 15 With the Minister to guide, this is easy for His Highness. 16 It is a trainer's acceptance·of·poor·material which reveals the inferiority·of·(his)·intelligence. 17 This is the same neck- lace·of·jewels His Majesty gave to the princess at the time·of· (her)·departure. 18 Remember your own remark to [prati] me on seeing·the·portrait. 19 He gave his·own·daughter to Vatsarāja though (she was) being·wooed·by·me. 20 Free all prisoners including Yajñasena's·brother-in-law. 21 Forgive (me) what I did without·informing Your Majesty. 22 We too are busying ourselves upon our·own·work. 23 Go into the picture·gallery quiet(ly) with Manoramā and stay watching our·acting. 24 Oh (you [f.] who are) conscious·only·of·the pangs·of·your·own·heart (while) ignorant·of·another's·suffer- ing—see, (I) scold you. 25 Well, say what [kim] is to be done with [gen.] this villain. 26 This mendicant Jīvasiddhi who, employed·by·Rākṣasa, had Parvateśvara killed by a poison·girl shall after proclamation of this same crime be banished in dis- grace from the city. 27 When (you had) thus discovered·the· grounds·for·the·disloyalty·of these (people) [use loc. abs. with predicative bahuvrīhi], why did Your Excellency not swiftly take countermeasures? 28 Gautama, who is so ill-disposed to us [who has:] as to have enraged Her Majesty? 29 Worthy Cārudatta, do *you have in relation to [saha] the daughter of this worthy (lady) (any) attachment, affection or fondness? 30 Reverend (sir), in (the course of) some altercation [of:] between that (woman) who today at Court acknowledged defeat at my hands [mattaḥ] and myself, she taunted me [f.] ['you are boasting . . .':] with boasting as if I had [past. act. part.] seduced Marīci.

Exercise 12

For convenience, 'must' represents a gerundive in **tavya**, 'should' one in **ya** or **anīya**.

Grammatical practice: 1 they are doing 2 he hates 3 the two go 4 let him do 5 you two abide 6 are you listening? 7 they abide 8 we do 9 listen 10 hating, the two abide

1 Ah, Vṛṣala occupies the throne! 2 One·should·not·go· against Divaspati's command, friend. 3 You too [make your own office not·void:] be about your affairs. 4 He must be here, where (there is) this crowd·of·people. 5 Because° the house °is·decrepit, the door creaks. 6 Have *you two (ladies) ever witnessed this? 7 And the gold·box here you must guard by night, and Vardhamānaka by day. 8 I won't let go before you look at my heart's·beloved [f.] painted on the rock. 9 One should of course salute (all) deities. 10 Let the two of us just listen attentive(ly). 11 Here is that hero, [become·an object·of·speech for you:] (now) within range of your voice. 12 So I'll [make her debtless:] discharge her debt. 13 And now, in returning, dear·Rāma must inévitably see in the Pañcavaṭī·forest the places (that were) witness·to·the·intimacies· of·his·sojourn·with·his·bride. 14 As my heart declares, Gautama is free·from·the·poison. 15 Frivolous (girl), (you) must not go a single step further [padāt padam api] from this place without·giving (me) this rosary. 16 [Let there abide:] Never mind this un·instructed wretch. 17 What, has Śaṅkhacūḍa (by) coming (here) made·fruitless my wish? 18 How am I indeed to distract myself, whose·desires·are·(so)· hard·to·win? 19 Then [while I [f.] having fainted was regaining consciousness (*present tense*), she became one·whose· sight·was·hard·to·win:] when I came round after my swoon, she had vanished from sight. 20 Rather, since [iti] a guest is senior to anyone, it is *you who should be honoured by us. 21 Ho there students! Turn this horse away (by) surrounding it and beating (it) off with clods of earth. 22 Worthy lady, with the Nāgānanda to be acted, why these quite uncalled for tears? [*use impersonal passive of* rud] 23 And from the fact

that (there is) this violent gale which·has·shaken·the·crags·of·
the·Malaya·mountain, I surmise that the king·of·the·birds is
at hand [āsannī˘bhūta]. 24 And complacent (as I was),
I made that same (woman) mistress of my·[own]·money,
my·house, my·household [gaṇaḥ], my·person and my·life.
25 Then, when the ruler·of·Siṃhala, though often petitioned
by us on·(our)·master's·behalf because of (our) belief·in·that·
(prophecy), in his avoidance of [*pres. part. of* parihṛ] dis-
tress·of·mind to Queen Vāsavadattā refused to give her (i.e.
the girl, in marriage), (we) contrived a report that Her Majesty
had been burnt [by:] in the fire at Lāvāṇaka, and despatched
Bābhravya to him. 26 How inspiring of cónfidence [viśvas-
anīya] is (his) form, though resplendent. 27 And this (man),
obviously, must be her son, for·whose·sake she is crying. 28
So (by) coming and personally playing [his own role:] the
part of himself, let him enjoy the delight·of·a·meeting. 29
But the decorations previously·worn·by·Parvateśvara (being)
of·merit should be conferred only on brahmins of·merit.
30 Until I come (back) after going to the city and having
[kṛ] a drink·of·wine in·the·company·of·my·friends, you [*f.*]
should [be not·negligent upon:] look after the house.

Exercise 13

Grammatical practice: 1 of that (man) 2 sacrifice 3 he
obstructs 4 they two buy 5 let them know 6 in those
(men) 7 give that [*n.*] 8 we two obstruct 9 those (women)
sacrifice 10 buy those two

1 Take this box. 2 Where, I wonder, will there be water? 3
If (it is) not a secret, I should like to hear the cause·of·(your)·
grief 4 Why, you will be [vṛt] right beside·me. 5 Oh, thére
is the woman. 6 Manoramā, is it true what Vasantaka says?
7 You know, dear child, how to distract Her Majesty (when
she is) féeling depressed. 8 People are taking (it) in this way.
9 Then what is that man going to say to (his) friends, poor
fellow? 10 If you are *really* going back, you should [arh] take
me too to the hermitage. 11 The workings of men's·fortunes
are indeed inscrutable, since I have reached such a pass.

12 So, Vṛṣala, we have been summoned to be rebuked? 13
Reverend sir, why do you say [**abhidhā**] so? 14 Poison is
difficult to turn·into·medicine. 15 Highness, if Śakaṭadāsa
wrote it [the letter *m*.], then *I* wrote it. 16 Give me leave (to
go), dear child [*f*.]. 17 So I will go in here and find out
news·of·Candanadāsa from someone. 18 And it is strange
that, although understanding (this to be) so, I [*f*.] cannot
restrain my own mental turmoil. 19 Highness, those are *not*
the peaks·of·the·Malaya·mountain. 20 How is this proper
for *you even to consider [with:] in your mind, let alone
declare or look upon? 21 I will try (to see to it) that that
selfsame harlot [will unite you with your own wealth:] restores
your wealth to you. 22 So let Your Highness don this. 23
What, are the very ones who are ready to appease Candragupta
by killing·me providing my bodyguard? 24 That man is the
noble·Cārudatta after all—how could he have done this misdeed? 25 Lakṣmaṇa dear child, the reverend Vālmīki has
invited us to see his·own·work [being] performed by the
nymphs. 26 Shame (on you, you) fool! Why did you scare
her by laughing (so) loudly that she flew up and went somewhere else? 27 But a heart (that has) inclined in one direction
cannot be made to incline in another. Therefore I dare not
accept her. 28 Are you worried that Mataṅga is going to
snatch the kingdom? If so, what of it? Why, it is for·the·sake·
of·others that I protect everything, starting with my·own·per-
son [**sva:śarīra˘taḥ prabhṛti**]. But that (I) don't give it (to
him) of my own accord is out of regard·for·my·father. 29
How [does:] can an audience pass over the works of those·
whose·fame·is·widespread such·as·Bhāsa·Saumilla·and·Kavi-
putra, and have respect for the activity of Kālidāsa, a con-
temporary·writer? 30 If this same girl [**sā iyam**] [is of·un-
shakeable·resolve:] continues to be stubborn, all these people
will [having·no·other·course:] have no choice but to fast to
death right here.

Exercise 14

Use the imperfect tense where possible, except in 28 and the
first part of 15.

Grammatical practice: 1 we two led   2 they may lead   3 of
two better (things)   4 you *pl.* hurried   5 I obstructed   6 they
may hate   7 you two abided   8 we may see the two elder
(men)   9 you were elder   10 they would be better

1 In falling to [*loc.*] the ground it might make a noise.   2 So I
should like to hear who you are.   3 There he saw one of the
two mating curlews being shot by a huntsman.   4 Here is my
younger brother actually arrived, having·assumed·the·role·of·
Yaugandharāyaṇa.   5 Destiny would at long last indeed be
acting·rightly, if it should join this pair suited·to·each·other.
6   As   if   fearful·of·the·falling·of·a·shower·of·Love's·sharp·
arrows, the slender·body [**gātra:yaṣṭi** *f.*] trembled.   7 Now
is Mālatī especially·attractive.   8 If only the vile Rākṣasa may
be captured.   9 But because of my ugliness I had the sobriquet
'Virūpaka'.   10 She was immediately summoned together
with her mother by the king.   11 Why, your elder sister here
is in distress—so embrace her.   12 But with you denounced,
all our·family would be ruined.   13 And Haṃsa, Lord·of·the
second·Gandharva·family, made her his beloved wife as (did)
the Ocean·of·Milk Mandākinī.   14 What may (a man who is)
being beaten not say?   15 But what she did on coming there,
what she said, how [*use* **kim**] she behaved [everything (being)
absent·minded I [*f.*] did not notice:] I was so absent-minded
that I did not notice at all.   16 No other (thing) is more·
wholly·evil [**pāpiṣṭha˜tama**] than suicide.   17 Your Majesty,
we had great hope(s) that your·servant Rāgamañjarī, whose·
character·accomplishments·and·skill·are·suited·to·her·beauty,
would fulfil (our) wishes.   18 The purse·proud Arthapati,
[having·bits·of·rag·as·remnants:] reduced to rags, was banished
in·front·of·all·the·townsfolk.   19 And feeling compassion I
said, 'Come virtuous lady, let me [*opt.*] take you to the home·
of·your·beloved,' and proceeded three·or·four steps.   20 Say
now what is in your mind, Gautama.   21 Otherwise, perhaps,
on suddenly seeing me in·such·a·condition my parents might
abandon life.   22 And Rumaṇvant, having set my ^elder
^brother Jayavarman over [*loc.*] the Kosalas, is in fact coming
by slow stages accompanying his whole·army (which has been)

wounded·in·battle.　23 If only I were able to effect the rescue of even one serpent by [*abl.*] giving·my·own·body.　24 So thus with·my·plans·accomplished I made Rāgamañjarī's· house full·of·gold·and·jewels.　25 Where are (you) going, abandoning a person dearer even than life?　26 And Candra-gupta might accept (him) because he is in fact an hereditary (servant). In which case [**evaṃ sati**] His Highness would not trust us [too:] either.　27 I gave half·of·it to the gaming-master and his assistants, appropriated half, and rose; and there rose (with me) the delighted [**harṣa:garbha**] acclamations of those·who·were·there.　28 (I) did not say (anything) because I was going to congratulate Her Majesty when this mission was actually accomplished [*loc. abs.*].　29 Vṛṣala, if Malayaketu's escape·had·not·been·connived·at [*loc. abs. with bahuvrihi*], (we) should have had [a twofold course:] two courses: he might have been either suppressed or presented with the half·of·the·kingdom already·promised. Now [**tāvat**] in sup-pressing him, (our) signature would have been given [*p.p. with* **as**] [to the ingratitude that [**iti**] Parvataka was murdered by us:] to a confession of having treacherously murdered Parvataka.　30 And we [two] got up and with·washed·faces performed the morning rites, and (as we were) strolling through the town (which was) in·a·turmoil·at·our·deeds, we heard a clamour in the houses·of·the·bride·and·groom.

Supplementary Exercises: Key

Exercise 2a

1 nāryaḥ khalv asminn udyāne tapasvibhiḥ sakopaṃ gṛhād ānītāḥ 2 asmin khalv ûdyāne nāryas tapasvibhir gṛhāt sakopam ānītāḥ 3 ānītāḥ sakopaṃ khalu nāryo gṛhād udyāne ʾsmiṃs tapasvibhiḥ 4 ānītā asmin nārya udyāne sakopaṃ khalu tapasvibhir gṛhāt 5 tapasvibhiḥ khalu sakopaṃ gṛhān nāryo ʾsminn udyāna ānītāḥ 6 sakopaṃ khalu gṛhāt tapasvibhir asmin nārya ānītā udyāne 7 asminn ānītā gṛhāt khalv ûdyāne nāryaḥ sakopaṃ tapasvibhiḥ 8 udyāne gṛhād asmin sakopaṃ khalv ānītās tapasvibhir nāryaḥ

Exercise 2b

1 evaṃ vadanti 2 gāyataḥ 3 api/kiṃ smarasi? 4 adhunā kiṃ pṛcchatha? 5 paśyāmaḥ 6 na likhāmi 7 kathaṃ, gacchati? 8 ‘nṛtyantʾ îty avagacchāmi 9 kva bhramathaḥ? 10 adhunā jayanti 11 ita āgacchataḥ 12 atra tiṣṭhāvaḥ 13 paśyasi cɩ âvagacchasi ca 14 ‘kva gacchasɩ?’ îti pṛcchantɩ îva 15 na punar avagacchatha 16 adhunā nɩ ôpaviśāmaḥ 17 adya kim atrɩ êcchathaḥ? 18 tatra punar api vasantɩ îti na praviśāmaḥ 19 punar adhunā śocata iva 20 evaṃ punar icchāmaḥ 21 na smarāmɩ îti pṛcchāmi

Exercise 3

1 śiṣyāḥ, māṃ kva nayatha? 2 ‘api jīvati sa brāhmaṇa?’ iti punar api narau pṛcchanti 3 śobhanau sūrya;candrau 4

jalaṃ ka icchati? 5 sūryam adya bālā na paśyanti 6 vanam (āvāṃ) praviśāvaḥ 7 vayam api parvatān gacchāmaḥ 8 bālāḥ, likhaty ācāryaḥ 9 katham, brāhmaṇaṃ māṃ pṛcchasi? 10 bhojanaṃ tau bālāv icchataḥ 11 ācārya;śiṣyā vismitās tiṣṭhanti 12 ācārya, svalpaṃ tat kṣetram 13 'te kva gacchanti paṇḍitā?' ity asmān pṛcchati 14 brāhmaṇā api tan na smaranti 15 tad api n̍ âvagacchāmaḥ 16 duḥkhaṃ nayati narān krodhaḥ 17 tān paṇḍitān adhunā kaḥ smarati? 18 bāla iva phalam atra na paśyati 19 kiṃ tvaṃ Makarandaḥ? 20 bāla, kim evaṃ māṃ vadasi?

Exercise 4

1 ramaṇīyam etan nagaram 2 kiṃ tatr̍ aîva gacchāmi? 3 eṣa vayasyaiḥ saha gṛhaṃ praviśati 4 gatā bālāḥ— aham api gacchāmi 5 ānītau jīvitāv eva paṇḍitau 6 priya vayasya, etat pṛcchāmi—kiṃ madīyaiḥ putraiḥ kṛtam (iti)? 7 vismṛtāni tvayā prathamāny eva vacanāni 8 katham, mām eva pṛcchasi? 9 alaṃ viṣādena 10 śīghraṃ vā ̍śvaṃ śobhanaṃ v)̍ êcchanti 11 na punar dṛṣṭau devena madīyāv eva putrau 12 vanam āgato)̍pi śiṣyān na paśyati 13 deva, pariśrāntā ete prayatnena 14 adbhuta eva jano madīyair vayasyair gṛham ānītaḥ 15 ten̍ aîvi aîtad udyānaṃ kṛtam 16 deva, n̍ aîtan mayā likhitam 17 deva, prathamam atr̍ āgatair apy asmābhiḥ pariśrāntā vayasyā iti n̍ aîva dṛṣṭam

Exercise 5

1 deva, jitāḥ smaḥ 2 asti vaḥ krodhasyɩ âvasaraḥ 3 kṣetrebhyo)̍yam asmābhir ānītaḥ 4 gṛhaṃ tyaktvā vaneṣu putraiḥ saha bhramati 5 priya vayasya kvɩ âsi? 6 gṛham anyad gatvā pṛcchāmaḥ 7 pariśrāntaḥ khalu kumāraḥ 8 adbhutaḥ ko)̍yaṃ sarveṣām āvegaḥ? 9 iha na kiṃcit sukhāyɩ aîva 10 api dṛṣṭas tvayā Kusumapure Stanakalaśaḥ? 11 andhā muhūrtaṃ bhūtvā sarvam idānīṃ paśyanti 12 'asty anyasmin deśe)̍ndhaḥ kaścit kumāra' iti bālān vadati 13 pariśrāntā iva smaḥ 14 Mārīcas te darśanam icchati 15 kiṃ kumārasyɩ âpy eka eva putraḥ? 16 mitrayor āvegāt pāpaṃ kiṃcid

avagacchāmi 17 kasyı êdaṃ pustakam? 18 hā na
kaścid atra 19 'ayam eva sa pāpa' ity uktvā kāṇo gṛhītaḥ
20 mārga eva pādapo nipatitaḥ 21 lekha eva madīyo na
bhavati 22 kim etat? kva gatas tava mayy adbhuto
ınurāgaḥ? 23 katham, māṃ dṛṣṭvā ıpi parityajya gato ısi?
24 sarveṣām evı âsmākam ayaṃ niścayaḥ

Exercise 6

1 deva, kuta iyaṃ kanyakā? 2 Ūrmilāṃ pṛcchaty āryā 3
idam ārya:Cāṇakyasya gṛham 4 pramāṇa-sūtraṃ me
vismṛtam 5 Vṛṣala, kim-arthaṃ vayam āhūtāḥ? 6 hanta,
śaila-śikharād gaganam utpatya bāṇair mām abhivarṣati
7 sā mayā tubhyaṃ pradattā 8 dūrı:âtītaḥ khalı ûpadeśa-
kālaḥ 9 tāta-saṃdeśeın aîvı âsmi tvat-sakāśam ihı āgataḥ
10 dṛṣṭam etaj jīrṇı:ôdyānam 11 aham api mudrāṃ na
prayacchāmi 12 aye, puruṣa-dvayaṃ suptam 13 bhadre,
satyaṃ tad evı êdaṃ suvarṇa-bhāṇḍam? 14 deva, jitā
ınayā ıham 15 mayā ıpy etat kasmiṃścit paritoṣa-sthāne
Siddhārthakāya dattam 16 idānīm api tvam evı âsyāḥ
prabhavasi 17 visṛṣṭaś ca Vāmadevı-âbhimantrito medhyo ıśvaḥ 18 tena citrakareın âsmad-upadiṣṭam āryasya
caritam asyāṃ vīthikāyām abhilikhitam 19 bhadra, kim
ayam evı aîkaḥ Kaumudī-mahotsava-pratiṣedhaś Candraguptasya Cāṇakyaṃ prati kopa-kāraṇam, utı ânyad
apy asti? 20 katham, apriya-nivedanān mayıı aîtām
avasthāṃ gamitau [or nītau]? athavā viṣadhara-vadanād
viṣam antareṇa kim anyan niṣkrāmati?

Exercise 7

1 su:viditam etan mama 2 Vetravati, na khalv antarā
dṛṣṭā tvayā devī Vasumatī? 3 klinne vāsasī Vasantase-
nāyāḥ 4 katham, Rākṣasena ghātitas tāto, na Cāṇakyena?
5 pratyāsīdati gṛha-gamana-kālaḥ 6 Bābhravya, sadṛśıı
îyaṃ rāja-putryā 7 deva, evam amātya-pariṣade nivedayāmi 8 aty: ākulaṃ kathayasi 9 Pṛthvī:Bhāgīrathī-
bhyām abhyupapannıı āryā 10 na gatā khalu sā tayā
diśā? 11 an:āryaḥ para-dāra-vyavahāraḥ 12 athı êmaṃ
divasa-śeṣam ucita:vyāpāra-parāṅmukhena cetasā kva nu
khalu yāpayāmi? 13 darśaneın aîvı âtrabhavatīnāṃ

puraskṛto ›smi   14 ārya, kim a:vidita ev› âyaṃ devasya
Candraguptasya   Kaumudī-mahotsava-pratiṣedhaḥ?   15
'ujjhita':śabdena janitaṃ naḥ kutūhalam   16 ahaṃ tvayā
mārga-gata eva tāḍitaḥ   17 katham, akṛtv› aîva prasādaṃ
gatā devī?   18 yāvad anuyātrikān atidūre tapo-vanasya
niveśayāmi   19 kim atrabhavatyoḥ karṇa-pathaṃ n›
āyātaṃ Śakuntalā-pratyādeśa-kaulīnam?   20 anena mat-
priy›-âbhiyogena smārayasi me pūrva: śiṣyāṃ Saudā-
manīm   21 tad yāvad asmin viṣama: daśā-pariṇāma-
sulabhe bhagna:śīlā-tale muhūrtam upaviśāmi   22 puṃ-
ścali, tvad-gataṃ apacāraṃ suhṛdo me varṇayanti   23
iyaṃ hi kā ›pi kanyakā sva:cetas› aîva parikalpy› ālikhitā,
na tu dṛṣṭa:pūrvā 24 mādhavī-latā-maṇḍapaṃ gatvā priya-
tamā-saṃket›-âvasaraṃ pratipālayāvaḥ

Exercise 8

1 namo ›smai kaṣṭa:tapase   2 ete kumārasy› ājñā-›nan-
taram eva pratinivṛttāḥ sarve rājānaḥ   3 eṣā kusum›-
âvacaya-vyagra:hastā sakhyās te paricārikā Candrikā
samāgacchati   4 yāvad ātmānam ācchādya tiṣṭhāmi   5
n› âyaṃ pratīkāro ›sya pāpmanaḥ   6 Śambūko nāma
dhūma-paḥ śūdro ›sminn eva Janasthāne tapaś carati   7
tad yāvad asya dur:ātmanaḥ Kumbhīnasī-putrasy› ôn-
mūlanāya Śatrughnaṃ preṣayāmi   8 dur:labham atr›
ânunayaṃ paśyāmi   9 uddhṛta:viṣāda:śalyaḥ kathayāmi
10 katham, anyad ev› êdaṃ prekṣaṇīyakaṃ saṃvṛttam
11 itaretar›-ânurāgo hi dāra-karmaṇi parārdhyaṃ maṅgalam   12 vidita:vṛttānto ›pi kiṃ māṃ pṛcchasi?   13
ten› aîva c› êdaṃ Caitrarathaṃ nām› âti:manoharaṃ
kānanaṃ nirmitam   14 sarvaḥ khalu kāntam ātmānaṃ
paśyati   15 a:saṃvijñāta:pada-nibandhanaṃ tama iva
praviśāmi   16 svayam eva Sugāṅga:prāsāda-gatena
deven› âvalokitam a:pravṛtta:Kaumudī-mahotsavaṃ
Kusumapuram   17 āḥ, ka eṣa pāpo ›smākam antarāyaḥ
saṃvṛttaḥ?   18 āryeṇ› aîvaṃ sarvato niruddha:ceṣṭā-
prasarasya mama bandhanam iva rājyaṃ, na rājyam
iva   19 samāpta: japo ›smi   20 gṛhīt›:âbhiprāyo ›si Vasan-
takena   21 kiṃ:nāmadheyaṃ tasyā mitram?   22 deva,
prayoga:pradhānaṃ hi nāṭya-śāstram   23 idānīṃ
saphala:pariśramo ›smi saṃvṛttaḥ

Exercise 9

1 Mitrāvaso, svāgatam 2 nipuṇo bhavān 3 ete tvarā-
mahe 4 tataḥ kim uktavatī 5 bahuśas tu pariṣadā
pūrveṣāṃ kavīnāṃ dṛṣṭaḥ prayogabandhaḥ 6 abhivādaye bhavantau 7 rāja-sutā ca śvaśura-kule vartate 8
sādhu, Kosala-pate, sādhu 9 ke bhavatyau, kā cı êyam? 10
priyāṃ Mālatīṃ prati nir_āśaḥ saṃvṛtto ısmi 11 na
khalu yuktaḥ sakhī:jana evaṃvidhaḥ kopı-ânubandhaḥ
12 sakhe, samyag gṛhītavān asi 13 śrutaṃ bhavadbhiḥ?
14 idaṃ kasyı âpi sādhor an:āvṛta:pakṣa-dvāraṃ geham
15 vayasya, saṃlāpa iva vartate 16 diṣṭyā Śakaṭadāsaṃ
praty apanīto me vikalpaḥ 17 rājan, svādhīna:kuśalāḥ
khalu siddhi˜mantaḥ 18 kiṃ:nimittaṃ punar ime saṃ-
ghāta-mṛtyavo jātāḥ? 19 kiṃ tatrı aîva prativasati? na
tapo-vanaṃ gataḥ, pratijñāṃ vā na punaḥ samārūḍhavān?
20 māpayitvā karma samārabhe 21 aho vighnavatyaḥ
prārthita-siddhayaḥ 22 sādhu, vayasya—nipuṇam upa-
krāntam. idānīṃ dur:adhigama:siddhāv apy asminn
ārambhe vayam āśaṃsāmahe 23 Susaṃgate, katham
aham iha:stho bhavatyā jñātaḥ? 24 diṣṭyā putra-vijayena
dampatī vardhete 25 Bhagavati, etat prahṛṣṭa:Nandanı-
âbhinanditena rājñā Padmāvatı-īśvareṇa Bhūrivasoḥ
pratyakṣam abhilikhya pattram āyuṣmato Mādhavasya
preṣitam 26 kiṃ tv āhitı:âgner nı ânyenı âgninā saṃskāro
vihitaḥ. ato ıgnihotra-śaraṇād agnīn ādāyı ātmānam
uddīpayāmaḥ 27 stanya-tyāgāt pareṇa dāraka-dvayaṃ
ca tasyāḥ Prācetasasya maharṣer Gaṅgā: devī
svayam arpitavatī 28 atrı ântare brāhmaṇena mṛtaṃ putram āropya rāja-dvāri sı_ôras-tāḍam abrahmaṇyam
udghoṣitam

Exercise 10

1 svāgatam. ito niṣīdatam 2 nūnam an:apatya˜tā māṃ
vatsalayati 3 katham, aparāddhas tapasvinām asmi? 4
tad enāṃ āhūyı āgaccha 5 sarvam idaṃ mama nṛśaṃ-
sasyı âsamīkṣya:kāri˜tāyā vijṛmbhitam 6 vijayetāṃ
kumārau 7 anena ca patatā strī vyāpāditā 8 bho mahıı:
ātman, narakı-ânala-jvālā-ıvalīḍham ivı ātmānaṃ
manyamāno duḥkhaṃ tiṣṭhāmi 9 amba, tvam api nivartasvı
êdānīm 10 aho saṃdīpanāny akṣarāṇi 11 pakṣapātināv

anayor aham devī ca 12 Vardhamānaka, parivartaya pravahaṇam—sakhe Maitreya, avatāraya Vasantasenām 13 vatsa, a:vitathı aîṣā bhāratī te bhavatu 14 mahati rāja-kule ratna-bāhulyān na durlabho bhūṣaṇānāṃ saṃvādaḥ 15 alam alam upālambhena. upakāriṇī tavı êyam 16 'rājñī':śabda-bhājanam ātmānam api cintayatu bhavatī 17 anyā api durvinītena Manmathenı ônmatta˘tāṃ nītā nāryaḥ 18 aho vaicitryam ārya:Cāṇakya-nīteḥ 19 mṛṣyantv idānīṃ Lavasya bāliśa˘tāṃ tāta-pādāḥ 20 dhiṅ mām upanata:śreyo-ıvamāninam 21 tataḥ sakala:nāga-loka-vināśa-śaṅkinā nāga-rājena Vāsukinā Garutmān abhihitaḥ 22 Mādhavasena-sacivaṃ Sumatiṃ mamı âgrajam avagaccha 23 Jayasene, karma-siddhāv āśu pratipattim ānaya 24 na khalu viditās te tatra nivasantaś Cāṇakya:hatakena? 25 mayā ıpi cı aînāṃ devī-haste sa_gauravaṃ nikṣipatā yuktam evı ânuṣṭhitam 26 tātas tv an:apatya˘tayā suta-janmı-âtiriktena mahotsavena majjanmı âbhinanditavān 27 mamı âpy ante Puru-vaṃśa-śriya eṣa vṛttāntaḥ 28 bhagavan, imām ājñākarīṃ vo Gāndharveṇa vidhinı ôpayamya kasya cit kālasya bandhubhir ānītāṃ smṛti-śaithilyāt pratyādiśann, aparāddho ısmi tatrabhavato yuṣmad-gotrasya Kaṇvasya. paścād enām aṅgurīyaka-darśanād ūḍha:pūrvām avagato ısmi 29 sa ca kṣapaṇaka-liṅga-dhārī Nanda-vaṃśa-vadha-pratijñā-ınantaram eva Kusumapuram upanīya sarva: Nandı˘âmātyaiḥ saha sakhyaṃ grāhitaḥ

Exercise 11

1 tad dīyatām eṣā mudrā 2 su:janaḥ sa rāja:ṛṣiḥ śrūyate 3 namo Yogācāryāya, yasyı âhaṃ prathamaḥ śiṣyaḥ 4 vatsa Lava, saṃhriyatām astram 5 katham, māṃ parityajya tapo-vanaṃ yātau pitarau? 6 bhavatā punaḥ kva gamyate? 7 nanu sa eṣa yasya haste mātṛ-ṣvasā te pattrikām anupreṣitavatī 8 idānīṃ devyāṃ prasannāyāṃ Sāgarikā-cintı aîva kevalaṃ māṃ bādhate 9 kas trātā tava putraka? 10 śīghram anusṛtya gṛhyatāṃ dur:ātmā Śakaṭadāsaḥ 11 aye, dakṣiṇena vṛkṣa-vāṭikām, ālāpa iva śrūyate 12 Susaṃgate, krīḍā_mātram evı aîtat 13 Kāṇe-līmātaḥ, asti kiṃ cic cihnaṃ yad upalakṣayasi? 14 Vasantaka, pratyudgamya praveśyatāṃ Vasubhūtiḥ 15 amātye

netari, sulabham etat kumārasya 16 vinetur adravya-
parigraha eva buddhi-lāghavaṃ prakāśayati 17 sꣲ aîvꣲ
êyaṃ ratna-mālā yā devena rāja-putryai prasthāna-kāle
dattā 18 smaryatām ālekhya-darśane māṃ praty ātmano
vacanam 19 mat-prārthyamānā ꣲpy anena sva:duhitā
Vatsarājāya dattā 20 Yajñasena-śyālam urīkṛtya
mucyantāṃ sarve bandhana-sthāḥ 21 kṣamyatāṃ yan
mayā devasyꣲ â:nivedya kṛtam 22 vayam api sva:
karmaṇy abhiyujyāmahe 23 nibhṛtena citra-śālāṃ
praviśya Manoramayā sahꣲ âsman-nṛttaṃ paśyatā sthīyatām 24 ayi sva:citta-vedanā-mātra-vedini para-vyathā-
ꣲnabhijñe, iyam upālabhyase 25 nanꣲ ûcyatāṃ kim asya
pāpasyꣲ ânuṣṭhīyatām 26 ya eṣa kṣapaṇako Jīvasiddhī
Rākṣasa-prayukto viṣa-kanyayā Parvateśvaraṃ ghātitavān, sa enam eva doṣaṃ prakhyāpya sa‿nikāraṃ nagarān
nirvāsyatām 27 evam eteṣu parijñāṭ‿âparāga‿hetuṣu,
kṣipram eva kasmān na prativihitam āryeṇa? 28
Gautama, ka evaṃ vimukho ꣲsmākaṃ yena caṇḍī‾kṛtā
devī? 29 ārya Cārudatta, asti bhavato ꣲsyā āryāyā duhitrā
saha prasaktiḥ praṇayaḥ prītir vā? 30 bhagavan, yayā ꣲdya
rāja-kule mattaḥ parājayo ꣲbhyupetas, tasyāś ca mama
ca kasmiṃś cit saṃgharṣe 'Marīcim āvarjitavatꣲ îva
ślāghasa' iti tayā ꣲsmy aham adhikṣiptā

Exercise 12

1 aye, siṃhāsanam adhyāste Vṛṣalaḥ 2 vayasya, an:
atikramaṇīyā Divaspater ājñā 3 tvam api svam adhi-
kāram a:śūnyaṃ kuru 4 atra tena bhavitavyaṃ, yatrꣲ
êyaṃ janapada-samavāyaḥ 5 jīrṇa‾tvād gṛhasya virauti
kapāṭam 6 bhavatībhyāṃ kadācid etat pratyakṣīkṛtam?
7 idaṃ ca suvarṇa-bhāṇḍaṃ rakṣitavyaṃ tvayā rātrau,
Vardhamānakenꣲ âpi divā 8 na tāvan muñcāmi yāvan
mama hṛdaya-vallabhāṃ śilāyām ālikhitāṃ na paśyasi
9 vandyāḥ khalu devatāḥ 10 avahitau śṛṇuvas tāvat
11 eṣa te vāg-viṣayī‾bhūtaḥ sa vīraḥ 12 tad aham enām
an:ṛṇāṃ karomi 13 adhunā ca pratinivartamānena
Rāma:bhadreṇa niyatam eva Pañcavaṭī-vane vadhū-
sahavāsa-viśrambha-sākṣiṇaḥ pradeśā draṣṭavyāḥ 14
yathā me hṛdayam ācaṣṭe, tathā nir‿viṣo Gautamaḥ 15
cañcale, pradeśād asmād imām akṣamālām a:dattvā
padāt padam api na gantavyam 16 āstām ayam a:śikṣito

varākaḥ 17 katham, viphalī‾kṛto me manorathaḥ Śaṅ-khacūḍeṇ āgacchatā? 18 mayā khalu durlabha:prār-thanaḥ katham ātmā vinodayitavyaḥ 19 tato ɪhaṃ moham upagatā yāvat saṃjñām upalabhe, tāvad iyaṃ durlabha:darśanā saṃvṛttā 20 nanu sarvasyɪ âbhyāgato gurur iti bhavān evɪ âsmākaṃ pūjyaḥ 21 bho baṭavaḥ, parivṛtya loṣṭair apaghnantaḥ parāvartayaṭ aīnam aśvan 22 ārye, Nāgānande nāṭayitavye kim idam a:kāraṇam eva rudyate? 23 yathā cɪ âyaṃ calita:Malayɪ‾âcala‾śilā‾cayaḥ pracaṇḍo nabhasvāṃs, tathā tarkayāmy 'āsanni‾ bhūtaḥ pakṣi-rāja' iti 24 subhagaṃmanyena ca mayā sva:dhanasya sva:gṛhasya sva:gaṇasya sva:dehasya sva: jīvitasya ca sɪɪ aîvɪ ēśvarī kṛtā 25 tatas tat-pratyayād asmābhiḥ svāmy-arthaṃ bahuśaḥ prārthyamāneɪɪ âpi Siṃhaɪɪ-ēśvareṇa devyā Vāsavadattāyāś citta-khedaṃ pariharatā yadā na dattā, tadā Lāvāṇakena vahninā devī dagdhɪɪ êti prasiddhim utpādya tad-antikaṃ Bābhravyaḥ prahitaḥ 26 aho dīptimato ɪpi viśvasanīya‾tā vapuṣaḥ. 27 nūnam aneɪ âpy asyāḥ sutena bhavitavyaṃ, yad-artham ākrandati 28 tad āgatya svayam eva svāṃ bhū-mikāṃ kurvāṇaḥ samāgamɪ: ôtsavam anubhavatu 29 kiṃ tu Parvateśvara-dhṛta:pūrvāṇi bhūṣaṇāni guṇavanti guṇavadbhya eva brāhmaṇebhyaḥ pratipādanīyāni 30 yāvad ahaṃ nagaraṃ gatvā suhṛt-sameto madhu-pānaṃ kṛtvɪɪ āgacchāmi tāvad a:pramattayā gṛhe tvayā bhāvyam

Exercise 13

1 gṛhāṇ aîtad bhāṇḍam 2 kva nu khalu salilaṃ bhaviṣ-yati? 3 na ced rahasyam, icchāmi śrotuṃ śoka-hetum 4 nanu mat-samīpa eva vartiṣyase 5 aye, iyam asau yoṣit 6 Manorame, satyam idaṃ yad Vasantako ɪbhidhatte? 7 jānāsi vatsa durmanāyamānāṃ devīṃ vinodayitum 8 evaṃ jano gṛhṇāti 9 tataḥ suhṛdbhyaḥ kim asau kath-ayiṣyati tapasvī? 10 yadi satyam eva nivartase, mām apy āśramaṃ netum arhasi 11 puruṣa-bhāgyānām acintyāḥ khalu vyāpārā yad aham īdṛśīṃ daśām anuprāptaḥ 12 Vṛṣala, upālabdhuṃ tarhi vayam āhūtāḥ? 13 bhagavan, kasmād evam abhidhatse? 14 duṣkaraṃ viṣam auṣadhī‾ kartum 15 kumāra, yadi Śakaṭadāsena likhitas tadā mayɪɪ aîva likhitaḥ 16 vatse, anujānīhi mām 17 tad atra praviśya kutaś cic Candanadāsa-vṛttāntam upalapsye 18

citraṃ cɪ êdaṃ yad aham evam avagacchanty api na
śaknomy ātmano vikāram upasaṃhartum 19 kumāra, nɪ
aîvɪ âmī Malayɪ:âcala-sānavaḥ 20 katham etad yuktaṃ
bhavato manasā ɪpi cintayituṃ, kiṃ punar ākhyātum
īkṣituṃ vā? 21 nijena dyumnenɪ āsāv veśyā yathā tvāṃ
yojayiṣyati, tathā yatiṣye 22 tad etat paridhattāṃ kumāraḥ 23 kathaṃ, ya eva mad-vināśena Candraguptam
ārādhayitum udyatās, ta eva māṃ parivṛṇvanti? 24 ārya:
Cārudattaḥ khalv asau—katham idam akāryaṃ kariṣyati?
25 vatsa Lakṣmaṇa, bhagavatā Vālmīkinā sva:kṛtim
apsarobhiḥ prayuɪyamānāṃ draṣṭum upanimantritāḥ
smaḥ 26 dhiṅ mūrkha, kim uccair hasatā tvayɪ êyam
uttrāsitā yenɪ ôḍḍīyɪ ânyatra kvɪ âpi gatā 27 kiṃ tu na
śakyate cittam anyataḥ pravṛttam anyataḥ pravartayitum.
ato nɪ âham enāṃ pratigrahītum utsahe 28 kiṃ Mataṅgo
rājyaṃ hariṣyatɪ îti śaṅkase? yady evaṃ, tataḥ kim? nanu
sva:śarīra˜taḥ prabhṛti parɪ-ârtham eva sarvaṃ mayā
paripālyate. yat tu svayaṃ na dīyate, tat tātɪ-ânurodhāt
29 prathita:yaśasāṃ Bhāsa;Saumilla;Kaviputrɪ:ādīnāṃ
prabandhān atikramya vartamāna:kaveḥ Kālidāsasya
kriyāyāṃ kathaṃ pariṣado bahumānaḥ? 30 sā ced iyam
ahārya:niścayā, sarva eṣa jano ɪtrɪ aîvɪ ân:anya:gatir
an:aśanena saṃsthāsyate

Exercise 14

1 bhūmau patacɪ chabdam utpādayet 2 tat kas tvam
iti śrotum icchāmi 3 tatra yugma-cāriṇoḥ krauñcayor
ekaṃ vyādhena vidhyamānam apaśyat 4 eṣa mama
kanīyān bhrātā gṛhīta:Yaugandharāyaṇa-bhūmikaḥ prāpta
eva 5 cirāt khalu yukta-kārī vidhiḥ syād, yadi yugalam
etad anyonyɪ-ânurūpaṃ ghaṭayet 6 Makaradhvaja-
niśita:śara-nikara-nipāta-trastɪ êvɪ âkampata gātra:yaṣṭiḥ
7 samprati ramaṇīya˜tarā Mālatī 8 api nāma dur:ātmā
Rākṣaso gṛhyeta 9 vairūpyāt tu mama 'Virūpaka' iti
prasiddhir āsīt 10 sā sadya eva rājñā saha jananyā
samāhūyata 11 nanv iyaṃ jyāyasī te bhaginī duḥkham
āste—tat pariṣvajasvɪ aînām 12 tvayi tv apadiṣṭe sarvam
asmat-kuṭumbam avasīdet 13 tāṃ ca dvitīya:
Gandharva˜kulɪ-âdhipatir Haṃso Mandākinīm iva kṣīra-
sāgaraḥ praṇayinīm akarot 14 tāḍyamānaḥ kiṃ na brūyāt?
15 tayā tu tatrɪ āgatya kiṃ kṛtaṃ, kim abhihitaṃ, kim

ācestitam iti śūnya: hṛdayā sarvaṃ nı âlakṣayam 16 nı
ânyat pāpiṣṭha˜tamam ātma-tyāgāt 17 deva, yuṣmad-dāsī
Rāgamañjarī rūpı-ânurūpa: śīla; śilpa; kauśalā pūrayiṣyati
manorathān ity āsīd asmākam mahaty āśā 18 paṭaccara-
ccheda: śeṣo ırthapatir artha-mattaḥ sarva:paurajana-
samakṣaṃ niravāsyata 19 dayamānaś cı âham abravam,
'ehi sādhvi, tvāṃ nayeyaṃ tvat-priyı-āvasatham' iti tri;
caturāṇi padāny udacalam 20 Gautama, vadı êdānīṃ yat
te manasi vartate 21 anyathā kadācid īdṛg: avasthaṃ
māṃ sahasıı aîvı ālokya pitarau jīvitaṃ jahyātām 22
Rumaṇvān api Kosaleṣu mad-bhrātaraṃ jyāyāṃsaṃ
Jayavarmāṇaṃ sthāpayitvā samara-vraṇitam aśeṣa:
balam anuvartamānaḥ śanaiḥ śanair āgacchaty eva 23
api nāma śaknuyām ahaṃ sva:śarīra-dānād ekasyı âpi
phaṇabhṛtaḥ prāṇa-rakṣāṃ kartum 24 tad evaṃ siddha:
saṃkalpo Rāgamañjarī-gṛhaṃ hema; ratna-pūrṇam
akaravam 25 kva prāṇebhyo ıpi vallabha˜taraṃ janaṃ
vihāya gamyate? 26 Candragupto ıpi 'pitṛ-paryāyı-āgata
evı âyam' ity aṅgīkuryāt. evaṃ saty asmāsv api kumāro
na viśvaset 27 tad-ardhaṃ sabhikāya sabhyebhyaś ca
dattvā ırdhaṃ svīkṛtyı ôdatiṣṭham. udatiṣṭhaṃś ca tatra:
gatānāṃ harṣa: garbhāḥ praśaṃsı-ālāpāḥ 28 siddha evı
âsmin prayojane devīṃ diṣṭyā vardhayiṣyāmı îti nı ôktam
29 Vṛṣala, Malayaketav an:upekṣiṭ: âpakramaṇe dvayī
gatiḥ syāt—nigṛhyeta vā pūrva: pratiśrutaṃ rājyı-ârdhaṃ
vā pratipādyeta. nigrahe tāvad asya, Parvatako ısmābhir
vyāpādita iti kṛtaghnatāyāḥ svahasto dattaḥ syāt 30
utthāya ca dhauta: vaktrau pragetanāni maṅgalāny
anuṣṭhāyı âsmat-karma-tumulaṃ puram anuvicarantāv
aśṛnuva vara; vadhū-gṛheṣu kolāhalam

Grammatical Practice: Keys

6 1 kanyābhyaḥ 2 Ūrmilāyāḥ 3 āryābhyām 4 Sīte
   5 mudrāsu 6 kanyāṃ paśyati 7 tābhyaḥ 8 anayā/
   etayā mudrayā 9 ime/ete tiṣṭhataḥ 10 tasyām

7 1 suhṛdi 2 manobhiḥ 3 nadyoḥ 4 devyai 5 dik
   tiṣṭhati 6 suhṛdbhyaḥ 7 nadīḥ paśyati 8 manāṃsi
   tiṣṭhanti 9 diśe 10 nadīṣu

8 1 rājan 2 nāmabhyaḥ 3 rājā tiṣṭhati 4 ātmane

5 rājñe 6 nāmabhyām 7 rājānau paśyati 8 āt-
manām 9 rājasu 10 nāmnī/nāmanī tiṣṭhataḥ

9 1 tvarethe 2 agnaye 3 bhavatā 4 śucyoḥ 5 śuci-
noḥ 6 tvarante 7 mṛdūnām 8 bhavataḥ paśyati 9
śucīni tiṣṭhanti 10 tvarete bhavantau

10 1 gacchata 2 tapasviṣu 3 vadhvāḥ 4 nayatoḥ 5
strīḥ/strīyaḥ paśya 6 nayate tapasvine 7 mahāntas
tiṣṭhantu 8 tapasvinaḥ, tvaradhvam 9 bhuvi 10
gāyantau gacchatām

11 1 kartṛbhyām 2 svasṝḥ paśyati 3 pitṝṇām 4 nīyā-
vahe 5 mātaraṃ paśyati 6 svasāras tiṣṭhanti 7
kartuḥ 8 mātarau nīyetām 9 svasaḥ 10 pitre

12 1 kurvanti 2 dveṣṭi 3 itaḥ 4 karotu 5 āsāthe 6
śṛṇoṣi 7 āsate 8 kurmaḥ 9 śṛṇu 10 dviṣantāv
āsāte

13 1 amuṣya 2 juhudhi 3 ruṇaddhi 4 krīṇītaḥ 5 jān-
antu 6 amīṣu 7 ado dehi 8 rundhvaḥ 9 amūr
juhvati 10 amū krīṇīhi

14 1 anayāva 2 nayeyuḥ 3 śreyasoḥ 4 atvaradhvam
5 aruṇadham 6 dviṣyuḥ 7 āsāthām 8 jyāyāṃsau
paśyema 9 jyāyān āsīḥ 10 śreyāṃsaḥ syuḥ